THE
CONCISE OXFORD
DICTIONARY OF
QUOTATIONS

THE
CONCISE OXFORD
DICTIONARY
OF
QUOTATIONS

WORLD BOOKS : LONDON

This edition published by
World Books, 1971
by arrangement with Oxford University Press

PRINTED IN GREAT BRITAIN

CONTENTS

PUBLISHER'S FOREWORD

The Oxford Dictionary of Quotations, published in 1941, quickly established itself as a standard work of reference and was seven times reprinted with occasional revisions. In 1953 a second edition appeared, which has also been reprinted. The compilers of *The Concise Oxford Dictionary of Quotations* have had the latest revised impression before them in preparing this abridgement.

The *Concise O.D.Q.* is not to be considered as displacing, superseding, or providing even a tolerable substitute for its parent volume. A comparison between the thousand large pages of the *Dictionary* and the many fewer small pages of the present volume will make this clear enough. The *Concise O.D.Q.* has been undertaken to meet the demand for a shorter dictionary containing such quotations as might be used daily by the 'man in the street' rather than by the literary specialist. The intention has been to reduce, not to add; but some additions have nevertheless been made, with the idea of keeping the work up to date, from sources as far apart as Lord Hewart, Dorothy Parker, Adlai Stevenson, and Beatrix Potter.

The Oxford Dictionary of Quotations is graced by an introduction from the late Bernard Darwin. 'Quotation brings to many people one of the intensest joys of living', he begins, and even the members of the Amen House committee who have spent many hours weighing one quotation against another—to test their merits for possible inclusion in this book—rose from their labours with the love of quotation unimpaired. Few can emulate Bernard Darwin's dexterity with a quotation; but others beside leader-writers and crossword zealots will turn to these pages with enthusiasm, for dictionaries of quotations are fields of paradise for the browser. It is the hope of the compilers that the joy of this book will remain intense in its concise form.

One further warning may be added: proverbs and phrases are not included either in this dictionary or in its parent volume, but they are fully dealt with in the *Oxford Dictionary of English Proverbs*.

SIR J. E. E. DALBERG ACTON, FIRST BARON ACTON 1834–1902

1 Power tends to corrupt and absolute power corrupts absolutely.
Letter in Life of Mandell Creighton (1904), i. 372

SAMUEL ADAMS 1722–1803

2 A Nation of shop-keepers are very seldom so disinterested.
Oration said to have been delivered at Philadelphia, 1776, p. 10 (*see also* 151:15, 217:12)

JOSEPH ADDISON 1672–1719

3 And, pleas'd th' Almighty's orders to perform,
Rides in the whirl-wind, and directs the storm. *The Campaign,* l. 291

4 'Tis not in mortals to command success,
But we'll do more, Sempronius; we'll deserve it. *Cato,* ii. 43

5 When vice prevails, and impious men bear sway,
The post of honour is a private station.
Ib. 140

6 From hence, let fierce contending nations know
What dire effects from civil discord flow. *Ib.* iv. 111

7 Thus I live in the world rather as a spectator of mankind than as one of the species. *The Spectator,* No. 1

8 When I am in a serious humour, I very often walk by myself in Westminster Abbey. *Ib.* No. 26

9 I have often thought, says Sir Roger, it happens very well that Christmas should fall out in the Middle of Winter. *Ib.* No. 269

10 The Knight in the triumph of his heart made several reflections on the greatness of the *British* Nation; as, that one *Englishman* could beat three *Frenchmen*; that we cou'd never be in danger of Popery so long as we took care of our fleet; that the *Thames* was the noblest river in *Europe*; that *London Bridge* was a greater piece of work than any of the Seven Wonders of the World; with many other honest prejudices which naturally cleave to the heart of a true *Englishman*.
Ib. No. 383

11 The spacious firmament on high,
With all the blue ethereal sky.
The Spectator, No. 465. Ode

12 Soon as the evening shades prevail,
The moon takes up the wondrous tale,
And nightly to the listening Earth
Repeats the story of her birth. *Ib.*

13 Whilst all the stars that round her burn,
And all the planets, in their turn,
Confirm the tidings as they roll,
And spread the truth from pole to pole. *Ib.*

14 In Reason's ear they all rejoice,
And utter forth a glorious Voice,
For ever singing as they shine,
'The Hand that made us is Divine.'
Ib.

15 If we may believe our logicians, man is distinguished from all other creatures by the faculty of laughter.
Ib. No. 494

16 'We are always doing', says he, 'something for Posterity, but I would fain see Posterity do something for us.'
Ib. No. 583

THOMAS ADY c. 1655

17 Matthew, Mark, Luke, and John,
The Bed be blest that I lie on.
Four angels to my bed,
Four angels round my head,
One to watch, and one to pray,
And two to bear my soul away.
Quoted in part by Ady in *A Candle in the Dark* (1656)

AESOP c. 550 B.C.

18 Beware that you do not lose the substance by grasping at the shadow.
Fables. The Dog and the Shadow

19 The gods help them that help themselves. *Ib. Hercules and the Waggoner*

20 It is not only fine feathers that make fine birds.
Ib. The Jay and the Peacock

21 Don't count your chickens before they are hatched.
Ib. The Milkmaid and her Pail

AGATHON 447?–401 B.C.

22 Even God cannot change the past.
Attr. by Aristotle in The Nicomachean Ethics, vi.

CHARLES HAMILTON AÏDÉ
1830–1906

1 I sit beside my lonely fire,
  And pray for wisdom yet—
For calmness to remember
  Or courage to forget.
  Remember or Forget

ALFRED AINGER 1837–1904

2 No flowers, by request.
  At a dinner given to the contributors to the Dict. of Nat. Biog., 8 July 1897: his summary of their editor's instructions.

ARTHUR CAMPBELL AINGER
1841–1919

3 God is working His purpose out as
    year succeeds to year,
God is working His purpose out and
    the time is drawing near;
Nearer and nearer draws the time, the
    time that shall surely be,
When the earth shall be fill'd with the
    glory of God as the waters cover the
    sea.
    God is Working His Purpose Out
    (1894)

ALCUIN 735–804

4 Vox populi, vox dei.
  The voice of the people is the voice
    of God.
  Letter to Charlemagne, A.D. 800.
  Works, Epis. 127

HENRY ALDRICH 1648–1710

5 If all be true that I do think,
There are five reasons we should drink;
Good wine—a friend—or being dry—
Or lest we should be by and by—
Or any other reason why.
    Reasons for Drinking

ALEXANDER 356–323 B.C.

6 εἰ μὴ Ἀλέξανδρος ἤμην, Διογένης ἂν ἤμην.
  If I were not Alexander, I would be
    Diogenes.
  Plutarch, *Life of Alexander*, xiv. 3

CECIL FRANCES ALEXANDER
1818–1895

7 All things bright and beautiful,
  All creatures great and small,
All things wise and wonderful,
  The Lord God made them all.
    All Things Bright and Beautiful
    (1848)

8 The rich man in his castle,
  The poor man at his gate,
God made them, high or lowly,
  And order'd their estate.   *Ib.*

9 Do no sinful action,
  Speak no angry word;
Ye belong to Jesus,
  Children of the Lord.
    Do No Sinful Action (1848)

10 Once in royal David's city
  Stood a lowly cattle shed,
Where a Mother laid her Baby
  In a manger for His bed:
Mary was that Mother mild.
Jesus Christ her little Child.
    Once in Royal David's City (1848)

11 We are but little children weak
  Not born in any high estate.
    We are but Little Children Weak
    (1850)

SIR WILLIAM ALEXANDER, EARL OF STIRLING 1567?–1640

12 The weaker sex, to piety more prone.
    Doomsday, Hour v, lv

HENRY ALFORD 1810–1871

13 Come, ye thankful people, come,
  Raise the song of Harvest-home:
All is safely gathered in,
  Ere the winter storms begin.
    Come, Ye Thankful People, Come
    (1844)

14 Ten thousand times ten thousand,
  In sparkling raiment bright.
    Ten Thousand Times Ten Thousand (1867)

ABBÉ D'ALLAINVAL 1700–1753

15 L'embarras des richesses.
  The more alternatives, the more
    difficult the choice.
    Title of Comedy (1726)

GRANT ALLEN 1848–1899

16 The Woman who Did.
    Title of Novel (1895)

WILLIAM ALLINGHAM
1824–1889

17 Up the airy mountain,
  Down the rushy glen,
We daren't go a-hunting,
  For fear of little men.   *The Fairies*

18 Four ducks on a pond,
  A grass-bank beyond,
A blue sky of spring,
White clouds on the wing:
What a little thing
  To remember for years—
  To remember with tears!   *A Memory*

ST. AMBROSE c. 340–397

1 Si fueris Romae, Romano vivito more;
Si fueris alibi, vivito sicut ibi.

> If you are at Rome live in the
> Roman style; if you are else-
> where live as they live elsewhere.
> *Quoted by Jeremy Taylor, Ductor
> Dubitantium, I. i. 5*

MAXWELL ANDERSON 1888–1959

2 What Price Glory, *Title of Play* (1924)

SIR NORMAN ANGELL 1874–1967

3 The Great Illusion
> *Title of book on the futility of war*

ARCHIBALD DOUGLAS, FIFTH EARL OF ANGUS 1449?–1514

4 I shall bell the cat.
> *Attr. by J. Man in Buchanan's
> Rerum Scoticarum Historia
> (1762), bk. xii, § 41, note*

ANONYMOUS

English

5 A beast, but a just beast.
> *Of Dr. Temple, Headmaster of
> Rugby, 1857–69*

6 Absence makes the heart grow fonder.
> Davison, *Poetical Rhapsody* (1602)
> (*see 19:3*)

7 Adam
Had 'em.
> *On the Antiquity of Microbes.
> (Said to be the shortest poem.)*

8 All present and correct.
> *King's Regulations (Army). Re-
> port of the Orderly Sergeant to the
> Officer of the Day*

9 An abomination unto the Lord, but
a very present help in time of trouble.
[A lie.]
> (*Cf. Proverbs xii. 22; the second
> half is from Psalms xlvi. 1*)

10 An Austrian army, awfully arrayed,
Boldly by battery besieged Belgrade;
Cossack commanders cannonading
come,
Dealing destruction's devastating
doom.
> *Siege of Belgrade. The Trifler, 1817*

11 A place within the meaning of the Act.
> *The Betting Act*

12 Appeal from Philip drunk to Philip
sober.
> *See Valerius Maximus, Facta et
> Dicta Memorabilia (c. A.D. 15),
> bk. vi, ch. ii*

13 Are we downhearted? No!
> *Expression much used by British
> soldiers in War of 1914–18, prob-
> ably based on remark of Joseph
> Chamberlain, q.v.*

14 As I sat on a sunny bank,
On Christmas Day in the morning,
I spied three ships come sailing by.
> *Carol: As I sat on a Sunny Bank.
> Oxford Book of Carols*

15 A swarm of bees in May
Is worth a load of hay;
A swarm of bees in June
Is worth a silver spoon;
A swarm of bees in July
Is not worth a fly. *Old Rhyme*

16 Begone, dull care! I prithee begone
from me!
Begone, dull care, you and I shall
never agree. *Begone Dull Care*

17 Be happy while y'er leevin,
For y'er a lang time deid.
> *Scottish Motto for a house. Notes
> and Queries, 7 Dec. 1901, p. 469*

18 Born 1820, still going strong.
> *Advertisement for Johnnie Walker
> Whisky*

19 Bovril prevents that sinking feeling.
> *Advertisement*

20 Christmas is coming, the geese are
getting fat,
Please to put a penny in the old man's
hat;
If you haven't got a penny, a ha'penny
will do,
If you haven't got a ha'penny, God
bless you! *Beggar's Rhyme*

21 Come, landlord, fill the flowing bowl
Until it doth run over. . . .
For to-night we'll merry be,
To-morrow we'll be sober.
> *Come, Landlord, Fill the Flowing
> Bowl. Oxford Song Book*

22 Come lasses and lads, get leave of
your dads,
And away to the Maypole hie,
For every he has got him a she,
And the fiddler's standing by.
For Willie shall dance with Jane,
And Johnny has got his Joan,
To trip it, trip it, trip it, trip it, trip
it up and down.
> *Come Lasses and Lads (c. 1670).
> Oxford Song Book*

23 Conduct . . . to the prejudice of good
order and military discipline.
> *Army Act, § 40*

1 Dear Sir, Your astonishment's odd:
  I am always about in the Quad.
     And that's why the tree
      Will continue to be,
  Since observed by Yours faithfully,
     God.
      Reply to limerick on Idealism,
      'There was once a man who said
      "God . . ." ' *(see 129:2)*

2 Dollar Diplomacy.
      Term applied to Secretary Knox's
      activities in securing opportunities
      for the investment of American
      capital abroad, particularly in
      Latin America and China. See
      Harper's Weekly, 23 Apr. 1910,
      p. 8.

3 Dr. Williams' pink pills for pale people.
      Advertisement

4 Early one morning, just as the sun was
    rising,
  I heard a maid sing in the valley be-
    low:
  'Oh, don't deceive me; Oh, never leave
    me!
  How could you use a poor maiden so?'
      Early One Morning. Oxford Song
      Book

5 Earned a precarious living by taking
  in one another's washing.
      In The Commonweal, *6 Aug.*
      1887, William Morris suggested
      that this was an invention of Mark
      Twain's

6 Esau selleth his birthright for a mess
  of potage.
      Genevan Bible: chapter-heading to
      Genesis, ch. 25

7 An intelligent Russian once remarked
  to us, 'Every country has its own constitution; ours is absolutism mode-
  rated by assassination.'
      Georg Herbert, Count Münster,
      Political Sketches of the State of
      Europe, 1814–1867, ed. 1868, p.
      19

8 Frankie and Johnny were lovers, my
  gawd, how they could love,
  Swore to be true to each other, true
    as the stars above;
  He was her man, but he done her
    wrong.   *Frankie and Johnny, st. 1*

9 From ghoulies and ghosties and long-
    leggety beasties
  And things that go bump in the night,
    Good Lord, deliver us! *Cornish*

10 God be in my head,
  And in my understanding;

  God be in my eyes,
  And in my looking;

God be in my mouth,
And in my speaking;

God be in my heart,
And in my thinking;

God be at my end,
And at my departing. *Sarum Missal*

11 God rest you merry, Gentlemen,
  Let nothing you dismay.
      Carol: God Rest You Merry.
      Oxford Book of Carols

12 O tidings of comfort and joy.   *Ib.*

13 God's own country.
      Sir St. V. Troubridge (Notes and
      Queries, *26 Sept. 1942) quotes*
      from Sir W. Craigie's Dictionary
      of American English:
      'A special part of the U.S. or
      the country as a whole, viewed
      nostalgically as almost a para-
      dise.'
      The earliest example without 'own'
      given is 1865, the earliest with
      'own' is 1921

14 Great Chatham with his sabre drawn
  Stood waiting for Sir Richard
    Strachan;
  Sir Richard, longing to be at 'em,
  Stood waiting for the Earl of Chatham.
      At Walcheren, 1809

15 Greensleeves was all my joy,
    Greensleeves was my delight,
  Greensleeves was my heart of gold,
    And who but Lady Greensleeves?
      A new Courtly Sonnet of the Lady
      Greensleeves, to the new tune of
      'Greensleeves'. From *A Handful*
      of Pleasant Delites (1584)

16 Ha-ha-ha, you and me,
  Little brown jug, don't I love thee.
      The Little Brown Jug. Oxford
      Song Book

17 Here lies Fred,
  Who was alive and is dead:
  Had it been his father,
  I had much rather;
  Had it been his brother,
  Still better than another;
  Had it been his sister,
  No one would have missed her;
  Had it been the whole generation,
  Still better for the nation:
  But since 'tis only Fred,
  Who was alive and is dead,—
  There's no more to be said.
      Horace Walpole, *Memoirs of*
      George II (1847), vol. i, p. 436

18 Here we come a-wassailing. *Old Song*

19 Here we come gathering nuts in May
    Nuts in May,
  On a cold and frosty morning.
      Children's Song

1 He that fights and runs away
  May live to fight another day.
      Musarum Deliciae, collected by
      Sir John Mennes and Dr. James
      Smith, 1656

2 He won't be happy till he gets it.
      Advertisement for Pears' Soap

3 Hierusalem, my happy home,
  When shall I come to thee?
  When shall my sorrows have an end,
  Thy joys when shall I see?
      Hierusalem. See *Songs of Praise*
      Discussed

4 'How different, how very different
  from the home life of our own dear
  Queen!'
      Irvin S. Cobb, *A Laugh a Day*
      As Cleopatra, Sarah Bernhardt
      stabbed the slave who bore to her
      the tidings of Mark Antony's
      defeat at Actium; she stormed,
      raved, wrecked some of the scenery
      in her frenzy and finally, as the
      curtain fell, dropped in a shud-
      dering, convulsive heap.
      As the applause died, a middle-
      aged British matron was heard to
      say to her neighbour: 'How
      different, how very different from
      the home life of our own dear
      Queen!' (Victoria).

5 I feel no pain dear mother now
  But oh, I am so dry!
  O take me to a brewery
  And leave me there to die.
      C. Fox-Smith's *Book of Shanties*
      (1927)

6 If you your lips would keep from slips
  Of five things have a care:
  To whom you speak, of whom you
    speak,
  And how, and when, and where.
      Quoted in Augustus Hare, *Story*
      of My Life

7 I know two things about the horse,
  And one of them is rather coarse.
      The Week-End Book

8 In Dublin's fair city, where girls are so
    pretty,
  I first set my eyes on sweet Molly
    Malone,
  As she wheeled her wheelbarrow
    through streets broad and narrow,
  Crying, Cockles and mussels! alive,
    alive, oh!
      Cockles and Mussels. Oxford
      Song Book

9 In good King Charles's golden days,
  When loyalty no harm meant;
  A furious High-Churchman I was,
  And so I gain'd preferment.
  Unto my flock I daily preach'd,
  Kings are by God appointed,

And damned are those who dare resist,
  Or touch the Lord's Anointed.
  And this is law, I will maintain,
  Unto my dying day, Sir,
  That whatsoever King shall reign,
  I will be the Vicar of Bray, Sir!
      The Vicar of Bray. Brit. Musical
      Miscellany (1734), i

10 I saw three ships a-sailing there,
    —A-sailing there, a-sailing there,
  Jesu, Mary and Joseph they bare
    On Christ's Sunday at morn.
      I saw three ships. Oxford Book of
      Carols

11 I sing of a maiden
    That is makeless;
  King of all kings
    To her son she ches.
      Carol: I Sing of a Maiden (15th
      cent.). *Oxford Book of Carols*

12 The children of Lord Lytton organized
  a charade. The scene displayed a
  Crusader knight returning from the
  wars. At his gate he was welcomed by
  his wife to whom he recounted his
  triumphs and the number of heathen
  he had slain. His wife, pointing to a
  row of dolls of various sizes, replied
  with pride, 'And I too, my lord, have
  not been idle'.
      G. W. E. Russell's *Collections*
      and Recollections, ch. 31

13 It's a long time between drinks.
      The Governor of South Carolina re-
      quired the return of a fugitive slave.
      The Governor of North Carolina
      hesitated because of powerful
      friends of the fugitive. He gave a
      banquet to his official brother. The
      Governor of South Carolina in a
      speech demanded the return of the
      slave and ended with 'What do
      you say?' The Governor of North
      Carolina replied as above

14 It is good to be merry and wise,
  It is good to be honest and true,
  It is best to be off with the old love,
  Before you are on with the new.
      Songs of England and Scotland.
      London (1835), vol. ii, p. 73

15 It's love, it's love that makes the
  world go round.
      Chansons Nationales et Popu-
      laires de France, vol. ii, p. 180

16 I wish I were single again.
      I Married a Wife (19th cent.)

17 Jesus Christ is risen to-day,
  Our triumphant holy day;
  Who did once upon the cross
  Suffer to redeem our loss.
      Hallelujah!
      Jesus Christ is Risen To-day.
      From a Latin Hymn of the 15th
      cent. Translator unknown

1 King Charles the First walked and
  talked
  Half an hour after his head was cut off.
      See Peter Puzzlewell, *A Choice
      Collection of Riddles, Charades
      and Rebusses* (1792)

2 Like a fine old English gentleman,
  All of the olden time.
      The Fine Old English Gentleman.
      Oxford Song Book

3 Lizzie Borden took an axe
  And gave her mother forty whacks;
  When she saw what she had done
  She gave her father forty-one!
      *After an American murder trial of
      the 1890's in which Miss Borden
      was acquitted of murdering her
      father and stepmother*

4 Love me little, love me long,
  Is the burden of my song.
      Love me Little, Love me Long
      (1569–70)

5 March winds and April showers
  Bringeth vo'th May flowers.
      West Somerset Word-Book, ed.
      Frederick Thomas Elworthy
      (1886), March

6 Miss Buss and Miss Beale
  Cupid's darts do not feel.
  How different from us,
  Miss Beale and Miss Buss.
      *Of the Headmistress of the North
      London Collegiate School and the
      Principal of the Ladies' College,
      Cheltenham. 19th cent.*

7 Most Gracious Queen, we thee implore
  To go away and sin no more,
  But if that effort be too great,
  To go away at any rate.
      *Epigram on Queen Caroline,
      1820. Quoted in Lord Colchester's
      Diary, 15 Nov. 1820; sent to him
      by Francis Burton*

8 Multiplication is vexation,
  Division is as bad;
  The Rule of three doth puzzle me,
  And Practice drives me mad.
      Elizabethan MS. dated 1570

9 My name is George Nathaniel Curzon,
  I am a most superior person.
      *The Masque of Balliol, composed
      by and current among members of
      Balliol College in the late 1870's
      (see also 20:5, 219:19 and 20)*

10 My face is pink, my hair is sleek,
   I dine at Blenheim once a week.
       Ib. (a later addition)

11 Now I lay me down to sleep;
   I pray the Lord my soul to keep.
   If I should die before I wake,
   I pray the Lord my soul to take.
       *First printed in a late edition of the
       New England Primer, 1781*

12 O Death, where is thy sting-a-ling-a-
   ling,
   O Grave, thy victoree?
   The bells of Hell go ting-a-ling-a-ling
   For you but not for me.
       *Song popular in the British Army,
       1914–18*

13 O God, if there be a God, save my soul,
   if I have a soul!
       *Prayer of a common soldier
       before the battle of Blenheim (see
       Notes and Queries, clxxiii. 264).
       Quoted in Newman's Apologia*

14 Oh, Shenandoah, I long to hear you.
   Away, you rolling river,
   Oh, Shenandoah, I long to hear you.
   Away, I'm bound to go
   'Cross the wide Missouri.
       Shenandoah. Oxford Song Book

15 Oh! the oak, and the ash, and the
   bonny ivy-tree,
   They flourish at home in my own
   country.
       O The Oak and The Ash (c.
       1650). *Oxford Song Book*

16 Oh, 'tis my delight on a shining night,
   in the season of the year.
       *The Lincolnshire Poacher. Oxford
       Song Book*

17 Oh, 'twas in the broad Atlantic,
   'Mid the equinoctial gales,
   That a young fellow fell overboard
   Among the sharks and whales.
   And down he went like a streak of
   light,
   So quickly down went he,
   Until he came to a mer-ma-id
   At the bottom of the deep blue sea.
   Singing, Rule Britannia, Britannia,
   rule the waves!
   Britons never, never, never shall be
   mar-ri-ed to a mer-ma-id
   At the bottom of the deep blue sea.
       *Oh! 'Twas in the Broad Atlantic.
       Oxford Song Book.*

18 Oh! where is my wandering boy to-
   night?
   The boy who was bravest of all.
       Oh! Where is My Boy To-night?

19 Old soldiers never die;
   They only fade away!
       *War song of the British Soldiers,
       1914–18*

20 One Friday morn when we set sail,
   And our ship not far from land,
   We there did espy a fair pretty maid,
   With a comb and a glass in her hand.
   While the raging seas did roar,
   And the stormy winds did blow,
   And we jolly sailor-boys were all up
   aloft
   And the land-lubbers lying down
   below.
       The Mermaid. Oxford Song Book

1 O No John! No John! No John! No!
   O No, John. Oxford Song Book

2 O Paddy dear, an' did ye hear the news
   that's goin' round?
   The shamrock is by law forbid to grow
   on Irish ground!
   No more St. Patrick's Day we'll keep,
   his colour can't be seen,
   For there's a cruel law agin the
   wearin' o' the Green!
   *The Wearin' o' the Green.
   (Famous street ballad, later added
   to by Boucicault.)*

3 Please to remember the Fifth of
   November,
   Gunpowder Treason and Plot.
   *Traditional since seventeenth cent.
   (see also 157:12)*

4 O ye'll tak' the high road, and I'll
   tak' the low road,
   And I'll be in Scotland afore ye,
   But me and my true love will never
   meet again,
   On the bonnie, bonnie banks o' Loch
   Lomon'.
   *The Bonnie Banks o' Loch
   Lomon'. Oxford Song Book*

5 She was poor but she was honest,
   And her parents was the same,
   Till she met a city feller,
   And she lost her honest name.
   *1914–18 War song. There are
   many versions*

6 Its the same the whole world over,
   Its the poor wot gets the blame,
   Its the rich wot gets the pleasure,
   Ain't it all a blooming shame.   *Ib.*

7 Some talk of Alexander, and some of
   Hercules;
   Of Hector and Lysander, and such
   great names as these;
   But of all the world's brave heroes,
   there's none that can compare
   With a tow, row, row, row, row, row,
   for the British Grenadier.
   The British Grenadiers

8 Spheres of influence.
   *'Spheres of action', found in Earl
   Granville's letter to Count Mün-
   ster, 29 Apr. 1885. Hertslet's
   Map of Africa by Treaty, 3rd
   edn., p. 868 (see 132:2)*

9 Sumer is icumen in
   Lhude sing cuccu!
   Groweth sed, and bloweth med,
   And springth the wude nu.
   Cuckoo Song (c. 1250)

10 Swing low, sweet chariot—
   Comin' for to carry me home;
   I looked over Jordan and what did I
   see?
   A band of angels comin' after me—
   Comin' for to carry me home.
   American Negro Spiritual (c. 1850)

11 That schoolgirl complexion.
   Advertisement for Palmolive Soap

12 The almighty dollar is the only object
   of worship.
   *Philadelphia Public Ledger,
   2 Dec. 1836*

13 The animals went in one by one,
   There's one more river to cross.
   *One More River. Oxford Song
   Book*

14 The Campbells are comin', oho, oho.
   *The Campbells are Comin' (c.
   1715). Oxford Song Book*

15 The eternal triangle.
   Book review in The Daily Chronicle, *5 Dec. 1907*

16 The girl I left behind me.
   *Title of song (c. 1759). Oxford Song
   Book*

17 The holly and the ivy,
   When they are both full grown,
   Of all the trees that are in the wood,
   The holly bears the crown:
   The rising of the sun
   And the running of the deer,
   The playing of the merry organ,
   Sweet singing in the choir.
   *The Holly and the Ivy. Oxford
   Book of Carols*

18 The King over the Water.
   Jacobite Toast, eighteenth cent.

19 The ministry of all the talents.
   *A name given ironically to Gren-
   ville's coalition of 1806; also
   applied to later coalitions*

20 And Vilikins and his Dinah
   Lie a-buried in one grave.
   In Henry Mayhew's The Wander-
   ing Minstrels *(1834)*

21 The noble Duke of York,
   He had ten thousand men,
   He marched them up to the top of the
   hill,
   And he marched them down again.
   And when they were up, they were up,
   And when they were down, they were
   down,
   And when they were only half way up,
   They were neither up nor down.
   *The Noble Duke of York, first
   printed in A. Rackham, Mother
   Goose (1913)*

22 There is a lady sweet and kind,
   Was never face so pleased my mind;
   I did but see her passing by,
   And yet I love her till I die.
   *Found on back of leaf 53 of
   'Popish Kingdome or reigne of
   Antichrist', in Latin verse by
   Thomas Naogeorgus, and Eng-
   lished by Barnabe Googe. Printed
   1570. See Notes and Queries, 9th
   series, x. 427*

1 There is a tavern in the town,
  And there my dear love sits him down,
  And drinks his wine 'mid laughter free,
  And never, never thinks of me.
  Fare thee well, for I must leave thee,
  Do not let this parting grieve thee,
  And remember that the best of
    friends must part.

  Adieu, adieu, kind friends, adieu,
    adieu, adieu,
  I can no longer stay with you.
  I'll hang my harp on a weeping
    willow-tree,
  And may the world go well with
    thee.
  There is a Tavern in the Town.
  Oxford Song Book

2 There's nae luck about the house,
    There's nae luck at a',
  There's nae luck about the house
    When our gudeman's awa'.
  The Mariner's Wife

3 There was an old man of Boulogne,
  Who sang a most topical song.
    It wasn't the words
    Which frightened the birds,
  But the horrible double entendre.
  Langford Reed, *The Limerick
    Book*, p. 51

4 There was a young lady of Riga,
  Who rode with a smile on a tiger;
    They returned from the ride
    With the lady inside,
  And the smile on the face of the tiger.
  Ib. p. 103

5 They came as a boon and a blessing to
    men,
  The Pickwick, the Owl, and the
    Waverley pen.   *Advertisement*

6 To change the name, and not the
    letter,
  Is a change for the worse, and not for
    the better.
  Book of Days (ed. Robert
    Chambers, 1802–71), vol. i, June,
    p. 723

7 Wash me in the water
  That you washed the colonel's daugh-
    ter
  And I shall be whiter
  Than the whitewash on the wall.
  *Song popular among the British
    troops in France, 1914–18*

8 We don't want to fight; but, by Jingo,
    if we do,
  We won't go to the front ourselves,
    but we'll send the mild Hindoo.
  *1878 parody, on hearing that
    Indian troops were being sent to
    Malta to help the English.*
  G. W. E. Russell's *Collections
    and Recollections*, ch. 28

9 We hold these truths to be self-evi-
    dent, that all men are created equal,
    that they are endowed by their Creator
    with certain unalienable rights, that
    among these are life, liberty, and the
    pursuit of happiness.
  *The American Declaration of In-
    dependence, 4 July 1776 (see
    113:2)*

10 Western wind, when wilt thou blow,
    The small rain down can rain?
  Christ, if my love were in my arms
    And I in my bed again!
  Oxford Book of 16th Cent. Verse

11 What did you do in the Great War,
  daddy?
  Recruiting placard, 1914–18 War

12 What shall we do with the drunken
    sailor?
  Early in the morning?
  Hoo-ray and up she rises
  Early in the morning.
  *What shall we do with the Drunken
    Sailor? Oxford Song Book*

13 When Adam delved, and Eve span,
  Who was then a gentleman?
  *Text of Ball's revolutionary ser-
    mon at Blackheath in Wat Tyler's
    Rebellion, 1381. See J. R. Green,
    Short Hist. (1893), ii. 484 (see
    99:11)*

14 When Johnny Comes Marching Home
  Again.
  Title of Song. Oxford Song Book

15 When the wind is in the east,
  'Tis neither good for man nor beast;
  When the wind is in the north,
  The skilful fisher goes not forth;
  When the wind is in the south,
  It blows the bait in the fishes' mouth;
  When the wind is in the west,
  Then 'tis at the very best.
  *See J. O. Halliwell, Popular
    Rhymes (1849)*

16 Workers of the world, unite!
  *Common form of 'Working men
    of all countries, unite!' This is the
    English Translation (1888) by
    Samuel Moore, revised by Engels,
    of 'Proletarier aller Länder,
    vereinigt euch!' which concludes
    The Communist Manifesto
    (1848), by Marx and Engels, and
    is quoted as the final words of the
    programme of the Communist
    International (1928). Another
    common form is 'Proletarians of
    the world, unite!'*

17 Worth a guinea a box.
  Advertisement for Beecham's Pills

French

1 An army marches on its stomach.
> *Attr. to Napoleon in, e.g.,*
> Windsor Magazine (1904) p. 268
>
> Probably condensed from a long
> passage in Las Cases, *Mémo-*
> *rial de Ste-Hélène* (Nov. 1816)

2 Ça ira.
> Untranslatable phrase, meaning
> 'That will certainly happen'. *Re-*
> *frain of French Revolutionary Song*

3 Cet animal est très méchant,
Quand on l'attaque il se défend.
> This animal is very mischievous;
> when it is attacked it defends it-
> self.
> *La Ménagerie, by Théodore*
> *P. K. (1868)*

4 Chevalier sans peur et sans reproche.
> Knight without fear and without
> blemish.
> *Description in contemporary*
> *chronicles of Pierre Bayard,*
> *1476–1524*

5 Il ne faut pas être plus royaliste que le
roi.
> One must not be more royalist than
> the king.
> *Phrase originated under Louis*
> *XVI. Chateaubriand, La Monar-*
> *chie selon la Charte (ed. 1876),*
> *p. 94*

6 Le monde est plein de fous, et qui n'en
veut pas voir
Doit se tenir tout seul, et casser son
miroir.
> The world is full of fools, and he who
> would not see it
> Should live alone and smash his
> mirror.
> *An adaptation from an original*
> *form attributed to Claude Le*
> *Petit (1640–1665) in Discours*
> *Satiriques (1686)*

7 Liberté! Égalité! Fraternité!
> Liberty! Equality! Fraternity!
> *Phrase of unknown origin dating*
> *from before the French Revolu-*
> *tion. Aulard in Études et Leçons*
> *sur la Révolution Française (6e*
> *série) gives the first official use of*
> *the phrase in the motion passed*
> *by the Club des Cordeliers (30*
> *June 1793): 'que les proprié-*
> *taires seront invités, . . . de faire*
> *peindre sur la façade de leurs*
> *maisons, en gros caractères, ces*
> *mots: Unité, indivisibilité de la*
> *République, Liberté, Égalité,*
> *Fraternité ou la mort.'*
> *(Journal de Paris, No. 182)*

8 Retournons à nos moutons.
> Let us return to our sheep. (Let us
> get back to the subject.)
> *Maistre Pierre Pathelin, l. 1191*

9 Taisez-vous! Méfiez-vous! Les oreilles
ennemies vous écoutent.
> Be quiet! Be on your guard!
> Enemy ears are listening to you.
> *Official Notice in France in 1915*

10 Tout passe, tout casse, tout lasse.
> Everything passes, everything
> perishes, everything palls.
> *Cahier, Quelques six mille pro-*
> *verbes*

Greek

11 μηδὲν ἄγαν.
> Nothing in excess.
> *Written up in the temple at Delphi*
> *by Cleobulus, according to some*
> *accounts. Quoted by Plato in*
> *Protagoras, 343 b*

12 γνῶθι σεαυτόν.
> From the gods comes the saying
> 'Know thyself'.
> *Juvenal, Satires, xi. 27. The*
> *saying was written up in the*
> *temple of Delphi*

Italian

13 Se non è vero, è molto ben trovato.
> If it is not true, it is a happy in-
> vention.
> *Apparently a common saying in*
> *the sixteenth century. Found in*
> *Giordano Bruno (1585) in the*
> *above form, and in Antonio Doni*
> *(1552) as 'Se non è vero, egli*
> *è stato un bel trovato'*

Latin

14 Adeste, fideles,
Laeti triumphantes;
Venite, venite in Bethlehem.
> O come, all ye faithful,
> Joyful and triumphant,
> O come, ye, O come ye to Bethle-
> hem.
> *French or German hymn of eigh-*
> *teenth cent. Trans. by Oakeley in*
> *Murray's Hymnal (1852). See*
> *Songs of Praise Discussed*

15 Ad majorem Dei gloriam.
> To the greater glory of God.
> *Motto of the Society of Jesus*

16 Ave Caesar, morituri te salutant.
> Hail Caesar; those who are about to
> die salute you.
> *Salutation of Roman gladiators on*
> *entering the arena*

1 Et in Arcadia ego.

> *Inscription on a tomb, frequently reproduced in paintings, e.g. by Guercino, Poussin, and Reynolds*

Usually translated: 'And I too [the occupant of the tomb] was in Arcadia.' But perhaps rather, 'I too [the tomb itself] am in Arcadia': even in Arcadia there am I (Death). (See E. Panofsky in *Philosophy and History*: essays presented to E. Cassirer (1936).)

2 Gaudeamus igitur,
Juvenes dum sumus
Post jucundam juventutem,
Post molestam senectutem,
Nos habebit humus.

> Let us live then and be glad
> While young life's before us
> After youthful pastime had,
> After old age hard and sad,
> Earth will slumber o'er us.
> *Medieval students' song, traced to 1267, but revised in the eighteenth cent.*

3 Nemo me impune lacessit.

> No one provokes me with impunity.
> *Motto of the Crown of Scotland and of all Scottish regiments*

4 Orare est laborare, laborare est orare.

> To pray is to work, to work is to pray.
> *See* Notes and Queries, 6th series, vol. xi, p. 477

5 Quidquid agas, prudenter agas, et respice finem.

> Whatever you do, do cautiously, and look to the end.
> *Gesta Romanorum*, cap. 103. init.

6 Te Deum laudamus.

> We praise thee, O God.
> *First words and title of Canticle attr. to St. Ambrose*

7 Tempora mutantur, et nos mutamur in illis.

> Times change, and we change with them.
> Harrison, *Description of Britain* (1577), part III, ch. iii, p. 99.

CHRISTOPHER ANSTEY
1724–1805

8 How he welcomes at once all the world and his wife,
And how civil to folk he ne'er saw in his life.

> *Ib.* (1766), *letter 13*, A Public Breakfast

THOMAS APPLETON 1812–1884

9 Good Americans, when they die, go to Paris.

> O. W. Holmes, *Autocrat of the Breakfast Table*, ch. 6

ARABIAN NIGHTS

10 Who will change old lamps for new ones? . . . new lamps for old ones?

> *The History of Aladdin*

11 Open Sesame!

> *The History of Ali Baba*

ARCHIMEDES 287–212 B.C.

12 εὕρηκα.

> Eureka! (I have found!)
> Vitruvius Pollio, *De Architectura*, ix. 215

13 δός μοι ποῦ στῶ καὶ κινῶ τὴν γῆν.

> Give me but one firm spot on which to stand, and I will move the earth.
> Pappus Alexandr., *Collectio*, lib. viii, prop. 10, § xi (ed. Hultsch, Berlin, 1878)

COMTE D'ARGENSON 1652–1721

14 L'ABBÉ GUYOT DESFONTAINES: Il faut que je vive.

> D'ARGENSON: Je n'en vois pas la nécessité.

> DESFONTAINES: I must live.
> D'ARGENSON: I do not see the necessity.
> Voltaire, *Alzire, Discours Préliminaire* (see *178:1*)

ARISTOTLE 384–322 B.C.

15 ἄνθρωπος φύσει πολιτικὸν ζῷον.

> Man is by nature a political animal.
> *Politics*, i. 2. 9. 1253 *a* (ed. W. L. Newman)

16 ἔστιν οὖν τραγῳδία μίμησις πράξεως σπουδαίας καὶ τελείας μέγεθος ἐχούσης . . . δι' ἐλέου καὶ φόβου περαίνουσα τὴν τῶν τοιούτων παθημάτων κάθαρσιν.

> A tragedy is the imitation of an action that is serious and also, as having magnitude, complete in itself . . . with incidents arousing pity and fear, wherewith to accomplish its purgation of such emotions.
> *Poetics*, 6. 1449 *b*. Trans. by Bywater

17 Amicus Plato, sed magis amica veritas

> Plato is dear to me, but dearer still is truth.
> *Original ascribed to Aristotle*

SIR JOHN ARKWRIGHT
1872–1954

1 O valiant hearts who to your glory
   came.   *Hymn*

ROBERT ARMIN *fl.* 1610

2 A flea in his ear.
                Foole upon Foole (1605), c. 3

JOHN ARMSTRONG 1709–1779

3 Of right and wrong he taught
   Truths as refin'd as ever Athens heard;
   And (strange to tell!) he practis'd
      what he preach'd.
            Art of Preserving Health (1744),
            bk. iv, l. 303

4 'Tis not too late to-morrow to be
   brave.   *Ib.* l. 460

SIR EDWIN ARNOLD 1832–1904

5   Nor ever once ashamed
      So we be named
   Press-men; Slaves of the Lamp;
      Servants of Light.
            The Tenth Muse, st. 18

GEORGE ARNOLD 1834–1865

6 The living need charity more than the
   dead.   *The Jolly Old Pedagogue*

MATTHEW ARNOLD 1822–1888

7 And we forget because we must
   And not because we will.   *Absence*

8 The Sea of Faith
   Was once, too, at the full, and round
      earth's shore
   Lay like the folds of a bright girdle
      furl'd.
   But now I only hear
   Its melancholy, long, withdrawing
      roar,
   Retreating, to the breath
   Of the night-wind, down the vast edges
      drear
   And naked shingles of the world.
            Dover Beach, l. 21

9 And we are here as on a darkling plain
   Swept with confused alarms of struggle
      and flight,
   Where ignorant armies clash by night.
            Ib. l. 35

10 Come, dear children, let us away;
   Down and away below.
            The Forsaken Merman, l. 1

11 Where great whales come sailing by,
   Sail and sail, with unshut eye,
   Round the world for ever and aye.
            Ib. l. 41

12 Children dear, was it yesterday
   (Call yet once) that she went away?
            Ib. l. 48

13 Singing, 'Here came a mortal,
   But faithless was she!
   And alone dwell for ever
   The kings of the sea.'
            The Forsaken Merman, l. 120

14 Who saw life steadily, and saw it
      whole:
   The mellow glory of the Attic stage;
   Singer of sweet Colonus, and its child.
            *Sonnet to a Friend: 'Who prop,
            thou ask'st.'*

15 Wandering between two worlds, one
      dead,
   The other powerless to be born.
            The Grande Chartreuse, l. 85

16 He bears the seed of ruin in himself.
            Merope, l. 856

17 We cannot kindle when we will
      The fire which in the heart resides,
   The spirit bloweth and is still,
      In mystery our soul abides:
   But tasks in hours of insight will'd
   Can be through hours of gloom fulfill'd.
            Morality, st. 1

18 Listen, Eugenia—
   How thick the bursts come crowding
      through the leaves!
   Again—thou hearest!
   Eternal Passion!
   Eternal Pain!   *Philomela*, l. 28

19 Strew on her roses, roses,
      And never a spray of yew.
   In quiet she reposes:
      Ah! would that I did too.
            Requiescat

20 Others abide our question. Thou art
      free.
   We ask and ask: Thou smilest and art
      still,
   Out-topping knowledge.   *Shakespeare*

21 Truth sits upon the lips of dying men.
            Sohrab and Rustum, l. 656

22 Go, for they call you, Shepherd, from
      the hill.   *The Scholar-Gipsy*, l. 1

23 All the live murmur of a summer's day.
            Ib. l. 20

24 Crossing the stripling Thames at
      Bab-lock-hithe,
      Trailing in the cool stream thy
         fingers wet,
      As the slow punt swings round.
            Ib. l. 74

25 Thou waitest for the spark from
      heaven! and we,
   Light half-believers in our casual
      creeds   *Ib.* l. 171

26 This strange disease of modern life.
            Ib. l. 203

27 Still nursing the unconquerable hope,
      Still clutching the inviolable shade.
            Ib. l. 211

1 And that sweet City with her dreaming
    spires,
  She needs not June for beauty's
    heightening.   *Thyrsis*, l. 19

2 So have I heard the cuckoo's parting
    cry,
  From the wet field, through the
    vext garden-trees,
  Come with the volleying rain and
    tossing breeze:
  'The bloom is gone, and with the
    bloom go I.'   *Ib.* l. 57

3 [Oxford] [Beautiful city! so venerable,
  so lovely, so unravaged by the fierce
  intellectual life of our century, so
  serene! . . . whispering from her
  towers the last enchantments of the
  Middle Age.] . . . Home of lost causes,
  and forsaken beliefs, and unpopular
  names, and impossible loyalties!
          Essays in Criticism, First Series,
          Preface

4 Philistinism!—We have not the expression in English. Perhaps we have
  not the word because we have so
  much of the thing.   *Ib. Heinrich Heine*

5 In poetry, no less than in life, he is 'a
  beautiful and ineffectual angel, beating in the void his luminous wings in
  vain'.   *Ib. Second Series, Shelley*
  [Quoting his own sentence in his
  essay on Byron, *Essays in Criticism, Second Series*]

6 The pursuit of perfection, then, is the
  pursuit of sweetness and light . . .
  He who works for sweetness and light
  united, works to make reason and the
  will of God prevail.
          Culture and Anarchy, p. 47

7 Miracles do not happen.
          Literature and Dogma, preface to
          1883 edition, last words

8 The true meaning of religion is thus
  not simply morality, but morality
  touched by emotion.   *Ib.* ch. 1, § 2

9 Conduct is three-fourths of our life
  and its largest concern.   *Ib.* § 3

10 Let us put into their 'Eternal' and
  'God' no more science than they [the
  Hebrew writers] did:—the enduring
  power, not ourselves, which makes for
  righteousness.   *Ib.* § 5

11 But there remains the question: what
  righteousness really is. The method
  and secret and sweet reasonableness
  of Jesus.   *Ib.* ch. xii, § 2

SAMUEL JAMES ARNOLD
                              1774–1852

12 Our ships were British oak,
  And hearts of oak our men.
          Death of Nelson

THOMAS ARNOLD 1795–1842

13 My object will be, if possible, to form
  Christian men, for Christian boys I
  can scarcely hope to make.
          *Letter, in 1828, on appointment
          to Headmastership of Rugby*

**GEORGE ASAF [GEORGE H.
POWELL]** 1880–1951

14 What's the use of worrying?
      It never was worth while,
  So, pack up your troubles in your old
    kit-bag,
  And smile, smile, smile.
          *Pack Up Your Troubles in Your
          Old Kit-Bag*

**JOHN DUNNING, BARON
ASHBURTON** 1731–1783

15 The influence of the Crown has increased, is increasing, and ought to be
  diminished.
          *Motion passed in the House of
          Commons, 1780*

**HERBERT HENRY ASQUITH,
EARL OF OXFORD** 1852–1928

16 Wait and see.
          *Phrase used repeatedly in speeches
          in 1910.* Spender and Cyril
          Asquith's *Life of Lord Oxford
          and Asquith*, vol. i, p. 275

SIR JACOB ASTLEY 1579–1652

17 O Lord! thou knowest how busy I
  must be this day: if I forget thee, do
  not thou forget me.
          *Prayer before the Battle of Edge-
          hill* (Sir Philip Warwick,
          Memoires, 1701, p. 229)

EDWARD L. ATKINSON
and
APSLEY CHERRY-GARRARD

18 A very gallant gentleman.
          *Inscription on the burial place of
          Capt. L. E. G. Oates in the
          Antarctic, Nov. 1912. Being al-
          most crippled, he walked to his
          death in a blizzard to enable his
          companions to proceed on their
          journey more quickly.*

JOHN AUBREY 1626–1697

19 When he killed a calf he would do it in
  a high style, and make a speech.
          Brief Lives. William Shakespeare

20 Anno 1670 not far from Cirencester
  was an apparition. Being demanded
  whether a good spirit or a bad? returned no answer but disappeared with
  a curious Perfume and most melodious
  Twang. Mr. W. Lilley believes it was
  a Farie.   *Ib. Nicholas Towes*

ÉMILE AUGIER 1820–1889

1 La nostalgie de la boue.

Homesickness for the gutter.
Le Mariage d'Olympe, I. i

ST. AUGUSTINE 354–430

2 Fecisti nos ad te et inquietum est cor nostrum, donec requiescat in te.

Thou hast created us for thyself, and our heart cannot be quieted till it may find repose in thee.
Confessions, bk. i, ch. i. Trans. by Watts

3 Da mihi castitatem et continentiam, sed noli modo.

Give me chastity and continency, but do not give it yet.
Ib. bk. viii, ch. 7

4 Tolle lege, tolle lege.

Take up and read, take up and read.
Ib. ch. 12

5 Da quod iubes et iube quod vis. Imperas nobis continentiam.

Give what thou commandest, and command what thou wilt.
Thou imposest continency upon us.
Ib. ch. 29

6 Securus iudicat orbis terrarum.

The verdict of the world is conclusive.
Contra Epist. Parmen. iii. 24

7 Salus extra ecclesiam non est.

No salvation exists outside the church.
De Bapt. IV, c. xvii. 24, referring back to St. Cyprian's 'Habere non potest Deum patrem qui ecclesiam non habet matrem' (He cannot have God for his Father who has not the church for his mother), *De Cath. Eccl. Unitate.* vi

8 Audi partem alteram.

Hear the other side.
De Duabus Animabus, XIV. ii

9 Ama et fac quod vis.

Love and do what you will.
Popular version of St. Augustine's 'Dilige et quod vis fac' (Love and do what you will), *In Epist. Johann. Hom.* vii. 8

10 Multi quidem facilius se abstinent ut non utantur, quam temperent ut bene utantur.

To many, total abstinence is easier than perfect moderation.
On the Good of Marriage, xxi

11 Roma locuta est; causa finita est.

Rome has spoken; the case is concluded.
Sermons, bk. i

JANE AUSTEN 1775–1817

12 An egg boiled very soft is not unwholesome. [*Mr. Woodhouse.*]
Emma, ch. 3

13 One half of the world cannot understand the pleasures of the other. [*Emma.*]
Ib. ch. 9

14 A basin of nice smooth gruel, thin, but not too thin.
Ib. ch. 12

15 Let other pens dwell on guilt and misery.
Mansfield Park, ch. 48

16 'And what are you reading, Miss —?' 'Oh! it is only a novel!' replies the young lady: while she lays down her book with affected indifference, or momentary shame.—'It is only Cecilia, or Camilla, or Belinda:' or, in short, only some work in which the most thorough knowledge of human nature, the happiest delineation of its varieties, the liveliest effusions of wit and humour are conveyed to the world in the best chosen language.
Northanger Abbey, ch. 5

17 Sir Walter Elliot, of Kellynch-hall, in Somersetshire, was a man who, for his own amusement, never took up any book but the Baronetage; there he found occupation for an idle hour, and consolation in a distressed one; . . . this was the page at which the favourite volume always opened: ELLIOT OF KELLYNCH-HALL.
Persuasion, ch. 1

18 It is a truth universally acknowledged, that a single man in possession of a good fortune, must be in want of a wife.
Pride and Prejudice, ch. 1

19 You have delighted us long enough. [*Mr. Bennet.*]
Ib. ch. 18

20 Nobody is on my side, nobody takes part with me: I am cruelly used, nobody feels for my poor nerves. [*Mrs. Bennet.*]
Ib. ch. 20

21 Lady Middleton . . . exerted herself to ask Mr. Palmer if there was any news in the paper.
'No, none at all,' he replied, and read on.
Sense and Sensibility, ch. 19

ALFRED AUSTIN 1835–1913

22 Across the wires the electric message came:
'He is no better, he is much the same.'
On the Illness of the Prince of Wales, afterwards Edward VII. Attr. to Austin, but probably not his. *See* J. Lewis May in the *Dublin Review*, July 1937

WILLIAM EDMONDSTOUNE AYTOUN 1813–1865

1 They bore within their breasts the grief
    That fame can never heal—
The deep, unutterable woe
    Which none save exiles feel.
          The Island of the Scots, xii

2 Fhairshon swore a feud
    Against the clan M'Tavish;
Marched into their land
    To murder and to rafish;
For he did resolve
    To extirpate the vipers,
With four-and-twenty men
    And five-and-thirty pipers.
        The Massacre of the Macpherson, i

3 Fhairshon had a son,
    Who married Noah's daughter,
And nearly spoiled ta Flood,
    By trinking up ta water: *Ib.* vii

4 Come hither, Evan Cameron!
    Come, stand beside my knee.
        The Execution of Montrose, i

FRANCIS BACON 1561–1626

5 All good moral philosophy is but an handmaid to religion.
    Advancement of Learning, II, xxii, 14

6 Pyrrhus, when his friends congratulated to him his victory over the Romans, under the conduct of Fabricius, but with great slaughter of his own side, said to them again: 'Yes, but if we have such another victory, we are undone.'   *Apothegms* 193

7 Silence is the virtue of fools.
    De Dignitate et Augmentis Scientiarium, pt. 1, bk. vii, ch. 31 (ed. 1640, trans. Gilbert Watts)

8 There is no excellent beauty that hath not some strangeness in the proportion.   *Essays*, 43. *Of Beauty*

9 Mahomet made the people believe that he would call a hill to him, and from the top of it offer up his prayers for the observers of his law. The people assembled: Mahomet called the hill to come to him again and again; and when the hill stood still, he was never a whit abashed, but said, 'If the hill will not come to Mahomet, Mahomet will go to the hill.' *Ib.* 12. *Of Boldness*

10 A wise man will make more opportunities than he finds.
    Ib. 52. *Of Ceremonies and Respects*

11 In things that are tender and unpleasing, it is good to break the ice by some whose words are of less weight, and to reserve the more weighty voice to come in as by chance.
        Essays, 22. *Of Cunning*

12 Men fear death as children fear to go in the dark; and as that natural fear in children is increased with tales, so is the other.   *Ib.* 2. *Of Death*

13 Lookers-on many times see more than gamesters.
    Ib. 48. *Of Followers and Friends*

14 A crowd is not company, and faces are but a gallery of pictures, and talk but a tinkling cymbal, where there is no love.   *Ib.* 27. *Of Friendship*

15 Cure the disease and kill the patient.
                      Ib.

16 God Almighty first planted a garden; and, indeed, it is the purest of human pleasures.   *Ib.* 46. *Of Gardens*

17 He that hath wife and children hath given hostages to fortune; for they are impediments to great enterprises, either of virtue or mischief.
    Ib. 8. *Of Marriage and Single Life*

18 Wives are young men's mistresses, companions for middle age, and old men's nurses.   *Ib.*

19 He was reputed one of the wise men that made answer to the question when a man should marry? 'A young man not yet, an elder man not at all.' *Ib.*

20 Children sweeten labours, but they make misfortunes more bitter.
    Ib. 7. *Of Parents and Children*

21 Revenge is a kind of wild justice, which the more man's nature runs to, the more ought law to weed it out.
            Ib. 4. *Of Revenge*

22 Money is like muck, not good except it be spread.
    Ib. 15. *Of Seditions and Troubles*

23 The remedy is worse than the disease.
                      Ib.

24 Studies serve for delight, for ornament, and for ability.
             Ib. 50. *Of Studies*

25 Some books are to be tasted, others to be swallowed, and some few to be chewed and digested; that is, some books are to be read only in parts; others to be read but not curiously; and some few to be read wholly, and with diligence and attention. Some books also may be read by deputy, and extracts made of them by others. *Ib.*

26 Reading maketh a full man; conference a ready man and writing an exact man.   *Ib.*

27 Histories make men wise; poets, witty; the mathematics, subtile; natural philosophy, deep; moral,

grave; logic and rhetoric, able to contend.
Essays, 50. Of Studies

1 There is a superstition in avoiding superstition. *Ib. 17. Of Superstition*

2 Neither is money the sinews of war (as it is trivially said).
Ib. 29. Of The True Greatness of Kingdoms

3 Thus much is certain; that he that commands the sea is at great liberty, and may take as much and as little of the war as he will. *Ib.*

4 Travel, in the younger sort, is a part of education; in the elder, a part of experience. He that travelleth into a country before he hath some entrance into the language, goeth to school, and not to travel.
Ib. 18. Of Travel

5 What is truth? said jesting Pilate; and would not stay for an answer.
Ib. 1. Of Truth

6 It is the wisdom of the crocodiles, that shed tears when they would devour.
Ib. 23. Of Wisdom for a Man's Self

7 He is the fountain of honour.
Essay of a King

8 Lucid intervals and happy pauses.
History of King Henry VII, par. 3

9 I have taken all knowledge to be my province.
Letter to Lord Burleigh, 1592

10 Opportunity makes a thief.
Letter to the Earl of Essex, 1598

11 There are four classes of Idols which beset men's minds. To these for distinction's sake I have assigned names —calling the first class, Idols of the Tribe; the second, Idols of the Cave; the third, Idols of the Market-place; the fourth, Idols of the Theatre.
Novum Organon, Aphor. xxxix. Trans. Spedding

12 Nam et ipsa scientia potestas est.
Knowledge itself is power.
Religious Meditations. Of Heresies

13 De Sapientia Veterum.
The wisdom of the ancients.
Title of Work. Trans. Sir Arthur Gorges, 1619

14 Who then to frail mortality shall trust,
But limns the water, or but writes in dust. *The World*

15 What then remains, but that we still should cry,
Not to be born, or being born, to die? *Ib.*

KARL BAEDEKER 1801–1859

16 Oxford is on the whole more attractive than Cambridge to the ordinary visitor; and the traveller is therefore recommended to visit Cambridge first, or to omit it altogether if he cannot visit both.
Baedeker's Great Britain (1887), 30. From London to Oxford

WALTER BAGEHOT 1826–1877

17 It has been said that England invented the phrase, 'Her Majesty's Opposition'.
The English Constitution, ch. i. The Cabinet

18 The *Times* has made many ministries. *Ib.*

CHARLES BRUCE BAIRNSFATHER 1888–1959

19 Well, if you knows of a better 'ole, go to it.
Fragments from France, No. 1 (1915)

HENRY WILLIAMS BAKER 1821–1877

20 The King of Love my Shepherd is, Whose goodness faileth never.
Hymns Ancient and Modern. The King of Love my Shepherd is (1868)

MICHAEL BAKUNIN 1814–1876

21 We wish, in a word, equality—equality in fact as corollary, or, rather, as primordial condition of liberty. From each according to his faculties, to each according to his needs; that is what we wish sincerely and energetically.
Declaration signed by forty-seven anarchists on trial after the failure of their uprising at Lyons in 1870. See J. Morrison Davidson, The Old Order and the New (1890) (see 140:15)

STANLEY BALDWIN, EARL BALDWIN 1867–1947

22 When you think about the defence of England you no longer think of the chalk cliffs of Dover. You think of the Rhine. That is where our frontier lies to-day.
Speech, House of Commons, 30 July 1934

ARTHUR JAMES BALFOUR FIRST EARL OF BALFOUR, 1848–1930

23 Defence of philosophic doubt.
Article in Mind (1878)

1 Frank Harris ... said ...: 'The fact is,
Mr. Balfour, all the faults of the age
come from Christianity and journalism.' 'Christianity, of course, but
why journalism?'
    Autobiography of Margot Asquith,
    vol. i, ch. 10

BALLADS

2 In Scarlet town, where I was born,
There was a fair maid dwellin',
Made every youth cry *Well-a-way!*
Her name was Barbara Allen.
    The Oxford Book of Ballads.
    Barbara Allen's Cruelty

3 'But I hae dream'd a dreary dream,
Beyond the Isle of Sky;
I saw a dead man win a fight,
And I think that man was I.'
    Ib. Chevy Chase (xix in the Scot-
    tish version, but not included in the
    Oxford Book version)

4 Clerk Saunders and may Margaret
Walk'd owre yon garden green;
And deep and heavy was the love
That fell thir twa between.

'A bed, a bed,' Clerk Saunders said,
'A bed for you and me!'
'Fye na, fye na,' said may Margaret,
''Till anes we married be!'
    Ib. Clerk Saunders

5 She hadna sail'd a league, a league,
A league but barely three,
Till grim, grim grew his countenance
And gurly grew the sea.
    Ib. The Daemon Lover

6 Goodman, you've spoken the foremost
word!
Get up and bar the door.
    Ib. Get Up and Bar the Door

7 I wish I were where Helen lies,
Night and day on me she cries;
O that I were where Helen lies,
On fair Kirkconnell lea!

Curst be the heart that thought the
thought,
And curst the hand that fired the shot,
When in my arms burd Helen dropt,
And died to succour me!
    Ib. Helen of Kirkconnell

8 'What gat ye to your dinner, Lord
Randal, my Son?
What gat ye to your dinner, my
handsome young man?'
'I gat eels boil'd in broo'; mother,
make my bed soon,
For I'm weary wi' hunting, and fain
wald lie down.' *Ib. Lord Randal*

9 When captains couragious whom
death could not daunte,
Did march to the siege of the city of
Gaunt
They mustered their soldiers by two
and by three,
And the foremost in battle was Mary
Ambree.
    The Oxford Book of Ballads.
    Mary Ambree

10 Yestreen the Queen had four Maries,
The night she'll hae but three;
There was Marie Seaton, and Marie
Beaton,
And Marie Carmichael, and me.
    Ib. The Queen's Maries

11 There are twelve months in all the
year,
As I hear many men say,
But the merriest month in all the year
Is the merry month of May.
    Ib. Robin Hood and the Widow's
    Three Sons

12 The king sits in Dunfermline town
Drinking the blude-red wine.
    Ib. Sir Patrick Spens

13 'To Noroway, to Noroway,
To Noroway o'er the faem;
The king's daughter o' Noroway,
'Tis thou must bring her hame.' *Ib.*

14 I saw the new moon late yestreen
Wi' the auld moon in her arm;
And if we gang to sea, master,
I fear we'll come to harm.'   *Ib.*

15 And lang, lang may the maidens sit
Wi' their gowd kames in their hair,
A-waiting for their ain dear loves!
For them they'll see nae mair. *Ib.*

16 And till seven years were gane and
past,
True Thomas on earth was never
seen. *Ib. Thomas the Rhymer,* xx

17 There were three ravens sat on a tree,
They were as black as they might be.
The one of them said to his make,
'Where shall we our breakfast take?'
    Ib. The Three Ravens

18 All the trees they are so high,
The leaves they are so green,
The day is past and gone, sweet-
heart,
That you and I have seen.
It is cold winter's night,
You and I must bide alone:
Whilst my pretty lad is young
And is growing.
    Ib. The Trees so High

19 As I was walking all alane,
I heard twa corbies[1] making a mane:
The tane unto the tither did say,
'Where sall we gang and dine the day?'
    Ib. The Twa Corbies

    [1] corbies = ravens

1 'The wind doth blow to-day, my love,
    And a few small drops of rain;
I never had but one true love;
    In cold grave she was lain.
            The Oxford Book of Ballads.
            The Unquiet Grave

2 O waly, waly, up the bank,
    And waly, waly, doun the brae,
And waly, waly, yon burn-side,
    Where I and my Love wont to gae!
            Ib. Waly, Waly

3 But had I wist, before I kist,
    That love had been sae ill to win,
I had lock'd my heart in a case o'
    gowd,
And pinn'd it wi' a siller pin.   *Ib.*

4 'Tom Pearse, Tom Pearse, lend me
    your grey mare,
All along, down along, out along, lee.
For I want for to go to Widdicombe
    Fair,
Wi' Bill Brewer, Jan Stewer, Peter
    Gurney, Peter Davey, Dan'l Whid-
    don, Harry Hawk,
        Old Uncle Tom Cobbleigh and
            all.
        Old Uncle Tom Cobbleigh and
            all.'   *Ib. Widdicombe Fair*

EDWARD BANGS *fl.* 1775

5 Yankee Doodle, keep it up,
    Yankee Doodle dandy;
Mind the music and the step,
    And with the girls be handy.
        Yankee Doodle; or Father's Re-
        turn to Camp. See Nicholas
        Smith, *Stories of Great National*
        Songs

6 Yankee Doodle came to town
    Riding on a pony;
Stuck a feather in his cap
    And called it Macaroni.   *Ib.*

THÉODORE DE BANVILLE
                            1823–1891

7 Nous n'irons plus aux bois, les lauriers
    sont coupés.
        We will go no more to the woods,
        the laurel-trees are cut.
        Les Cariatides, Les Stalactites
        (*Nursery rhyme, earlier than Ban-*
        ville)

ANNA LETITIA BARBAULD
                            1743–1825

8   Life! we've been long together,
Through pleasant and through cloudy
        weather;
    'Tis hard to part when friends are
        dear,
Perhaps 'twill cost a sigh, a tear;

Then steal away, give little warning;
    Choose thine own time;
Say not 'Good-night'; but in some
        brighter clime
Bid me 'Good-morning'.
                            Ode to Life

REV. RICHARD HARRIS
BARHAM 1788–1845

9 What Horace says is,
    Eheu fugaces
    Anni labuntur, Postume, Postume!
Years glide away, and are lost to me,
    lost to me!
        The Ingoldsby Legends. Epigram:
        Eheu fugaces

10 What *was* to be done?—'twas per-
        fectly plain
That they could not well hang the
        man over again;
What *was* to be done?—The man was
        dead!
Nought *could* be done—nought could
        be said;
So—my Lord Tomnoddy went home
        to bed!
        Ib. Hon. Mr. Sucklethumbkin's
        Story

11 The Jackdaw sat on the Cardinal's
        chair!
Bishop, and abbot, and prior were
        there;
    Many a monk, and many a friar,
    Many a knight, and many a squire,
With a great many more of lesser
        degree,—
In sooth a goodly company;
And they served the Lord Primate on
        bended knee.
            Never, I ween,
            Was a prouder seen,
Read of in books, or dreamt of in
        dreams,
Than the Cardinal Lord Archbishop
        of Rheims!
        Ib. The Jackdaw of Rheims

12 And six little Singing-boys,—dear
        little souls!
In nice clean faces, and nice white
        stoles.   *Ib.*

13 Never was heard such a terrible curse!
    But what gave rise to no little sur-
        prise,
Nobody seem'd one penny the worse!
                            Ib.

14 Heedless of grammar, they all cried,
    'That's him!'   *Ib.*

15   A German,
Who smoked like a chimney.
                    Ib. Lay of St. Odille

16 So put that in your pipe, my Lord
    Otto, and smoke it!   *Ib.*

1 'Twas in Margate last July, I walk'd
    upon the pier,
  I saw a little vulgar Boy—I said,
    'What make you here?'
      The Ingoldsby Legends. Mis-
      adventures at Margate

2 He had no little handkerchief to wipe
  his little nose!   *Ib.*

3 But when the Crier cried, 'O Yes!' the
  people cried, 'O No!'   *Ib.*

4 He smiled and said, 'Sir, does your
  mother know that you are out?'   *Ib.*

5 They were a little less than 'kin', and
  rather more than 'kind'.
                           Ib. Nell Cook

SABINE BARING-GOULD
                           1834-1924

6 Now the day is over,
    Night is drawing nigh,
  Shadows of the evening
    Steal across the sky.
      Hymns Ancient and Modern.
      Now the Day is Over

7 Onward, Christian soldiers,
    Marching as to war,
  With the Cross of Jesus
    Going on before.
      Ib. Onward, Christian Soldiers

8 Through the night of doubt and sorrow
  Onward goes the pilgrim band,
  Singing songs of expectation,
  Marching to the Promised Land.
      Ib. Tr. from the Danish of B. S.
      Ingemann, 1789–1862. Through
      the Night of Doubt and Sorrow

9 Brother clasps the hand of brother,
  Stepping fearless through the night.
                                    Ib.

WILLIAM BARNES 1801–1886

10 An' there vor me the apple tree
   Do lean down low in Linden Lea.
      My Orcha'd in Linden Lea

11 Since I noo mwore do zee your feäce.
      The Wife A-Lost

RICHARD BARNFIELD 1574–1627

12 As it fell upon a day,
   In the merry month of May,
   Sitting in a pleasant shade,
   Which a grove of myrtles made,
   Beasts did leap and birds did sing,
   Trees did grow and plants did spring,
   Everything did banish moan,
   Save the nightingale alone.
   She, poor bird, as all forlorn,
   Lean'd her breast up-till a thorn,
   And there sung the dolefull'st ditty
   That to hear it was great pity.
   Fie, fie, fie, now would she cry;
   Tereu, Tereu, by and by.
      Poems: in Divers Humors, An Ode

13 King Pandion, he is dead,
   All thy friends are lapp'd in lead.
      Poems: in Divers Humors, An Ode

PHINEAS T. BARNUM 1810–1891

14 There's a sucker born every minute.
                                    Attr.

SIR JAMES MATTHEW BARRIE
                           1860–1937

15 His lordship may compel us to be
   equal upstairs, but there will never be
   equality in the servants' hall.
      The Admirable Crichton, Act I

16 I don't want to be a might-have-been!
      Dear Brutus, Act II

17 Never ascribe to an opponent motives
   meaner than your own.
      'Courage', Rectorial Address, St.
      Andrews, 3 May 1922

18 Courage is the thing. All goes if
   courage goes.   *Ib.*

19 When the first baby laughed for the
   first time, the laugh broke into a
   thousand pieces and they all went
   skipping about, and that was the
   beginning of fairies. *Peter Pan, Act I*

20 Every time a child says 'I don't believe
   in fairies' there is a little fairy somewhere that falls down dead.   *Ib.*

21 To die will be an awfully big adven-
   ture.   *Ib. Act III*

22 Do you believe in fairies? . . . If you
   believe, clap your hands! *Ib. Act IV*

23 The Twelve-pound Look.
                           Title of Play

24 It's a sort of bloom on a woman. If
   you have it [charm], you don't need
   to have anything else; and if you
   don't have it, it doesn't much matter
   what else you have.
      What Every Woman Knows, Act I

25 There are few more impressive sights
   in the world than a Scotsman on the
   make.   *Ib. Act II*

GEORGE BARRINGTON b. 1755

26 True patriots we; for be it understood,
   We left our country for our country's
   good.
      Prologue for the opening of the
      Playhouse, Sydney, New South
      Wales, 16 Jan. 1796. The com-
      pany was composed of convicts.

EDGAR BATEMAN
                           nineteenth century

27 Wiv a ladder and some glasses,
   You could see to 'Ackney Marshes,
   If it wasn't for the 'ouses in between.
      If it wasn't for the 'ouses in
      between

RICHARD BAXTER 1615–1691

1 I preach'd as never sure to preach
again,
And as a dying man to dying men!
*Love Breathing Thanks and
Praise*, pt. ii

2 In necessary things, unity; in doubt-
ful things, liberty; in all things,
charity.   *Motto*

THOMAS HAYNES BAYLY
1797–1839

3 Absence makes the heart grow fonder,
Isle of Beauty, Fare thee well!
Isle of Beauty (see 3:6)

4 The mistletoe hung in the castle hall,
The holly branch shone on the old oak
wall.   *The Mistletoe Bough*

5 She wore a wreath of roses,
The night that first we met.
She Wore a Wreath of Roses

6 Gaily the Troubadour
Touch'd his guitar.
Welcome Me Home

PIERRE-AUGUSTIN DE
BEAUMARCHAIS 1732–1799

7 Je me presse de rire de tout, de peur
d'être obligé d'en pleurer.

I make myself laugh at everything,
for fear of having to weep.
Le Barbier de Séville, I. ii

8 Parce que vous êtes un grand seigneur,
vous vous croyez un grand génie! . . .
Vous vous êtes donné la peine de
naître, et rien de plus.

Because you are a great lord, you
believe yourself to be a great
genius! . . . You took the trouble
to be born, but no more.
Mariage de Figaro, v. iii

FRANCIS BEAUMONT 1584–1616

9 What things have we seen,
Done at the Mermaid! heard words
that have been
So nimble, and so full of subtil flame,
As if that every one from whence they
came,
Had meant to put his whole wit in
a jest,
And had resolv'd to live a fool, the rest
Of his dull life.   *Letter to Ben Jonson*

FRANCIS BEAUMONT 1584–1616
and
JOHN FLETCHER 1579–1625

10 You are no better than you should be.
The Coxcomb, IV. iii

11 I care not two-pence.   *Ib.* v. i

12 It is always good
When a man has two irons in the fire.
The Faithful Friends, I. ii

13 Let's meet, and either do, or die.
The Island Princess, II. ii

14 Deeds, not words shall speak me.
The Lovers' Progress, III. vi

15 I find the medicine worse than the
malady.   *Ib.* ii

16 Faith, Sir, he went away with a flea
in 's ear.   *Ib.* IV. iii

17 I'll put on my considering cap.
The Loyal Subject, II. i

18 I'll put a spoke among your wheels.
The Mad Lover, III. vi

19 Those have most power to hurt us that
we love.   *The Maid's Tragedy*, V. iv

20 All your better deeds
Shall be in water writ, but this in
marble.   *The Nice Valour*, V. iii

21 'Tis virtue, and not birth that makes
us noble.
Great actions speak great minds, and
such should govern.
The Prophetess, II. iii

22 I'll have a fling.
Rule a Wife and have a Wife,
III. v

23 Kiss till the cow comes home.
Scornful Lady, II. ii

24 Daisies smell-less, yet most quaint.
Two Noble Kinsmen, I. i

25 Though I say't, that should not say't.
Wit at Several Weapons, II. ii

26 Whistle and she'll come to you.
Wit Without Money, IV. iv

27 Let the world slide.   *Ib.* v. ii

LORD BEAVERBROOK 1879–1964

28 Responsible for this work of development were 'the boys in the back
rooms' who 'do not sit in the lime-
light, but are the men who do the
work'.
Glasgow Herald 24 March 1941,
p. 6, col. 4 (report of broadcast
by Lord Beaverbrook)

CARL BECKER 1873–1945

29 Twice tricked by the British into a
European war in order to pull their
chestnuts out of the fire.
Progress and Power (1935)

THOMAS BECON 1512–1567

30 For when the wine is in, the wit is out.
Catechism, 375

THOMAS LOVELL BEDDOES
1798–1851

1 If there were dreams to sell,
  What would you buy?
Some cost a passing bell;
  Some a light sigh,
That shakes from Life's fresh crown
  Only a roseleaf down.
If there were dreams to sell,
  Merry and sad to tell,
And the crier rung the bell,
  What would you buy?
                    Dream-Pedlary

BEDE 673–735

2 'Such,' he said, 'O King, seems to me
the present life of men on earth, in
comparison with that time which to us
is uncertain, as if when on a winter's
night you sit feasting with your ealdor-
men and thegns,—a single sparrow
should fly swiftly into the hall, and
coming in at one door, instantly fly
out through another. In that time in
which it is indoors it is indeed not
touched by the fury of the winter, but
yet, this smallest space of calmness
being passed almost in a flash, from
winter going into winter again, it is
lost to your eyes. Somewhat like this
appears the life of man; but of what
follows or what went before, we are
utterly ignorant.'
        Ecclesiastical History, bk. ii, ch. 13

BERNARD ELLIOTT BEE
1823–1861

3 Let us determine to die here, and we
will conquer. There is Jackson standing like a stone wall. Rally behind the
Virginians.
        First Battle of Bull Run, 1861.
        Poore, *Reminiscences of Metro-*
        polis, ii. 85.

HENRY CHARLES BEECHING
1859–1919

4 With lifted feet, hands still,
I am poised, and down the hill
Dart, with heedful mind;
The air goes by in a wind.
        Going Down Hill on a Bicycle

5 First come I; my name is Jowett.
There's no knowledge but I know it.
I am Master of this college:
What I don't know isn't knowledge.
        The Masque of Balliol, composed
        by and current among members of
        Balliol College in the late 1870's
        (see also 6:9, 219:19 and 20)

SIR MAX BEERBOHM 1872–1956

6 Most women are not so young as they
are painted.   *A Defence of Cosmetics*

7 To give an accurate and exhaustive
account of that period would need a
far less brilliant pen than mine.   *1880*

8 Not that I had any special reason for
hating school. Strange as it may seem
to my reader, I was not unpopular
there. I was a modest, good-humoured
boy. It was Oxford that has made me
insufferable.   *Going back to School*

9 The Nonconformist Conscience makes
cowards of us all.
        King George the Fourth

10 'Ah, say that again,' she murmured.
'Your voice is music.'
  He repeated his question.
  'Music!' she said dreamily; and such
is the force of habit that 'I don't', she
added, 'know anything about music,
really. But I know what I like.'
        Zuleika Dobson, ch. 16

APHRA BEHN 1640–1689

11 Faith, Sir, we are here to-day, and
gone to-morrow.
        The Lucky Chance, IV

12 Beauty unadorn'd.
        The Rover, Part II, IV. ii

W. H. BELLAMY *nineteenth century*

13 Old Simon the Cellarer keeps a rare
  store
Of Malmsey and Malvoisie.
        Song: Simon the Cellarer

JOACHIM DU BELLAY 1515–1560

14 France, mère des arts, des armes et
des loix.
  France, mother of arts, of warriors,
    and of laws.   *Sonnets*

15 Heureux qui comme Ulysse a fait un
beau voyage.
  Happy the wanderer, like Ulysses,
    who has come happily home at
    last.   *Ib.*

HILAIRE BELLOC 1870–1953

16 Your little hands were made to take
The better things and leave the worse
  ones:
They also may be used to shake
The massive paws of elder persons.
        Bad Child's Book of Beasts, dedi-
        cation

17 When people call this beast to mind,
They marvel more and more
At such a little tail behind,
So large a trunk before.
        Ib. The Elephant

18 I shoot the Hippopotamus
With bullets made of platinum,
Because if I use leaden ones
His hide is sure to flatten 'em.
        Ib. The Hippopotamus

1 The nicest child I ever knew
Was Charles Augustus Fortescue.
Cautionary Tales. Charles Augustus Fortescue

2 Godolphin Horne was nobly born;
He held the human race in scorn.
Ib. Godolphin Horne

3 The chief defect of Henry King
Was chewing little bits of string,
Ib. Henry King

4 'Oh, my friends, be warned by me,
That breakfast, dinner, lunch, and tea
Are all the human frame requires . . .'
With that, the wretched child expires.
Ib.

5 Lord Lundy from his earliest years
Was far too freely moved to tears.
Ib. Lord Lundy

6 Towards the age of twenty-six,
They shoved him into politics.   *Ib.*

7 We had intended you to be
The next Prime Minister but three:
The stocks were sold; the Press was
squared;
The Middle Class was quite prepared.
But as it is! . . . My language fails!
Go out and govern New South Wales!
Ib.

8 Matilda told such Dreadful Lies,
It made one Gasp and Stretch one's
Eyes;
Her Aunt, who, from her Earliest
Youth,
Had kept a Strict Regard for Truth,
Attempted to Believe Matilda:
The effort very nearly killed her.
Ib. Matilda

9 For every time she shouted 'Fire!'
They only answered 'Little liar!'   *Ib.*

10 It happened that a few Weeks later
Her Aunt was off to the Theatre
To see that Interesting Play
The Second Mrs. Tanqueray.   *Ib.*

11 She was not really bad at heart,
But only rather rude and wild;
She was an aggravating child.
Ib. Rebecca

12 From quiet homes and first beginning,
Out to the undiscovered ends,
There's nothing worth the wear of
winning,
But laughter and the love of friends.
Dedicatory Ode

13 The moon on the one hand, the dawn
on the other:
The moon is my sister, the dawn is my
brother.
The moon on my left and the dawn
on my right.
My brother, good morning: my sister,
good night.   *The Early Morning*

14 They died to save their country and
they only saved the world.
The English Graves

15 When I am dead, I hope it may be
said:
'His sins were scarlet, but his books
were read.'   *Epigrams. On his Books*

16 Of this bad world the loveliest and the
best
Has smiled and said 'Good Night,'
and gone to rest.
Ib. On a Dead Hostess

17 I said to Heart, 'How goes it?' Heart
replied:
'Right as a Ribstone Pippin!' But it
lied.   *Ib. The False Heart*

18 The accursed power which stands on
Privilege
(And goes with Women, and Cham-
pagne, and Bridge)
Broke—and Democracy resumed her
reign:
(Which goes with Bridge, and Women
and Champagne).
Ib. On a Great Election

19 The Devil, having nothing else to do,
Went off to tempt my Lady Poltagrue.
My Lady, tempted by a private whim,
To his extreme annoyance, tempted
him.
*Ib. On Lady Poltagrue, a Public
Peril*

20 Remote and ineffectual Don
That dared attack my Chesterton.
Lines to a Don

21 Don different from those regal Dons!
With hearts of gold and lungs of
bronze,
Who shout and bang and roar and
bawl
The Absolute across the hall,
Or sail in amply billowing gown.
Enormous through the Sacred Town.
Ib.

22 The Llama is a woolly sort of fleecy
hairy goat,
With an indolent expression and an
undulating throat
Like an unsuccessful literary man.
*More Beasts for Worse Children.
The Llama*

23 I had an aunt in Yucatan
Who bought a Python from a man
And kept it for a pet.
She died, because she never knew
These simple little rules and few;—
The Snake is living yet.
Ib. The Python

24 When I am living in the Midlands
That are sodden and unkind

the great hills of the South Country
Come back into my mind.
The South Country

1 If I ever become a rich man,
　Or if ever I grow to be old,
I will build a house with deep thatch
　To shelter me from the cold,
And there shall the Sussex songs be
　　sung
And the story of Sussex told.
I will hold my house in the high wood
　Within a walk of the sea,
And the men that were boys when I
　was a boy
Shall sit and drink with me.
The South Country

2 Do you remember an Inn,
　Miranda? *Tarantella*

3 The fleas that tease in the high Pyre-
　nees. *Ib.*

JULIEN BENDA 1868–1956

4 La trahison des clercs.

　The treason of the educated classes.
Attr.

ENOCH ARNOLD BENNETT
1867–1931

5 Journalists say a thing that they know
isn't true, in the hope that if they keep
on saying it long enough it *will* be
true. *The Title*, Act II

S. R. BENNETT 1836–1898

6 In the sweet by-and-by,
　We shall meet on that beautiful shore.
*Sacred Songs and Solos. Sweet
By-and-By*

ARTHUR CHRISTOPHER
BENSON 1862–1925

7 Land of Hope and Glory, Mother of
　the Free,
How shall we extol thee, who are born
　of thee?
Wider still and wider shall thy bounds
　be set;
God who made thee mighty, make
　thee mightier yet.
Song from Pomp and Circumstance *by* Elgar, op. 39, No. 1

JEREMY BENTHAM 1748–1832

8 The greatest happiness of the greatest
number is the foundation of morals
and legislation. (*see 112:10*)
The Commonplace Book (Works,
vol. x, p. 142)

EDMUND CLERIHEW BENTLEY
1875–1956

9 The art of Biography
Is different from Geography.
Geography is about maps,
But Biography is about chaps.
Biography for Beginners

10 What I like about Clive
Is that he is no longer alive.
There is a great deal to be said
For being dead.
Biography for Beginners. Clive

11 John Stuart Mill
By a mighty effort of will
Overcame his natural bonhomie
And wrote 'Principles of Political
　Economy.' *Ib. John Stuart Mill*

12 Sir Christopher Wren
Said, 'I am going to dine with some
　men.
If anybody calls
Say I am designing St. Paul's.'
Ib. Sir Christopher Wren

13 George the Third
Ought never to have occurred.
One can only wonder
At so grotesque a blunder.
More Biographies. George the Third

THOMAS BENTLEY 1693?–1742

14 No man is demolished but by himself.
A Letter to Mr. Pope, 1735

PIERRE-JEAN DE BÉRANGER
1780–1857

15 Nos amis, les ennemis.

　Our friends, the enemy.
L'Opinion de ces demoiselles

BISHOP GEORGE BERKELEY
1685–1753

16 Westward the course of empire takes
　its way;
The four first acts already past,
A fifth shall close the drama with the
　day:
Time's noblest offspring is the last.
*On the Prospect of Planting Arts
and Learning in America*

IRVING BERLIN 1888–

17 Come on and hear, come on and hear,
Alexander's Ragtime Band.
Alexander's Ragtime Band

WILLIAM BAYLE BERNARD
1807–1875

18 A Storm in a Teacup.
Title of farce (1854)

RICHARD BETHELL, BARON
WESTBURY 1800–1873

19 His Lordship says he will turn it over
in what he is pleased to call his mind.
Nash, *Life of Westbury*, i. 158

THEOBALD VON BETHMANN HOLLWEG 1856–1921

1 Just for a word—'neutrality', a word which in wartime has so often been disregarded, just for a scrap of paper— Great Britain is going to make war.
To Sir Edward Goschen, 4 Aug. 1914. Dispatch by Sir Edward Goschen to the British Foreign Office

JACOB BEULER *nineteenth century*

2 If I had a donkey wot wouldn't go, D'ye think I'd wollop him? no, no, no.
Music Hall Song (c. 1822)

WILLIAM, LORD BEVERIDGE 1879–1963

3 The object of government in peace and in war is not the glory of rulers or of races, but the happiness of the common man. *Social Insurance*

HOLY BIBLE

Old Testament

4 In the beginning God created the heaven and the earth. *Genesis* i. 1

5 And God said, Let there be light: and there was light. *Ib.* 3

6 Fiat lux.
Let there be light. *Ib.* 3 (Vulgate)

7 And God saw that it was good. *Ib.* 10

8 Male and female created he them. *Ib.* 27

9 Be fruitful, and multiply, and replenish the earth. *Ib.* 28

10 But of the tree of the knowledge of good and evil, thou shalt not eat of it: for in the day that thou eatest thereof thou shalt surely die. *Ib.* ii. 17

11 It is not good that the man should be alone; I will make him an help meet for him. *Ib.* 18

12 And the Lord God caused a deep sleep to fall upon Adam, and he slept: and he took one of his ribs, and closed up the flesh instead thereof;
And the rib, which the Lord God had taken from man, made he a woman. *Ib.* 21

13 Bone of my bones, and flesh of my flesh. *Ib.* 23

14 Therefore shall a man leave his father and his mother, and shall cleave unto his wife: and they shall be one flesh. *Ib.* 24

15 And they sewed fig leaves together, and made themselves aprons [breeches in *Genevan Bible*, 1560].
And they heard the voice of the Lord God walking in the garden in the cool of the day. *Genesis* iii. 7

16 In the sweat of thy face shalt thou eat bread. *Ib.* 19

17 For dust thou art, and unto dust shalt thou return. *Ib.*

18 Am I my brother's keeper? *Ib.* iv. 9

19 Dwelt in the land of Nod. *Ib.* 16

20 And Noah begat Shem, Ham, and Japheth. *Ib.* v. 32

21 There were giants in the earth in those days. *Ib.* vi. 4

22 Whoso sheddeth man's blood, by man shall his blood be shed. *Ib.* ix. 6

23 I do set my bow in the cloud. *Ib.* 13

24 Even as Nimrod the mighty hunter before the Lord. *Ib.* x. 9

25 His hand will be against every man, and every man's hand against him. *Ib.* xvi. 12

26 But his wife looked back from behind him, and she became a pillar of salt. *Ib.* xix. 26

27 And he sold his birthright unto Jacob. *Ib.* xxv. 33

28 Behold, Esau my brother is a hairy man, and I am a smooth man. *Ib.* xxvii. 11

29 And he [Jacob] dreamed, and behold a ladder set up on the earth, and the top of it reached to heaven: and behold the angels of God ascending and descending on it. *Ib.* xxviii. 12

30 And Jacob served seven years for Rachel; and they seemed unto him but a few days, for the love he had to her. *Ib.* xxix. 20

31 Mizpah; for he said, The Lord watch between me and thee, when we are absent one from another. *Ib.* xxxi

32 Now Israel loved Joseph more than all his children, because he was the son of his old age; and he made him a coat of many colours. *Ib.* xxxvii. 3

33 Behold, this dreamer cometh. *Ib.* 19

34 Jacob saw that there was corn in Egypt. *Ib.* xlii. 1

35 Bring down my gray hairs with sorrow to the grave. *Ib.* 38

36 Ye shall eat the fat of the land. *Ib.* xlv. 18

37 I have been a stranger in a strange land. *Exodus* ii. 22

38 Behold, the bush burned with fire, and the bush was not consumed. *Ib.* iii. 2

1 Put off thy shoes from off thy feet,
for the place whereon thou standest
is holy ground.   *Exodus* iii. 5

2 A land flowing with milk and honey;
unto the place of the Canaanites, and
the Hittites, and the Amorites, and
the Perizzites, and the Hivites, and
the Jebusites.   *Ib.* 8

3 I AM THAT I AM.   *Ib.* 14

4 Darkness which may be felt.
                          Ib. x. 21

5 With your loins girded, your shoes on
your feet, and your staff in your hand;
and ye shall eat it in haste; it is the
Lord's passover.   *Ib.* xii. 11

6 Would to God we had died by the
hand of the Lord in the land of
Egypt, when we sat by the flesh pots,
and when we did eat bread to the full.
                          Ib. xvi. 3

7 Life for life,
Eye for eye, tooth for tooth, hand for
hand, foot for foot,
Burning for burning, wound for
wound, stripe for stripe.   *Ib.* xxi. 23

8 A stiffnecked people.   *Ib.* xxxiii. 3

9 Joshua the son of Nun.   *Ib.* 11

10 There shall no man see me, and live.
                          Ib. 20

11 Let him go for a scapegoat into the
wilderness.   *Leviticus* xvi. 10

12 Thou shalt love thy neighbour as thyself.   *Ib.* xix. 18; *St. Matthew* xix. 19

13 The Lord bless thee, and keep thee:
The Lord make his face shine upon
thee, and be gracious unto thee:
The Lord lift up his countenance upon
thee, and give thee peace.
                          Numbers vi. 24

14 Sent to spy out the land.   *Ib.* xiii. 16

15 Smote him with the edge of the sword.
                          Ib. xxi. 24

16 Be sure your sin will find you out.
                          Ib. xxxii. 23

17 Man doth not live by bread only, but
by every word that proceedeth out of
the mouth of the Lord doth man live.
                      Deuteronomy viii. 3

18 A dreamer of dreams.   *Ib.* xiii. 1

19 The wife of thy bosom.   *Ib.* 6

20 Thou shalt not muzzle the ox when
he treadeth out the corn.   *Ib.* xxv. 4

21 Cursed be he that removeth his
neighbour's landmark.   *Ib.* xxvii. 17

22 In the waste howling wilderness.
                          Ib. xxxii. 10

23 Jeshurun waxed fat, and kicked.
                          Ib. 15

24 As thy days, so shall thy strength be.
                      Deuteronomy xxxiii. 25

25 The eternal God is thy refuge, and
underneath are the everlasting arms.
                          Ib. 27

26 Be strong and of a good courage; be
not afraid, neither be thou dismayed:
for the Lord thy God is with thee,
whithersoever thou goest.   *Joshua* i. 9

27 Hewers of wood and drawers of water.
                          Ib. ix. 21

28 The stars in their courses fought
against Sisera.   *Judges* v. 20

29 She brought forth butter in a lordly
dish.   *Ib.* 25

30 Faint, yet pursuing.   *Ib.* viii. 4

31 Out of the eater came forth meat, and
out of the strong came forth sweetness.
                          Ib. xiv. 14

32 He smote them hip and thigh.
                          Ib. xv. 8

33 From Dan even to Beer-sheba.
                          Ib. xx. 1

34 The people arose as one man.   *Ib.* 8

35 Intreat me not to leave thee, or to
return from following after thee: for
whither thou goest, I will go; and
where thou lodgest, I will lodge: thy
people shall be my people, and thy
God my God: *Ruth* i. 16

36 The flower of their age.
                      1 Samuel ii. 33

37 Speak, Lord; for thy servant heareth.
                          Ib. iii. 9

38 Quit yourselves like men.   *Ib.* iv. 9

39 I-chabod, saying, The glory is departed from Israel.   *Ib.* 21

40 God save the king.   *Ib.* x. 24

41 A man after his own heart.
                          Ib. xiii. 14

42 Agag came unto him delicately. And
Agag said, Surely the bitterness of
death is past.   *Ib.* xv. 32

43 Now he was ruddy, and withal of a
beautiful countenance, and goodly to
look to.   *Ib.* xvi. 12

44 Go, and the Lord be with thee.
                          Ib. xvii. 37

45 Saul hath slain his thousands, and
David his ten thousands.   *Ib.* xviii. 7

46 I have played the fool.   *Ib.* xxvi. 21

47 The beauty of Israel is slain upon thy
high places: how are the mighty fallen!
Tell it not in Gath, publish it not in
the streets of Askelon.   *2 Samuel* i. 19

48 Saul and Jonathan were lovely and
pleasant in their lives, and in their
death they were not divided: they

1 were swifter than eagles, they were stronger than lions. *2 Samuel* i. 23

1 How are the mighty fallen in the midst of the battle! O Jonathan, thou wast slain in thine high places.
I am distressed for thee, my brother Jonathan: very pleasant hast thou been unto me: thy love to me was wonderful, passing the love of women. How are the mighty fallen, and the weapons of war perished! *Ib.* 25

2 Smote him under the fifth rib.
Ib. ii. 23

3 The poor man had nothing, save one little ewe lamb. *Ib.* xii. 3

4 Would God I had died for thee, O Absalom, my son, my son!
Ib. xviii. 33

5 The sweet psalmist of Israel.
Ib. xxiii. 1

6 Went in jeopardy of their lives. *Ib.* 17

7 A proverb and a byword among all people. *1 Kings* ix. 7

8 Behold, the half was not told me.
Ib. x. 7

9 Ivory, and apes, and peacocks. *Ib.* 22

10 My father hath chastised you with whips, but I will chastise you with scorpions. *Ib.* xii. 11

11 He slept with his fathers. *Ib.* xiv. 20

12 There ariseth a little cloud out of the sea, like a man's hand. *Ib.* xviii. 44

13 Sat down under a juniper tree.
Ib. xix. 4

14 But the Lord was not in the wind: and after the wind an earthquake; but the Lord was not in the earthquake:
And after the earthquake a fire: but the Lord was not in the fire: and after the fire a still small voice. *Ib.* 11

15 Elijah passed by him, and cast his mantle upon him. *Ib.* 19

16 Feed him with bread of affliction and with water of affliction, until I come in peace. *Ib.* xxii. 27

17 And a certain man drew a bow at a venture, and smote the king of Israel between the joints of the harness.
Ib. 34

18 I bow myself in the house of Rimmon.
2 Kings v. 18

19 Is thy servant a dog, that he should do this great thing? *Ib.* viii. 13

20 The driving is like the driving of Jehu, the son of Nimshi; for he driveth furiously. *Ib.* ix. 20

21 She painted her face, and tired her head, and looked out at a window.
Ib. 30

22 Thou trustest upon the staff of this bruised reed, even upon Egypt, on which if a man lean, it will go into his hand, and pierce it. *2 Kings* xviii. 21

23 He died in a good old age, full of days, riches, and honour.
1 Chronicles xxix. 28

24 And the Lord said unto Satan, Whence comest thou? Then Satan answered the Lord, and said, From going to and fro in the earth, and from walking up and down in it. *Job* i. 7

25 Doth Job fear God for naught? *Ib.* 9

26 The Lord gave, and the Lord hath taken away; blessed be the name of the Lord. *Ib.* 21

27 Curse God, and die. *Ib.* ii. 9

28 There the wicked cease from troubling, and there the weary be at rest.
Ib. iii. 17

29 Man is born unto trouble, as the sparks fly upward. *Ib.* v. 7

30 Canst thou by searching find out God?
Ib. xi. 7

31 Man that is born of a woman is of few days, and full of trouble. *Ib.* xiv. 1

32 Miserable comforters are ye all.
Ib. xvi. 2

33 I am escaped with the skin of my teeth. *Ib.* xix. 20

34 Oh that my words were now written! oh that they were printed in a book!
Ib. 23

35 I know that my redeemer liveth, and that he shall stand at the latter day upon the earth. *Ib.* 25

36 Seeing the root of the matter is found in me. *Ib.* 28

37 The price of wisdom is above rubies.
Ib. xxviii. 18

38 My desire is . . . that mine adversary had written a book. *Ib.* xxxi. 35

39 Who is this that darkeneth counsel by words without knowledge?
Ib. xxxviii. 2

40 Gird up now thy loins like a man. *Ib.* 3

41 Where wast thou when I laid the foundations of the earth? *Ib.* 4

42 When the morning stars sang together, and all the sons of God shouted for joy. *Ib.* 7

43 Canst thou bind the sweet influences of Pleiades, or loose the bands of Orion? *Ib.* 31

44 He saith among the trumpets, Ha, ha; and he smelleth the battle afar off, the thunder of the captains, and the shouting. *Ib.* xxxix. 25

1 Behold now behemoth, which I made with thee; he eateth grass as an ox.
Job xl. 15

2 Canst thou draw out leviathan with an hook?   *Ib.* xli. 1

3 Dominus illuminatio mea.
The Lord is my light.
Psalms xxvii. 1 (Vulgate)

4 Nisi dominus frustra.
Except the Lord keep the city the watchman waketh but in vain.
Ib. cxxvii. 1 (Vulgate) abridged
(*Motto of the City of Edinburgh*)

For psalms in the Book of Common Prayer see Prayer Book

5 Surely in vain the net is spread in the sight of any bird.   *Proverbs* i. 17

6 Length of days is in her right hand; and in her left hand riches and honour.
Ib. iii. 16

7 Her ways are ways of pleasantness, and all her paths are peace.   *Ib.* 17

8 Go to the ant, thou sluggard; consider her ways, and be wise.   *Ib.* vi. 6

9 Yet a little sleep, a little slumber, a little folding of the hands to sleep.
Ib. 10

10 As an ox goeth to the slaughter.
Ib. vii. 22

11 Stolen waters are sweet, and bread eaten in secret is pleasant.   *Ib.* ix. 17

12 In the multitude of counsellors there is safety.   *Ib.* xi. 14

13 Hope deferred maketh the heart sick.
Ib. xiii. 12

14 The way of transgressors is hard.
Ib. 15

15 He that spareth his rod hateth his son.
Ib. 24

16 A soft answer turneth away wrath.
Ib. xv. 1

17 A merry heart maketh a cheerful countenance.   *Ib.* 13

18 Better is a dinner of herbs where love is, than a stalled ox and hatred therewith.   *Ib.* 17

19 A word spoken in due season, how good is it!   *Ib.* 23

20 Pride goeth before destruction, and an haughty spirit before a fall.
Ib. xvi. 18

21 There is a friend that sticketh closer than a brother.   *Ib.* xviii. 24

22 Train up a child in the way he should go: and when he is old, he will not depart from it.   *Ib.* xxii. 6

23 Look not thou upon the wine when it is red, when it giveth his colour in the cup.   *Proverbs* xxiii. 31

24 Heap coals of fire upon his head.
Ib. xxv. 22

25 As cold waters to a thirsty soul, so is good news from a far country.   *Ib.* 25

26 Answer a fool according to his folly.
Ib. xxvi. 5

27 As a dog returneth to his vomit, so a fool returneth to his folly.   *Ib.* 11

28 Boast not thyself of to morrow; for thou knowest not what a day may bring forth.   *Ib.* xxvii. 1

29 The wicked flee when no man pursueth: but the righteous are bold as a lion.   *Ib.* xxviii. 1

30 Where there is no vision, the people perish.   *Ib.* xxix. 18

31 The way of an eagle in the air; the way of a serpent upon a rock; the way of a ship in the midst of the sea; and the way of a man with a maid.   *Ib.* xxx. 19

32 Who can find a virtuous woman? for her price is far above rubies.
Ib. xxxi. 10

33 Her children arise up, and call her blessed.   *Ib.* 28

34 Vanity of vanities, saith the Preacher, vanity of vanities; all is vanity.
What profit hath a man of all his labour which he taketh under the sun? One generation passeth away, and another generation cometh.
Ecclesiastes i. 2

35 The thing that hath been, it is that which shall be; and that which is done is that which shall be done: and there is no new thing under the sun.   *Ib.* 8

36 All is vanity and vexation of spirit.
Ib. 14

37 He that increaseth knowledge increaseth sorrow.   *Ib.* 18

38 To every thing there is a season, and a time to every purpose under the heaven:
A time to be born, and a time to die.
Ib. iii. 1

39 As the crackling of thorns under a pot, so is the laughter of a fool.   *Ib.* vii. 6

40 Be not righteous over much.   *Ib.* 16

41 God hath made man upright; but they have sought out many inventions.
Ib. 29

42 There is no discharge in that war.
Ib. viii. 8

43 A man hath no better thing under the sun, than to eat, and to drink, and to be merry.   *Ib.* 15

1 A living dog is better than a dead lion.
Ecclesiastes ix. 4

2 Whatsoever thy hand findeth to do, do it with thy might; for there is no work, nor device, nor knowledge, nor wisdom, in the grave, whither thou goest. *Ib.* 10

3 The race is not to the swift, nor the battle to the strong. *Ib.* 11

4 He that diggeth a pit shall fall into it. *Ib.* x. 8

5 Cast thy bread upon the waters: for thou shalt find it after many days. *Ib.* xi. 1

6 In the place where the tree falleth, there it shall be. *Ib.* 3

7 Remember now thy Creator in the days of thy youth, while the evil days come not, nor the years draw nigh, when thou shalt say, I have no pleasure in them; *Ib.* xii. 1

8 Or ever the silver cord be loosed, or the golden bowl be broken, or the pitcher be broken at the fountain, or the wheel broken at the cistern.
Then shall the dust return to the earth as it was: and the spirit shall return unto God who gave it. *Ib.* xii. 6

9 Of making many books there is no end; and much study is a weariness of the flesh. *Ib.* 12

10 Fear God, and keep his commandments: for this is the whole duty of man. *Ib.* 13

11 The song of songs, which is Solomon's. *The Song of Solomon* i. 1

12 I am black, but comely, O ye daughters of Jerusalem, as the tents of Kedar, as the curtains of Solomon. *Ib.* 5

13 I am the rose of Sharon, and the lily of the valleys. *Ib.* ii. 1

14 His banner over me was love. *Ib.* 4

15 Stay me with flagons, comfort me with apples: for I am sick of love.
His left hand is under my head, and his right hand doth embrace me. *Ib.* 5

16 Rise up, my love, my fair one, and come away.
For, lo, the winter is past, the rain is over and gone;
The flowers appear on the earth; the time of the singing of birds is come, and the voice of the turtle is heard in our land. *Ib.* 10

17 Take us the foxes, the little foxes, that spoil the vines. *Ib.* 15

18 My beloved is mine, and I am his: he feedeth among the lilies.
Until the day break, and the shadows flee away. *Ib.* 16

19 Who is she that looketh forth as the morning, fair as the moon, clear as the sun, and terrible as an army with banners. *The Song of Solomon* vi. 10

20 Many waters cannot quench love, neither can the floods drown it: if a man would give all the substance of his house for love, it would utterly be contemned. *Ib.* viii. 7

21 Though your sins be as scarlet, they shall be as white as snow. *Isaiah* i. 18

22 They shall beat their swords into plowshares, and their spears into pruninghooks: nation shall not lift up sword against nation, neither shall they learn war any more. *Ib.* ii. 4

23 Grind the faces of the poor. *Ib.* iii. 15

24 My wellbeloved hath a vineyard in a very fruitful hill. *Ib.* v. i

25 Woe unto them that join house to house, that lay field to field, till there be no place. *Ib.* 8

26 Woe unto them that call evil good, and good evil. *Ib.* 20

27 In the year that king Uzziah died I saw also the Lord sitting upon a throne, high and lifted up, and his train filled the temple.
Above it stood the seraphims: each one had six wings; with twain he covered his face, and with twain he covered his feet, and with twain he did fly.
And one cried unto another, and said, Holy, holy, holy, is the Lord of hosts: the whole earth is full of his glory.
And the posts of the door moved at the voice of him that cried, and the house was filled with smoke.
Then said I, Woe is me! for I am undone; because I am a man of unclean lips, and I dwell in the midst of a people of unclean lips. *Ib.* vi. 1

28 Whom shall I send, and who will go for us? Then said I, Here am I; send me. *Ib.* 8

29 Then said I, Lord, how long? *Ib.* 11

30 Behold, a virgin shall conceive, and bear a son, and shall call his name Immanuel. *Ib.* vii. 14

31 The people that walked in darkness have seen a great light; they that dwell in the land of the shadow of death, upon them hath the light shined. *Ib.* ix. 2

32 For unto us a child is born, unto us a son is given: and the government shall be upon his shoulder: and his name shall be called Wonderful, Counsellor, The mighty God, The everlasting Father, The Prince of Peace.
Of the increase of his government and peace there shall be no end. *Ib.* 6

1 And there shall come forth a rod out
of the stem of Jesse, and a Branch
shall grow out of his roots:
And the spirit of the Lord shall rest
upon him, the spirit of wisdom and
understanding, the spirit of counsel
and might, the spirit of knowledge and
of the fear of the Lord.   *Isaiah* xi. 1

2 The wolf also shall dwell with the
lamb, and the leopard shall lie down
with the kid; and the calf and the
young lion and the fatling together;
and a little child shall lead them.
Ib. 6

3 for the earth shall be full of the knowledge of the Lord, as the waters cover
the sea.   *Ib.* 9

4 How art thou fallen from heaven, O
Lucifer, son of the morning!
Ib. xiv. 12

5 Watchman, what of the night?
Watchman, what of the night?
The watchman said, The morning
cometh, and also the night.
Ib. xxi. 11

6 Let us eat and drink; for to morrow
we shall die.   *Ib.* xxii. 13

7 For precept must be upon precept,
precept upon precept; line upon line,
line upon line; here a little, and there
a little.   *Ib.* xxviii. 10

8 The bread of adversity.   *Ib.* xxx. 20

9 This is the way, walk ye in it. *Ib.* 21
The wilderness and the solitary place
shall be glad for them; and the desert
shall rejoice, and blossom as the rose.
Ib. xxxv. 1

10 Set thine house in order.
Ib. xxxviii. 1

11 Comfort ye, comfort ye my people,
saith your God. Speak ye comfortably
to Jerusalem, and cry unto her, that
her warfare is accomplished. *Ib.* xl. 1

12 The voice of him that crieth in the
wilderness, Prepare ye the way of the
Lord, make straight in the desert a
highway for our God.
Every valley shall be exalted, and
every mountain and hill shall be made
low: and the crooked shall be made
straight, and the rough places plain:
And the glory of the Lord shall be revealed, and all flesh shall see it together: for the mouth of the Lord
hath spoken it.   *Ib.* 3

13 The voice said, Cry. And he said,
What shall I cry? All flesh is grass,
and all the goodliness thereof is as the
flower of the field:
The grass withereth, the flower fadeth:
because the spirit of the Lord bloweth
upon it: surely the people is grass.
Ib. 6

14 He shall feed his flock like a shepherd:
he shall gather the lambs with his arm,
and carry them in his bosom, and shall
gently lead those that are with young.
Isaiah xl. 11

15 But they that wait upon the Lord shall
renew their strength: they shall
mount up with wings as eagles; they
shall run, and not be weary; and they
shall walk, and not faint.
Ib. xlviii. 31

16 A bruised reed shall he not break, and
the smoking flax shall he not quench.
Ib. xlii. 3

17 There is no peace, saith the Lord, unto
the wicked.   *Ib.* 22

18 How beautiful upon the mountains
are the feet of him that bringeth good
tidings, that publisheth peace; that
bringeth good tidings of good, that
publisheth salvation; that saith unto
Zion, Thy God reigneth!   *Ib.* lii. 7

19 For they shall see eye to eye, when the
Lord shall bring again Zion.
Break forth into joy, sing together, ye
waste places of Jerusalem: for the
Lord hath comforted his people, he
hath redeemed Jerusalem.   *Ib.* 8

20 He is despised and rejected of men;
a man of sorrows, and acquainted with
grief: and we hid as it were our faces
from him; he was despised, and we
esteemed him not.
Surely he hath borne our griefs, and
carried our sorrows.   *Ib.* liii. 3

21 But he was wounded for our trans-
gressions, he was bruised for our ini-
quities: the chastisement of our peace
was upon him; and with his stripes we
are healed.
All we like sheep have gone astray; we
have turned every one to his own way;
and the Lord hath laid on him the
iniquity of us all.
He was oppressed, and he was afflicted,
yet he opened not his mouth: he is
brought as a lamb to the slaughter,
and as a sheep before her shearers is
dumb, so he openeth not his mouth.
Ib. 5

22 He was cut off out of the land of the
living.   *Ib.* 8

23 He was numbered with the transgressors.   *Ib.* 12

24 Seek ye the Lord while he may be
found, call ye upon him while he is
near.   *Ib.* lv. 6

25 For my thoughts are not your
thoughts, neither are your ways my
ways, saith the Lord.   *Ib.* 8

26 Peace to him that is far off, and to
him that is near.   *Ib.* lvii. 19

1 Arise, shine; for thy light is come, and the glory of the Lord is risen upon thee.
Isaiah lx. 1

2 To bind up the brokenhearted, to proclaim liberty to the captives, and the opening of the prison to them that are bound;
Ib. lxi. 1

3 For, behold, I create new heavens and a new earth.
Ib. lxv. 17

4 Saying, Peace, peace; when there is no peace.
Jeremiah vi. 14

5 Is there no balm in Gilead?
Ib. viii. 22

6 Can the Ethiopian change his skin, or the leopard his spots?
Ib. xiii. 23

7 The heart is deceitful above all things, and desperately wicked.
Ib. xvii. 9

8 Is it nothing to you, all ye that pass by? behold, and see if there be any sorrow like unto my sorrow.
Lamentations i. 12

9 The wormwood and the gall.
Ib. iii. 19

10 It is good for a man that he bear the yoke in his youth.
Ib. 27

11 As is the mother, so is her daughter.
Ezekiel xvi. 44

12 The fathers have eaten sour grapes, and the children's teeth are set on edge.
Ib. xviii. 2

13 When the wicked man turneth away from his wickedness that he hath committed, and doeth that which is lawful and right, he shall save his soul alive.
Ib. 27

14 The valley which was full of bones.
Ib. xxxvii. 1

15 Can these bones live?
Ib. 3

16 The sound of the cornet, flute, harp, sackbut, psaltery, dulcimer, and all kinds of musick.
Daniel iii. 5

17 Cast into the midst of a burning fiery furnace.
Ib. 6

18 MENE, MENE, TEKEL, UPHARSIN.
This is the interpretation of the thing: MENE; God hath numbered thy kingdom, and finished it.
TEKEL; Thou art weighed in the balances, and art found wanting.
PERES; Thy kingdom is divided, and given to the Medes and Persians.
Ib. v. 25

19 The Ancient of days.
Ib. vii. 9

20 They have sown the wind, and they shall reap the whirlwind.
Hosea viii. 7

21 I will restore to you the years that the locust hath eaten.
Joel ii. 25

22 And it shall come to pass afterward, that I will pour out my spirit upon all flesh; and your sons and your daughters shall prophesy, your old men shall dream dreams, your young men shall see visions.
Joel ii. 28

23 Multitudes in the valley of decision.
Ib. iii. 14

24 A firebrand plucked out of the burning.
Amos iv. 11

25 Come, and let us cast lots, that we may know for whose cause this evil is upon us. So they cast lots, and the lot fell upon Jonah.
Jonah i. 7

26 Jonah was in the belly of the fish three days and three nights.
Ib. 17

27 They shall sit every man under his vine and under his fig tree.
Micah iv. 4

28 But thou, Beth-lehem Ephratah, though thou be little among the thousands of Judah, yet out of thee shall he come forth unto me that is to be ruler in Israel.
Ib. v. 2

29 What doth the Lord require of thee, but to do justly, and to love mercy, and to walk humbly with thy God?
Ib. vi. 8

Apocrypha

30 I shall light a candle of understanding in thine heart, which shall not be put out.
2 Esdras xiv. 25

31 Magna est veritas et praevalet.
Great is Truth, and mighty above all things.
3 Esdras iv. 41 (Vulgate)

32 But the souls of the righteous are in the hand of God, and there shall no torment touch them.
The Wisdom of Solomon iii. 1

33 For though they be punished in the sight of men, yet is their hope full of immortality.
And having been a little chastised, they shall be greatly rewarded: for God proved them, and found them worthy for himself.
Ib. 4

34 And in the time of their visitation they shall shine, and run to and fro like sparks among the stubble.
Ib. 7

35 He that toucheth pitch shall be defiled therewith.
Ecclesiasticus xiii. 1

36 Leave off first for manners' sake.
Ib. xxxi. 17

37 Let us now praise famous men, and our fathers that begat us.
Ib. xliv. 1

38 And some there be, which have no memorial.
Ib. 9

39 When he was at the last gasp.
2 Maccabees vii. 9

New Testament

1 There came wise men from the east to Jerusalem,
Saying, Where is he that is born King of the Jews? for we have seen his star in the east, and are come to worship him. *St. Matthew* ii. 1

2 They presented unto him gifts; gold, and frankincense, and myrrh. *Ib.* 11

3 Repent ye: for the kingdom of heaven is at hand. *Ib.* iii. 2

4 The voice of one crying in the wilderness, Prepare ye the way of the Lord, make his paths straight. *Ib.* 3

5 O generation of vipers, who hath warned you to flee from the wrath to come? *Ib.* 7

6 And now also the axe is laid unto the root of the trees. *Ib.* 10

7 This is my beloved Son, in whom I am well pleased. *Ib.* 17

8 Man shall not live by bread alone, but by every word that proceedeth out of the mouth of God. *Ib.* iv. 4

9 Thou shalt not tempt the Lord thy God. *Ib.* 7

10 Fishers of men. *Ib.* 19

11 Blessed are the poor in spirit: for theirs is the kingdom of heaven.
Blessed are they that mourn: for they shall be comforted.
Blessed are the meek: for they shall inherit the earth.
Blessed are they which do hunger and thirst after righteousness: for they shall be filled.
Blessed are the merciful: for they shall obtain mercy.
Blessed are the pure in heart: for they shall see God.
Blessed are the peacemakers: for they shall be called the children of God. *Ib.* v. 3

12 Ye are the salt of the earth: but if the salt have lost his savour, wherewith shall it be salted? *Ib.* 13

13 Ye are the light of the world. A city that is set on an hill cannot be hid. *Ib.* 14

14 Let your light so shine before men, that they may see your good works. *Ib.* 16

15 Think not that I am come to destroy the law, or the prophets: I am come not to destroy, but to fulfil. *Ib.* 17

16 Till thou hast paid the uttermost farthing. *Ib.* 26

17 Let your communication be, Yea, yea; Nay, nay. *Ib.* 37

18 Resist not evil: but whosoever shall smite thee on thy right cheek, turn to him the other also. *St. Matthew* v. 39

19 He maketh his sun to rise on the evil and on the good, and sendeth rain on the just and on the unjust. *Ib.* 45

20 When thou doest alms, let not thy left hand know what thy right hand doeth. *Ib.* vi. 3

21 Use not vain repetitions, as the heathen do: for they think that they shall be heard for their much speaking. *Ib.* 7

22 After this manner therefore pray ye: Our Father which art in heaven, Hallowed be thy name.
Thy kingdom come. Thy will be done in earth, as it is in heaven.
Give us this day our daily bread.
And forgive us our debts, as we forgive our debtors.
And lead us not into temptation, but deliver us from evil: For thine is the kingdom, and the power, and the glory, for ever. Amen. *Ib.* 9

23 Lay not up for yourselves treasures upon earth, where moth and rust doth corrupt, and where thieves break through and steal. *Ib.* 19

24 Lay up for yourselves treasures in heaven. *Ib.* 20

25 Where your treasure is, there will your heart be also. *Ib.* 21

26 No man can serve two masters. *Ib.* 24

27 Ye cannot serve God and mammon. *Ib.*

28 Consider the lilies of the field, how they grow; they toil not, neither do they spin:
And yet I say unto you, That even Solomon in all his glory was not arrayed like one of these. *Ib.* 28

29 Take therefore no thought for the morrow: for the morrow shall take thought for the things of itself. Sufficient unto the day is the evil thereof. *Ib.* 34

30 Judge not, that ye be not judged. *Ib.* vii. 1

31 Why beholdest thou the mote that is in thy brother's eye, but considerest not the beam that is in thine own eye? *Ib.* 3

32 Neither cast ye your pearls before swine. *Ib.* 6

33 Ask, and it shall be given you; seek, and ye shall find; knock, and it shall be opened unto you. *Ib.* 7

34 Or what man is there of you, whom if his son ask bread, will he give him a stone? *Ib.* 9

1 Wide is the gate, and broad is the way, that leadeth to destruction, and many there be that go in thereat.
St. Matthew vii. 13

2 Strait is the gate, and narrow is the way, which leadeth unto life, and few there be that find it. *Ib.* 14

3 Beware of false prophets, which come to you in sheep's clothing, but inwardly they are ravening wolves.
Ib. 15

4 By their fruits ye shall know them.
Ib. 20

5 I am a man under authority, having soldiers under me: and I say to this man, Go, and he goeth; and to another, Come, and he cometh; and to my servant, Do this, and he doeth it. *Ib.* viii. 9

6 But the children of the kingdom shall be cast out into outer darkness: there shall be weeping and gnashing of teeth.
Ib. 12

7 The foxes have holes, and the birds of the air have nests; but the Son of man hath not where to lay his head.
Ib. 20

8 Let the dead bury their dead. *Ib.* 22

9 Sitting at the receipt of custom.
Ib. ix. 9

10 Why eateth your Master with publicans and sinners? *Ib.* 11

11 Neither do men put new wine into old bottles. *Ib.* 17

12 When ye depart out of that house or city, shake off the dust of your feet.
Ib. x. 14

13 Be ye therefore wise as serpents, and harmless as doves. *Ib.* 16

14 The very hairs of your head are all numbered. *Ib.* 30

15 I came not to send peace, but a sword.
Ib. 34

16 He that findeth his life shall lose it: and he that loseth his life for my sake shall find it. *Ib.* 39

17 Whosoever shall give to drink unto one of these little ones a cup of cold water only in the name of a disciple, verily I say unto you, he shall in no wise lose his reward. *Ib.* 42

18 What went ye out into the wilderness to see? A reed shaken with the wind?
Ib. xi. 3

19 We have piped unto you, and ye have not danced; we have mourned unto you, and ye have not lamented. *Ib.* 17

20 Come unto me, all ye that labour and are heavy laden, and I will give you rest. *Ib.* 28

21 For my yoke is easy, and my burden is light. *St. Matthew* xi. 30

22 He that is not with me is against me.
Ib. xii. 30

23 Empty, swept, and garnished. *Ib.* 44

24 Then goeth he, and taketh with himself seven other spirits more wicked than himself, and they enter in and dwell there: and the last state of that man is worse than the first. *Ib.* 45

25 Some seeds fell by the wayside.
Ib. xiii. 4

26 An enemy hath done this. *Ib.* 28

27 The kingdom of heaven is like to a grain of mustard seed. *Ib.* 31

28 One pearl of great price. *Ib.* 46

29 A prophet is not without honour, save in his own country, and in his own house. *Ib.* 57

30 They be blind leaders of the blind. And if the blind lead the blind, both shall fall into the ditch. *Ib.* xv. 14

31 The dogs eat of the crumbs which fall from their masters' table. *Ib.* 27

32 The signs of the times. *Ib.* xvi. 3

33 Thou art Peter, and upon this rock I will build my church; and the gates of hell shall not prevail against it.
Ib. 18

34 Get thee behind me, Satan. *Ib.* 23

35 What is a man profited, if he shall gain the whole world, and lose his own soul? *Ib.* 26

36 If ye have faith as a grain of mustard seed, ye shall say unto this mountain, Remove hence to yonder place; and it shall remove. *Ib.* xvii. 20

37 Except ye be converted, and become as little children, ye shall not enter into the kingdom of heaven.
Ib. xviii. 3

38 But whoso shall offend one of these little ones which believe in me, it were better for him that a millstone were hanged about his neck, and that he were drowned in the depth of the sea.
Ib. 6

39 If thine eye offend thee, pluck it out, and cast it from thee. *Ib.* 9

40 For where two or three are gathered together in my name, there am I in the midst of them. *Ib.* 20

41 What therefore God hath joined together, let not man put asunder.
Ib. xix. 6

42 Thou shalt love thy neighbour as thyself. *Ib.* 19

1 It is easier for a camel to go through the eye of a needle, than for a rich man to enter into the kingdom of God.
St. Matthew xix. 24

2 With men this is impossible; but with God all things are possible.   *Ib.* 26

3 But many that are first shall be last; and the last shall be first.   *Ib.* 30

4 Borne the burden and heat of the day.
Ib. xx. 12

5 I will give unto this last, even as unto thee.
Is it not lawful for me to do what I will with mine own?   *Ib.* 14

6 For many are called, but few are chosen.   *Ib.* xxii. 14

7 Render therefore unto Cæsar the things which are Cæsar's.   *Ib.* 21

8 Blind guides, which strain at a gnat, and swallow a camel.   *Ib.* xxiii. 24

9 Whited sepulchres, which indeed appear beautiful outward, but are within full of dead men's bones.
Ib. 27

10 Wars and rumours of wars.
Ib. xxiv. 6

11 For nation shall rise against nation, and kingdom against kingdom.   *Ib.* 7

12 Abomination of desolation.   *Ib.* 15

13 Wheresoever the carcase is, there will the eagles be gathered together.
Ib. 28

14 Well done, thou good and faithful servant.   *Ib.* xxv. 21

15 Unto every one that hath shall be given, and he shall have abundance: but from him that hath not shall be taken away even that which he hath.
Ib. 29

16 I was a stranger, and ye took me in: Naked, and ye clothed me: I was sick, and ye visited me: I was in prison, and ye came unto me.   *Ib.* 35

17 Inasmuch as ye have done it unto one of the least of these my brethren, ye have done it unto me.   *Ib.* 40

18 What will ye give me, and I will deliver him unto you? And they covenanted with him for thirty pieces of silver.   *Ib.* xxvi. 15

19 This night, before the cock crow, thou shalt deny me thrice.   *Ib.* 34

20 If it be possible, let this cup pass from me.   *Ib.* 39

21 The spirit indeed is willing, but the flesh is weak.   *Ib.* 41

22 Hail, master; and kissed him.   *Ib.* 49

23 All they that take the sword shall perish with the sword.   *Ib.* 52

24 He saved others; himself he cannot save.   *St. Matthew* xxvii. 42

25 Eli, Eli, lama sabachthani? . . . My God, my God, why hast thou forsaken me?   *Ib.* 46

26 The sabbath was made for man, and not man for the sabbath.
St. Mark ii. 27

27 If a house be divided against itself, that house cannot stand.   *Ib.* iii. 25

28 He that hath ears to hear, let him hear.   *Ib.* iv. 9

29 My name is Legion: for we are many.
Ib. v. 9

30 Clothed, and in his right mind.   *Ib.* 15

31 I see men as trees, walking.   *Ib.* viii. 24

32 For what shall it profit a man, if he shall gain the whole world, and lose his own soul?   *Ib.* 36

33 Lord, I believe; help thou mine unbelief.   *Ib.* ix. 24

34 Suffer the little children to come unto me, and forbid them not: for of such is the kingdom of God.   *Ib.* x. 14

35 And there came a certain poor widow, and she threw in two mites.   *Ib.* xii. 42

36 Hail, thou that art highly favoured, the Lord is with thee: blessed art thou among women.   *St. Luke* i. 28

37 My soul doth magnify the Lord,
And my spirit hath rejoiced in God my Saviour.
For he hath regarded the low estate of his handmaiden: for, behold, from henceforth all generations shall call me blessed.   *Ib.* 46

38 He hath shewed strength with his arm; he hath scattered the proud in the imagination of their hearts.
He hath put down the mighty from their seats, and exalted them of low degree.
He hath filled the hungry with good things; and the rich he hath sent empty away.   *Ib.* 51

39 To give light to them that sit in darkness and in the shadow of death, to guide our feet into the way of peace.
Ib. 79

40 Because there was no room for them in the inn.   *Ib.* ii. 7

41 And, lo, the angel of the Lord came upon them, and the glory of the Lord shone round about them: and they were sore afraid.   *Ib.* 9

42 Be not afraid; for behold, I bring you good tidings of great joy.   *Ib.* 10

43 Glory to God in the highest, and on earth peace, good will toward men.
Ib. 14

1 Lord, now lettest thou thy servant depart in peace, according to thy word. *St. Luke* ii. 29

2 Physician, heal thyself. *Ib.* iv. 23

3 Judge not, and ye shall not be judged. *Ib.* vi. 37

4 Peace be to this house. *Ib.* x. 5

5 For the labourer is worthy of his hire. *Ib.* 7

6 Fell among thieves. *Ib.* 30

7 He passed by on the other side. *Ib.* 31

8 Go, and do thou likewise. *Ib.* 37

9 But Martha was cumbered about much serving. *Ib.* 40

10 When a strong man armed keepeth his palace, his goods are in peace. *Ib.* xi. 21

11 All his armour wherein he trusted. *Ib.* 22

12 Woe unto you, lawyers! for ye have taken away the key of knowledge. *Ib.* 52

13 Are not five sparrows sold for two farthings, and not one of them is forgotten before God? *Ib.* xii. 6

14 Friend, go up higher. *Ib.* xiv. 10

15 For whosoever exalteth himself shall be abased; and he that humbleth himself shall be exalted. *Ib.* 11

16 I have married a wife, and therefore I cannot come. *Ib.* 20

17 The poor, and the maimed, and the halt, and the blind. *Ib.* 21

18 Go out into the highways and hedges, and compel them to come in. *Ib.* 23

19 Rejoice with me; for I have found my sheep which was lost. *Ib.* xv. 6

20 Joy shall be in heaven over one sinner that repenteth, more than over ninety and nine just persons, which need no repentance. *Ib.* 7

21 Wasted his substance with riotous living. *Ib.* 13

22 I will arise and go to my father, and will say unto him, Father, I have sinned against heaven, and before thee,
And am no more worthy to be called thy son: make me as one of thy hired servants. *Ib.* 18

23 Bring hither the fatted calf, and kill it. *Ib.* 23

24 This my son was dead, and is alive again; he was lost, and is found. *Ib.* 24

25 I cannot dig; to beg I am ashamed. *Ib.* xvi. 3

26 Make to yourselves friends of the mammon of unrighteousness. *St. Luke* xvi. 9

27 The crumbs which fell from the rich man's table. *Ib.* 21

28 Carried by the angels into Abraham's bosom. *Ib.* 22

29 Between us and you there is a great gulf fixed. *Ib.* 26

30 It were better for him that a millstone were hanged about his neck, and he cast into the sea. *Ib.* xvii. 2

31 The kingdom of God is within you. *Ib.* 21

32 Remember Lot's wife. *Ib.* 32

33 God, I thank thee, that I am not as other men are. *Ib.* xviii. 11

34 God be merciful to me a sinner. *Ib.* 13

35 If these should hold their peace, the stones would immediately cry out. *Ib.* xix. 40

36 In your patience possess ye your souls. *Ib.* xxi. 19

37 Nevertheless, not my will, but thine, be done. *Ib.* xxii. 42

38 For if they do these things in a green tree, what shall be done in the dry? *Ib.* xxiii. 31

39 Father, forgive them; for they know not what they do. *Ib.* 34

40 Lord, remember me when thou comest into thy kingdom. *Ib.* 42

41 To day shalt thou be with me in paradise. *Ib.* 43

42 Father, into thy hands I commend my spirit. *Ib.* 46

43 In the beginning was the Word, and the Word was with God, and the Word was God. *St. John* i. 1

44 And the light shineth in darkness; and the darkness comprehended it not. *Ib.* 5

45 He came unto his own, and his own received him not. *Ib.* 11

46 And the Word was made flesh, and dwelt among us. *Ib.* 14

47 Who coming after me is preferred before me, whose shoe's latchet I am not worthy to unloose. *Ib.* 27

48 Can there any good thing come out of Nazareth? *Ib.* 46

49 Woman, what have I to do with thee? mine hour is not yet come. *Ib.* ii. 4

50 The wind bloweth where it listeth, and thou hearest the sound thereof, but canst not tell whence it cometh, and whither it goeth. *Ib.* iii. 8

1 God so loved the world, that he gave his only begotten Son, that whosoever believeth in him should not perish, but have everlasting life. *St. John* iii. 16

2 God is a Spirit: and they that worship him must worship him in spirit and in truth. *Ib.* iv. 24

3 Rise, take up thy bed, and walk. *Ib.* v. 8

4 What are they among so many? *Ib.* vi. 9

5 Him that cometh to me I will in no wise cast out. *Ib.* 37

6 He that is without sin among you, let him first cast a stone at her. *Ib.* viii. 7

7 Neither do I condemn thee: go, and sin no more. *Ib.* 11

8 The truth shall make you free. *Ib.* 32

9 There is no truth in him. *Ib.* 44

10 He is a liar, and the father of it. *Ib.*

11 The night cometh, when no man can work. *Ib.* ix. 4

12 The good shepherd giveth his life for the sheep. *Ib.* x. 11

13 I am the resurrection, and the life. *Ib.* xi. 25

14 It is expedient for us, that one man should die for the people. *Ib.* 50

15 The poor always ye have with you. *Ib.* xii. 8

16 Let not your heart be troubled: ye believe in God, believe also in me. *Ib.* xiv. 1

17 In my Father's house are many mansions. *Ib.* 2

18 I go to prepare a place for you. *Ib.*

19 I am the way, the truth, and the life: no man cometh unto the Father, but by me. *Ib.* 6

20 Greater love hath no man than this, that a man lay down his life for his friends. *Ib.* xv. 13

21 Quo vadis? Whither goest thou? *Ib.* xvi. 5 (Vulgate) and the Apocryphal *Acts of Peter*

22 In the world ye shall have tribulation: but be of good cheer; I have overcome the world. *Ib.* 33

23 Pilate saith unto him, What is truth? *Ib.* xviii. 38

24 Now Barabbas was a robber. *Ib.* 40

25 Ecce homo.
Behold the man. *Ib.* xix. 5 (Vulgate)

26 What I have written I have written. *Ib.* 22

27 Woman, behold thy son! . . .
Behold thy mother! *St. John* xix. 26

28 Consummatum est.
It is finished. *Ib.* 30 (Vulgate)

29 Noli me tangere.
Touch me not. *Ib.* xx. 17 (Vulgate)

30 The disciple whom Jesus loved. *Ib.* xxi. 20

31 A rushing mighty wind. *The Acts of the Apostles* ii. 2

32 Silver and gold have I none; but such as I have give I thee. *Ib.* iii. 6

33 We ought to obey God rather than men. *Ib.* v. 29

34 Breathing out threatenings and slaughter. *Ib.* ix. 1

35 Saul, Saul, why persecutest thou me? *Ib.* 4

36 It is hard for thee to kick against the pricks. *Ib.* 5

37 Full of good works. *Ib.* 36

38 God is no respecter of persons. *Ib.* x. 34

39 Come over into Macedonia, and help us. *Ib.* xvi. 9

40 Certain lewd fellows of the baser sort. *Ib.* xvii. 5

41 These that have turned the world upside down. *Ib.* 6

42 Ye men of Athens, I perceive that in all things ye are too superstitious.
For as I passed by, and beheld your devotions, I found an altar with this inscription, TO THE UNKNOWN GOD. Whom therefore ye ignorantly worship, him declare I unto you. *Ib.* 22

43 For in him we live, and move, and have our being. *Ib.* 28

44 Gallio cared for none of those things. *Ib.* xviii. 17

45 All with one voice about the space of two hours cried out, Great is Diana of the Ephesians. *Ib.* xix. 34

46 It is more blessed to give than to receive. *Ib.* xx. 35

47 A citizen of no mean city. *Ib.* xxi. 39

48 I appeal unto Cæsar. *Ib.* xxv. 11

49 Hast thou appealed unto Cæsar? unto Cæsar shalt thou go. *Ib.* 12

50 Paul, thou art beside thyself; much learning doth make thee mad. *Ib.* xxvi. 24

51 Almost thou persuadest me to be a Christian. *Ib.* 28

52 The just shall live by faith. *The Epistle of Paul to the Romans* i. 17

1 Let us do evil, that good may come.
Romans iii. 8

2 Who against hope believed in hope.
Ib. iv. 18

3 Shall we continue in sin, that grace
may abound? *Ib.* vi. 1

4 Christ being raised from the dead
dieth no more; death hath no more
dominion over him. *Ib.* 9

5 The wages of sin is death. *Ib.* 23

6 For the good that I would I do not:
but the evil which I would not, that
I do. *Ib.* vii. 19

7 For ye have not received the spirit of
bondage again to fear; but ye have
received the Spirit of adoption,
whereby we cry, Abba, Father.
Ib. viii. 15

8 All things work together for good to
them that love God. *Ib.* 28

9 If God be for us, who can be against
us? *Ib.* 31

10 For I am persuaded, that neither
death, nor life, nor angels, nor principalities, nor powers, nor things present, nor things to come,
Nor height, nor depth, nor any other
creature, shall be able to separate us
from the love of God, which is in
Christ Jesus our Lord. *Ib.* 38

11 Vengeance is mine; I will repay, saith
the Lord. *Ib.* xii. 19

12 Be not overcome of evil, but overcome
evil with good. *Ib.* 21

13 The powers that be are ordained of
God. *Ib.* xxiii. 1

14 Now it is high time to awake out of
sleep: for now is our salvation nearer
than when we believed.
The night is far spent, the day is at
hand: let us therefore cast off the
works of darkness, and let us put on
the armour of light. *Ib.* 11

15 Absent in body, but present in spirit.
*The First Epistle of Paul to the
Corinthians* v. 3

16 It is better to marry than to burn.
Ib. vii. 9

17 I am made all things to all men.
Ib. ix. 22

18 All things are lawful for me, but all
things are not expedient. *Ib.* x. 23

19 For the earth is the Lord's, and the
fulness thereof. *Ib.* 26

20 Though I speak with the tongues of
men and of angels, and have not
charity, I am become as sounding
brass, or a tinkling cymbal. *Ib.* xiii. 1

21 Though I have all faith, so that I could
remove mountains, and have not
charity, I am nothing.
And though I bestow all my goods to
feed the poor, and though I give my
body to be burned, and have not
charity, it profiteth me nothing.
Charity suffereth long, and is kind;
charity envieth not; charity vaunteth
not itself, is not puffed up,
Doth not behave itself unseemly,
seeketh not her own, is not easily
provoked, thinketh no evil;
Rejoiceth not in iniquity, but rejoiceth in the truth;
Beareth all things, believeth all
things, hopeth all things, endureth all
things.
Charity never faileth: but whether
there be prophecies, they shall fail;
whether there be tongues, they shall
cease; whether there be knowledge, it
shall vanish away.
For we know in part, and we prophesy
in part. *1 Corinthians* xiii. 2

22 When I was a child, I spake as a
child, I understood as a child, I
thought as a child: but when I became
a man, I put away childish things.
For now we see through a glass,
darkly; but then face to face; now
I know in part; but then shall I know
even as also I am known.
And now abideth faith, hope, charity,
these three; but the greatest of these
is charity. *Ib.* xiii. 11

23 Let all things be done decently and in
order. *Ib.* xiv. 40

24 Last of all he was seen of me also, as
of one born out of due time. *Ib.* xv. 8

25 The last enemy that shall be destroyed
is death. *Ib.* 26

26 Let us eat and drink; for to morrow
we die. *Ib.* 32

27 Evil communications corrupt good
manners. *Ib.* 33

28 The first man is of the earth, earthy.
Ib. 47

29 Behold, I shew you a mystery; We
shall not all sleep, but we shall all be
changed,
In a moment, in the twinkling of an
eye, at the last trump. *Ib.* 51

30 For this corruptible must put on in-
corruption, and this mortal must put
on immortality. *Ib.* 53

31 O death, where is thy sting? O grave,
where is thy victory? *Ib.* 55

32 Quit you like men, be strong.
Ib. xvi. 13

1 Not of the letter, but of the spirit: for the letter killeth, but the spirit giveth life.
The Second Epistle of Paul to the Corinthians iii. 6

2 God loveth a cheerful giver.   *Ib.* ix. 7

3 For ye suffer fools gladly, seeing ye yourselves are wise.   *Ib.* xi. 19

4 There was given to me a thorn in the flesh, the messenger of Satan to buffet me.   *Ib.* xii. 7

5 The right hands of fellowship.
The Epistle of Paul to the Galatians ii. 9

6 Ye are fallen from grace.   *Ib.* v. 4

7 But the fruit of the Spirit is love, joy, peace, longsuffering, gentleness, goodness, faith,
Meekness, temperance.   *Ib.* 22

8 Be not deceived; God is not mocked: for whatsoever a man soweth, that shall he also reap.   *Ib.* vi. 7

9 To be strengthened with might by his Spirit in the inner man.
The Epistle of Paul to the Ephesians iii. 16

10 Carried about with every wind of doctrine.   *Ib.* iv. 14

11 We are members one of another.
Ib. 25

12 Be ye angry, and sin not: let not the sun go down upon your wrath.   *Ib.* 26

13 Put on the whole armour of God.
Ib. vi. 11

14 For we wrestle not against flesh and blood, but against principalities, against powers, against the rulers of the darkness of this world, against spiritual wickedness in high places.
Wherefore take unto you the whole armour of God, that ye may be able to withstand in the evil day, and having done all, to stand.   *Ib.* 12

15 Given him a name which is above every name:
That at the name of Jesus every knee should bow.
The Epistle of Paul to the Philippians ii. 9

16 Work out your own salvation with fear and trembling.   *Ib.* 12

17 Whose God is their belly, and whose glory is in their shame.   *Ib.* iii. 19

18 Rejoice in the Lord alway: and again I say, Rejoice.   *Ib.* iv. 4

19 The peace of God, which passeth all understanding.   *Ib.* 7

20 Whatsoever things are true, whatsoever things are honest, whatsoever things are just, whatsoever things are pure, whatsoever things are lovely, whatsoever things are of good report; if there be any virtue, and if there be any praise, think on these things.
Philippians iv. 8

21 I can do all things through Christ which strengtheneth me.   *Ib.* 13

22 Set your affection on things above, not on things on the earth.
The Epistle of Paul to the Colossians iii. 2

23 Labour of love.
The First Epistle of Paul to the Thessalonians i. 3

24 Prove all things; hold fast that which is good.   *Ib.* v. 21

25 Be not weary in well doing.
The Second Epistle of Paul to the Thessalonians iii. 13

26 Not greedy of filthy lucre.
The First Epistle of Paul to Timothy iii. 3

27 Old wives' fables.   *Ib.* iv. 7

28 Drink no longer water, but use a little wine for thy stomach's sake and thine often infirmities.   *Ib.* v. 23

29 For we brought nothing into this world, and it is certain we can carry nothing out.   *Ib.* vi. 7

30 The love of money is the root of all evil.   *Ib.* 10

31 Fight the good fight of faith, lay hold on eternal life.   *Ib.* 12

32 Rich in good works.   *Ib.* 18

33 I have fought a good fight, I have finished my course, I have kept the faith.
The Second Epistle of Paul to Timothy iv. 7

34 Unto the pure all things are pure.
The Epistle of Paul to Titus i. 15

35 Wherefore seeing we also are compassed about with so great a cloud of witnesses, let us lay aside every weight, and the sin which doth so easily beset us, and let us run with patience the race that is set before us,
Looking unto Jesus the author and finisher of our faith.
The Epistle of Paul to the Hebrews xii. 1

36 Whom the Lord loveth he chasteneth.
Ib. 6

37 Be not forgetful to entertain strangers; for thereby some have entertained angels unawares.   *Ib.* xiii. 1

38 Jesus Christ the same yesterday, and to day, and for ever.   *Ib.* 8

39 Faith without works is dead.
The General Epistle of James ii. 20

1 Ye have heard of the patience of Job.
James v. 11

2 Let your yea be yea; and your nay, nay.
Ib. 12

3 All flesh is as grass, and all the glory of man as the flower of grass. The grass withereth, and the flower thereof falleth away.
The First Epistle General of Peter i. 24

4 Honour all men. Love the brotherhood. Fear God. Honour the king.
Ib. ii. 17

5 Giving honour unto the wife, as unto the weaker vessel.
Ib. iii. 7

6 Charity shall cover the multitude of sins.
Ib. iv. 8

7 Be sober, be vigilant; because your adversary the devil, as a roaring lion, walketh about, seeking whom he may devour.
Ib. v. 8

8 If we say that we have no sin, we deceive ourselves, and the truth is not in us.
The First Epistle General of John i. 8

9 He that loveth not knoweth not God; for God is love.
Ib. iv. 8

10 No man hath seen God at any time.
Ib. 12

11 There is no fear in love; but perfect love casteth out fear.
Ib. 18

12 If a man say, I love God, and hateth his brother, he is a liar: for he that loveth not his brother whom he hath seen, how can he love God whom he hath not seen?
Ib. 20

13 I am Alpha and Omega, the beginning and the ending, saith the Lord.
The Revelation of John the Divine i. 8

14 Be thou faithful unto death, and I will give thee a crown of life.
Ib. ii. 10

15 Behold, I stand at the door, and knock.
Ib. iii. 20

16 They were full of eyes within: and they rest not day and night, saying, Holy, holy, holy, Lord God Almighty, which was, and is, and is to come.
Ib. iv. 8

17 And I looked, and behold a pale horse: and his name that sat on him was Death.
Ib. vi. 8

18 God shall wipe away all tears from their eyes.
Ib. vii. 17

19 And there were stings in their tails.
Ib. ix. 10

20 And that no man might buy or sell, save he that had the mark, or the name of the beast, or the number of his name.
Revelation xiii. 17

21 Babylon is fallen, is fallen, that great city.
Ib. xiv. 8

22 MYSTERY, BABYLON THE GREAT, THE MOTHER OF HARLOTS AND ABOMINATIONS OF THE EARTH.
And I saw the woman drunken with the blood of the saints.
Ib. xvii. 5

23 The key of the bottomless pit.
Ib. xx. 1

24 And the sea gave up the dead which were in it.
Ib. 13

25 And I saw a new heaven and a new earth: for the first heaven and the first earth were passed away; and there was no more sea.
And I John saw the holy city, new Jerusalem, coming down from God out of heaven, prepared as a bride adorned for her husband.
Ib. xxi. 1

26 And God shall wipe away all tears from their eyes; and there shall be no more death, neither sorrow, nor crying, neither shall there be any more pain: for the former things are passed away.
And he that sat upon the throne said, Behold, I make all things new. And he said unto me, Write: for these words are true and faithful.
Ib. 4

27 I will give unto him that is athirst of the fountain of the water of life freely.
Ib. 6

28 The twelve gates were twelve pearls.
Ib. 21

ISAAC BICKERSTAFFE
1735?–1812?

29 There was a jolly miller once,
Lived on the river Dee;
He worked and sang from morn till night;
No lark more blithe than he.
Love in a Village, I. v

30 And this the burthen of his song,
For ever us'd to be,
I care for nobody, not I,
If no one cares for me.
Ib.

31 We all love a pretty girl—under the rose.
Ib. II. ii

32 In every port he finds a wife.
Thomas and Sally (1761), ii

EDWARD HENRY BICKERSTETH 1825–1906

33 Peace, perfect peace, in this dark world of sin?
The Blood of Jesus whispers peace within.
Songs in the House of Pilgrimage (1875)

JOSH BILLINGS
see HENRY WHEELER SHAW

LAURENCE BINYON 1869–1943

1 With proud thanksgiving, a mother
   for her children,
   England mourns for her dead across
   the sea.   *Poems for the Fallen*

2 They shall grow not old, as we that
   are left grow old:
   Age shall not weary them, nor the
   years condemn.
   At the going down of the sun and in
   the morning
   We will remember them.   *Ib.*

OTTO VON BISMARCK 1815–1898

3 Nach Canossa gehen wir nicht.
   We will not go to Canossa.
        Speech, Reichstag, 14 May 1872

4 Blut und Eisen.
   Blood and iron.
        *Speech, Prussian House of Depu-
        ties, 28 Jan. 1886*
   (Legt eine möglichst starke mili-
   tärische Kraft . . . in die Hand des
   Königs von Preussen, dann wird er
   die Politik machen können, die Ihr
   wünscht; mit Reden und Schützen-
   festen und Leidern macht sie sich
   nicht, sie macht sich nur durch
   Blut und Eisen.
   Place in the hands of the King of
   Prussia the strongest possible
   military power, then he will be
   able to carry out the policy you
   wish; this policy cannot succeed
   through speeches, and shooting-
   matches, and songs; it can only
   be carried out through blood and
   iron.)

VALENTINE BLACKER 1778–1823

5 'Put your trust in God, my boys, and
   keep your powder dry.'
        Oliver's Advice

SIR WILLIAM BLACKSTONE
                    1723–1780

6 The king never dies.
        *Commentaries on the Laws of
        England*, bk. i. 7

7 That the king can do no wrong, is a
   necessary and fundamental principle
   of the English constitution. *Ib.* iii. 17

8 It is better that ten guilty persons
   escape than one innocent suffer.
        Ib. iv. 27

CHARLES DUPEE BLAKE
                    1846–1903

9 Rock-a-bye-baby on the tree top,
   When the wind blows the cradle will
   rock,

When the bough bends the cradle will
fall,
Down comes the baby, cradle and all.
        Attr. But see Oxford Dictionary
        of Nursery Rhymes

WILLIAM BLAKE 1757–1827

10 To see a World in a Grain of Sand,
   And a Heaven in a Wild Flower,
   Hold Infinity in the palm of your hand,
   And Eternity in an hour.
        Auguries of Innocence

11 A Robin Redbreast in a Cage
   Puts all Heaven in a Rage.   *Ib.*

12 The harlot's cry from street to street
   Shall weave old England's winding
   sheet.   *Ib.*

13 'What,' it will be questioned, 'when
   the sun rises, do you not see a round
   disc of fire somewhat like a guinea?'
   'O no, no, I see an innumerable company of the heavenly host crying,
   "Holy, Holy, Holy is the Lord God
   Almighty!"'
        Descriptive Catalogue, 1810. *The
        Vision of Judgment*

14 [On Cromek]
   A petty sneaking knave I knew—
   O! Mr. Cr—, how do ye do?
        On Friends and Foes, xxi

15 Great things are done when men and
   mountains meet,
   This is not done by jostling in the
   street.   *Gnomic Verses*, i

16 And did those feet in ancient time
   Walk upon England's mountains
   green?
   And was the holy Lamb of God
   On England's pleasant pastures seen?

   And did the Countenance Divine
   Shine forth upon our clouded hills?
   And was Jerusalem builded here
   Among these dark Satanic mills?

   Bring me my bow of burning gold!
   Bring me my arrows of desire!
   Bring me my spear! O clouds, unfold!
   Bring me my chariot of fire!

   I will not cease from Mental Fight,
   Nor shall my Sword sleep in my hand,
   Till we have built Jerusalem,
   In England's green & pleasant Land.
        Milton, preface

17 Mock on, mock on, Voltaire, Rous-
   seau;
   Mock on, mock on, 'tis all in vain!
   You throw the sand against the wind,
   And the wind blows it back again.
        Mock on, mock on, Voltaire

18 Hear the voice of the Bard!
   Who present, past, and future sees.
        Songs of Experience, introduction

1 Tyger! Tyger! burning bright
In the forests of the night,
What immortal hand or eye
Could frame thy fearful symmetry?
Songs of Experience. The Tyger

2 And what shoulder, and what art,
Could twist the sinews of thy heart?
And when thy heart began to beat,
What dread hand? and what dread
feet?

What the hammer? What the chain?
In what furnace was thy brain?
What the anvil? what dread grasp
Dare its deadly terrors clasp?   *Ib.*

3 Did he who made the Lamb make
thee?   *Ib.*

4 Tyger! Tyger! burning bright
In the forests of the night,
What immortal hand or eye,
Dare frame thy fearful symmetry? *Ib.*

5 Love seeketh not itself to please,
Nor for itself hath any care,
But for another gives its ease,
And builds a Heaven in Hell's despair.
Ib. The Clod and the Pebble

6 Love seeketh only Self to please,
To bind another to its delight,
Joys in another's loss of ease,
And builds a Hell in Heaven's despite.
Ib.

7 Ah, Sun-flower! weary of time,
Who countest the steps of the Sun;
Seeking after that sweet golden clime,
Where the traveller's journey is done.
Ib. Ah, Sun-Flower!

8 Piping down the valleys wild,
Piping songs of pleasant glee,
On a cloud I saw a child,
And he laughing said to me:

'Pipe a song about a Lamb!'
So I piped with merry cheer.
'Piper, pipe that song again;'
So I piped: he wept to hear.

'Drop thy pipe, thy happy pipe;
Sing thy songs of happy cheer:'
So I sang the same again,
While he wept with joy to hear.

'Piper, sit thee down and write
In a book, that all may read.'
So he vanish'd from my sight,
And I pluck'd a hollow reed.

And I made a rural pen,
And I stain'd the water clear,
And I wrote my happy songs
Every child may joy to hear.
Songs of Innocence, introduction

9 Little Lamb, who made thee?
Ib. The Lamb

10 My mother bore me in the southern
wild,
And I am black, but O! my soul is
white;

White as an angel is the English child,
But I am black, as if bereav'd of light.
*Songs of Innocence. The Little
Black Boy*

11 When the voices of children are heard
on the green,
And laughing is heard on the hill.
Ib. Nurse's Song

12 To Mercy, Pity, Peace, and Love
All pray in their distress.
Ib. The Divine Image

13 For Mercy has a human heart,
Pity a human face,
And Love, the human form divine,
And Peace, the human dress.
Ib.

14 Can I see another's woe,
And not be in sorrow too?
Can I see another's grief,
And not seek for kind relief?
Ib. On Another's Sorrow

15 Energy is Eternal Delight.
*The Marriage of Heaven and Hell:
The Voice of the Devil*

16 The reason Milton wrote in fetters
when he wrote of Angels and God, and
at liberty when of Devils and Hell, is
because he was a true Poet, and of the
Devil's party without knowing it.
Ib. note

17 A fool sees not the same tree that a
wise man sees.   *Ib. Proverbs of Hell*

18 Eternity is in love with the produc-
tions of time.   *Ib.*

19 If the fool would persist in his folly
he would become wise.   *Ib.*

20 Damn braces. Bless relaxes.   *Ib.*

21 If the doors of perception were
cleansed everything would appear to
man as it is, infinite.
The Marriage of Heaven and Hell

PHILIPP BLISS 1838–1876

22 Hold the fort, for I am coming.
*The Charm. Ho, My Comrades,
See the Signal!*

23 Pull for the shore, sailor, pull for the
shore!
Heed not the rolling waves, but bend to
the oar.
*Sacred Songs and Solos. The Life-
boat*

**GEBHARD LEBERECHT
BLÜCHER** 1742–1819

24 Was für plündern!
What a place to plunder!
*On his visit to London in 1814.
Attr.*

EDMUND BLUNDEN 1896–

25 Undertones of War   *Title of Book*

BOETHIUS 480?–524

1 For truly in adverse fortune the worst sting of misery is to *have been* happy.
> *Consolation of Philosophy*, bk. ii, prose 4 (H. R. James's translation) (*see* 72:7)

NICOLAS BOILEAU 1636–1711

2 Enfin Malherbe vint, et, le premier en France,
Fit sentir dans les vers une juste cadence.

At last comes Malherbe and, the first to do so in France, makes verse run smoothly.
> *L'Art Poétique*, i. 131–2

HENRY ST. JOHN, VISCOUNT BOLINGBROKE 1678–1751

3 The Idea of a Patriot King.
> *Title of Book*

4 Truth lies within a little and certain compass, but error is immense.
> *Reflections upon Exile*

5 They make truth serve as a stalking-horse to error.
> *On the Study of History*, letter 1

CARRIE JACOBS BOND 1862–1946

6 And we find at the end of a perfect day
The soul of a friend we've made.
> *A Perfect Day*, st. 2

'GENERAL' WILLIAM BOOTH 1829–1912

7 This Submerged Tenth—is it, then, beyond the reach of the nine-tenths in the midst of whom they live.
> *In Darkest England* (1890), I. ii. 23

GEORGE BORROW 1803–1881

8 There's night and day, brother, both sweet things; sun, moon, and stars, brother, all sweet things; there's likewise a wind on the heath. Life is very sweet, brother; who would wish to die?
> *Lavengro*, ch. 25

9 Youth will be served, every dog has his day, and mine has been a fine one.
> *Ib.* ch. 92

MARÉCHAL BOSQUET 1810–1861

10 C'est magnifique, mais ce n'est pas la guerre.

It is magnificent, but it is not war.
> *Remark on the Charge of the Light Brigade, 1854*

JOHN COLLINS BOSSIDY 1860–1928

11 And this is good old Boston,
The home of the bean and the cod,
Where the Lowells talk to the Cabots,
And the Cabots talk only to God.
> *On the Aristocracy of Harvard*

BOULAY DE LA MEURTHE 1761–1840

12 C'est pire qu'un crime, c'est une faute.

It is worse than a crime, it is a blunder.
> *On hearing of the execution of the Duc d'Enghien, 1804*

FRANCIS WILLIAM BOURDILLON 1852–1921

13 The night has a thousand eyes,
And the day but one;
Yet the light of the bright world dies,
With the dying sun.

The mind has a thousand eyes,
And the heart but one;
Yet the light of a whole life dies,
When love is done.   *Light*

CHARLES, BARON BOWEN 1835–1894

14 The rain it raineth on the just
And also on the unjust fella:
But chiefly on the just, because
The unjust steals the just's umbrella.
> Walter Sichel, *Sands of Time*

EDWARD ERNEST BOWEN 1836–1901

15 Forty years on, when afar and asunder
Parted are those who are singing to-day.
> *Forty Years On. Harrow School Song*

16 Follow up! Follow up! Follow up!
Follow up! Follow up!
Till the field ring again and again,
With the tramp of the twenty-two men,
Follow up!   *Ib.*

JOHN BRADFORD 1510?–1555

17 But for the grace of God there goes John Bradford.
> *Exclamation on seeing some criminals taken to execution. Dict. of Nat. Biog.*

JOHN BRAHAM 1774?–1856

18 England, home and beauty.
> *The Americans* (1811). Song, *The Death of Nelson*

HARRY BRAISTED
nineteenth century

1   If you want to win her hand,
Let the maiden understand
That she's not the only pebble on the
beach.
*You're Not the Only Pebble on
the Beach*

REV. JAMES BRAMSTON
1694?–1744

2   What's not destroy'd by Time's
devouring hand?
Where's Troy, and where's the Maypole in the Strand?
Art of Politics, l. 71

RICHARD BRATHWAITE
1588?–1673

3   To Banbury came I, O profane one!
Where I saw a Puritane-one
Hanging of his cat on Monday,
For killing of a mouse on Sunday.
Barnabee's Journal, pt. i

NICHOLAS BRETON 1545?–1626?

4   We rise with the lark and go to bed
with the lamb.
The Court and the Country, par. 8

5   A Mad World, My Masters.
Title of Dialogue (1635)

ROBERT BRIDGES 1844–1930

6   I love all beauteous things,
I seek and adore them;
God hath no better praise,
And man in his hasty days
Is honoured for them.
I Love All Beauteous Things

7   When men were all asleep the snow
came flying,
In large white flakes falling on the
city brown,
Stealthily and perpetually settling
and loosely lying.
London Snow

8   Whither, O splendid ship, thy white
sails crowding,
Leaning across the bosom of the ur-
gent West,
That fearest nor sea rising, nor sky
clouding,
Whither away, fair rover, and what
thy quest? *A Passer-By*

JOHN BRIGHT 1811–1889

9   My opinion is that the Northern
States will manage somehow to muddle
through.
During the American Civil War.
Quoted in Justin McCarthy,
Reminiscences (1899)

10   The angel of death has been abroad
throughout the land; you may almost
hear the beating of his wings.
*Speech, House of Commons,
23 Feb. 1855*

11   I am for 'Peace, retrenchment, and
reform', the watchword of the great
Liberal party 30 years ago.
Ib. Birmingham, 28 Apr. 1859

12   England is the mother of Parliaments.
Ib. 18 Jan. 1865

EMILY BRONTË 1818–1848

13   No coward soul is mine,
No trembler in the world's storm-
troubled sphere:
I see Heaven's glories shine,
And faith shines equal, arming me
from fear. *Last Lines*

14   Vain are the thousand creeds
That move men's hearts: unutterably
vain;
Worthless as withered weeds,
Or idlest froth amid the boundless
main. *Ib.*

15   Cold in the earth—and fifteen wild
Decembers,
From those brown hills, have melted
into spring. *Remembrance*

RUPERT BROOKE 1887–1915

16   Blow out, you bugles, over the rich
Dead!
There's none of these so lonely and
poor of old,
But, dying, has made us rarer gifts
than gold.
These laid the world away; poured out
the red
Sweet wine of youth; gave up the
years to be
Of work and joy, and that unhoped
serene,
That men call age; and those who
would have been,
Their sons, they gave, their immor-
tality. *The Dead*

17   The cool kindliness of sheets, that soon
Smooth away trouble; and the rough
male kiss of blankets.
The Great Lover

18   The benison of hot water. *Ib.*

19   Fish say, they have their stream and
pond;
But is there anything beyond?
Heaven

20   One may not doubt that, somehow,
good
Shall come of water and of mud;
And, sure, the reverent eye must see
A purpose in liquidity. *Ib.*

C

1 But somewhere, beyond space and time,
  Is wetter water, slimier slime;   *Heaven*

2 Immense, of fishy form and mind,
  Squamous, omnipotent, and kind;
  And under that Almighty Fin,
  The littlest fish may enter in.   *Ib.*

3 Unfading moths, immortal flies,
  And the worm that never dies.
  And in that Heaven of all their wish,
  There shall be no more land, say fish.
                                         Ib.

4 Breathless, we flung us on the windy hill,
  Laughed in the sun, and kissed the lovely grass.   *The Hill*

5 Here tulips bloom as they are told;
  Unkempt about those hedges blows
  An English unofficial rose.
                The Old Vicarage, Grantchester

6 Curates, long dust, will come and go
  On lissom, clerical, printless toe;
  And oft between the boughs is seen
  The sly shade of a Rural Dean.   *Ib.*

7 God; I will pack, and take a train,
  And get me to England once again;
  For England's the one land, I know,
  Where men with splendid hearts may go;
  And Cambridgeshire, of all England,
  The shire for men who understand;
  And of *that* district I prefer
  The lovely hamlet Grantchester.   *Ib.*

8 For Cambridge people rarely smile,
  Being urban, squat, and packed with guile.   *Ib.*

9 Stands the Church clock at ten to three?
  And is there honey still for tea?   *Ib.*

10 Now, God be thanked Who has matched us with His hour,
  And caught our youth, and wakened us from sleeping.   *Peace*

11 If I should die, think only this of me:
  That there's some corner of a foreign field
  That is for ever England. There shall be
  In that rich earth a richer dust concealed;
  A dust whom England bore, shaped, made aware,
  Gave, once, her flowers to love, her ways to roam,
  A body of England's, breathing English air,
  Washed by the rivers, blest by suns of home.
  And think, this heart, all evil shed away,
  A pulse in the eternal mind, no less
  Gives somewhere back the thoughts by England given.
  Her sights and sounds; dreams happy as her day;

And laughter, learnt of friends; and gentleness,
In hearts at peace, under an English heaven.   *The Soldier*

THOMAS BROOKS 1608–1680

12 For (magna est veritas et prævalebit) great is truth, and shall prevail.
        The Crown and Glory of Christianity (1662), p. 407

JOHN BROWN 1715–1766

13 Altogether upon the high horse.
        *Letter to Garrick, 27 Oct. 1765.
        Correspondence of Garrick* (1831), vol. i, p. 205

JOHN BROWN 1800–1859

14 I, John Brown, am now quite certain that the crimes of this guilty land will never be purged away but with blood.
        *Last Statement, 2 Dec. 1859.
        R. J. Hinton, John Brown and His Men*

THOMAS BROWN 1663–1704

15 A little before you made a leap into the dark.   *Letters from the Dead*

16 I do not love you, Dr. Fell,
  But why I cannot tell;
  But this I know full well,
  I do not love you, Dr. Fell.
        (Trans. of Martial, *Epigrams*, i. 32.) *Works* (1719), vol. iv, p. 113

THOMAS EDWARD BROWN
                                    1830–1897

17 A garden is a lovesome thing, God wot!
                                    My Garden

18 Not God! in gardens! when the eve is cool?
  Nay, but I have a sign;
  'Tis very sure God walks in mine. *Ib.*

CHARLES FARRAR BROWNE
see ARTEMUS WARD

SIR THOMAS BROWNE 1605–1682

19 I love to lose myself in a mystery; to pursue my reason to an O *altitudo!*
        Religio Medici, pt. i, § 10

20 Charity begins at home, is the voice of the world.   *Ib.* pt. ii, § 4

21 For the world, I count it not an inn, but an hospital, and a place, not to live, but to die in.   *Ib.* § 12

22 There is surely a piece of divinity in us, something that was before the elements, and owes no homage unto the sun.   *Ib.*

1 What song the Syrens sang, or what name Achilles assumed when he hid himself among women, though puzzling questions, are not beyond all conjecture. *Urn Burial, ch. 5*

WILLIAM BROWNE 1591–1643

2 Underneath this sable hearse
Lies the subject of all verse,
Sidney's sister, Pembroke's mother;
Death, ere thou hast slain another,
Fair and learn'd, and good as she,
Time shall throw a dart at thee.
Epitaph. On the Countess of Pembroke

SIR WILLIAM BROWNE 1692–1774

3 The King to Oxford sent a troop of horse,
For Tories own no argument but force:
With equal skill to Cambridge books he sent,
For Whigs admit no force but argument.
Reply to Trapp's epigram 'The King, observing with judicious eyes' (see 234:3)
Nichols' Literary Anecdotes, vol. iii, p. 330

ELIZABETH BARRETT BROWNING 1806–1861

4 Earth's crammed with heaven,
And every common bush afire with God; *Aurora Leigh, bk. vii*

5 What was he doing, the great god Pan,
Down in the reeds by the river?
A Musical Instrument

ROBERT BROWNING 1812–1889

6 On the earth the broken arcs; in the heaven, a perfect round.
Abt Vogler, ix

7 The high that proved too high, the heroic for earth too hard,
The passion that left the ground to lose itself in the sky,
Are music sent up to God by the lover and the bard;
Enough that he heard it once: we shall hear it by and by. *Ib. x*

8 Ah, but a man's reach should exceed his grasp,
Or what's a heaven for?
Andrea del Sarto

9 Just when we're safest, there's a sun-set-touch,
A fancy from a flower-bell, some one's death,

A chorus-ending from Euripides,
And that's enough for fifty hopes and fears,—
The grand Perhaps.
Bishop Blougram's Apology

10 Gigadibs the literary man. *Ib.*

11 Oh, the little more, and how much it is!
And the little less, and what worlds away! *By the Fireside, xxxix*

12 Kentish Sir Byng stood for his King,
Bidding the crop-headed Parliament swing:
And, pressing a troop unable to stoop
And see the rogues flourish and honest folk droop,
Marched them along, fifty-score strong,
Great-hearted gentlemen, singing this song.
Cavalier Tunes, 1. Marching Along

13 Boot, saddle, to horse, and away!
Ib. 3. Boot and Saddle

14 Dauntless the slug-horn to my lips I set,
And blew.
Childe Roland to the Dark Tower came. Childe Roland, xxxiv

15 How sad and bad and mad it was—
But then, how it was sweet!
Confessions

16 Stung by the splendour of a sudden thought. *A Death in the Desert, l. 59*

17 He said, 'What's time? leave now for dogs and apes!
Man has Forever
A Grammarian's Funeral, l. 83

18 That low man seeks a little thing to do,
Sees it and does it:
This high man, with a great thing to pursue,
Dies ere he knows it.
That low man goes on adding one to one,
His hundred's soon hit:
This high man, aiming at a million,
Misses an unit.
That, has the world here—should he need the next,
Let the world mind him!
This, throws himself on God, and unperplext
Seeking shall find Him. *Ib. l. 113*

19 He settled *Hoti's* business—let it be!—
Properly based *Oun*—
Gave us the doctrine of the enclitic *De*,
Dead from the waist down.
Ib. l. 129

20 This is Ancona, yonder is the sea.
The Guardian Angel

1 Oh, to be in England
   Now that April's there,
And whoever wakes in England
   Sees, some morning, unaware,
That the lowest boughs and the
   brushwood sheaf
   Round the elm-tree bole are in tiny
   leaf,
While the chaffinch sings on the or-
   chard bough
   In England—now!
        Home-thoughts, from Abroad

2 Nobly, nobly Cape St. Vincent to the
   North-west died away;
Sunset ran, one glorious blood-red,
   reeking into Cadiz Bay.
        Home-thoughts, from the Sea

3 'Here and here did England help me:
   how can I help England?'—say,
Whoso turns as I, this evening, turn
   to God to praise and pray,
While Jove's planet rises yonder,
   silent over Africa.   *Ib.*

4   'With this same key
Shakespeare unlocked his heart' once
   more!
Did Shakespeare? If so, the less Shakespeare he!   *House*, x

5 I sprang to the stirrup, and Joris, and
   he;
I galloped, Dirck galloped, we galloped
   all three.
        How they brought the Good News
        from Ghent to Aix

6 You know, we French stormed Ratis-
   bon.   *Incident of the French Camp*

7 'You're wounded!' 'Nay,' the soldier's
   pride
Touched to the quick, he said:
'I'm killed, Sire!' And his chief beside
Smiling the boy fell dead.   *Ib.*

8 Escape me?
   Never—
Beloved!   *Life in a Love*

9 Just for a handful of silver he left us,
   Just for a riband to stick in his coat.
        The Lost Leader

10 We that had loved him so, followed
   him, honoured him,
   Lived in his mild and magnificent
   eye,
   Learned his great language, caught his
   clear accents,
   Made him our pattern to live and to
   die!   *Ib.*

11 Shakespeare was of us, Milton was
   for us,
   Burns, Shelley, were with us—they
   watch from their graves!   *Ib.*

12 Never glad confident morning again!
        Ib.

13 Ah, did you once see Shelley plain,
   And did he stop and speak to you
And did you speak to him again?
   How strange it seems, and new!
        Memorabilia

14 That's my last Duchess painted on
the wall.   *My Last Duchess*, I. i

15 Never the time and the place
   And the loved one all together!
        Never the Time and the Place

16 Round the Cape of a sudden came the
   sea,
And the sun looked over the mountain's rim;
And straight was a path of gold for
   him,
And the need of a world of men for me.
        Parting at Morning

17 It was roses, roses, all the way.
        The Patriot

18 Hamelin Town's in Brunswick,
   By famous Hanover city;
The river Weser, deep and wide,
   Washes its walls on the southern
   side.
        The Pied Piper of Hamelin, st. i

19   Shrieking and squeaking
In fifty different sharps and flats.
        Ib. ii

20 Anything like the sound of a rat
Makes my heart go pit-a-pat!   *Ib.* iv

21 In did come the strangest figure!
        Ib. v

22 So munch on, crunch on, take your
   nuncheon,
Breakfast, supper, dinner, luncheon.
        Ib. vii

23 So, Willy, let me and you be wipers
Of scores out with all men, especially
   pipers!   *Ib.* xv

24 The year's at the spring,
And day's at the morn;
Morning's at seven;
The hill-side's dew-pearled;
The lark's on the wing;
The snail's on the thorn:
   God's in his heaven—
All's right with the world!
        Pippa Passes, pt. I

25 In the morning of the world,
When earth was nigher heaven than
   now.   *Ib.* pt. III

26   Who fished the murex up?
What porridge had John Keats?
        Popularity

27   All her hair
In one long yellow string I wound
Three times her little throat around,
And strangled her. No pain felt she;
I am quite sure she felt no pain.
        Porphyria's Lover

1 And all night long we have not stirred,
And yet God has not said a word! *Ib.*

2 Fear death?—to feel the fog in my throat,
The mist in my face. *Prospice*

3 Where he stands, the Arch Fear in a visible form. *Ib.*

4 Grow old along with me!
The best is yet to be,
The last of life, for which the first was made:
Our times are in His hand
Who saith, 'A whole I planned,
Youth shows but half; trust God: see all, nor be afraid!'
Rabbi ben Ezra, i

5 Time's wheel runs back or stops:
potter and clay endure. *Ib.* xxvii

6 O lyric Love, half angel and half bird
And all a wonder and a wild desire.
The Ring and the Book, bk. 1, l. 1391

7 Gr-r-r- there go, my heart's abhorrence!
Water your damned flower-pots, do!
Soliloquy of the Spanish Cloister

8 The sin I impute to each frustrate ghost
Is—the unlit lamp and the ungirt loin,
Though the end in sight was a vice, I say. *The Statue and the Bust*

9 Greet the unseen with a cheer.
Summum Bonum (Asolando), epilogue

10 One who never turned his back but marched breast forward,
Never doubted clouds would break,
Never dreamed, though right were worsted, wrong would triumph,
Held we fall to rise, are baffled to fight better,
Sleep to wake. *Ib.*

11 What of soul was left, I wonder, when the kissing had to stop?
A Toccata of Galuppi's, xiv

12 Dear dead women, with such hair, too—what's become of all the gold
Used to hang and brush their bosoms?
I feel chilly and grown old. *Ib.* xv

13 What's become of Waring
Since he gave us all the slip?
Waring, I. i

GEORGE BRYAN BRUMMELL
1778–1840

14 Who's your fat friend? [Of the Prince of Wales.]
Gronow, *Reminiscences* (1862), p. 63

WILLIAM JENNINGS BRYAN
1860–1925

15 You shall not press down upon the brow of labor this crown of thorns, you shall not crucify mankind upon a cross of gold.
Speech at the National Democratic Convention, Chicago, 1896

WILLIAM CULLEN BRYANT
1794–1878

16 They seemed
Like old companions in adversity.
A Winter Piece, l. 26

ROBERT WILLIAMS BUCHANAN 1841–1901

17 The Fleshly School of Poetry.
Title of article in The Contemporary Review, *Oct. 1871. (Applied to Swinburne, William Morris, D. G. Rossetti, and others.)*

GEORGE VILLIERS, SECOND DUKE OF BUCKINGHAM
1628–1687

18 The world is made up for the most part of fools and knaves.
To Mr. Clifford, on his Humane Reason

19 Ay, now the plot thickens very much upon us. *The Rehearsal* III. i

HENRY J. BUCKOLL 1803–1871

20 Lord, behold us with Thy blessing
Once again assembled here.
Psalms and Hymns for the Use of Rugby School Chapel. Lord, Behold us with Thy Blessing

21 Lord, dismiss us with Thy blessing,
Thanks for mercies past receive.
Ib. Lord, Dismiss us with Thy Blessing

GEORGES-LOUIS LECLERC DE BUFFON 1707–1788

22 Le style est l'homme même.
Style is the man himself.
Discours sur le Style

23 Le génie n'est qu'une grande aptitude à la patience.
Genius is only a great aptitude for patience.
Attr. to Buffon by Hérault de Séchelles in Voyage à Montbard

ARTHUR BULLER 1874–1944

24 There was a young lady named Bright,
Whose speed was far faster than light;

She set out one day
In a relative way,
And returned home the previous night.
Limerick in Punch, *19 Dec. 1923*

ALFRED BUNN 1796?–1860

1 Alice, where art thou?   *Title of Song*

2 I dreamt that I dwelt in marble halls,
With vassals and serfs at my side.
Bohemian Girl, Act II

JOHN BUNYAN 1628–1688

3 As I walk'd through the wilderness of
this world.   *Pilgrim's Progress, pt. i*

4 The name of the slough was Despond.
Ib.

5 The gentleman's name was Mr.
Wordly-Wise-Man.   *Ib.*

6 And behold there was a very stately
palace before him, the name of which
was Beautiful.   *Ib.*

7 The valley of Humiliation.   *Ib.*

8 A foul Fiend coming over the field to
meet him; his name is Apollyon.   *Ib.*

9 It beareth the name of Vanity-Fair,
because the town where 'tis kept, is
lighter than vanity.   *Ib.*

10 Hanging is too good for him, said Mr.
Cruelty.   *Ib.*

11 A castle, called Doubting-Castle, the
owner whereof was Giant Despair.
Ib.

12 They came to the Delectable Mountains.   *Ib.*

13 Sleep is sweet to the labouring man.
Ib.

14 So I awoke, and behold it was a dream.
Ib.

15 A man that could look no way but
downwards, with a muckrake in his
hand.   *Ib. pt. ii*

16 One Great-heart.   *Ib.*

17 He that is down need fear no fall,
He that is low no pride.
He that is humble ever shall
Have God to be his guide.
*Ib. Shepherd Boy's Song in the
Valley of Humiliation*

18 An ornament to her profession.   *Ib.*

19 Whose name is Valiant-for-Truth. *Ib.*

20 Who would true valour see,
Let him come hither;
One here will constant be,
Come wind, come weather.
There's no discouragement
Shall make him once relent
His first avow'd intent
To be a pilgrim.
Then fancies flee away!

I'll fear not what men say,
I'll labour night and day
To be a pilgrim.
*Pilgrim's Progress, pt. ii.
Shepherd Boy's Song in the Valley
of Humiliation*

21 Mr. Standfast.   *Ib.*

22 My sword, I give to him that shall
succeed me in my pilgrimage, and my
courage and skill to him that can get
it. [Mr. *Valiant-for-Truth.*]   *Ib.*

23 So he passed over, and all the trumpets
sounded for him on the other side.   *Ib.*

GELETT BURGESS 1866–1951

24 I never saw a Purple Cow,
I never hope to see one;
But I can tell you, anyhow,
I'd rather see than be one!
*Burgess Nonsense Book. The
Purple Cow*

25 Ah, yes! I wrote the 'Purple Cow'—
I'm sorry, now, I wrote it!
But I can tell you anyhow,
I'll kill you if you quote it!   *Ib.*

REV. JOHN WILLIAM BURGON
1813–1888

26 A rose-red city—'half as old as Time'!
Petra, l. 132

EDMUND BURKE 1729–1797

27 Parliament is not a *congress* of ambas-
sadors from different and hostile interests; which interests each must
maintain, as an agent and advocate,
against other agents and advocates;
but parliament is a *deliberative* assembly of *one* nation, with *one* interest, that of the whole; where, not
local purposes, not local prejudices
ought to guide, but the general good,
resulting from the general reason of
the whole. You choose a member indeed; but when you have chosen him,
he is not member of Bristol, but he is
a member of *parliament.*
*Speech to the Electors of Bristol,
3 Nov. 1774*

28 Young man, there is America—which
at this day serves for little more than
to amuse you with stories of savage
men, and uncouth manners; yet shall,
before you taste of death, show itself
equal to the whole of that commerce
which now attracts the envy of the
world.
*Speech on Conciliation with
America, 22 Mar. 1775*

29 The use of force alone is but *temporary.*
It may subdue for a moment; but it
does not remove the necessity of sub-
duing again: and a nation is not
governed, which is perpetually to be
conquered.   *Ib.*

1 All protestantism, even the most cold and passive, is a sort of dissent. But the religion most prevalent in our northern colonies is a refinement on the principle of resistance: it is the dissidence of dissent, and the protestantism of the Protestant religion.
Speech on Conciliation with America, 22 Mar. 1775

2 I do not know the method of drawing up an indictment against an whole people. *Ib.*

3 It is the love of the people; it is their attachment to their government, from the sense of the deep stake they have in such a glorious institution, which gives you your army and your navy, and infuses into both that liberal obedience, without which your army would be a base rabble, and your navy nothing but rotten timber. *Ib.*

4 Magnanimity in politics is not seldom the truest wisdom; and a great empire and little minds go ill together. *Ib.*

5 By adverting to the dignity of this high calling, our ancestors have turned a savage wilderness into a glorious empire: and have made the most extensive, and the only honourable conquests, not by destroying, but by promoting the wealth, the number, the happiness of the human race. *Ib.*

6 My hold of the colonies is in the close affection which grows from common names, from kindred blood, from similar privileges, and equal protection. These are ties which, though light as air, are as strong as links of iron. *Ib.*

7 Corrupt influence, which is itself the perennial spring of all prodigality, and of all disorder; which loads us, more than millions of debt; which takes away vigour from our arms, wisdom from our councils, and every shadow of authority and credit from the most venerable parts of our constitution.
Speech on the Economical Reform, 1780

8 The people are the masters. *Ib.*

9 A rapacious and licentious soldiery.
Speech on Fox's East India Bill, 1783

10 An event has happened, upon which it is difficult to speak, and impossible to be silent.
Impeachment of Warren Hastings, 5 May 1789

11 I impeach him in the name of the people of India, whose rights he has trodden under foot, and whose country he has turned into a desert. Lastly, in the name of human nature itself, in the name of both sexes, in the name of every age, in the name of every rank, I impeach the common enemy and oppressor of all!
Impeachment of Warren Hastings, as recorded by Macaulay in his essay on Warren Hastings

12 Well stored with pious frauds, and, like most discourses of the sort, much better calculated for the private advantage of the preacher than the edification of the hearers.
Observations on a Publication, 'The present state of the nation'

13 People will not look forward to posterity, who never look backward to their ancestors.
Reflections on the Revolution in France

14 It is now sixteen or seventeen years since I saw the Queen of France, then the Dauphiness, at Versailles; and surely never lighted on this orb, which she hardly seemed to touch, a more delightful vision. I saw her just above the horizon, decorating and cheering the elevated sphere she just began to move in,—glittering like the morning star, full of life, and splendour, and joy. . . . Little did I dream that I should have lived to see disasters fallen upon her in a nation of gallant men, in a nation of men of honour, and of cavaliers. I thought ten thousand swords must have leaped from their scabbards to avenge even a look that threatened her with insult. But the age of chivalry is gone. That of sophisters, economists, and calculators, has succeeded; and the glory of Europe is extinguished for ever. *Ib.*

15 Vice itself lost half its evil, by losing all its grossness. *Ib.*

16 Superstition is the religion of feeble minds. *Ib.*

17 And having looked to government for bread, on the very first scarcity they will turn and bite the hand that fed them.
Thoughts and Details on Scarcity

18 Somebody has said, that a king may make a nobleman, but he cannot make a gentleman.
Letter to Wm. Smith, 29 Jan. 1795

19 Not merely a chip of the old 'block', but the old block itself.
On Pitt's First Speech, 1781

BISHOP GILBERT BURNET
1643–1715

20 There was a sure way never to see it lost, and that was to die in the last ditch.
History of his own Times (1715), i. 457 (1766)

1 He [Halifax] had said he had known many kicked down stairs, but he never knew any kicked up stairs before.
Original Memoirs, c. 1697

JOHN BURNS 1858–1943

2 Every drop of the Thames is liquid 'istory.
Attr. by Sir Frederick Whyte, K.C.S.I.

ROBERT BURNS 1759–1796

3 Ae fond kiss, and then we sever.
Ae Fond Kiss

4 But to see her was to love her, Love but her, and love for ever. *Ib.*

5 Had we never lov'd sae kindly, Had we never lov'd sae blindly, Never met—or never parted, We had ne'er been broken-hearted. *Ib.*

6 Should auld acquaintance be forgot, And never brought to mind?
Auld Lang Syne

7 We'll tak a cup o' kindness yet, For auld lang syne. *Ib.*

8 And there's a hand, my trusty fiere, And gie's a hand o' thine. *Ib.*

9 To make a happy fire-side clime To weans and wife, That's the true pathos and sublime Of human life. *To Dr. Blacklock*

10 Bonnie wee thing, cannie wee thing, Lovely wee thing, wert thou mine, I wad wear thee in my bosom, Lest my jewel it should tine.
The Bonnie Wee Thing

11 Gin a body meet a body Coming through the rye; Gin a body kiss a body, Need a body cry?
Coming through the Rye (taken from an old song The Bob-tailed Lass)

12 They never sought in vain that sought the Lord aright!
The Cottar's Saturday Night, vi

13 I wasna fou, but just had plenty.
Death and Dr. Hornbook, iii

14 On ev'ry hand it will allow'd be, He's just—nae better than he should be.
A Dedication to Gavin Hamilton, l. 25

15 The De'il's Awa' Wi' the Exciseman.
Title of Song

16 The rank is but the guinea's stamp; The man's the gowd for a' that!
For a' that and a' that

17 A man's a man for a' that. *Ib.*

18 Go fetch to me a pint o' wine, An' fill it in a silver tassie.
Go Fetch to Me a Pint

19 Green grow the rashes O, Green grow the rashes O; The sweetest hours that e'er I spend, Are spent amang the lasses O!
Green Grow the Rashes

20 John Anderson my jo, John, When we were first acquent, Your locks were like the raven, Your bonny brow was brent.
John Anderson My Jo

21 Now we maun totter down, John, And hand in hand we'll go, And sleep thegither at the foot, John Anderson, my jo. *Ib.*

22 There were three kings into the east, Three kings both great and high; And they hae sworn a solemn oath John Barleycorn should die.
John Barleycorn

23 O wad some Pow'r the giftie gie us To see oursels as others see us! It wad frae mony a blunder free us, And foolish notion. *To a Louse*

24 Man's inhumanity to man Makes countless thousands mourn!
Man was made to Mourn

25 Wee, sleekit, cow'rin', tim'rous beastie, O what a panic's in thy breastie! Thou need na start awa sae hasty, Wi' bickering brattle! I wad be laith to rin an' chase thee, Wi' murd'ring pattle!
To a Mouse

26 The best laid schemes o' mice an' men Gang aft a-gley. *Ib.*

27 My heart's in the Highlands, my heart is not here; My heart's in the Highlands a-chasing the deer; Chasing the wild deer, and following the roe, My heart's in the Highlands, wherever I go.
My Heart's in the Highlands

28 O, my Luve's like a red red rose That's newly sprung in June: O my Luve's like the melodie That's sweetly play'd in tune.
My Love is like a Red Red Rose

29 If there's a hole in a' your coats, I rede you tent it: A chield's amang you taking notes, And, faith, he'll prent it.
On Captain Grose's Peregrinations

30 Scots, wha hae wi' Wallace bled, Scots, wham Bruce has aften led, Welcome to your gory bed, Or to victorie.

Now's the day, and now's the hour; See the front o' battle lour! See approach proud Edward's power— Chains and slaverie!
Scots, Wha Hae

1 Liberty's in every blow!
   Let us do or die!
            Scots, Wha Hae

2 The mirth and fun grew fast and
furious.   *Tam O'Shanter, l. 143*

3 O whistle, and I'll come to you, my
   lad:
  O whistle, and I'll come to you, my
   lad:
  Tho' father and mither and a' should
   gae mad,
  O whistle, and I'll come to you, my
   lad.
      *Whistle, and I'll come to you, my
      Lad*

4 Ye banks and braes o' bonny Doon,
  How can ye bloom sae fresh and
   fair?
  How can ye chant, ye little birds,
  And I sae weary fu' o' care?
     *Ye Banks and Braes o' Bonny
     Doon*

5 Thou minds me o' departed joys,
  Departed never to return.   *Ib.*

6 Don't let the awkward squad fire over
me.
   A. Cunningham's *Works of
   Burns; with his Life* (1834), vol. i,
   p. 344

BENJAMIN HAPGOOD BURT
nineteenth century

7 When you're all dressed up and no
place to go.   *Title of Song*

ROBERT BURTON 1577–1640

8 I had no time to lick it into form, as
she [a bear] doth her young ones.
   *Anatomy of Melancholy, Demo-
   critus to the Reader*

9 What is a ship but a prison?
       Ib. pt. ii, § 3, memb. 4

10 To these crocodile's tears, they will
add sobs, fiery sighs, and sorrowful
countenance.
   Ib. pt. iii, § 2, memb. 2, subsect. 4

11 England is a paradise for women, and
hell for horses: Italy a paradise for
horses, hell for women, as the diverb
goes.   *Ib. § 3, memb. 1, subsect. 2*

12 One religion is as true as another.
      Ib. § 4, memb. 2, subsect. 1

13 Be not solitary, be not idle.
        Ib. Last words

COMTE DE BUSSY-RABUTIN
1681–1693

14 L'absence est à l'amour ce qu'est au
feu le vent; il éteint le petit, il
allume le grand.
   Absence is to love what wind is to

fire; it extinguishes the small, it en-
kindles the great.
   *Histoire amoureuse des Gaules,
   Maximes d'Amours*

BISHOP JOSEPH BUTLER
1692–1752

15 Things and actions are what they are,
and the consequences of them will be
what they will be: why then should we
desire to be deceived?
    Fifteen Sermons. No. 7, § 16

SAMUEL BUTLER 1612–1680

16 What ever sceptic could inquire for;
  For every why he had a wherefore.
      Hudibras, pt. i, c. 1, l. 131

17 He knew what's what, and that's as
  high
  As metaphysic wit can fly. *Ib. l. 149*

18 'T was Presbyterian true blue.
           Ib. l. 189

19 Compound for sins, they are inclin'd to
  By damning those they have no mind
  to.   *Ib. l. 213*

20 He ne'er consider'd it, as loth
  To look a gift-horse in the mouth.
          Ib. l. 483

21 Quoth Hudibras, I smell a rat;
  Ralpho, thou dost prevaricate.
          Ib. l. 815

22 Through perils both of wind and limb,
  Through thick and thin she follow'd
  him.   *Ib. c. 2, l. 369*

23   I'll make the fur
  Fly 'bout the ears of the old cur.
          Ib. l. 277

24 These reasons made his mouth to
water.   *Ib. l. 379*

25 Then while the honour thou hast got
  Is spick and span-new, piping hot.
          Ib. l. 398

26 Love is a boy, by poets styl'd,
  Then spare the rod, and spoil the
  child.   *Ib. pt. ii, c. 1, l. 844*

27 Have always been at daggers-drawing,
  And one another clapper-clawing.
         Ib. c. 2, l. 79

28   As the ancients
  Say wisely, Have a care o' th' main
   chance,
  And look before you ere you leap;
  For, as you sow, you are like to reap.
          Ib. l. 501

29 Doubtless the pleasure is as great
  Of being cheated, as to cheat.
  As lookers-on feel most delight,
  That least perceive a juggler's sleight,
  And still the less they understand,
  The more th' admire his sleight of
  hand.   *Ib. c. 3, l. 1*

1 To swallow gudgeons ere th'are
    catch'd,
  And count their chickens ere th'are
    hatch'd.
              Hudibras, pt. ii, c. 3, l. 923

2 For in what stupid age or nation
  Was marriage ever out of fashion?
              Ib. pt. iii, c. 1, l. 817

3 He that complies against his will,
  Is of his own opinion still.
              Ib. c. 3, l. 547

4 All love at first, like generous wine,
  Ferments and frets until 'tis fine;
  But when 'tis settled on the lee,
  And from th' impurer matter free,
  Becomes the richer still the older,
  And proves the pleasanter the colder.
              Miscellaneous Thoughts

SAMUEL BUTLER 1835–1902

5 Genius . . . has been defined as a
  supreme capacity for taking trouble.
  . . . It might be more fitly described
  as a supreme capacity for getting its
  possessors into trouble of all kinds
  and keeping them therein so long as
  the genius remains.
              Notebooks, Genius, i

6 The phrase 'unconscious humour' is
  the one contribution I have made to
  the current literature of the day.
              *Ib. The Position of a Homo Unius
              Libri. Myself and 'Unconscious
              Humour'*

7 An honest God's the noblest work of
  man.
              *Further Extracts from the Note-
              books* (1934), p. 26. *See also
              Festing Jones, Memoir* (1919),
              vol. i, p. 212.

8 The advantage of doing one's praising
  for oneself is that one can lay it on so
  thick and exactly in the right places.
              The Way of All Flesh, ch. 34

9 There's many a good tune played on
  an old fiddle.   *Ib.* ch. 61

10 O God! Oh Montreal!
              Psalm of Montreal

WILLIAM BUTLER 1535–1618

11 Doubtless God could have made a
   better berry [strawberry], but doubtless God never did.
              Walton, *Compleat Angler*, pt. i,
              ch. 5

JOHN BYROM 1692–1763

12 Some say, that Signor Bononcini,
   Compar'd to Handel's a mere ninny;

Others aver, to him, that Handel
Is scarcely fit to hold a candle.
Strange! that such high dispute shou'd
  be
'Twixt Tweedledum and Tweedledee.
              *Epigram on the Feuds between
              Handel and Bononcini*

13 I shall prove it—as clear as a whistle.
              Epistle to Lloyd, I. xii

14 Christians awake, salute the happy
   morn,
   Whereon the Saviour of the world was
   born.   *Hymn for Christmas Day*

15 God bless the King, I mean the Faith's
   Defender;
   God bless—no harm in blessing—the
   Pretender;
   But who Pretender is, or who is King,
   God bless us all—that's quite another
   thing.   *To an Officer in the Army*

GEORGE GORDON BYRON, LORD BYRON 1788–1824

16 In short, he was a perfect cavaliero,
   And to his very valet seem'd a hero.
              Beppo, xxxiii

17 His heart was one of those which most
   enamour us,
   Wax to receive, and marble to retain.
              Ib. xxxiv

18 Mark! where his carnage and his conquests cease!
   He makes a solitude, and calls it—
   peace!   *Bride of Abydos,* c. II. xx

19 Hark! to the hurried question of
   Despair:
   'Where is my child?'—an echo answers
   —'Where?'   *Ib.* xxvii

20 War, war is still the cry, 'War even
   to the knife!'
              Childe Harold, c. I. lxxxvi

21 A schoolboy's tale, the wonder of an
   hour!   *Ib.* c. II. ii

22 Where'er we tread 'tis haunted, holy
   ground.   *Ib.* lxxxviii

23 There was a sound of revelry by night,
   And Belgium's capital had gather'd
     then
   Her beauty and her chivalry, and
     bright
   The lamps shone o'er fair women and
     brave men;
   A thousand hearts beat happily; and
     when
   Music arose with its voluptuous
     swell,
   Soft eyes look'd love to eyes which
     spake again,
   And all went merry as a marriage
     bell;
   But hush! hark! a deep sound strikes
   like a rising knell!   *Ib.* c. III. xxi

1 Did ye not hear it?—No; 'twas but the
      wind,
      Or the car rattling o'er the stony
         street;
      On with the dance! let joy be uncon-
         fined;
      No sleep till morn, when Youth and
         Pleasure meet
   To chase the glowing Hours with
      flying feet.
                  Childe Harolde, c. III. xxii

2 Arm! Arm! it is—it is—the cannon's
      opening roar!   *Ib.*

3 He rush'd into the field, and, foremost
      fighting, fell.   *Ib.*

4 Yet, Freedom! yet thy banner, torn,
      but flying,
      Streams like the thunder-storm *against*
      the wind.   *Ib.* c. IV. xcviii

5 He reck'd not of the life he lost nor
      prize,
      But where his rude hut by the Danube
         lay,
      There were his young barbarians all
         at play,
      There was their Dacian mother—he,
         their sire,
      Butcher'd to make a Roman holiday.
                              Ib. cxli

6 While stands the Coliseum, Rome
      shall stand;
      When falls the Coliseum, Rome shall
         fall;
      And when Rome falls—the World.
                              Ib. cxlv

7 There is a pleasure in the pathless
      woods,
      There is a rapture on the lonely shore,
      There is society, where none intrudes,
      By the deep sea, and music in its roar:
      I love not man the less, but Nature
         more,
      From these our interviews, in which
         I steal
      From all I may be, or have been before,
      To mingle with the Universe, and feel
      What I can ne'er express, yet cannot
         all conceal.   *Ib.* clxxviii

8 Roll on, thou deep and dark blue
      Ocean—roll!
      Ten thousand fleets sweep over thee
         in vain;   *Ib.* clxxix

9 Eternal spirit of the chainless mind!
      Brightest in dungeons, Liberty! thou
         art.   *Sonnet on Chillon*

10 Her stature tall—I hate a dumpy
      woman.   *Don Juan*, c. I. lxi

11 What men call gallantry, and gods
      adultery,
      Is much more common where the
         climate's sultry.   *Ib.* lxiii

12 A little still she strove, and much
      repented,
      And whispering 'I will ne'er consent'—
         consented.   *Ib.* cxvii

13 'Tis sweet to hear the watch-dog's
      honest bark
      Bay deep-mouth'd welcome as we
         draw near home;
      'Tis sweet to know there is an eye
         will mark
      Our coming, and look brighter when
         we come.   *Don Juan*, c. I. cxxiii

14 Man's love is of man's life a thing
      apart,
      'Tis woman's whole existence.
                              Ib. cxciv

15 Let us have wine and women, mirth
      and laughter,
      Sermons and soda-water the day after.
                        Ib. c. II. clxxviii

16 He was the mildest manner'd man
      That ever scuttled ship or cut a
         throat,
      With such true breeding of a gentle-
         man,
      You never could divine his real
         thought.   *Ib.* c. III. xli

17 The isles of Greece, the isles of Greece!
      Where burning Sappho loved and
         sung,
      Where grew the arts of war and peace,
      Where Delos rose, and Phœbus
         sprung!
      Eternal summer gilds them yet,
      But all, except their sun, is set.
                              Ib. lxxxvi. 1

18 The mountains look on Marathon—
      And Marathon looks on the sea;
      And musing there an hour alone,
      I dream'd that Greece might still be
         free.   *Ib.* 3

19 A king sate on the rocky brow
      Which looks o'er sea-born Salamis;
      And ships, by thousands, lay below,
      And men in nations;—all were his!
      He counted them at break of day—
      And when the sun set where were they?
                              Ib. 4

20 Earth! render back from out thy breast
   A remnant of our Spartan dead!
   Of the three hundred grant but three,
   To make a new Thermopylæ!   *Ib.* 7

21 Fill high the cup with Samian wine!
                        Ib. lxxxvi. 9

22 And if I laugh at any mortal thing,
   'Tis that I may not weep.   *Ib.* c. IV. iv

23 A lady in the case.   *Ib.* c. V. xix

24 That all-softening, overpowering knell,
   The tocsin of the soul—the dinner-bell.
                              Ib. xlix

25 John Keats, who was kill'd off by one
      critique,
   Just as he really promised something
      great,
   If not intelligible, without Greek
   Contrived to talk about the Gods of
      late,

Much as they might have been supposed to speak.
Poor fellow! His was an untoward
fate;
'Tis strange the mind, that very fiery
particle,
Should let itself be snuff'd out by an
article.   *Don Juan, c.* XI. lx

1 A finish'd gentleman from top to toe.
          Ib. c. XII. lxxxiv

2 'Tis strange—but true; for truth is
always strange;
Stranger than fiction.   *Ib. c.* XIV. ci

3 With just enough of learning to mis-
quote.
          *English Bards and Scotch Re-
          viewers* l. 66

4 Or lend fresh interest to a twice-told
tale.   *Hints from Horace,* l. 184

5 Though women are angels, yet wed-
lock's the devil.
          Hours of Idleness. To Eliza

6 Who killed John Keats?
'I,' says the Quarterly,
So savage and Tartarly;
''Twas one of my feats.'   *John Keats*

7 Oh, talk not to me of a name great in
story;
The days of our youth are the days of
our glory;
And the myrtle and ivy of sweet
two-and-twenty
Are worth all your laurels, though
ever so plenty.
          *Stanzas Written on the Road be-
          tween Florence and Pisa*

8 I am the very slave of circumstance
And impulse—borne away with every
breath!   *Sardanapalus,* iv. i

9 The Assyrian came down like the wolf
on the fold,
And his cohorts were gleaming in
purple and gold;
And the sheen of their spears was like
stars on the sea,
When the blue wave rolls nightly on
deep Galilee.
          Destruction of Sennacherib

10 For the Angel of Death spread his
wings on the blast.   *Ib.*

11 And the might of the Gentile, unsmote
by the sword,
Hath melted like snow in the glance of
the Lord!   *Ib.*

12 She walks in beauty, like the night
Of cloudless climes and starry
skies;
          *Hebrew Melodies. She Walks in
          Beauty*

13 So, we'll go no more a roving
So late into the night,
Though the heart be still as loving,
And the moon be still as bright.
          So, We'll Go No More a Roving

14 For the sword outwears its sheath,
And the soul wears out the breast.
And the heart must pause to breathe,
And love itself have rest.   *Ib.*

15 Though the night was made for loving,
And the day returns too soon,
Yet we'll go no more a-roving
By the light of the moon.   *Ib.*

16 When we two parted
In silence and tears,
Half broken-hearted
To sever for years,
Pale grew thy cheek and cold,
Colder thy kiss.
          When We Two Parted

17 If I should meet thee
After long years,
How should I greet thee?—
With silence and tears.   *Ib.*

18 As he [Lord Byron] himself briefly
described it in his Memoranda, 'I
awoke one morning and found myself famous.'—Moore's *Life of Byron*
(1830), vol. i, p. 347 (referring to the
instantaneous success of *Childe
Harold*)

JAMES BRANCH CABELL 1879–

19 The optimist proclaims that we live
in the best of all possible worlds; and
the pessimist fears this is true.
          The Silver Stallion, bk. iv, ch. 26

AUGUSTUS CAESAR
          63 B.C.–A.D. 14

20 Quintili Vare, legiones redde.
Quintilius Varus, give me back my
legions.
          Suetonius, *Divus Augustus,* 23

21 Urbem . . . excoluit adeo, ut iure sit
gloriatus marmoream se relinquere,
quam latericiam accepisset.
He so improved the city that he
justly boasted that he found it
brick and left it marble. *Ib.* 28

22 Ad Graecas Kalendas soluturos.
They will pay at the Greek Kalends.
          Ib. 87

JULIUS CAESAR 102?–44 B.C.

23 Gallia est omnis divisa in partes tres.
Gaul as a whole is divided into three
parts.   *De Bello Gallico,* I. i

1 Et tu, Brute?
  You also, Brutus?
      *Of unknown origin. Quoted by
      Shakespeare, 'Julius Caesar',
      III. i, perhaps from the (lost) Latin
      play 'Caesar Interfectus', prob-
      ably from 'The True Tragedie
      of Richard Duke of York.'
      'Some have written that as M.
      Brutus came running upon him,
      he said "καὶ σύ, τέκνον", "and
      you, my son." '*
          (Holland's *Suetonius*, p. 33)

2 Veni, vidi, vici.
  I came, I saw, I conquered.
      *Suetonius, Divus Julius, xxxvii.
      2.
      (Inscription displayed in Caesar's
      Pontic triumph, or, according to
      Plutarch, l. 2, written in a letter
      by Caesar, announcing the victory
      of Zela which concluded the Pontic
      campaign)*

3 Iacta alea est.
  The die is cast.   Ib. xxxii
      At the crossing of the Rubicon

CALIGULA A.D. 12–41
4 Utinam populus Romanus unam
  cervicem haberet!
      Would that the Roman people had
      but one neck!
          Suetonius, Life of Caligula, 30

CALLIMACHUS *fl.* 250 B.C.
5 μέγα βιβλίον μέγα κακόν.
  Great book, great evil.
      *Proverb derived from Calli-
      machus, Fragments, 359*

CHARLES STUART CALVERLEY
                1831–1884
6 The farmer's daughter hath soft
  brown hair;
      (*Butter and eggs and a pound of
      cheese*)
  And I met with a ballad, I can't say
  where,
  Which wholly consisted of lines like
  these.   *Ballad*

7 A bare-legg'd beggarly son of a gun.
      The Cock and the Bull

8 Life is with such all beer and skittles;
  They are not difficult to please
  About their victuals.   *Contentment*

9 Sweet, when the morn is grey;
  Sweet, when they've cleared away
  Lunch; and at close of day
  Possibly sweetest. *Ode to Tobacco*

**PIERRE-JACQUES, BARON DE
CAMBRONNE** 1770–1842
10 La Garde meurt, mais ne se rend pas.
   The Guards die but do not surrender.
      *Attr. to Cambronne when called
      upon to surrender by Col. Halkett.
      Cambronne denied the saying at
      a banquet at Nantes, 1835*

WILLIAM CAMDEN 1551–1623
11 My friend, judge not me,
   Thou seest I judge not thee.
   Betwixt the stirrup and the ground
   Mercy I asked, mercy I found.
      *Remains. Epitaph for a Man
      Killed by Falling from His Horse*

**JANE MONTGOMERY
CAMPBELL** 1817–1878
12 We plough the fields, and scatter
   The good seed on the land,
   But it is fed and watered
   By God's Almighty Hand;
   He sends the snow in winter,
   The warmth to swell the grain,
   The breezes and the sunshine,
   And soft refreshing rain.
   All good gifts around us
   Are sent from Heaven above,
   Then thank the Lord, O thank the
   Lord,
   For all His love.
      *We Plough the Fields. Trans. from
      the German. C. S. Bere's Gar-
      land of Songs*

THOMAS CAMPBELL 1777–1844
13 O leave this barren spot to me!
   Spare, woodman, spare the beechen
   tree.   *The Beech-Tree's Petition*

14 To live in hearts we leave behind
   Is not to die.   *Hallowed Ground*

15 On Linden, when the sun was low,
   All bloodless lay the untrodden snow,
   And dark as winter was the flow
   Of Iser, rolling rapidly.   *Hohenlinden*

16 'Tis the sunset of life gives me mysti-
   cal lore,
   And coming events cast their shadows
   before.   *Lochiel's Warning*

17 A chieftain to the Highlands bound
   Cries, 'Boatman, do not tarry!
   And I'll give thee a silver pound
   To row us o'er the ferry.'
          Lord Ullin's Daughter

18 'O, I'm the chief of Ulva's isle,
   And this Lord Ullin's daughter.'
                              Ib.

1 'Come back! come back!' he cried in
  grief
    Across the stormy water:
  'And I'll forgive your Highland chief,
  My daughter! oh my daughter!'
                    Lord Ullin's Daughter

2 With Freedom's lion-banner
  Britannia rules the waves.
                    Ode to the Germans

3 'Tis distance lends enchantment to the
  view,
  And robes the mountain in its azure
  hue.   *Pleasures of Hope*, pt. i, l. 7

4 The proud, the cold untroubled heart
  of stone,
  That never mused on sorrow but its
  own.   *Ib.* l. 185

5 Hope, for a season, bade the world
  farewell,
  And Freedom shrieked—as Kosciusko
  fell!   *Ib.* l. 381

6 Ye Mariners of England
  That guard our native seas,
  Whose flag has braved, a thousand
  years,
  The battle and the breeze—
  Your glorious standard launch again
  To match another foe!
  And sweep through the deep,
  While the stormy winds do blow,—
  While the battle rages loud and long,
  And the stormy winds do blow.
                    Ye Mariners of England

7 Britannia needs no bulwarks,
  No towers along the steep;
  Her march is o'er the mountain waves,
  Her home is on the deep.   *Ib.*

8 The meteor flag of England
  Shall yet terrific burn,
  Till danger's troubled night depart
  And the star of peace return.   *Ib.*

9 Now Barabbas was a publisher.
                    Often attr. to Byron

THOMAS CAMPION d. 1620

10 Good thoughts his only friends,
     His wealth a well-spent age,
   The earth his sober inn
     And quiet pilgrimage.
                    A Book of Airs, xviii

11 There is a garden in her face,
   Where roses and white lilies grow;
   A heav'nly paradise is that place,
   Wherein all pleasant fruits do flow.
   There cherries grow, which none may
   buy
   Till 'Cherry ripe' themselves do cry.
                    Fourth Book of Airs, vii

GEORGE CANNING 1770–1827

12 In matters of commerce the fault of
   the Dutch
     Is offering too little and asking too
     much.

The French are with equal advantage
content,
So we clap on Dutch bottoms just
twenty per cent.
        *Dispatch, in Cipher, To Sir
        Charles Bagot, English Ambas-
        sador at The Hague, 31 Jan. 1826*

13 A steady patriot of the world alone,
   The friend of every country but his
   own. [The Jacobin.]
                    New Morality, l. 113

14 Give me the avowed, erect and manly
   foe;
   Firm I can meet, perhaps return the
   blow;
   But of all plagues, good Heaven, thy
   wrath can send,
   Save me, oh, save me, from the candid
   friend.   *Ib.* l. 207

15 Pitt is to Addington
   As London is to Paddington.
                    The Oracle, c. 1803–4

16 A sudden thought strikes me, let us
   swear an eternal friendship.
                    The Rovers, I. i

17 (*Pitt:*)
   When our perils are past, shall our
   gratitude sleep?
   No,—here's to the pilot that
   weathered the storm.
                    *Song for the inauguration of the
                    Pitt Club, 25 May 1802*

18 I called the New World into existence,
   to redress the balance of the Old.
                    Speech, 12 Dec. 1826

FRANCESCO CARACCIOLI
                    1752–1799

19 Il y a en Angleterre soixante sectes
   religieuses différentes, et une seule
   sauce.
     In England there are sixty different
     religions, and only one sauce.
                    Attr.

THOMAS CAREW 1595?–1639?

20 Here lies a King that rul'd, as he
   thought fit
   The universal monarchy of wit;
   Here lies two Flamens, and both those
   the best:
   Apollo's first, at last the true God's
   priest.   *Elegy on the Death of Donne*

21 An untimely grave.
                    *Inscription on Tomb of the Duke
                    of Buckingham*

HENRY CAREY 1693?–1743

22 God save our gracious king!
   Long live our noble king!
     God save the king!
                    God Save the King

1 Confound their politics,
  Frustrate their knavish tricks.   *Ib.*

2 Of all the girls that are so smart
  There's none like pretty Sally,
  She is the darling of my heart,
  And she lives in our alley.
                          Sally in our Alley

3 When she is by I leave my work,
  (I love her so sincerely)
  My master comes like any Turk,
  And bangs me most severely.   *Ib.*

4 Of all the days that's in the week
  I dearly love but one day—
  And that's the day that comes be-
      twixt
  A Saturday and Monday.   *Ib.*

THOMAS CARLYLE 1795–1881

5 The three great elements of modern
  civilization, Gunpowder, Printing, and
  the Protestant Religion.
            *Critical   and   Miscellaneous
            Essays,* vol. i. *State of German
            Literature*

6 To the very last, he [Napoleon] had
  a kind of idea; that, namely, of
  La carrière ouverte aux talents, The
  tools to him that can handle them.
            Ib. vol. iv. *Sir Walter Scott*

7 A witty statesman said, you might
  prove anything by figures.
            Ib. Chartism, ch. 2

8 In epochs when cash payment has become the sole nexus of man to man.
            Ib. ch. 6

9 'Genius' (which means transcendent
  capacity of taking trouble, first of all).
            Frederick the Great, bk. iv, ch. 3

10 Happy the people whose annals are
   blank in history-books!
            Ib. bk. xvi, ch. 1

11 A whiff of grapeshot.
            History of the French Revolution,
            pt. 1, bk. v, ch. 3

12 The seagreen Incorruptible. [Robes-
   pierre.]   *Ib.* pt. II, ch. 4

13 No great man lives in vain. The history of the world is but the biography of great men.
            Heroes and Hero Worship, i. *The
            Hero as Divinity*

14 The true University of these days is a
   collection of books.
            Ib. v. *The Hero as Man of
            Letters*

15 Burke said there were Three Estates
   in Parliament; but, in the Reporters'
   Gallery yonder, there sat a *Fourth
   Estate* more important far than they
   all.   *Ib.*

16 A Parliament speaking through reporters to Buncombe and the twenty-
   seven millions mostly fools.
            Latter-Day Pamphlets No. 6.
            Parliaments

17 The unspeakable Turk should be immediately struck out of the question.
            Letter to G. Howard, 24 Nov. 1876

18 Transcendental moonshine.
            Life of John Sterling, pt. i, ch. 15

19 Captains of industry.
            Past and Present, bk. iv, title of
            ch. 4

20 Man is a tool-using animal. . . .
   Without tools he is nothing, with
   tools he is all.
            Sartor Resartus, bk. i, ch. 5

21 I don't pretend to understand the
   Universe—it's a great deal bigger
   than I am. . . . People ought to be
   modester.
            Remark to Wm. Allingham. D. A.
            Wilson's and D. Wilson Mac-
            Arthur *Carlyle in Old Age*

22 Macaulay is well for a while, but one
   wouldn't *live* under Niagara.
            Remark. R. M. Milnes's *Note-
            book* (1838)

23 Who never ate his bread in sorrow,
   Who never spent the darksome hours
   Weeping and watching for the morrow
   He knows ye not, ye heavenly Powers.
            Translation of Goethe's *Wilhelm
            Meister's Apprenticeship,* bk. ii,
            ch. 13

24 MARGARET FULLER:
   I accept the universe.
   CARLYLE:
   Gad! she'd better!   *Attr.*

DALE CARNEGIE 1888–1955

25 How to win Friends and influence
   People.   *Title of Book*

JULIA CARNEY 1823–1908

26 Little drops of water, little grains of
      sand,
   Make the mighty ocean, and the
      pleasant land.
   So the little minutes, humble though
      they be,
   Make the mighty ages of eternity.
            Little Things. (Attr. also to E. C.
            Brewer, D. C. Colesworthy, and
            F. S. Osgood)

JOSEPH EDWARDS CARPENTER
1813–1885

27 What are the wild waves saying
      Sister, the whole day long,
   That ever amid our playing,
      I hear but their low lone song?
            What are the Wild Waves Saying?

LEWIS CARROLL [CHARLES LUTWIDGE DODGSON] 1832–1898

1 What I tell you three times is true.
> *Hunting of the Snark*, Fit 1.
> *The Landing*

2 He would answer to 'Hi!' or to any
> loud cry,
> Such as 'Fry me!' or 'Fritter-my-
> wig!'   *Ib.*

3 His intimate friends called him
> 'Candle-ends',
> And his enemies, 'Toasted-cheese'
>   *Ib.*

4 But oh, beamish nephew, beware of
> the day,
> If your Snark be a Boojum! For
> then
> You will softly and suddenly vanish
> away,
> And never be met with again!
> *Ib.* Fit 3. *The Baker's Tale*

5 They sought it with thimbles, they
> sought it with care;
> They pursued it with forks and
> hope;
> They threatened its life with a rail-
> way-share;
> They charmed it with smiles and
> soap.
> *Ib.* Fit 5. *The Beaver's Lesson*

6 For the Snark *was* a Boojum, you see.
> *Ib.* Fit 8. *The Vanishing*

7 He thought he saw an Elephant,
> That practised on a fife:
> He looked again, and found it was
> A letter from his wife.
> 'At length I realize,' he said,
> 'The bitterness of life!'
> *Sylvie and Bruno*, ch. 5

8 He thought he saw a Rattlesnake
> That questioned him in Greek,
> He looked again and found it was
> The Middle of Next Week.
> 'The one thing I regret,' he said,
> 'Is that it cannot speak!'   *Ib.* ch. 6

9 He thought he saw a Banker's Clerk
> Descending from the bus:
> He looked again, and found it was
> A Hippopotamus:
> 'If this should stay to dine,' he said,
> 'There won't be much for us.'
>   *Ib.* ch. 7

10 'What is the use of a book', thought
> Alice, 'without pictures or conver-
> sations?'   *Alice in Wonderland*, ch. 1

11 Do cats eat bats? . . . Do bats eat
> cats?   *Ib.*

12 'Curiouser and curiouser!' cried Alice.
>   *Ib.* ch. 2

13 How doth the little crocodile
> Improve his shining tail,
> And pour the waters of the Nile
> On every golden scale!   *Ib.*

14 'I'll be judge, I'll be jury,' said cun-
> ning old Fury;
> 'I'll try the whole cause, and con-
> demn you to death.'
> *Alice in Wonderland*, ch. 3

15 The Duchess! The Duchess!
> O my dear paws! Oh my fur and whis-
> kers!   *Ib.* ch. 4

16 'You are old, Father William,' the
> young man said,
> 'And your hair has become very
> white;
> And yet you incessantly stand on your
> head—
> Do you think, at your age, it is
> right?'
>
> 'In my youth,' Father William replied
> to his son.
> 'I feared it might injure the brain;
> But now that I'm perfectly sure I have
> none,
> Why, I do it again and again.'
>   *Ib.* ch. 5

17 'I have answered three questions, and
> that is enough,'
> Said his father; 'don't give yourself
> airs!
> Do you think I can listen all day to
> such stuff?
> Be off, or I'll kick you downstairs!'
>   *Ib.*

18 'If everybody minded their own
> business,' said the Duchess in a hoarse
> growl, 'the world would go round a
> deal faster than it does.' *Ib.* ch. 6

19 Speak roughly to your little boy,
> And beat him when he sneezes;
> He only does it to annoy,
> Because he knows it teases.   *Ib.*

20 For he can thoroughly enjoy
> The pepper when he pleases!   *Ib.*

21 This time it vanished quite slowly,
> beginning with the end of the tail, and
> ending with the grin, which remained
> some time after the rest of it had gone.
> [The Cheshire Cat.]   *Ib.*

22 'Then you should say what you mean,'
> the March Hare went on. 'I do,'
> Alice hastily replied; 'at least—at
> least I mean what I say—that's the
> same thing, you know.'
> 'Not the same thing a bit!' said the
> Hatter. 'Why, you might just as well
> say that "I see what I eat" is the same
> thing as "I eat what I see!" '
>   *Ib.* ch. 7

23 'It was the *best* butter,' the March
> Hare meekly replied.   *Ib.*

24 Twinkle, twinkle, little bat!
> How I wonder what you're at!
> Up above the world you fly!
> Like a teatray in the sky.   *Ib.*

1 The Queen was in a furious passion,
and went stamping about, and shouting, 'Off with his head!' or 'Off with
her head!' about once in a minute.
Alice in Wonderland, ch. 8

2 'A cat may look at a king,' said Alice.
Ib.

3 And the moral of that is—'Oh, 'tis
love, 'tis love, that makes the world
go round!'   *Ib.* ch. 9

4 Take care of the sense, and the sounds
will take care of themselves.   *Ib.*

5 I only took the regular course . . .
the different branches of Arithmetic—
Ambition, Distraction, Uglification,
and Derision.   *Ib.*

6 'That's the reason they're called
lessons,' the Gryphon remarked: 'because they lessen from day to day.' *Ib.*

7 'Will you walk a little faster?' said
a whiting to a snail,
'There's a porpoise close behind us,
and he's treading on my tail.'
Ib. ch. 10

8 Will you, won't you, will you, won't
you, will you join the dance?   *Ib.*

9 The further off from England the
nearer is to France—
Then turn not pale, beloved snail,
but come and join the dance.   *Ib.*

10 'Tis the voice of the lobster; I heard
him declare,
'You have baked me too brown, I
must sugar my hair.'   *Ib.*

11 Soup of the evening, beautiful Soup!
Ib.

12 The Queen of Hearts, she made some
tarts,
All on a summer day:
The Knave of Hearts, he stole those
tarts,
And took them quite away!
Ib. ch. 11

13 'Where shall I begin, please your
Majesty?' he asked.
'Begin at the beginning,' the King
said, gravely, 'and go on till you
come to the end: then stop.'   *Ib.*

14 'Twas brillig, and the slithy toves
Did gyre and gimble in the wabe;
All mimsy were the borogoves,
And the mome raths outgrabe.

'Beware the Jabberwock, my son!
The jaws that bite, the claws that
catch!
Beware the Jubjub bird, and shun
The frumious Bandersnatch!'

He took his vorpal sword in hand:
Long time the manxome foe he
sought—
So rested he by the Tumtum tree,
And stood awhile in thought.

And as in uffish thought he stood,
The Jabberwock, with eyes of flame,
Came whiffling through the tulgey
wood,
And burbled as it came!

One, two! One, two! And through and
through
The vorpal blade went snicker-
snack!
He left it dead, and with its head
He went galumphing back.

'And hast thou slain the Jabberwock?
Come to my arms, my beamish boy!
O frabjous day! Callooh! Callay!'
He chortled in his joy.
Through the Looking-Glass, ch. 1

15 Curtsey while you're thinking what
to say. It saves time.   *Ib.* ch. 2

16 Speak in French when you can't think
of the English for a thing.   *Ib.*

17 Now, *here* you see, it takes all the
running *you* can do, to keep in the
same place. If you want to get somewhere else, you must run at least
twice as fast as that!   *Ib.*

18 Tweedledum and Tweedledee
Agreed to have a battle;
For Tweedledum said Tweedledee
Had spoiled his nice new rattle.

Just then flew down a monstrous crow,
As black as a tar-barrel;
Which frightened both the heroes so,
They quite forgot their quarrel.
Ib. ch. 4

19 'Contrariwise,' continued Tweedledee,
'if it was so, it might be; and if it
were so, it would be: but as it isn't,
it ain't. That's logic.'   *Ib.*

20 The sun was shining on the sea,
Shining with all his might:
He did his very best to make
The billows smooth and bright—
And this was odd, because it was
The middle of the night.
Ib. The Walrus and the Carpenter

21 The Walrus and the Carpenter
Were walking close at hand;
They wept like anything to see
Such quantities of sand:
'If this were only cleared away,'
They said, 'it would be grand!'

'If seven maids with seven mops
Swept it for half a year,
Do you suppose,' the Walrus said,
'That they could get it clear?'
'I doubt it,' said the Carpenter,
And shed a bitter tear.   *Ib.*

22 'The time has come,' the Walrus said,
'To talk of many things:
Of shoes—and ships—and sealing
wax—
Of cabbages—and kings—
And why the sea is boiling hot—
And whether pigs have wings.' *Ib.*

1 But answer came there none—
  And this was scarcely odd because
    They'd eaten every one.
          Through the Looking-Glass.
          The Walrus and the Carpenter

2 'Let's fight till six, and then have
  dinner,' said Tweedledum.   *Ib.*

3 The rule is, jam to-morrow and jam
  yesterday—but never jam to-day.
                          Ib. ch. 5

4 They gave it me,—for an un-birthday
  present.   *Ib.* ch. 6

5 'There's glory for you!' 'I don't know
  what you mean by "glory",' Alice
  said. 'I meant, "there's a nice knock-
  down argument for you!"' 'But
  "glory" doesn't mean "a nice knock-
  down argument",' Alice objected.
  'When I use a word,' Humpty Dumpty
  said in a rather scornful tone, 'it means
  just what I choose it to mean,—
  neither more nor less.'   *Ib.*

6 I said it very loud and clear;
  I went and shouted in his ear.

  But he was very stiff and proud;
  He said 'You needn't shout so loud!'

  And he was very proud and stiff;
  He said 'I'd go and wake them, if——'
                              Ib.

7 You see it's like a portmanteau—there
  are two meanings packed up into one
  word.   *Ib.*

8 He's an Anglo-Saxon Messenger—
  and those are Anglo-Saxon attitudes.
                          Ib. ch. 7

9 It's as large as life, and twice as
  natural!   *Ib.*

10 The [White] Knight said . . . 'It's my
   own invention.'   *Ib.*

11 I'll tell thee everything I can:
   There's little to relate.
   I saw an aged, aged man,
   A-sitting on a gate.   *Ib.*

12 He said, 'I hunt for haddocks' eyes
   Among the heather bright,
   And work them into waistcoat-buttons
   In the silent night.   *Ib.*

13 I sometimes dig for buttered rolls,
   Or set limed twigs for crabs;
   I sometimes search the grassy knolls
   For wheels of hansom-cabs.' *Ib.*

14 Or madly squeeze a right-hand foot
   Into a left-hand shoe.   *Ib.*

15 'Speak when you're spoken to!' the
   Red Queen sharply interrupted her.
                          Ib. ch. 9

16 It isn't etiquette to cut any one you've
   been introduced to. Remove the joint.
                              Ib.

WILLIAM HERBERT CARRUTH
1859–1924

17 Some call it evolution,
   And others call it God.
          *Each In His Own Tongue, and
          Other Poems* (1908)

PHOEBE CARY 1824–1871

18 And though hard be the task,
   'Keep a stiff upper lip'.
              Keep a Stiff Upper Lip

HARRY CASTLING

19 What-Ho! She bumps!   *Title of Song*

20 Let's all go down the Strand.
                      Title of Song

REV. EDWARD CASWALL
1814–1878

(As *adapted* in 'Hymns Ancient and
Modern'):

21 Days and moments quickly flying,
     Blend the living with the dead;
   Soon will you and I be lying
     Each within our narrow bed.
          *Hymns and Poems. Days and
          Moments Quickly Flying*

22 Earth has many a noble city;
   Bethlehem, thou dost all excel.
          Ib. Earth Has Many a Noble City

23 Jesu, the very thought of Thee
   With sweetness fills the breast.
              *Ib. Jesu, The Very Thought of
              Thee* (trans. from Latin)

CATO THE ELDER 234–149 B.C.

24 Delenda est Carthago.
          Carthage must be destroyed.
                      Plutarch, *Life of Cato*

CATULLUS 84?–54? B.C.

25 Lugete, O Veneres Cupidinesque,
   Et quantum est hominum venusti-
     orum.
   Passer mortuus est meae puellae,
   Passer, deliciae meae puellae.

     Come, all ye Loves and Cupids,
       haste
     To mourn, and all ye men of taste;
     My lady's sparrow, O, he's sped,
     The bird my lady loved is dead!
          Carmina, iii, trans. by Sir W.
          Marris

26 Vivamus, mea Lesbia, atque amemus,
   Rumoresque senum severiorum
   Omnes unius aestimemus assis.
   Soles occidere et redire possunt:
   Nobis cum semel occidit brevis lux
   Nox est perpetua una dormienda.

     Lesbia mine, let's live and love!
     Give no doit for tattle of
     Crabbed old censorious men;

Suns may set and rise again,
But when our short day takes flight
Sleep we must one endless night.
Carmina, v

1 Da mi basia mille.
Kiss me times a thousand o'er. *Ib.*

2 Odi et amo: quare id faciam, fortasse requiris.
Nescio, sed fieri sentio et excrucior.
I hate, I love—the cause thereof
Belike you ask of me:
I do not know, but feel 'tis so,
And I'm in agony. *Ib.* lxxxv

3 Accipe fraterno multum manantia fletu,
Atque in perpetuum, frater, ave atque vale.
A brother's tears have wet them o'er and o'er;
And so, my brother, hail, and farewell evermore! *Ib.* ci

EDITH CAVELL 1865–1915

4 I realize that patriotism is not enough.
I must have no hatred or bitterness towards anyone.
Last Words, 12 Oct. 1915. The Times, 23 Oct. 1915

ROBERT CECIL
see SALISBURY

THOMAS OF CELANO c. 1250

5 Dies irae, dies illa
Solvet saeclum in favilla,
Teste David cum Sibylla.
Day of wrath and doom impending,
David's word with Sibyl's blending
Heaven and earth in ashes ending!
Analecta Hymnica, liv, p. 269.
(Trans. by Dr. W. J. Irons in *The English Hymnal*)

SUSANNAH CENTLIVRE
1667?–1723

6 The real Simon Pure.
Bold Stroke for a Wife, v. i.

7 And lash the vice and follies of the age.
The Man's Bewitched, prologue

MIGUEL DE CERVANTES
1547–1616

8 El Caballero de la Triste Figura.
The Knight of the Sorrowful Countenance.
Don Quixote, pt. i, ch. 19. *Trans. by* Smollett

9 La mejor salsa del mundo es el hambre.
The best sauce in the world is hunger. *Ib.* pt. ii, ch. 5

10 Muchos pocos hacen un mucho.
Many a pickle makes a mickle.
Don Quixote, pt. ii, ch. 7

11 Dos linages sólos hay en el mundo, como decía una abuela mia, que son el tenir y el no tenir.
There are but two families in the world, as my grandmother used to say, the Haves and the Have-nots. *Ib.* ch. 20

PATRICK REGINALD CHALMERS
1872–1942

12 What's lost upon the roundabouts we pulls up on the swings!
Green Days and Blue Days: Roundabouts and Swings

JOSEPH CHAMBERLAIN
1836–1914

13 Provided that the City of London remains as it is at present, the clearing-house of the world.
Speech, Guildhall, London, 19 Jan. 1904

14 We are not downhearted. The only trouble is, we cannot understand what is happening to our neighbours.
Ib. Smethwick, 18 Jan. 1906

NEVILLE CHAMBERLAIN
1869–1940

15 In war, whichever side may call itself the victor, there are no winners, but all are losers.
Speech at Kettering, 3 July 1938

16 I believe it is peace for our time . . . peace with honour.
Radio Speech after Munich Agreement. 1 Oct. 1938

CHARLES HADDON
CHAMBERS 1860–1921

17 The long arm of coincidence.
Captain Swift, Act II

JOHN CHANDLER 1806–1876

18 Conquering kings their titles take
From the foes they captive make:
Jesu, by a nobler deed,
From the thousands He hath freed.
As in Hymns Ancient and Modern. Conquering Kings Their Titles Take, trans. from Latin

GEORGE CHAPMAN 1559?–1634?

19 Speed his plough.
Bussy D'Ambois, I. i

20 And let a scholar all Earth's volumes carry,
He will be but a walking dictionary.
Tears of Peace, l. 266

CHARLES II OF GREAT BRITAIN
1630–1685

1 It is upon the navy under the Providence of God that the safety, honour, and welfare of this realm do chiefly attend.   *Articles of War.* Preamble

2 Better than a play.
(*On the Debates in the House of Lords on Lord Ross's Divorce Bill, 1670.*) A. Bryant, *King Charles II*

3 Let not poor Nelly starve.
Burnet, *History of My Own Time,* vol. ii, bk. iii, ch. 17

4 Brother, I am too old to go again to my travels.
Hume's *History of Great Britain,* vol. ii (1757), ch. 7

5 He had been, he said, an unconscionable time dying; but he hoped that they would excuse it.
Macaulay's *Hist. England* (1849), vol. i, ch. 4, p. 437.

CHARLES V 1500–1558

6 Je parle espagnol à Dieu, italien aux femmes, français aux hommes et allemand à mon cheval.

To God I speak Spanish, to women Italian, to men French, and to my horse—German.   *Attr.*

EARL OF CHATHAM
see WILLIAM PITT

THOMAS CHATTERTON
1752–1770

7 O' synge untoe mie roundelaie,
O! droppe the brynie teare wythe mee,
Daunce ne moe atte hallie daie,
Lycke a reynynge ryver bee;
   Mie love ys dedde,
   Gon to hys death-bedde,
   Al under the wyllowe-tree.
Mynstrelles Songe

GEOFFREY CHAUCER 1340?–1400

8 Whanne that Aprille with his shoures sote
The droghte of Marche hath perced to the rote.
Canterbury Tales. Prologue, l. 1

9 And smale fowles maken melodye,
That slepen al the night with open yë,
(So priketh hem nature in hir corages):
Than longen folk to goon on pilgrimages.   *Ib.* l. 9

10 He was a verray parfit gentil knight.
Ib. l. 72

11 He was as fresh as is the month of May.   *Ib.* l. 92

12 Ful wel she song the service divyne,
Entuned in hir nose ful semely;
And Frensh she spak ful faire and fetisly,
After the scole of Stratford atte Bowe,
For Frensh of Paris was to hir unknowe.
Canterbury Tales. Prologue, l. 122

13 A Clerk ther was of Oxenford also.
Ib. l. 285

14 And gladly wolde he lerne, and gladly teche.   *Ib.* l. 308

15 No-wher so bisy a man as he ther nas,
And yet he semed bisier than he was.
Ib. l. 321

16 She was a worthy womman al hir lyve,
Housbondes at chirche-dore she hadde fyve,   *Ib.* l. 459

17 The smyler with the knyf under the cloke.   *Ib.* l. 1141

18 What is this world? what asketh men to have?
Now with his love, now in his colde grave
Allone, with-outen any companye.
Ib. Knightes Tale, l. 1919

19 So was hir joly whistle wel y-wet.
Ib. The Reves Tale, l. 235

20 The bacoun was nat fet for hem, I trowe,
That som men han in Essex at Dunmowe.
Ib. The Prologue of the Wyves' Tale of Bathe, l. 217

21 Farwel my book and my devocion.
Legend of Good Women. Prologue, l. 29

22 And she was fair as is the rose in May.
Ib. Legend of Cleopatra, l. 34

23 Thou shalt make castels than in Spayne,
And dreme of joye, al but in vayne.
Romaunt of the Rose, B. l. 2573

24 Til crowes feet be growe under your yë.   *Troilus and Criseyde,* ii, l. 403

25 And we shal speke of thee som-what, I trowe,
Whan thou art goon, to do thyne eres glowe!   *Ib.* l. 1021

26 It is nought good a sleping hound to wake.   *Ib.* iii, l. 764

27 Right as an aspes leef she gan to quake.   *Ib.* l. 1200

28 Oon ere it herde, at the other out it wente.   *Ib.* iv, l. 434

29 But manly set the world on sixe and sevene;
And, if thou deye a martir, go to hevene.   *Ib.* l. 622

30 For tyme y-lost may not recovered be.
Ib. l. 1283

1 Go, litel book, go litel myn tragedie.
Troilus and Criseyde, iv, l. 1786

2 O yonge fresshe folkes, he or she.
Ib. l. 1835

PHILIP DORMER STANHOPE, EARL OF CHESTERFIELD 1694–1773

3 Unlike my subject will I frame my song,
It shall be witty and it sha'n't be long.
Epigram on 'Long' Sir Thomas Robinson. D.N.B.

4 The picture plac'd the busts between,
Adds to the thought much strength;
Wisdom and Wit are little seen,
But Folly's at full length.
Wit and Wisdom of Lord Chesterfield. Epigrams. On the Picture of Richard Nash . . . between the Busts of . . . Newton and . . . Pope . . . at Bath. (Attr. also to Mrs. Jane Brereton)

5 There is a Spanish proverb, which says very justly, Tell me whom you live with, and I will tell you who you are. *Letter to his Son, 9 Oct. 1747*

6 Take the tone of the company that you are in. *Ib.*

7 Do as you would be done by is the surest method that I know of pleasing.
Ib. 16 Oct. 1747

8 I recommend you to take care of the minutes: for hours will take care of themselves. *Ib. 6 Nov. 1747*

9 It must be owned, that the Graces do not seem to be natives of Great Britain; and I doubt, the best of us here have more of rough than polished diamond. *Ib. 18 Nov. 1748*

10 Idleness is only the refuge of weak minds. *Ib. 20 July 1749*

11 A chapter of accidents.
Ib. 16 Feb. 1753

12 Religion is by no means a proper subject of conversation in a mixed company.
Undated Letter to his Godson, No. 112

GILBERT KEITH CHESTERTON 1874–1936

13 Talk about the pews and steeples
And the cash that goes therewith!
But the souls of Christian peoples . . .
Chuck it, Smith!
Antichrist, or the Reunion of Christendom

14 I tell you naught for your comfort,
Yea, naught for your desire,

Save that the sky grows darker yet
And the sea rises higher.
Ballad of the White Horse, bk. i

15 For the great Gaels of Ireland
Are the men that God made mad,
For all their wars are merry,
And all their songs are sad. *Ib. bk. ii*

16 When fishes flew and forests walked
And figs grew upon thorn,
Some moment when the moon was blood
Then surely I was born.
With monstrous head and sickening cry
And ears like errant wings,
The devil's walking parody
On all four-footed things.
The Donkey

17 Fools! For I also had my hour;
One far fierce hour and sweet:
There was a shout about my ears,
And palms before my feet. *Ib.*

18 White founts falling in the courts of the sun,
And the Soldan of Byzantium is smiling as they run. *Lepanto*

19 Don John of Austria is going to the war. *Ib.*

20 From all the easy speeches
That comfort cruel men.
O God of Earth and Altar

21 Before the Roman came to Rye or out to Severn strode,
The rolling English drunkard made the rolling English road.
The Rolling English Road

22 That night we went to Birmingham by way of Beachy Head. *Ib.*

23 For there is good news yet to hear and fine things to be seen,
Before we go to Paradise by way of Kensal Green. *Ib.*

24 Smile at us, pay us, pass us; but do not quite forget.
For we are the people of England, that never have spoken yet.
The Secret People

25 God made the wicked Grocer
For a mystery and a sign,
That men might shun the awful shop
And go to inns to dine.
Song Against Grocers

26 They haven't got no noses,
The fallen sons of Eve.
The Song of Quoodle

27 And goodness only knowses
The Noselessness of Man. *Ib.*

28 And Noah he often said to his wife when he sat down to dine,
'I don't care where the water goes if it doesn't get into the wine.'
Wine and Water

1 The human race, to which so many of
my readers belong . . .
The Napoleon of Notting Hill,
ch. 1

2 Hardy went down to botanize in the
swamp, while Meredith climbed towards the sun. Meredith became, at his
best, a sort of daintily dressed Walt
Whitman: Hardy became a sort of
village atheist brooding and blas-
pheming over the village idiot.
The Victorian Age in Literature,
ch. 2

ALBERT CHEVALIER 1861–1923

3 'Wot's the good of Hanyfink? Why—
Nuffink!'   *Cockney Complaint*

4 We've been together now for forty
years,
An' it don't seem a day too much;
There ain't a lady livin' in the land
As I'd 'swop' for my dear old Dutch!
My Old Dutch

5 Knocked 'em in the Old Kent Road.
Title of Song

DAVID CHRISTY 1802–?

6 Cotton is King.   *Title of Book* (1855)

CHARLES CHURCHILL 1731–1764

7   Be England what she will,
With all her faults, she is my country
still.   *The Farewell,* l. 27

8 Just to the windward of the law.
The Ghost, bk. iii, l. 56

9 By different methods different men
excel;
But where is he who can do all things
well?
Epistle to William Hogarth, l. 573

10 Keep up appearances; there lies the
test;
The world will give thee credit for
the rest.   *Night,* l. 311

11 Who often, but without success, have
pray'd
For apt Alliteration's artful aid.
The Prophecy of Famine, l. 85

LORD RANDOLPH SPENCER CHURCHILL 1849–1894

12 Ulster will fight; Ulster will be right.
Letter, 7 May 1886

13 The old gang. [Members of the Con-
servative Government.]
*Speech, House of Commons,
7 Mar. 1878*

14 An old man in a hurry. [Gladstone.]
*Ib. To the Electors of South Pad-
dington, June 1886*

15 All great men make mistakes. Napo-
leon forgot Blücher, I forgot Goschen.
*Leaves from the Notebooks of
Lady Dorothy Nevill,* p. 21

16 The duty of an Opposition is to
oppose.
*1830. Quoted by Lord Randolph
Churchill. W. S. Churchill, Lord
Randolph Churchill* (1906), vol.
i, ch. 5

17 (*Decimal points:*) I never could make
out what those damned dots meant.
Ib. vol. ii, p. 184

SIR WINSTON CHURCHILL 1874–1965

18 It cannot in the opinion of His
Majesty's Government be classified as
slavery in the extreme acceptance of
the word without some risk of termi-
nological inexactitude.
*Speech, House of Commons,
22 Feb. 1906*

19 The maxim of the British people is
'Business as usual'.
Speech at Guildhall, 9 Nov. 1914

20 I would say to the House, as I said
to those who have joined this Government, 'I have nothing to offer but
blood, toil, tears and sweat'.
*Speech, House of Commons,
13 May 1940*

21 We shall not flag or fail. We shall fight
in France, we shall fight on the seas
and oceans, we shall fight with growing
confidence and growing strength in the
air, we shall defend our island, whatever the cost may be, we shall fight
on the beaches, we shall fight on the
landing grounds, we shall fight in the
fields and in the streets, we shall
fight in the hills; we shall never
surrender.   *Ib. 4 June 1940*

22 Let us therefore brace ourselves to our
duty and so bear ourselves that if
the British Commonwealth and Empire
lasts for a thousand years men will
still say, 'This was their finest hour.'
Ib. 18 June 1940

23 Never in the field of human conflict
was so much owed by so many to so
few.
Ib. 20 Aug. 1940

24 Give us the tools, and we will finish
the job.
*Radio Broadcast. (Addressing
President Roosevelt.) 9 Feb. 1941*

25 What kind of people do they [the
Japanese] think we are?
*Speech to U.S. Congress, 24 Dec.
1941*

1 When I warned them [the French Government] that Britain would fight on alone whatever they did, their Generals told their Prime Minister and his divided Cabinet: 'In three weeks England will have her neck wrung like a chicken.'
Some chicken! Some neck!
Speech to the Canadian Parliament, 30 Dec. 1941

2 This is not the end. It is not even the beginning of the end. But it is, perhaps, the end of the beginning.
Speech at the Mansion House, 10 Nov. 1942. (Of the Battle of Egypt)

3 I have not become the King's First Minister in order to preside over the liquidation of the British Empire. *Ib.*

4 The soft under-belly of the Axis.
Report on the War Situation, House of Commons, 11 Nov. 1942

5 An iron curtain is drawn down upon their front. We do not know what is going on behind.
Telegram to President Truman, 12 May 1945. (Printed in W. S. Churchill, Triumph and Tragedy (1954), p. 498.) But see also 94 : 11 and 234 : 5.

COLLEY CIBBER 1671–1757

6 Off with his head—so much for Buckingham.
Richard III, altered, IV. iii

7 Conscience avaunt, Richard's himself again: *Ib.*

8 Perish the thought! *Ib.* v

9 Stolen sweets are best.
The Rival Fools, Act 1

10 This business will never hold water.
She Would and She Would Not, Act IV

MARCUS TULLIUS CICERO 106–43 B.C.

11 Salus populi suprema est lex.
The good of the people is the chief law. *De Legibus, III. iii. 8*

12 'Ipse dixit.' 'Ipse' autem erat Pythagoras.
'He himself said it', and this 'he himself', it seems, was Pythagoras.
De Natura Deorum, I. v. 10

13 Summum bonum.
The highest good.
De Officiis, I. ii. 5

14 Cedant arma togae, concedat laurea laudi.
Let wars yield to peace, laurels to paeans. *De Officiis, I. xxii. 82*

15 Numquam se minus otiosum esse quam cum otiosus, nec minus solum quam cum solus esset.
Never less idle than when wholly idle, nor less alone than when wholly alone. *Ib. III. i. 1*

16 Quousque tandem abutere, Catilina, patientia nostra?
How long will you abuse our patience, Catiline?
In Catilinam, I. i. 1

17 O tempora, O mores!
O what times, O what habits! *Ib.*

18 Civis Romanus sum.
I am a Roman citizen.
In Verrem, v. lvii. 147

19 Oderint, dum metuant.
Let them hate so long as they fear.
Philippic, I. 14 (quoted from the tragedian Accius)

20 Quod di omen avertant.
May the gods avert this omen.
Ib. III. xiv. 35

21 Silent enim leges inter arma.
Laws are inoperative in war.
Pro Milone, IV. xi

22 Cui bono.
To whose profit. *Ib. XII. xxxii*

23 Ne quid res publica detrimenti caperet.
That no harm come to the state.
Ib. XXVI. lxx, quoting the senatorial 'ultimate decree', beginning 'caveant consules' (let the consuls see to it).

24 O fortunatam natam me consule Romam!
O happy Rome, born when I was consul! *Quoted in Juvenal, x. 122*

EDWARD HYDE, EARL OF CLARENDON 1609–1674

25 Without question, when he [Hampden] first drew the sword, he threw away the scabbard.
History of the Rebellion, ed. W. Dunn Macray (1888), III. vii. 84

26 So enamoured on peace that he would have been glad the King should have bought it at any price. *Ib. 233*

JOHN CLARKE *fl.* 1639

27 Home is home, though it be never so homely.
Parœmiologia Anglo-Latina (1639)

SAMUEL LANGHORNE CLEMENS
see MARK TWAIN

**STEPHEN GROVER
CLEVELAND** 1837–1908

1 I have considered the pension list of
the republic a roll of honour.
*Veto of Dependent Pension Bill,
5 July 1888*

ROBERT CLIVE, LORD CLIVE
1725–1774

2 By God, Mr. Chairman, at this
moment I stand astonished at my own
moderation!
*Reply during Parliamentary
cross-examination, 1773*

ARTHUR HUGH CLOUGH
1819–1861

3 How pleasant it is to have money,
heigh-ho!
How pleasant it is to have money.
Dipsychus, pt. I. iv

4 'There is no God,' the wicked saith,
'And truly it's a blessing,
For what he might have done with us
It's better only guessing.' *Ib.* v.

5 Thou shalt have one God only; who
Would be at the expense of two?
The Latest Decalogue

6 Thou shalt not kill; but need'st not
strive
Officiously to keep alive. *Ib.*

7 Do not adultery commit;
Advantage rarely comes of it. *Ib.*

8 Thou shalt not steal; an empty feat,
When it's so lucrative to cheat. *Ib.*

9 Thou shalt not covet; but tradition
Approves all forms of competition.
Ib.

10 Say not the struggle naught availeth,
The labour and the wounds are vain,
The enemy faints not, nor faileth,
And as things have been, things
remain.

If hopes were dupes, fears may be
liars;
It may be, in yon smoke concealed,
Your comrades chase e'en now the
fliers,
And, but for you, possess the field.

For while the tired waves, vainly
breaking,
Seem here no painful inch to gain,
Far back through creeks and inlets
making
Comes silent, flooding in, the main.

And not by eastern windows only,
When daylight comes, comes in the
light,
In front the sun climbs slow, how
slowly,
But westward, look, the land is
bright.
*Say Not the Struggle Naught
Availeth*

11 That out of sight is out of mind
Is true of most we leave behind.
*Songs in Absence, That Out of
Sight*

12 Where lies the land to which the ship
would go!
Far, far ahead, is all her seamen know.
And where the land she travels from?
Away,
Far, far behind, is all that they can
say. *Ib. Where Lies the Land*

SIR WILLIAM LAIRD CLOWES
1856–1905

13 The Glorious First of June.
Page-heading in The Royal
Navy: a History (1899), vol. iv,
p. 225. Taken from explanatory
pamphlet accompanying Cleve-
ley's prints of the action: *Two
prints . . . representing the
Glorious and Memorable Action
of the First of June 1794*

WILLIAM COBBETT 1762–1835

14 But what is to be the fate of the great
wen [London] of all? The monster,
called . . . 'the metropolis of the
empire'? *Rural Rides, 1821*

**CHARLES COBORN
[C. W. McCALLUM]** 1852–1945

15 Two lovely black eyes,
Oh! what a surprise!
Only for telling a man he was wrong,
Two lovely black eyes!
Two Lovely Black Eyes

ALISON COCKBURN 1713–1794

16 For the flowers of the forest are
withered away.
The Flowers of the Forest

DESMOND F. T. COKE 1879–1931

17 His blade struck the water a full
second before any other . . . until . . .
as the boats began to near the
winning-post, his own was dipping
into the water *twice* as often as any
other.
*Sandford of Merton (1903), ch.
xii. Often quoted as* 'All rowed fast
but none so fast as stroke', *and
attr. to* Ouida.

SIR EDWARD COKE 1552–1634

1 For a man's house is his castle, *et domus sua cuique est tutissimum refugium.*
Institutes: Commentary upon Littleton. Third Institute, cap. 73

HARTLEY COLERIDGE 1796–1849

2 She is not fair to outward view
As many maidens be;
Her loveliness I never knew
Until she smiled on me.
Oh! then I saw her eye was bright,
A well of love, a spring of light.
Song. She is not Fair

MARY ELIZABETH COLERIDGE 1861–1907

3 We were young, we were merry, we were very, very wise,
And the door stood open at our feast,
When there passed us a woman with the West in her eyes,
And a man with his back to the East.
Unwelcome

SAMUEL TAYLOR COLERIDGE 1772–1834

4 It is an ancient Mariner,
And he stoppeth one of three.
'By thy long grey beard and glittering eye,
Now wherefore stopp'st thou me?'
The Ancient Mariner, pt. i

5 He holds him with his skinny hand,
'There was a ship,' quoth he.
'Hold off! unhand me, grey-beard loon!'
Eftsoons his hand dropt he.

He holds him with his glittering eye—
The Wedding-Guest stood still,
And listens like a three years' child:
The Mariner hath his will. *Ib.*

6 The Sun came up upon the left,
Out of the sea came he!
And he shone bright, and on the right
Went down into the sea. *Ib.*

7 The Wedding-Guest here beat his breast,
For he heard the loud bassoon. *Ib.*

8 The ice was here, the ice was there,
The ice was all around:
It cracked and growled, and roared and howled,
Like noises in a swound! *Ib.*

9 And a good south wind sprung up behind;
The Albatross did follow,
And every day, for food or play,
Came to the mariner's hollo! *Ib.*

10 'God save thee, ancient Mariner!
From the fiends that plague thee thus!—
Why look'st thou so?—With my cross-bow
I shot the Albatross.
The Ancient Mariner, pt. i

11 We were the first that ever burst
Into that silent sea. *Ib.* pt. ii

12 All in a hot and copper sky,
The bloody Sun, at noon,
Right up above the mast did stand,
No bigger than the Moon. *Ib.*

13 As idle as a painted ship
Upon a painted ocean. *Ib.*

14 Water, water, every where,
And all the boards did shrink;
Water, water, every where,
Nor any drop to drink.

The very deep did rot: O Christ!
That ever this should be!
Yea, slimy things did crawl with legs
Upon the slimy sea.

I bit my arm, I sucked the blood,
And cried, A sail! a sail! *Ib.* pt. iii

15 The Sun's rim dips; the stars rush out:
At one stride comes the dark;
With far-heard whisper, o'er the sea,
Off shot the spectre-bark. *Ib.*

16 The hornèd Moon, with one bright star
Within the nether tip. *Ib.*

17 Each turned his face with a ghastly pang,
And cursed me with his eye. *Ib.*

18 'I fear thee, ancient Mariner!
I fear thy skinny hand!
And thou art long, and lank, and brown,
As is the ribbed sea-sand.' *Ib.* pt. iv

19 Alone, alone, all, all alone,
Alone on a wide wide sea!
And never a saint took pity on
My soul in agony. *Ib.*

20 And a thousand thousand slimy things
Lived on; and so did I. *Ib.*

21 An orphan's curse would drag to hell
A spirit from on high;
But oh! more horrible than that
Is the curse in a dead man's eye. *Ib.*

22 The moving Moon went up the sky,
And no where did abide:
Softly she was going up,
And a star or two beside. *Ib.*

23 Oh Sleep! it is a gentle thing,
Beloved from pole to pole,
To Mary Queen the praise be given!
She sent the gentle sleep from Heaven,
That slid into my soul. *Ib.* pt. v

1 The silly buckets on the deck,
  That had so long remained,
  I dreamt that they were filled with
      dew;
  And when I awoke, it rained.
              The Ancient Mariner, pt. v.

2 We were a ghastly crew.   *Ib.*

3 It ceased; yet still the sails made on
  A pleasant noise till noon,
  A noise like of a hidden brook
  If the leafy month of June,
  That to the sleeping woods all night
  Singeth a quiet tune.   *Ib.*

4 Quoth he, 'The man hath penance
      done,
  And penance more will do.'   *Ib.*

5 Like one, that on a lonesome road
  Doth walk in fear and dread,
  And having once turned round walks on,
  And turns no more his head;
  Because he knows, a frightful fiend
  Doth close behind him tread.
                              Ib. pt. vi

6 O sweeter than the marriage-feast,
  'Tis sweeter far to me,
  To walk together to the kirk
  With a goodly company.
  To walk together to the kirk,
  And all together pray,
  While each to his great Father bends,
  Old men, and babes, and loving friends
  And youths and maidens gay!
                              Ib. pt. vii

7 He prayeth well, who loveth well
  Both man and bird and beast.

  He prayeth best, who loveth best
  All things both great and small;
  For the dear God who loveth us,
  He made and loveth all.   *Ib.*

8 A sight to dream of, not to tell!
                    Christabel, pt. i

9 In Köhln, a town of monks and bones,
  And pavements fang'd with murderous
      stones
  And rags, and hags, and hideous
      wenches;
  I counted two and seventy stenches,
  All well defined, and several stinks!
  Ye Nymphs that reign o'er sewers and
      sinks,
  The river Rhine, it is well known,
  Doth wash your city of Cologne;
  But tell me, Nymphs, what power
      divine
  Shall henceforth wash the river
      Rhine?   *Cologne*

10 His jacket was red and his breeches
      were blue,
  And there was a hole where the tail
      came through. *The Devil's Thoughts*

11 With Donne, whose muse on drome-
      dary trots,
  Wreathe iron pokers into true-love
      knots.   *On Donne's Poetry*

12 What is an Epigram? a dwarfish whole,
  Its body brevity, and wit its soul.
                              Epigram

13 Swans sing before they die—'twere
      no bad thing
  Did certain persons die before they
      sing.
          Epigram on a Volunteer Singer

14 In Xanadu did Kubla Khan
  A stately pleasure-dome decree:
  Where Alph, the sacred river, ran
  Through caverns measureless to man
  Down to a sunless sea.
  So twice five miles of fertile ground
  With walls and towers were girdled
      round:
  And there were gardens bright with
      sinuous rills,
  Where blossomed many an incense-
      bearing tree;
  And here were forests ancient as the
      hills,
  Enfolding sunny spots of greenery.
  But oh! that deep romantic chasm
      which slanted
  Down the green hill athwart a cedarn
      cover!
  A savage place! as holy and enchanted
  As e'er beneath a waning moon was
      haunted
  By woman wailing for her demon-
      lover!
  And from this chasm, with ceaseless
      turmoil seething,
  As if this earth in fast thick pants
      were breathing,
  A mighty fountain momently was
      forced.   *Kubla Khan*

15 And 'mid these dancing rocks at once
      and ever
  It flung up momently the sacred river.
  Five miles meandering with a mazy
      motion
  Through wood and dale the sacred
      river ran,
  Then reached the caverns measureless
      to man,
  And sank in tumult to a lifeless ocean:
  And 'mid this tumult Kubla heard
      from far
  Ancestral voices prophesying war!

    The shadow of the dome of pleasure
    Floated midway on the waves;
    Where was heard the mingled
        measure
    From the fountain and the caves.
  It was a miracle of rare device,
  A sunny pleasure-dome with caves of
      ice!

    A damsel with a dulcimer
    In a vision once I saw:
    It was an Abyssinian maid,
    And on her dulcimer she played,
    Singing of Mount Abora.

Could I revive within me
Her symphony and song,
To such a deep delight 'twould win me,
That with music loud and long,
I would build that dome in air,
That sunny dome! those caves of ice!
And all who heard should see them there,
And all should cry, Beware! Beware!
His flashing eyes, his floating hair!
Weave a circle round him thrice,
And close your eyes with holy dread,
For he on honey-dew hath fed,
And drunk the milk of Paradise.
Kubla Khan

1 Trochee trips from long to short.
Metrical Feet

2 Iambics march from short to long;—
With a leap and a bound the swift
Anapaests throng. *Ib.*

3 Like some poor nigh-related guest,
That may not rudely be dismist;
Yet hath outstay'd his welcome while,
And tells the jest without the smile.
Youth and Age

4 He who begins by loving Christianity
better than Truth will proceed by
loving his own sect or church better
than Christianity, and end by loving
himself better than all.
*Aids to Reflection: Moral and
Religious Aphorisms,* xxv

5 That willing suspension of disbelief
for the moment, which constitutes
poetic faith.
Biographia Literaria, ch. 14

6 Summer has set in with its usual
severity.
*Remark quoted in Lamb's Letter
to V. Novello, 9 May 1826*

7 To see him [Kean] act, is like reading
Shakespeare by flashes of lightning.
Table Talk, 27 Apr. 1823

8 I wish our clever young poets would
remember my homely definitions of
prose and poetry; that is, prose =
words in their best order;—poetry =
the *best* words in the best order.
Ib. 12 July 1827

JESSE COLLINGS 1831–1920

9 Three acres and a cow.
*Phrase used in his land-reform
propaganda of 1885.*

MORTIMER COLLINS 1827–1876

10 A man is as old as he's feeling,
A woman as old as she looks.
The Unknown Quantity

WILLIAM COLLINS 1721–1759

11 If aught of oaten stop, or pastoral
song,
May hope, O pensive Eve, to soothe
thine ear. *Ode to Evening*

12 Now air is hush'd, save where the
weak-ey'd bat,
With short shrill shriek flits by on
leathern wing,
Or where the beetle winds
His small but sullen horn *Ib.*

13 Hamlets brown, and dim-discover'd
spires. *Ib.*

14 How sleep the brave, who sink to rest,
By all their country's wishes blest!
Ode Written in the Year 1746

15 By fairy hands their knell is rung,
By forms unseen their dirge is sung;
There Honour comes, a pilgrim grey,
To bless the turf that wraps their clay
And Freedom shall awhile repair,
To dwell a weeping hermit there! *Ib*

GEORGE COLMAN 1732–1794

16 Love and a cottage! Eh, Fanny! Ah,
give me indifference and a coach and
six! *The Clandestine Marriage,* I. ii

GEORGE COLMAN 1762–1836

17 Mum's the word.
Battle of Hexham, II. i

18 Lord help you! Tell 'em Queen Anne's
dead. *Heir-at-Law,* I. i

19 Oh, London is a fine town,
A very famous city,
Where all the streets are paved with
gold,
And all the maidens pretty. *Ib.* ii

20 Not to be sneezed at. *Ib.* II. i

21 Says he, 'I am a handsome man, but
I'm a gay deceiver.'
Love Laughs at Locksmiths, Act II,
Song

22 Johnson's style was grand and
Gibbon's elegant; the stateliness of
the former was sometimes pedantic,
and the polish of the latter was oc-
casionally finical. Johnson marched to
kettle-drums and trumpets; Gibbon
moved to flutes and hautboys: Johnson hewed passages through the Alps,
while Gibbon levelled walks through
parks and gardens.
Random Records (1830), i. 121

23 His heart runs away with his head.
Who Wants a Guinea?, I. i

24 When taken, To be well shaken.
*My Nightgown and Slippers.
Newcastle Apothecary*

CHARLES CALEB COLTON
1780?–1832

1 When you have nothing to say, say
nothing.   *Lacon*, vol. i, No. 183

2 Man is an embodied paradox, a bundle
of contradictions.
Ib. No. 408

WILLIAM CONGREVE 1670–1729

3 She lays it on with a trowel.
The Double Dealer, III. x

4 See how love and murder will out.
Ib. IV. vi

5 If I can give that Cerberus a sop, I
shall be at rest for one day.
Love for Love, I. iv

6 I warrant you, if he danced till dooms-
day, he thought I was to pay the piper.
Ib. II. v

7 Has he not a rogue's face? . . . a
hanging-look to me . . . has a damn'd
Tyburn-face, without the benefit o'
the Clergy. . . .   *Ib.* vii

8 Oh fie, Miss, you must not kiss and
tell.   *Ib.* x

9 Music has charms to sooth a savage
breast.   *The Mourning Bride*, I. i

10 Heav'n has no rage, like love to hatred
turn'd,
Nor Hell a fury, like a woman
scorn'd.   *Ib.* III. viii

11 Now am I slap-dash down in the
mouth.   *The Old Bachelor*, IV. ix

12 Well, Sir Joseph, you have such a
winning way with you.   *Ib.* v. vii

13 SHARPER.
Thus grief still treads upon the
heels of pleasure:
Marry'd in haste, we may repent at
leisure.
SETTER.
Some by experience find those
words mis-plac'd:
At leisure marry'd, they repent in
haste.   *Ib.* viii *and* ix

14 O Sleep, why dost thou leave me?
Why thy visionary joys remove?
O Sleep, again deceive me,
To my arms restore my wand'ring
Love.   *Semele*, II. ii

15 Alack he's gone the way of all flesh.
Squire Bickerstaff Detected. (Attr.
to Congreve)

16 Say what you will, 'tis better to be
left than never to have been loved.
The Way of the World, II. i

17 Here she comes i' faith full sail, with
her fan spread and streamers out, and
a shoal of fools for tenders.   *Ib.* iv

18 I nauseate walking; 'tis a country
diversion, I loath the country.   *Ib.*

19 These articles subscrib'd, if I continue
to endure you a little longer, I may
by degrees dwindle into a wife.
The Way of the World, IV. v

20 O horrid provisos!   *Ib.*

T. W. CONNOR *nineteenth century*

21 She was one of the early birds,
And I was one of the worms.
She Was A Dear Little Dickie-bird

CONSTANTINE c. 274–337

22 In hoc signo vinces.
In this sign shalt thou conquer.
Words of Constantine's vision.
Eusebius, *Life of Constantine*, i. 28

ELIZA COOK 1818–1889

23 I love it, I love it; and who shall dare
To chide me for loving that old arm-
chair?   *The Old Arm-chair*

CALVIN COOLIDGE 1872–1933

24 He said he was against it.
*On being asked what had been said
by a clergyman who preached on
sin*

25 The business of America is business.
*Speech before Society of American
Newspaper Editors*, 17 Jan. 1925

JAMES FENIMORE COOPER
1789–1851

26 The Last of the Mohicans.
Title of Novel

BISHOP RICHARD CORBET
1582–1635

27 Farewell rewards and fairies.
The Fairy's Farewell

FRANCES CROFTS CORNFORD
1886–1960

28 O fat white woman whom nobody
loves,
Why do you walk through the fields in
gloves,
.   .   .   .
Missing so much and so much?
To a Fat Lady Seen from a Train

MME CORNUEL 1605–1694

29 Il n'y a point de héros pour son valet
de chambre.
No man is a hero to his valet.
Lettres de Mlle Aissé, xii, 13
August 1728

CORONATION SERVICE

1 We present you with this Book, the
most valuable thing that this world
affords. Here is wisdom; this is the
royal Law; these are the lively Oracles
of God.
The Presenting of the Holy Bible

WILLIAM JOHNSON CORY
1823–1892

2 They told me, Heraclitus, they told
me you were dead,
They brought me bitter news to hear
and bitter tears to shed. *Heraclitus*

3   How often you and I
Had tired the sun with talking and
sent him down the sky.   *Ib.*

4 A handful of grey ashes, long long
ago at rest.   *Ib.*

ÉMILE COUÉ 1857–1926

5 Tous les jours, à tous points de vue,
je vais de mieux en mieux.

Every day, in every way, I am getting better and better.
Formula in his clinic at Nancy

VICTOR COUSIN 1792–1867

6 L'art pour l'art.

Art for art's sake.
Lecture at the Sorbonne

THOMAS COVENTRY, BARON
COVENTRY 1578–1640

7 The wooden walls are the best walls
of this kingdom.
*Speech to the Judges, 17 June
1635, given in Rushworth's Hist.
Coll. (1680), vol. ii, p. 297.*

NOEL COWARD 1899–

8 Mad dogs and Englishmen go out in
the mid-day sun;
The Japanese don't care to, the
Chinese wouldn't dare to;
Hindus and Argentines sleep firmly
from twelve to one,
But Englishmen detest a siesta.
Mad Dogs and Englishmen

9 Don't put your daughter on the stage,
Mrs. Worthington.   *Title of Song*

10 Dance, Little Lady.   *Ib.*

11 Twentieth-Century Blues.   *Ib.*

12 Poor Little Rich Girl.   *Ib.*

13 Don't let's be beastly to the Germans.
Ib.

14 In Which We Serve.   *Title of Film*

15 Strange how potent cheap music is.
Private Lives, Act I

16 Very flat, Norfolk.   *Ib.*

17 Certain women should be struck
regularly, like gongs.   *Ib. Act* II

ABRAHAM COWLEY 1618–1667

18 God the first garden made, and the
first city Cain   *The Garden*

19 Life is an incurable disease.
To Dr. Scarborough, vi

WILLIAM COWPER 1731–1800

20 Regions Caesar never knew
Thy posterity shall sway,
Where his eagles never flew,
None invincible as they.   *Boadicea*

21 John Gilpin was a citizen
Of credit and renown,
A train-band captain eke was he
Of famous London town.
John Gilpin

22 To-morrow is our wedding-day,
And we will then repair
Unto the Bell at Edmonton
All in a chaise and pair.   *Ib.*

23 I am a linen-draper bold,
As all the world doth know,
And my good friend the calender
Will lend his horse to go.   *Ib.*

24   O'erjoy'd was he to find
That, though on pleasure she was bent,
She had a frugal mind.   *Ib.*

25   And all agog
To dash through thick and thin!   *Ib.*

26 John Gilpin at his horse's side
Seiz'd fast the flowing mane,
And up he got, in haste to ride,
But soon came down again.   *Ib.*

27 Away went Gilpin, neck or nought,
Away went hat and wig!   *Ib*

28 The dogs did bark, the children
scream'd.
Up flew the windows all;
And ev'ry soul cried out—Well done!
As loud as he could bawl.

Away went Gilpin—who but he?
His fame soon spread around—
He carries weight! he rides a race!
'Tis for a thousand pound!   *Ib.*

29 My hat and wig will soon be here—
They are upon the road.   *Ib.*

30 Said John—It is my wedding-day,
And all the world would stare,
If wife should dine at Edmonton
And I should dine at Ware.   *Ib.*

31 Now let us sing—Long live the king,
And Gilpin long live he;
And, when he next doth ride abroad,
May I be there to see!   *Ib.*

1 Beware of desp'rate steps. The darkest
day
(Live till to-morrow) will have pass'd
away.   *The Needless Alarm*, l. 132

2 What peaceful hours I once enjoy'd!
How sweet their mem'ry still!
But they have left an aching void,
The world can never fill.
Olney Hymns, 1

3 Hark, my soul! it is the Lord;
'Tis thy Saviour, hear his word;
Jesus speaks, and speaks to thee;
'Say, poor sinner, lov'st thou me?'
Ib. 18

4 'Can a woman's tender care
Cease, towards the child she bare?
Yes, she may forgetful be,
Yet will I remember thee.'   *Ib.*

5 God moves in a mysterious way
His wonders to perform;
He plants his footsteps in the sea,
And rides upon the storm.   *Ib.* 35

6 Ye fearful saints fresh courage take,
The clouds ye so much dread
Are big with mercy, and shall break
In blessings on your head.   *Ib.*

7 The poplars are fell'd, farewell to the
shade
And the whispering sound of the cool
colonnade.   *The Poplar-Field*

8 Talks of darkness at noon-day.
Progress of Error, l. 451

9 Toll for the brave—
The brave! that are no more:
All sunk beneath the wave,
Fast by their native shore.
Loss of the Royal George

10 Toll for the brave—
Brave Kempenfelt is gone.   *Ib.*

11 His sword was in the sheath,
His fingers held the pen,
When Kempenfelt went down
With twice four hundred men.   *Ib.*

12 As if the world and they were hand
and glove.   *Table Talk*, l. 173

13 I sing the Sofa.
The Task, bk. i, *The Sofa*, l. 1

14 God made the country, and man made
the town.   *Ib.* l. 749

15 England, with all thy faults, I love
thee still—
My country!
Ib. bk. ii, *The Timepiece*, l. 206

16 Variety's the very spice of life,
That gives it all its flavour.
Ib. l. 606

17 I was a stricken deer, that left the
herd
Long since.
Ib. bk. iii, *The Garden*, l. 108

18 Now stir the fire, and close the shutters
fast,
Let fall the curtains, wheel the sofa
round,
And, while the bubbling and loud-
hissing urn
Throws up a steamy column, and the
cups,
That cheer but not inebriate, wait
on each,
So let us welcome peaceful ev'ning in.
The Task, bk. iv, *The Winter
Evening*, l. 34

19 I am monarch of all I survey,
My right there is none to dispute;
*Verses Supposed to be Written by
Alexander Selkirk*

GEORGE CRABBE 1754–1832

20 And mighty folios first, a lordly band,
Then quartos, their well-order'd ranks
maintain,
And light octavos fill a spacious plain;
See yonder, ranged in more frequented
rows,
A humbler band of duodecimos.
The Library, l. 128

21 When from the cradle to the grave
I look,
Mine I conceive a melancholy book.
The Parish Register, pt. iii,
Burials, l. 21

22 When the coarse cloth she saw, with
many a stain,
Soil'd by rude hinds who cut and came
again.
Tales, vii, *The Widow's Tale*,
l. 25

23 I sought the simple life that Nature
yields.   *The Village*, bk. i, l. 110

STEPHEN CRANE 1871–1900

24 The Red Badge of Courage.   *Title*

ARCHBISHOP THOMAS
CRANMER 1489–1556

25 This hand hath offended.
Strype's *Memorials of Cranmer*
(1694), vol. iii

RICHARD CRASHAW 1612?–1649

26 By all the eagle in thee, all the dove.
*The Flaming Heart upon the
Book of Saint Teresa*, l. 95

27 Whoe'er she be,
That not impossible she
That shall command my heart and
me;
Wishes to His Supposed Mistress

MRS. EDMUND CRASTER d. 1874

1 The Centipede was happy quite,
Until the Toad in fun
Said 'Pray which leg goes after which?'
And worked her mind to such a pitch,
She lay distracted in the ditch
Considering how to run.   *Attr.*

JULIA CRAWFORD *fl.* 1835

2 Kathleen Mavourneen! the grey dawn
is breaking,
The horn of the hunter is heard on
the hill;
The lark from her light wing the bright
dew is shaking;
Kathleen Mavourneen! what, slumbering still?
Oh! hast thou forgotten how soon we
must sever?
Oh! hast thou forgotten this day we
must part?
It may be for years, and it may be
for ever,
Oh! why art thou silent, thou voice
of my heart?
Kathleen Mavourneen. Metropolitan Magazine, London, 1835

BISHOP MANDELL CREIGHTON
1843–1901

3 No people do so much harm as those
who go about doing good.
Life (1904), vol. ii, p. 503

JOHN WILSON CROKER
1780–1857

4 A game which a sharper once played
with a dupe, entitled, 'Heads I win,
tails you lose.'   *Croker Papers,* iii. 59

OLIVER CROMWELL 1599–1658

5 Such men as had the fear of God before
them and as made some conscience of
what they did . . . the plain russet-coated captain that knows what he
fights for and loves what he knows.
*Letter of Sept. 1643. In Carlyle,
Letters and Speeches of Oliver
Cromwell*

6 I beseech you, in the bowels of Christ,
think it possible you may be mistaken.
*Letter to the General Assembly of
the Church of Scotland, 3 Aug.
1650*

7 The dimensions of this mercy are
above my thoughts. It is, for aught I
know, a crowning mercy.
*Letter for the Honourable William
Lenthall, 4 Sept. 1651*

8 Not what they want but what is good
for them.   *Attr. remark*

9 Mr. Lely, I desire you would use all
your skill to paint my picture truly
like me, and not flatter me at all;
but remark all these roughnesses,
pimples, warts, and everything as you
see me, otherwise I will never pay
a farthing for it.
Remark, Walpole's *Anecdotes of
Painting,* ch. 12

10 Take away these baubles.
Remark, Sydney Papers (1825),
p. 141

11 It is not fit that you should sit here
any longer! . . . you shall now give
place to better men.
*Speech to the Rump Parliament,
22 Jan. 1654*

12 Necessity hath no law. Feigned necessities, imaginary necessities, . . . are
the greatest cozenage that men can put
upon the Providence of God, and make
pretences to break known rules by.
*Speech to Parliament, 12 Sept.
1654*

13 My design is to make what haste I can
to be gone.
Last Words. Morley, *Life,* v,
ch. 10

JOHANN CRÜGER 1598–1662

14 Nun danket alle Gott.
Now thank we all our God.   *Hymn*

BISHOP RICHARD CUMBERLAND 1631–1718

15 It is better to wear out than to rust
out.
G. Horne, *The Duty of Contending for the Faith*

ALLAN CUNNINGHAM 1784–1842

16 A wet sheet and a flowing sea,
A wind that follows fast
And fills the white and rustling sail
And bends the gallant mast.
A Wet Sheet and a Flowing Sea

JOHN PHILPOT CURRAN
1750–1817

17 The condition upon which God hath
given liberty to man is eternal vigilance; which condition if he break,
servitude is at once the consequence of
his crime, and the punishment of his
guilt.
*Speech on the Right of Election
of Lord Mayor of Dublin,
10 July 1790*

HARRY DACRE *fl.* 1892

1 Daisy, Daisy, give me your answer, do!
  I'm half crazy, all for the love of you!
  It won't be a stylish marriage,
  I can't afford a carriage,
  But you'll look sweet upon the seat
  Of a bicycle made for two!   *Daisy Bell*

CHARLES ANDERSON DANA
1819–1897

2 When a dog bites a man that is not
  news, but when a man bites a dog
  that is news.
        *What is News? The New York
        Sun, 1882*

SAMUEL DANIEL 1562–1619

3 Unless above himself he can
  Erect himself, how poor a thing is
  man!
        *To the Lady Margaret, Countess
        of Cumberland,* xii

DANTE ALIGHIERI 1265–1321

4 Nel mezzo del cammin di nostra vita.
        In the middle of the road of our life.
        Divine Comedy. Inferno, i.

5 Lasciate ogni speranza voi ch'entrate!
        All hope abandon, ye who enter
        here.   *Ib.* iii. 9

6 Il gran rifiuto.
        The great refusal.   *Ib.* 60

7 Nessun maggior dolore,
  Che ricordarsi del tempo felice
  Nella miseria.
        There is no greater sorrow than to
        recall a time of happiness in misery.
                Ib. v. 121

GEORGES JACQUES DANTON
1759–1794

8 De l'audace, et encore de l'audace,
  et toujours de l'audace!
        Boldness, and again boldness, and
        always boldness!
        *Speech to the Legislative Com-
        mittee of General Defence, 2 Sept.
        1792. Le Moniteur, 4 Sept. 1792*

CHARLES ROBERT DARWIN
1809–1882

9 I have called this principle, by which
  each slight variation, if useful, is
  preserved, by the term of Natural
  Selection.
        The Origin of Species, ch. 3

CHARLES DAVENANT 1656–1714

10 Custom, that unwritten law,
   By which the people keep even kings
   in awe.   *Circe,* II. iii

SIR WILLIAM DAVENANT
1606–1668

11 I shall sleep like a top.
        The Rivals, Act III

JOHN DAVIDSON 1857–1909

12 A runnable stag, a kingly crop.
        A Runnable Stag

WILLIAM HENRY DAVIES
1870–1940

13 What is this life if, full of care,
   We have no time to stand and stare?
        Leisure

STEPHEN DECATUR 1779–1820

14 Our country! In her intercourse with
   foreign nations, may she always be
   in the right; but our country, right
   or wrong.
        A. S. Mackenzie, *Life of Decatur,*
        ch. xiv.

MARQUISE DU DEFFAND
1697–1780

15 La distance n'y fait rien; il n'y a que
   le premier pas qui coûte.
        The distance is nothing; it is only
        the first step that is difficult.
        *Remark on the legend that St.
        Denis, carrying his head in his
        hands, walked two leagues. Letter
        to d'Alembert, 7 July 1763*

DANIEL DEFOE 1661?–1731

16 The good die early, and the bad die
   late.
        *Character of the late Dr. S.
        Annesley*

17 I takes my man Friday with me.
        *The Life and Adventures of
        Robinson Crusoe,* pt. i

THOMAS DEKKER 1570?–1641?

18 Art thou poor, yet hast thou golden
   slumbers?
        Oh sweet content!
   Art thou rich, yet is thy mind per-
   plexed?
        Oh, punishment!
   Dost thou laugh to see how fools are
   vexed
   To add to golden numbers, golden
   numbers?
   O, sweet content, O, sweet, O, sweet
   content!
        Work apace, apace, apace, apace;
        Honest labour bears a lovely face;
   Then hey nonny, nonny; hey nonny,
   nonny.   *Patient Grissil,* Act I

1 Golden slumbers kiss your eyes,
Smiles awake you when you rise:
Sleep, pretty wantons, do not cry,
And I will sing a lullaby:
Rock them, rock them, lullaby.
Patient Grissil, Act IV. ii

WALTER DE LA MARE 1873–1956

2 Oh, no man knows
Through what wild centuries
Roves back the rose. *All That's Past*

3 Look thy last on all things lovely,
Fare Well, iii

4 'Is there anybody there?' said the
traveller,
Knocking on the moonlit door.
The Listeners

5 'Tell them I came, and no one answered,
That I kept my word,' he said. *Ib.*

6 Ay, they heard his foot upon the
stirrup,
And the sound of iron on stone,
And how the silence surged softly
backward,
When the plunging hoofs were gone.
Ib.

7 It's a very odd thing—
As odd as can be—
That whatever Miss T. eats
Turns into Miss T. *Miss T.*

8 Three jolly Farmers
Once bet a pound
Each dance the others would
Off the ground. *Off the Ground*

9 Slowly, silently, now the moon
Walks the night in her silver shoon.
Silver

10 Some one came knocking
At my wee, small door;
Some one came knocking,
I'm sure—sure—sure. *Some One*

THOMAS, LORD DENMAN
1779–1854

11 Trial by jury itself, instead of being
a security to persons who are accused,
will be a delusion, a mockery, and a
snare.
Judgement in O'Connell v. *the
Queen, 4 Sept. 1844*

CLARENCE JAMES DENNIS
1876–1938

12 Me name is Mud.
*The Sentimental Bloke: A Spring
Song*, st. 2 (1916)

JOHN DENNIS 1657–1734

13 Damn them! They will not let my play
run, but they steal my thunder!
W. S. Walsh, *Handy-Book of
Literary Curiosities*

THOMAS DE QUINCEY 1785–1859

14 Murder Considered as One of the
Fine Arts. *Title of Essay*

RENÉ DESCARTES 1596–1650

15 Cogito, ergo sum.
I think, therefore I am.
Le Discours de la Méthode

PHILIPPE NÉRICAULT dit
DESTOUCHES 1680–1754

16 Les absents ont toujours tort.
The absent are always in the wrong.
L'Obstacle imprévu, I. vi

CHARLES DIBDIN 1745–1814

17 In every mess I finds a friend,
In every port a wife.
Jack in his Element

18 But the standing toast that pleased
the most
Was—The wind that blows, the ship
that goes,
And the lass that loves a sailor!
The Round Robin

19 Here, a sheer hulk, lies poor Tom
Bowling,
The darling of our crew.
Tom Bowling

THOMAS JOHN DIBDIN
1771–1841

20 Oh! what a snug little Island,
A right little, tight little Island!
The Snug Little Island

CHARLES DICKENS 1812–1870

21 Jarndyce and Jarndyce still drags its
dreary length before the Court, peren-
nially hopeless. *Bleak House*, ch. 1

22 This is a London particular. . . . A fog,
miss. *Ib.* ch. 3

23 Educating the natives of Borrio-
boola-Gha, on the left bank of the
Niger. [*Mrs. Jellyby.*] *Ib.* ch. 4

24 'Not to put too fine a point upon it'—
a favourite apology for plain-speaking
with Mr. Snagsby. *Ib.* ch. 11

25 He wos wery good to me, he wos! [*Jo.*]
Ib.

26 'It is', says Chadband, 'the ray of
rays, the sun of suns, the moon of
moons, the star of stars. It is the
light of Terewth.' *Ib.* ch. 25

27 England has been in a dreadful state
for some weeks. Lord Coodle would go
out, and Sir Thomas Doodle wouldn't
come in, and there being nobody in

Great Britain (to speak of) except Coodle and Doodle, there has been no Government. *Bleak House*, ch. 40

1 A smattering of everything, and a knowledge of nothing. [*Minerva House*.]
Sketches by Boz. Tales, ch. 3. *Sentiment*

2 O let us love our occupations,
Bless the squire and his relations,
Live upon our daily rations,
And always know our proper stations.
The Chimes, 2nd Quarter

3 'Glod bless us every one!' said Tiny Tim, the last of all.
A Christmas Carol, stave 3

4 It *was* a turkey! He could never have stood upon his legs, that bird. He would have snapped 'em off short in a minute, like sticks of sealing-wax.
Ib., stave 5

5 'I am a lone lorn creetur',' were Mrs. Gummidge's words, . . . 'and everythink goes contrairy with me.'
David Copperfield, ch. 3

6 Barkis is willin'. *Ib.* ch. 5

7 I have known him [Micawber] come home to supper with a flood of tears, and a declaration that nothing was now left but a jail; and go to bed making a calculation of the expense of putting bow-windows to the house, 'in case anything turned up,' which was his favourite expression. *Ib.* ch. 11

8 Annual income twenty pounds, annual expenditure nineteen nineteen six, result happiness. Annual income twenty pounds, annual expenditure twenty pounds ought and six, result misery. [*Mr. Micawber*.] *Ib.* ch. 12

9 I am well aware that I am the 'umblest person going. . . . My mother is likewise a very 'umble person. We live in a numble abode. [*Uriah Heep*.]
Ib. ch. 16

10 The mistake was made of putting some of the trouble out of King Charles's head into my head. *Ib.* ch. 17

11 I only ask for information. [*Miss Rosa Dartle*.] *Ib.* ch. 20

12 Accidents will occur in the best-regulated families; and in families not regulated by that pervading influence which sanctifies while it enhances the —a—I would say, in short, by the influence of Woman, in the lofty character of Wife, they may be expected with confidence, and must be borne with philosophy. [*Mr. Micawber*.] *Ib.* ch. 28

13 Mrs. Crupp had indignantly assured him that there wasn't room to swing a cat there; but, as Mr. Dick justly observed to me, sitting down on the foot of the bed, nursing his leg, 'You know, Trotwood, I don't want to swing a cat. I never do swing a cat. Therefore, what does that signify to me!' *David Copperfield*, ch. 35

14 It's only my child-wife. [*Dora*.]
Ib. ch. 44

15 'Wal'r, my boy,' replied the Captain, 'in the Proverbs of Solomon you will find the following words, "May we never want a friend in need, nor a bottle to give him!" When found, make a note of.' [*Captain Cuttle*.]
Dombey and Son, ch. 15

16 On the Rampage, Pip, and off the Rampage, Pip; such is Life! [*Joe Gargery*.] *Great Expectations*, ch. 15

17 You don't object to an aged parent, I hope? [*Wemmick*.] *Ib.* ch. 25

18 Whatever was required to be done, the Circumlocution Office was beforehand with all the public departments in the art of perceiving—HOW NOT TO DO IT. *Little Dorrit*, bk. i, ch. 10

19 Father is rather vulgar, my dear. The word Papa, besides, gives a pretty form to the lips. Papa, potatoes, poultry, prunes and prism, are all very good words for the lips; especially prunes and prism. [*Mrs. General*.]
Ib. bk. ii, ch. 5

20 With affection beaming in one eye, and calculation shining out of the other. [*Mrs. Todgers*.]
Martin Chuzzlewit, ch. 8

21 'Mrs. Harris,' I says, 'leave the bottle on the chimley-piece, and don't ask me to take none, but let me put my lips to it when I am so dispoged.' [*Mrs. Gamp*.] *Ib.* ch. 19

22 Some people . . . may be Rooshans, and others may be Prooshans; they are born so, and will please themselves. Them which is of other naturs thinks different. [*Mrs. Gamp*.] *Ib.*

23 He'd make a lovely corpse. [*Mrs. Gamp*.] *Ib.* ch. 25

24 'Bother Mrs. Harris!' said Betsey Prig. . . . 'I don't believe there's no sich a person!' *Ib.* ch. 49

25 EDUCATION.—At Mr. Wackford Squeers's Academy, Dotheboys Hall, at the delightful village of Dotheboys, near Greta Bridge in Yorkshire, Youth are boarded, clothed, booked, furnished with pocket-money, provided with all necessaries, instructed in all languages living and dead, mathematics, orthography, geometry, astronomy, trigonometry, the use of the globes, algebra, single stick (if re-

quired), writing, arithmetic, fortification, and every other branch of classical literature. Terms, twenty guineas per annum. No extras, no vacations, and diet unparalleled.
Nicholas Nickleby, ch. 3

1 Here's richness! [*Mr. Squeers.*]
Ib. ch. 5

2 C-l-e-a-n, clean, verb active, to make bright, to scour. W-i-n, win, d-e-r, der, winder, a casement. When the boy knows this out of the book, he goes and does it. [*Mr. Squeers.*]   *Ib.* ch. 8

3 As she frequently remarked when she made any such mistake, it would be all the same a hundred years hence. [*Mrs. Squeers.*]   *Ib.* ch. 9

4 Language was not powerful enough to describe the infant phenomenon.
Ib. ch. 23

5 All is gas and gaiters. [*The Gentleman in the Small-clothes.*]   *Ib.* ch. 49

6 He has gone to the demnition bow-wows. [*Mr. Mantalini.*]   *Ib.* ch. 64

7 Oliver Twist has asked for more! [*Bumble.*]   *Oliver Twist*, ch. 2

8 Known by the *sobriquet* of 'The Artful Dodger.'   *Ib.* ch. 8

9 'Hard,' replied the Dodger. 'As nails,' added Charley Bates.   *Ib.* ch. 9

10 'If the law supposes that,' said Mr. Bumble . . . 'the law is a ass—a idiot.'
Ib. ch. 51

11 The question [with Mr. Podsnap] about everything was, would it bring a blush into the cheek of the young person?
Our Mutual Friend, bk. i, ch. 11

12 I think . . . that it is the best club in London. [*Mr. Tremlow, on the House of Commons.*]   *Ib.* bk. ii, ch. 3

13 Queer Street is full of lodgers just at present. [*Fledgeby.*]   *Ib.* bk. iii, ch. 1

14 He'd be sharper than a serpent's tooth, if he wasn't as dull as ditch water. [*Fanny Cleaver.*]   *Ib.* ch. 10

15 He had used the word in its Pickwickian sense. . . . He had merely considered him a humbug in a Pickwickian point of view. [*Mr. Blotton.*]
Pickwick Papers, ch. 1

16 Kent, sir—everybody knows Kent—apples, cherries, hops, and women. [*Jingle.*]   *Ib.* ch. 2

17 I wants to make your flesh creep. [*The Fat Boy.*]   *Ib.* ch. 8

18 'It's always best on these occasions to do what the mob do.' 'But suppose there are two mobs?' suggested Mr. Snodgrass. 'Shout with the largest,' replied Mr. Pickwick.   *Ib.* ch. 13

19 'Can I unmoved see thee dying
On a log,
Expiring frog!' [*Mrs. Leo Hunter.*]
Pickwick Papers, ch. 15

20 Mr. Weller's knowledge of London was extensive and peculiar.   *Ib.* ch. 20

21 Be wery careful o' vidders all your life. [*Mr. Weller.*]   *Ib.*

22 Keep yourself *to* yourself. [*Mr. Raddle.*]   *Ib.* ch. 32

23 She's a swellin' wisibly before my wery eyes. [*Mr. Weller.*]   *Ib.* ch. 33

24 Chops and Tomata sauce. Yours, Pickwick.   *Ib.* ch. 34

25 Put it down a we, my Lord, put it down a we. [*Mr. Weller.*]   *Ib.*

26 'Little to do, and plenty to get, I suppose?' said Sergeant Buzfuz, with jocularity.
'Oh, quite enough to get, sir, as the soldier said ven they ordered him three hundred and fifty lashes,' replied Sam.
'You must not tell us what the soldier, or any other man, said, sir,' interposed the judge; 'it's not evidence.'   *Ib.*

27 'Yes, I have a pair of eyes,' replied Sam, 'and that's just it. If they wos a pair o' patent double million magnifyin' gas microscopes of hextra power, p'raps I might be able to see through a flight o' stairs and a deal door; but bein' only eyes, you see my wision's limited.'   *Ib.*

28 Oh Sammy, Sammy, vy worn't there a alleybi! [*Mr. Weller.*]   *Ib.*

29 Miss Bolo rose from the table considerably agitated, and went straight home, in a flood of tears and a Sedan chair.   *Ib.* ch. 35

30 A friendly swarry, consisting of a boiled leg of mutton with the usual trimmings.   *Ib.* ch. 37

31 'That 'ere young lady,' replied Sam. 'She knows wot's wot, she does.'   *Ib.*

32 The have-his-carcase, next to the perpetual motion, is vun of the blessedest things as wos ever made. [*Sam Weller.*]
Ib. ch. 43

33 Anythin' for a quiet life, as the man said wen he took the sitivation at the lighthouse. [*Sam Weller.*]   *Ib.*

34 It is a far, far better thing that I do, than I have ever done; it is a far, far better rest that I go to, than I have ever known. [*Sydney Carton.*]
A Tale of Two Cities, bk. iii, ch. 15

JOHN DICKINSON 1732–1808

1 Then join in hand brave Americans
all,
By uniting we stand, by dividing we
fall.
*The Liberty Song. Memoirs of the
Historical Soc. of Pennsylvania,*
vol. xiv

DENIS DIDEROT 1713–1784

2 L'esprit de l'escalier.
Staircase wit.
*An untranslatable phrase, the
meaning of which is that one only
thinks on one's way downstairs of
the smart retort one might have
made in the drawing-room.
Paradoxe sur le Comédien*

WENTWORTH DILLON, EARL OF ROSCOMMON 1633?–1685

3 The multitude is always in the wrong.
Essay on Translated Verse, l. 183

DIOGENES *fl. c.* 380 B.C.

4 Alexander . . . asked him if he lacked
anything. 'Yea,' said he, 'that I do:
that you stand out of my sun a little.'
Plutarch, *Life of Alexander,* 14
(North's translation)

BENJAMIN DISRAELI, EARL OF BEACONSFIELD 1804–1881

5 Though I sit down now, the time
will come when you will hear me.
Maiden Speech, 7 Dec. 1837.
Meynell, *Disraeli,* i. 43

6 The Continent will not suffer England
to be the workshop of the world.
*Speech, House of Commons,
15 Mar. 1838*

7 The right hon. Gentleman [Sir Robert
Peel] caught the Whigs bathing, and
walked away with their clothes.
Ib. 28 Feb. 1845

8 Is man an ape or an angel? Now I am
on the side of the angels.
*Ib. at Meeting of Society for In-
creasing Endowments of Small
Livings in the Diocese of Oxford,
25 Nov. 1864*

9 As I sat opposite the Treasury Bench
the ministers reminded me of one of
those marine landscapes not very
unusual on the coasts of South America. You behold a range of exhausted
volcanoes. *Ib. Manchester, 3 Apr. 1872*

10 Lord Salisbury and myself have
brought you back peace—but a peace
I hope with honour.
*Ib. House of Commons, 16 July
1878*

11 A sophistical rhetorician, inebriated
with the exuberance of his own ver-
bosity. [Gladstone.]
*Speech at Banquet in Riding School,
Knightsbridge, 27 July 1878*

12 Damn your principles! Stick to your
party.
*Attr. Remark to Bulwer Lytton
(Latham, Famous Sayings)*

13 There is no reason to doubt the story
which represents him as using more
than once, in conversation with Her
Majesty on literary subjects, the
words: 'We authors, Ma'am.'
Monypenny and Buckle, *Life of
Disraeli,* v. 49

14 She is an excellent creature, but she
never can remember which came first,
the Greeks or the Romans. [Of his
wife.] G. W. E. Russell, *Collections and
Recollections,* ch. 1

15 Everyone likes flattery; and when you
come to Royalty you should lay it on
with a trowel.
Remark to Matthew Arnold. Ib. ch. 23

16 His Christianity was muscular.
Endymion, bk. i, ch. 14

17 Time is the great physician.
Ib. bk. vi, ch. 9

18 The blue ribbon of the turf. [The
Derby.]
Life of Lord George Bentinck,
ch. 26

19 Every woman should marry—and no
man. *Lothair,* ch. 30

20 Little things affect little minds.
Sybil, bk. iii, ch. 2

21 I was told that the Privileged and the
People formed Two Nations.
Ib. bk. iv, ch. 8

22 The microcosm of a public school.
Vivian Grey, bk. i, ch. 2

23 A *dark* horse, which had never been
thought of, and which the careless
St. James had never even observed in
the list, rushed past the grand stand
in sweeping triumph.
The Young Duke, bk. ii, ch. 5

HENRY AUSTIN DOBSON
1840–1921

24 I intended an Ode,
And it turned to a Sonnet.
It began *à la mode,*
I intended an Ode;
But Rose crossed the road
In her latest new bonnet;
I intended an Ode;
And it turned to a Sonnet.
Rose-Leaves

CHARLES LUTWIDGE DODGSON
see LEWIS CARROLL

JOHN DONNE 1571?–1631

1 All other things, to their destruction draw,
Only our love hath no decay;
This, no to-morrow hath, nor yester-day,
Running it never runs from us away,
But truly keeps his first, last, ever-lasting day. *The Anniversary*

2 For God's sake hold your tongue, and let me love. *The Canonization*

3 She, and comparisons are odious.
Elegies, No. 8. *The Comparison*

4 No Spring, nor Summer beauty hath such grace,
As I have seen in one Autumnal face.
Ib. No. 9. *The Autumnal*

5 O my America! my new-found-land.
Ib. No. 19. *On Going to Bed*

6 Where, like a pillow on a bed,
A pregnant bank swelled up, to rest
The violet's reclining head,
Sat we two, one another's best.
The Extasy

7 I wonder by my troth, what thou, and I
Did, till we lov'd? were we not wean'd till then?
But suck'd on country pleasures, childishly? *The Good-Morrow*

8 At the round earth's imagined corners, blow
Your trumpets, Angels, and arise, arise. *Holy Sonnets*, vii

9 Death be not proud, though some have called thee
Mighty and dreadful, for, thou art not so,
For, those, whom thou think'st, thou dost overthrow,
Die not, poor death. *Ib.* x

10 One short sleep past, we wake eternally,
And death shall be no more; death, thou shalt die. *Ib.*

11 What if this present were the world's last night? *Ib.* xiii

12 Batter my heart, three person'd God; for, you
As yet but knock, breathe, shine, and seek to mend. *Ib.* xiv

13 I long to talk with some old lover's ghost,
Who died before the god of love was born. *Love's Deity*

14 A bracelet of bright hair about the bone. *The Relic*

15 Sweetest love, I do not go,
For weariness of thee,
Nor in hope the world can show
A fitter Love for me;
But since that I
Must die at last, 'tis best,
To use my self in jest
Thus by feigned deaths to die. *Song*

16 Go, and catch a falling star,
Get with child a mandrake root,
Tell me, where all past years are,
Or who cleft the Devil's foot.
Song, Go and Catch a Falling Star

17 And swear
No where
Lives a woman true and fair. *Ib.*

18 Busy old fool, unruly Sun,
Why dost thou thus,
Through windows, and through curtains call on us?
Must to thy motions lovers' seasons run? *The Sun Rising*

19 I am two fools, I know,
For loving, and for saying so
In whining Poetry. *The Triple Fool*

20 Dull sublunary lovers' love
(Whose soul is sense) cannot admit
Absence, because it doth remove
Those things which elemented it.
A Valediction Forbidding Mourning

21 But I do nothing upon my self, and yet I am mine own *Executioner.*
Devotions

22 No man is an *Island*, entire of it self.
Ib.

23 Any man's *death* diminishes *me*, because I am involved in *Mankind*;
And therefore never send to know for whom the *bell* tolls; It tolls for *thee.*
Ib.

24 John Donne, Anne Donne, Un-done.
Letter to his Wife

WILLIAM DOUGLAS 1672–1748

25 And for bonnie Annie Laurie
I'd lay me doun and dee.
Annie Laurie

ERNEST DOWSON 1867–1900

26 I have been faithful to thee, Cynara! in my fashion. *Non Sum Qualis Eram*

27 I have forgot much, Cynara! gone with the wind,
Flung roses, roses, riotously, with the throng,
Dancing, to put thy pale, lost lilies out of mind. *Ib.*

SIR ARTHUR CONAN DOYLE
1859–1930

1 What of the bow?
The bow was made in England:
Of true wood, of yew-wood,
The wood of English bows.
Song of the Bow

2 It is quite a three-pipe problem.
The Adventures of Sherlock Holmes. The Red-Headed League

3 To Sherlock Holmes she [Irene Adler] is always *the* woman.
Ib. Scandal in Bohemia

4 It is a capital mistake to theorize before one has data. *Ib.*

5 You know my methods, Watson.
The Memoirs of Sherlock Holmes. The Crooked Man

6 'Excellent!' I [Dr. Watson] cried. 'Elementary,' said he [Holmes]. *Ib.*

7 'It is my duty to warn you that it will be used against you,' cried the Inspector, with the magnificent fair play of the British criminal law.
Ib. Dancing Men

8 He [Professor Moriarty] is the Napoleon of crime. *Ib. The Final Problem*

9 These are much deeper waters than I had thought. *Ib. Reigate Squires*

10 A long shot, Watson; a very long shot!
Ib. Silver Blaze

11 'Is there any point to which you would wish to draw my attention?'
'To the curious incident of the dog in the night-time.'
'The dog did nothing in the night-time.'
'That was the curious incident,' remarked Sherlock Holmes. *Ib.*

12 Good old Watson! You are the one fixed point in a changing age.
His Last Bow. His Last Bow.

13 But here, unless I am mistaken, is our client. *Ib. Wisteria Lodge*

14 There is but one step from the grotesque to the horrible. *Ib.*

15 An experience of women which extends over many nations and three separate continents. *The Sign of Four*

16 How often have I said to you that when you have eliminated the impossible, whatever remains, *however improbable*, must be the truth? *Ib.*

17 The vocabulary of 'Bradshaw' is nervous and terse but limited.
The Valley of Fear

18 Mediocrity knows nothing higher than itself, but talent instantly recognizes genius. *Ib.*

19 The Baker Street irregulars. *Ib.*

20 London, that great cesspool into which all the loungers of the Empire are irresistibly drained.
A Study in Scarlet

21 'Wonderful!' I [Dr. Watson] ejaculated. 'Commonplace,' said Holmes.
Ib.

SIR FRANCIS HASTINGS CHARLES DOYLE 1810–1888

22 Last night, among his fellow roughs, He jested, quaff'd, and swore.
The Private of the Buffs

23 *To-day*, beneath the foeman's frown, He stands in Elgin's place, Ambassador from Britain's crown And type of all her race. *Ib.*

24 His creed no parson ever knew, For this was still his 'simple plan,' To have with clergymen to do As little as a Christian can.
The Unobtrusive Christian

SIR FRANCIS DRAKE 1540?–1596

25 There is plenty of time to win this game, and to thrash the Spaniards too. *Attr. in the* Dict. of Nat. Biog.

'The tradition goes, that Drake would needs see the game up; but was soon prevail'd on to go and play out the rubber with the Spaniards.' W. Oldys' *Life of Ralegh* in Ralegh's *Hist. of the World* (1736)

26 I remember Drake, in the vaunting style of a soldier, would call the Enterprise [of Cadiz, 1587] the singeing of the King of Spain's Beard.
Bacon, *Considerations touching a War with Spain* (Harleian Misc. (1745), vol. v, p. 85, col. 1)

27 I must have the gentleman to haul and draw with the mariner, and the mariner with the gentleman. . . . I would know him, that would refuse to set his hand to a rope, but I know there is not any such here.
Corbett, *Drake and the Tudor Navy*, i. 249

MICHAEL DRAYTON 1563–1631

28 Fair stood the wind for France When we our sails advance, Nor now to prove our chance Longer will tarry.
To the Cambro-Britons. Agincourt

29 Since there's no help, come let us kiss and part. *Sonnets*, lxi

WILLIAM DRENNAN 1754–1820

30 The men of the Emerald Isle. *Erin*

THOMAS DRUMMOND 1797–1840

1 Property has its duties as well as its rights.
Letter to the Earl of Donoughmore, 22 May 1838

JOHN DRYDEN 1631–1700

2 In pious times, ere priestcraft did begin,
Before polygamy was made a sin.
Absalom and Achitophel, pt. i, l. 1

3 And, wide as his command,
Scatter'd his Maker's image through the land. *Ib.* l. 9

4 The Jews, a headstrong, moody, murmuring race
As ever tried the extent and stretch of grace,
God's pampered people, whom, debauched with ease,
No king could govern nor no God could please. *Ib.* l. 45

5 A fiery soul, which working out its way,
Fretted the pigmy body to decay:
And o'er informed the tenement of clay. *Ib.* l. 156

6 Great wits are sure to madness near alli'd,
And thin partitions do their bounds divide. *Ib.* l. 163

7 But far more numerous was the herd of such
Who think too little and who talk too much. *Ib.* l. 533

8 A man so various that he seem'd to be
Not one, but all mankind's epitome.
Stiff in opinions, always in the wrong;
Was everything by starts, and nothing long:
But, in the course of one revolving moon,
Was chemist, fiddler, statesman, and buffoon. *Ib.* l. 545

9 During his office treason was no crime,
The sons of Belial had a glorious time. *Ib.* l. 597

10 Doeg, though without knowing how or why,
Made still a blund'ring kind of melody;
Spurr'd boldly on, and dash'd through thick and thin,
Through sense and nonsense, never out nor in. *Ib.* pt. ii, l. 412

11 None but the brave deserves the fair.
Alexander's Feast, l. 15

12 Drinking is the soldier's pleasure.
Ib. l. 57

13 All For Love, or the World Well Lost.
Title of Play

14 A knock-down argument; 'tis but a word and a blow. *Amphitryon*, I. i

15 Whistling to keep myself from being afraid. *Amphitryon*, III. i

16 From harmony, from heavenly harmony
This universal frame began:
From harmony to harmony
Through all the compass of the notes it ran,
The diapason closing full in Man.
St. Cecilia's Day, i

17 The soft complaining flute. *Ib.* iv

18 The trumpet shall be heard on high,
The dead shall live, the living die,
And Music shall untune the sky.
Ib. Grand Chorus

19 I am as free as nature first made man,
Ere the base laws of servitude began,
When wild in woods the noble savage ran.
The Conquest of Granada, pt. i, I. i

20 Here lies my wife: here let her lie!
Now she's at rest, and so am I.
Epitaph Intended for Dryden's Wife

21 He had brought me to my last dregs;
I was fighting as low as ever was Squire Widdrington.
An Evening's Love, II. i

22 Either to be wholly slaves or wholly free.
The Hind and the Panther, pt. ii, l. 285

23 Fairest Isle, all isles excelling,
Seat of pleasures, and of loves;
Venus here will choose her dwelling,
And forsake her Cyprian groves.
King Arthur, v. Song of Venus

24 The rest to some faint meaning make pretence,
But Shadwell never deviates into sense.
Some beams of wit on other souls may fall,
Strike through and make a lucid interval;
But Shadwell's genuine night admits no ray,
His rising fogs prevail upon the day.
Mac Flecknoe, l. 19

25 I am to be married within these three days; married past redemption.
Marriage à la Mode, I. i

26 But treason is not own'd when 'tis descried;
Successful crimes alone are justified.
The Medal, l. 207

27 And Antony, who lost the world for love.
Palamon and Arcite, bk. ii, l. 607

28 Like pilgrims to th' appointed place we tend;
The world's an inn, and death the journey's end. *Ib.* bk. iii, l. 887

1   There is a pleasure sure,
In being mad, which none but mad-
men know!
                    The Spanish Friar, I. i

2   We must beat the iron while it is hot,
but we may polish it at leisure.
                    Dedication of the Aeneis

3   He was the man who of all modern,
and perhaps ancient poets, had the
largest and most comprehensive soul.
. . . He was naturally learn'd; he
needed not the spectacles of books to
read Nature; he looked inwards, and
found her there. . . . He is many times
flat, insipid; his comic wit degenerat-
ing into clenches, his serious swelling
into bombast. But he is always great,
when some occasion is presented to
him. [Shakespeare.]
                    Essay of Dramatic Poesy

4   The consideration of this made Mr.
Hales of Eaton say, that there was
no subject of which any poet ever
writ, but he would produce it much
better done in Shakespeare.   *Ib.*

5   What judgment I had increases rather
than diminishes; and thoughts, such
as they are, come crowding in so fast
upon me, that my only difficulty is
to choose or reject; to run them into
verse or to give them the other
harmony of prose.   *Preface to Fables*

6   'Tis sufficient to say [of Chaucer],
according to the proverb, that here is
God's plenty.   *Ib.*

7   He [Chaucer] is a perpetual fountain
of good sense.   *Ib.*

GEORGE DUFFIELD 1818–1888

8   Stand up!—stand up for Jesus!
                    *The Psalmist. Stand Up, Stand
                    Up for Jesus*

ALEXANDRE DUMAS 1802–1870

9   Cherchons la femme.
        Let us look for the woman.
                    Les Mohicans de Paris, vol. ii,
                    ch. 2
        (Cherchez la femme. Attr. to Joseph
        Fouché.)

10   Tous pour un, un pour tous.
        All for one, one for all.
                    Les Trois Mousquetaires, passim

MARÉCHAL DUMOURIEZ
                    1739–1823

11   Les courtisans qui l'entourent n'ont
rien oublié et n'ont rien appris.
        The courtiers who surround him

have forgotten nothing and learnt
nothing.
        *Of Louis XVIII, at the time of the
        Declaration of Verona, Sept. 1795.
        Examen. See also* Talleyrand

WILLIAM DUNBAR 1465?–1530?

12   Timor mortis conturbat me.
                    Lament for the Makaris

13   London, thou art of townes A *per se.*
                    London, 1. 1

14   London, thou art the flower of cities
all!
Gemme of all joy, jasper of jocunditie.
                    Ib. 1. 16

JAMES DUPORT 1606–1679

15   Quem Juppiter vult perdere dementat
prius.
        Whom God would destroy He first
        sends mad.

THOMAS D'URFEY 1653–1723

16   Neighbours o'er the Herring Pond.
                    Pills to Purge Melancholy (1719),
                    vol. ii, p. 333. *Fable of the Lady,
                    the Lurcher, and the Marrow-
                    Puddings*, xiv

SIR EDWARD DYER c. 1540–1607

17   My mind to me a kingdom is,
    Such present joys therein I find,
That it excels all other bliss
    That earth affords or grows by kind.
Though much I want which most
    would have,
Yet still my mind forbids to crave.
                    My Mind to Me a Kingdom Is

JOHN DYER 1700?–1758

18   A little rule, a little sway,
A sunbeam in a winter's day,
Is all the proud and mighty have
Between the cradle and the grave.
                    Grongar Hill, 1. 89

JOHN DYER *fl.* 1714

19   And he that will this health deny,
Down among the dead men let him lie.
                    Toast: Here's a Health to the King

MARIA EDGEWORTH 1767–1849

20   Well! some people talk of morality,
and some of religion, but give me a
little snug property.
                    The Absentee, ch. 2

21   Come when you're called;
And do as you're bid;
Shut the door after you;
And you'll never be chid.
                    The Contrast, ch. 1

THOMAS ALVA EDISON
1847–1931

1 Genius is one per cent. inspiration and ninety-nine per cent. perspiration.
Newspaper Interview. Life (1932), ch. 24

JAMES EDMESTON 1791–1867

2 Lead us, Heavenly Father, lead us
O'er the world's tempestuous sea;
Guard us, guide us, keep us, feed us,
For we have no help but Thee.
Sacred Lyrics, Set 2. Lead Us, Heavenly Father

EDWARD III OF ENGLAND
1312–1377

3 Let the boy win his spurs.
Of the Black Prince at Crécy, 1345

4 Also say to them, that they suffre hym this day to wynne his spurres, for if god be pleased, I woll this iourney be his, and the honoure therof.
Lord Berners, *Froissart's Chron.* (1812), I. cxxx. 158.

EDWARD VIII OF GREAT BRITAIN 1894–

5 I have found it impossible to carry the heavy burden of responsibility and to discharge my duties as King as I would wish to do without the help and support of the woman I love.
Broadcast, 11 Dec. 1936

JONATHAN EDWARDS 1629–1712

6 The bodies of those that made such a noise and tumult when alive, when dead, lie as quietly among the graves of their neighbours as any others.
Procrastination

OLIVER EDWARDS 1711–1791

7 I have tried too in my time to be a philosopher; but, I don't know how, cheerfulness was always breaking in.
Boswell's *Johnson,* 17 Apr. 1778

'GEORGE ELIOT' [MARY ANN CROSS] 1819–1880

8 I'm not denyin' the women are foolish: God Almighty made 'em to match the men. *Adam Bede,* ch. 53

9 The happiest women, like the happiest nations, have no history.
The Mill on the Floss, bk. vi, ch. 3

THOMAS STEARNS ELIOT 1888–1965

10 Time present and time past
Are both perhaps present in time future,
And time future contained in time past. *Burnt Norton*

11 In the seventeenth century a dissociation of sensibility set in from which we have never recovered. *Essay on Dryden*

12 We are the hollow men
We are the stuffed men
Leaning together. *The Hollow Men*

13 This is the way the world ends
Not with a bang but a whimper. *Ib.*

14 When the evening is spread out against the sky
Like a patient etherized upon a table.
Love Song of J. Alfred Prufrock

15 In the room the women come and go
Talking of Michelangelo. *Ib.*

16 The yellow fog that rubs its back upon the window-panes. *Ib.*

17 I have measured out my life with coffee spoons. *Ib.*

18 I should have been a pair of ragged claws
Scuttling across the floors of silent seas. *Ib.*

19 I grow old . . . I grow old . . .
I shall wear the bottoms of my trousers rolled. *Ib.*

20 I am aware of the damp souls of housemaids
Sprouting despondently at area gates.
Morning at the Window

21 The last temptation is the greatest treason:
To do the right deed for the wrong reason. *Murder in the Cathedral,* pt. 1

22 The nightingales are singing near
The Convent of the Sacred Heart
And sang within the bloody wood
When Agamemnon cried aloud.
Sweeney Among the Nightingales

23 April is the cruellest month, breeding
Lilacs out of the dead land, mixing
Memory and desire, stirring
Dull roots with spring rain.
The Waste Land, i. *The Burial of the Dead*

24 And I will show you something different from either
Your shadow at morning striding behind you,
Or your shadow at evening rising to meet you
I will show you fear in a handful of dust. *Ib.*

1 O the moon shone bright on Mrs.
    Porter
  And on her daughter
  They wash their feet in soda water.
        The Waste Land, iii. The Fire Sermon

2 When lovely woman stoops to folly
    and
  Paces about her room again, alone,
  She smoothes her hair with automatic
    hand,
  And puts a record on the gramophone.
        Ib.

3 Webster was much possessed by death.
        Whispers of Immortality

QUEEN ELIZABETH I 1533–1603

4 'Twas God the word that spake it,
  He took the Bread and brake it;
  And what the word did make it;
  That I believe, and take it.
        *Answer on being asked her opinion
        of Christ's presence in the Sacra-
        ment.* S. Clarke's *Marrow of
        Ecclesiastical History*, pt. ii, *Life
        of Queen Elizabeth* (ed. 1675)

5 The queen of Scots is this day leichter
  of a fair son, and I am but a barren
  stock.
        *Memoirs of Sir James Melville
        (1549–93)*

6 God may forgive you, but I never can.
  [To the Countess of Nottingham.]
        The Queen . . . crying to her that
        God might pardon her, but she
        never could.
        Hume, *History of England under
        the House of Tudor*, vol. ii, ch. 7

7 If thy heart fails thee, climb not at
  all.
        *Lines written on a window after
        Sir Walter Ralegh's line* 'Fain
        would I climb, yet fear I to fall.'
        Fuller, *Worthies of England*,
        vol. i, p. 419

8 Semper eadem.   *Motto*

9 I know I have the body of a weak and
  feeble woman, but I have the heart
  and stomach of a king, and of a king
  of England too; and think foul scorn
  that Parma or Spain, or any prince of
  Europe, should dare to invade the
  borders of my realm.
        *Speech to the Troops at Tilbury
        on the Approach of the Armada,
        1588*

10 Must! Is *must* a word to be addressed
   to princes? Little man, little man!
   thy father, if he had been alive, durst
   not have used that word.
        To Robert Cecil. On her death-bed.
        J. R. Green, *A Short History of
        the English People*, ch. vii

JOHN ELLERTON 1826–1893

11 The day Thou gavest, Lord, is ended,
   The darkness falls at Thy behest.
        *A Liturgy for Missionary Meet-
        ings. The Day Thou Gavest*

JANE ELLIOT 1727–1805

12 I've heard them lilting, at the ewe
     milking.
   Lasses a' lilting, before dawn of day;
   But now they are moaning, on ilka
     green loaning;
   The flowers of the forest are a' wede
     away.   *The Flowers of the Forest*

GEORGE ELLIS
see SIR GREGORY GANDER

RALPH WALDO EMERSON
                                    1803–1882

13 If the red slayer think he slays,
   Or if the slain think he is slain,
   They know not well the subtle ways
   I keep, and pass, and turn again.
        Brahma

14 By the rude bridge that arched the
     flood,
   Their flag to April's breeze unfurled,
   Here once the embattled farmers
     stood,
   And fired the shot heard round the
     world.
        *Hymn Sung at the Completion
        of the Concord Monument*

15 The hand that rounded Peter's dome,
   And groined the aisles of Christian
     Rome,
   Wrought in a sad sincerity;
   Himself from God he could not free;
   He builded better than he knew;—
   The conscious stone to beauty grew.
        The Problem

16 Art is a jealous mistress.
        Conduct of Life. Wealth

17 The louder he talked of his honour,
   the faster we counted our spoons.
        Ib. Worship

18 There is properly no history; only
     biography.   *Essays, i. History*

19 All mankind love a lover. *Ib. v. Love*

20 In skating over thin ice, our safety is
   in our speed.   *Ib. vii. Prudence*

21 Is it so bad, then, to be misunderstood? Pythagoras was misunderstood, and Socrates, and Jesus, and
   Luther, and Copernicus, and Galileo,
   and Newton, and every pure and wise
   spirit that ever took flesh. To be great
   is to be misunderstood.
        Ib. ii. Self-Reliance

1 I have heard with admiring submission the experience of the lady who declared that the sense of being well-dressed gives a feeling of inward tranquillity which religion is powerless to bestow. [Miss C. F. Forbes, 1817–1911.]
> *Letters and Social Aims. Social Aims*

2 Hitch your wagon to a star.
> *Society and Solitude. Civilization*

3 We boil at different degrees.
> *Ib. Eloquence*

4 If a man write a better book, preach a better sermon, or make a better mouse-trap than his neighbour, tho' he build his house in the woods, the world will make a beaten path to his door.
> *Mrs. Sarah S. B. Yule (1856–1916) credits the quotation to Emerson in her Borrowings (1889), stating in The Docket, Feb. 1912, that she copied this in her handbook from a lecture delivered by Emerson. The 'mouse-trap' quotation was the occasion of a long controversy, owing to Elbert Hubbard's claim to its authorship.*

ENNIUS 239–169 B.C.

5 Unus homo nobis cunctando restituit rem.
> One man by delaying saved the state for us.
> *Cicero, De Senectute, iv. 10*

HENRY ERSKINE 1746–1817

6 In the garb of old Gaul, wi' the fire of old Rome. *In the Garb of Old Gaul*

THOMAS ERSKINE, BARON ERSKINE 1750–1823

7 The uncontrouled licentiousness of a brutal and insolent soldiery.
> *Report (1796) of Erskine's defence of William Stone*

HENRI ESTIENNE 1531–1598

8 Si jeunesse savoit; si vieillesse pouvoit.
> If youth knew; if age could.
> *Les Prémices, Épigramme cxci*

EUCLID *fl. c.* 300 B.C.

9 Quod erat demonstrandum (trans. from the Greek).
> Which was to be proved.

10 A line is length without breadth.

EURIPIDES 485?–406? B.C.

11 ἡ γλῶσσ' ὀμώμοχ', ἡ δὲ φρὴν ἀνώμοτος.
> 'Twas but my tongue, 'twas not my soul that swore.
> *Hippolytus, 612. Trans. by Gilbert Murray*

ABEL EVANS 1679–1737

12 Under this stone, Reader, survey Dead Sir John Vanbrugh's house of clay.
Lie heavy on him, Earth! for he Laid many heavy loads on thee!
> *Epitaph on Sir John Vanbrugh, Architect of Blenheim Palace*

WILLIAM NORMAN EWER 1885–

13 How odd
Of God
To choose
The Jews. *How Odd*

FREDERICK WILLIAM FABER 1814–1863

14 My God, how wonderful Thou art!
Thy majesty how bright,
How beautiful Thy mercy-seat
In depths of burning light!
> *Jesus and Mary. My God, How Wonderful Thou Art!*

ROBERT FABYAN *d.* 1513

15 Finally he paid the debt of nature.
> *Chronicles*, pt. ii, xli

LUCIUS CARY, VISCOUNT FALKLAND 1610?–1643

16 When it is not necessary to change, it is necessary not to change.
> *A Speech concerning Episcopacy* [delivered 1641]. *A Discourse of Infallibility* (1660)

AUGUST HEINRICH HOFF-MANN VON FALLERSLEBEN 1798–1874

17 Deutschland, Deutschland über alles.
> Germany, Germany over all.
> *Title of Song*

GEORGE FARQUHAR 1678–1707

18 My Lady Bountiful.
> *The Beaux' Stratagem*, I. i

19 He answered the description the page gave to a T, Sir.
> *Love and a Bottle*, IV. iii

REV. FREDERICK WILLIAM FARRAR 1831–1903

20 Russell, let me always call you Edwin, and call me Eric.
> *Eric, or Little by Little*, pt. i, ch. 4

GUY FAWKES 1570–1606

1 Desperate diseases require desperate
remedies.
  (Gunpowder plot) *Dict. of Nat.
  Biog.*

EUGENE FIELD 1850–1895

2 Listen to my tale of woe.
                    The Little Peach

3 Wynken, Blynken, and Nod one night
  Sailed off in a wooden shoe—
  Sailed on a river of crystal light,
  Into a sea of dew.
      Wynken, Blynken, and Nod

HENRY FIELDING 1707–1754

4 One of my illustrious predecessors.
  *Covent-Garden Journal, No. 3,
  11 Jan. 1752*

5 I am as sober as a Judge.
  Don Quixote in England, III. xiv

6 Oh! The roast beef of England,
  And old England's roast beef.
      The Grub Street Opera, III. iii

7 Public schools are the nurseries of all
  vice and immorality.
      Joseph Andrews, bk. iii, ch. 5

8 Some folks rail against other folks,
  because other folks have what some
  folks would be glad of.
          Ib. bk. iv, ch. 6

9 An amiable weakness.
      Tom Jones, bk. x, ch. 8

10 To sun my self in Huncamunca's eyes.
   Tom Thumb the Great, I. iii

11 The dusky night rides down the sky,
   And ushers in the morn;
   The hounds all join in glorious cry,
   The huntsman winds his horn:
   And a-hunting we will go.
           A-Hunting We Will Go

L'ABBÉ EDGEWORTH DE FIRMONT 1745–1807

12 Fils de Saint Louis, montez au ciel.
   Son of Saint Louis, ascend to heaven.
   *Attr. words to Louis XVI as he
   mounted the steps of the guillotine
   at his execution, 1793. No docu-
   mentary proof at all.*

JOHN ARBUTHNOT FISHER, LORD FISHER 1841–1920

13 Sack the lot!
       The Times, 2 Sept. 1919

ALBERT H. FITZ

14 You are my honey, honey-suckle,
   I am the bee.
       The Honey-Suckle and the Bee

EDWARD FITZGERALD
1809–1883

15 Awake! for Morning in the Bowl of
   Night
   Has flung the Stone that puts the
   Stars to Flight:
     And Lo! the Hunter of the East has
     caught
   The Sultan's Turret in a Noose of
   Light.   *Omar Khayyám*, ed. 1, i

16 Iram indeed is gone with all its Rose,
   And Jamshyd's Sev'n-ring'd Cup
   where no one knows;
   But still the Vine her ancient Ruby
   yields,
   And still a Garden by the Water
   blows.   *Ib.* ed. 1, v

17 Come, fill the Cup, and in the Fire
   of Spring
   The Winter Garment of Repentance
   fling:
     The Bird of Time has but a little
     way
   To fly—and Lo! the Bird is on the
   Wing.   *Ib.* ed. 1, vii

18 Here with a Loaf of Bread beneath the
   bough,
   A Flask of Wine, a Book of Verse—
   and Thou
     Beside me singing in the Wilder-
     ness—
   And Wilderness is Paradise enow.
               Ib. ed. 1, xi

19 A Book of Verses underneath the
   Bough,
   A Jug of Wine, a Loaf of Bread—and
   Thou
     Beside me singing in the Wilder-
     ness—
   Oh, Wilderness were Paradise enow!
               Ib. ed. 4, xii

20 Ah, take the Cash in hand and
   waive the Rest;
   Oh, the brave Music of a *distant*
   Drum!   *Ib.* ed. 1, xii

21 Ah, take the Cash, and let the
   Credit go,
   Nor heed the rumble of a distant
   Drum!   *Ib.* ed. 4, xiii

22 Think, in this batter'd Caravanserai
   Whose Doorways are alternate Night
   and Day,
   How Sultan after Sultan with his
   Pomp
   Abode his Hour or two, and went his
   way.   *Ib.* ed. 1, xv

23 Think, in this batter'd Caravanserai
   Whose Portals are alternate Night and
   Day,
   How Sultan after Sultan with his
   Pomp
   Abode his destin'd Hour, and went his
   way.   *Ib.* ed. 4, xvii

1 They say the Lion and the Lizard keep
  The Courts where Jamshyd gloried
      and drank deep:
    And Bahram, that great Hunter—
        the Wild Ass
  Stamps o'er his Head, and he lies fast
      asleep.
                    Omar Khayyám, ed. 1, xvii

2 I sometimes think that never blows so
      red
  The Rose as where some buried Caesar
      bled;
    That every Hyacinth the Garden
        wears
  Dropt in her Lap from some once
      lovely Head.
                    Ib. ed. 1, xviii; ed. 4, xix

3 Ah, my Belovéd, fill the Cup that
      clears
  To-DAY of past Regrets and Future
      Fears:
    To-morrow!—Why, To-morrow I
        may be
  Myself with Yesterday's Sev'n
      thousand Years.
                    Ib. ed. 1, xx; ed. 4, xxi

4 Lo! some we loved, the loveliest and
      best
  That Time and Fate of all their
      Vintage prest,
    Have drunk their Cup a Round or
        two before,
  And one by one crept silently to Rest.
                    Ib. ed. 1, xxi

5 Ah, make the most of what we yet
      may spend,
  Before we too into the Dust descend;
    Dust into Dust, and under Dust, to
        lie,
  Sans Wine, sans Song, sans Singer,
      and—sans End!
                    Ib. ed. 1, xxiii; ed. 4, xxiv

6 Oh, come with old Khayyám, and
      leave the Wise
  To talk; one thing is certain, that Life
      flies;
    One thing is certain, and the Rest
        is Lies;
  The Flower that once hath blown
      for ever dies.   *Ib.* ed. 1, xxvi

7 Myself when young did eagerly fre-
      quent
  Doctor and Saint, and heard great
      argument
    About it and about: but evermore
  Came out by the same Door as in
      I went.   *Ib.* xxvii

8 Ah, fill the Cup:—what boots it to
      repeat
  How Time is slipping underneath our
      Feet:
    Unborn To-MORROW, and dead
        YESTERDAY,
  Why fret about them if To-DAY be
      sweet!
                    Ib. ed. 1, xxxvii. Not in ed. 4

9 One Moment in Annihilation's Waste,
  One Moment, of the Well of Life to
      taste—
    The Stars are setting and the Cara-
        van
  Starts for the Dawn of Nothing—Oh,
      make haste!
                    Omar Khayyám, ed. 1, xxxviii

10 'Tis all a Chequer-board of Nights and
      Days
  Where Destiny with Men for Pieces
      plays:
    Hither and thither moves, and
        mates, and slays,
  And one by one back in the Closet
      lays.   *Ib.* ed. 1, xlix

11 The Ball no question makes of Ayes
      and Noes,
  But Here or There as strikes the
      Player goes;
    And He that toss'd you down into
        the Field,
  He knows about it all—HE knows—
      HE knows!   *Ib.* ed. 4, lxx

12 The Moving Finger writes; and, hav-
      ing writ,
  Moves on: nor all thy Piety nor Wit
    Shall lure it back to cancel half a
        Line,
  Nor all thy Tears wash out a Word of
      it.   *Ib.* ed. 1, li
  [Ed. 4, lxxi, reads 'your' instead of
  'thy'.]

13 And that inverted Bowl we call The
      Sky,
  Whereunder crawling coop't we live
      and die,
    Lift not thy hands to It for help—
        for It
  Rolls impotently on as Thou or I.
                    Ib. lii

14 Said one—'Folks of a surly Tapster
      tell,
  And daub his Visage with the Smoke
      of Hell;
    They talk of some strict Testing of
        us—Pish!
  He's a Good Fellow, and 'twill all be
      well.'   *Ib.* lxiv; ed. 4, lxxxviii

15 Indeed the Idols I have loved so long
  Have done my credit in this World
      much wrong:
    Have drown'd my Glory in a
        Shallow Cup
  And sold my Reputation for a Song.
                    Ib. ed. 4, xciii

16 And much as Wine has play'd the
      Infidel,
  And robb'd me of my Robe of Honour
      —Well,
    I often wonder what the Vintners
        buy
  One half so precious as the Goods they
      sell.   *Ib.* ed. 1, lxxi

1 Ah Love! could thou and I with Fate
conspire
To grasp this sorry Scheme of Things
entire,
  Would not we shatter it to bits—
and then
Re-mould it nearer to the Heart's
Desire!
    Omar Khayyám, ed. 1, xxiii

2 Ah, Moon of my Delight who know'st
no wane,
The Moon of Heav'n is rising once
again:
  How oft hereafter rising shall she
look
Through this same Garden after me—
in vain!   *Ib.* ed. 1, lxxiv

3 And when Thyself with shining Foot
shall pass
Among the Guests Star-scattered on
the Grass,
  And in thy joyous Errand reach the
Spot
Where I made one—turn down an
empty Glass!   *Ib.* ed. 1, lxxv

4 And when like her, O Saki, you shall
pass.   *Ib.* ed. 4, ci

JAMES ELROY FLECKER
1884–1915

5 The dragon-green, the luminous, the
dark, the serpent-haunted sea.
    *The Gates of Damascus. West
Gate*

6 How splendid in the morning glows
the lily; with what grace he throws
His supplication to the rose.
    Hassan, I. i

7   For one night or the other night
Will come the Gardener in white, and
gathered flowers are dead, Yasmin.
    Ib. ii

8 For lust of knowing what should not
be known,
We take the Golden Road to Samar-
kand.   *Ib.* v. ii

9 It was so old a ship—who knows, who
knows?
  And yet so beautiful, I watched in
vain
To see the mast burst open with a
rose,
And the whole deck put on its leaves
again.   *The Old Ships*

10 A ship, an isle, a sickle moon—
  With few but with how splendid
stars
The mirrors of the sea are strewn
Between their silver bars.
    A Ship, an Isle, and a Sickle Moon

MARJORIE FLEMING 1803–1811

11 O lovely O most charming pug
Thy graceful air and heavenly mug....
His noses cast is of the roman
He is a very pretty weoman
I could not get a rhyme for roman
And was oblidged to call it weoman.
    Poems

ANDREW FLETCHER OF
SALTOUN 1655–1716

12 I knew a very wise man so much of
Sir Chr—'s sentiment, that he believed if a man were permitted to
make all the ballads, he need not care
who should make the laws of a nation.
    *Letter to the Marquis of Montrose,
and Others. Political Works*

JOHN FLORIO 1553?–1625

13 England is the paradise of women, the
purgatory of men, and the hell of
horses.   *Second Frutes*

MARÉCHAL FOCH 1851–1929

14 Mon centre cède, ma droite recule,
situation excellente. J'attaque!
  My centre is giving way, my right
is in retreat; situation excellent.
I shall attack.
    Sir G. Aston, *Biography of Foch*
(1929), ch. 13, p. 122

JEAN DE LA FONTAINE
1621–1695

15 Aide-toi, le ciel t'aidera.
  Help yourself, and heaven will help
you.
    Fables, vi. 18. *Le Chartier Em-
bourbé*

16 Je plie et ne romps pas.
  I bend and I break not.
    Ib. i. 22. *Le Chêne et le Roseau*

17 Il connaît l'univers et ne se connaît
pas.
  He knows the world and does not
know himself.
    Ib. viii. 26. *Démocrite et les
Abdéritains*

18 La raison du plus fort est toujours la
meilleure.
  The reason of the strongest is always the best.
    Ib. i. 10. *Le Loup et l'Agneau*

SAMUEL FOOTE 1720–1777

19 So she went into the garden to cut a
cabbage-leaf, to make an apple-pie;
and at the same time a great she-bear,
coming up the street, pops its head
into the shop. 'What! no soap?' So

he died, and she very imprudently married the barber; and there were present the Picninnies, and the Joblillies, and the Garyalies, and the grand Panjandrum himself, with the little round button at top, and they all fell to playing the game of catch as catch can, till the gun powder ran out at the heels of their boots.

> In Maria Edgeworth, *Harry and Lucy Concluded*

1 He is not only dull in himself, but the cause of dullness in others.
> Remark. Boswell's *Life of Johnson,* ed. Powell, iv, p. 178. Parody of Shakespeare, *Henry IV, Part II,* I. ii. 7

HENRY FORD 1863–1947

2 History is bunk.
> In the witness-box during his libel suit v. the Chicago Tribune, July 1919

JOHN FORD 1586–1639?

3 'Tis Pity She's a Whore. *Title of Play*

LENA GUILBERT FORD d. 1916?

4 Keep the home fires burning, while your hearts are yearning,
Though your lads are far away they dream of home;
There's a silver lining through the dark cloud shining;
Turn the dark cloud inside out, till the boys come home.
> *Keep the Home Fires Burning*

HOWELL FORGY 1908–

5 Praise the Lord, and pass the ammunition.
> Attr. when a Naval Lt., at Pearl Harbour, 7 Dec. 1941

E. M. FORSTER 1879–

6 Only connect. *Howard's End,* ch. xxii

VENANTIUS FORTUNATUS c. 535–c. 600

7 Vexilla regis prodeunt
Fulget crucis mysterium.

The royal banners forward go
The cross shines forth in mystic glow.
> *Durham Rituale.* Trans. by J. M. Neale

STEPHEN COLLINS FOSTER 1826–1864

8 I come down dah wid my hat caved in,
Doodah! doodah!
I go back home wid a pocket full of tin,
Oh! doodah day!

Gwine to run all night!
Gwine to run all day!
I'll bet my money on de bob-tail nag,
Somebody bet on de bay.
> *Camptown Races*

9 De blind hoss stick'n in a big mud hole,
Doodah! doodah!
Can't touch de bottom wid a ten-foot pole,
Oh! doodah day! *Ib.*

10 Weep no more, my lady,
Oh! weep no more to-day!
We will sing one song for the old Kentucky Home,
For the old Kentucky Home far away. *My Old Kentucky Home*

11 'Way down upon de Swanee Ribber,
Far, far away,
Dere's where my heart is turning ebber:
Dere's where de old folks stay.
All up and down de whole creation
Sadly I roam,
Still longing for de old plantation,
And for de old folks at home.
> *Old Folks at Home (Swanee Ribber)*

12 I'm coming, I'm coming,
For my head is bending low,
I hear their gentle voices calling
'Poor old Joe.' *Poor Old Joe*

13 He had no wool on de top of his head,
In de place where de wool ought to grow. *Uncle Ned*

14 Dere's no more hard work for poor old Ned,
He's gone whar de good niggers go.
> *Ib.*

15 I dream of Jeanie with the light brown hair.
> *Jeanie With the Light Brown Hair*

16 Beautiful Dreamer *Song Title*

CHARLES JAMES FOX 1749–1806

17 How much the greatest event it is that ever happened in the world! and how much the best!
> On the Fall of the Bastille. Letter to Fitzpatrick, *30 July 1789.* Russell's *Life and Times of C. J. Fox,* vol. ii, p. 361

FRANÇOIS Iᴱᴿ 1494–1547

18 Tout est perdu fors l'honneur.

All is lost save honour.
> Traditional words in a letter to his mother after his defeat at Pavia, 1525. The actual words were: 'De toutes choses ne m'est demeuré que l'honneur et la vie qui est saulve.' *Collection des Documents Inédits sur l'Histoire de France,* vol. i (1847), p. 129

BENJAMIN FRANKLIN 1706–1790

1 Remember, that time is money.
> *Advice to Young Tradesman, 1748. Writings*, vol. ii.

2 No nation was ever ruined by trade.
> *Essays. Thoughts on Commercial Subjects*

3 There never was a good war, or a bad peace. *Letter to Quincy, 11 Sept. 1783*

4 But in this world nothing can be said to be certain, except death and taxes.
> *Letter to Jean Baptiste Le Roy, 13 Nov. 1789. Writings*, vol. x

5 A little neglect may breed mischief, . . . for want of a nail, the shoe was lost; for want of a shoe the horse was lost; and for want of a horse the rider was lost.
> *Maxims . . . Prefixed to* Poor Richard's Almanac (1758)

6 We must indeed all hang together, or, most assuredly, we shall all hang separately.
> *Remark to John Hancock, at Signing of the Declaration of Independence, 4 July 1776*

FREDERICK THE GREAT
1712–1786

7 Ihr Racker, wollt ihr ewig leben?
> Rascals, would you live for ever?
> *When the Guards hesitated, at Kolin, 18 June 1757*

JOHN HOOKHAM FRERE
1769–1846

8 The feather'd race with pinions skim the air—
> Not so the mackerel, and still less the bear!
> *Progress of Man*, l. 34. *Poetry of the Anti-Jacobin* (1799)

ROBERT FROST 1875–1963

9 My apple trees will never get across
> And eat the cones under his pines,
> I tell him.
> He only says, 'Good fences make good neighbours.'
> *North of Boston. Mending Wall*

JAMES ANTHONY FROUDE
1818–1894

10 Wild animals never kill for sport. Man is the only one to whom the torture and death of his fellow-creatures is amusing in itself.
> *Oceana*, ch. 5

THOMAS FULLER 1608–1661

11 Worldly wealth he cared not for, desiring only to make both ends meet. [Of Edmund Grindall.]
> *Worthies of England. Worthies of Cumberland*

ROSE FYLEMAN 1877–1957

12 There are fairies at the bottom of our garden. *Fairies and Chimneys. Fairies*

THOMAS GAINSBOROUGH
1727–1788

13 We are all going to heaven, and Vandyke is of the company.
> *Attr. Last Words.* Boulton, *Thomas Gainsborough*, ch. 9

GAIUS *fl. c.* 110–c. 180

14 Damnosa hereditas.
> Ruinous inheritance. *Inst.* ii. 163

GALILEO GALILEI 1564–1642

15 E pur si muove.
> But it does move.
> *Attr. to Galileo after his recantation in 1632. The Earliest appearance of the phrase is 1761 (see E. R. Hull,* Galileo), *and it is generally conceded to be apocryphal.*

SIR GREGORY GANDER [GEORGE ELLIS] 1745–1815

16 Snowy, Flowy, Blowy,
> Showery, Flowery, Bowery,
> Hoppy, Croppy, Droppy,
> Breezy, Sneezy, Freezy.
> *The Twelve Months*

AUGUSTUS P. GARDNER
1865–1918

17 Wake up, America.
> *Speech, 16 Oct. 1916*

DAVID GARRICK 1717–1779

18 Come, cheer up, my lads! 'tis to glory we steer,
> To add something more to this wonderful year;
> To honour we call you, not press you like slaves,
> For who are so free as the sons of the waves?
> Heart of oak are our ships,
> Heart of oak are our men:
> We always are ready;
> Steady, boys, steady;
> We'll fight and we'll conquer again and again. *Heart of Oak*

1 Here lies Nolly Goldsmith, for shortness call'd Noll,
Who wrote like an angel, but talk'd
like poor Poll.
Impromptu Epitaph

2 A fellow-feeling makes one wond'rous
kind.
*An Occasional Prologue on Quit-
ting the Theatre, 10 June 1776*

WILLIAM LLOYD GARRISON
1805–1879

3 I am in earnest—I will not equivocate
—I will not excuse—I will not retreat
a single inch—and I will be heard!
*Salutatory Address of The Libera-
tor, 1 Jan. 1831*

SIR SAMUEL GARTH 1661–1719

4 A barren superfluity of words.
The Dispensary, c. 2, l. 95

ELIZABETH CLEGHORN
GASKELL 1810–1865

5 Get her a flannel waistcoat and flannel
drawers, ma'am, if you wish to keep
her alive. But my advice is, kill the
poor creature at once. [*Capt. Brown on
Miss Betsey Barker's cow.*]
Cranford, ch. 1

GAVARNI 1801–1866

6 Les enfants terribles.
The embarrassing young.
Title of a series of prints

JOHN GAY 1685–1732

7 ⠀⠀⠀⠀I rage, I melt, I burn,
The feeble God has stabb'd me to the
heart. ⠀⠀⠀*Acis and Galatea, ii*

8 O ruddier than the cherry,
O sweeter than the berry. ⠀⠀*Ib.*

9 Do you think your mother and I
should have liv'd comfortably so long
together, if ever we had been married?
*The Beggar's Opera, Act I, sc.
viii, air vii*

10 O Polly, you might have toy'd and
kist,
By keeping men off, you keep them
on. ⠀⠀⠀⠀⠀⠀*Ib. air ix*

11 Well, Polly; as far as one woman can
forgive another, I forgive thee.
Ib.

12 The comfortable estate of widowhood,
is the only hope that keeps up a wife's
spirits. ⠀⠀⠀⠀⠀*Ib. x*

13 Away, hussy. Hang your husband and
be dutiful. ⠀⠀⠀⠀*Ib. xii*

14 ⠀⠀I sipt each flower,
I chang'd ev'ry hour,
But here ev'ry flower is united
*The Beggar's Opera, Act I, sc.
xiii, air xv*

15 If with me you'd fondly stray
Over the hills and far away. ⠀*Ib. air xvi*

16 O what pain it is to part! ⠀*Ib. air xvii*

17 Fill ev'ry glass, for wine inspires us,
And fires us
With courage, love and joy.
Women and wine should life employ.
Is there aught else on earth desirous?
Ib. II, ii, air xix

18 If the heart of a man is deprest with
cares,
The mist is dispell'd when a woman
appears. ⠀⠀⠀*Ib. iii, air xxi*

19 Youth's the season made for joys,
Love is then our duty.
Ib. iv, air xxii

20 So he that tastes woman, woman,
woman,
He that tastes woman, ruin meets.
Ib. viii, air xxvi

21 How happy could I be with either,
Were t'other dear charmer away!
But while ye thus tease me together,
To neither a word will I say.
Ib. xiii, air xxxv

22 She who has never lov'd, has never
liv'd. ⠀⠀⠀*The Captives, II. i*

23 If e'er your heart has felt the tender
passion
You will forgive this just, this pious
fraud. ⠀⠀⠀⠀*Ib. IV. x*

24 Behold the bright original appear.
Epistle to a Lady, l. 85

25 One always zealous for his country's
good. ⠀⠀⠀⠀*Ib. l. 118*

26 Life is a jest; and all things show it.
I thought so once; but now I know it.
My Own Epitaph

27 Whence is thy learning? Hath thy toil
O'er books consum'd the midnight
oil?
Fables. Series 1, introduction, l. 15

28 Where there is life, there's hope, he
cried,
Then why such haste? so groan'd and
died.
*Ib. xxvii. The Sick Man and the
Angel, l. 49*

29 And when a lady's in the case,
You know, all other things give place.
*Ib. l. The Hare and Many Friends,
l. 41*

30 All in the Downs the fleet was moor'd,
The streamers waving in the wind,
When black-ey'd Susan came aboard.
*Sweet William's Farewell to Black-
Ey'd Susan*

1 They'll tell thee, sailors, when away,
   In ev'ry port a mistress find.
      *Sweet William's Farewell to Black-
      Eyed Susan*

SIR ERIC GEDDES 1875–1937

2 We will get everything out of her
   [Germany] that you can squeeze out
   of a lemon and a bit more. . . . I will
   squeeze her until you can hear the
   pips squeak.
      *Speech at the Drill Hall, Cam-
      bridge, 9 Dec. 1918*

DAVID LLOYD GEORGE, EARL OF DWYFOR 1863–1945

3 What is our task? To make Britain
   a fit country for heroes to live in.
      *Speech, Wolverhampton, 24 Nov.
      1918*

GEORGE I OF GREAT BRITAIN 1660–1727

4 I hate all Boets and Bainters.
      Campbell, *Lives of the Chief
      Justices*, ch. 30, Lord Mansfield

GEORGE II OF GREAT BRITAIN 1683–1760

5 Non, j'aurai des maîtresses.

   No, I shall have mistresses.
      *Reply to Queen Caroline when, as
      she lay dying, she urged him to
      marry again. Her reply to this
      was* 'Ah! mon Dieu! cela n'em-
      pêche pas'. Hervey, *Memoirs of
      George the Second (1848), vol. ii.*

6 Oh! he is mad, is he? Then I wish he
   would *bite* some other of my generals.
      *Reply to one who complained that
      General Wolfe was a madman.* F.
      Thackeray, *History of William
      Pitt*, vol. i, ch. 15, note

GEORGE III OF GREAT BRITAIN 1738–1820

7 Born and educated in this country
   I glory in the name of Briton.
      Speech from the Throne, 1760

8 'Was there ever', cried he, 'such stuff
   as great part of Shakespeare? Only
   one must not say so! But what think
   you?—what?—Is there not sad stuff?
   what?—what?
      *To Fanny Burney (in her Diary,
      19 Dec. 1785)*

GEORGE V OF GREAT BRITAIN 1865–1936

9 Wake up, England.
      *Title of a reprint in 1911 of a
      speech made by the King when
      Prince of Wales in the Guildhall
      on 5 Dec. 1901 on his return from
      a tour of the Empire*

EDWARD GIBBON 1737–1794

10 I sighed as a lover, I obeyed as a son.
      Autobiography (World's Classics
      ed.), p. 83

11 Crowds without company, and dissi-
   pation without pleasure.   *Ib.* p. 90

12 It was at Rome, on the 15th of Oc-
   tober, 1764, as I sat musing amidst
   the ruins of the Capitol, while the
   barefoot friars were singing vespers in
   the Temple of Jupiter, that the idea
   of writing the decline and fall of the
   city first started to my mind.
      Ib. p. 160

13 My English text is chaste, and all
   licentious passages are left in the
   decent obscurity of a learned language.
      Ib. p. 212

14 Titus Antoninus Pius. . . . His reign
   is marked by the rare advantage of
   furnishing very few materials for
   history; which is, indeed, little more
   than the register of the crimes, follies,
   and misfortunes of mankind.
      *Decline and Fall of the Roman
      Empire*, ch. 3

STELLA GIBBONS 1902–

15 Something nasty in the woodshed.
      Cold Comfort Farm, passim

FRED GILBERT 1850–1903

16 At Trinity Church I met my doom.
      Title of Song

17   As I walk along the Bois Bou-long,
         With an independent air,
      You can hear the girls declare,
         'He must be a millionaire';
   You can hear them sigh and wish to die,
   You can see them wink the other eye
   At the man who broke the Bank at
         Monte Carlo.
      *The Man Who Broke the Bank at
      Monte Carlo*

SIR HUMPHREY GILBERT 1539?–1583

18 We are as near to heaven by sea as by
   land!
      Hakluyt's Voyages, iii (1600),
      p. 159

SIR WILLIAM SCHWENCK GILBERT 1836–1911

19 He had often eaten oysters, but had
   never had enough.
      The Bab Ballads. Etiquette

20 The padre said, 'Whatever have you
   been and gone and done?'
      Ib. Gentle Alice Brown

1 Which is pretty, but I don't know
   what it means.   *The Bab Ballads.*
                   Gentle Alice Brown

2 Then they began to sing
   That extremely lovely thing,
   'Scherzando! ma non troppo ppp.'   Ib.

3 Oh, I am a cook and a captain bold,
   And the mate of the *Nancy* brig,
   And a bo'sun tight, and a midshipmite,
   And the crew of the captain's gig.
                   Ib. The Yarn of the 'Nancy Bell'

4 In all the woes that curse our race
   There is a lady in the case.
                   Fallen Fairies, II

5 He led his regiment from behind—
   He found it less exciting.
                   The Gondoliers, I

6 That celebrated,
   Cultivated,
   Underrated
        Nobleman,
   The Duke of Plaza Toro!   Ib.

7 Of that there is no manner of doubt—
   No probable, possible shadow of
        doubt—
   No possible doubt whatever.   Ib.

8 Oh, 'tis a glorious thing, I ween,
   To be a regular Royal Queen!
   No half-and-half affair, I mean,
   But a right-down regular Royal
   Queen!   Ib.

9 All shall equal be.
   The Earl, the Marquis, and the Dook,
   The Groom, the Butler, and the Cook,
   The Aristocrat who banks with Coutts,
   The Aristocrat who cleans the boots.
                   Ib.

10   But the privilege and pleasure
       That we treasure beyond measure
   Is to run on little errands for the
       Ministers of State.   *Ib.* II

11 With the gratifying feeling that our
   duty has been done!   Ib.

12 Take a pair of sparkling eyes.   Ib.

13 Dukes were three a penny.   Ib.

14 When every one is somebodee,
   Then no one's anybody.   Ib.

15 For I'm to be married to-day—
        to-day—
   Yes, I'm to be married to-day!
                   Iolanthe, I

16 Bow, bow, ye lower middle classes!
   Bow, bow, ye tradesmen, bow, ye
   masses.   Ib.

17 The Law is the true embodiment
   Of everything that's excellent.
   It has no kind of fault or flaw,
   And I, my Lords, embody the Law.
                   Ib.

18 A pleasant occupation for
   A rather susceptible Chancellor!   Ib.

19 Hearts just as pure and fair
   May beat in Belgrave Square
   As in the lowly air
        Of Seven Dials.   *Iolanthe*

20 When I went to the Bar as a very
        young man,
   (Said I to myself, said I).   Ib.

21 I often think it's comical
        How Nature always does contrive
   That every boy and every gal,
   That's born into the world alive,
   Is either a little Liberal,
        Or else a little Conservative!   Ib.

22 The House of Peers, throughout the
        war,
   Did nothing in particular,
        And did it very well:
   Yet Britain set the world ablaze
   In good King George's glorious days!
                   Ib.

23 When you're lying awake with a dis-
   mal headache, and repose is taboo'd
        by anxiety,
   I conceive you may use any language
        you choose to indulge in, without
        impropriety.   Ib.

24 For you dream you are crossing the
        Channel, and tossing about in a
        steamer from Harwich—
   Which is something between a large
        bathing machine and a very small
        second class carriage.   Ib.

25 And you're giving a treat (penny ice
        and cold meat) to a party of friends
        and relations—
   They're a ravenous horde—and they
        all came on board at Sloane Square
        and South Kensington Stations.
   And bound on that journey you find
        your attorney (who started that
        morning from Devon);
   He's a bit undersized, and you don't
        feel surprised when he tells you he's
        only eleven.   Ib.

26 Faint heart never won fair lady!
   Nothing venture, nothing win—
   Blood is thick, but water's thin—
   In for a penny, in for a pound—
   It's Love that makes the world go
        round!   Ib.

27 A wandering minstrel I—
   A thing of shreds and patches,
   Of ballads, songs and snatches,
   And dreamy lullaby!   *The Mikado,* I

28 I can trace my ancestry back to a
   protoplasmal primordial atomic glo-
   bule. Consequently, my family pride
   is something in-conceivable. I can't
   help it. I was born sneering.   Ib.

29 It revolts me, but I do it!   Ib.

30 As some day it may happen that a
        victim must be found,
        I've got a little list—I've got a little
        list

Of society offenders who might well
    be under ground
And who never would be missed—
    who never would be missed!
                        The Mikado, I

1 The idiot who praises, with en-
   thusiastic tone,
   All centuries but this, and every
   country but his own.   *Ib.*

2 Three little maids from school are we,
   Pert as a schoolgirl well can be,
   Filled to the brim with girlish glee.
                                  Ib.

3 Three little maids who, all unwary,
   Come from a ladies' seminary. *Ib.*

4 Modified rapture!   *Ib.*

5 Awaiting the sensation of a short,
      sharp shock,
   From a cheap and chippy chopper on
      a big black block.   *Ib.*

6 For he's going to marry Yum-Yum—
                        Yum-Yum. *Ib.*

7 Here's a how-de-doo!   *Ib.*

8 My object all sublime
   I shall achieve in time—
   To let the punishment fit the crime—
   The punishment fit the crime. *Ib.* II

9 The billiard sharp whom any one
      catches,
         His doom's extremely hard—
         He's made to dwell—
         In a dungeon cell
   On a spot that's always barred.
   And there he plays extravagant
      matches
         In fitless finger-stalls
         On a cloth untrue
         With a twisted cue
   And elliptical billiard balls. *Ib.*

10 I drew my snickersnee!   *Ib.*

11 I have a left shoulder-blade that is
    a miracle of loveliness. People come
    miles to see it. My right elbow has a
    fascination that few can resist. *Ib.*

12 Something lingering, with boiling oil
    in it, I fancy.   *Ib.*

13 Merely corroborative detail, intended
    to give artistic verisimilitude to an
    otherwise bald and unconvincing
    narrative.   *Ib.*

14 The flowers that bloom in the spring,
                        Tra la,
    Have nothing to do with the case.
                                  Ib.

15 I've got to take under my wing,
                        Tra la,
    A most unattractive old thing,
                        Tra la,
    With a caricature of a face.
    And that's what I mean when I say,
      or I sing,
    'Oh bother the flowers that bloom in
      the spring.'   *Ib.*

16 On a tree by a river a little tom-tit
    Sang 'Willow, titwillow, titwillow!'
    And I said to him, 'Dicky-bird, why
      do you sit
    Singing 'Willow, titwillow, titwillow?'
                        The Mikado, II

17 'Is it weakness of intellect, birdie?'
      I cried,
    'Or a rather tough worm in your little
      inside?'
    With a shake of his poor little head
      he replied,
    'Oh, willow, titwillow, titwillow!'
                                  Ib.

18 Twenty love-sick maidens we,
    Love-sick all against our will.
                        Patience, I

19 When I first put this uniform on. *Ib.*

20 If you're anxious for to shine in the
    high aesthetic line as a man of
    culture rare.   *Ib.*

21 You must lie upon the daisies and
    discourse in novel phrases of your
    complicated state of mind,
    The meaning doesn't matter if it's
    only idle chatter of a transcendental
    kind.
         And everyone will say,
         As you walk your mystic way,
    'If this young man expresses himself
      in terms too deep for *me*,
    Why, what a very singularly deep
    young man this deep young man
    must be!'   *Ib.*

22 Then a sentimental passion of a vege-
    table fashion must excite your
    languid spleen,
    An attachment à la Plato for a bash-
    ful young potato, or a not too
    French French bean!
    Though the Philistines may jostle, you
    will rank as an apostle in the high
    aesthetic band,
    If you walk down Piccadilly with a
    poppy or a lily in your medieval
    hand.
         And everyone will say,
         As you walk your flowery way,
    'If he's content with a vegetable love
      which would certainly not suit *me*,
    Why, what a most particularly pure
    young man this pure young man
    must be!'   *Ib.*

23 Prithee, pretty maiden—prithee, tell
    me true.   *Ib.*

24 Prithee, pretty maiden, will you
      marry me?
    (Hey, but I'm hopeful, willow, willow,
      waly!)
    I may say, at once, I'm a man of
      propertee—
         Hey willow waly O!
         Money, I despise it;
         Many people prize it,
         Hey willow waly O!   *Ib.*

1 There will be too much of me
In the coming by and by! *Patience, II*

2 Sing 'Hey to you—good day to you'—
Sing 'Bah to you—ha! ha! to you'—
Sing 'Booh to you—pooh, pooh to
you.' *Ib.*

3 Francesca di Rimini, miminy, piminy,
Je-ne-sais-quoi young man! *Ib.*

4 A greenery-yallery, Grosvenor Gallery,
Foot-in-the-grave young man! *Ib.*

5 I'm called Little Buttercup—dear
Little Buttercup,
Though I could never tell why.
H.M.S. Pinafore, I

6 I am the Captain of the *Pinafore*;
And a right good captain too! *Ib.*

7 And I'm never, never sick at sea!
What, never?
No, never!
What, *never?*
Hardly ever!
He's hardly ever sick at sea!
Then give three cheers, and one cheer
more,
For the hardy Captain of the *Pinafore!*
Ib.

8 I never use a big, big D. *Ib.*

9 And so do his sisters, and his cousins
and his aunts!
His sisters and his cousins,
Whom he reckons up by dozens,
And his aunts! *Ib.*

10 When I was a lad I served a term
As office boy to an Attorney's firm.
I cleaned the windows and I swept the
floor,
And I polished up the handle of the
big front door.
I polished up that handle so care-
fullee
That now I am the Ruler of the
Queen's Navee! *Ib.*

11 Stick close to your desks and never
go to sea,
And you all may be Rulers of the
Queen's Navee! *Ib.*

12 It was the cat! *Ib. II*

13 He is an Englishman!
For he himself has said it,
And it's greatly to his credit,
That he is an Englishman! *Ib.*

14 For he might have been a Roosian,
A French, or Turk, or Proosian,
Or perhaps Ital-ian!
But in spite of all temptations
To belong to other nations,
He remains an Englishman! *Ib.*

15 The other, upper crust,
A regular patrician. *Ib.*

16 It is, it is a glorious thing
To be a Pirate King.
Pirates of Penzance, I

17 Poor wandering one!
Though thou hast surely strayed,
Take heart of grace,
Thy steps retrace,
Poor wandering one!
Pirates of Penzance, I

18 I am the very model of a modern
Major-General. *Ib.*

19 I'm very good at integral and differ-
ential calculus;
I know the scientific names of beings
animalculous. *Ib.*

20 When the foeman bares his steel,
Tarantara, tarantara!
We uncomfortable feel,
Tarantara. *Ib. II*

21 When constabulary duty's to be done,
The policeman's lot is not a happy one.
Ib.

22 When the enterprising burglar's not
a-burgling. *Ib.*

23 When the coster's finished jumping on
his mother—
He loves to lie a-basking in the sun.
Ib.

24 You must stir it and stump it,
And blow your own trumpet,
Or trust me, you haven't a chance.
Ruddigore, I

25 He combines the manners of a Marquis
with the morals of a Methodist. *Ib.*

26 When he's excited he uses language
that would make your hair curl. *Ib.*

27 Desperate deeds of derring do. *Ib. II*

28 Some word that teems with hidden
meaning—like Basingstoke. *Ib.*

29 This particularly rapid, unintelligible
patter
Isn't generally heard, and if it is it
doesn't matter. *Ib.*

30 I was a pale young curate then.
The Sorcerer, I

31 Oh! My name is John Wellington
Wells,
I'm a dealer in magic and spells. *Ib.*

32 If anyone anything lacks,
He'll find it all ready in stacks,
If he'll only look in
On the resident Djinn,
Number seventy, Simmery Axe! *Ib.*

33 So I fell in love with a rich attorney's
Elderly ugly daughter.
Trial by Jury

34 She may very well pass for forty-three
In the dusk with a light behind her!
Ib.

35 For now I am a Judge
And a good Judge too. *Ib.*

36 'Tis ever thus with simple folk—an
accepted wit has but to say 'Pass the
mustard', and they roar their ribs
out! *The Yeomen of the Guard*

JAMES GILLRAY 1757–1815

1 Political Ravishment, or, The Old
Lady of Threadneedle Street in
Danger.　　*Title of Caricature, 1797*

WILLIAM EWART GLADSTONE
1809–1898

2 You cannot fight against the future.
Time is on our side.
　　Speech on the Reform Bill, 1866

3 [The Turks] one and all, bag and
baggage, shall, I hope, clear out from
the province they have desolated and
profaned.
　　*Speech, House of Commons,
7 May 1877*

4 Out of the range of practical politics.
　　Ib. at Dalkeith, 26 Nov. 1879

5 All the world over, I will back the
masses against the classes.
　　Ib. Liverpool, 28 June 1886

HANNAH GLASSE *fl.* 1747

6 Take your hare when it is cased. . . .
　　Art of Cookery
　　Usually misquoted as 'First catch
　　your hare'.

WILLIAM HENRY, DUKE OF
GLOUCESTER 1743–1805

7 Another damned, thick, square book!
Always scribble, scribble, scribble!
Eh! Mr. Gibbon?
　　Best's Literary Memorials. (Bos-
well's *Johnson*, vol. ii, p. 2, n.)

JOHN A. GLOVER-KINDE d. 1918

8 I Do Like To Be Beside the Seaside.
　　Title of Song (1909)

ALFRED DENIS GODLEY
1856–1925

9 What is this that roareth thus?
Can it be a Motor Bus?
Yes, the smell and hideous hum
Indicat Motorem Bum
　　　·　　　·　　　·
How shall wretches live like us
Cincti Bis Motoribus?
Domine, defende nos
Contra hos Motores Bos!
　　The Motor Bus. Letter to
　　C.R.L.F., 10 Jan. 1914

WILLIAM GODWIN 1756–1836

10 The log was burning brightly,
'Twas a night that should banish all
　sin,
For the bells were ringing the Old
　Year out,
And the New Year in.
　　The Miner's Dream of Home

JOSEF GOEBBELS 1897–1945

11 Wenn das deutsche Volk die Waffen
niederlegte, würden die Sowjets, auch
nach den Abmachungen zwischen
Roosevelt, Churchill und Stalin, ganz
Ost- und Südosteuropa zuzüglich des
grössten Teiles des Reiches besetzen.
Vor diesem einschliesslich der Sowjet-
union riesigen Territorium würde sich
sofort ein eiserner Vorhang herunter-
senken.

　　Should the German people lay down
　　its arms, the agreement between
　　Roosevelt, Churchill and Stalin
　　would allow the Soviets to occupy
　　all Eastern and South-eastern
　　Europe together with the major
　　part of the Reich. An iron cur-
　　tain would at once descend on
　　this territory which, including
　　the Soviet Union, would be of
　　enormous dimensions.
　　　Das Reich, 25 February 1945.
　　　Cf. Mrs. Philip Snowden, *Through
　　　Bolshevik Russia* (1920), ii, p. 32.
　　　We were behind the 'iron curtain'
　　　at last!
See also 63:5 and 234:5

HERMANN GOERING 1893–1946

12 Guns will make us powerful; butter
will only make us fat.
　　Radio Broadcast, summer of 1936
See also Hanns Johst

JOHANN WOLFGANG VON
GOETHE 1749–1832

13 Meine Ruh' ist hin,
Mein Herz ist schwer.

　　My peace is gone,
　　My heart is heavy.
　　　Faust, pt. i. Gretchen am Spinnrad

14 Die Tat ist alles, nicht der Ruhm.

　　The deed is everything, its repute
　　nothing.　　*Ib. pt. ii. Großer Vorhof*

15 Über allen Gipfeln
Ist Ruh'.

　　Over all the mountain tops is peace.
　　　Wanderers Nachtlied

16 Kennst du das Land, wo die Zitronen
　blühn?
Im dunkeln Laub die Gold-Orangen
　glühn,
Ein sanfter Wind vom blauen Himmel
　weht,
Die Myrte still und hoch der Lorbeer
　steht—
Kennst du es wohl?
　　　　　　Dahin! Dahin!
Möcht ich mit dir, o mein Geliebter,
　ziehn!

　　Know you the land where the
　　lemon-trees bloom? In the dark

foliage the gold oranges glow; a soft wind hovers from the sky, the myrtle is still and the laurel stands tall—do you know it well? There, there, I would go, O my beloved, with thee!
Wilhelm Meisters Lehrjahre, III. i

1 Mehr Licht!
  More light!
  Attr. dying words. (Actually: 'Macht doch den zweiten Fensterladen auch auf, damit mehr Licht hereinkomme': 'Open the second shutter, so that more light can come in.')

OLIVER GOLDSMITH 1728–1774

2 For he who fights and runs away
  May live to fight another day;
  But he who is in battle slain
  Can never rise and fight again.
      Art of Poetry on a New Plan. Written by Newbery, revised by Goldsmith

3 Sweet Auburn! loveliest village of the plain.   *The Deserted Village*, l. 1

4 Ill fares the land, to hast'ning ills a prey,
  Where wealth accumulates, and men decay;
  Princes and lords may flourish, or may fade;
  A breath can make them, as a breath has made;
  But a bold peasantry, their country's pride,
  When once destroy'd, can never be supplied.   *Ib.* l. 51

5 The watchdog's voice that bay'd the whisp'ring wind,
  And the loud laugh that spoke the vacant mind.   *Ib.* l. 121

6 A man he was to all the country dear,
  And passing rich with forty pounds a year;   *Ib.* l. 141

7 Truth from his lips prevail'd with double sway,
  And fools, who came to scoff, remain'd to pray.   *Ib.* l. 179

8 In arguing too, the parson own'd his skill,
  For e'en though vanquish'd, he could argue still;

  And still they gaz'd, and still the wonder grew,
  That one small head could carry all he knew.   *Ib.* l. 211

9 Man wants but little here below,
  Nor wants that little long.
      Edwin and Angelina, or The Hermit

10 Good people all, of every sort,
  Give ear unto my song;
  And if you find it wond'rous short,
  It cannot hold you long.
      Elegy on the Death of a Mad Dog

11 That still a godly race he ran,
  Whene'er he went to pray.   *Ib.*

12 The naked every day he clad,
  When he put on his clothes.   *Ib.*

13 And in that town a dog was found,
  As many dogs there be,
  Both mongrel, puppy, whelp, and hound,
  And curs of low degree.   *Ib.*

14 The dog, to gain some private ends,
  Went mad and bit the man.   *Ib.*

15 And swore the dog had lost his wits,
  To bite so good a man.   *Ib.*

16 The man recover'd of the bite,
  The dog it was that died.   *Ib.*

17 Who, born for the Universe, narrow'd his mind,
  And to party gave up what was meant for mankind.
      [Edmund Burke] *Retaliation*, l. 31

18 Who, too deep for his hearers, still went on refining,
  And thought of convincing, while they thought of dining.
      [Edmund Burke] *Ib.* l. 35

19 When they talk'd of their Raphaels, Correggios, and stuff,
  He shifted his trumpet, and only took snuff.   [Reynolds] *Ib.* l. 145

20 Let schoolmasters puzzle their brain,
  With grammar, and nonsense, and learning,
  Good liquor, I stoutly maintain,
  Gives genius a better discerning.
      She Stoops to Conquer, I. i, song

21 When lovely woman stoops to folly
  And finds too late that men betray,
  What charm can soothe her melancholy,
  What art can wash her guilt away?
  The only art her guilt to cover,
  To hide her shame from every eye,
  To give repentance to her lover,
  And wring his bosom—is to die.
      Song. From *The Vicar of Wakefield*, ch. 29

22 I'm now no more than a mere lodger in my own house.
      The Good-Natured Man, I

23 She stoops to conquer.   *Title of play*

24 I love everything that's old; old friends, old times, old manners, old books, old wines.
      She Stoops to Conquer, I

25 The very pink of perfection.   *Ib.*

26 This is Liberty-Hall, gentlemen.   *Ib.* II

1 As for murmurs, mother, we grumble
a little now and then, to be sure. But
there's no love lost between us.
She Stoops to Conquer, IV

2 By the living jingo, she was all of a
muck of sweat.
The Vicar of Wakefield, ch. 9

3 There is no arguing with Johnson; for
when his pistol misses fire, he knocks
you down with the butt end of it.
*Remark. Boswell's Life of John-
son, 26 Oct. 1769*

4 [To Johnson who was laughing when
he said that the little fishes in a
proposed fable should talk like little
fishes.]
Why, Dr. Johnson, this is not so
easy as you seem to think; for if
you were to make little fishes
talk, they would talk like whales.
Ib. 27 Apr. 1773

SAMUEL GOLDWYN 1882–

5 In two words: im-possible.
*Quoted in Alva Johnson, The
Great Goldwyn*

ADAM LINDSAY GORDON
1833–1870

6 Life is mostly froth and bubble,
Two things stand like stone,
Kindness in another's trouble,
Courage in your own.
Ye Wearie Wayfarer, Fytte 8

GEORGE JOACHIM, FIRST
VISCOUNT GOSCHEN 1831–1907

7 We have stood alone in that which is
called isolation—our splendid isolation, as one of our colonial friends
was good enough to call it. [See G. E.
Foster.]
Speech at Lewes, 26 Feb. 1896

RICHARD GRAFTON ?–1572?

8 Thirty days hath November,
April, June, and September,
February hath twenty-eight alone,
And all the rest have thirty-one.
*Abridgement of the Chronicles of
England (1570), introductory
matter, sig. 1 ¶ j. b*

HARRY GRAHAM 1874–1936

9 Auntie, did you feel no pain
Falling from that willow-tree?
Would you do it, please, again?
Cos my friend here didn't see.
*Ruthless Rhymes for Heartless
Homes. Appreciation*

10 O'er the rugged mountain's brow
Clara threw the twins she nursed,
And remarked, 'I wonder now
Which will reach the bottom first?'
*Ruthless Rhymes for Heartless Homes.
Calculating Clara*

11 Aunt Jane observed, the second time
She tumbled off a bus,
The step is short from the Sublime
To the Ridiculous. *Ib. Equanimity*

12 'There's been an accident!' they said,
'Your servant's cut in half; he's dead!'
'Indeed!' said Mr. Jones, 'and please
Send me the half that's got my keys.'
Ib. Mr. Jones

13 Billy, in one of his nice new sashes,
Fell in the fire and was burnt to ashes;
Now, although the room grows chilly,
I haven't the heart to poke poor Billy.
Ib. Tender-Heartedness

14 When Baby's cries grew hard to bear
I popped him in the Frigidaire.
I never would have done so if
I'd known that he'd be frozen stiff.
My wife said: 'George, I'm so unhappé!
Our darling's now completely *frappé!*
*More Ruthless Rhymes. L'Enfant
Glacé*

15 When Mrs. Gorm (Aunt Eloise)
Was stung to death by savage bees,
Her husband (Prebendary Gorm)
Put on his veil and took the swarm.
He's publishing a book, next May,
On 'How to Make Bee-keeping Pay'.
Ib. Opportunity

KENNETH GRAHAME 1859–1932

16 Believe me, my young friend, there is
nothing—absolutely nothing—half so
much worth doing as simply messing
about in boats.
The Wind in the Willows, ch. 1

17 The clever men at Oxford
Know all that there is to be
knowed.
But they none of them know one half
as much
As intelligent Mr. Toad. *Ib.* ch. x

SIR ROBERT GRANT 1779–1838

18 The Ancient of Days,
Pavilioned in splendour,
And girded with praise.
*Bickersteth's Church Psalmody.
O Worship the King*

19 His chariots of wrath The deep
thunder clouds form,
And dark is his path On the wings of
the storm. *Ib.*

20 Frail children of dust,
And feeble as frail. *Ib.*

ULYSSES SIMPSON GRANT
1822–1885

1 No terms except unconditional and immediate surrender can be accepted. I propose to move immediately upon your works.
To Simon Bolivar Buckner, whom he was besieging in Fort Donelson, 16 Feb. 1862

JOHN WOODCOCK GRAVES
1795–1886

2 D'ye ken John Peel with his coat so gray?
D'ye ken John Peel at the break of day?
D'ye ken John Peel when he's far far away
With his hounds and his horn in the morning?
'Twas the sound of his horn called me from my bed,
And the cry of his hounds has me oft-times led;
For Peel's view-hollo would waken the dead,
Or a fox from his lair in the morning.
John Peel

ROBERT GRAVES 1895–

3 Goodbye to all that.   *Title of book*

THOMAS GRAY 1716–1771

4 Ruin seize thee, ruthless King!
Confusion on thy banners wait,
Tho' fann'd by Conquest's crimson wing
They mock the air with idle state.
The Bard, I. i

5 Weave the warp, and weave the woof,
The winding-sheet of Edward's race.
Give ample room, and verge enough
The characters of hell to trace.
Ib. II. i

6 Youth on the prow, and Pleasure at the helm;   *Ib.* ii

7 Ye towers of Julius, London's lasting shame,
With many a foul and midnight murther fed.   *Ib.* iii

8 The curfew tolls the knell of parting day,
The lowing herd wind slowly o'er the lea,
The ploughman homeward plods his weary way,
And leaves the world to darkness and to me.

Now fades the glimmering landscape on the sight,
And all the air a solemn stillness holds,

Save where the beetle wheels his droning flight,
And drowsy tinklings lull the distant folds.
Elegy Written in a Country Churchyard, i–ii

9 Save that from yonder ivy-mantled tow'r,
The moping owl does to the moon complain.   *Ib.* iii

10 Each in his narrow cell for ever laid,
The rude forefathers of the hamlet sleep.   *Ib.* iv

11 The breezy call of incense-breathing Morn,
The swallow twitt'ring from the straw-built shed,
The cock's shrill clarion, or the echoing horn,
No more shall rouse them from their lowly bed.   *Ib.* v

12 Let not ambition mock their useful toil,
Their homely joys, and destiny obscure;
Nor grandeur hear with a disdainful smile,
The short and simple annals of the poor.

The boast of heraldry, the pomp of pow'r,
And all that beauty, all that wealth e'er gave,
Awaits alike th' inevitable hour,
The paths of glory lead but to the grave.   *Ib.* viii–ix

13 Can storied urn or animated bust
Back to its mansion call the fleeting breath?
Can honour's voice provoke the silent dust,
Or flatt'ry soothe the dull cold ear of death?   *Ib.* xi

14 Hands, that the rod of empire might have sway'd,
Or wak'd to ecstasy the living lyre.   *Ib.* xii

15 Full many a gem of purest ray serene,
The dark unfathom'd caves of ocean bear:
Full many a flower is born to blush unseen,
And waste its sweetness on the desert air.

Some village-Hampden, that with dauntless breast
The little tyrant of his fields withstood;
Some mute inglorious Milton here may rest,
Some Cromwell guiltless of his country's blood.   *Ib.* xiv–xv

1 Far from the madding crowd's ig-
noble strife,
  Their sober wishes never learn'd to
    stray;
Along the cool sequester'd vale of life
They kept the noiseless tenor of
  their way.
    *Elegy Written in a Country
    Churchyard, xix*

2 What female heart can gold despise?
What cat's averse to fish?
    *Ode on the Death of a Favourite
    Cat*

3 A fav'rite has no friend!   *Ib.*

4 Not all that tempts your wand'ring
eyes
  And heedless hearts, is lawful prize;
Nor all, that glisters, gold.   *Ib.*

5 Ye distant spires, ye antique towers,
  That crown the wat'ry glade.
    *Ode on a Distant Prospect of
    Eton College, l. 1*

6 Urge the flying ball.   *Ib. l. 30*

7 Still as they run they look behind,
  They hear a voice in every wind,
    And snatch a fearful joy. *Ib. l. 38*

8 Alas regardless of their doom,
  The little victims play!
No sense have they of ills to come,
  Nor care beyond to-day.   *Ib. l. 51*

9 To each his suff'rings: all are men,
  Condemn'd alike to groan;
The tender for another's pain,
  Th' unfeeling for his own. *Ib. l. 91*

10 . . . Where ignorance is bliss
  'Tis folly to be wise.   *Ib. l. 99*

11 He saw; but blasted with excess of
light,
Closed his eyes in endless night.
[Milton.]
    The Progress of Poesy, iii. 2

ROBERT GREENE 1560?–1592

12 Friar Bacon and Friar Bungay.
    Title of Play

13 For there is an upstart crow, beauti-
fied with our feathers, that with his
tiger's heart wrapped in a player's
hide, supposes he is as well able to
bumbast out a blank verse as the best
of you; and being an absolute *Iohannes
fac totum*, is in his own conceit the
only Shake-scene in a country.
    *The Groatsworth of Wit Bought
    with a Million of Repentance*

GREGORY I 540–604

14 Responsum est, quod Angli vocaren-
tur. At ille: 'Bene,' inquit; 'nam et
angelicam habent faciem, et tales

angelorum in caelis decet esse co-
heredes.'
  They answered that they were
  called Angles. 'It is well,' he said,
  'for they have the faces of angels,
  and such should be the co-heirs
  of the angels in heaven.'
  Traditionally quoted: 'Non Angli
  sed Angeli.'
    Bede, *Historia Ecclesiastica*, II. i

STEPHEN GRELLET 1773–1855

15 I expect to pass through this world but
once; any good thing therefore that
I can do, or any kindness that I can
show to any fellow-creature, let me
do it now; let me not defer or neglect
it, for I shall not pass this way again.
    *Attr. 'Treasure Trove', collected
    by John o' London, 1925.* Many
    other claimants to authorship

**FULKE GREVILLE, FIRST
BARON BROOKE** 1554–1628

16 Fulke Greville, Servant to Queen
Elizabeth, Councillor to King James,
and Friend to Sir Philip Sidney.
    *Epitaph Written for Himself, on
    his Monument in Warwick*

**EDWARD, VISCOUNT GREY OF
FALLODON** 1862–1933

17 The lamps are going out all over
Europe; we shall not see them lit
again in our lifetime.
    *3 Aug. 1914. Twenty-Five Years,
    vol. ii, ch. 18*

GEORGE GROSSMITH 1847–1912
and
WALTER WEEDON GROSSMITH
1854–1919

18 I left the room with silent dignity, but
caught my foot in the mat.
    The Diary of a Nobody, ch. 12

19 What's the matter with Gladstone?
He's all right.   *Ib. ch. 17*

PHILIP GUEDALLA 1889–1944

20 The work of Henry James has always
seemed divisible by a simple dynastic
arrangement into three reigns:
James I, James II, and the Old Pretender.
    *Collected Essays, vol. iv. Men of
    Letters: Mr. Henry James*

YVETTE GUILBERT 1867–1944

21 Linger longer Lucy,
Linger longer Lou.   *Song*

TEXAS GUINAN 1884–1933

1 Fifty million Frenchmen can't be
wrong.
*Attr. New York World-Telegram,
21 Mar. 1931*

DOROTHY FRANCES GURNEY
1858–1932

2 The kiss of the sun for pardon,
The song of the birds for mirth,
One is nearer God's Heart in a garden
Than anywhere else on earth.
God's Garden

HADRIAN A.D. 76–138

3 Animula vagula blandula,
Hospes comesque corporis,
Quae nunc abibis in loca
Pallidula rigida nudula,
Nec ut soles dabis iocos!

Little soul, wandering, pleasant,
guest and companion of the body,
into what places wilt thou now
go, pale, stiff, naked, nor wilt thou
play any longer as thou art wont.
Duff, Minor Latin Poems (Loeb,
1934), 445

DOUGLAS HAIG, EARL HAIG
1861–1928

4 Every position must be held to the
last man: there must be no retirement.
With our backs to the wall, and be-
lieving in the justice of our cause, each
one of us must fight on to the end.
*Order to the British Troops,
12 Apr. 1918. The Times, 13 Apr.*

SARAH JOSEPHA HALE
1788–1879

5 Mary had a little lamb,
Its fleece was white as snow,
And everywhere that Mary went
The lamb was sure to go.

'What makes the lamb love Mary so?'
The eager children cry.
'Oh, Mary loves the lamb, you know,'
The teacher did reply.
*Poems for Our Children. Mary's
Little Lamb*

CHARLES SPRAGUE HALL
fl. 1860

6 John Brown's body lies a mould'ring
in the grave,
His soul is marching on!
*John Brown's Body. Nicholas
Smith's Stories of Great National
Songs*

BISHOP JOSEPH HALL 1574–1656

7 All his dealings are square, and above
the board.
Virtues and Vices (1608), bk. 1,
p. 15

OWEN HALL [JAMES DAVIS]
d. 1907

8 Tell me, pretty maiden, are there any
more at home like you?
Florodora, Act II

**FRIEDRICH HALM [FRANZ VON
MÜNCH-BELLINGHAUSEN]**
1806–1871

9 Mein Herz ich will dich fragen:
Was ist denn Liebe? Sag'!—
'Zwei Seelen und ein Gedanke,
Zwei Herzen und ein Schlag!'

What love is, if thou wouldst be
taught,
Thy heart must teach alone,—
Two souls with but a single thought,
Two hearts that beat as one.
Der Sohn der Wildnis, Act II
ad fin. Trans. by Maria Lovell
in *Ingomar the Barbarian*

OSCAR HAMMERSTEIN II
1895–1960

10 The last time I saw Paris, her heart
was warm and gay,
I heard the laughter of her heart in
every street café.
Song. The Last Time I Saw Paris

RICHARD ROLLE DE HAMPOLE
1290?–1349

11 When Adam dalfe and Eve spane
So spire if thou may spede,
Whare was than the pride of man,
That nowe merres his mede?
*Religious Pieces in Prose and
Verse,* vii. *Early English Text
Society, Original Series,* No. 26.
*An altered form was used by John
Ball* (d. 1381) *as the text of his
revolutionary sermon on the out-
break of the Peasants' Revolt,
1381:*
When Adam delved, and Eve
span,
Who was then a gentleman?

MINNY MAUD HANFF *fl.* 1900

12 Since then they called him Sunny Jim.
*Sunny Jim. Advertisement for
Force, a breakfast food.*

KATHERINE HANKEY 1834–1911

13 Tell me the old, old story,
Of unseen things above.
*The Story Wanted. Tell Me the
Old, Old Story*

SIR WILLIAM HARCOURT
1827–1904

1 We are all Socialists now.
    See Fabian Essays (*1889*) *ed.*
    Shaw (p. 194 in 1948 edition)

E. J. HARDY 1849–1920

2 How To Be Happy Though Married.
    Title of Book (1910)

THOMAS HARDY 1840–1928

3 William Dewy, Tranter Reuben,
    Farmer Ledlow late at plough,
 Robert's kin, and John's, and Ned's,
 And the Squire, and Lady Susan, lie
    in Mellstock churchyard now!
                        Friends Beyond

4 Only a man harrowing clods
    In a slow silent walk
 With an old horse that stumbles and
    nods
    Half asleep as they stalk.

 Only thin smoke without flame
    From the heaps of couch grass;
 Yet this will go onward the same
    Though Dynasties pass.

 Yonder a maid and her wight
    Come whispering by:
 War's annals will cloud into night
    Ere their story die.
        *In Time of 'The Breaking of
        Nations'*

5 This is the weather the cuckoo likes,
    And so do I.   *Weathers*

6 When I set out for Lyonnesse,
    A hundred miles away.
        When I Set Out for Lyonnesse

7 When I came back from Lyonnesse
    With magic in my eyes.   *Ib.*

8 Life's Little Ironies.   *Title*

9   Michael Henchard's Will.
    That Elizabeth-Jane Farfrae be not
      told of my death, or made to
      grieve on account of me.
        & that I be not buried in consecrated
          ground.
        & that no sexton be asked to toll
          the bell.
        & that nobody is wished to see my
          dead body.
        & that no murners walk behind me
          at my funeral.
        & that no flours be planted on my
          grave.
        & that no man remember me.
    To this I put my name.
        The Mayor of Casterbridge, ch. 45

10 The President of the Immortals (in
    Æschylean phrase) had ended his
    sport with Tess.
        Tess of the D'Urbervilles, ch. 59

JULIUS CHARLES HARE 1795–1855
and
AUGUSTUS WILLIAM HARE
1792–1834

11 Man without religion is the creature
    of circumstances.
            Guesses at Truth, Series 1

MAURICE EVAN HARE 1889–1967

12 There once was a man who said,
        'Damn!
    It is borne in upon me I am
        An engine that moves
        In predestinate grooves,
    I'm not even a bus I'm a tram.'
        *Written, as above, at St. John's
        College, Oxford, in 1905*

WILLIAM HARGREAVES d. 1941

13 I'm Burlington Bertie:
    I rise at ten-thirty.
        Burlington Bertie. First Sung by
        Ella Shields in October 1914 at
        the Argyle Theatre, Birkenhead.

SIR JOHN HARINGTON
1561–1612

14 Treason doth never prosper: what's
        the reason?
    For if it prosper, none dare call it
        treason.
        Epigrams, bk. iv, No. 5. *Of
        Treason*

CHARLES K. HARRIS 1865–1930

15 After the ball is over.   *After the Ball*

16 Somewhere the sun is shining.
                        Somewhere

CLIFFORD HARRIS d. 1949

17 You called me Baby Doll a year ago.
                    A Broken Doll.

JOEL CHANDLER HARRIS
1848–1908

18 A contrapshun what he call a Tar-
    Baby.
        *Uncle Remus. Legends of the
        Old Plantation, ch. 2. Tar-Baby
        Story*

19 Tar-baby ain't sayin' nuthin', en
    Brer Fox, he lay low.   *Ib.*

20 Bred en bawn in a brier-patch!
                        Ib. ch. 4

1 Oh, whar shill we go w'en de great day
comes,
Wid de blowin' er de trumpits en de
bangin' er de drums?
How many po' sinners'll be kotched
out late
En find no latch ter de golden gate?
Uncle Remus. His Songs, i

FRANCIS BRETT HART *or* BRET HARTE 1839–1902

2 If, of all words of tongue and pen,
The saddest are, 'It might have been,'
More sad are these we daily see:
'It is, but hadn't ought to be!'
Mrs. Judge Jenkins

3 Which I wish to remark,
And my language is plain,
That for ways that are dark
And for tricks that are vain,
The heathen Chinee is peculiar,
Which the same I would rise to explain.
*Plain Language from Truthful
James*

4 And he smiled a kind of sickly smile,
and curled up on the floor,
And the subsequent proceedings interested him no more.
The Society upon the Stanislaus

MINNIE LOUISE HASKINS 1875–1957

5 And I said to the man who stood at
the gate of the year: 'Give me a light
that I may tread safely into the unknown.' And he replied: 'Go out into
the darkness and put your hand into
the hand of God. That shall be to you
better than light and safer than a
known way.'
*God Knows. Quoted by King
George VI in a Christmas Broadcast, 25 Dec. 1939*

ROBERT STEPHEN HAWKER 1803–1875

6 And have they fixed the where and
when?
And shall Trelawny die?
Here's twenty thousand Cornish men
Will know the reason why!
*Song of the Western Men. The
last three lines have existed since
the imprisonment by James II,
1688, of the seven Bishops, including Trelawny, Bishop of Bristol.*

SIR ANTHONY HOPE HAWKINS *see* ANTHONY HOPE

LORD CHARLES HAY ?–1760

7 Gentlemen of the French Guard, fire
first! (Messieurs les gardes françaises,
tirez.)
Battle of Fontenoy, 1745. E.
Fournier, *L'Esprit dans l'Histoire* (1883), ch. 52, p. 349

IAN HAY [JOHN HAY BEITH] 1876–1952

8 Funny peculiar, or funny ha-ha?
The Housemaster, Act III

WILLIAM HAZLITT 1778–1830

9 His worst is better than any other
person's best.
English Literature, ch. xiv. *Sir
Walter Scott*

10 He [Coleridge] talked on for ever;
and you wished him to talk on for
ever.
Lectures on the English Poets.
Lecture viii, *On the Living Poets*

11 Give me the clear blue sky over my
head, and the green turf beneath my
feet, a winding road before me, and
a three hours' march to dinner—and
then to thinking! It is hard if I cannot
start some game on these lone heaths.
Table Talk, xix. *On Going a
Journey*

12 The English (it must be owned) are
rather a foul-mouthed nation.
Ib. xxii. *On Criticism*

13 We can scarcely hate anyone that we
know. *Ib.*

BISHOP REGINALD HEBER 1783–1826

14 Brightest and best of the sons of the
morning!
Dawn on our darkness and lend us
Thine aid!
Hymns, &c. Brightest and Best

15 From Greenland's icy mountains,
From India's coral strand,
Where Afric's sunny fountains
Roll down their golden sand.
*Ib. From Greenland's Icy Moun-
tains*

16 What though the spicy breezes
Blow soft o'er Ceylon's isle;
Though every prospect pleases,
And only man is vile:

In vain with lavish kindness
The gifts of God are strown;
The heathen in his blindness
Bows down to wood and stone.
*This is the most familiar version.
Bishop Heber originally wrote
'The savage in his blindness'.
He altered this, and also altered
'Ceylon's' to 'Java's'. Ib.*

1 Holy, Holy, Holy; Lord God Al-
mighty!
Early in the morning our song shall
rise to Thee:
Holy, Holy, Holy! Merciful and
Mighty;
God in Three Persons, Blessed Trinity!

Holy, Holy, Holy; all the Saints adore
Thee,
Casting down their golden crowns
around the glassy sea.
Hymns, &c. Holy, Holy, Holy!

GEORG WILHELM HEGEL
1770–1831

2 What experience and history teach is
this—that people and governments
never have learned anything from
history, or acted on principles deduced
from it.
Philosophy of History. Introduction. Used by Shaw in his
Revolutionist's Handbook and in
the Preface to *Heartbreak House*

HEINRICH HEINE 1797–1856

3 Ich grolle nicht, und wenn das Herz
auch bricht.

I do not murmur, even if my heart
break.
Buch der Lieder. Title of Song

4 Ich weiss nicht, was soll es bedeuten,
Dass ich so traurig bin;
Ein Märchen aus alten Zeiten,
Das kommt mir nicht aus dem Sinn.

I know not why I am so sad; I
cannot get out of my head a
fairy-tale of olden times.
Die Lorelei

5 Auf Flügeln des Gesanges.
On the wings of song. *Title of Song*

6 Dieu me pardonnera. C'est son métier.
God will pardon me. It is His trade.
On his Deathbed

FELICIA DOROTHEA HEMANS
1793–1835

7 The boy stood on the burning deck
Whence all but he had fled;
The flame that lit the battle's wreck
Shone round him o'er the dead.
Casabianca

8 There came a burst of thunder sound—
The boy—oh! where was he? *Ib.*

9 They grew in beauty, side by side,
They fill'd one home with glee;—
Their graves are sever'd, far and wide,
By mount, and stream, and sea.
The Graves of a Household

10 He Never Smiled Again! *Title of poem*

11 The stately homes of England,
How beautiful they stand!
Amidst their tall ancestral trees,
O'er all the pleasant land.
The Homes of England

12 In the busy haunts of men.
Tale of the Secret Tribunal, pt. i,
l. 203

WILLIAM ERNEST HENLEY
1849–1903

13 Out of the night that covers me,
Black as the Pit from pole to pole,
I thank whatever gods may be
For my unconquerable soul.

In the fell clutch of circumstance,
I have not winced nor cried aloud:
Under the bludgeonings of chance
My head is bloody, but unbowed.
Echoes, iv. *Invictus. In Mem.*
R. T. H. B.

14 It matters not how strait the gate,
How charged with punishments the
scroll,
I am the master of my fate:
I am the captain of my soul.   *Ib.*

15 Or ever the Knightly years were gone
With the old world to the grave,
I was a King in Babylon
And you were a Christian Slave.
Ib. xxxvii. *To W. A.*

16 What have I done for you,
England, my England?
What is there I would not do,
England, my own?
For England's Sake, iii. *Pro Rege*
Nostro

17 Ever the faith endures,
England, my England:—
'Take and break us: we are yours,
England, my own!
Life is good, and joy runs high
Between English earth and sky;
Death is death; but we shall die
To the Song on your bugles blown,
England.'   *Ib.*

HENRI IV 1553–1610

18 Je veux qu'il n'y ait si pauvre paysan
en mon royaume qu'il n'ait tous les
dimanches sa poule au pot.

I want there to be no peasant in
my kingdom so poor that he is
unable to have a chicken in his
pot ever Sunday.
Hardouin de Péréfixe, *Hist. de*
Henry le Grand (1681)

1 Pends-toi, brave Crillon; nous avons combattu à Arques et tu n'y étais pas.

Hang yourself, brave Crillon; we fought at Arques and you were not there.

Traditional form given by Voltaire to a letter of Henri to Crillon. Lettres missives de Henri IV, Collection des documents inédits de l'histoire de France, vol. iv (1847), p. 848

2 Paris vaut bien une messe.

Paris is well worth a mass.

Attr. either to Henry IV or to his minister Sully, in conversation with Henry. Caquets de l'Accouchée, 1622

3 The wisest fool in Christendom.

Of James I of England. Remark attr. to Henry IV and Sully. The French is not known

MATTHEW HENRY 1662–1714

4 Many a dangerous temptation comes to us in gay, fine colours, that are but skin-deep.
Commentaries, Genesis iii. 1

5 To their own second and sober thoughts. *Ib. Job vi. 29*

6 They that die by famine die by inches.
Ib. Ps. lix. 15

7 Men of polite learning and a liberal education. *Ib. Acts x. 1*

8 All this and heaven too.
Life of Philip Henry, p. 70

PATRICK HENRY 1736–1799

9 Caesar had his Brutus—Charles the First, his Cromwell—and George the Third—('Treason,' cried the Speaker) . . . *may profit by their example. If this* be treason, make the most of it.
Speech in the Virginia Convention, 1765. W. Wirt's Patrick Henry (1818), p. 65

10 I know not what course others may take; but as for me, give me liberty, or give me death!
Ib. 23 Mar. 1775. W. Wirt's Patrick Henry (1818), p. 123.

PHILIP HENRY 1631–1696

11 They are not amissi, but praemissi.
[Not lost, but gone before.]
Matthew Henry, Life of Philip Henry, ch. 5 (ed. 1825), p. 111

HENRY II OF ENGLAND
1133–1189

12 Who will free me from this turbulent priest? [Becket.] *History books*

13 What a parcel of fools and dastards have I nourished in my house, that not one of them will avenge me of this one upstart clerk!
K. Norgate, in Dict. of Nat. Biog.

HENRY VIII OF ENGLAND
1491–1547

14 [Anne of Cleves.] The King found her so different from her picture . . . that . . . he swore they had brought him a Flanders mare.
Smollett, Hist. of England (ed. 3, 1759), vi. 68

HERACLEITUS *fl.* 513 B.C.

15 πάντα ῥεῖ, οὐδὲν μένει.

All is flux, nothing is stationary.
Alluded to by Aristotle in De Caelo, 3. 1. 18 (ed. Weise) and elsewhere

SIR ALAN PATRICK HERBERT
1890–

16 Let 's stop somebody from doing something! *Let 's Stop Somebody*

17 Holy Deadlock.
Title of a novel satirizing the Divorce Law

GEORGE HERBERT 1593–1633

18 Let all the world in ev'ry corner sing
My God and King.
The heav'ns are not too high,
His praise may thither fly;
The earth is not too low,
His praises there may grow.
Let all the world in ev'ry corner sing
My God and King.
The Church with psalms must shout,
No door can keep them out:
But above all, the heart
Must bear the longest part.
The Temple. Antiphon

19 I struck the board, and cried, 'No more;
I will abroad.' *Ib. The Collar*

20 Methought I heard one calling, 'Child';
And I replied, 'My Lord.'
Ib.

21 Teach me, my God and King,
In all things Thee to see,
And what I do in any thing
To do it as for Thee.

A man that looks on glass,
On it may stay his eye;
Or if he pleaseth, through it pass,
And then the heaven espy.
Ib. The Elixir

22 A servant with this clause
Makes drudgery divine;
Who sweeps a room as for Thy laws
Makes that and th' action fine. *Ib.*

1 Love bade me welcome; yet my soul
    drew back,
        Guilty of dust and sin.
But quick-ey'd Love, observing me
    grow slack
        From my first entrance in,
Drew nearer to me, sweetly questioning
    If I lack'd any thing.
                The Temple. Love

2 King of glory, King of peace,
        I will love Thee;
And, that love may never cease,
    I will move Thee.
                Ib. Praise

3 Sev'n whole days, not one in seven,
        I will praise Thee;
In my heart, though not in heaven,
    I can raise Thee.   *Ib.*

4 The God of love my Shepherd is,
And He that doth me feed,
While He is mine, and I am His,
What can I want or need?
                Ib. 23rd Psalm

5 Lord, make me coy and tender to
    offend.   *Ib. Unkindness*

6 Sweet day, so cool, so calm, so bright,
The bridal of the earth and sky,
The dew shall weep thy fall to-night;
    For thou must die.
                Ib. Virtue

7 Sweet spring, full of sweet days and
    roses,
A box where sweets compacted lie. *Ib.*

ROBERT HERRICK 1591–1674

8 Cherry ripe, ripe, ripe, I cry,
Full and fair ones; come and buy:
If so be, you ask me where
They do grow? I answer, there,
Where my Julia's lips do smile;
There's the land, or cherry-isle.
                Hesperides. Cherry Ripe

9 Get-up, sweet Slug-a-bed, and see
The dew bespangling herb and tree.
                Ib. Corinna's Going a-Maying

10 Fair daffodils, we weep to see
You haste away so soon:
As yet the early-rising sun
Has not attain'd his noon.
        Stay, stay,
Until the hasting day
        Has run
But to the even-song;
And, having pray'd together, we
Will go with you along.
                Ib. Daffodils

11 A sweet disorder in the dress
Kindles in clothes a wantonness:
A lawn about the shoulders thrown
Into a fine distraction:
An erring lace, which here and there
Enthrals the crimson stomacher:
A cuff neglectful, and thereby
Ribbands to flow confusedly:

A winning wave (deserving note)
In the tempestuous petticoat:
A careless shoe-string, in whose tie
I see a wild civility:
Do more bewitch me, than when Art
Is too precise in every part.
                Hesperides. Delight in Disorder

12 You say, to me-wards your affection's
    strong;
Pray love me little, so you love me long.
                Ib. Love me Little, Love me Long

13 Her eyes the glow-worm lend thee,
The shooting-stars attend thee;
        And the elves also,
        Whose little eyes glow,
Like the sparks of fire, befriend thee.

No Will-o'-th'-Wisp mislight thee;
Nor snake, or slow-worm bite thee:
        But on, on thy way
        Not making a stay,
Since ghost there's none to affright
    thee.   *Ib. The Night-Piece, to Julia*

14 Gather ye rosebuds while ye may,
Old Time is still a-flying:
And this same flower that smiles to-day,
To-morrow will be dying.
                *Ib. To Virgins, to Make Much of
                Time*

15 Whenas in silks my Julia goes,
Then, then (methinks) how sweetly
    flows
That liquefaction of her clothes.

Next, when I cast mine eyes and see
That brave vibration each way free;
O how that glittering taketh me!
                Ib. Upon Julia's Clothes

16 Here a little child I stand,
Heaving up my either hand;
Cold as paddocks though they be,
Here I lift them up to Thee,
For a benison to fall
On our meat, and on us all. Amen.
                *Noble Numbers. Another Grace for
                a Child*

JAMES HERVEY 1714–1758

17 E'en crosses from his sov'reign hand
Are blessings in disguise.
                *Works. Reflections on a Flower-
                Garden*

HESIOD c. 735 B.C.

18 πλέον ἥμισυ παντός.
        The half is greater than the whole.
                Works and Days, 40

GORDON HEWART, LORD
HEWART 1870–1943

19 Justice should not only be done, but
manifestly and undoubtedly be seen
to be done.
                *Rex v. Sussex Justices, 9 Nov.
                1923 (King's Bench Reports,
                1924, vol. i, p. 259)*

THOMAS HEYWOOD d. 1650?

1 Seven cities warr'd for Homer, being
  dead,
  Who, living, had no roof to shroud his
  head.
    Hierarchie of the Blessed Angels

2 Pack, clouds, away, and welcome day,
  With night we banish sorrow;
  Sweet air blow soft, mount larks aloft
  To give my Love good-morrow!
    Pack, Clouds, Away, st. 1

3 A Woman Killed with Kindness.
    Title of Play

WILLIAM EDWARD HICKSON
1803–1870

4 'Tis a lesson you should heed,
  Try, try again.
  If at first you don't succeed,
  Try, try again.   *Try and Try Again*

'DR. BREWSTER HIGLEY'
nineteenth century

5 Oh give me a home where the buffalo
  roam,
  Where the deer and the antelope play,
  Where seldom is heard a discouraging
  word
  And the skies are not cloudy all day.
    Home on the Range (1873)

HIPPOCRATES c. 460–357 B.C.

6 ὁ βίος βραχύς, ἡ δὲ τέχνη μακρή.
   The life so short, the craft so long
   to learn.
     Aphorisms, I. i. Trans. by
     Chaucer

ADOLF HITLER 1889–1945

7 My patience is now at an end.
    Speech, 26 Sept. 1938

8 It is the last territorial claim which I
  have to make in Europe.   *Ib.*

THOMAS HOBBES 1588–1679

9 No arts; no letters; no society; and
  which is worst of all, continual fear
  and danger of violent death; and the
  life of man, solitary, poor, nasty,
  brutish, and short.
    Leviathan, pt. i, ch. 13

10 I am about to take my last voyage,
   a great leap in the dark.
     Last Words. Watkins, *Anecdotes
     of Men of Learning*

JOHN CAM HOBHOUSE, BARON BROUGHTON 1786–1869

11 When I invented the phrase 'His
   Majesty's Opposition' [Canning] paid
   me a compliment on the fortunate hit.
     Recollections of a Long Life, ii,
     ch. 12

EDWARD WALLIS HOCH
1849–1925

12 There is so much good in the worst of
   us,
   And so much bad in the best of us,
   That it hardly becomes any of us
   To talk about the rest of us.
     Good and Bad. Attr. to many
     other authors

RALPH HODGSON 1871–1962

13 'Twould ring the bells of Heaven
   The wildest peal for years,
   If Parson lost his senses
   And people came to theirs,
   And he and they together
   Knelt down with angry prayers
   For tamed and shabby tigers
   And dancing dogs and bears,
   And wretched, blind, pit ponies,
   And little hunted hares.
     Poems. The Bells of Heaven

14 Time, you old gypsy man,
     Will you not stay,
   Put up your caravan
     Just for one day?
     Ib. Time, You Old Gypsy Man

HEINRICH HOFFMAN 1809–1874

15 Augustus was a chubby lad;
   Fat ruddy cheeks Augustus had:
   And everybody saw with joy
   The plump and hearty, healthy boy.
   He ate and drank as he was told,
   And never let his soup get cold.
   But one day, one cold winter's day,
   He screamed out, 'Take the soup
     away!
   O take the nasty soup away!
   I won't have any soup to-day.'
     Struwwelpeter. Augustus

16 Here is cruel Frederick, see!
   A horrid wicked boy was he.
     Ib. Cruel Frederick

17 Let me see if Philip can
   Be a little gentleman;
   Let me see, if he is able
   To sit still for once at table.
     Ib. Fidgety Philip

18 But fidgety Phil,
   He won't sit still;
   He wriggles
   And giggles,
   And then, I declare,
   Swings backwards and forwards,
   And tilts up his chair.   *Ib.*

E

1 It almost makes me cry to tell
What foolish Harriet befell.
Struwwelpeter. Harriet and the Matches

2 Look at Little Johnny there,
Little Johnny Head-In-Air!
Ib. Johnny Head-in-Air

3 The door flew open, in he ran,
The great, long, red-legged scissor-
man. *Ib. The Little Suck-a-Thumb*

4 'Ah!' said Mamma, 'I knew he'd come
To naughty little Suck-a-Thumb.' *Ib.*

5 Anything to me is sweeter
Than to see Shock-headed Peter.
Ib. Shock-Headed Peter

JAMES HOGG 1770–1835

6 We'll o'er the water, we'll o'er the sea,
We'll o'er the water to Charlie;
Come weel, come wo, we'll gather and
go,
And live or die wi' Charlie.
Jacobite Relics of Scotland, ii. 76.
O'er the Water to Charlie

7 'Twas on a Monday morning,
Right early in the year,
That Charlie came to our town,
The young Chevalier.
And Charlie he's my darling,
My darling, my darling,
And Charlie he's my darling,
The young Chevalier.
Ib. 93. *The Young Chevalier*

8 Will you no come back again?
Better lo'ed you'll never be,
And will you no come back again?
Ib. 195. *Will You No Come Back
Again?*

9 My love she's but a lassie yet.
Title of Song

JOHN HAYNES HOLMES 1879–

10 The universe is not hostile, nor yet
is it friendly. It is simply indifferent.
Sensible Man's View of Religion

OLIVER WENDELL HOLMES
1809–1894

11 We love the precepts for the teacher's
sake.
*Poems. A Rhymed Lesson
(Urania)*

12 Man wants but little drink below,
But wants that little strong.
Ib. A Song of other Days. Parody
on Goldsmith

13 Man has his will,—but woman has her
way.
*The Autocrat of the Breakfast-
Table*, ch. 1

JOHN HOME 1722–1808

14 My name is Norval; on the Grampian
hills
My father feeds his flocks; a frugal
swain,
Whose constant cares were to increase
his store. *Douglas*, II. i

HOMER c. 900 B.C.

15 μῆνιν ἄειδε, θεά, Πηληϊάδεω Ἀχιλῆος
οὐλομένην, ἣ μυρί' Ἀχαιοῖς ἄλγε' ἔθηκε.

The wrath of Peleus' son, the direful
spring
Of all the Grecian woes, O Goddess,
sing! *Iliad*, i. 1. Trans. by Pope

16 ἄνδρα μοι ἔννεπε, Μοῦσα, πολύτροπον.

Tell me, Muse, of the man of many
wiles. [Odysseus.] *Odyssey*, i. 1

17 πολλῶν δ' ἀνθρώπων ἴδεν ἄστεα καὶ νόον
ἔγνω.

He saw the cities of many men, and
knew their mind. *Ib.* 3

WILLIAM HONE 1780–1842

18 John Jones may be described as 'one
of the *has* beens'.
Every-Day Book, vol. ii, p. 820

THOMAS HOOD 1799–1845

19 It was not in the winter
Our loving lot was cast!
It was the time of roses,
We plucked them as we passed!
Ballad: It Was Not in the Winter

20 One more Unfortunate,
Weary of breath,
Rashly importunate,
Gone to her death!
Take her up tenderly,
Lift her with care;
Fashion'd so slenderly,
Young, and so fair!
The Bridge of Sighs

21 Two stern-faced men set out from
Lynn,
Through the cold and heavy mist;
And Eugene Aram walked between,
With gyves upon his wrist.
The Dream of Eugene Aram

22 Ben Battle was a soldier bold,
And used to war's alarms:
But a cannon-ball took off his legs,
So he laid down his arms!
Faithless Nelly Gray

23 His death, which happen'd in his
berth,
At forty-odd befell:
They went and told the sexton, and
The sexton toll'd the bell.
Faithless Sally Brown

1 I remember, I remember,
The house where I was born,
The little window where the sun
Came peeping in at morn.
I Remember

2 He never spoils the child and spares
the rod,
But spoils the rod and never spares
the child.
The Irish Schoolmaster, xii

3 With fingers weary and worn,
With eyelids heavy and red,
A woman sat, in unwomanly rags,
Plying her needle and thread—
Stitch! stitch! stitch!
In poverty, hunger, and dirt.
The Song of the Shirt

4 Oh! God! that bread should be so
dear,
And flesh and blood so cheap!   *Ib.*

5 There are three things which the public will always clamour for sooner or
later: namely, Novelty, novelty,
novelty.
*Announcement for Comic Annual
for 1836*

ELLEN STURGIS HOOPER
1816–1841

6 I slept, and dreamed that life was
Beauty;
I woke, and found that life was Duty.
Life a Duty

HERBERT CLARK HOOVER
1874–1964

7 The American system of rugged indi-
vidualism.
*Campaign speech, New York,
22 Oct. 1928*

ANTHONY HOPE [SIR
ANTHONY HOPE HAWKINS]
1863–1933

8 His foe was folly and his weapon wit.
*Inscription on the tablet to W. S.
Gilbert, Victoria Embankment,
London* (1915)

LAURENCE HOPE [ADELA
FLORENCE NICOLSON] 1865–1904

9 Pale hands I loved beside the Shali-
mar,
Where are you now? Who lies beneath
your spell?
*Indian Love Lyrics. Pale Hands
I Loved*

10 Less than the dust beneath thy chariot
wheel,
Less than the weed that grows beside
thy door,
Less than the rust that never stained
thy sword,

Less than the need thou hast in life of
me,
Even less am I.
*Indian Love Lyrics. Less than the
Dust*

GERARD MANLEY HOPKINS
1844–1889

11 Towery city and branchy between
towers.   *Duns Scotus' Oxford*

12 The world is charged with the grandeur of God.   *God's Grandeur*

13 Elected Silence, sing to me
And beat upon my whorlèd ear,
Pipe me to pastures still and be
The music that I care to hear.
The Habit of Perfection

14 Glory be to God for dappled things.
Pied Beauty

15 All things counter, original, spare,
strange;
Whatever is fickle, freckled (who
knows how?)
With swift, slow; sweet, sour; adazzle,
dim;
He fathers-forth whose beauty is past
change:
Praise him.   *Ib.*

16 Look at the stars! look, look up at the
skies!
O look at all the fire-folk sitting in the
air!
The bright boroughs, the circle-cita-
dels there!   *The Starlight Night*

17 I caught this morning morning's
minion, kingdom of daylight's dau-
phin, dapple-dawn-drawn Falcon.
The Windhover

HORACE 65–8 B.C.

18 Inceptis gravibus plerumque et magna
professis
Purpureus, late qui splendeat, unus
et alter
Adsuitur pannus.
Often on a work of grave purpose
and high promises is tacked a
purple patch or two to give an
effect of colour.   *Ars Poetica,* 14

19 Proicit ampullas et sesquipedalia
verba.
Throws aside his paint-pots and his
words a foot and a half long.
Ib. 97

20 Si vis me flere, dolendum est
Primum ipsi tibi.
If you wish to draw tears from me,
you must first feel pain yourself.
Ib. 102

21 Parturient montes, nascetur ridiculus
mus.
Mountains will be in labour, the
birth will be a single laughable
little mouse.   *Ib.* 139

1 Semper ad eventum festinat et in
medias res
Non secus ac notas auditorem rapit.

He ever hastens to the issue, and
hurries his hearers into the
midst of the story as if they knew
it before.   *Ars Poetica*, 148.

2 Laudator temporis acti   *Ib.* 173
Inclined to praise the way the world
went.

3 Indignor quandoque bonus dormitat
Homerus.

But if Homer, usually good, nods
for a moment, I think it shame.
Ib. 359

4 Ut pictura poesis.

As with the painter's work, so with
the poet's.   *Ib.* 361

5 Nonumque prematur in annum.

Let it be kept quiet till the ninth
year.   *Ib.* 388

6 Si possis recte, si non, quocumque
modo rem.

Money by right means if you can,
if not, by any means, money.
Epistles, I. i. 66

7 Dimidium facti qui coepit habet:
sapere aude.

He who has begun his task has half
done it. Have the courage to be
wise.   *Ib.* ii. 40

8 Naturam expellas furca, tamen usque
recurret.

If you drive nature out with a pitchfork, she will soon find a way back.
Ib. x. 24

9 Caelum non animum mutant qui
trans mare currunt.
Strenua nos exercet inertia: navibus
atque
Quadrigis petimus bene vivere. Quod
petis hic est,
Est Ulubris, animus si te non deficit
aequus.

They change their sky, not their
soul, who run across the sea.
We work hard at doing nothing:
we seek happiness in yachts and
four-horse coaches. What you
seek is here—is at Ulubrae—if
an even soul does not fail you.
Ib. xi. 27

10 Concordia discors.
Harmony in discord.   *Ib.* xii. 19

11 Principibus placuisse viris non ultima
laus est.
Non cuivis homini contingit adire
Corinthum.

To have found favour with leaders
of mankind is not the meanest of
glories. It is not every one that
can get to Corinth.   *Ib.* xvii. 35

12 Si foret in terris, rideret Democritus.

If he were on earth, Democritus
would laugh at the sight.
Epistles, II. i. 194

13 Quid te exempta iuvat spinis de
pluribus una?
Vivere si recte nescis, decede peritis.
Lusisti satis, edisti satis atque bibisti:
Tempus abire tibi est.

How does it relieve you to pluck one
thorn out of many? If you do not
know how to live aright, make
way for those who do. You have
played enough, have eaten and
drunk enough. It is time for you
to leave the scene.   *Ib.* ii. 212

14 Beatus ille, qui procul negotiis,
Ut prisca gens mortalium,
Paterna rura bubus exercet suis,
Solutus omni faenore.

Happy the man who far from
schemes of business, like the early
generations of mankind, ploughs
and ploughs again his ancestral
land with oxen of his own breeding, with no yoke of usury on
his neck!
Epodes, ii. I. Trans. by Wickham

15 Nil mortalibus ardui est.

No height is too arduous for mortal
men.   *Odes*, I. iii. 37

16 Pallida Mors aequo pulsat pede pau-
perum tabernas
Regumque turris.

Pale Death with impartial foot
knocks at the doors of poor men's
hovels and of kings' palaces.
Ib. iv. 13

17 Vitae summa brevis spem nos vetat
incohare longam.

Life's short span forbids us to enter
on far-reaching hopes.   *Ib.* 15

18 Quis multa gracilis te puer in rosa
Perfusus liquidis urget odoribus
Grato, Pyrrha, sub antro?
Cui flavam religas comam,
Simplex munditiis?

What delicate stripling is it, Pyrrha,
that now, steeped in liquid perfumes, is wooing thee on the
heaped rose-leaves in some
pleasant grot? For whose eyes
dost thou braid those flaxen
locks, so trim, so simple? *Ib.* v. 1

19 Nil desperandum Teucro duce et
auspice Teucro.

No lot is desperate under Teucer's
conduct and Teucer's star.
Ib. vii. 27

1 Quid sit futurum cras fuge quaerere et
Quem Fors dierum cumque dabit
lucro
Appone.

What shall be to-morrow, think not
of asking. Each day that Fortune
gives you, be it what it may, set
down for gain.   *Odes*, I. ix. 13

2 Tu ne quaesieris, scire nefas.

Pray, ask not,—such knowledge is
not for us.   *Ib*. xi. 1

3   Dum loquimur, fugerit invida
Aetas: carpe diem, quam minimum
credula postero.

Even while we speak, Time, the
churl, will have been running.
Snatch the sleeve of to-day and
trust as little as you may to
to-morrow.   *Ib*. 7

4 O matre pulchra filia pulchrior.

O fairer daughter of a fair mother.
          Ib. xvi. 1

5 Integer vitae scelerisque purus.

He that is unstained in life and
pure from guilt.   *Ib*. xxii. 1

6 Dulce ridentem Lalagen amabo,
Dulce loquentem.

Still shall I love Lalage and her
sweet laughter, Lalage and her
sweet prattle.   *Ib*. 23

7 Quis desiderio sit pudor aut modus
Tam cari capitis?

What shame or measure should
there be in grief for one so dear?
          Ib. xxiv. 1

8 Nunc est bibendum, nunc pede libero
Pulsanda tellus.

Now we must drink, now beat the
earth with free step.
          Ib. xxxvii. 1

9 Persicos odi, puer, apparatus.

Persian luxury, boy, I hate.
          Ib. xxxviii. 1

10 Aequam memento rebus in arduis
Servare mentem.

Remember when life's path is steep
to keep your mind even.
          Ib. II. iii. 1

11 Omnes eodem cogimur.

We all are driven one road. *Ib*. 25

12 Ille terrarum mihi praeter omnis
Angulus ridet.

That nook of earth's surface has a
smile for me before all other
places.   *Ib*. vi. 13

13 Auream quisquis mediocritatem
Diligit.

Whoso loves well the golden mean.
          Ib. x. 5

14 Eheu fugaces, Postume, Postume,
Labuntur anni.

Ah me, Postumus, Postumus, the
fleeting years are slipping by.
          Odes, II. xiv. 1

15   Credite posteri.

Believe it, after-years! *Ib*. xix. 2

16 Odi profanum vulgus et arceo;
Favete linguis; carmina non prius
Audita Musarum sacerdos
Virginibus puerisque canto.

I hate the uninitiate crowd and
bid them avaunt. Listen all in
silence! Strains unheard before
I, the Muses' hierophant, now
chant to maidens and to boys.
          Ib. III. i. 1

17 Post equitem sedet atra Cura.

Black Care mounts on the horse-
man's pillion.   *Ib*. 40

18 Dulce et decorum est pro patria mori.

To die for fatherland is a sweet
thing and becoming. *Ib*. ii. 13

19 Iustum et tenacem propositi virum
Non civium ardor prava iubentium,
Non vultus instantis tyranni
Mente quatit solida.

The just man and firm of purpose,
not the heat of fellow citizens
clamouring for what is wrong, nor
presence of threatening tyrant
can shake in his rocklike soul.
          Ib. iii. 1

20 Fratresque tendentes opaco
Pelion imposuisse Olympo.

The brothers who strove to leave
Pelion set on the top of leafy
Olympus.   *Ib*. iv. 51

21 Vis consili expers mole ruit sua.

Force without mind falls by its
own weight.   *Ib*. 65

22 Delicta maiorum immeritus lues.

For the sins of your sires albeit you
had no hand in them, you must
suffer.   *Ib*. vi. 1

23 Aetas parentum peior avis tulit
Nos nequiores, mox daturos
Progeniem vitiosiorem.

Our sires' age was worse than our
grandsires'. We their sons are
more worthless than they: so in
our turn we shall give the world a
progeny yet more corrupt. *Ib*. 46

24 O fons Bandusiae splendidior vitro.

O spring of Bandusia, more brilliant
than glass.   *Ib*. xiii. 1

25 Non ego hoc ferrem calidus iuventa
Consule Planco.

I should not have borne it in my
youth's hot blood when Plancus
was consul.   *Ib*. xiv. 27

1 Magnas inter opes inops.

> A pauper in the midst of wealth.
> *Odes*, III. xvi. 28

2 Vixi puellis nuper idoneus
Et militavi non sine gloria;
> Nunc arma defunctumque bello
> Barbiton hic paries habebit.

> Though that life is past, I was but
> now still meet for ladies' love,
> and fought my battles not with-
> out glory. Now my armour and
> the lute, whose campaigns are
> over, will hang here on yonder
> wall.   *Ib.* xxvi. 1

3 Non omnis moriar.

> I shall not all die.   *Ib.* xxx, 6

4   Non sum qualis eram bonae
Sub regno Cinarae. Desine, dulcium
Mater saeva Cupidinum.

> I am other than I was when poor
> Cinara was queen. Try no more,
> 'imperious mother of sweet loves'.
> *Ib.* IV. i. 3

5 Diffugere nives, redeunt iam gramina
campis
> Arboribusque comae.

> The snows have scattered and fled;
> already the grass comes again in
> the fields and the leaves on the
> trees.   *Ib.* vii. 1

6 Damna tamen celeres reparant caele-
stia lunae:
> Nos ubi decidimus
Quo pater Aeneas, quo Tullus dives
et Ancus,
> Pulvis et umbra sumus.

> Yet change and loss in the heavens
> the swift moons make up again.
> For us, when we have descended
> where is father Aeneas, where
> are rich old Tullus and Ancus,
> we are but some dust and a
> shadow.   *Ib.* 13

7 Misce stultitiam consiliis brevem:
> Dulce est desipere in loco.

> Mix with your sage counsels some
> brief folly. In due place to forget
> one's wisdom is sweet. *Ib.* xii. 27

8   Mutato nomine de te
Fabula narratur.

> Change but the name, and it is of
> yourself that tale is told.
> *Satires*, I. i. 69. Trans. by Wickham

9 Hoc genus omne.

> All their kith and kin.   *Ib.* ii. 2

10 Stans pede in uno.

> Without effort.   *Ib.* iv. 10

11 Etiam disiecti membra poetae.

> Even in his dismembered state, the
> limbs of a poet.   *Ib.* 62

12   Credat Iudaeus Apella,
Non ego.

> Apella the Jew must believe it,
> not I.   *Satires*, v. 100

13 O noctes cenaeque deum!

> O nights and suppers of gods!
> *Ib.* II. vi. 65

RICHARD MONCKTON MILNES, BARON HOUGHTON 1809–1885

14 A fair little girl sat under a tree,
Sewing as long as her eyes could see;
Then smoothed her work, and folded
it right,
And said, 'Dear work! Good Night!
Good Night!'
> *Good Night and Good Morning*

ALFRED EDWARD HOUSMAN 1859–1936

15 Loveliest of trees, the cherry now
Is hung with bloom along the bough,
And stands about the woodland ride
Wearing white for Eastertide.

Now, of my threescore years and ten,
Twenty will not come again,
And take from seventy springs a
score,
It only leaves me fifty more.

And since to look at things in bloom
Fifty springs are little room,
About the woodlands I will go
To see the cherry hung with snow.
> *A Shropshire Lad*, ii

16 When I was one-and-twenty
I heard a wise man say,
'Give crowns and pounds and guineas
But not your heart away.' *Ib.* xiii

17 When I was one-and-twenty
I heard him say again,
'The heart out of the bosom
Was never given in vain;
'Tis paid with sighs a plenty
And sold for endless rue.'
And I am two-and-twenty,
And oh, 'tis true, 'tis true.   *Ib.*

18 Oh, when I was in love with you,
Then I was clean and brave,
And miles around the wonder grew
How well did I behave.   *Ib.* xiv

19 In summertime on Bredon
The bells they sound so clear;
Round both the shires they ring them
In steeples far and near,
A happy noise to hear.

Here of a Sunday morning
My love and I would lie,
And see the coloured counties,
And hear the larks so high
About us in the sky.   *Ib.* xxi

1 The bells they sound on Bredon,
   And still the steeples hum.
   'Come all to church, good people,'—
   Oh, noisy bells, be dumb;
   I hear you, I will come.
                    A Shropshire Lad, xxi

2 The lads that will die in their glory
   and never be old.   *Ib.* xxiii

3 Is my team ploughing,
   That I was used to drive? *Ib.* xxvii

4 The goal stands up, the keeper
   Stands up to keep the goal.   *Ib.*

5 Into my heart an air that kills
   From yon far country blows.
   What are those blue remembered hills,
   What spires, what farms are those?

   That is the land of lost content,
   I see it shining plain,
   The happy highways where I went
   And cannot come again.   *Ib.* xl

6 Many a rose-lipt maiden
   And many a lightfoot lad.   *Ib.* liv

7 Malt does more than Milton can,
   To justify God's ways to man.
                             Ib. lxii

8 We'll to the woods no more,
   The laurels all are cut.
              Last Poems, introductory.

9 I, a stranger and afraid
   In a world I never made.   *Ib.* xii

10 The candles burn their sockets,
   The blinds let through the day,
   The young man feels his pockets
   And wonders what's to pay.
                             Ib. xxi

11 These, in the day when heaven was
        falling,
   The hour when earth's foundations
        fled,
   Followed their mercenary calling
   And took their wages and are dead.

   Their shoulders held the sky sus-
        pended;
   They stood, and earth's foundations
        stay;
   What God abandoned, these defended,
   And saved the sum of things for
        pay.
        Ib. xxxvii. *Epitaph on an Army
        of Mercenaries*

**BISHOP WILLIAM WALSHAM
HOW** 1823–1897

12 For all the Saints who from their
        labours rest,
   Who Thee by faith before the world
        confess'd,
   Thy name, O Jesu, be for ever blest,
                             Alleluia!
        Earl Nelson's *Hymns For Saints'
        Days: For All the Saints*

13 O Lord, stretch forth thy mighty
        hand
   And guard and bless our fatherland.
        Church Hymns (1871). *To Thee,
        Our God, We Fly*

14 O Jesu, thou art standing
   Outside the fast-closed door.
        Psalms and Hymns, 1867

JULIA WARD HOWE 1819–1910

15 Mine eyes have seen the glory of the
        coming of the Lord:
   He is trampling out the vintage where
        the grapes of wrath are stored.
        *Battle Hymn of the American
        Republic*

16 As He died to make men holy, let us
   die to make men free.   *Ib.*

MARY HOWITT 1799–1888

17 Buttercups and daisies,
   Oh, the pretty flowers.
        Buttercups and Daisies

18 'Will you walk into my parlour?' said
        a spider to a fly:
   ''Tis the prettiest little parlour that
        ever you did spy.'
        The Spider and the Fly

EDMOND HOYLE 1672–1769

19 When in doubt, win the trick.
        *Hoyle's Games. Whist. Twenty-
        four Short Rules for Learners*

ELBERT HUBBARD 1859–1915

20 Life is just one damned thing after
        another.
        A Thousand and One Epigrams,
        p. 137

THOMAS HUGHES 1822–1896

21 It's more than a game. It's an insti-
        tution. [Cricket.]
        Tom Brown's Schooldays, pt. ii,
        ch. 7

DAVID HUME 1711–1776

22 Never literary attempt was more un-
        fortunate than my Treatise of Human
        Nature. It fell *dead-born from the press.*
        My Own Life, ch. 1

**MARGARET WOLFE HUNGER-
FORD** 1855?–1897

23 Beauty is in the eye of the beholder.
        Quoted in Molly Bawn (1878)
        (*see* 238:2)

G. W. HUNT *fl.* 1878

1 We don't want to fight, but, by jingo
     if we do,
  We've got the ships, we've got the
     men, we've got the money too.
                    We Don't Want to Fight. Music
                    Hall Song, 1878

JAMES HENRY LEIGH HUNT
                              1784–1859

2 Abou Ben Adhem (may his tribe
     increase!)
  Awoke one night from a deep dream of
     peace
                    Abou Ben Adhem and the Angel

3   'I pray thee then,
  Write me as one that loves his fellow-
     men.'   *Ib.*

4 Jenny kissed me when we met,
  Jumping from the chair she sat in;
  Time, you thief, who love to get
  Sweets into your list, put that in:
  Say I'm weary, say I'm sad,
  Say that health and wealth have
     missed me,
  Say I'm growing old, but add,
  Jenny kissed me.   *Rondeau*

5 Stolen sweets are always sweeter,
  Stolen kisses much completer,
  Stolen looks are nice in chapels,
  Stolen, stolen, be your apples.
                    Song of Fairies Robbing an Or-
                    chard

6 The two divinest things this world
     has got,
  A lovely woman in a rural spot!
                    The Story of Rimini

7 This Adonis in loveliness was a cor-
  pulent man of fifty. [The Prince
  Regent.]
                    The Examiner, 22 Mar. 1812

ANNE HUNTER 1742–1821

8 My mother bids me bind my hair
     With bands of rosy hue,
  Tie up my sleeves with ribbons rare,
     And lace my bodice blue.
                    My Mother Bids Me Bind My
                    Hair

JOHN HUSS 1373–1415

9 O sancta simplicitas!
  O holy simplicity!
                    At the stake, seeing an old peasant
                    bringing a faggot to throw on the
                    pile. Zincgreff-Weidner, *Apo-*
                    phthegmata (Amsterdam, 1653),
                    pt. iii, p. 383. Geo. Büchmann,
                    Geflügelte Worte (1898), p. 509

FRANCIS HUTCHESON 1694–1746

10 That action is best, which procures
   the greatest happiness for the greatest
   numbers.
                    Inquiry into the Original of our
                    Ideas of Beauty and Virtue,
                    Treatise II. *Concerning Moral*
                    Good and Evil, sec. 3, § 8 (*see*
                    22:8)

THOMAS HENRY HUXLEY
                              1825–1895

11 It is the customary fate of new truths
   to begin as heresies and to end as
   superstitions.
                    Science and Culture, xii. *The*
                    Coming of Age of the Origin of
                    Species

12 I took thought, and invented what I
   conceived to be the appropriate title
   of 'agnostic'.
                    Science and Christian Tradition,
                    ch. 7

EDWARD HYDE

see EARL OF CLARENDON

HENRIK IBSEN 1828–1906

13 The minority is always right.
                    An Enemy of the People, Act IV

14 One should never put on one's best
   trousers to go out to battle for freedom
   and truth.   *Ib.* Act V

15 Vine-leaves in his hair.
                    Hedda Gabler, Act II

WASHINGTON IRVING
                              1783–1859

16 The almighty dollar, that great object
   of universal devotion throughout our
   land, seems to have no genuine de-
   votees in these peculiar villages.
                    Wolfert's Roost. The Creole Vil-
                    lage

RICHARD JAGO 1715–1781

17 With leaden foot time creeps along
      While Delia is away.
                    Absence: With Leaden Foot

JAMES I OF ENGLAND AND VI
OF SCOTLAND 1566–1625

18 Dr. Donne's verses are like the peace
   of God; they pass all understanding.
                    Saying recorded by Archdeacon
                    Plume (1630–1704)

WILLIAM JAMES 1842–1910

1 [Letter to H. G. Wells.] A symptom of the moral flabbiness born of the exclusive worship of the bitch-goddess SUCCESS.
1906 in Letters, *ed. Henry James (1920), ii, 260*

THOMAS JEFFERSON 1743–1826

2 We hold these truths to be sacred and undeniable; that all men are created equal and independent, that from that equal creation they derive rights inherent and inalienable, among which are the preservation of life, and liberty, and the pursuit of happiness.
Original draft for the Declaration of Independence *(see 8:9)*

3 The tree of liberty must be refreshed from time to time with the blood of patriots and tyrants. It is its natural manure.
Letter to W. S. Smith, 13 Nov. 1787

4 No duty the Executive had to perform was so trying as to put the right man in the right place.
J. B. MacMaster, History of the People of the U.S. *vol. ii, ch. 13, p. 586*

FRANCIS, LORD JEFFREY
1773–1850

5 This will never do.
On Wordsworth's 'Excursion'. Edinburgh Review, *Nov. 1814, p. 1*

JEROME KLAPKA JEROME
1859–1927

6 Love is like the measles; we all have to go through it.
Idle Thoughts of an Idle Fellow. *On Being in Love*

7 George goes to sleep at a bank from ten to four each day, except Saturdays, when they wake him up and put him outside at two.
Three Men in a Boat, *ch. 2*

8 I like work: it fascinates me. I can sit and look at it for hours. I love to keep it by me: the idea of getting rid of it nearly breaks my heart.
Ib. ch. 15

9 The Passing of the Third Floor Back.
Title of Play

DOUGLAS WILLIAM JERROLD
1803–1857

10 Mrs. Caudle's Curtain Lectures.
Title of Book

11 Love's like the measles—all the worse when it comes late in life.
Wit and Opinions of Douglas Jerrold *(1859), p. 6. A Philanthropist*

12 We love peace, as we abhor pusillanimity; but not peace at any price. There is a peace more destructive of the manhood of living man than war is destructive of his material body. Chains are worse than bayonets.
A Charitable Man, *p. 155. Peace*

PHILANDER CHASE JOHNSON
1866–1939

13 Cheer up, the worst is yet to come.
Shooting Stars. *See* Everybody's Magazine, *May 1920*

SAMUEL JOHNSON 1709–1784

14 *Johnson:* I had no notion that I was wrong or irreverent to my tutor.
Boswell: That, Sir, was great fortitude of mind.
Johnson: No, Sir: stark insensibility.
Boswell's Life of Johnson, *vol. i, p. 60. 5 Nov. 1728*

15 Sir, we are a nest of singing birds.
Ib. p. 75. 1730

16 If you call a dog *Hervey,* I shall love him.
Ib. p. 106. 1737

17 A man may write at any time, if he will set himself doggedly to it.
Ib. p. 203. Mar. 1750

18 [Of F. Lewis]
Sir, he lived in London, and hung loose upon society.
Ib. p. 226. 1750

19 [On being knocked up at 3 a.m. by Beauclerk and Langton]
What, is it you, you dogs! I'll have a frisk with you.
Ib. p. 250. 1752

20 I had done all I could; and no man is well pleased to have his all neglected, be it ever so little.
Ib. p. 261. Letter to Lord Chesterfield, 7 Feb. 1755

21 The shepherd in Virgil grew at last acquainted with Love, and found him a native of the rocks.
Ib.

22 Is not a Patron, my Lord, one who looks with unconcern on a man struggling for life in the water, and, when he has reached ground, encumbers him with help? The notice which you have been pleased to take of my labours, had it been early, had been kind; but it has been delayed till I am indifferent, and cannot enjoy it; till I am solitary, and cannot impart it; till I am known, and do not want it.
Ib.

1 [Of Lord Chesterfield]
This man I thought had been a Lord among wits; but, I find, he is only a wit among Lords. Boswell's *Life of Johnson*, vol. i, p. 266. *1754*

2 [Of Lord Chesterfield's *Letters*]
They teach the morals of a whore, and the manners of a dancing master. *Ib.*

3 [When asked by a lady why he defined 'pastern' as the 'knee' of a horse, in his Dictionary]
Ignorance, madam, pure ignorance.
Ib. p. 293. *1755*

4 Lexicographer: a writer of dictionaries, a harmless drudge.
Ib. p. 296. *1755*

5 A man, Sir, should keep his friendship in constant repair. *Ib.* p. 300. *1755*

6 No man will be a sailor who has contrivance enough to get himself into a jail; for being in a ship is being in a jail, with the chance of being drowned. . . . A man in a jail has more room, better food, and commonly better company.
Ib. p. 348. *16 Mar. 1759*

7 *Boswell*: I do indeed come from Scotland, but I cannot help it.
Johnson: That, Sir, I find, is what a very great many of your countrymen cannot help. *Ib.* p. 392. *16 May 1763*

8 [On Dr. Blair's asking whether any man of a modern age could have written *Ossian*]
Yes, Sir, many men, many women, and many children.
Ib. p. 396. *24 May 1763*

9 He insisted on people praying with him; and I'd as lief pray with Kit Smart as any one else.
Ib. p. 397. *24 May 1763*

10 [Of Kit Smart]
He did not love clean linen; and I have no passion for it. *Ib.*

11 [Of literary criticism]
You may scold a carpenter who has made you a bad table, though you cannot make a table. It is not your trade to make tables.
Ib. p. 409. *25 June 1763*

12 [Of Dr. John Campbell]
I am afraid he has not been in the inside of a church for many years; but he never passes a church without pulling off his hat. This shews that he has good principles.
Ib. p. 418. *1 July 1763*

13 Norway, too, has noble wild prospects; and Lapland is remarkable for prodigious noble wild prospects. But, Sir, let me tell you, the noblest prospect which a Scotchman ever sees, is the high road that leads him to England!
Ib. p. 425. *6 July 1763*

14 A man ought to read just as inclination leads him; for what he reads as a task will do him little good.
Boswell's *Life of Johnson*, vol. i, p. 428. *14 July 1763*

15 Your levellers wish to level *down* as far as themselves; but they cannot bear levelling *up* to themselves.
Ib. p. 448. *21 July 1763*

16 Sir, it is no matter what you teach them [children] first, any more than what leg you shall put into your breeches first.
Ib. p. 452. *26 July 1763*

17 Why, Sir, Sherry [Thomas Sheridan] is dull, naturally dull; but it must have taken him a great deal of pains to become what we now see him. Such an excess of stupidity, Sir, is not in Nature. *Ib.* p. 453. *28 July 1763*

18 [Of Thomas Sheridan's influence on the English language]
Sir, it is burning a farthing candle at Dover, to shew light at Calais.
Ib. p. 454. *28 July 1763*

19 Sir, a woman's preaching is like a dog's walking on his hinder legs. It is not done well; but you are surprised to find it done at all.
Ib. p. 463. *31 July 1763*

20 I look upon it, that he who does not mind his belly will hardly mind anything else.
Ib. p. 467. *5 Aug. 1763*

21 [Talking of Bishop Berkeley's theory of the non-existence of matter, Boswell observed that though they were satisfied it was not true, they were unable to refute it. Johnson struck his foot against a large stone, till he rebounded from it, saying]
I refute it *thus*.
Ib. p. 471. *6 Aug. 1763*

22 [Of Sir John Hawkins]
A very unclubable man.
Ib. p. 480 n. *1764*

23 It was not for me to bandy civilities with my Sovereign.
Ib. vol. ii, p. 35. *Feb. 1767*

24 Sir, We *know* our will is free, and *there's* an end on't.
Ib. p. 82. *16 Oct. 1769*

25 Inspissated gloom. *Ib.*

26 I would not *coddle* the child.
Ib. p. 101. *26 Oct.* 1769

27 A gentleman who had been very unhappy in marriage, married immediately after his wife died: Johnson said, it was the triumph of hope over experience. *Ib.* p. 128. *1770*

28 [To Sir Adam Fergusson]
Sir, I perceive you are a vile Whig.
Ib. p. 170. *31 Mar. 1772*

1 [Quoting a college tutor]
Read over your compositions, and where ever you meet with a passage which you think is particularly fine, strike it out.
Boswell's *Life of Johnson*, vol. ii, p. 237. *30 Apr. 1773*

2 I think the full tide of human existence is at Charing-Cross.
Ib. p. 337. *2 Apr. 1775*

3 Most vices may be committed very genteelly: a man may debauch his friend's wife genteelly: he may cheat at cards genteelly.
Ib. p. 340. *6 Apr. 1775*

4 Patriotism is the last refuge of a scoundrel. *Ib.* p. 348. *7 Apr. 1775*

5 In lapidary inscriptions a man is not upon oath. *Ib.* p. 407. *1775*

6 Sir, it is a great thing to dine with the Canons of Christ-Church.
Ib. p. 445. *20 Mar. 1776*

7 There is nothing which has yet been contrived by man, by which so much happiness is produced as by a good tavern or inn.
Ib. p. 452. *21 Mar. 1776*

8 No man but a blockhead ever wrote, except for money.
Ib. vol. iii, p. 19. *5 Apr. 1776*

9 'Sir, what is poetry?'
'Why, Sir, it is much easier to say what it is not. We all *know* what light is; but it is not easy to *tell* what it is.'
Ib. p. 38. *12 Apr. 1776*

10 Dine with Jack Wilkes, Sir! I'd as soon dine with Jack Ketch.
Ib. p. 66. (This has been circulated as if actually said by Johnson; when the truth is, it was only supposed by me. *Boswell's note, Ib.* p. 66. *May 1776*)

11 Olivarii Goldsmith, Poetae, Physici, Historici, Qui nullum fere scribendi genus non tetigit, Nullum quod tetigit non ornavit.
To Oliver Goldsmith, A Poet, Naturalist, and Historian, who left scarcely any style of writing untouched, and touched none that he did not adorn.
Ib. p. 82. *22 June 1776.* Epitaph on Goldsmith

12 If I had no duties, and no reference to futurity, I would spend my life in driving briskly in a post-chaise with a pretty woman.
Ib. p. 162. *19 Sept. 1777*

13 Depend upon it, Sir, when a man knows he is to be hanged in a fortnight, it concentrates his mind wonderfully.
Ib. p. 167. *19 Sept. 1777*

14 No, Sir, when a man is tired of London, he is tired of life; for there is in London all that life can afford.
Boswell's *Life of Johnson*, vol. iii, p. 178. *20 Sept. 1777*

15 John Wesley's conversation is good, but he is never at leisure. He is always obliged to go at a certain hour. This is very disagreeable to a man who loves to fold his legs and have out his talk as I do.
Ib. p. 230. *31 Mar. 1778*

16 Every man thinks meanly of himself for not having been a soldier, or not having been at sea.
Ib. p. 265. *10 Apr. 1778*

17 Johnson had said that he could repeat a complete chapter of 'The Natural History of Iceland', from the Danish of Horrebow, the whole of which was exactly thus:—'CHAP. LXXII. *Concerning snakes.* 'There are no snakes to be met with throughout the whole island.'
Ib. p. 279. *13 Apr. 1778*

18 As the Spanish proverb says, 'He, who would bring home the wealth of the Indies, must carry the wealth of the Indies with him.' So it is in travelling; a man must carry knowlege with him, if he would bring home knowledge.
Ib. p. 302. *17 Apr. 1778*

19 I have always said, the first Whig was the Devil.
Ib. p. 326. *28 Apr. 1778*

20 Claret is the liquor for boys; port for men; but he who aspires to be a hero must drink brandy.
Ib. p. 381. *7 Apr. 1779*

21 *Boswell:* Is not the Giant's-Causeway worth seeing?
Johnson: Worth seeing? yes; but not worth going to see.
Ib. p. 410. *12 Oct. 1779*

22 If you are idle, be not solitary; if you are solitary, be not idle.
Ib. p. 415. *Letter to Boswell, 27 Oct. 1779*

23 This merriment of parsons is mighty offensive.
Ib. vol. iv, p. 76. *Mar. 1781*

24 [At the sale of Thrale's brewery]
We are not here to sell a parcel of boilers and vats, but the potentiality of growing rich, beyond the dreams of avarice. *Ib.* p. 87. *6 Apr. 1781*

25 'The woman had a bottom of good sense.'
The word *'bottom'* thus introduced, was so ludicrous, . . . that most of us could not forbear tittering . . .
Where's the merriment? . . . I say the *woman* was *fundamentally* sensible.'
Ib. p. 99. *20 Apr. 1781*

1 [To Maurice Morgann who asked him whether he reckoned Derrick or Smart the better poet]
Sir, there is no settling the point of precedency between a louse and a flea.
    Boswell's *Life of Johnson*, vol. iv, p. 192. *1783*

2 When I observed he was a fine cat, saying, 'why yes, Sir, but I have had cats whom I liked better than this'; and then as if perceiving Hodge to be out of countenance, adding, 'but he is a very fine cat, a very fine cat indeed.'   *Ib.* p. 197. *1783*

3 Clear your *mind* of cant.
    Ib. p. 221. *15 May 1783*

4 Boswell is a very clubable man.
    Ib. p. 254 n. *1783*

5 [To Miss Hannah More, who had expressed a wonder that the poet who had written *Paradise Lost* should write such poor Sonnets]
Milton, Madam, was a genius that could cut a Colossus from a rock; but could not carve heads upon cherry-stones.   *Ib.* p. 305. *13 June 1784*

6 [On Sir Joshua Reynolds's observing that the real character of a man was found out by his amusements]
Yes, Sir; no man is a hypocrite in his pleasures.   *Ib.* p. 316. *June 1784*

7 Blown about by every wind of criticism.   *Ib.* p. 319. *June 1784*

8 Sir, I look upon every day to be lost, in which I do not make a new acquaintance.   *Ib.* p. 374. *Nov. 1784*

9 If the man who turnips cries,
  Cry not when his father dies,
  'Tis a proof that he had rather
  Have a turnip than his father.
    Johnsonian Miscellanies, vol. i, p. 193. *Burlesque of Lopez de Vega's lines, 'Se acquien los leones vence,' &c.*

10 What is written without effort is in general read without pleasure.
    Ib. vol. ii, p. 309

11 As with my hat upon my head
   I walk'd along the Strand,
   I there did meet another man
     With his hat in his hand.
    Ib. Anecdotes by George Steevens, p. 315

12 Fly fishing may be a very pleasant amusement; but angling or float fishing I can only compare to a stick and a string, with a worm at one end and a fool at the other.
    Attr. to Johnson by Hawker in Instructions to Young Sportsmen (1859), p. 197. *Not found in his works. See* Notes and Queries, *11 Dec.* 1915

13 To make dictionaries is dull work.
    Dictionary of the English Language. Dull. 8

14 *Excise.* A hateful tax levied upon commodities.   *Ib.*

15 *Net.* Anything reticulated or decussated at equal distances, with interstices between the intersections. *Ib.*

16 *Oats.* A grain, which in England is generally given to horses, but in Scotland supports the people.   *Ib.*

17 *Patron.* Commonly a wretch who supports with insolence, and is paid with flattery.   *Ib.*

18 *Pension.* An allowance made to anyone without an equivalent. In England it is generally understood to mean pay given to a state hireling for treason to his country.   *Ib.*

19 *Whig.* The name of a faction.   *Ib.*

20 When two Englishmen meet, their first talk is of the weather.
    The Idler, No. 11

21 The father of English criticism.
[Dryden]
    Lives of the English Poets (1905), ed. G. B. Hill, vol. i, *Dryden*, § 193, p. 410

22 But what are the hopes of man! I am disappointed by that stroke of death, which has eclipsed the gaiety of nations and impoverished the public stock of harmless pleasure. [Garrick's death.]
    Ib. vol. ii, *Edmund Smith*, § 76, p. 21

23 Human life is everywhere a state in which much is to be endured, and little to be enjoyed.   *Rasselas*, ch. 11

24 Marriage has many pains, but celibacy has no pleasures.   *Ib.* ch. 26

25 Example is always more efficacious than precept.   *Ib.* ch. 29

26 Notes are often necessary, but they are necessary evils.
    Shakespeare (1765), preface.

27 This mournful truth is ev'rywhere confess'd,
Slow rises worth by poverty depress'd.
    London, l. 176

28 The stage but echoes back the public voice.
The drama's laws the drama's patrons give,
For we that live to please, must please to live.
    Prologue at the Opening of Drury Lane

1 Let observation with extensive view,
Survey mankind, from China to Peru;
Remark each anxious toil, each eager
strife,
And watch the busy scenes of crowded
life. *Vanity of Human Wishes*, l. 1

2 Deign on the passing world to turn
thine eyes,
And pause awhile from letters to be
wise;
There mark what ills the scholar's
life assail,
Toil, envy, want, the patron, and the
jail.
See nations slowly wise, and meanly
just,
To buried merit raise the tardy bust.
Ib. l. 157

3 His fall was destined to a barren
strand,
A petty fortress, and a dubious hand;
He left the name, at which the world
grew pale,
To point a moral, or adorn a tale.
Ib. l. 219

JOHN BENN JOHNSTONE
1803–1891

4 I want you to assist me in forcing her
on board the lugger; once there, I'll
frighten her into marriage.

(*Since quoted as*: Once aboard the
lugger and the maid is mine.)
The Gipsy Farmer

HANNS JOHST 1890–

5 Wenn ich Kultur höre . . . entsichere
ich meinen Browning.

Whenever I hear the word culture,
I release the safety catch on my
revolver.
Schlageter (1934), Act I, sc. i.
Attr. to Goering in the form, When
I hear anyone talk of culture I
reach for my revolver.

AL JOLSON 1886–1950

6 You ain't heard nothin' yet, folks.
*Remark in the first talking film,
'The Jazz Singer', July 1927*

JOHN PAUL JONES 1747–1792

7 I have not yet begun to fight.
*Remark on being hailed to know
whether he had struck his flag as
his ship was sinking, 23 Sept.
1779. De Koven's* Life and Letters
of J. P. Jones, *vol. i*

BEN JONSON 1573–1637

8 Fortune, that favours fools.
The Alchemist, prologue

9 Thou look'st like Anti-Christ in that
lewd hat! *The Alchemist*, Act IV

10 Slow, slow, fresh fount, keep time
with my salt tears:
Yet, slower, yet; O faintly, gentle
springs:
List to the heavy part the music bears,
Woe weeps out her division, when
she sings. *Cynthia's Revels*, I. i

11 Queen and huntress, chaste and fair,
Now the sun is laid to sleep,
Seated in thy silver chair,
State in wonted manner keep:
Hesperus entreats thy light,
Goddess, excellently bright.
Ib. v. iii

12 I remember the players have often
mentioned it as an honour to Shakespeare that in his writing (whatsoever
he penned) he never blotted out a
line. My answer hath been 'Would he
had blotted a thousand'. Which they
thought a malevolent speech. I had
not told posterity this, but for their
ignorance, who chose that circumstance to commend their friend by
wherein he most faulted; and to
justify mine own candour: for I
loved the man, and do honour his
memory, on this side idolatry, as
much as any.
*Discoveries. De Shakespeare Nos-
trati. Augustus in Haterium*

13 Alas, all the castles I have, are built
with air, thou know'st.
Eastward Ho!, II. ii. 226

14 Helter skelter, hang sorrow, care'll
kill a cat, up-tails all, and a louse for
the hangman.
Every Man in his Humour, I. iii

15 I have it here in black and white.
Ib. IV. ii

16 It must be done like lightning. *Ib.* V

17 There shall be no love lost.
Every Man out of his Humour,
II. i

18 Follow a shadow, it still flies you,
Seem to fly it, it will pursue:
So court a mistress, she denies you;
Let her alone, she will court you.
Say, are not women truly, then,
Styl'd but the shadows of us men?
The Forest, vii. *Song: That Women
are but Men's Shadows*

19 Drink to me only with thine eyes,
And I will pledge with mine;
Or leave a kiss but in the cup,
And I'll not look for wine.
The thirst that from the soul doth rise
Doth ask a drink divine;
But might I of Jove's nectar sup,
I would not change for thine.

I sent thee late a rosy wreath,
  Not so much honouring thee,
As giving it a hope that there
  It could not wither'd be.
But thou thereon didst only breathe,
  And sent'st it back to me;
Since when it grows and smells, I
  swear,
Not of itself, but thee.
                    The Forest, ix. To Celia

1 Ramp up my genius, be not retro-
    grade;
  But boldly nominate a spade a spade.
                    The Poetaster, v. i

2 This is Mab, the Mistress-Fairy
  That doth nightly rob the dairy.
                    The Satyr

3 This figure that thou here seest put,
  It was for gentle Shakespeare cut,
  Wherein the graver had a strife
  With Nature, to out-do the life:
  O could he but have drawn his wit
  As well in brass, as he has hit
  His face; the print would then surpass
  All that was ever writ in brass:
  But since he cannot, reader, look
  Not on his picture, but his book.
                    *On the Portrait of Shakespeare,
                    To the Reader*

4   Soul of the Age!
  The applause! delight! the wonder of
    our stage!
  My Shakespeare, rise; I will not lodge
    thee by
  Chaucer, or Spenser, or bid Beaumont
    lie
  A little further, to make thee a room:
  Thou art a monument, without a
    tomb,
  And art alive still, while thy book
    doth live,
  And we have wits to read, and praise
    to give.
                    *To the Memory of My Beloved,
                    the Author, Mr. William Shake-
                    speare*

5 Marlowe's mighty line.   *Ib.*

6 And though thou hadst small Latin,
    and less Greek.   *Ib.*

7 He was not of an age, but for all time!
                              Ib.

8 For a good poet's made, as well as
    born.   *Ib.*

9 Sweet Swan of Avon! what a sight it
    were
  To see thee in our waters yet appear,
  And make those flights upon the banks
    of Thames,
  That so did take Eliza, and our James!
                              Ib.

10   Hark you, John Clay, if you have
  Done any such thing, tell troth and
    shame the devil.
                    Tale of a Tub, II. i

11 Have you seen but a bright lily grow,
  Before rude hands have touch'd it?
  Have you mark'd but the fall o' the
    snow
  Before the soil hath smutch'd it?

  O so white! O so soft! O so sweet is she!
                    *Underwoods Celebration of Cha-
                    ris, IV. Her Triumph*

12 Come, my Celia, let us prove,
  While we can, the sports of love.
                    Volpone, III. v

13 Suns, that set, may rise again;
  But if once we lose this light,
  'Tis with us perpetual night.   *Ib.*

14 O rare Ben Jonson.
                    *Epitaph written on his tombstone
                    in Westminster Abbey, by Jack
                    Young. See Aubrey's Brief Lives,
                    Ben Jonson*

DOROTHEA JORDAN 1762–1816

15 'Oh where, and Oh! where is your
    Highland laddie gone?'
  'He's gone to fight the French, for
    King George upon the throne,
  And it's Oh! in my heart, how I wish
    him safe at home!'
                    The Blue Bells of Scotland. Prop-
                    erly *The Blue Bell of Scotland*
                    but popularly known as *Blue
                    Bells*

BENJAMIN JOWETT 1817–1893

16 The lie in the Soul is a true lie.
                    *From the Introduction to his
                    translation of* Plato's *Republic,*
                    bk. ii

JAMES JOYCE 1882–1941

17 A portrait of the artist as a young
  man.   *Title of Book*

JULIAN THE APOSTATE
                              c. 331–363

18 Vicisti, Galilæe.
    Thou hast conquered, O Galilean.
                    Dying words. Latin translation
                    of Theodoret, *Hist. Eccles.* iii. 20

JUVENAL A.D. 60–c. 130

19 Si natura negat, facit indignatio
  versum.
    If nature denies the power, indig-
    nation would give birth to verses.
                    Satires, i. 79. Trans. by Lewis
                    Evans.

1 Quidquid agunt homines, votum timor
ira voluptas
Gaudia discursus nostri farrago libelli
est.

> All that men are engaged in, their
> wishes, fears, anger, pleasures,
> joys, and varied pursuits, form
> the hotch-potch of my book.
> *Satires*, i. 85

2 Nemo repente fuit turpissimus.

> No one ever reached the climax of
> vice at one step.   *Ib.* ii. 83

3 Haud facile emergunt quorum virtuti-
bus obstat
Res angusta domi.

> Difficult indeed is it for those to
> emerge from obscurity whose
> noble qualities are cramped by
> narrow means at home.
> *Ib.* iii. 164

4 Rara avis in terris nigroque simillima
cycno.

> A rare bird on the earth and very
> like a black swan.   *Ib.* vi. 165

5 'Pone seram, prohibe.' Sed quis custo-
diet ipsos
Custodes? Cauta est et ab illis incipit
uxor.

> 'Put on a lock! keep her in confine-
> ment!' But who is to guard the
> guards themselves? Your wife is
> as cunning as you, and begins
> with them.   *Ib.* 347

6   Tenet insanabile multos
Scribendi cacoethes et aegro in corde
senescit.

> An inveterate itch of writing, now
> incurable, clings to many, and
> grows old in their distempered
> body.   *Ib.* vii. 51

7   Verbosa et grandis epistula venit
A Capreis.

> A wordy and lengthy epistle came
> from Capreae.   *Ib.* x. 71

8   Duas tantum res anxius optat,
Panem et circenses.

> Limits its [i.e. the Roman people's]
> anxious longings to two things
> only—bread, and the games of the
> circus.   *Ib.* 80

9 Orandum est ut sit mens sana in
corpore sano.

> Your prayer must be that you may
> have a sound mind in a sound
> body.   *Ib.* 356

IMMANUEL KANT 1724–1804

10 Zwei Dinge erfüllen das Gemüth mit
immer neuer und zunehmender Be-
wunderung und Ehrfurcht, je öfter
und anhaltender sich das Nach-
denken damit beschäftigt: der be-
stirnte Himmel über mir, und das
moralische Gesetz in mir.

> Two things fill the mind with ever-
> increasing wonder and awe, the
> more often and the more in-
> tensely the mind of thought is
> drawn to them: the starry
> heavens above me and the moral
> law within me.
> *Critique of Practical Reason*, con-
> clusion

11 There is . . . but one categorical im-
perative: 'Act only on that maxim
whereby thou canst at the same time
will that it should become a universal
law.'

> *Trans. by* A. D. Lindsay, *from*
> *Fundamental Principles of . . .*
> *Morals*, p. 421

12 I ought, therefore I can.   *Attr.*

ALPHONSE KARR 1808–1890

13 Plus ça change, plus c'est la même
chose.

> The more things change, the more
> they are the same.
> *Les Guêpes, Jan. 1849*, vi

14 Si l'on veut abolir la peine de mort en
ce cas, que MM. les assassins commencent.

> If we are to abolish the death
> penalty, I should like to see the
> first step taken by our friends the
> murderers.   *Ib.*

TED KAVANAGH 1892–1958

15 It's that man again.
>   B.B.C., *Itma* programmes

DENIS KEARNEY 1847–1907

16 Horny-handed sons of toil.
>   *Speech. San Francisco, c. 1878*

JOHN KEATS 1795–1821

17 Season of mists and mellow fruitful-
ness,
Close bosom-friend of the maturing
sun;
Conspiring with him how to load and
bless
With fruit the vines that round the
thatch-eaves run.   *To Autumn*

18 Who hath not seen thee oft amid thy
store?
Sometimes whoever seeks abroad may
find
Thee sitting careless on a granary floor,
Thy hair soft-lifted by the winnowing
wind;

Or on a half-reap'd furrow sound
  asleep,
Drows'd with the fume of poppies,
  while thy hook
Spares the next swath and all its
  twined flowers.   *To Autumn*

1 A thing of beauty is a joy for ever:
  Its loveliness increases; it will never
  Pass into nothingness; but still will
    keep
  A bower quiet for us, and a sleep
  Full of sweet dreams, and health,
    and quiet breathing.
                  Endymion, bk. i, l. 1

2 St. Agnes' Eve—Ah, bitter chill it was!
  The owl, for all his feathers, was
    a-cold;
  The hare limp'd trembling through the
    frozen grass,
  And silent was the flock in woolly
    fold.   *The Eve of Saint Agnes*, i

3 The silver, snarling trumpets 'gan to
    chide.   *Ib.* iv

4 A casement high and triple-arch'd
    there was,
  All garlanded with carven imag'ries
  Of fruits, and flowers, and bunches of
    knot-grass,
  And diamonded with panes of quaint
    device,
  Innumerable of stains and splendid
    dyes,
  As are the tiger-moth's deep-damask'd
    wings;
  And in the midst, 'mong thousand
    heraldries,
  And twilight saints, and dim em-
    blazonings,
  A shielded scutcheon blush'd with
    blood of queens and kings.
                              Ib. xxiv

5 And they are gone: aye, ages long ago
  These lovers fled away into the storm.
                              Ib. xlii

6 Ever let the fancy roam,
  Pleasure never is at home. *Fancy*, l. 1

7   No stir of air was there,
  Not so much life as on a summer's day
  Robs not one light seed from the
    feather'd grass,
  But where the dead leaf fell, there did
    it rest.   *Hyperion*, bk. i, l. 7

8 So the two brothers and their murder'd
    man
  Rode past fair Florence.
                      Isabella, xxvii

9 I stood tip-toe upon a little hill.
                              Title

10 Oh what can ail thee, Knight at arms
  Alone and palely loitering;
  The sedge is wither'd from the lake,
  And no birds sing.
                La Belle Dame Sans Merci

11 I see a lily on thy brow,
  With anguish moist and fever dew;
  And on thy cheek a fading rose
  Fast withereth too.
              La Belle Dame Sans Merci

12 She look'd at me as she did love,
  And made sweet moan.   *Ib.*

13 And there I shut her wild, wild eyes
  With kisses four.
            Ib. (Ld. Houghton's version)

14   La belle Dame sans Merci
  Hath thee in thrall!   *Ib.*

15 Love in a hut, with water and a crust,
  Is—Love, forgive us!—cinders, ashes,
    dust;
  Love in a palace is perhaps at last
  More grievous torment than a hermit's
    fast.   *Lamia*, pt. ii, l. 1

16 Philosophy will clip an Angel's wings.
                          Ib. l. 234

17 Souls of poets dead and gone,
  What Elysium have ye known,
  Happy field or mossy cavern,
  Choicer than the Mermaid Tavern?
  Have ye tippled drink more fine
  Than mine host's Canary wine?
            Lines on the Mermaid Tavern

18 Thou still unravish'd bride of quiet-
    ness,
  Thou foster-child of silence and slow
    time.   *Ode on a Grecian Urn*

19 Heard melodies are sweet, but those
    unheard
  Are sweeter; therefore, ye soft pipes,
    play on;
  Not to the sensual ear, but, more
    endear'd,
  Pipe to the spirit ditties of no tone. *Ib.*

20 For ever wilt thou love, and she be
    fair!   *Ib.*

21 Who are these coming to the sacrifice?
  To what green altar, O mysterious
    priest,
  Lead'st thou that heifer lowing at the
    skies,
  And all her silken flanks with garlands
    drest?
  What little town by river or sea shore,
  Or mountain-built with peaceful cita-
    del,
  Is emptied of this folk, this pious
    morn?   *Ib.*

22 O Attic shape! Fair attitude!   *Ib.*

23 'Beauty is truth, truth beauty,'—
    that is all
  Ye know on earth, and all ye need to
    know.   *Ib.*

24 She dwells with Beauty—Beauty that
    must die;
  And Joy, whose hand is ever at his lips
  Bidding adieu; and aching Pleasure
    nigh,
  Turning to Poison while the bee-
    mouth sips:

Ay, in the very temple of delight
Veil'd Melancholy has her sovran
    shrine.
Though seen of none save him whose
    strenuous tongue
Can burst Joy's grape against his
    palate fine;
His soul shall taste the sadness of her
    might,
And be among her cloudy trophies
    hung.   *Ode on Melancholy*

1 My heart aches, and a drowsy numb-
        ness pains
   My sense.   *Ode to a Nightingale*

2 'Tis not through envy of thy happy lot,
   But being too happy in thine happi-
        ness,—
      That thou, light-winged Dryad of the
        trees,
        In some melodious plot
   Of beechen green, and shadows num-
        berless,
   Singest of summer in full-throated
        ease.   *Ib.*

3 O, for a draught of vintage! that hath
        been
   Cool'd a long age in the deep-delved
        earth,
   Tasting of Flora and the country
        green,
   Dance, and Provençal song, and sun-
        burnt mirth!
   O for a beaker full of the warm South,
   Full of the true, the blushful Hippo-
        crene,
   With beaded bubbles winking at the
        brim,
   And purple-stained mouth;
   That I might drink, and leave the
        world unseen,
   And with thee fade away into the
        forest dim.   *Ib.*

4 Fade far away, dissolve, and quite
        forget
   What thou among the leaves hast
        never known,
   The weariness, the fever, and the fret,
   Here, where men sit and hear each
        other groan.   *Ib.*

5 Fast fading violets cover'd up in
        leaves;
   And mid-May's eldest child,
   The coming musk-rose, full of dewy
        wine,
   The murmurous haunt of flies on
        summer eves.   *Ib.*

6 Darkling I listen; and, for many a
        time
   I have been half in love with easeful
        Death,
   Call'd him soft names in many a
        mused rhyme,
   To take into the air my quiet breath;

Now more than ever seems it rich to
    die,
To cease upon the midnight with no
    pain,
While thou art pouring forth thy soul
    abroad
    In such an ecstasy!
Still wouldst thou sing, and I have
    ears in vain—
To thy high requiem become a sod.

Thou wast not born for death, im-
    mortal Bird!
No hungry generations tread thee
    down;
The voice I hear this passing night
    was heard
In ancient days by emperor and
    clown:
Perhaps the self-same song that found
    a path
Through the sad heart of Ruth, when
    sick for home,
She stood in tears amid the alien corn;
    The same that oft-times hath
Charm'd magic casements, opening on
    the foam
Of perilous seas, in faery lands forlorn.
                    Ode to a Nightingale

7 Forlorn! the very word is like a bell
   To toll me back from thee to my sole
        self!
   Adieu! the fancy cannot cheat so well
   As she is fam'd to do, deceiving elf.
   Adieu! adieu! thy plaintive anthem
        fades
   Past the near meadows, over the still
        stream,
   Up the hill-side; and now 'tis buried
        deep
        In the next valley-glades:
   Was it a vision, or a waking dream?
   Fled is that music:—Do I wake or
        sleep?   *Ib.*

8 Bright star, would I were steadfast
        as thou art—
   Not in lone splendour hung aloft the
        night
   And watching, with eternal lids apart,
   Like nature's patient, sleepless Ere-
        mite,
   The moving waters at their priestlike
        task
   Of pure ablution round earth's human
        shores.   *Sonnet. Bright Star*

9 Much have I travell'd in the realms of
        gold,
   And many goodly states and kingdoms
        seen;
   Round many western islands have I
        been
   Which bards in fealty to Apollo hold.
   Oft of one wide expanse had I been
        told
   That deep-brow'd Homer ruled as his
        demesne;
   Yet did I never breathe its pure serene

Till I heard Chapman speak out loud
  and bold:
Then felt I like some watcher of the
  skies
When a new planet swims into his ken;
Or like stout Cortez when with eagle
  eyes
He star'd at the Pacific—and all his
  men
Look'd at each other with a wild
  surmise—
Silent, upon a peak in Darien.
    *Sonnets. On First Looking into
    Chapman's Homer*

1 Glory and loveliness have pass'd away.
    Ib. To Leigh Hunt

2 To one who has been long in city pent;
'Tis very sweet to look into the fair
And open face of heaven.
    Ib. To One Who Has Been Long

3 When I have fears that I may cease to
  be
Before my pen has glean'd my teeming
  brain.   *Ib. When I Have Fears*

4 When I behold upon the night's
  starr'd face,
Huge cloudy symbols of a high
  romance.   *Ib.*

5   Then on the shore
Of the wide world I stand alone, and
  think
Till love and fame to nothingness do
  sink.   *Ib.*

6 In a drear-nighted December,
Too happy, happy tree,
Thy branches ne'er remember
Their green felicity.
    *Stanzas. In a Drear-nighted
    December*

7 I am certain of nothing but the holiness of the heart's affections and the
  truth of imagination—what the imagination seizes as beauty must be truth
  —whether it existed before or not.
    *Letters (ed. M. B. Forman), 31.
    To Benjamin Bailey, 22 Nov.
    1817*

8 O for a life of sensations rather than
  of thoughts!   *Ib.*

9 There is an awful warmth about my
  heart like a load of immortality.
    *Ib. 87. To J. H. Reynolds, 22
    Sept. 1818*

10 I think I shall be among the English
  Poets after my death.
    *Ib. 94. To George and Georgiana
    Keats, 14 Oct. 1818*

11 You, I am sure, will forgive me for
  sincerely remarking that you might
  curb your magnanimity, and be more
  of an artist, and load every rift of
  your subject with ore.
    Ib. 227. To Shelley, Aug. 1820

12 Here lies one whose name was writ in
  water.
    Epitaph. Lord Houghton, *Life
    of Keats,* ii. 91

JOHN KEBLE 1792–1866

13 New every morning is the love
Our wakening and uprising prove.
    The Christian Year. Morning

14 The trivial round, the common task,
Would furnish all we ought to ask;
Room to deny ourselves; a road
To bring us, daily, nearer God.   *Ib.*

15 And help us, this and every day,
To live more nearly as we pray.   *Ib.*

16 Sun of my soul! Thou Saviour dear,
It is not night if Thou be near.
    Ib. Evening

17 Like infant slumbers, pure and light.
    Ib.

18 There is a book, who runs may read,
  Which heavenly truth imparts,
And all the lore its scholars need,
  Pure eyes and Christian hearts.
    Ib. Septuagesima

19 Bless'd are the pure in heart,
For they shall see our God.
    Ib. The Purification

20 The voice that breathed o'er Eden.
    Poems. Holy Matrimony

THOMAS KELLY 1769–1854

21 The Head that once was crowned with
  thorns
Is crowned with glory now.
    *Hymns on Various Passages of
    Scripture (1820). The Head that
    Once Was Crowned*

THOMAS À KEMPIS 1380–1471

22 Nam homo proponit, sed Deus dis-
  ponit.
    Man proposes but God disposes.
      Imitatio Christi, Bk. 1, ch. xix.
      § 2

23 Sic transit gloria mundi.
    O, how quickly doth the glory of
      the world pass away!
        Ib. ch. iii. § 6

JOHN KEMPTHORNE 1775–1838

24 Praise the Lord! ye heavens adore
  Him,
  Praise Him, Angels in the height;
Sun and moon, rejoice before Him,
  Praise Him, all ye stars and light.
    *Hymns of Praise. For Foundling
    Apprentices (1796). Praise the
    Lord! Ye Heavens Adore Him*

BISHOP THOMAS KEN 1637–1711

1 Awake my soul, and with the sun
Thy daily stage of duty run;
Shake off dull sloth, and joyful rise
To pay thy morning sacrifice.
Morning Hymn (1709). *Awake My Soul*

2 Teach me to live, that I may dread
The grave as little as my bed.
Evening Hymn. Glory to Thee My God This Night

3 Praise God, from whom all blessings flow,
Praise Him, all creatures here below,
Praise Him above, ye heavenly host,
Praise Father, Son, and Holy Ghost.
Morning and Evening Hymn

JOSEPH KESSELRING 1902–

4 Arsenic and Old Lace.
Title of Play (1941)

WILLIAM KETHE d. 1608?

5 All people that on earth do dwell,
Sing to the Lord with cheerful voice;
Him serve with fear, His praise forth tell,
Come ye before Him, and rejoice.

The Lord, ye know, is God indeed;
Without our aid He did us make.
Daye's Psalter (1560). *All People That on Earth*

6 For it is seemly so to do.   *Ib.*

FRANCIS SCOTT KEY 1779–1843

7 'Tis the star-spangled banner; O long may it wave
O'er the land of the free, and the home of the brave!
The Star-Spangled Banner

JOYCE KILMER 1888–1918

8 I think that I shall never see
A poem lovely as a tree.
Poems, Essays, and Letters (1917), i. *Trees*

9 Poems are made by fools like me,
But only God can make a tree.   *Ib.*

BENJAMIN FRANKLIN KING
1857–1894

10 Nothing to do but work,
Nothing to eat but food,
Nothing to wear but clothes
To keep one from going nude.
The Pessimist

BISHOP HENRY KING 1592–1669

11 But hark! My pulse like a soft drum
Beats my approach, tells thee I come;
And slow howe'er my marches be,
I shall at last sit down by thee.
The Exequy

STODDARD KING 1889–1933

12 There's a long, long trail a-winding
Into the land of my dreams,
Where the nightingales are singing
And a white moon beams:
There's a long, long night of waiting
Until my dreams all come true;
Till the day when I'll be going down
That long long trail with you.
The Long, Long Trail

ALEXANDER WILLIAM KING-LAKE 1809–1891

13 Soon the men of the column began to
see that though the scarlet line was
slender, it was very rigid and exact.
Invasion of the Crimea, vol. ii, p. 455

CHARLES KINGSLEY 1819–1875

14 Be good, sweet maid, and let who can be clever;
Do lovely things, not dream them, all day long;
And so make Life, and Death, and that For Ever,
One grand sweet song.
A Farewell. To C. E. G.

15 What we can we will be,
Honest Englishmen.
Do the work that's nearest,
Though it's dull at whiles,
Helping, when we meet them,
Lame dogs over stiles.
Letter to Thomas Hughes

16 Welcome, wild North-easter!
Shame it is to see
Odes to every zephyr;
Ne'er a verse to thee.
Ode to the North-East Wind

17 I once had a sweet little doll, dears,
The prettiest doll in the world;
Her cheeks were so red and so white, dears,
And her hair was so charmingly curled.
Songs from The Water Babies. My Little Doll

18 When all the world is young, lad,
And all the trees are green;
And every goose a swan, lad,
And every lass a queen;
Then hey for boot and horse, lad,
And round the world away:
Young blood must have its course, lad,
And every dog his day.

When all the world is old, lad,
And all the trees are brown;
And all the sport is stale, lad,
And all the wheels run down;
Creep home, and take your place
  there,
The spent and maimed among:
God grant you find one face there,
You loved when all was young.
Songs from The Water Babies.
Young and Old

1 'O Mary, go and call the cattle home,
  and call the cattle home,
And call the cattle home,
Across the sands of Dee:'
The western wind was wild and dank
  with foam,
And all alone went she.
The Sands of Dee

2 Three fishers went sailing away to the
  west,
Away to the west as the sun went
  down;
Each thought on the woman who
  loved him the best,
And the children stood watching
  them out of the town.
The Three Fishers

3 For men must work, and women must
  weep. *Ib.*

4 To be discontented with the divine
discontent, and to be ashamed with
the noble shame, is the very germ
and first upgrowth of all virtue.
Health and Education (1874),
p. 20

5 Mrs. Bedonebyasyoudid is coming.
The Water Babies, ch. 5

6 The loveliest fairy in the world; and
her name is Mrs. Doasyouwouldbe-
doneby. *Ib.*

7 More ways of killing a cat than
choking her with cream.
Westward Ho!, ch. 20

8 Some say that the age of chivalry is
past, that the spirit of romance is
dead. The age of chivalry is never past,
so long as there is a wrong left unre-
dressed on earth.
Life (1879), vol. ii, ch. 28

RUDYARD KIPLING 1865–1936

9 When you've shouted 'Rule Britannia', when you've sung 'God save
the Queen',
When you've finished killing Kruger
with your mouth.
The Absent-Minded Beggar

10 He's an absent-minded beggar, and
his weaknesses are great. *Ib.*

11 Duke's son—cook's son—son of a
hundred Kings—
(Fifty thousand horse and foot going
to Table Bay!) *Ib.*

12 Rolling down the Ratcliffe Road
drunk and raising Cain.
The Ballad of the 'Bolivar'

13 Oh, East is East, and West is West,
and never the twain shall meet,
Till Earth and Sky stand presently at
God's great Judgment Seat;
But there is neither East nor West,
Border, nor Breed, nor Birth,
When two strong men stand face to
face, though they come from the
ends of the earth!
The Ballad of East and West

14 And a woman is only a woman, but
a good cigar is a Smoke.
The Betrothed

15 'Oh, where are you going to, all you
Big Steamers,
With England's own coal, up and
down the salt seas?'
'We are going to fetch you your bread
and your butter,
Your beef, pork, and mutton, eggs,
apples, and cheese.' *Big Steamers*

16 We're foot—slog—slog—slog—slog-
gin' over Africa—
Foot—foot—foot—foot—sloggin' over
Africa—
(Boots — boots — boots — boots —
movin' up an' down again!)
There's no discharge in the war!
Boots

17 Land of our birth, we pledge to thee
Our love and toil in the years to be;
When we are grown and take our
place,
As men and women with our race.

Father in Heaven who lovest all,
Oh, help Thy children when they call;
That they may build from age to age
An undefilèd heritage.

Teach us to bear the yoke in youth,
With steadfastness and careful truth;
That, in our time, Thy Grace may give
The truth whereby the nations live.
The Children's Song

18 Teach us delight in simple things,
And mirth that has no bitter springs;
Forgiveness free of evil done,
And love to all men 'neath the sun!

Land of our birth, our faith, our pride,
For whose dear sake our fathers died;
O Motherland, we pledge to thee
Head, heart, and hand through the
years to be! *Ib.*

19 Gold is for the mistress—silver for the
maid—
Copper for the craftsman cunning at
his trade.
'Good!' said the Baron, sitting in his
hall,
'But Iron—Cold Iron—is master of
them all.' *Cold Iron*

1 Our father Adam sat under the Tree
   and scratched with a stick in the
   mould;
  And the first rude sketch that the
   world had seen was joy to his
   mighty heart.
  Till the Devil whispered behind the
   leaves, 'It's pretty, but is it Art?'
       *The Conundrum of the Work-
       shops*

2 'For they're hangin' Danny Deever,
   you can hear the Dead March play,
  The Regiment's in 'ollow square—
   they're hangin' 'im to-day;
  They've taken of 'is buttons off an'
   cut 'is stripes away,
  An' they're hangin' Danny Deever in
   the mornin'.'   *Danny Deever*

3 The 'eathen in 'is blindness bows down
   to wood an' stone;
  'E don't obey no orders unless they is
   'is own;
  'E keeps 'is side-arms awful: 'e leaves
   'em all about,
  An' then comes up the Regiment an'
   pokes the 'eathen out. *The 'Eathen*

4 Winds of the World, give answer!
   They are whimpering to and fro—
  And what should they know of Eng-
   land who only England know?
         The English Flag

5 When the Himalayan peasant meets
   the he-bear in his pride,
  He shouts to scare the monster, who
   will often turn aside.
  But the she-bear thus accosted rends
   the peasant tooth and nail
  For the female of the species is more
   deadly than the male.
      The Female of the Species

6 To the legion of the lost ones, to the
   cohort of the damned.
         Gentlemen Rankers

7 Gentlemen-rankers out on the spree,
  Damned from here to Eternity.   *Ib.*

8 Our England is a garden that is full of
   stately views,
  Of borders, beds and shrubberies and
   lawns and avenues,
  With statues on the terraces and peacocks strutting by;
  But the Glory of the Garden lies in
   more than meets the eye.
       The Glory of the Garden

9 Our England is a garden, and such
   gardens are not made
  By singing:—'Oh, how beautiful!' and
   sitting in the shade,
  While better men than we go out and
   start their working lives
  At grubbing weeds from gravel paths
   with broken dinner-knives.   *Ib.*

10 Oh, Adam was a gardener, and God
    who made him sees
  That half a proper gardener's work is
    done upon his knees,
  So when your work is finished, you
    can wash your hands and pray
  For the Glory of the Garden, that it
    may not pass away!
  And the Glory of the Garden it shall
    never pass away!
        The Glory of the Garden

11 You may talk o' gin an' beer
  When you're quartered safe out 'ere,
  An' you're sent to penny-fights an'
    Aldershot it;
  But when it comes to slaughter
  You will do your work on water,
  An' you'll lick the bloomin' boots of
    'im that's got it.   *Gunga Din*

12 Though I've belted you an' flayed you,
  By the livin' Gawd that made you,
  You're a better man than I am,
    Gunga Din!   *Ib.*

13 There are nine and sixty ways of
    constructing tribal lays,
  And—every—single—one—of—them
    —is—right! *In the Neolithic Age*

14 If you can keep your head when all
    about you
    Are losing theirs and blaming it on
     you,
  If you can trust yourself when all men
    doubt you,
    But make allowance for their doubt-
     ing too;
  If you can wait and not be tired by
    waiting,
    Or being lied about, don't deal in lies,
  Or being hated, don't give way to
    hating,
    And yet don't look too good, nor
    talk too wise:

  If you can dream—and not make
    dreams your master;
    If you can think—and not make
    thoughts your aim;
  If you can meet with Triumph and
    Disaster
    And treat those two impostors just
    the same.   *If*

15 If you can make one heap of all your
    winnings
    And risk it on one turn of pitch-
    and-toss,
  And lose, and start again at your
    beginnings
    And never breathe a word about
    your loss.   *Ib.*

16 If you can talk with crowds and keep
    your virtue,
    Or walk with Kings—nor lose the
    common touch,
  If neither foes nor loving friends can
    hurt you,
    If all men count with you, but none
    too much;

If you can fill the unforgiving minute
    With sixty seconds' worth of dis-
      tance run,
Yours is the Earth and everything
    that's in it,
    And—which is more—you'll be a
      Man, my son!   *If*

1 Then ye returned to your trinkets;
    then ye contented your souls
    With the flannelled fools at the
      wicket or the muddied oafs at the
      goals.   *The Islanders*

2 The Camel's hump is an ugly lump
    Which well you may see at the Zoo;
    But uglier yet is the Hump we get
    From having too little to do.
        *Just-So Stories. How the Camel
        Got his Hump*

3 We get the Hump—
    Cameelious Hump—
    The Hump that is black and blue! *Ib.*

4 The cure for this ill is not to sit still,
    Or frowst with a book by the fire;
    But to take a large hoe and a shovel
      also,
    And dig till you gently perspire. *Ib.*

5 Old Man Kangaroo first, Yellow-Dog
    Dingo behind.
        *Ib. Sing-Song of Old Man Kan-
        garoo*

6 'Confound Romance!' . . . And all un-
      seen
    Romance brought up the nine-fifteen.
                The King

7 I've taken my fun where I've found it,
    An' now I must pay for my fun,
    For the more you 'ave known o' the
      others
    The less will you settle to one;
    An' the end of it's sittin' an' thinkin',
    An' dreamin' Hell-fires to see.
    So be warned by my lot (which I
      know you will not),
    An' learn about women from me!
              The Ladies

8 For the Colonel's Lady an' Judy
    O'Grady
    Are sisters under their skins!   *Ib.*

9 Now this is the Law of the Jungle—
    as old and as true as the sky.
          The Law of the Jungle

10 Ye thought? Ye are not paid to think.
            McAndrew's Hymn

11 By the old Moulmein Pagoda, lookin'
    eastward to the sea,
    There's a Burma girl a-settin', and
      I know she thinks o' me;
    For the wind is in the palm-trees, an'
      the temple-bells they say:
    'Come you back, you British soldier;
      come you back to Mandalay!'
    Come you back to Mandalay,
    Where the old Flotilla lay;

Can't you 'ear their paddles chunkin'
    from Rangoon to Mandalay?
On the road to Mandalay,
Where the flyin'-fishes play,
An' the dawn comes up like thunder
    outer China 'crost the Bay!
              Mandalay

12 An' I seed her first a-smokin' of a
    whackin' white cheroot,
    An' a-wastin' Christian kisses on an
      'eathen idol's foot.   *Ib.*

13 But that's all shove be'ind me—long
    ago an' fur away,
    An' there ain' no 'buses runnin' from
      the Bank to Mandalay;
    An' I'm learnin' 'ere in London wot
      the ten-year soldier tells:
    'If you've 'eard the East a-callin',
      you won't never 'eed naught else.'
                  Ib.

14 I am sick o' wastin' leather on these
    gritty pavin'-stones,
    An' the blasted English drizzle wakes
      the fever in my bones;
    Tho' I walks with fifty 'ousemaids
      outer Chelsea to the Strand,
    An' they talks a lot o' lovin', but wot
      do they understand?
    Beefy face an' grubby 'and—
    Law! Wot do they understand?
    I've a neater, sweeter maiden in a
      cleaner, greener land!   *Ib.*

15 Ship me somewheres east of Suez,
    where the best is like the worst,
    Where there aren't no Ten Command-
      ments, an' a man can raise a thirst:
    For the temple-bells are callin', an'
      it's there that I would be—
    By the old Moulmein Pagoda, looking
      lazy at the sea.   *Ib.*

16 If I were hanged on the highest hill,
    Mother o' mine, O mother o' mine!
    I know whose love would follow me
      still,
    Mother o' mine, O mother o' mine!
            Mother O' Mine

17 And the epitaph drear: 'A Fool lies
    here who tried to hustle the East.'
      Naulahka, heading of ch. 5

18 The Saxon is not like us Normans.
    His manners are not so polite.
        Norman and Saxon

19 A Nation spoke to a Nation,
    A Throne sent word to a Throne:
    'Daughter am I in my mother's house,
    But mistress in my own.
        Our Lady of the Snows

20 The toad beneath the harrow knows
    Exactly where each tooth-point goes;
    The butterfly upon the road
    Preaches contentment to that toad.
          Pagett M.P.

21 Pagett, M.P., was a liar, and a fluent
    liar therewith.   *Ib.*

1 Can't! Don't! Sha'n't! Won't!
Pass it along the line!
Somebody's pack has slid from his back,
'Wish it were only mine!
Somebody's load has tipped off in the road—
Cheer for a halt and a row!
Urrh! Yarrh! Grr! Arrh!
Somebody's catching it now!
Parade-Song of the Camp-Animals. Commissariat Camels

2 Brothers and Sisters, I bid you beware
Of giving your heart to a dog to tear.
The Power of the Dog

3 God of our fathers, known of old,
Lord of our far-flung battle-line,
Beneath whose awful Hand we hold
Dominion over palm and pine—
Lord God of Hosts, be with us yet,
Lest we forget—lest we forget!

4 The tumult and the shouting dies;
The Captains and the Kings depart:
Still stands Thine ancient sacrifice,
An humble and a contrite heart.
Lord God of Hosts, be with us yet,
Lest we forget—lest we forget!
Recessional

5 Lo, all our pomp of yesterday
Is one with Nineveh and Tyre!   *Ib.*

6 If, drunk with sight of power, we loose
Wild tongues that have not Thee in awe,
Such boastings as the Gentiles use,
Or lesser breeds without the Law. *Ib.*

7 For heathen heart that puts her trust
In reeking tube and iron shard,
All valiant dust that builds on dust,
And, guarding, calls not Thee to guard,
For frantic boast and foolish word—
Thy mercy on Thy People, Lord!   *Ib.*

8 And I've lost Britain, and I've lost Gaul,
And I've lost Rome and, worst of all,
I've lost Lalage!   *Rimini*

9 Shillin' a day,
Bloomin' good pay—
Lucky to touch it, a shillin' a day!
Shillin' a Day

10 Them that asks no questions isn't told a lie.
Watch the wall, my darling, while the Gentlemen go by!
Five and twenty ponies
Trotting through the dark—
Brandy for the Parson,
'Baccy for the Clerk;
Laces for a lady, letters for a spy,
Watch the wall, my darling, while the Gentlemen go by!
A Smuggler's Song

11 I am all that ever went with evening dress!   *The Song of the Banjo*

12 If blood be the price of admiralty,
Lord God, we ha' paid in full!
The Song of the Dead, ii

13 Through the Jungle very softly flits a shadow and a sigh—
He is Fear, O ha' Little Hunter, he is Fear!
The Song of the Little Hunter

14 Mithras, God of the Morning, our trumpets waken the Wall!
'Rome is above the Nations, but Thou art over all!' *A Song to Mithras*

15 'Let us now praise famous men—
Men of little showing—
For their work continueth,
And their work continueth,
Broad and deep continueth,
Greater than their knowing!
Stalky & Co. A School Song

16 A Jelly-bellied Flag-flapper.   *Ib.*

17 You may carve it on his tombstone, you may cut it on his card,
That a young man married is a young man marred.
The Story of the Gadsbys

18 God gives all men all earth to love,
But, since man's heart is small,
Ordains for each one spot shall prove
Belovèd over all.
Each to his choice, and I rejoice
The lot has fallen to me
In a fair ground—in a fair ground—
Yea, Sussex by the sea!   *Sussex*

19 One man in a thousand, Solomon says,
Will stick more close than a brother.
The Thousandth Man

20 Oh, it's Tommy this, an' Tommy that, an' 'Tommy, go away';
But it's 'Thank you, Mister Atkins,' when the band begins to play.
Tommy

21 It's Tommy this, an' Tommy that, an' 'Chuck him out, the brute!'
But it's 'Saviour of 'is country' when the guns begin to shoot.   *Ib.*

22 Then it's Tommy this, an' Tommy that, an' 'Tommy 'ow's yer soul?'
But it's 'Thin red line of 'eroes' when the drums begin to roll.   *Ib.*

23 We aren't no thin red 'eroes, nor we aren't no blackguards too.
But single men in barricks, most remarkable like you;
An' if sometimes our conduck isn't all your fancy paints,
Why, single men in barricks don't grow into plaster saints.   *Ib.*

24 Of all the trees that grow so fair,
Old England to adorn,
Greater are none beneath the Sun,
Than Oak, and Ash, and Thorn.
A Tree Song

1 A fool there was and he made his
     prayer
     (Even as you and I!)
  To a rag and a bone and a hank of hair
  (We called her the woman who did not
     care)
  But the fool he called her his lady
     fair—
  (Even as you and I!)   *The Vampire*

2 They shut the road through the woods
  Seventy years ago.
          The Way Through the Woods

3 Steadily cantering through
     The misty solitudes,
  As though they perfectly knew
  The old lost road through the woods—
  But there is no road through the
     woods!   *Ib.*

4 When 'Omer smote 'is bloomin' lyre,
  'E'd 'eard men sing by land an' sea;
  An' what 'e thought 'e might require,
  'E went an' took—the same as me!
          *When 'Omer Smote. (Barrack-
          Room Ballads: Introduction)*

5 Take up the White Man's burden—
     Send forth the best ye breed—
  Go, bind your sons to exile
     To serve your captives' need;
  To wait in heavy harness
     On fluttered folk and wild—
  Your new-caught, sullen peoples,
     Half-devil and half-child.
          The White Man's Burden

6 'Ave you 'eard o' the Widow at
     Windsor
  With a hairy gold crown on 'er 'ead?
  She 'as ships on the foam—she 'as
     millions at 'ome,
  An' she pays us poor beggars in red.
          The Widow at Windsor

7 Down to Gehenna or up to the Throne,
  He travels the fastest who travels
     alone.   *The Winners*

8 When the 'arf-made recruity goes out
     to the East
  'E acts like a babe an' 'e drinks like
     a beast,
  An' 'e wonders because 'e is frequent
     deceased
  Ere 'e's fit for to serve as a soldier.
          The Young British Soldier

9 Good hunting!
          The Jungle Book. Kaa's Hunting

10 We be of one blood, thou and I.   *Ib.*

11 Most 'scruciating idle.
          *Just-So Stories. How the Camel
          Got His Hump*

12 'Humph yourself!'
     And the Camel humphed himself.
                                     Ib.

13 An Elephant's Child—who was full of
     'satiable curiosity.
          Ib. The Elephant's Child

14 The great grey-green, greasy Lim-
  popo River, all set about with fever-
  trees.
          *Just-So Stories. The Elephant's
          Child*

15 Led go! You are hurtig be!   *Ib.*

16 The Cat. He walked by himself, and
  all places were alike to him.
          *Ib. The Cat That Walked By
          Himself*

17 He went back through the Wet Wild
  Woods, waving his wild tail, and
  walking by his wild lone. But he never
  told anybody.   *Ib.*

18 What's the good of argifying?
          *Life's Handicap. On Greenhow
          Hill*

19 The Light that Failed.   *Title of Novel*

20 But that is another story.
          *Plain Tales from the Hills. Three
          and an Extra*

21 Lalun is a member of the most ancient
  profession in the world.
          Soldiers Three. On the City Wall

22 Steady the Buffs.
          *Ib. The Gadsbys. Poor Dear
          Mamma*

23 I gloat! Hear me gloat!
          Stalky & Co., ch. i

24 Your Uncle Stalky.   *Ib.*

25 Once upon a time there was a Man and
  his Wife and a Tertium Quid.
          *Wee Willie Winkie. At the Pit's
          Mouth*

26 Gawd knows, an' 'E won't split on a
  pal. *Ib. Drums of the Fore and Aft*

FRIEDRICH VON KLINGER
1752–1831
27 Sturm und Drang.
     Storm and stress.
          Title of Play (1775)

CHARLES KNIGHT
28 Here we are! here we are!! here we
     are again!!!
  There's Pat and Mac and Tommy and
     Jack and Joe.
  When there's trouble brewing,
  When there's something doing,
  Are we downhearted?
  No! let 'em all come!
          *Here We Are! Here We Are
          Again!!*

MARY KNOWLES 1733–1807
29 He [Dr. Johnson] gets at the substance of a book directly; he tears
  out the heart of it.
          Boswell's *Johnson* (ed. 1934),
          vol. iii, p. 284. *15 Apr. 1778*

JOHN KNOX 1505–1572

1 The First Blast of the Trumpet Against the Monstrous Regiment of Women.
Title of Pamphlet (1558)

RONALD ARBUTHNOT KNOX
1888–1957

2 There was once a man who said 'God
    Must think it exceedingly odd
        If he finds that this tree
        Continues to be
    When there's no one about in the Quad.'
Attr. Langford Reed, The Limerick Book

ARTHUR J. LAMB 1870–1928

3 She's a bird in a gilded cage.
Song (1900)

LADY CAROLINE LAMB
1785–1828

4 Mad, bad, and dangerous to know.
Of Byron, in her Journal

CHARLES LAMB 1775–1834

5 I am, in plainer words, a bundle of prejudices—made up of likings and dislikings.
Essays of Elia. Imperfect Sympathies

6 'A clear fire, a clean hearth, and the rigour of the game.' This was the celebrated wish of old Sarah Battle (now with God), who, next to her devotions, loved a good game at whist.
Ib. Mrs. Battle's Opinions on Whist

7 I mean your *borrowers of books*—those mutilators of collections, spoilers of the symmetry of shelves, and creators of odd volumes.
Ib. The Two Races of Men

8 I could forgive a man for not enjoying Milton; but I would not call that man my friend who should be offended with 'the divine chit-chat of Cowper'.
Quoting Coleridge's own phrase in Letter to Coleridge, 5 Dec. 1796

9 The scene for the most part laid in a Brothel. O tempora, O mores! but as friend Coleridge said when he was talking bawdy to Miss — 'to the pure all things are pure'.
Letter to Southey, July 1798

10 I came home . . . hungry as a hunter.
Letter to Coleridge, probably 16 or 17 Apr. 1800

11 A little thin, flowery border round, neat, not gaudy.
Letter to Wordsworth, June 1806

12 His face when he repeats his verses hath its ancient glory, an Archangel a little damaged. [Coleridge.]
Letter to W. Wordsworth, 26 Apr. 1816

13 You are knee deep in clover.
Letter to C. C. Clarke, Dec. 1828

14 When my sonnet was rejected, I exclaimed, 'Damn the age; I will write for Antiquity!'
Letter to B. W. Procter, 22 Jan. 1829

15 The greatest pleasure I know, is to do a good action by stealth, and to have it found out by accident.
Table Talk by the late Elia. The Athenaeum, 4 Jan. 1834

16 I have had playmates, I have had companions,
In my days of childhood, in my joyful school-days,—
All, all are gone, the old familiar faces.
The Old Familiar Faces

17 I do not [know the lady]; but damn her at a venture.
E. V. Lucas, Charles Lamb (1905), vol. i, p. 320, note

JOHN GEORGE LAMBTON, FIRST EARL OF DURHAM
1792–1840

18 . . . one of his sublimities . . . too good to be lost . . . he said he considered £40,000 a year a moderate income—such a one as a man *might jog on with.*
The Creevey Papers (13 Sept. 1821), ii. 32

WALTER SAVAGE LANDOR
1775–1864

19 Ah, what avails the sceptred race!
Ah, what the form divine!
What every virtue, every grace!
Rose Aylmer, all were thine.
Rose Aylmer

20 I strove with none; for none was worth my strife;
    Nature I loved, and, next to Nature, Art;
I warmed both hands before the fire of life;
    It sinks, and I am ready to depart.
Finis

21 Mother, I cannot mind my wheel. *Title*

22 There are no fields of amaranth on this side of the grave: there are no voices, O Rhodopè! that are not soon mute, however tuneful: there is no name, with whatever emphasis of passionate love repeated, of which the echo is not faint at last.
Imaginary Conversations, Æsop and Rhodope, ii

ANDREW LANG 1844–1912

1 The surge and thunder of the Odyssey.
  *As One that for a Weary Space
  has Lain*

2 If the wild bowler thinks he bowls,
    Or if the batsman thinks he's
    bowled,
  They know not, poor misguided souls,
    They too shall perish unconsoled.
  I am the batsman and the bat,
  I am the bowler and the ball,
  The umpire, the pavilion cat,
    The roller, pitch, and stumps, and
    all.
    Brahma (in imitation of Emer-
    son)

FREDERICK LANGBRIDGE
                              1849–1923

3 Two men look out through the same
  bars:
  One sees the mud, and one the stars.
    *A Cluster of Quiet Thoughts
    (1896) (Religious Tract Society
    Publication)*

WILLIAM LANGLAND
                              1330?–1400?

4 In a somer seson whan soft was the
  sonne.
    *The Vision of William concerning
    Piers the Plowman* (ed. Skeat),
    B Text, Prologue, l. 1.

**ARCHBISHOP STEPHEN
LANGTON** d. 1228

5   Veni, Sancte Spiritus,
  Et emitte coelitus
  Lucis tuae radium.

    Come, thou holy Paraclete,
    And from thy celestial seat
    Send thy light and brilliancy.
      Trans. by J. M. Neale

BISHOP HUGH LATIMER
                              1485?–1555

6 Be of good comfort Master Ridley,
  and play the man. We shall this day
  light such a candle by God's grace in
  England, as (I trust) shall never be
  put out.
    Foxe, *Actes and Monuments*
    (1570), p. 1937

SIR HARRY LAUDER 1870–1950

7 I love a lassie.   *Title of Song*

8 Just a wee deoch-an-doris
  Before we gang awa' . . .
  If you can say, 'It's a braw, bricht,
  moonlicht nicht',
  Ye're a' richt, ye ken.   *Song*

9 Keep right on to the end of the road.
                                 Song

10 O! it's nice to get up in the mornin'
   But it's nicer to lie in bed.   *Song*

11 Roamin' in the Gloamin'.
                              Title of Song

STEPHEN BUTLER LEACOCK
                              1869–1944

12 Lord Ronald . . . flung himself upon
   his horse and rode madly off in all
   directions.
     *Nonsense Novels. Gertrude the
     Governess*

13 A pie may be produced any number of
   times.
     *Literary Lapses. Boarding House
     Geometry*

14 The landlady can be reduced to her
   lowest terms by a series of proposi-
   tions.   *Ib.*

EDWARD LEAR 1812–1888

15 There was an Old Man with a beard,
   Who said, 'It is just as I feared!—
     Two Owls and a Hen,
     Four Larks and a Wren,
   Have all built their nests in my beard!'
                         Book of Nonsense

16 There was an old man who said,
   'Hush!
   I perceive a young bird in this bush!'
     When they said, 'Is it small?'
     He replied, 'Not at all!'
   It is four times as big as the bush!'
                                       Ib.

17 'How pleasant to know Mr. Lear!'
     Who has written such volumes of
     stuff!
   Some think him ill-tempered and
     queer,
   But a few think him pleasant
     enough. *Nonsense Songs*, preface

18 His body is perfectly spherical,
   He weareth a runcible hat.   *Ib.*

19 On the coast of Coromandel
   Where the early pumpkins blow,
     In the middle of the woods
   Lived the Yonghy-Bonghy-Bò.
   Two old chairs, and half a candle,—
   One old jug without a handle,—
     These were all his worldly goods.
     *Ib. The Courtship of the Yonghy-
     Bonghy-Bò*

20 When awful darkness and silence reign
   Over the great Gromboolian plain,
     Through the long, long wintry
     nights.
   When the angry breakers roar
   As they beat on the rocky shore;—
   When Storm-clouds brood on the
     towering heights
     Of the Hills of the Chankly Bore.
     *Ib. The Dong with the Luminous
     Nose*

1 'The Dong!—the Dong!
  The wandering Dong through the forest goes!
  The Dong!—the Dong!
  The Dong with the Luminous Nose!'
  Nonsense Songs. The Dong with the Luminous Nose

2 And who so happy,—O who,
  As the Duck and the Kangaroo?
  Ib. The Duck and the Kangaroo

3 O My agèd Uncle Arly!
  Sitting on a heap of Barley
    Thro' the silent hours of night,—
  Close beside a leafy thicket:—
  On his nose there was a Cricket,—
  In his hat a Railway-Ticket;—
    (But his shoes were far too tight.)
      Ib. Incidents in the Life of my Aged Uncle Arly

4 Far and few, far and few,
  Are the lands where the Jumblies live;
  Their heads are green, and their hands are blue,
  And they went to sea in a Sieve.
      Ib. The Jumblies

5 In spite of all their friends could say,
  On a winter's morn, on a stormy day,
  In a Sieve they went to sea! *Ib.*

6 The Owl and the Pussy-Cat went to sea
  In a beautiful pea-green boat.
  They took some honey, and plenty of money,
  Wrapped up in a five-pound note.
  The Owl looked up to the Stars above
  And sang to a small guitar,
  'O lovely Pussy! O Pussy, my love,
  What a beautiful Pussy you are.'
      Ib. The Owl and the Pussy-Cat

7 Pussy said to the Owl, 'You elegant fowl!
  How charmingly sweet you sing!
  O let us be married! too long we have tarried:
  But what shall we do for a ring?'
  They sailed away for a year and a day,
  To the land where the Bong-tree grows,
  And there in a wood a Piggy-wig stood
  With a ring at the end of his nose.
      Ib.

8 'Dear Pig, are you willing to sell for one shilling
  Your ring?' Said the Piggy, 'I will'.
      Ib.

9 They dined on mince, and slices of quince,
    Which they ate with a runcible spoon;
  And hand in hand, on the edge of the sand,
  They danced by the light of the moon. *Ib.*

10 The Pobble who has no toes
   Had once as many as we;
   When they said, 'Some day you may lose them all';—
   He replied,—'Fish fiddle de-dee!'
       Nonsense Songs. The Pobble Who Has No Toes

11 His Aunt Jobiska made him drink
   Lavender water tinged with pink,
   For she said, 'The world in general knows
   There's nothing so good for a Pobble's toes!' *Ib.*

12 He has gone to fish, for his Aunt Jobiska's
   Runcible Cat with crimson whiskers! *Ib.*

13   It's a fact the whole world knows,
   That Pobbles are happier without their toes. *Ib.*

14 Who, or why, or which, or what,
   Is the Akond of Swat?
       Ib. 1888 edn. The Akond of Swat

15 There was an old man of Thermopylae,
   Who never did anything properly;
   But they said, 'If you choose
   To boil eggs in your shoes,
   You shall never remain in Thermopylae.'
       One Hundred Nonsense Pictures and Rhymes

MARY ELIZABETH LEASE
                                   1853–1933

16 Kansas had better stop raising corn and begin raising hell. **Attr.**

HENRY LEE 1756–1818

17 First in war, first in peace, first in the hearts of his fellow citizens.
       Resolution in the House of Representatives on the death of Washington, 26 Dec. 1799

NATHANIEL LEE 1653?–1692

18 When Greeks joined Greeks, then was the tug of war!
       The Rival Queens, IV. ii

CHARLES GODFREY LELAND
                                   1824–1903

19 Hans Breitmann gife a barty—
   Vhere ish dat barty now?
       Hans Breitmann's Party

WILLIAM LENTHALL 1591–1662

20 I have neither eye to see, nor tongue to speak here, but as the House is pleased to direct me.
       Rushworth's *Historical Collections, iv. 238*

SIR ROGER L'ESTRANGE
1616–1704

1 It is with our passions as it is with fire
and water, they are good servants, but
bad masters.
> *Æsop's Fables*, no. 38, *Reflection*

GEORGE LEVESON-GOWER, EARL GRANVILLE 1815–1891

2 Spheres of action.
> *Letter to Count Münster, 29 Apr.
1885* (Sir Edward Hertslet, *Map
of Africa by Treaty* (1894),
vol. ii, p. 596) (*see* 7:8)

DUC DE LÉVIS 1764–1830

3 Noblesse oblige.
> Nobility carries its obligations.
> *Maximes et réflexions*

GEORGE LEYBOURNE d. 1884

4 O, he flies through the air with the
greatest of ease,
This daring young man on the flying
trapeze.
> *The Man on the Flying Trapeze*

CHARLES-JOSEPH, PRINCE DE LIGNE 1735–1814

5 Le congrès ne marche pas, il danse.
> The Congress makes no progress;
but it dances.
> *Comment on the Congress of
Vienna to Comte Auguste de La
Garde-Chambonas*. La Garde-
Chambonas, *Souvenirs du Con-
grès de Vienne, 1814–1815*, ch. 1

ABRAHAM LINCOLN 1809–1865

6 The ballot is stronger than the bullet.
> *Speeches and Letters* (1907).
Speech, 19 May 1856

7 'A house divided against itself cannot
stand.' I believe this government
cannot endure permanently, half
slave and half free.
> *Ib. Speech, 16 June 1858*

8 Fourscore and seven years ago our
fathers brought forth upon this continent a new nation, conceived in
liberty, and dedicated to the pro-
position that all men are created equal.
Now we are engaged in a great civil
war, testing whether that nation, or
any nation so conceived and so dedicated, can long endure. We are met
on a great battlefield of that war.
We have come to dedicate a portion of
that field as a final resting-place of
those who here gave their lives that
that nation might live. It is altogether
fitting and proper that we should do
this. But in a larger sense we cannot
dedicate, we cannot consecrate, we
cannot hallow this ground. The brave
men, living and dead, who struggled
here, have consecrated it far above our
power to add or detract. The world
will little note, nor long remember,
what we say here, but it can never
forget what they did here. It is for us,
the living, rather to be dedicated here
to the unfinished work they have thus
far so nobly advanced. It is rather for
us to be here dedicated to the great
task remaining before us, that from
these honoured dead we take increased
devotion to that cause for which they
here gave the last full measure of
devotion; that we here highly resolve
that the dead shall not have died in
vain, that this nation, under God,
shall have a new birth of freedom;
and that government of the people,
by the people, and for the people,
shall not perish from the earth.
> *Address at Dedication of National
Cemetery at Gettysburg, 19 Nov.
1863*

9 With malice toward none; with
charity for all; with firmness in the
right, as God gives us to see the right.
> *Ib. Second Inaugural Address,
4 Mar. 1865*

10 You can fool all the people some of
the time, and some of the people all
the time, but you can not fool all the
people all of the time.
> *Attr. words in a speech at Clinton,
8 Sept. 1858*. N. W. Stephenson,
Autobiography of A. Lincoln
(1927). *Attr. also to Phineas
Barnum, 1810–91*

11 It is not best to swap horses while
crossing the river.
> *Reply to National Union League,
9 June 1864*. J. E. Nicolay and
J. Hay, *Abraham Lincoln*, bk. ix

12 People who like this sort of thing will
find this the sort of thing they like.
> *Judgement on a book*. G. W. E.
Russell, *Collections and Recollections*, ch. 30

GEORGE LINLEY 1798–1865

13 Among our ancient mountains,
And from our lovely vales,
Oh, let the prayer re-echo:
'God bless the Prince of Wales!'
> *Poems. God Bless the Prince of
Wales*

SIR THOMAS LITTLETON
1422–1481

14 [From] time whereof the memory of
man runneth not to the contrary.
> *Tenures* (?1481), § 170

LIVY 59 B.C.,–A.D. 17

1 Vae victis.

Woe to the vanquished.
History, v. xlviii. 9

MARIE LLOYD 1870–1922

2 A little of what you fancy does you
good. *Title of Song*

3 I'm one of the ruins that Cromwell
knocked about a bit. *Ib.*

4 Oh, mister porter, what shall I do?
Ib. (*words actually by* Thomas Le
Brunn)

ROBERT LLOYD 1733–1764

5 Slow and steady wins the race.
Poems. The Hare and the Tortoise

JOHN LOCKE 1632–1704

6 New opinions are always suspected,
and usually opposed, without any
other reason but because they are not
already common.
*Essay on the Human Under-
standing*, dedicatory epistle.

7 It is one thing to show a man that he
is in an error, and another to put him
in possession of truth.
Ib. bk. iv, ch. 7, sec. 11

8 All men are liable to error; and most
men are, in many points, by passion or
interest, under temptation to it.
Ib. ch. 20, sec. 17

**FREDERICK LOCKER-
LAMPSON** 1821–1895

9 If you lift a guinea-pig up by the tail
His eyes drop out! *A Garden Lyric*

THOMAS LODGE 1558?–1625

10 Devils are not so black as they are
painted. *A Margarite of America*

**JACK LONDON [JOHN
GRIFFITH LONDON]** 1876–1916

11 The Call of the Wild. *Title*

**HENRY WADSWORTH
LONGFELLOW** 1807–1882

12 I shot an arrow into the air,
It fell to earth, I knew not where.
The Arrow and the Song

13 Thou, too, sail on, O Ship of State!
Sail on, O Union, strong and great!
Humanity with all its fears,
With all the hopes of future years,
Is hanging breathless on thy fate!
The Building of the Ship

14 The bards sublime,
Whose distant footsteps echo
Through the corridors of Time.
The Day is Done

15 The cares that infest the day
Shall fold their tents, like the Arabs,
And as silently steal away. *Ib.*

16 This is the forest primeval.
Evangeline, introduction, l. 1

17 The shades of night were falling fast,
As through an Alpine village passed
A youth, who bore, 'mid snow and ice,
A banner with the strange device,
Excelsior! *Excelsior*

18 'O stay,' the maiden said, 'and rest
Thy weary head upon this breast!' *Ib.*

19 'Beware the pine-tree's withered
branch!
Beware the awful avalanche!' *Ib.*

20 A traveller, by the faithful hound,
Half-buried in the snow was found.
Ib.

21 I like that ancient Saxon phrase, which
calls
The burial-ground God's-Acre!
God's-Acre

22 The heights by great men reached and
kept
Were not attained by sudden flight,
But they, while their companions
slept,
Were toiling upward in the night.
The Ladder of Saint Augustine

23 Standing, with reluctant feet,
Where the brook and river meet,
Womanhood and childhood fleet!
Maidenhood

24 A boy's will is the wind's will,
And the thoughts of youth are long,
long thoughts. *My Lost Youth*

25 Listen, my children, and you shall hear
Of the midnight ride of Paul Revere,
On the eighteenth of April in Seventy-
five. *Paul Revere's Ride*

26 Tell me not, in mournful numbers,
Life is but an empty dream!
For the soul is dead that slumbers,
And things are not what they seem.

Life is real! Life is earnest!
And the grave is not its goal;
Dust thou art, to dust returnest,
Was not spoken of the soul.
A Psalm of Life

27 Lives of great men all remind us
We can make our lives sublime,
And, departing, leave behind us
Footprints on the sands of time. *Ib.*

28 Let us, then, be up and doing,
With a heart for any fate;
Still achieving, still pursuing,
Learn to labour and to wait. *Ib.*

1 There is no flock, however watched
      and tended,
    But one dead lamb is there!
  There is no fireside, howsoe'er de-
      fended,
    But has one vacant chair!
                              Resignation

2 Though the mills of God grind slowly,
      yet they grind exceeding small;
  Though with patience he stands wait-
      ing, with exactness grinds he all.
          *Retribution. From the Sinnge-
          dichte of Friedrich von Logau*

3 Beside the ungather'd rice he lay,
    His sickle in his hand.
                        The Slave's Dream

4 By the shores of Gitche Gumee,
    By the shining Big-Sea-Water,
    Stood the wigwam of Nokomis,
    Daughter of the Moon, Nokomis.
  Dark behind it rose the forest,
    Rose the black and gloomy pine-trees,
    Rose the firs with cones upon them;
  Bright before it beat the water,
    Beat the clear and sunny water,
    Beat the shining Big-Sea-Water.
          The Song of Hiawatha, iii. *Hia-
          watha's Childhood*

5 Ewa-yea! my little owlet!
  Who is this, that lights the wigwam?
  With his great eyes lights the wigwam?
                                      Ib.

6 From the waterfall he named her,
    Minnehaha, Laughing Water.
          Ib. iv. *Hiawatha and Mudje-
          keewis*

7 As unto the bow the cord is,
    So unto the man is woman;
  Though she bends him, she obeys him,
  Though she draws him, yet she
      follows;
  Useless each without the other!
                Ib. x. *Hiawatha's Wooing*

8 Onaway! Awake, beloved!
                Ib. xi. *Hiawatha's Wedding*

  Ships that pass in the night, and
      speak each other in passing;
  Only a signal shown and a distant
      voice in the darkness;
  So on the ocean of life we pass and
      speak one another,
  Only a look and a voice; then darkness
      again and a silence.
          Tales of a Wayside Inn, pt. III.
          The Theologian's Tale. Elizabeth,
          iv

0 Under the spreading chestnut tree
    The village smithy stands;
  The smith, a mighty man is he,
    With large and sinewy hands;
  And the muscles of his brawny arms
  Are strong as iron bands.
                    The Village Blacksmith

11 Something   attempted,   something
        done,
    Has earned a night's repose.
                      The Village Blacksmith

12 It was the schooner Hesperus,
      That sailed the wintry sea;
  And the skipper had taken his little
        daughter,
    To bear him company.
                  The Wreck of the Hesperus

13 But the father answered never a word,
    A frozen corpse was he.   *Ib.*

14 There was a little girl
    Who had a little curl
  Right in the middle of her forehead,
    When she was good
  She was very, very good,
  But when she was bad she was horrid.
          B. R. T. Machetta, *Home Life of
          Longfellow*

ANITA LOOS 1893–

15 Gentlemen Prefer Blondes.
                            Title of Novel

LOUIS XIV 1638–1715

16 Il n'y a plus de Pyrénées.
    The Pyrenees have ceased to exist.
          *At the accession of his grandson
          to the throne of Spain, 1700. Attr.
          by Voltaire in Siècle de Louis
          XIV, ch. 28*

17 L'État c'est moi.
    I am the State.
          *Attr. remark before the Parlement
          de Paris, 13 Apr. 1655. Dulaure,
          Histoire de Paris*

LOUIS XVIII 1755–1824

18 L'exactitude est la politesse des rois.
    Punctuality is the politeness of
        kings.   *Attr.*

RICHARD LOVELACE 1618–1658

19 Stone walls do not a prison make
      Nor iron bars a cage;
  Minds innocent and quiet take
      That for an hermitage;
  If I have freedom in my love,
      And in my soul am free;
  Angels alone, that soar above,
      Enjoy such liberty.
                      To Althea, From Prison

20 Tell me not (Sweet) I am unkind,
      That from the nunnery
  Of thy chaste breast, and quiet mind,
      To war and arms I fly.
  True; a new mistress now I chase,
      The first foe in the field;
  And with a stronger faith embrace
      A sword, a horse, a shield.

Yet this inconstancy is such,
  As you too shall adore;
I could not love thee (Dear) so much,
  Lov'd I not honour more.
        To Lucasta, Going to the Wars

JAMES RUSSELL LOWELL
                            1819–1891

1 You've a darned long row to hoe.
    The Biglow Papers, First Series,
    No. 1

2 I *don't* believe in princerple,
  But O, I *du* in interest.
    Ib. No. 6. *The Pious Editor's
    Creed*

3 Once to every man and nation comes
    the moment to decide,
In the strife of Truth with Falsehood,
    for the good or evil side.
                  The Present Crisis

4 New occasions teach new duties: Time
  makes ancient good uncouth;
They must upward still, and onward,
  who would keep abreast of Truth.
                           Ib.

LUCAN A.D. 39–65

5 Stat magni nominis umbra.
    There stands the shadow of a
    glorious name.   *Works*, i. 135

6 Nil actum credens, dum quid super-
esset agendum.
    Thinking nothing done while any-
    thing remained to be done.
                     Ib. ii. 657

LUCRETIUS 99–55 B.C.

7 Tantum religio potuit suadere malo-
rum.
    Such evil deeds could religion
    prompt.
    De Rerum Natura, i. 101. Trans.
    by Bailey

8   Nil posse creari
De nilo
    Nothing can be created out of
    nothing.   *Ib.* 155

9 Inque brevi spatio mutantur saecla
animantum
Et quasi cursores vitai lampada
tradunt.
    And in a short space the tribes of
    living things are changed, and like
    runners hand on the torch of life.
                   Ib. ii. 78

MARTIN LUTHER 1483–1546

10 Ich kann nicht anders.
    I can do no other.
    *Speech at the Diet of Worms,
    18 Apr. 1521. On his monument
    at Worms*

11 Wer nicht liebt Wein, Weib und
    Gesang,
Der bleibt ein Narr sein Leben lang.

    Who loves not woman, wine, and song
    Remains a fool his whole life long.
        *Attr. to Luther. Written in the
        Luther room in the Wartburg, but
        no proof exists of its authorship*

12 Ein feste Burg ist unser Gott,
Ein gute Wehr und Waffen.

    A safe stronghold our God is still,
    A trusty shield and weapon.
        Klug'sches Gesangbuch (1529),
        Ein feste Burg. Trans. by Car-
        lyle

JOHN LYLY 1554?–1606

13 CAMPASPE:
Were women never so fair, men would
    be false.

  APELLES:
Were women never so false, men
    would be fond.   *Campaspe*, III. iii

14 Cupid and my Campaspe play'd
At cards for kisses, Cupid paid; *Ib.* v

15 Night hath a thousand eyes.
         Maides Metamorphose, III. i

HENRY FRANCIS LYTE 1793–1847

16 Abide with me; fast falls the eventide;
The darkness deepens; Lord, with me
    abide;
When other helpers fail, and comforts
    flee,
Help of the helpless, O, abide with me.

Swift to its close ebbs out life's little
    day;
Earth's joys grow dim, its glories pass
    away;
Change and decay in all around I see;
O Thou, who changest not, abide with
    me.   *Remains. Abide with Me*

17 I fear no foe with Thee at hand to
    bless;
Ills have no weight, and tears no
    bitterness;
Where is death's sting? Where, grave,
    thy victory?
I triumph still, if Thou abide with me.

Hold Thou Thy Cross before my clos-
    ing eyes;
Shine through the gloom, and point
    me to the skies;
Heaven's morning breaks, and earth's
    vain shadows flee;
In life, in death, O Lord, abide with
    me.   *Ib.*

EDWARD GEORGE BULWER-LYTTON, BARON LYTTON 1803–1873

1 Here Stanley meets,—how Stanley
  scorns, the glance!
  The brilliant chief, irregularly great,
  Frank, haughty, rash,—the Rupert
  of Debate.
                The New Timon, pt. I. vi

2 Beneath the rule of men entirely great
  The pen is mightier than the sword.
                Richelieu, II. ii

3 Poverty has strange bedfellows.
                The Caxtons, pt. iv, ch. 4

4 There is no man so friendless but what
  he can find a friend sincere enough to
  tell him disagreeable truths.
                What Will He Do With It?, bk.
                iii, ch. 15 (heading)

THOMAS BABINGTON MACAULAY, BARON MACAULAY 1800–1859

5 Attend, all ye who list to hear our
  noble England's praise;
  I tell of the thrice famous deeds she
  wrought in ancient days.
                The Armada

6 And the red glare on Skiddaw roused
  the burghers of Carlisle.   *Ib.*

7 For God! for the Cause! for the
  Church! for the laws!
  For Charles King of England, and
  Rupert of the Rhine!
                The Battle of Naseby

8 Lars Porsena of Clusium
    By the nine gods he swore
  That the great house of Tarquin
    Should suffer wrong no more.
  By the Nine Gods he swore it,
    And named a trysting day,
  And bade his messengers ride forth,
    East and west and south and north,
  To summon his array.
                Lays of Ancient Rome. Horatius, i

9 Then out spake brave Horatius,
    The Captain of the Gate:
  'To every man upon this earth
    Death cometh soon or late.
  And how can man die better
    Than facing fearful odds,
  For the ashes of his fathers,
    And the temples of his Gods?'
                Ib. xxvii

10 To save them from false Sextus
    That wrought the deed of shame.
                Ib. xxviii

11 'Now who will stand on either hand,
    And keep the bridge with me?'
                Ib. xxix

12 Then none was for a party;
    Then all were for the state;
  Then the great man helped the poor,
    And the poor man loved the great;
  Then lands were fairly portioned;
    Then spoils were fairly sold:
  The Romans were like brothers
    In the brave days of old.
                Lays of Ancient Rome. Horatius,
                xxxi

13 Was none who would be foremost
    To lead such dire attack;
  But those behind cried 'Forward!'
    And those before cried 'Back!'
                Ib. l

14 'Oh, Tiber! father Tiber!
    To whom the Romans pray,
  A Roman's life, a Roman's arms,
    Take thou in charge this day!'
                Ib. lix

15 And even the ranks of Tuscany
    Could scarce forbear to cheer.
                Ib. lx

16 With weeping and with laughter
    Still is the story told,
  How well Horatius kept the bridge
    In the brave days of old.   *Ib.* lxx

17 Those trees in whose dim shadow
    The ghastly priest doth reign,
  The priest who slew the slayer,
    And shall himself be slain.
                Ib. The Battle of Lake Regillus, x

18 The business of everybody is the business of nobody.
                *Historical Essays Contributed to
                the 'Edinburgh Review'. Hallam's
                Constitutional History* (Sept.
                1828)

19 The gallery in which the reporters sit
  has become a fourth estate of the
  realm.   *Ib.*

20 Every schoolboy knows who imprisoned Montezuma, and who
  strangled Atahualpa.
                Ib. Lord Clive (Jan. 1840)

21 When some traveller from New
  Zealand shall, in the midst of a vast
  solitude, take his stand on a broken
  arch of London Bridge to sketch the
  ruins of St. Paul's.
                Ib. Von Ranke (Oct. 1840)

22 The great Proconsul.
                Ib. Warren Hastings (Oct. 1841)

23 We know no spectacle so ridiculous as
  the British public in one of its periodical fits of morality.
                *Literary Essays contributed to the
                'Edinburgh Review'. Moore's Life
                of Lord Byron* (June 1830)

24 He was a rake among scholars, and a
  scholar among rakes. [Richard Steele.]
                Ib. Aikin's Life of Addison (July
                1843)

1 The Puritan hated bear-baiting, not because it gave pain to the bear, but because it gave pleasure to the spectators.
History of England, vol. i, ch. 2

2 There were gentlemen and there were seamen in the navy of Charles the Second. But the seamen were not gentlemen; and the gentlemen were not seamen. *Ib.* ch. 3

3 The English Bible, a book which, if everything else in our language should perish, would alone suffice to show the whole extent of its beauty and power.
Edinburgh Review, Jan. 1828. *On John Dryden*

4 Thank you, madam, the agony is abated. [Reply, aged four.]
Trevelyan's *Life and Letters of Macaulay*, ch. 1

5 I shall not be satisfied unless I produce something which shall for a few days supersede the last fashionable novel on the tables of young ladies.
Ib. ch. 9

JOSEPH McCARTHY d. 1944

6 You made me love you,
I didn't want to do it.
You Made Me Love You

GEORGE McCLELLAN 1826–1885

7 All quiet along the Potomac.
Attr. in the American Civil War

JOHN McCRAE d. 1918

8 We shall not sleep, though poppies grow
In Flanders fields.
In Flanders Fields. (*Punch*, vol. cxlix, 8 Dec. 1915)

GEORGE MACDONALD 1824–1905

9 Where did you come from, baby dear?
Out of the everywhere into here.
At the Back of the North Wind, xxxiii, *Song*

CHARLES MACKAY 1814–1889

10 Cheer! Boys, cheer! *Title of Song*

11 There's a good time coming, boys,
A good time coming.
The Good Time Coming

SIR JAMES MACKINTOSH 1765–1832

12 The Commons, faithful to their system, remained in a wise and masterly inactivity. *Vindiciæ Gallicæ*, § 1

IRENE RUTHERFORD McLEOD 1891–

13 I'm a lean dog, a keen dog, a wild dog, and alone. *Lone Dog*, st. 1

MAURICE DE MACMAHON 1808–1893

14 J'y suis, j'y reste.
Here I am, and here I stay.
Attr. remark at the taking of the Malakoff, 8 Sept. 1855

LEONARD McNALLY 1752–1820

15 This lass so neat, with smiles so sweet,
Has won my right good-will,
I'd crowns resign to call thee mine,
Sweet lass of Richmond Hill.
The Lass of Richmond Hill. E. Duncan, *Minstrelsy of England* (1905), i. 254. Attr. also to W. Upton in *Oxford Song Book*, and to W. Hudson in Baring-Gould, *English Minstrelsie* (1895), iii. 54

MAURICE DE MAETERLINCK 1862–1949

16 Il n'y a pas de morts.
There are no dead.
L'Oiseau bleu, IV. ii

MAGNA CARTA 1215

17 Nisi per legale iudicium parium suorum vel per legem terrae.
Except by the legal judgement of his peers or the law of the land.
Clause 39

ALFRED THAYER MAHAN 1840–1914

18 Those far distant, storm-beaten ships, upon which the Grand Army never looked, stood between it and the dominion of the world.
The Influence of Sea Power upon the French Revolution and Empire, 1793–1812 (1892), ii. 118

FRANCIS SYLVESTER MAHONY
see FATHER PROUT

JOSEPH DE MAISTRE 1753–1821

19 Toute nation a le gouvernement qu'elle mérite.
Every country has the government it deserves.
Lettres et Opuscules Inédits, i, p. 215, 15 August 1811

SIR THOMAS MALORY *fl.* 1470

20 The questing beast.
Le Morte D'Arthur, bk. ix, ch. 12

F

THOMAS ROBERT MALTHUS
1766–1834

1 Population, when unchecked, increases in a geometrical ratio. Subsistence only increases in an arithmetical ratio.
The Principle of Population, 1

W. R. MANDALE *nineteenth century*

2 Up and down the City Road,
In and out the Eagle,
That's the way the money goes—
Pop goes the weasel!
Pop Goes the Weasel

MRS. MARY DE LA RIVIERE MANLEY 1663–1724

3 No time like the present.
The Lost Lover, IV. i

LORD JOHN MANNERS, DUKE OF RUTLAND 1818–1906

4 Let wealth and commerce, laws and learning die,
But leave us still our old nobility!
England's Trust, pt. III, l. 227

WILLIAM MURRAY, EARL OF MANSFIELD 1705–1793

5 Consider what you think justice requires, and decide accordingly. But never give your reasons; for your judgement will probably be right, but your reasons will certainly be wrong.
Advice. Campbell's *Lives of the Chief Justices* (1874), vol. iv, p. 26

RICHARD MANT 1776–1848

6 Bright the vision that delighted
Once the sight of Judah's seer.
Ancient Hymns. Bright the Vision

WILLIAM LEARNED MARCY
1786–1857

7 To the victor belong the spoils of the enemy.
Parton's *Life of Jackson* (1860), vol. iii, p. 378

MARIE-ANTOINETTE 1755–1793

8 Qu'ils mangent de la brioche.
Let them eat cake.
On being told that her people had no bread. Attr. to Marie-Antoinette, but much older. Rousseau refers in his Confessions, *1740, to a similar remark, as a well-known saying*

CHRISTOPHER MARLOWE
1564–1593

9 My men, like satyrs grazing on the lawns,
Shall with their goat feet dance an antic hay.   *Edward II,* I. i. 59

10 MEPHISTOPHELES:
O by aspiring pride and insolence,
For which God threw him from the face of heaven.   *Faustus,* l. 303

11 Why this is hell, nor am I out of it:
Thinkst thou that I who saw the face of God,
And tasted the eternal joys of heaven,
Am not tormented with ten thousand hells
In being deprived of everlasting bliss!
Ib. l. 312

12 Was this the face that launch'd a thousand ships,
And burnt the topless towers of Ilium?
Sweet Helen, make me immortal with a kiss!
Her lips suck forth my soul: see, where it flies!
Come Helen, come give me my soul again.
Here will I dwell, for heaven be in these lips,
And all is dross that is not Helena.
Ib. l. 1328

13 O thou art fairer than the evening air,
Clad in the beauty of a thousand stars,
Brighter art thou than flaming Jupiter,
When he appeared to hapless Semele,
More lovely than the monarch of the sky
In wanton Arethusa's azured arms,
And none but thou shalt be my paramour.   *Ib.* l. 1341

14 Now hast thou but one bare hour to live,
And then thou must be damned perpetually:
Stand still you ever-moving spheres of heaven,
That time may cease, and midnight never come.
Fair nature's eye, rise, rise again and make
Perpetual day, or let this hour be but
A year, a month, a week, a natural day,
That Faustus may repent and save his soul.
O lente, lente currite noctis equi:
The stars move still, time runs, the clock will strike,
The devil will come, and Faustus must be damn'd.
O I'll leap up to my God: who pulls me down?
See see where Christ's blood streams in the firmament.
One drop would save my soul, half a drop, ah my Christ.   *Ib.* l. 1420

1 O soul, be changed into little water
    drops,
  And fall into the ocean, ne'er be found:
  My God, my God, look not so fierce on
    me.   *Faustus*, l. 1472

2 Cut is the branch that might have
    grown full straight,
  And burnèd is Apollo's laurel bough,
  That sometimes grew within this
    learned man.   *Ib.* l. 1478

3 Who ever loved that loved not at first
    sight?
      Hero and Leander. First Sestiad,
      l. 176

4 I count religion but a childish toy,
  And hold there is no sin but ignorance.
      The Jew of Malta, l. 14

5 And as their wealth increases, so en-
    close
  Infinite riches in a little room. *Ib.* l. 71

6 Come live with me, and be my love,
  And we will all the pleasures prove,
  That valleys, groves, hills and fields,
  Woods or steepy mountain yields.
      *The Passionate Shepherd to his
      Love*

7 By shallow rivers, to whose falls
  Melodious birds sing madrigals. *Ib.*

8 Jigging veins of rhyming mother wits.
      Conquests of Tamburlaine, Pro-
      logue

9 Is it not passing brave to be a King,
  And ride in triumph through Perse-
    polis?   *Ib.* pt. I, l. 758

10 Nature that fram'd us of four ele-
    ments,
  Warring within our breasts for regi-
    ment,
  Doth teach us all to have aspiring
    minds:
  Our souls, whose faculties can com-
    prehend
  The wondrous Architecture of the
    world:
  And measure every wand'ring planet's
    course,
  Still climbing after knowledge infinite,
  And always moving as the restless
    Spheres,
  Will us to wear ourselves and never
    rest,
  Until we reach the ripest fruit of all,
  That perfect bliss and sole felicity,
  The sweet fruition of an earthly
    crown.   *Ib.* l. 869

11 What is beauty saith my sufferings
    then?
  If all the pens that ever poets held,
  Had fed the feeling of their masters'
    thoughts,
  And every sweetness that inspir'd
    their hearts,
  Their minds, and muses on admired
    themes: *Ib.* l. 1941

12 Now walk the angels on the walls of
    heaven,
  As sentinels to warn th' immortal
    souls,
  To entertain divine Zenocrate.
      Conquests of Tamburlaine,
      pt. II, l. 2983

13 Holla, ye pampered Jades of Asia:
  What, can ye draw but twenty miles
    a day?   *Ib.* l. 3980

14 Tamburlaine, the Scourge of God,
    must die.   *Ib.* l. 4641

15 I'm arm'd with more than complete
    steel—
  The justice of my quarrel.
      Lust's Dominion, IV. iii.
      (*Authorship doubtful*)

**DONALD ROBERT PERRY
MARQUIS** 1878–1937

16 toujours gai, archy, toujours gai.
      archy's life of mehitabel, i. *the
      life of mehitabel the cat*

FREDERICK MARRYAT 1792–1848

17 If you please, ma'am, it was a very
    little one. [The nurse excusing her ille-
    gitimate baby.]
      Midshipman Easy, ch. 3

18 As savage as a bear with a sore head.
      The King's Own, ch. 26

19 I never knows the children. It's just
    six of one and half-a-dozen of the
    other.   *The Pirate*, ch. 4

20 I think it much better that . . . every
    man paddle his own canoe.
      Settlers in Canada, ch. 8

21 I haven't the gift of the gab, my sons
    —because I'm bred to the sea.
      The Old Navy, st. 1

MARTIAL b. A.D. 43

22 Non amo te, Sabidi, nec possum dicere
    quare:
      Hoc tantum possum dicere, non
      amo te.

      I do not love you, Sabidius, and I
      can't say why. This only I can
      say, I do not love you.
        Epigrammata, I. xxxii. Trans.
        by Ker

23 Laudant illa sed ista legunt.
      Those they praise, but they read
      the others.   *Ib.* IV. xlix

24 Rus in urbe.
      The country in town.   *Ib.* XII. lvii

ANDREW MARVELL 1621–1678

25 Where the remote Bermudas ride
  In th' ocean's bosom unespied.
      Bermudas

1 Echo beyond the Mexique Bay.
                              Bermudas

2 My love is of a birth as rare
As 'tis for object strange and high:
It was begotten by despair
Upon impossibility. *Definition of Love*

3 All this fair, and soft, and sweet,
Which scatteringly doth shine,
Shall within one Beauty meet,
And she be only thine.
        *Dialogue between the Resolved
        Soul and Created Pleasure*

4 How vainly men themselves amaze
To win the palm, the oak, or bays;
                              The Garden

5 Fair quiet, have I found thee here,
And Innocence thy Sister dear!   *Ib.*

6 What wond'rous life is this I lead!
Ripe apples drop about my head;
The luscious clusters of the vine
Upon my mouth do crush their wine;
The nectarine and curious peach,
Into my hands themselves do reach;
Stumbling on melons, as I pass,
Insnar'd with flow'rs, I fall on grass.
                                      Ib.

7 Annihilating all that's made
To a green thought in a green shade.
                                      Ib.

8 [*Charles I*]
He nothing common did or mean
Upon that memorable scene:
    But with his keener eye
    The axe's edge did try.
        *Horatian Ode upon Cromwell's
        Return from Ireland*, l. 57

9 But bowed his comely head,
Down as upon a bed.   *Ib.*

10 Who can foretell for what high cause
This darling of the Gods was born?
                      The Picture of Little T.C.

11 Had we but world enough, and time,
This coyness, Lady, were no crime.
We would sit down, and think which
    way
To walk, and pass our long love's day.
Thou by the Indian Ganges' side
Shouldst rubies find: I by the tide
Of Humber would complain. I would
Love you ten years before the Flood:
And you should if you please refuse
Till the conversion of the Jews.
My vegetable love should grow
Vaster than empires, and more slow.
                      To His Coy Mistress

12 But at my back I always hear
Time's wingèd chariot hurrying near.
And yonder all before us lie
Deserts of vast eternity.
Thy beauty shall no more be found;
Nor, in thy marble vault, shall sound
My echoing song: then worms shall
try

That long preserved virginity:
And your quaint honour turn to dust;
And into ashes all my lust.
The grave's a fine and private place,
But none I think do there embrace.
                      To His Coy Mistress

13 Thrice happy he who, not mistook,
Hath read in Nature's mystic book.
        *Upon Appleton House. To My
        Lord Fairfax*, lxxiii

KARL MARX 1818–1883

14 Die Proletarier haben nichts in ihr
zu verlieren als ihre Ketten. Sie
haben eine Welt zu gewinnen.
Proletarier aller Länder, vereinigt
euch!

    The workers have nothing to lose in
    this [revolution] but their chains.
    They have a world to gain.
    Workers of the world, unite!
        The Communist Manifesto
        (1848), last words

15 Jeder nach seinen Fähigkeiten, jedem
nach seinen Bedürfnissen.

    From each according to his abilities,
    to each according to his needs.
        Criticism of the Gotha programme
        (1875) (*see 15:21*)

16 Die Religion . . . ist das Opium des
Volkes.

    Religion . . . is the opium of the
    people.
        *Kritik der Hegelschen Rechts-
        philosophie*, Introduction

17 The dictatorship of the proletariat.
        '*Used more than once*', *according
        to Mr. and Mrs. Sidney Webb*

MARY TUDOR 1516–1558

18 When I am dead and opened, you
shall find 'Calais' lying in my heart.
        Holinshed, *Chron.* iii. 1160

JOHN MASEFIELD 1878–1967

19 Coming in solemn beauty like slow old
tunes of Spain.   *Beauty*

20 Quinquereme of Nineveh from distant
Ophir
Rowing home to haven in sunny Pales-
tine,
With a cargo of ivory,
And apes and peacocks,
Sandalwood, cedarwood, and sweet
white wine.   *Cargoes*

21 Dirty British coaster with a salt-
caked smoke stack,
Butting through the Channel in the
mad March days,
With a cargo of Tyne coal,
Road-rail, pig-lead,
Firewood, iron-ware, and cheap tin
trays.   *Ib.*

1 Oh some are fond of Spanish wine, and
   some are fond of French,
And some'll swallow tay and stuff fit
   only for a wench.
            Captain Stratton's Fancy

2 I must down to the seas again, to the
   lonely sea and the sky,
And all I ask is a tall ship and a star
   to steer her by,
And the wheel's kick and the wind's
   song and the white sail's shaking,
And a grey mist on the sea's face and
   a grey dawn breaking.   *Sea Fever*

3 I must down to the seas again, for the
   call of the running tide
Is a wild call and a clear call that may
   not be denied.   *Ib.*

4 I must down to the seas again, to the
   vagrant gypsy life,
To the gull's way and the whale's way
   where the wind's like a whetted
   knife;
And all I ask is a merry yarn from a
   laughing fellow-rover,
And quiet sleep and a sweet dream
   when the long trick's over.   *Ib.*

5 Friends and loves we have none, nor
   wealth nor blessed abode,
But the hope of the City of God at the
   other end of the road.   *The Seekers*

6 It's a warm wind, the west wind, full
   of birds' cries;
I never hear the west wind but tears
   are in my eyes.
For it comes from the west lands, the
   old brown hills,
And April's in the west wind, and
   daffodils.   *The West Wind*

WALT MASON 1862–1939

7 He's the Man Who Delivers the Goods.
   The Man Who Delivers the Goods

PHILIP MASSINGER 1583–1640

8 He that would govern others, first
   should be
The master of himself.
          The Bondman, I. iii

9   I am driven
Into a desperate strait and cannot
   steer
A middle course.
        Great Duke of Florence, III. i

10 A New Way to Pay Old Debts.
             Title of Play

11 What pity 'tis, one that can speak so
   well,
Should in his actions be so ill!
        Parliament of Love, III. iii

12 There are a thousand doors to let out
   life.   *Ib.* IV. ii

13   Serves and fears
The fury of the many-headed monster,
The giddy multitude.
       The Unnatural Combat, III. ii

CHARLES ROBERT MATURIN
1782–1824

14 'Tis well to be merry and wise,
'Tis well to be honest and true;
'Tis well to be off with the old love,
Before you are on with the new.
          Bertram. Motto

GEORGE LOUIS PALMELLA
BUSSON DU MAURIER 1834–1896

15 Life ain't all beer and skittles, and
   more's the pity; but what's the odds,
   so long as you're happy?
          Trilby, pt. 1

TERENTIANUS MAURUS
fl. c. A.D. 200

16 Pro captu lectoris habent sua fata
   libelli.
    The fate of books depends on the
    capacity of the reader.
    De Literis, Syllabis, &c., l. 1286

HUGHES MEARNS 1875–

17 As I was going up the stair
I met a man who wasn't there.
He wasn't there again to-day.
I wish, I wish he'd stay away.
      The Psychoed (Antigonish)

WILLIAM LAMB, VISCOUNT
MELBOURNE 1779–1848

18 I wish I was as cocksure of anything
   as Tom Macaulay is of everything.
    Earl Cowper's *Preface to Lord
    Melbourne's Papers* (1889), p. xii

19 I like the Garter; there is no damned
   merit in it.
      On the Order of the Garter

20 Things have come to a pretty pass
   when religion is allowed to invade the
   sphere of private life.
    *Remark on hearing an Evangelical
    Sermon.* G. W. E. Russell's
    Collections and Recollections, ch. 6

THOMAS MELLOR 1880–1926

21 I wouldn't leave my little wooden hut
   for you!
I've got one lover and I don't want
   two.
    *I Wouldn't Leave My Little
    Wooden Hut for You*

GEORGE MEREDITH 1828–1909

1 On a starred night Prince Lucifer up-
   rose.
   Tired of his dark dominion swung the
   fiend . . .
   He reached a middle height, and at
   the stars,
   Which are the brain of heaven, he
   looked, and sank.
   Around the ancient track marched,
   rank on rank,
   The army of unalterable law.
                    Lucifer in Starlight

2 Not till the fire is dying in the grate,
   Look we for any kinship with the
   stars.   *Modern Love, iv*

3 And if I drink oblivion of a day,
   So shorten I the stature of my soul.
                            Ib. xii

4   In tragic life, God wot,
   No villain need be! Passions spin the
   plot:
   We are betrayed by what is false
   within.   *Ib. xliii*

5 We saw the swallows gathering in the
   sky.   *Ib. xlvii*

6 The pilgrims of the year waxed very
   loud
   In multitudinous chatterings.   *Ib.*

7 Ah, what a dusty answer gets the soul
   When hot for certainties in this our
   life!   *Ib.*

8 Enter these enchanted woods,
           You who dare.
                The Woods of Westermain

9 Men may have rounded Seraglio Point:
   they have not yet doubled Cape Turk.
                Diana of the Crossways, ch. 1

10 You see he has a leg.
                    The Egoist, ch. 2

11 A dainty rogue in porcelain. *Ib. ch. 5*

12 I expect that Woman will be the last
   thing civilized by Man.
           The Ordeal of Richard Feverel,
           ch. 1

**OWEN MEREDITH [EDWARD
ROBERT BULWER, EARL OF
LYTTON]** 1831–1891

13 Genius does what it must, and Talent
   does what it can.
           Poems. Last words of a Sensitive
           Second-rate Poet

DIXON LANIER MERRITT 1879–

14 A wonderful bird is the pelican,
   His bill will hold more than his belican.
   He can take in his beak
   Food enough for a week,
   But I'm damned if I see how the
   helican.   *The Pelican*

JEAN MESSELIER
                    eighteenth century

15 Je voudrais, et ce sera le dernier et le
   plus ardent de mes souhaits, je
   voudrais que le dernier des rois fût
   étranglé avec les boyaux du dernier
   prêtre.

   I should like to see, and this will be
       the last and the most ardent of
       my desires, I should like to see
       the last king strangled with the
       guts of the last priest.
           In his Will, 1733, published by
           Voltaire

PRINCE METTERNICH 1773–1859

16 Italien ist ein geographischer Begriff.
   Italy is a geographical expression.
                Letter, 19 Nov. 1849

HUGO MEYNELL 1727–1808

17 The chief advantage of London is,
   that a man is always so near his
   burrow.
           Boswell's Johnson (ed. 1934),
           vol. iii, p. 379, 1 Apr. 1779

THOMAS MIDDLETON
                    1570?–1627

18 By many a happy accident.
           No Wit, No Help, Like a
           Woman's, IV. i. 66

19 Though I be poor, I'm honest.
                The Witch, III. ii

ALBERT MIDLANE 1825–1909

20 There's a Friend for little children
   Above the bright blue sky
           Good News for the Little Ones

JOHN STUART MILL 1806–1873

21 Unearned increment.
           Dissertations and Discussions, vol.
           iv, p. 299

22 The liberty of the individual must be
   thus far limited; he must not make
   himself a nuisance to other people.
                Liberty, ch. 3

23 The worth of a State, in the long run,
   is the worth of the individuals com-
   posing it.   *Ib.*

24 When the land is cultivated entirely
   by the spade and no horses are kept,
   a cow is kept for every three acres of
   land.
           Political Economy. A Treatise on
           Flemish Husbandry

EDNA ST. VINCENT MILLAY
1892–1950

1 My candle burns at both ends;
  It will not last the night;
  But oh, my foes, and oh, my friends—
  It gives a lovely light.   *Poems* (1923)

ALICE DUER MILLER 1874–1942

2 I am American bred,
  I have seen much to hate here—much
    to forgive,
  But in a world where England is
    finished and dead,
  I do not wish to live.
        The White Cliffs (1940)

MRS. EMILY MILLER 1833–1913

3 I love to hear the story
  Which angel voices tell.
        The Little Corporal. I Love to Hear

WILLIAM MILLER 1810–1872

4 Wee Willie Winkie
  Rins through the town,
  Upstairs and doon stairs
  In his nicht-gown,
  Tirling at the window,
  Crying at the lock,
  'Are the weans in their bed,
  For it's now ten o'clock?'
        Willie Winkie

A. J. MILLS

5 Just like the ivy I'll cling to you.
        Title of Song

REV. HENRY HART MILMAN
1791–1868

6 Ride on! ride on in majesty!
  In lowly pomp ride on to die.
        Hymns. Ride On!

ALAN ALEXANDER MILNE
1882–1956

7 They're changing guard at Bucking-
    ham Palace—
  Christopher Robin went down with
    Alice.
        *When We Were Very Young.
        Buckingham Palace*

8 John had
  Great Big
  Waterproof
  Boots on;
  John had a
  Great Big
  Waterproof
  Hat;
  John had a
  Great Big
  Waterproof
  Mackintosh.
  And that
  (Said John)
  Is That.   *Ib. Happiness*

9 James James
  Morrison Morrison
  Weatherby George Dupree
  Took great
  Care of his Mother
  Though he was only three.
        *When We Were Very Young.
        Disobedience*

10 You must never go down to the end of
  the town if you don't go down with
  me.   *Ib.*

11 *What* is the matter with Mary Jane?
  She's crying with all her might and
    main,
  And she won't eat her dinner—rice
    pudding again—
  What *is* the matter with Mary Jane?
        Ib. Rice Pudding

12 *What* is the matter with Mary Jane?
  She's perfectly well and she hasn't a
    pain
  And it's lovely rice pudding for dinner
    again!
  What *is* the matter with Mary Jane?
        Ib.

13 The King asked
  The Queen, and
  The Queen asked
  The Dairymaid:
  'Could we have some butter for
  The Royal slice of bread?'
        Ib. The King's Breakfast

14 I do like a little bit of butter to my
  bread!   *Ib.*

15 Little Boy kneels at the foot of the
    bed,
  Droops on the little hands, little gold
    head;
  Hush! Hush! Whisper who dares!
  Christopher Robin is saying his
    prayers.   *Ib. Vespers*

16 Isn't it funny
  How a bear likes honey?
  Buzz! Buzz! Buzz!
  I wonder why he does?
        Winnie-the-Pooh, ch. 1

17 I am a Bear of Very Little Brain, and
  long words Bother me.   *Ib.* ch. 4

18 Time for a little something.   *Ib.* ch. 6

ALFRED, LORD MILNER
1854–1925

19 [*The Peers and the Budget*] If we believe
  a thing to be bad, and if we have a
  right to prevent it, it is our duty to
  try to prevent it and to damn the
  consequences.
        Speech at Glasgow, 26 Nov. 1909

JOHN MILTON 1608–1674

20 What hath night to do with sleep?
        Comus, l. 122

1 Come, knit hands, and beat the ground,
In a light fantastic round. *Comus*, l. 143

2 How charming is divine philosophy!
Not harsh, and crabbed as dull fools suppose,
But musical as is Apollo's lute,
And a perpetual feast of nectared sweets,
Where no crude surfeit reigns.
Ib. l. 476

3 Sabrina fair,
Listen where thou art sitting
Under the glassy, cool, translucent wave,
In twisted braids of lilies knitting
The loose train of thy amber-dropping hair. *Ib.* l. 859

4 Hence, vain deluding joys,
The brood of Folly without father bred. *Il Penseroso*, l. 1

5 Hail divinest Melancholy. *Ib.* l. 12

6 Sweet bird, that shunn'st the noise of folly,
Most musical, most melancholy!
Ib. l. 61

7 Where glowing embers through the room
Teach light to counterfeit a gloom,
Far from all resort of mirth,
Save the cricket on the hearth.
Ib. l. 79

8 Sometime let gorgeous Tragedy
In sceptred pall come sweeping by,
Presenting Thebes, or Pelops' line,
Or the tale of Troy divine. *Ib.* l. 97

9 With antique pillars massy proof,
And storied windows richly dight,
Casting a dim religious light.
There let the pealing organ blow,
To the full-voiced quire below,
In service high, and anthems clear
As may, with sweetness, through mine ear,
Dissolve me into ecstasies,
And bring all Heaven before mine eyes. *Ib.* l. 158

10 Hence, loathed Melancholy,
Of Cerberus, and blackest Midnight born,
In Stygian cave forlorn,
'Mongst horrid shapes, and shrieks, and sights unholy.
L'Allegro, l. 1

11 So buxom, blithe, and debonair.
Ib. l. 24

12 Haste thee Nymph, and bring with thee
Jest and youthful jollity,
Quips and cranks, and wanton wiles,
Nods, and becks, and wreathed smiles.
Ib. l. 25

13 Sport that wrinkled Care derides,
And Laughter holding both his sides.
Come, and trip it as ye go
On the light fantastic toe.
L'Allegro, l. 31

14 Meadows trim with daisies pied,
Shallow brooks and rivers wide.
Towers, and battlements it sees
Bosom'd high in tufted trees,
Where perhaps some beauty lies,
The cynosure of neighbouring eyes.
Ib. l. 75

15 Of herbs, and other country messes,
Which the neat-handed Phyllis dresses. *Ib.* l. 85

16 To many a youth, and many a maid,
Dancing in the chequered shade.
And young and old come forth to play
On a sunshine holiday. *Ib.* l. 95

17 Then to the spicy nut-brown ale.
Ib. l. 100

18 Towered cities please us then,
And the busy hum of men. *Ib.* l. 117

19 And pomp, and feast, and revelry,
With mask, and antique pageantry,
Such sights as youthful poets dream,
On summer eves by haunted stream.
Then to the well-trod stage anon,
If Jonson's learnèd sock be on,
Or sweetest Shakespeare, Fancy's child,
Warble his native wood-notes wild,
And ever against eating cares,
Lap me in soft Lydian airs,
Married to immortal verse
Such as the meeting soul may pierce
In notes, with many a winding bout
Of linked sweetness long drawn out.
Ib. l. 127

20 Yet once more, O ye laurels, and once more
Ye myrtles brown, with ivy never sere,
I come to pluck your berries harsh and crude,
And with forc'd fingers rude,
Shatter your leaves before the mellowing year.
Bitter constraint and sad occasion dear
Compels me to disturb your season due,
For Lycidas is dead, dead ere his prime,
Young Lycidas and hath not left his peer.
Who would not sing for Lycidas? he knew
Himself to sing and build the lofty rhyme.
He must not float upon his watery bier
Unwept, and welter to the parching wind
Without the meed of some melodious tear. *Lycidas*, l. 1

21 Whom universal Nature did lament.
Ib. l. 60

1 Alas! what boots it with uncessant care
  To tend the homely, slighted, shep-
    herd's trade,
  And strictly meditate the thankless
    Muse?
Were it not better done, as others use,
To sport with Amaryllis in the shade,
Or with the tangles of Neæra's hair.
Fame is the spur that the clear spirit
    doth raise
(That last infirmity of noble mind)
To scorn delights, and live laborious
    days;
But the fair guerdon when we hope
    to find,
And think to burst out into sudden
    blaze,
Comes the blind Fury with th' ab-
    horred shears
And slits the thin-spun life.
                  Lycidas, 1. 64

2 Last came, and last did go,
The Pilot of the Galilean lake,
Two massy keys he bore of metals
    twain,
The golden opes, the iron shuts amain.
                  Ib. 1. 108

3   Their lean and flashy songs
Grate on their scrannel pipes of
    wretched straw,
The hungry sheep look up, and are not
    fed,
But, swoln with wind and the rank
    mist they draw,
Rot inwardly and foul contagion
    spread;
Besides what the grim wolf with privy
    paw
Daily devours apace, and nothing
    said.
But that two-handed engine at the
    door
Stands ready to smite once, and smite
    no more.   *Ib.* 1. 123

4 For Lycidas your sorrow is not dead,
Sunk though he be beneath the watery
    floor;
So sinks the day-star in the ocean bed,
And yet anon repairs his drooping
    head,
And tricks his beams, and with new
    spangled ore,
Flames in the forehead of the morning
    sky:
So Lycidas sunk low, but mounted
    high,
Through the dear might of Him that
    walked the waves.   *Ib.* 1. 166

5 At last he rose, and twitch'd his
    mantle blue;
To-morrow to fresh woods, and
    pastures new.   *Ib.* 1. 192

6 This is the month, and this the happy
    morn,
Wherein the Son of Heaven's eternal
    King,

Of wedded maid, and virgin mother
    born,
Our great redemption from above did
    bring;
For so the holy sages once did sing,
That He our deadly forfeit should
    release,
And with His Father work us a per-
    petual peace.
        Hymn. On the Morning of
        Christ's Nativity, 1. 1

7 It was the winter wild
  While the Heav'n-born child
All meanly wrapt in the rude manger
    lies,
  Nature in awe to him
  Had doff't her gawdy trim
With her great Master so to sympa-
    thize.   *Ib.* 1. 29

8 Time will run back, and fetch the age
    of gold.   *Ib.* 1. 135

9 Of Man's first disobedience, and the
    fruit
Of that forbidden tree, whose mortal
    taste
Brought death into the world, and all
    our woe,
With loss of Eden.
        Paradise Lost, bk. i, 1. 1

10 Things unattempted yet in prose or
    rhyme.   *Ib.* 1. 16

11   What in me is dark
Illumine, what is low raise and support;
That to the height of this great argu-
    ment
I may assert eternal Providence,
And justify the ways of God to Men.
                  Ib. 1. 22

12   Him the Almighty Power
Hurled headlong flaming from th'
    ethereal sky
With hideous ruin and combustion
    down
To bottomless perdition, there to
    dwell
In adamantine chains and penal fire
Who durst defy th' Omnipotent to
    arms.   *Ib.* 1. 44

13 No light, but rather darkness visible.
                  Ib. 1. 62

14   But O how fall'n! how changed
From him who, in the happy realms of
    light,
Clothed with transcendent brightness
    didst outshine
Myriads though bright.   *Ib.* 1, 84

15   What though the field be lost?
All is not lost; th' unconquerable will,
And study of revenge, immortal hate,
And courage never to submit or yield:
And what is else not to be overcome?
                  Ib. 1. 105

1 Fall'n Cherub, to be weak is miserable
Doing or suffering; but of this be sure,
To do aught good never will be our task,
But ever to do ill our sole delight.
                    Paradise Lost, bk. i, l. 157

2 The mind is its own place, and in it self
Can make a Heav'n of Hell, a Hell of Heav'n.   *Ib.* l. 254

3 Here we may reign secure, and in my choice
To reign is worth ambition though in hell:
Better to reign in hell, than serve in heav'n.   *Ib.* l. 261

4 Thick as autumnal leaves that strow the brooks
In Vallombrosa, where th' Etrurian shades
High over-arch'd imbower.   *Ib.* l. 302

5   And when night
Darkens the streets, then wander forth the sons
Of Belial, flown with insolence and wine.   *Ib.* l. 500

6 A shout that tore hell's concave, and beyond
Frighted the reign of Chaos and old Night.   *Ib.* l. 542

7   Who overcomes
By force, hath overcome but half his foe.   *Ib.* l. 648

8   Let none admire
That riches grow in hell; that soil may best
Deserve the precious bane.   *Ib.* l. 690

9   From morn
To noon he fell, from noon to dewy eve,
A summer's day; and with the setting sun
Dropt from the zenith like a falling star.   *Ib.* l. 742

10 Satan exalted sat, by merit raised
To that bad eminence;   *Ib.* bk. ii, l. 5

11 But all was false and hollow; though his tongue
Dropt manna, and could make the worse appear
The better reason.   *Ib.* l. 112

12 Who shall tempt with wand'ring feet
The dark unbottom'd infinite abyss
And through the palpable obscure find out
His uncouth way.   *Ib.* l. 404

13 With ruin upon ruin, rout on rout
Confusion worse confounded.
                            Ib. l. 995

14 So farewell hope, and with hope farewell fear,
Farewell remorse: all good to me is lost;
Evil be thou my Good.   *Ib.* bk. iv, l. 108

15 A heaven on earth.
            Paradise Lost, bk. iv, l. 208

16 For contemplation he and valour formed;
For softness she and sweet attractive grace,
He for God only, she for God in him:
His fair large front and eye sublime declared
Absolute rule.   *Ib.* l. 297

17 Adam, the goodliest man of men since born
His sons; the fairest of her daughters Eve.   *Ib.* l. 323

18 But wherefore thou alone? Wherefore with thee
Came not all hell broke loose?
                            Ib. l. 917

19 Hear all ye Angels, progeny of light,
Thrones, Dominations, Princedoms, Virtues, Powers.   *Ib.* bk. v, l. 600

20 Standing on earth, not rapt above the Pole,
More safe I sing with mortal voice, unchang'd
To hoarse or mute, though fall'n on evil days,
On evil days though fall'n, and evil tongues.
In darkness, and with dangers compass'd round,
And solitude; yet not alone, while thou
Visit'st my slumbers nightly, or when morn
Purples the east: still govern thou my song,
Urania, and fit audience find, though few:
But drive far off the barb'rous dissonance
Of Bacchus and his revellers.
                            Ib. bk. vii, l. 23

21 The sum of earthly bliss.
                    Ib. bk. viii, l. 522

22 As one who long in populous city pent,
Where houses thick and sewers annoy the air,
Forth issuing on a summer's morn to breathe
Among the pleasant villages and farms
Adjoin'd, from each thing met conceives delight.   *Ib.* bk. ix, l. 445

23 She fair, divinely fair, fit love for Gods.   *Ib.* l. 489

24 Demoniac frenzy, moping melancholy,
And moon-struck madness.
                    Ib. bk. xi, l. 485

25 The world was all before them, where to choose
Their place of rest, and Providence their guide:

They hand in hand with wandering
steps and slow
Through Eden took their solitary way.
Paradise Lost, bk. xii, l. 646

1 Of whom to be dispraised were no
small praise.
Paradise Regained, bk. iii, l. 56

2 Eyeless in Gaza, at the mill with
slaves.   *Samson Agonistes*, l. 41

3 O dark, dark, dark, amid the blaze
of noon,
Irrecoverably dark, total eclipse
Without all hope of day!   *Ib.* l. 80

4 To live a life half dead, a living death.
Ib. l. 100

5 But who is this, what thing of sea or
land?
Female of sex it seems,
That so bedeck'd, ornate, and gay,
Comes this way sailing
Like a stately ship
Of Tarsus, bound for th' isles
Of Javan or Gadier,
With all her bravery on, and tackle
trim,
Sails fill'd, and streamers waving,
Courted by all the winds that hold
them play,
An amber scent of odorous perfume
Her harbinger.   *Ib.* l. 710

6 O how comely it is, and how reviving
To the spirits of just men long opprest,
When God into the hands of their
deliverer
Puts invincible might,
To quell the mighty of the earth, th'
oppressor.   *Ib.* l. 1268

7 He's gone, and who knows how he may
report
Thy words by adding fuel to the
flame?   *Ib.* l. 1350

8 For evil news rides post, while good
news baits.   *Ib.* l. 1538

9   Samson hath quit himself
Like Samson, and heroically hath
finish'd
A life heroic.   *Ib.* l. 1709

10 Nothing is here for tears, nothing to
wail
Or knock the breast; no weakness, no
contempt,
Dispraise or blame; nothing but well
and fair,
And what may quiet us in a death so
noble.   *Ib.* l. 1721

11 His servants he with new acquist
Of true experience from this great
event
With peace and consolation hath dis-
miss'd,
And calm of mind all passion spent.
Ib. l. 1755

12 What needs my Shakespeare for his
honour'd bones,
The labour of an age in piled stones,
Or that his hallow'd relics should be
hid
Under a star-y-pointing pyramid?
Dear son of memory, great heir of
fame,
What need'st thou such weak witness
of thy name?
[Epitaph] on Shakespeare

13 Blest pair of Sirens, pledges of
Heaven's joy,
Sphere-born harmonious sisters, Voice
and Verse.   *At a Solemn Music*

14 Where the bright Seraphim in burning
row
Their loud up-lifted Angel trumpets
blow.   *Ib.*

15 All is, if I have grace to use it so,
As ever in my great Task-Master's eye.
*Sonnet ii. On his having arrived
at the age of twenty-three*

16 Avenge, O Lord, thy slaughtered
saints, whose bones
Lie scattered on the Alpine mountains
cold;
Ev'n them who kept thy truth so pure
of old,
When all our fathers worshipped
stocks and stones,
Forget not. In thy book record their
groans
Who were thy sheep, and in their
ancient fold
Slain by the bloody Piedmontese, that
rolled
Mother with infant down the rocks.
Ib. xv. *On the late Massacre in
Piedmont*

17 When I consider how my light is spent,
E're half my days, in this dark world
and wide,
And that one Talent which is death
to hide,
Lodg'd with me useless, though my
Soul more bent
To serve therewith my Maker, and
present
My true account, lest He returning
chide;
'Doth God exact day-labour, light
deny'd?'
I fondly ask; But Patience, to prevent
That murmur, soon replies, 'God doth
not need
Either man's work or his own gifts.
Who best
Bear his mild yoke, they serve him
best, his State
Is Kingly. Thousands at his bidding
speed
And post o'er Land and Ocean without
rest:
They also serve who only stand and
wait.'   *Ib.* xvi. *On His Blindness*

1 Methought I saw my late espousèd
Saint
Brought to me like Alcestis from the
grave.
    Sonnet xix. *On His Deceased Wife*

2 But O as to embrace me she inclined,
I waked, she fled, and day brought
back my night.   *Ib.*

3 New Presbyter is but old Priest writ
large.
    Ib. On the New Forcers of Con-
    science under the Long Parliament

4 For what can war but endless war still
breed?
    Ib. On the Lord General Fairfax

5   Peace hath her victories
No less renowned than war.
    Ib. [To the Lord General Crom-
    well, May 1652]

6 Fly, envious Time, till thou run out
thy race:
Call on the lazy leaden-stepping
hours.   *On Time,* l. 1

7 As good almost kill a man as kill a
good book: who kills a man kills a
reasonable creature, God's image;
but he who destroys a good book, kills
reason itself, kills the image of God,
as it were in the eye.   *Areopagitica*

8 A good book is the precious life-blood
of a master spirit, embalmed and
treasured up on purpose to a life
beyond life.   *Ib.*

9 I cannot praise a fugitive and clois-
tered virtue, unexercised and un-
breathed, that never sallies out and
sees her adversary, but slinks out of
the race, where that immortal garland
is to be run for, not without dust and
heat. Assuredly we bring not innocence into the world, we bring im-
purity much rather: that which puri-
fies us is trial, and trial is by what is
contrary.   *Ib.*

10 Methinks I see in my mind a noble
and puissant nation rousing herself
like a strong man after sleep, and
shaking her invincible locks. Methinks
I see her as an eagle mewing her
mighty youth, and kindling her un-
dazzled eyes at the full midday beam.
        Ib.

11 Let not England forget her prece-
dence of teaching nations how to live.
    The Doctrine and Discipline of
    Divorce

MISSAL

12 O felix culpa, quae talem ac tantum
meruit habere Redemptorem.

    O happy fault, which has deserved
    to have such and so mighty a
    Redeemer.
        'Exsultet' on Holy Saturday

EMILIO MOLA d. 1936

13 La quinta columna.

    The fifth column.
        Radio Address given when a
        General in the Spanish Civil
        War, 1936–1939

JEAN BAPTISTE POQUELIN,
called MOLIÈRE 1622–1673

14 Il faut manger pour vivre et non pas
vivre pour manger.

    One should eat to live, not live to
    eat.   *L'Avare,* III. v

15 M. JOURDAIN: Quoi? quand je dis:
'Nicole, apportez-moi mes pantoufles,
et me donnez mon bonnet de nuit',
c'est de la prose?
MAÎTRE DE PHILOSOPHIE: Oui, mon-
sieur.
M. JOURDAIN: Par ma foi! il y a plus
de quarante ans que je dis de la prose
sans que j'en susse rien.

    M. JOURDAIN: What? when I say:
    'Nicole, bring me my slippers, and
    give me my night-cap,' is that
    prose?
    PROFESSOR OF PHILOSOPHY: Yes, Sir.
    M. JOURDAIN: Good Heavens! For
    more than forty years I have been
    speaking prose without knowing
    it.
        Le Bourgeois Gentilhomme, II. iv

16 Tout ce qui n'est point prose est vers;
et tout ce qui n'est point vers est prose.

    All that is not prose is verse; and
    all that is not verse is prose.   *Ib.*

17 Que diable allait-il faire dans cette
galère?

    What the devil was he doing in that
    galley?
        Les Fourberies de Scapin, II. vii

18 Vous l'avez voulu, Georges Dandin,
vous l'avez voulu.

    You asked for it, George Dandin,
    you asked for it.
        Georges Dandin, I. ix

19 Oui, cela était autrefois ainsi, mais
nous avons changé tout cela.

    Yes, it used to be so, but we have
    changed all that.
        Le Médecin malgré lui, II. vi. *Said*
        by the pretended doctor to justify
        his mistake as to the relative
        positions of heart and liver.

20 Ils commencent ici [Paris] par faire
pendre un homme et puis ils lui font
procès.

    Here, in Paris, they hang a man first,
    and try him afterwards.
        Monsieur de Pourceaugnac, III. ii

**JOHN SAMUEL BEWLEY MON-
SELL** 1811–1875

1 Fight the good fight with all thy might,
  Christ is thy strength, and Christ thy
  right;
  Lay hold on life, and it shall be
  Thy joy and crown eternally.

  Run the straight race through God's
  good grace,
  Lift up thine eyes, and seek His Face;
  Life with its way before us lies,
  Christ is the path, and Christ the
  prize.
  *Hymns of Love and Praise. Fight
  of Faith*

MICHEL EYQUEM MONTAIGNE
1533–1592

2 [*Of his friend, Étienne de la Boétie*]
  Si l'on me presse de dire pourquoi je
  l'aimais, je sens que cela ne se peut
  exprimer qu'en répondant, Parce que
  c'était lui; parce que c'était moi.

  If you press me to say why I loved
  him, I can say no more than it
  was because he was he and I was
  I.   *Essais*, I. xxviii

3 La plus grande chose du monde c'est
  de savoir être à soi.

  The greatest thing in the world is
  to know how to be sufficient unto
  oneself.   *Ib.* xxxix

4 Que sais-je?
  What do I know?   *Ib.* II. xii

ROBERT MONTGOMERY
1807–1855

5 The soul aspiring pants its source to
  mount,
  As streams meander level with their
  fount.
  The Omnipresence of the Deity
  (ed. 1830), pt. i, l. 339

**JAMES GRAHAM, MARQUIS OF
MONTROSE** 1612–1650

6 He either fears his fate too much,
  Or his deserts are small,
  That puts it not unto the touch,
  To win or lose it all.
  My Dear and Only Love

PERCY MONTROSE
nineteenth century

7 In a cavern, in a canyon,
  Excavating for a mine,
  Dwelt a miner, Forty-niner,
  And his daughter, Clementine.
  Oh, my darling, oh my darling, oh
  my darling Clementine!
  Thou art lost and gone for ever, dread-
  ful sorry, Clementine. *Clementine*

8 Light she was and like a fairy,
  And her shoes were number nine;
  Herring boxes without topses,
  Sandals were for Clementine.
                          Clementine

9 But I kissed her little sister,
  And forgot my Clementine.   *Ib.*

EDWARD MOORE 1712–1757

10 This is adding insult to injuries.
  The Foundling, v. ii

11 I am rich beyond the dreams of
  avarice.   *The Gamester*, II. ii

THOMAS MOORE 1779–1852

12 Believe me, if all those endearing
  young charms,
  Which I gaze on so fondly to-day.
  Irish Melodies. Believe Me, if All

13 The harp that once through Tara's
  halls
  The soul of music shed,
  Now hangs as mute on Tara's walls
  As if that soul were fled.—
  So sleeps the pride of former days,
  So glory's thrill is o'er;
  And hearts, that once beat high for
  praise,
  Now feel that pulse no more.
  Ib. The Harp that Once

14 No, there's nothing half so sweet in
  life
  As love's young dream.
  Ib. Love's Young Dream

15 The Minstrel Boy to the war is gone,
  In the ranks of death you'll find
  him;
  His father's sword he has girded on,
  And his wild harp slung behind him.
  Ib. The Minstrel Boy

16 Oh! blame not the bard.
  Ib. Oh! Blame Not

17 She is far from the land where her
  young hero sleeps,
  And lovers are round her, sighing:
  But coldly she turns from their gaze,
  and weeps,
  For her heart in his grave is lying.
  Ib. She is Far

18 'Tis the last rose of summer
  Left blooming alone;
  All her lovely companions
  Are faded and gone.
  Ib. 'Tis the Last Rose

19 I never nurs'd a dear gazelle,
  To glad me with its soft black eye,
  But when it came to know me well,
  And love me, it was sure to die!
  *Lalla Rookh. The Fire-Wor-
  shippers*, i, l. 279

1 Oft, in the stilly night,
   Ere Slumber's chain has bound me,
Fond Memory brings the light
   Of other days around me;
     The smiles, the tears,
     Of boyhood's years,
The words of love then spoken;
     The eyes that shone,
     Now dimm'd and gone,
The cheerful hearts now broken!
    *National Airs. Oft in the Stilly
    Night*

2 Faintly as tolls the evening chime
Our voices keep tune and our oars
   keep time.
Soon as the woods on shore look dim,
We'll sing at St. Ann's our parting
   hymn.
Row, brothers, row, the stream runs
   fast,
The Rapids are near and the daylight's
   past.
    *Poems Relating to America.
    Canadian Boat Song*

THOMAS OSBERT MORDAUNT
1730–1809

3 Sound, sound the clarion, fill the fife,
  Throughout the sensual world pro-
   claim,
One crowded hour of glorious life
  Is worth an age without a name.
    *The Bee, 12 Oct. 1791. Verses
    Written During the War, 1756–
    1763*

SIR THOMAS MORE 1478–1535

4 I pray you, master Lieutenant, see me
safe up, and my coming down let me
shift for myself. [On mounting the
scaffold.]
    Roper, *Life of Sir Thomas More*
    (1935), p. 103

5 Pluck up thy spirits, man, and be not
afraid to do thine office; my neck is
very short; take heed therefore thou
strike not awry, for saving of thine
honesty. [To the Executioner.]
    Ib. p. 103

6 This hath not offended the king. [As
he drew his beard aside on placing his
head on the block.]
    Bacon, *Apophthegms*, 22

7 Yea, marry, now it is somewhat, for
now it is rhyme; before, it was neither
rhyme nor reason. [Advising an
author to put his ill-written work into
verse.]
    A. Cayley's *Memoirs of Sir Thos.
    More* (1808), vol. i, p. 247

8 They roll and rumble,
They turn and tumble,
  As pigges do in a poke.
    Works (1557), ¶ ii. 6. *How a
    Sergeant would learn to Play the
    Frere*

9 This is a fair tale of a tub told us of
his elects.
    Works (1557), p. 576. *Confutation
    of Tyndale's Answers*

THOMAS MORELL 1703–1784

10 See, the conquering hero comes!
Sound the trumpets, beat the drums!
    Joshua, pt. iii

AUGUSTUS DE MORGAN
1806–1871

11 Great fleas have little fleas upon their
  backs to bite 'em,
And little fleas have lesser fleas, and
  so *ad infinitum.*
    A Budget of Paradoxes (1872),
    p. 377

GEORGE POPE MORRIS
1802–1867

12 Woodman, spare that tree!
  Touch not a single bough!
In youth it sheltered me,
  And I'll protect it now.
    Woodman, Spare that Tree

WILLIAM MORRIS 1834–1896

13 The idle singer of an empty day.
    The Earthly Paradise. An Apology

14 Forget six counties overhung with
  smoke,
Forget the snorting steam and piston
  stroke,
Forget the spreading of the hideous
  town;
Think rather of the pack-horse on the
  down,
And dream of London, small and white
  and clean,
The clear Thames bordered by its
  gardens green.
    Ib. Prologue. *The Wanderers*, l. 1

THOMAS MORTON 1764?–1838

15 Approbation from Sir Hubert Stanley
is praise indeed.
    A Cure for the Heartache, v. ii

16 Always ding, dinging Dame Grundy
into my ears—what will Mrs. Grundy
zay? What will Mrs. Grundy think?
    Speed the Plough, I. i

JOHN LOTHROP MOTLEY
1814–1877

17 As long as he lived, he was the guiding-
star of a whole brave nation, and when
he died the little children cried in the
streets. [William of Orange.]
    Rise of the Dutch Republic, pt. vi,
    ch. vii

1 Give us the luxuries of life, and we will dispense with its necessities.
Remark. O. W. Holmes, *Autocrat of the Breakfast-Table*, ch. 6

PETER ANTHONY MOTTEUX
1660–1718

2 The devil was sick, the devil a monk wou'd be;
The devil was well, and the devil a monk he'd be.
Translation of Rabelais. *Gargantua and Pantagruel*, bk. iv, ch. 24

HENRY PHIPPS, EARL OF MULGRAVE 1755–1831

3 And toast before each martial tune—
'Howe, and the Glorious First of June!' *Our Line was Formed*

HECTOR HUGH MUNRO
see SAKI

C. W. MURPHY

4 Has anybody here seen Kelly?
Kelly from the Isle of Man?
Has Anybody Here seen Kelly?

FRED MURRAY

5 Carve a little bit off the top for me!
A Little Bit Off The Top

6 Our lodger's such a nice young man.
Title of Song

ALFRED DE MUSSET 1810–1857

7 Mon verre n'est pas grand mais je bois dans mon verre.

The glass I drink from is not large, but at least it is my own.
La Coupe et les lèvres

8 Le seul bien qui me reste au monde
Est d'avoir quelquefois pleuré.

The only good thing left to me
Is knowledge that I, too, have wept. *Poèmes*

9 Malgré moi l'infini me tourmente.

I can't help it, the idea of the infinite is a torment to me.
Premières Poésies, L'Espoir en Dieu

IAN NAIRN 1930–

10 By the end of the century Great Britain will consist of isolated oases of preserved monuments in a desert of wire, concrete roads, cosy plots and bungalows. . . . Upon this new Britain the REVIEW bestows a name in the hope that it will stick—SUBTOPIA.
Architectural Review (June 1955), p. 365

CAROLINA, BARONESS NAIRNE
1766–1845

11 Will ye no come back again?
Better lo'ed ye canna be,
Will ye no come back again?
Life and Songs (1869), *Bonnie Charlie's now awa'*

12 Charlie is my darling, my darling, my darling,
Charlie is my darling, the young Chevalier.
Ib. Charlie is My Darling

13 Wi' a hundred pipers an' a', an' a',
Wi' a hundred pipers an' a', an' a',
We'll up an' gie them a blaw, a blaw,
Wi' a hundred pipers an' a', an' a'.
Ib. The Hundred Pipers

SIR WILLIAM NAPIER 1785–1860

14 Then was seen with what a strength and majesty the British soldier fights.
History of the War in the Peninsula, bk. xii, ch. 6, *Albuera*

NAPOLEON I 1769–1821

15 L'Angleterre est une nation de boutiquiers.

England is a nation of shopkeepers.
Attr. by B. B. E. O'Meara, *Napoleon at St. Helena*, vol. ii. *The original is probably 'sono mercanti', a phrase of Paoli, quoted by Napoleon; see* Gourgaud, *Journal Inédit de Sainte-Hélène*, i. 69 (*see 1:2, 217:12*)

16 Tout soldat français porte dans sa giberne le bâton de maréchal de France.

Every French soldier carries in his cartridge-pouch the baton of a marshal of France.
E. Blaze, *La Vie Militaire sous l'Empire*, I. v

17 Quant au courage moral, il avait trouvé fort rare, disait-il, celui de deux heures après minuit; c'est-à-dire le courage de l'improviste.

As to moral courage, I have very rarely met with *the two o'clock in the morning courage*: I mean unprepared courage.
Las Cases, *Mémorial de Sainte-Hélène, Dec. 4–5, 1815*

18 La carrière ouverte aux talents.

The career open to talents.
O'Meara, *Napoleon in Exile* (1822), vol. i, p. 103

1 Soldats, songez que, du haut de ces
  pyramides, quarante siècles vous con-
  templent.
  > Think of it, soldiers; from the
  > summit of these pyramids, forty
  > centuries look down upon you.
  > *Speech to the Army of Egypt on*
  > *21 July 1798, before the Battle*
  > *of the Pyramids.* Gourgaud,
  > *Mémoires, Guerre d'Orient,* i,
  > p. 160

2 Du sublime au ridicule il n'y a qu'un
  pas.
  > There is only one step from the
  > sublime to the ridiculous.
  > *To De Pradt, Polish ambassador,*
  > *after the retreat from Moscow in*
  > *1812.* De Pradt, *Histoire de*
  > *l'Ambassade dans le grand-duché*
  > *de Varsovie en 1812* (ed. 1815),
  > p. 215.

3 Voilà le soleil d'Austerlitz
  > There rises the sun of Austerlitz.
  > *To his officers, before Moscow,*
  > *7 Sept. 1812*

4 Tête d'Armée.   *Last words*

THOMAS NASHE 1567–1601

5 Brightness falls from the air;
  Queens have died young and fair;
  Dust hath closed Helen's eye.
  I am sick, I must die.
  Lord have mercy on us.
  > *In Time of Pestilence*

6 Spring, the sweet spring, is the year's
  pleasant king;
  Then blooms each thing, then maids
  dance in a ring,
  Cold doth not sting, the pretty birds
  do sing:
  Cuckoo, jug-jug, pu-we, to-witta-
  woo!   *Spring*

JAMES MASON NEALE 1818–1866

7 All glory, laud, and honour
  To Thee, Redeemer, King,
  To whom the lips of children
  Made sweet Hosannas ring.
  > *All Glory, Laud, and Honour,*
  > trans. from Latin *Gloria, Laus et*
  > *Honor tibi sit.*

8 Around the throne of God a band
  Of glorious Angels always stand.
  > *Around the Throne of God.*
  > *Hymns for Children, First Series*
  > (1842)

9 Art thou weary, art thou languid,
  Art thou sore distressed?
  > *Art Thou Weary,* trans. from
  > Greek

10 Brief life is here our portion;
   Brief sorrow, short-lived care.
   > *Brief Life is here,* trans. from
   > Latin, *Hic breve Vivitur*

11 Christian, dost thou see them
   On the holy ground,
   How the troops of Midian
   Prowl and prowl around?
   > *Christian, Dost Thou See Them,*
   > trans. from Greek

12 Good Christian men, rejoice
   With heart, and soul, and voice.
   > *Good Christian Men,* Helmore
   > and Neale, *Carols for Christmas-*
   > *tide*

13 Good King Wenceslas look'd out,
   On the Feast of Stephen;
   When the snow lay round about,
   Deep and crisp and even.
   > *Good King Wenceslas.* Helmore
   > and Neale, *Carols for Christmas-*
   > *tide*

14 Jerusalem the golden,
   With milk and honey blest,
   Beneath thy contemplation
   Sink heart and voice opprest.
   > *Jerusalem the Golden,* trans.
   > from Latin, *Urbs Syon Aurea*

15 O come, O come, Emmanuel,
   And ransom captive Israel.
   > *O Come, O Come, Emmanuel,*
   > trans. from Latin, *Veni, Veni,*
   > *Emmanuel*

16 O happy band of pilgrims,
   Look upward to the skies,
   Where such a light affliction
   Shall win you such a prize!
   > *O Happy Band of Pilgrims.*
   > *Hymns of the Eastern Church*

HORATIO, VISCOUNT NELSON
1758–1805

17 Palmam qui meruit, ferat.
   > Let him who merits bear the palm.
   >   *Motto*

18 Sent Admiral Collingwood the Nelson
   touch.   *Private Diary,* 9 Oct. 1805

19 Before this time to-morrow I shall
   have gained a peerage, or Westminster
   Abbey.
   > *Battle of the Nile.* Southey's *Life*
   > *of Nelson,* ch. 5

20 I have only one eye,—I have a right
   to be blind sometimes: . . . I really do
   not see the signal!
   > *At the battle of Copenhagen. Ib.*

21 England expects every man will do
   his duty.
   > *At the battle of Trafalgar. Ib.*

22 This is too warm work, Hardy, to last
   long.   *Ib.*

23 Thank God, I have done my duty. *Ib.*

1 Kiss me, Hardy.
> At the battle of Trafalgar.
> Southey's Life of Nelson, ch. 5

2 Such a band of brothers [of his officers].
> Letter to Earl Howe, 8 Jan. 1799, about the battle of the Nile. See Henry V, iv. 3.

NERO A.D. 37–68

3 Qualis artifex pereo!
What an artist dies with me!
> Suetonius, Life of Nero, xlix. 1

SIR HENRY JOHN NEWBOLT
1862–1938

4 'Take my drum to England, hang et by the shore,
> Strike et when your powder's runnin' low;
> If the Dons sight Devon, I'll quit the port o' Heaven,
> An' drum them up the Channel as we drummed them long ago.'
> The Island Race. Drake's Drum

5 Drake he's in his hammock till the great Armadas come.
> (Capten, art tha sleepin' there below?)
> Slung atween the round shot, listenin' for the drum,
> An' dreamin' arl the time o' Plymouth Hoe.
> Call him on the deep sea, call him up the Sound,
> Call him when ye sail to meet the foe;
> Where the old trade's plyin' an' the old flag flyin'
> They shall find him ware an' wakin', as they found him long ago! Ib.

6 There's a breathless hush in the Close to-night—
> Ten to make and the match to win—
> A bumping pitch and a blinding light,
> An hour to play and the last man in.
> And it's not for the sake of a ribboned coat,
> Or the selfish hope of a season's fame,
> But his Captain's hand on his shoulder smote—
> 'Play up! play up! and play the game!' Ib. Vitaï Lampada

7 But cared greatly to serve God and the King,
> And keep the Nelson touch.
> Minora Sidera

JOHN HENRY, CARDINAL NEWMAN 1801–1890

8 It is very difficult to get up resentment towards persons whom one has never seen.
> Apologia pro Vita Sua (1864). Mr. Kingsley's Method of Disputation

9 There is such a thing as legitimate warfare: war has its laws; there are things which may fairly be done, and things which may not be done. . . . He has attempted (as I may call it) to poison the wells.
> Apologia pro Vita Sua (1864). Mr. Kingsley's Method of Disputation

10 I will vanquish, not my Accuser, but my judges.
> Ib. True Mode of meeting Mr. Kingsley

11 Trinity had never been unkind to me. There used to be much snap-dragon growing on the walls opposite my freshman's rooms there, and I had for years taken it as the emblem of my own perpetual residence even unto death in my University.
On the morning of the 23rd I left the Observatory. I have never seen Oxford since, excepting its spires, as they are seen from the railway.
> Ib. History of My Religious Opinions from 1841 to 1845

12 May He support us all the day long, till the shades lengthen, and the evening comes, and the busy world is hushed, and the fever of life is over, and our work is done! Then in His mercy may He give us a safe lodging, and a holy rest, and peace at the last.
> Sermon, 1834. Wisdom and Innocence

13 Firmly I believe and truly
> God is Three, and God is One;
> And I next acknowledge duly
> Manhood taken by the Son.
> The Dream of Gerontius

14 Praise to the Holiest in the height,
> And in the depth be praise;
> In all his words most wonderful,
> Most sure in all His ways. Ib.

15 Lead, kindly Light, amid the encircling gloom,
> Lead thou me on;
> The night is dark, and I am far from home,
> Lead thou me on.
> Keep Thou my feet; I do not ask to see
> The distant scene; one step enough for me.
> The Pillar of Cloud. Lead Kindly Light

16 And with the morn those Angel faces smile,
> Which I have loved long since, and lost awhile. Ib.

SIR ISAAC NEWTON 1642–1727

17 I do not know what I may appear to the world, but to myself I seem to have been only a boy playing on the seashore, and diverting myself in now and

then finding a smoother pebble or a prettier shell than ordinary, whilst the great ocean of truth lay all undiscovered before me.
Brewster's *Memoirs of Newton*, vol. ii, ch. 27

JOHN NEWTON 1725–1807

1 How sweet the name of Jesus sounds
In a believer's ear!
It soothes his sorrows, heals his wounds,
And drives away his fear.
Olney Hymns (1779), *How Sweet the Name*

2 Glorious things of thee are spoken,
Zion, city of our God.
Ib. Glorious Things of Thee

NICHOLAS I OF RUSSIA
1796–1855

3 Nous avons sur les bras un homme malade—un homme gravement malade.
We have on our hands a sick man—a very sick man.
[The sick man of Europe, the Turk.]
Parliamentary Papers. Accounts and Papers, vol. lxxi, pt. 5. *Eastern Papers*, p. 2. *Sir G. H. Seymour to Lord John Russell, 11 Jan. 1853*

4 Russia has two generals in whom she can confide—Generals Janvier and Février.
Punch, 10 Mar. 1853. Speech of the late Emperor of Russia

ADELA FLORENCE NICOLSON
see LAURENCE HOPE

FRIEDRICH WILHELM NIETZSCHE 1844–1900

5 Herren-Moral und Sklaven-Moral.
The morality of masters and the morality of slaves.
Jenseits von Gut und Böse

6 Ich lehre euch den Übermenschen. Der Mensch ist Etwas, das überwunden werden soll.
I teach you the superman. Man is something to be surpassed.
Thus Spake Zarathustra. Prologue

7 Blonde Bestie.
Blonde beast.
Zur Genealogie der Moral

THOMAS NOEL 1799–1861

8 Rattle his bones over the stones;
He's only a pauper, whom nobody owns!
Rhymes and Roundelays, The Pauper's Drive

CHRISTOPHER NORTH [JOHN WILSON] 1785–1854

9 His Majesty's dominions, on which the sun never sets.
Noctes Ambrosianae, No. 20 (Apr. 1829)

10 Laws were made to be broken.
Ib. No. 24 (May 1830)

SIR STAFFORD HENRY NORTHCOTE, EARL OF IDDESLEIGH 1818–1887

11 Argue as you please, you are nowhere, that grand old man, the Prime Minister, insists on the other thing.
Speech at Liverpool, 12 Apr. 1882

CAROLINE ELIZABETH SARAH NORTON 1808–1877

12 My beautiful, my beautiful! that standest meekly by,
With thy proudly-arched and glossy neck, and dark and fiery eye!
Fret not to roam the desert now, with all thy winged speed:
I may not mount on thee again!—thou'rt sold, my Arab steed!
The Arab's Farewell to His Steed

13 For death and life, in ceaseless strife,
Beat wild on this world's shore,
And all our calm is in that balm—
Not lost but gone before.
Not Lost but Gone Before

NOVALIS [FRIEDRICH VON HARDENBERG] 1772–1801

14 Ein Gott-betrunkener Mensch.
A God-intoxicated man.
Remark about Spinoza

IVOR NOVELLO 1893–1951

15 Keep the home fires burning.
Title and first line of Song

ALFRED NOYES 1880–1958

16 Go down to Kew in lilac-time, in lilac-time, in lilac-time;
Go down to Kew in lilac-time (it isn't far from London!)
And you shall wander hand in hand with love in summer's wonderland;
Go down to Kew in lilac-time (it isn't far from London!) *Barrel Organ*

1 The wind was a torrent of darkness
    among the gusty trees,
  The moon was a ghostly galleon tossed
    upon cloudy seas,
  The road was a ribbon of moonlight
    over the purple moor,
  And the highwayman came riding—
    Riding—riding—
  The highwayman came riding, up to
    the old inn-door. *The Highwayman*

NURSERY RHYMES

(Earliest known sources are given)

2 A was an apple-pie;
  B bit it;
  C cut it.
      Quoted by John Eachard, *Some
      Observations* (1671)

3 As I was going to St. Ives,
  I met a man with seven wives,
  Each wife had seven sacks,
  Each sack had seven cats,
  Each cat had seven kits:
  Kits, cats, sacks, and wives,
  How many were there going to St.
  Ives?   *Harley MS., 1316* (c. 1730)

4 Baa, baa, black sheep,
  Have you any wool?
  Yes, sir, yes, sir,
  Three bags full:
  One for the master,
  And one for the dame,
  And one for the little boy
  Who lives down the lane.
      *Tommy Thumb's Pretty Song
      Book* (c. 1744)

5 Boys and girls come out to play,
  The moon doth shine as bright as day.
      In William King, *Useful Trans-
      actions in Philosophy* (1708–9)

6 Bye, baby bunting,
  Daddy's gone a-hunting,
  Gone to get a rabbit skin
  To wrap the baby bunting in.
      Gammer Gurton's Garland (1784)

7 Cock a doodle doo!
  My dame has lost her shoe;
  My master's lost his fiddling-stick,
  And knows not what to do.
      *Quoted in The Most Cruel And
      Bloody Murder Committed by an
      Innkeepers Wife* (1606)

8 Come, let's to bed, says Sleepy-head;
  Tarry a while, says Slow;
  Put on the pot, says Greedy-gut,
  We'll sup before we go.
      Gammer Gurton's Garland (1784)

9 Cross-patch,
  Draw the latch,
  Sit by the fire and spin:
  Take a cup,
  And drink it up,
  Then call your neighbours in.
      Mother Goose's Melody (c. 1765)

10 Cry, baby, cry,
   Put your finger in your eye,
   And tell your mother it wasn't I.
       Nursery Rhymes, ed. J. O. Halli-
       well (1853)

11 Curly locks, Curly locks,
   Wilt thou be mine?
   Thou shalt not wash dishes
   Nor yet feed the swine.
   But sit on a cushion
   And sew a fine seam,
   And feed upon strawberries,
   Sugar and cream.
       Infant Institutes (1797)

12 Daffy-down-dilly is new come to
   town,
   With a yellow petticoat, and a green
   gown.   *Songs for the Nursery* (1805)

13 Ding, dong, bell,
   Pussy's in the well.
   Who put her in?
   Little Johnny Green.
       Mother Goose's Melody (c. 1765)

14 A frog he would a-wooing go.
   'Heigh ho!' says Rowley.
       In Thomas Ravenscroft, *Melis-
       mata* (1611)

15 Georgie Porgie, pudding and pie,
   Kissed the girls and made them cry;
   When the boys came out to play
   Georgie Porgie ran away.
       Nursery Rhymes, ed. J. O. Halli-
       well (1842)

16 Goosey goosey gander,
   Whither shall I wander?
   Upstairs and downstairs,
   And in my lady's chamber;
   There I met an old man
   That would not say his prayers;
   I took him by the left leg,
   And threw him down the stairs.
       Gammer Gurton's Garland (1784)

17 Hey diddle diddle,
   The cat and the fiddle,
   The cow jumped over the moon;
   The little dog laughed
   To see such sport,
   And the dish ran away with the spoon.
       Mother Goose's Melody (c. 1765)

18 Hickory, dickory, dock,
   The mouse ran up the clock,
   The clock struck one,
   The mouse ran down;
   Hickory, dickory, dock.
       *Tommy Thumb's Pretty Song
       Book* (c. 1744)

19 How many miles to Babylon?
   Threescore miles and ten.
   Can I get there by candle-light?
   Yes, and back again.
   If your heels are nimble and light,
   You may get there by candle-light.
       Songs for the Nursery (1805)

1 Humpty Dumpty sat on a wall,
Humpty Dumpty had a great fall;
All the king's horses,
And all the king's men,
Couldn't put Humpty together again.
       From MS. addition to a copy of
       Mother Goose's Melody (c. 1803)

2 I had a little nut tree, nothing would
it bear
But a silver nutmeg and a golden pear;
The king of Spain's daughter came to
visit me,
And all for the sake of my little nut
tree.
       Newest Christmas Box (c. 1797)

3 I like little pussy, her coat is so warm,
And if I don't hurt her, she'll do me
no harm.
So I'll not pull her tail, nor drive her
away,
But pussy and I very gently will play.
       Only True Mother Goose Melodies
       (Boston, c. 1843)

4 Jack and Jill went up the hill
To fetch a pail of water;
Jack fell down and broke his crown,
And Jill came tumbling after.
       Mother Goose's Melody (c. 1765)

5 Jack Sprat could eat no fat,
His wife could eat no lean;
And so between them both, you see,
They licked the platter clean.
       In John Clarke, Paroemiologia
       Anglo-Latina (1639)

6 The King of France went up the hill,
With forty thousand men;
The King of France came down the
hill,
And ne'er went up again.
       Quoted by James Howell in a
       letter to Sir James Crofts, 12 May
       1620

7 Ladybird, ladybird, fly away home,
Your house is on fire, and your children all gone.
       Tommy Thumb's Pretty Song
       Book (c. 1744)

8 The lion and the unicorn
Were fighting for the crown;
The lion beat the unicorn
All round about the town.
Some gave them white bread,
And some gave them brown;
Some gave them plum cake,
And sent them out of town.
       In William King, Useful Trans-
       actions in Philosophy (1708–9)

9 Little Bo-Peep has lost her sheep,
And can't tell where to find them;
Leave them alone, and they'll come
home,
And bring their tails behind them.
       Douce MS. (c. 1805)

10 Little boy blue, come blow up your
horn,
The sheep's in the meadow, the cow's
in the corn;
But where is the boy that looks after
the sheep?
He's under the haycock fast asleep.
Will you wake him? No, not I,
For if I do, he'll be sure to cry.
       The Famous Tommy Thumb's
       Little Story Book (c. 1760)

11 Little Jack Horner sat in the corner,
Eating a Christmas pie;
He put in his thumb, and pulled out a
plum,
And said, 'What a good boy am I!'
       Quoted by Henry Carey, Namby
       Pamby (c. 1720)

12 Little Polly Flinders
Sat among the cinders,
Warming her pretty little toes;
Her mother came and caught her,
And whipped her little daughter
For spoiling her nice new clothes.
       Original Ditties for the Nursery
       (c. 1805)

13 Little Tommy Tucker
Sings for his supper;
What shall we give him?
White bread and butter.
       Tommy Thumb's Pretty Song
       Book (c. 1744)

14 London bridge is broken down,
My fair lady.
       Quoted by Henry Carey, Namby
       Pamby (c. 1720)

15 The man in the wilderness asked me,
How many strawberries grow in the
sea?
I answered him, as I thought good,
As many as red herrings grow in the
wood.
       MS. addition, dated 1744, to the
       Bath Municipal Library's copy
       of The Whole Duty of Man (1733)

16 Mary, Mary, quite contrary,
How does your garden grow?
With silver bells, and cockle shells,
And pretty maids all in a row.
       Tommy Thumb's Pretty Song
       Book (c. 1744)

17 Monday's child is fair of face,
Tuesday's child is full of grace,
Wednesday's child is full of woe,
Thursday's child has far to go,
Friday's child is loving and giving,
Saturday's child works hard for its
living,
And a child that's born on the
Sabbath day
Is fair and wise and good and gay.
       Quoted by A. E. Bray, Traditions
       of Devonshire (1838), ii. 288

1 The north wind doth blow,
And we shall have snow,
And what will poor robin do then?
         Poor thing!
He'll sit in a barn,
To keep himself warm,
And hide his head under his wing.
         Poor thing!
   Songs for the Nursery (1805)

2 Old King Cole
Was a merry old soul,
And a merry old soul was he,
He called for his pipe,
And he called for his bowl,
And he called for his fiddlers three.
   Quoted by William King, *Useful Transactions in Philosophy* (1708–9)

3 Old Mother Hubbard
Went to the cupboard,
To get her poor dog a bone;
But when she came there
The cupboard was bare,
And so the poor dog had none.
   Sarah Catherine Martin, *The Comic Adventures of Old Mother Hubbard* (1805)

4 One a penny, two a penny, hot cross-buns;
If your daughters do not like them, give them to your sons.
   Christmas Box (1797)

5 One, two,
Buckle my shoe;
Three, four,
Knock at the door;
Five, six,
Pick up sticks.
Seven, eight,
Lay them straight;
Nine, ten,
A big fat hen.
   Songs for the Nursery (1805)

6 Oranges and lemons
Say the bells of St. Clement's.
   Tommy Thumb's Pretty Song Book (c. 1744)

7 When will you pay me?
Say the bells of Old Bailey.
When I grow rich,
Say the bells of Shoreditch.   *Ib.*

8 Here comes a candle to light you to bed,
Here comes a chopper to chop off your head.   *Ib.*

9 Pat-a-cake, pat-a-cake, baker's man,
Bake me a cake as fast as you can;
Pat it and prick it, and mark it with B,
Put it in the oven for baby and me.
   Quoted in Tom D'Urfey, *The Campaigners* (1698)

10 Pease-porridge hot, pease-porridge cold,
Pease-porridge in the pot, nine days old. *Newest Christmas Box* (c. 1797)

11 Peter Piper picked a peck of pickled pepper;
A peck of pickled pepper Peter Piper picked;
If Peter Piper picked a peck of pickled pepper,
Where's the peck of pickled pepper Peter Piper picked?
   Peter Piper's Practical Principles of Plain and Perfect Pronunciation (1819)

12 Please to remember
The Fifth of November,
   Gunpowder treason and plot;
We know no reason
Why gunpowder treason
   Should ever be forgot.
   Anonymous broadsheet (1826). *See* Wm. Hone, *The Every-Day Book* (1841) (*see also* 7:3)

13 Polly put the kettle on, we'll all have tea. [*Grip*.]   *Barnaby Rudge*, ch. 17

14 Pussy cat, pussy cat, where have you been?
I've been up to London to look at the queen.
Pussy cat, pussy cat, what did you there?
I frightened a little mouse under the chair. *Songs for the Nursery* (1805)

15 The Queen of Hearts
She made some tarts,
   All on a summer's day;
The Knave of Hearts
He stole the tarts,
   And took them clean away.
   The European Magazine (Apr. 1782)

16 Rain, rain, go away,
Come again another day.
   In James Howell, *Proverbs* (1659)

17 Ride a cock-horse to Banbury Cross,
To see a fine lady upon a white horse,
Rings on her fingers and bells on her toes,
And she shall have music wherever she goes.
   Gammer Gurton's Garland (1784)

18 See-saw, Margery Daw,
Jacky shall have a new master;
Jacky must have but a penny a day,
Because he can't work any faster.
   Mother Goose's Melody (c. 1765)

19 Simple Simon met a pieman
   Going to the fair:
Says Simple Simon to the pieman,
'Let me taste your ware.'
   Simple Simon (a chapbook advertisement, 1764)

1 Sing a song of sixpence,
     A pocket full of rye,
   Four and twenty blackbirds,
     Baked in a pie;
   When the pie was opened,
     The birds began to sing;
   Was not that a dainty dish
     To set before the king?

   The king was in his counting-house
     Counting out his money;
   The queen was in the parlour
     Eating bread and honey;
   The maid was in the garden
     Hanging out the clothes,
   There came a little blackbird,
     And snapped off her nose.
           *Tommy Thumb's Pretty Song
           Book (c. 1744)*

2 Solomon Grundy,
   Born on a Monday,
   Christened on Tuesday,
   Married on Wednesday,
   Took ill on Thursday,
   Worse on Friday,
   Died on Saturday,
   Buried on Sunday:
   This is the end
   Of Solomon Grundy.
           Nursery Rhymes, ed. J. O.
           Halliwell (1842)

3 Taffy was a Welshman, Taffy was a
     thief;
   Taffy came to my house and stole a
     piece of beef:
   I went to Taffy's house, Taffy was not
     at home;
   Taffy came to my house and stole a
     marrow-bone.
           Nancy Cock's Pretty Song Book
           (c. 1780)

4 Tell tale, tit!
   Your tongue shall be split,
   And all the dogs in the town
   Shall have a little bit.
           Nursery Rhymes, ed. J. O.
           Halliwell (1842)

5 There was a crooked man, and he
     walked a crooked mile,
   He found a crooked sixpence against a
     crooked stile:
   He bought a crooked cat, which caught
     a crooked mouse,
   And they all lived together in a little
     crooked house.   *Ib.*

6 There was an old woman who lived in
     a shoe,
   She had so many children she didn't
     know what to do;
   She gave them some broth without
     any bread,
   She whipped them all soundly and put
     them to bed.
           Gammer Gurton's Garland (1784)

7 Thirty days hath September,
   April, June, and November;
   All the rest have thirty-one,
   Excepting February alone,
   And that has twenty-eight days clear
   And twenty-nine in each leap year.
           Stevins MS. (c. 1555) (see 96:8)

8 This is the farmer sowing his corn,
   That kept the cock that crowed in the
     morn,
   That waked the priest all shaven and
     shorn,
   That married the man all tattered
     and torn,
   That kissed the maiden all forlorn,
   That milked the cow with the
     crumpled horn,
   That tossed the dog,
   That worried the cat,
   That killed the rat,
   That ate the malt
   That lay in the house that Jack built.
           *Nurse Truelove's New-Year's-
           Gift* (1755)

9 This little pig went to market;
   This little pig stayed at home;
   This little pig had roast beef;
   And this little pig had none;
   And this little pig cried, Wee, wee,
     wee!
   I can't find my way home.
           *The Famous Tommy Thumb's
           Little Story Book (c. 1760)*

10 Three blind mice, see how they run!
   They all ran after the farmer's wife,
   Who cut off their tails with a carving-
     knife,
   Did you ever see such a thing in your
     life
       As three blind mice?
           *In Thomas Ravenscroft, Deute-
           romelia (1609)*

11 Three wise men of Gotham
   Went to sea in a bowl:
   And if the bowl had been stronger,
   My song would have been longer.
           Mother Goose's Melody (c. 1765)

12 Tom he was a piper's son,
   He learned to play when he was
     young,
   But all the tune that he could play,
   Was 'Over the hills and far away.'
           Tom, the Piper's Son (c. 1795)

13 Tom, Tom, the piper's son,
   Stole a pig, and away he run;
   The pig was eat, and Tom was beat,
   And Tom went howling down the
     street.   *Ib.*

14 What are little boys made of?
   What are little boys made of?
   Frogs and snails, and puppy-dogs'
     tails;
   That's what little boys are made of.

What are little girls made of?
What are little girls made of?
Sugar and spice, and all that's nice;
That's what little girls are made of.
Nursery Rhymes, ed. J. O.
Halliwell (1844)

1 Where are you going to, my pretty
maid?
Quoted by William Pryce,
Archaeologia Cornu-Britannica
(1790)

2 'My face is my fortune, sir,' she said.
Ib.

3 'Nobody asked you, sir,' she said. *Ib.*

4 'Who killed Cock Robin?'
'I,' said the Sparrow,
'With my bow and arrow,
I killed Cock Robin.'
All the birds of the air fell a-sighing
and a-sobbing
When they heard of the death of poor
Cock Robin.
*Tommy Thumb's Pretty Song
Book (c.* 1744)

5 'Who saw him die?'
'I,' said the Fly,
'With my little eye,
I saw him die.'   *Ib.*

FREDERICK OAKELEY 1802–1880

6 O come, all ye faithful,
Joyful and triumphant,
O come ye, O come ye to Bethlehem.
O Come, All Ye Faithful, trans.
from Latin, *Adeste Fideles*

SEAN O'CASEY 1884–1964

7 The whole world is in a state of chassis.
Juno and the Paycock, I. i

ADOLPH S. OCHS 1858–1935

8 All the news that's fit to print.
Motto of the New York Times

JOHN O'KEEFFE 1747–1833

9 Amo, amas, I love a lass
Agreeable Surprise, II. ii. *Song:
Amo, Amas*

10 Fat, fair and forty were all the toasts
of the young men.   *Irish Minnie*, ii

11 You should always except the present
company.   *London Hermit*, I. ii

DENNIS O'KELLY 1720?–1787

12 Eclipse first, the rest nowhere.
Epsom, 3 May 1769. *Annals of
Sporting*, vol. ii, p. 271

BARONESS ORCZY [MRS. MON-TAGUE BARSTOW] 1865–1947

13 We seek him here, we seek him there,
Those Frenchies seek him everywhere.
Is he in heaven?—Is he in hell?
That demmed, elusive Pimpernel?
The Scarlet Pimpernel, ch. 12

META ORRED

14 In the gloaming, O, my darling!
When the lights are dim and low,
And the quiet shadows falling
Softly come and softly go.
In the Gloaming

GEORGE ORWELL [ERIC BLAIR] 1903–1950

15 All animals are equal, but some ani-mals are more equal than others.
Animal Farm, ch. 10

16 Big brother is watching you.
1984, pt. I, i

17 Double think means the power of
holding two contradictory beliefs in
one's mind simultaneously, and ac-cepting both of them.   *Ib.* pt. II, ix

ARTHUR WILLIAM EDGAR O'SHAUGHNESSY 1844–1881

18 We are the music makers,
We are the dreamers of dreams,
Ode: 'We are the Music Makers'

19 For each age is a dream that is dying,
Or one that is coming to birth.   *Ib.*

JOHN O'SULLIVAN 1813–1895

20 Our manifest destiny to overspread
the continent allotted by Providence
for the free development of our yearly
multiplying millions.
*U.S. Magazine and Democratic
Review*, vol. xvii, p. 5

JAMES OTIS 1725–1783

21 Taxation without representation is
tyranny.
*Watchword of the American
Revolution. Attr.*

THOMAS OTWAY 1652–1685

22 Oh woman! lovely woman! Nature
made thee
To temper man: we had been brutes
without you;
Venice Preserved, Act I, l. 337

SIR THOMAS OVERBURY
1581–1613

1 He disdains all things above his reach, and preferreth all countries before his own.
> *Miscellaneous Works. An Affectate Traveller*

OVID 43 B.C.–A.D. 18?

2 Cetera quis nescit?
> The rest who does not know?
> *Amores*, I. v. 25, Trans. by Showerman

3 Procul omen abesto!
> Far from us be the omen!
> *Ib.* xiv. 41

4 Iam seges est ubi Troia fuit.
> Now are fields of corn where Troy once was.   *Heroides*, I. i. 53

5 Rudis indigestaque moles.
> An unformed and confused mass.
> *Metamorphoses*, i. 7

6 Medio tutissimus ibis.
> You will go most safely in the middle.   *Ib.* ii. 137

7   Video meliora, proboque; Deteriora sequor.
> I see and approve better things, but follow worse.   *Ib.* vii. 20

8 Tempus edax rerum.
> Time the devourer of all things.
> *Ib.* xv. 234

9 Tu quoque.
> Thou also.   *Tristia*, ii. 39

JOHN OWEN 1560?–1622

10 Tempora mutantur nos et mutamur in illis:
Quomodo? fit semper tempore pejor homo.
> Times change, and we change with them too. How so?
> With time men only the more vicious grow.   *Epigrams*

THOMAS PAINE 1737–1809

11 The sublime and the ridiculous are often so nearly related, that it is difficult to class them separately. One step above the sublime, makes the ridiculous; and one step above the ridiculous, makes the sublime again.
> *Age of Reason* (1795), pt. II, p. 20

12 These are the times that try men's souls.
> *The American Crisis*, No. 1. *Writings* (1894), vol. i, p. 170

13 Government, even in its best state, is but a necessary evil; in its worst state, an intolerable one.
> *Common Sense*, ch. 1

14 The religion of humanity.
> *Attr. by Edmund Gosse*

REV. WILLIAM PALEY 1743–1805

15 Who can refute a sneer?
> *Moral Philosophy*, bk. v, ch. 9

HENRY JOHN TEMPLE, VISCOUNT PALMERSTON 1784–1865

16 Accidental and fortuitous concurrence of atoms.
> *Speech, House of Commons, 5 Mar. 1857*

17 Die, my dear Doctor, that's the last thing I shall do!   *Attr. last words*

DOROTHY PARKER 1893–

18 Men seldom make passes
At girls who wear glasses.
> *The Best of Dorothy Parker, News Item*

MARTIN PARKER d. 1656?

19 You gentlemen of England
Who live at home at ease,
How little do you think
On the dangers of the seas.
> *The Valiant Sailors (Early Naval Ballads* [Percy Society, 1841], p. 34)

20 But all's to no end, for the times will not mend
Till the king enjoys his own again.
> *Upon Defacing of Whitehall (The Loyal Garland,* 1671). Later title: *When the King Enjoys His Own Again.* Ritson's *Ancient Songs* (1792), p. 231

ROSS PARKER 1914–
and
HUGHIE CHARLES 1907–

21 There'll always be an England
While there's a country lane,
Wherever there's a cottage small
Beside a field of grain.
> *Song of Second World War* (1939)

THEODORE PARKER 1810–1860

22 A democracy, that is, a government of all the people, by all the people, for all the people; of course, a government after the principles of eternal justice, the unchanging law of God; for shortness' sake, I will call it the idea of freedom.
> *The American Idea. Speech at N.E. Anti-Slavery Convention, Boston, 29 May 1850. Discourses of Slavery* (1863), i

CHARLES STEWART PARNELL
1846–1891

1 No man has a right to fix the boundary of the march of a nation; no man has a right to say to his country—thus far shalt thou go and no further.
    Speech at Cork, 21 Jan. 1885

THOMAS PARNELL 1679–1718

2 We call it only pretty Fanny's way.
    Poems (1894). An Elegy, to an Old Beauty, l. 34

BLAISE PASCAL 1623–1662

3 Quand on voit le style naturel, on est tout étonné et ravi, car on s'attendait de voir un auteur, et on trouve un homme.

   When we encounter a natural style we are always astonished and delighted, for we expected to see an author, and find a man.
       Pensées, § i. 29

4 Le nez de Cléopatre: s'il eût été plus court, toute la face de la terre aurait changé.

   Had Cleopatra's nose been shorter, the whole history of the world would have been different.
       Ib. § ii. 162

5 Le silence éternel de ces espaces infinis m'effraie.

   The eternal silence of these infinite spaces [the heavens] terrifies me.
       Ib. § iii. 206

6 On mourra seul.

   We shall die alone.   *Ib.* 211

7 Le cœur a ses raisons que la raison ne connaît point.

   The heart has its reasons which reason knows nothing of.
       Ib. § iv. 277

8 L'homme n'est qu'un roseau, le plus faible de la nature; mais c'est un roseau pensant.

   Man is only a reed, the weakest thing in nature; but he is a thinking reed.   *Ib.* § vi. 347

WALTER HORATIO PATER
1839–1894

9 She is older than the rocks among which she sits; like the vampire, she has been dead many times, and learned the secrets of the grave; and has been a diver in deep seas, and keeps their fallen day about her; and trafficked for strange webs with Eastern merchants: and, as Leda, was the mother of Helen of Troy, and, as Saint Anne, the mother of Mary; and all this has been to her but as the sound of lyres and flutes, and lives only in the delicacy with which it has moulded the changing lineaments, and tinged the eyelids and the hands.
    The Renaissance. Leonardo da Vinci

10 All art constantly aspires towards the condition of music.
    Ib. The School of Giorgione

11 To burn always with this hard, gem-like flame, to maintain this ecstasy, is success in life.   *Ib. Conclusion*

ANDREW PATERSON 1864–1941

12 Once a jolly swagman camped by a billabong,
    Under the shade of a coolibah tree,
    And he sang as he sat and waited till his billy boiled
    'You'll come a-waltzing, Matilda, with me.'   *Waltzing Matilda*

COVENTRY PATMORE 1823–1896

13 For dear to maidens are their rivals dead.   *Amelia*, l. 135

14 I, singularly moved
    To love the lovely that are not beloved,
    Of all the Seasons, most
    Love Winter.
       The Unknown Eros, bk. I. iii. *Winter*, l. 1

15 My little Son, who look'd from thoughtful eyes
    And moved and spoke in quiet grown-up wise,
    Having my law the seventh time disobey'd,
    I struck him, and dismiss'd
    With hard words and unkiss'd,
    His Mother, who was patient, being dead.   *Ib.* x. *The Toys*, l. 1

JAMES PAYN 1830–1898

16 I had never had a piece of toast
    Particularly long and wide,
    But fell upon the sanded floor,
    And always on the buttered side.
       Chambers's Journal, 2 Feb. 1884

JOHN HOWARD PAYNE
1791–1852

17 Mid pleasures and palaces though we may roam,
    Be it ever so humble, there's no place like home;
    A charm from the sky seems to hallow us there,
    Which, seek through the world, is ne'er met with elsewhere.
    Home, home, sweet, sweet home!
    There's no place like home! there's no place like home!
       Clari, the Maid of Milan. Home, Sweet Home

THOMAS LOVE PEACOCK
1785–1866

1 The mountain sheep are sweeter,
    But the valley sheep are fatter;
  We therefore deemed it meeter
    To carry off the latter.
      *The Misfortunes of Elphin, ch.
      11. The War-Song of Dinas
      Vawr*

2 In a bowl to sea went wise men three,
    On a brilliant night in June:
  They carried a net, and their hearts
      were set
    On fishing up the moon.
      *The Wise Men of Gotham. Paper
      Money Lyrics*

WILLIAM PENN 1644–1718

3 No Cross, No Crown.
      Title of Pamphlet, 1669

SAMUEL PEPYS 1633–1703

4 And so to bed.   *Diary, 20 Apr. 1660*

5 I went out to Charing Cross, to see
  Major-general Harrison hanged,
  drawn, and quartered, which was done
  there, he looking as cheerful as any
  man could do in that condition.
      Ib. 13 Oct. 1660

6 My wife, who, poor wretch, is troubled
  with her lonely life. *Ib. 19 Dec. 1662*

7 Pretty witty Nell. [Nell Gwynne.]
      Ib. 3 Apr. 1665

CHARLES PERRAULT 1628–1703

8 'Anne, ma sœur Anne, ne vois-tu
  rien venir?' Et la sœur Anne lui
  répondit, 'Je ne vois rien que le
  soleil qui poudroye, et l'herbe qui
  verdoye.'

  'Anne, sister Anne, do you see any-
      thing coming?' And her sister
      Anne replied, 'I see nothing but
      the sun which makes a dust, and
      the grass looking green.'
      *Perrault, Histoires et contes du
      temps passé (1697). Trans. by
      R. Samber, 1764*

PERSIUS A.D. 34–62

9 Venienti occurrite morbo.
      Meet the disease at its first stage.
        Satires, iii. 64

10 De nihilo nihilum, in nihilum nil posse
   reverti.
      Nothing can come out of nothing,
      nothing can go back to nothing.
        Ib. 84. Trans. by Conington

MARÉCHAL PÉTAIN 1856–1951

11 Ils ne passeront pas.
      They shall not pass.
        Verdun, Feb. 1916

PETRONIUS d. c. A.D. 66

12 Cave canem.
      Beware of the dog.
        *Petronii Arbitri Satyricon, 29, 1.
        Found with picture of a dog on
        a mosaic floor in Pompeii.*

13 Abiit ad plures.
      He has joined the great majority.
        Cena Trimalchionis, xlii. 5

EDWARD JOHN PHELPS
1822–1900

14 The man who makes no mistakes does
   not usually make anything.
      *Speech at Mansion House, 24 Jan.
      1899*

WENDELL PHILLIPS 1811–1884

15 Every man meets his Waterloo at last.
      *Speeches (1880), Lecture at Brook-
      lyn, N.Y., 1 Nov. 1859*

EDEN PHILLPOTTS 1862–1960

16 His father's sister had bats in the
   belfry and was put away.
      Peacock House. My First Murder

WILLIAM PITT, EARL OF
CHATHAM 1708–1778

17 The atrocious crime of being a young
   man . . . I shall neither attempt to
   palliate or deny.
      *Speech, House of Commons,
      27 Jan. 1741*

18 Unlimited power is apt to corrupt the
   minds of those who possess it.
      Ib. House of Lords, 9 Jan. 1770

19 You cannot conquer America.
      Ib. 18 Nov. 1777

20 I invoke the genius of the Constitution!   *Ib.*

21 It was a saying of Lord Chatham, that
   the parks were the lungs of London.
      *William Windham, in a Speech
      in House of Commons, 30 June
      1808*

WILLIAM PITT 1759–1806

22 England has saved herself by her
   exertions, and will, as I trust, save
   Europe by her example.
      Speech, at the Guildhall, 1805

1 Roll up that map; it will not be
wanted these ten years.
> *On a map of Europe, after hear-
> ing the news of the Battle of
> Austerlitz.* Stanhope's *Life of
> the Rt. Hon. William Pitt* (1862),
> vol. iv, p. 369

2 Oh, my country! how I love my
country.   *Attr. last words. Ib.* p. 382

3 Oh, my country! how I leave my
country!
> *Attr. last words. Ib.* (1879),
> vol. iii, p. 391

4 My country! oh, my country!
> *Attr. last words.* G. Rose, *Diary,*
> 23 Jan. 1806

5 I think I could eat one of Bellamy's
veal pies.
> *Alternative attr. last words*

JAMES ROBINSON PLANCHÉ
1796–1880

6 It would have made a cat laugh.
> *Extravaganzas* (1879), *The Queen
> of the Frogs,* I. iv

PLATO c. 429–347 B.C.

7 Σωκράτη φησὶν ἀδικεῖν τούς τε νέους
διαφθείροντα καὶ θεοὺς οὓς ἡ πόλις νομίζει
οὐ νομίζοντα, ἕτερα δὲ δαιμόνια καινά.
> Socrates is charged with corrupting
> the youth of the city, and with
> rejecting the gods of Athens and
> introducing new divinities.
> *Apologia,* 24ᵇ 9

PLAUTUS B.C. 254–184

8 Quem di diligunt
Adulescens moritur.
> He whom the gods favour dies
> young.   *Bacchides* iv. 816

PLINY A.D. 23–79

9 Ex Africa semper aliquid novi.
> There is always something new from
> Africa. *Proverbial from Pliny:*
> Unde etiam vulgare Graeciae
> dictum 'semper aliquid novi
> Africam adferre'.
> Whence it is commonly said
> among the Greeks that 'Africa
> always offers something new'.
> *Naturalis Historia,* II. viii. 42

10 In vino veritas.
> Truth comes out in wine. *Proverbial
> from Pliny:* Vulgoque veritas iam
> attributa vino est.
> Now truth is commonly said to
> be in wine.   *Ib.* xiv. 141

11 Sal Atticum.
> Attic wit.   *Ib.* xxxi. 87

12 Nulla dies sine linea.
> Not a day without a line. *Prover-
> bial from Pliny:* Apelli fuit alioqui
> perpetua consuetudo numquam
> tam occupatam diem agendi, ut
> non lineam ducendo exerceret
> artem, quod ab eo in proverbium
> venit.
>
> It was moreover a regular habit
> of Apelles never to be so
> occupied in the business of the
> day that he could not practise
> his art by drawing a line, and
> this gave rise to the proverb.
> *Naturalis Historia,* xxxv. 36. 12

13 Ne supra crepidam sutor iudicaret.
> The cobbler should not judge above
> his last.   *Ib.* 85

EDGAR ALLAN POE 1809–1849

14 I was a child and she was a child,
In this kingdom by the sea;
But we loved with a love that was
more than love—
I and my Annabel Lee.   *Annabel Lee*

15 The fever call'd 'Living'
Is conquer'd at last.   *For Annie*

16 Helen, thy beauty is to me
Like those Nicean barks of yore,
That gently, o'er a perfumed sea,
The weary, wayworn wanderer bore
To his own native shore.

On desperate seas long wont to roam,
Thy hyacinth hair, thy classic face,
Thy Naiad airs have brought me
home
To the glory that was Greece
And the grandeur that was Rome.
> *To Helen,* l. 1

17 Take thy beak from out my heart, and
take thy form from off my door!
Quoth the Raven, 'Nevermore'.
> *The Raven,* xvii

JOHN POMFRET 1667–1703

18 We live and learn, but not the wiser
grow.   *Reason,* l. 112

MME DE POMPADOUR 1721–1764

19 Après nous le déluge.
> After us the deluge.
> Madame de Hausset, *Mémoires,*
> p. 19

JOHN POOLE 1786?–1872

20 I hope I don't intrude?
> *Paul Pry,* I. ii

ALEXANDER POPE 1688–1744

1 Poetic Justice, with her lifted scale,
  Where, in nice balance, truth with
      gold she weighs,
  And solid pudding against empty
      praise.   *The Dunciad*, bk. i, l. 52

2 May you, my Cam and Isis, preach it
      long!
  The Right Divine of Kings to govern
      wrong.   *Ib.* bk. iv, l. 187

3 Lo! thy dread empire, Chaos! is
      restor'd;
  Light dies before thy uncreating word;
  Thy hand, great Anarch! lets the
      curtain fall,
  And universal darkness buries all.
                             Ib. l. 653

4 Is it, in heav'n, a crime to love too
      well?
          Elegy to the Memory of an Un-
          fortunate Lady, l. 6

5 Is there no bright reversion in the sky,
  For those who greatly think, or
      bravely die?   *Ib.* l. 9

6 How happy is the blameless vestal's
      lot!
  The world forgetting, by the world
      forgot.   *Eloisa to Abelard*, l. 207

7 I am his Highness' dog at Kew;
  Pray tell me, sir, whose dog are you?
          Epigrams. On the Collar of a
          Dog which I gave to his Royal
          Highness

8 Nature and Nature's laws lay hid in
      night:
  God said, *Let Newton be!* and all was
      light.
          Epitaphs. Intended for Sir Isaac
          Newton

9 A little learning is a dang'rous thing;
  Drink deep, or taste not the Pierian
      spring.
          An Essay on Criticism, l. 215

10 True wit is nature to advantage
      dressed,
  What oft was thought, but n'er so well
      expressed.   *Ib.* l. 297

11 A needless Alexandrine ends the song,
  That, like a wounded snake, drags its
      slow length along.   *Ib.* l. 356

12 To err is human, to forgive, divine.
                             Ib. l. 525

13 For fools rush in where angels fear to
      tread.   *Ib.* l. 625

14 Hope springs eternal in the human
      breast;
  Man never is, but always to be
      blessed.
  The soul, uneasy, and confined from
      home,
  Rests and expatiates in a life to come.

Lo, the poor Indian! whose untutored
      mind
Sees God in clouds, or hears him in the
      wind;
His soul proud science never taught
      to stray
Far as the solar walk or milky way;
Yet simple nature to his hope has giv'n,
Behind the cloud-topped hill, an
      humbler heav'n.
          An Essay on Man. Epistle i, l. 95

15 Die of a rose in aromatic pain?
                             Ib. l. 200

16 The spider's touch how exquisitely
      fine!
  Feels at each thread, and lives along
      the line.   *Ib.* l. 217

17 And, spite of pride, in erring reason's
      spite,
  One truth is clear, Whatever is, is
      right.   *Ib.* l. 288

18 Know then thyself, presume not
      God to scan,
  The proper study of mankind is man.
  Placed on this isthmus of a middle
      state,
  A being darkly wise, and rudely
      great:
  With too much knowledge for the
      sceptic side.   *Ib.* Ep, ii, l. 3

19 Created half to rise, and half to fall;
  Great lord of all things, yet a prey to
      all;
  Sole judge of truth, in endless error
      hurled;
  The glory, jest, and riddle of the
      world!   *Ib.* l. 15

20 An honest man's the noblest work of
      God.   *Ib.* Ep. iv, l. 247

21 Thou wert my guide, philosopher, and
      friend.   *Ib.* l. 390

22 And you, brave Cobham! to the latest
      breath,
  Shall feel your ruling passion strong in
      death.
          Moral Essays, Ep. i, *To Lord*
          Cobham, l. 262

23 The ruling passion, be it what it will,
  The ruling passion conquers reason
      still.
          Ib. Ep. iii. *To Lord Bathurst*,
          l. 153

24 Rise, honest Muse! and sing the Man
      of Ross!   *Ib.* l. 250

25 Statesman, yet friend to truth! of soul
      sincere,
  In action faithful, and in honour
      clear;
  Who broke no promise, served no
      private end,
  Who gained no title, and who lost no
      friend.
          Ib. Ep. vii. *To Mr. Addison*, l. 67

1 Where'er you walk cool gales shall
fan the glade;
Trees, where you sit, shall crowd into
a shade;
Where'er you tread, the blushing
flow'rs shall rise,
And all things flourish where you turn
your eyes. *Pastorals, Summer*, l. 73

2 Fair tresses man's imperial race in-
snare,
And beauty draws us with a single
hair.
The Rape of the Lock, c. ii, l. 27

3 Here thou, great Anna! whom three
realms obey,
Dost sometimes counsel take—and
sometimes tea. *Ib.* c. iii, l. 7

4 As yet a child, nor yet a fool to fame,
I lisped in numbers, for the numbers
came.
*Epistles and Satires of Horace
Imitated. Prologue, Epistle to
Dr. Arbuthnot*, l. 127

5 This long disease, my life. *Ib.* l. 132

6 Damn with faint praise, assent with
civil leer,
And, without sneering, teach the rest
to sneer;
Willing to wound, and yet afraid to
strike,
Just hint a fault, and hesitate dislike.
Alike reserved to blame, or to commend. *Ib.* l. 201

7 Let Sporus tremble.—A. What? that
thing of silk,
Sporus, that mere white curd of ass's
milk?
Satire or sense, alas! can Sporus feel?
Who breaks a butterfly upon a wheel?
Ib. l. 305

8 Yet let me flap this bug with gilded
wings
This painted child of dirt, that stinks
and stings. *Ib.* l. 309

9 Wit that can creep, and pride that
licks the dust. *Ib.* l. 333

10 There St. John mingles with my
friendly bowl
The feast of reason and the flow of
soul.
*Ib. I. Hor. II, Sat. 1. To Mr.
Fortescue*, l. 127

11 For I, who hold sage Homer's rule the
best,
Welcome the coming, speed the going
guest.
*Ib. II. Hor. II, Sat. 2. To Mr.
Bethel*, l. 159. (In *Odyssey*, xv.
83, with 'parting' for 'going'.)

12 There still remains to mortify a wit,
The many-headed monster of the pit.
On Paradise Lost, l. 304

13 Let humble Allen, with an awkward
shame,
Do good by stealth, and blush to find
it fame.
On Paradise Lost, Epilogue, Dial. i, l. 136

14 Happy the man whose wish and care
A few paternal acres bound,
Content to breathe his native air,
In his own ground. *Ode on Solitude*

15 This is the Jew
That Shakspeare drew.
*Of Macklin's performance of
Shylock, 14 Feb. 1741.* Baker,
Reed, & Jones, *Biographia
Dramatica* (1812), vol. 1, pt. ii,
p. 469

16 'Blessed is the man who expects
nothing, for he shall never be disappointed', was the ninth beatitude
which a man of wit (who, like a man
of wit, was a long time in gaol) added
to the eighth.
Letters. To Fortescue, 23 Sept. 1725

RICHARD PORSON 1759–1808

17 The Germans in Greek
Are sadly to seek:
Not five in five score,
But ninety-five more:
All, save only Herman,
And Herman's a German.
M. L. Clarke, Life of Porson,
ch. vii

18 I went to Frankfort, and got drunk
With that most learn'd professor,
Brunck;
I went to Worts, and got more drunken
With that more learn'd professor,
Ruhnken.
Faceti& Cantabrigienses (1825)

BEILBY PORTEUS 1731–1808

19 War its thousands slays, Peace its
ten thousands. *Death*, l. 179

20 Teach him how to live,
And, oh! still harder lesson! how to
die. *Ib.* l. 319

FRANCIS POTT 1832–1909

21 The strife is o'er, the battle done;
Now is the Victor's triumph won;
O let the song of praise be sung.
Alleluia!
*The Strife is O'er. Hymns fitted
to the Order of Common Prayer
(1861), trans. of Latin Finita
Iam Sunt Praelia*

BEATRIX POTTER 1866–1943

22 Once upon a time there were four
little Rabbits, and their names were
Flopsy, Mopsy, Cotton-tail, and Peter.
The Tale of Peter Rabbit

POTTER—BOOK OF COMMON PRAYER

166

1 No more twist!
The Tailor of Gloucester

2 It is said that the effect of eating too much lettuce is 'soporific'.
The Tale of the Flopsy Bunnies

STEPHEN POTTER 1900–

3 Gamesmanship. *Book Title*

JOHN O'CONNOR POWER

4 The mules of politics: without pride of ancestry, or hope of posterity.
Quoted in H. H. Asquith's Memories and Reflections, i. 123

WINTHROP MACKWORTH PRAED 1802–1839

5 His talk was like a stream, which runs
With rapid change from rocks to roses:
It slipped from politics to puns,
It passed from Mahomet to Moses;
Beginning with the laws which keep
The planets in their radiant courses,
And ending with some precept deep
For dressing eels, or shoeing horses.
The Vicar

THE BOOK OF COMMON PRAYER

6 A Table of the Moveable Feasts.
Section Heading in Introductory Pages, p. xxxi

7 Dearly beloved brethren, the Scripture moveth us in sundry places to acknowledge and confess our manifold sins and wickedness.
Morning Prayer. Priest's Opening Exhortation

8 We have erred, and strayed from thy ways like lost sheep.
Ib. General Confession

9 We have left undone those things which we ought to have done; And we have done those things which we ought not to have done; And there is no health in us. *Ib.*

10 A godly, righteous, and sober life. *Ib.*

11 And forgive us our trespasses, As we forgive them that trespass against us.
Ib. The Lord's Prayer

12 The noble army of martyrs.
Ib. Te Deum Laudamus

13 Give peace in our time, O Lord.
Because there is none other that fighteth for us, but only thou, O God.
Ib. Versicles

14 The author of peace and lover of concord, in knowledge of whom standeth our eternal life, whose service is perfect freedom.
Ib. Second Collect, for Peace

15 Neither run into any kind of danger.
Morning Prayer. Third Collect, for Grace

16 In Quires and Places where they sing.
Ib. Rubric after Third Collect

17 When two or three are gathered together in thy Name thou wilt grant their requests.
Ib. Prayer of St. Chrysostom

18 From whom all holy desires, all good counsels, and all just works do proceed. *Evening Prayer. Second Collect*

19 That peace which the world cannot give. *Ib.*

20 Lighten our darkness, we beseech thee, O Lord; and by thy great mercy defend us from all perils and dangers of this night. *Ib. Third Collect*

21 Have mercy upon us miserable sinners.
The Litany

22 Envy, hatred, and malice, and all uncharitableness. *Ib.*

23 Deceits of the world, the flesh, and the devil. *Ib.*

24 Agony and bloody Sweat. *Ib.*

25 The kindly fruits of the earth, so as in due time we may enjoy them. *Ib.*

26 Our Mediator and Advocate.
Prayers and Thanksgivings, upon Several Occasions. 'O God, whose nature and property'

27 All sorts and conditions of men.
Ib. Prayer for All Conditions of Men

28 All who profess and call themselves Christians. *Ib.*

29 Any ways afflicted, or distressed, in mind, body, or estate. *Ib.*

30 A happy issue out of all their afflictions. *Ib.*

31 Our creation, preservation, and all the blessings of this life.
Ib. Thanksgiving. A General Thanksgiving

32 For the means of grace, and for the hope of glory. *Ib.*

33 Cast away the works of darkness, and put upon us the armour of light, now in the time of this mortal life.
Collects. 1st Sunday in Advent

34 Hear them, read, mark, learn, and inwardly digest them.
Ib. 2nd Sunday in Advent

35 The unruly wills and affections of sinful men.
Ib. 4th Sunday after Easter

36 We may so pass through things temporal, that we finally lose not the things eternal.
Ib. 4th Sunday after Trinity

1 Such good things as pass man's understanding.
Collects. 6th Sunday after Trinity

2 The author and giver of all good things. *Ib. 7th Sunday after Trinity*

3 An open and notorious evil liver.
Holy Communion: Introductory Rubric

4 Unto whom all hearts be open, all desires known, and from whom no secrets are hid. *Ib. Collect for Purity*

5 Thou shalt have none other gods but me. *Ib. 1st Commandment*

6 Incline our hearts to keep this law.
Ib. Response to Commandments

7 Thou shalt not make to thyself any graven image, nor the likeness of any thing that is in heaven above, or in the earth beneath, or in the water under the earth. Thou shalt not bow down to them, nor worship them: for I the Lord thy God am a jealous God, and visit the sins of the fathers upon the children unto the third and fourth generation. *Ib. 2nd Commandment*

8 Thou shalt not take the Name of the Lord thy God in vain.
Ib. 3rd Commandment

9 Remember that thou keep holy the Sabbath-day. Six days shalt thou labour, and do all that thou hast to do; but the seventh day is the Sabbath of the Lord thy God.
Ib. 4th Commandment

10 The stranger that is within thy gates.
Ib.

11 In six days the Lord made heaven and earth, the sea, and all that in them is, and rested the seventh day. *Ib.*

12 Honour thy father and thy mother; that thy days may be long in the land which the Lord thy God giveth thee.
Ib. 5th Commandment

13 Thou shalt do no murder.
Ib. 6th Commandment

14 Thou shalt not commit adultery.
Ib. 7th Commandment

15 Thou shalt not steal.
Ib. 8th Commandment

16 Thou shalt not bear false witness against thy neighbour.
Ib. 9th Commandment

17 Thou shalt not covet thy neighbour's wife, nor his servant, nor his maid, nor his ox, nor his ass, nor any thing that is his. *Ib. 10th Commandment*

18 All things visible and invisible.
Ib. Nicene Creed

19 One Catholick and Apostolick Church.
Ib.

20 The whole state of Christ's Church militant here in earth.
Holy Communion: Prayer for the Church Militant

21 All them, who in this transitory life are in trouble, sorrow, need, sickness, or any other adversity. *Ib.*

22 Ye that do truly and earnestly repent you of your sins, and are in love and charity with your neighbours, and intend to lead a new life.
Ib. The Invitation

23 It is meet and right so to do.
Ib. Versicles

24 This our bounden duty and service.
Ib. Prayer of Oblation, 1

25 The peace of God, which passeth all understanding. *Ib. The Blessing*

26 Be amongst you and remain with you always. *Ib.*

27 All the changes and chances of this mortal life.
Ib. Collects after the Offertory, 1

28 Prevent us, O Lord, in all our doings.
Ib. 4

29 All our works begun, continued, and ended in thee. *Ib.*

30 Grant that the old Adam in this Child may be so buried, that the new man may be raised up in him.
Publick Baptism of Infants. Invocation of Blessing on the Child

31 Ministration of Baptism to Such as are of Riper Years. *Title*

32 What is your name?

N. or *M.*

Who gave you this name?

My Godfathers and Godmothers in my Baptism; wherein I was made a member of Christ, the child of God, and an inheritor of the kingdom of heaven.

What did your Godfathers and Godmothers then for you?

They did promise and vow three things in my name. First, that I should renounce the devil and all his works, the pomps and vanity of this wicked world, and all the sinful lusts of the flesh. Secondly, that I should believe all the Articles of the Christian Faith. And thirdly, that I should keep God's holy will and commandments, and walk in the same all the days of my life. *The Catechism*

33 My duty towards God, and my duty towards my Neighbour. *Ib.*

34 To keep my hands from picking and stealing, and my tongue from evil-speaking, lying, and slandering. *Ib.*

1 To learn and labour truly to get mine own living, and to do my duty in that state of life, unto which it shall please God to call me.   *The Catechism*

2 An outward and visible sign of an inward and spiritual grace.   *Ib.*

3 Being now come to the years of discretion.   *Confirmation*

4 Defend, O Lord, this thy child [or this thy servant] with thy heavenly grace that *he* may continue thine for ever; and daily increase in thy holy Spirit more and more, until *he* come unto thy everlasting kingdom.   *Ib.*

5 If any of you know cause, or just impediment, why these two persons should not be joined together in holy Matrimony, ye are to declare it. This is the first time of asking.   *Solemnization of Matrimony. The Banns*

6 First, it was ordained for the procreation of children.   *Ib.*

7 A remedy against sin.   *Ib.*

8 Such persons as have not the gift of continency.   *Ib.*

9 Let him now speak, or else hereafter for ever hold his peace.   *Ib.*

10 Wilt thou have this woman to thy wedded wife, to live together after God's ordinance in the holy estate of Matrimony?   *Ib. Betrothal*

11 Forsaking all other, keep thee only unto her, so long as ye both shall live.   *Ib.*

12 To have and to hold from this day forward, for better for worse, for richer for poorer, in sickness and in health, to love and to cherish, till death us do part, according to God's holy ordinance; and thereto I plight thee my troth.   *Ib.*

13 To love, cherish, and to obey.   *Ib.*

14 With this Ring I thee wed, with my body I thee worship, and with all my worldly goods I thee endow.   *Ib. The Wedding*

15 Those whom God hath joined together let no man put asunder.   *Ib. The Prayer*

16 Unto God's gracious mercy and protection we commit thee.   *Visitation of the Sick*

17 The inner man.   *Ib.*

18 Laid violent hands upon themselves.   *Burial of the Dead. Introductory Rubric*

19 In the midst of life we are in death.   *Ib. First Anthem*

20 We therefore commit *his* body to the ground; earth to earth, ashes to ashes, dust to dust; in sure and certain hope of the Resurrection to Eternal life.   *Burial of the Dead. First Anthem*

21 Why do the heathen so furiously rage together: and why do the people imagine a vain thing?   *Psalms ii. 1*

22 Out of the mouth of very babes and sucklings hast thou ordained strength, because of thine enemies: that thou mightest still the enemy, and the avenger.   *Ib. viii. 2*

23 What is man, that thou art mindful of him: and the son of man, that thou visitest him?   *Ib. 4*

24 The fowls of the air, and the fishes of the sea.   *Ib. 8*

25 Up, Lord, and let not man have the upper hand.   *Ib. ix. 19*

26 The fool hath said in his heart: There is no God.   *Ib. xiv. 1*

27 Lord, who shall dwell in thy tabernacle: or who shall rest upon thy holy hill?
Even he, that leadeth an uncorrupt life: and doeth the thing which is right, and speaketh the truth from his heart.   *Ib. xv. 1*

28 Keep me as the apple of an eye: hide me under the shadow of thy wings.   *Ib. xvii. 8*

29 The heavens declare the glory of God: and the firmament sheweth his handywork.
One day telleth another: and one night certifieth another.   *Ib. xix. 1*

30 In them hath he set a tabernacle for the sun: which cometh forth as a bridegroom out of his chamber, and rejoiceth as a giant to run his course. It goeth forth from the uttermost part of the heaven, and runneth about unto the end of it again: and there is nothing hid from the heat thereof.   *Ib.*

31 Let the words of my mouth, and the meditation of my heart: be alway acceptable in thy sight,
O Lord, my strength, and my redeemer.   *Ib. 14*

32 Some put their trust in chariots, and some in horses: but we will remember the name of the Lord our God.   *Ib. xx. 7*

33 Thou hast given him his heart's desire: and hast not denied him the request of his lips.   *Ib. xxi. 2*

34 Many oxen are come about me: fat bulls of Basan close me in on every side.   *Ib. xxii. 12*

1 Deliver my soul from the sword: my darling from the power of the dog. Save me from the lion's mouth: thou hast heard me also from the horns of the unicorns.   *Psalms* xxii. 20

2 The Lord is my shepherd: therefore can I lack nothing.
He shall feed me in a green pasture: and lead me forth beside the waters of comfort.
He shall convert my soul: and bring me forth in the paths of righteousness, for his Name's sake.
Yea, though I walk through the valley of the shadow of death, I will fear no evil: for thou art with me; thy rod and thy staff comfort me.
Thou shalt prepare a table before me against them that trouble me: thou hast anointed my head with oil, and my cup shall be full.
But thy loving-kindness and mercy shall follow me all the days of my life: and I will dwell in the house of the Lord for ever.   *Ib.* xxiii

3 The earth is the Lord's, and all that therein is: the compass of the world, and they that dwell therein.
          Ib. xxiv. 1

4 Lift up your heads, O ye gates, and be ye lift up, ye everlasting doors: and the King of glory shall come in.
          Ib. 7

5 Who is the King of glory: even the Lord of hosts, he is the King of glory.
          Ib. 10

6 O remember not the sins and offences of my youth.   *Ib.* xxv. 6

7 I should utterly have fainted: but that I believe verily to see the goodness of the Lord in the land of the living.   *Ib.* xxvii. 15

8 Give thanks unto him for a remembrance of his holiness.
For his wrath endureth but the twinkling of an eye, and in his pleasure is life: heaviness may endure for a night, but joy cometh in the morning.   *Ib.* xxx. 4

9 Into thy hands I commend my spirit.
          Ib. xxxi. 6

10 I am clean forgotten, as a dead man out of mind.   *Ib.* 14

11 Sing unto the Lord a new song: sing praises lustily unto him with a good courage.   *Ib.* xxxiii. 3

12 Eschew evil, and do good: seek peace, and ensue it.   *Ib.* xxxiv. 14

13 I have been young, and now am old: and yet saw I never the righteous forsaken, nor his seed begging their bread.   *Ib.* xxxvii. 25

14 I myself have seen the ungodly in great power: and flourishing like a green bay-tree.   *Psalms* xxxvii. 36

15 Like as the hart desireth the waterbrooks: so longeth my soul after thee, O God.   *Ib.* xlii. 1

16 One deep calleth another, because of the noise of the water-pipes: all thy waves and storms are gone over me.
          Ib. 9

17 While mine enemies that trouble me cast me in the teeth.   *Ib.* 12

18 My heart is inditing of a good matter: I speak of the things which I have made unto the King.
My tongue is the pen of a ready writer.   *Ib.* xlv. 1

19 The King's daughter is all glorious within: her clothing is of wrought gold.
          Ib. 14

20 God is our hope and strength: a very present help in trouble.
Therefore will we not fear, though the earth be moved: and though the hills be carried into the midst of the sea.   *Ib.* xlvi. 1

21 He maketh wars to cease in all the world: he breaketh the bow, and knappeth the spear in sunder, and burneth the chariots in the fire.
Be still then, and know that I am God.
          Ib. 9

22 God is gone up with a merry noise: and the Lord with the sound of the trump.   *Ib.* xlvii. 5

23 Walk about Sion, and go round about her: and tell the towers thereof.
          Ib. xlviii. 11

24 Man being in honour hath no understanding: but is compared unto the beasts that perish.   *Ib.* xlix. 20

25 Behold, I was shapen in wickedness: and in sin hath my mother conceived me.   *Ib.* li. 5

26 Thou shalt purge me with hyssop, and I shall be clean: thou shalt wash me, and I shall be whiter than snow.
          Ib. 7

27 Make me a clean heart, O God: and renew a right spirit within me. *Ib.* 10

28 For thou desirest no sacrifice, else would I give it thee: but thou delightest not in burnt-offerings.
The sacrifice of God is a troubled spirit: a broken and contrite heart, O God, shalt thou not despise. *Ib.* 16

29 Even like the deaf adder that stoppeth her ears;
Which refuseth to hear the voice of the charmer; charm he never so wisely.   *Ib.* lviii. 4

G

1 They grin like a dog, and run about through the city.   *Psalms* lix. 6

2 Moab is my wash-pot; over Edom will I cast out my shoe.   *Ib.* lx. 8

3 The folds shall be full of sheep: the valleys also shall stand so thick with corn, that they shall laugh and sing.   *Ib.* lxv. 14

4 God be merciful unto us, and bless us: and shew us the light of his countenance, and be merciful unto us.
That thy way may be known upon earth: thy saving health among all nations.   *Ib.* lxvii. 1

5 Then shall the earth bring forth her increase: and God, even our own God, shall give us his blessing.   *Ib.* 6

6 Let God arise, and let his enemies be scattered: let them also that hate him flee before him.   *Ib.* lxviii. 1

7 Thou art gone up on high, thou hast led captivity captive, and received gifts for men.   *Ib.* 18

8 The zeal of thine house hath even eaten me.   *Ib.* lxix. 9

9 His enemies shall lick the dust.   *Ib.* lxxii. 9

10 For promotion cometh neither from the east, nor from the west: nor yet from the south.   *Ib.* lxxv. 7

11 A faithless and stubborn generation.   *Ib.* lxxviii. 9

12 So the Lord awaked as one out of sleep: and like a giant refreshed with wine.
He smote his enemies in the hinder parts: and put them to a perpetual shame.   *Ib.* 66

13 O how amiable are thy dwellings: thou Lord of hosts!
My soul hath a desire and longing to enter into the courts of the Lord: my heart and my flesh rejoice in the living God.
Yea, the sparrow hath found her an house, and the swallow a nest where she may lay her young: even thy altars, O Lord of hosts, my King and my God.   *Ib.* lxxxiv. 1

14 Who going through the vale of misery use it for a well: and the pools are filled with water.
They will go from strength to strength.   *Ib.* 6

15 For one day in thy courts: is better than a thousand. I had rather be a door-keeper in the house of my God: than to dwell in the tents of ungodliness.   *Ib.* 10

16 Lord, thou hast been our refuge from one generation to another.   *Ib.* xc. 1

17 For a thousand years in thy sight are but as yesterday: seeing that is past as a watch in the night.
As soon as thou scatterest them they are even as a sleep: and fade away suddenly like the grass.
In the morning it is green, and groweth up: but in the evening it is cut down, dried up, and withered.
          Psalms xc. 4

18 For when thou art angry all our days are gone: we bring our years to an end, as it were a tale that is told.
The days of our age are threescore years and ten; and though men be so strong that they come to fourscore years: yet is their strength then but labour and sorrow; so soon passeth it away, and we are gone.   *Ib.* 9

19 For he shall deliver thee from the snare of the hunter: and from the noisome pestilence.
He shall defend thee under his wings, and thou shalt be safe under his feathers: his faithfulness and truth shall be thy shield and buckler.
Thou shalt not be afraid for any terror by night: nor for the arrow that flieth by day.
For the pestilence that walketh in darkness: nor for the sickness that destroyeth in the noon-day.
A thousand shall fall beside thee, and ten thousand at thy right hand: but it shall not come nigh thee. *Ib.* xci. 3

20 There shall no evil happen unto thee: neither shall any plague come nigh thy dwelling.
For he shall give his angels charge over thee: to keep thee in all thy ways.
They shall bear thee in their hands: that thou hurt not thy foot against a stone.   *Ib.* 10

21 Shew ourselves glad in him with psalms.   *Ib.* xcv. 2

22 In his hand are all the corners of the earth: and the strength of the hills is his also.
The sea is his, and he made it: and his hands prepared the dry land.   *Ib.* 4

23 O come, let us worship and fall down: and kneel before the Lord our Maker.   *Ib.* 6

24 For he is the Lord our God: and we are the people of his pasture, and the sheep of his hand.   *Ib.* 7

25 To-day if ye will hear his voice, harden not your hearts: as in the provocation, and as in the day of temptation in the wilderness.   *Ib.* 8

26 When your fathers tempted me: proved me, and saw my works. *Ib.* 9

1 The days of man are but as grass: for he flourisheth as a flower of the field. For as soon as the wind goeth over it, it is gone: and the place thereof shall know it no more. *Psalms* ciii. 15

2 Wine that maketh glad the heart of man: and oil to make him a cheerful countenance. *Ib.* civ. 15

3 Man goeth forth to his work, and to his labour: until the evening. *Ib.* 23

4 So is the great and wide sea also: wherein are things creeping innumerrable, both small and great beasts.
There go the ships, and there is that Leviathan: whom thou hast made to take his pastime therein.
These wait all upon thee: that thou mayest give them meat in due season. *Ib.* 25

5 Whose feet they hurt in the stocks: the iron entered into his soul. *Ib.* cv. 18

6 Their soul abhorred all manner of meat: and they were even hard at death's door. *Ib.* cvii. 18

7 They that go down to the sea in ships: and occupy their business in great waters;
These men see the works of the Lord: and his wonders in the deep. *Ib.* 23

8 They reel to and fro, and stagger like a drunken man: and are at their wit's end.
So when they cry unto the Lord in their trouble: he delivereth them out of their distress. *Ib.* 27

9 Then are they glad, because they are at rest: and so he bringeth them unto the haven where they would be. *Ib.* 30

10 The Lord said unto my Lord: Sit thou on my right hand, until I make thine enemies thy footstool. *Ib.* cx. 1

11 The fear of the Lord is the beginning of wisdom: a good understanding have all they that do thereafter; the praise of it endureth for ever. *Ib.* cxi. 10

12 The mountains skipped like rams: and the little hills like young sheep. *Ib.* cxiv. 4

13 They have mouths, and speak not: eyes have they, and see not.
They have ears, and hear not: noses have they, and smell not.
They have hands, and handle not: feet have they, and walk not: neither speak they through their throat. *Ib.* cxv. 5

14 I said in my haste, All men are liars. *Ib.* cxvi. 10

15 The same stone which the builders refused: is become the head-stone in the corner. *Ib.* cxviii. 22

16 I will lift up mine eyes unto the hills: from whence cometh my help. *Psalms* cxxi. 1

17 The Lord himself is thy keeper: the Lord is thy defence upon thy right hand;
So that the sun shall not burn thee by day: neither the moon by night. *Ib.* 5

18 The Lord shall preserve thy going out, and thy coming in: from this time forth for evermore. *Ib.* 8

19 I was glad when they said unto me: We will go into the house of the Lord. *Ib.* cxxii. 1

20 O pray for the peace of Jerusalem: they shall prosper that love thee.
Peace be within thy walls: and plenteousness within thy palaces. *Ib.* 6

21 Turn our captivity, O Lord: as the rivers in the south.
They that sow in tears: shall reap in joy.
He that now goeth on his way weeping, and beareth forth good seed: shall doubtless come again with joy, and bring his sheaves with him. *Ib.* cxxvi. 5

22 Except the Lord build the house: their labour is but lost that build it.
Except the Lord keep the city: the watchman waketh but in vain. *Ib.* cxxvii. 1

23 Like as the arrows in the hand of the giant: even so are the young children.
Happy is the man that hath his quiver full of them: they shall not be ashamed when they speak with their enemies in the gate. *Ib.* 5

24 Thy wife shall be as the fruitful vine upon the walls of thine house.
Thy children like the olive-branches round about thy table. *Ib.* cxxviii. 3

25 Out of the deep have I called unto thee, O Lord: Lord, hear my voice. *Ib.* cxxx. 1

26 Behold, how good and joyful a thing it is, brethren, to dwell together in unity! *Ib.* cxxxiii. 1

27 His mercy endureth for ever. *Ib.* cxxxvi. 1

28 By the waters of Babylon we sat down and wept: when we remembered thee, O Sion.
As for our harps, we hanged them up: upon the trees that are therein.
For they that led us away captive required of us then a song, and melody, in our heaviness: Sing us one of the songs of Sion.
How shall we sing the Lord's song in a strange land?

If I forget thee, O Jerusalem: let my right hand forget her cunning.
If I do not remember thee, let my tongue cleave to the roof of my mouth: yea, if I prefer not Jerusalem in my mirth.   *Psalms* cxxxvii. 1

1 If I take the wings of the morning and remain in the uttermost parts of the sea;
Even there also shall thy hand lead me: and thy right hand shall hold me.
If I say, Peradventure the darkness shall cover me: then shall my night be turned to day.
Yea, the darkness is no darkness with thee, but the night is as clear as the day: the darkness and light to thee are both alike.   *Ib.* cxxxix. 8

2 I will give thanks unto thee, for I am fearfully and wonderfully made. *Ib.* 13

3 The Lord is gracious, and merciful: long-suffering, and of great goodness.   *Ib.* cxlv. 8

4 O put not your trust in princes, nor in any child of man: for there is no help in them.   *Ib.* cxlvi. 2

5 The Lord careth for the strangers; he defendeth the fatherless and widow: as for the way of the ungodly, he turneth it upside down.   *Ib.* 9

6 Young men and maidens, old men and children, praise the Name of the Lord: for his Name only is excellent, and his praise above heaven and earth.   *Ib.* cxlviii. 12

7 To bind their kings in chains: and their nobles with links of iron.   *Ib.* cxlix. 8

8 Praise him upon the well-tuned cymbals: praise him upon the loud cymbals.
Let every thing that hath breath: praise the Lord.   *Ib.* cl. 5

9 Such as pass on the seas upon their lawful occasions.
          Forms of Prayer to be Used at Sea. 'O Eternal Lord God'

10 We therefore commit his body to the deep, to be turned into corruption, looking for the resurrection of the body (when the Sea shall give up her dead).
          Ib. At the Burial of their Dead at Sea

11 Come, Holy Ghost, our souls inspire, And lighten with celestial fire.
Thou the anointing Spirit art, Who dost thy seven-fold gifts impart.
          Ordering of Priests. Veni, Creator Spiritus

12 All things necessary to salvation.
          Articles of Religion, vi. Of the Sufficiency of the Holy Scriptures

13 Of Works of Supererogation.
          Articles of Religion. Title of Article xiv

14 Understanded of the people.
          Ib. xxiv. *Of Speaking in the Congregation*

15 It is lawful for Christian men, at the commandment of the Magistrate, to wear weapons, and serve in the wars.
          Ib. Of the Civil Magistrates

16 Table of Kindred and Affinity.   *Title*

17 A Man may not marry his Grandmother.   *Table of Kindred*

ARCHIBALD PHILIP PRIMROSE, EARL OF ROSEBERY
see ROSEBERY

MATTHEW PRIOR 1664–1721

18 All jargon of the schools.
          On Exod. iii. 14. I am that I am. An Ode, l. 65

19 No longer shall the bodice, aptly lac'd
From thy full bosom to thy slender waist,
That air and harmony of shape express,
Fine by degrees and beautifully less.
          Henry and Emma, l. 427

20 I never strove to rule the roast, She ne'er refus'd to pledge my toast.
          Turtle and Sparrow, l. 334

21 A Rechabite poor Will must live, And drink of Adam's ale.
          The Wandering Pilgrim, iii

ADELAIDE ANN PROCTER
1825–1864

22 Seated one day at the organ, I was weary and ill at ease,
And my fingers wandered idly Over the noisy keys.
          Legends and Lyrics. A Lost Chord

23 But I struck one chord of music, Like the sound of a great Amen.
          Ib.

PROTAGORAS c. 481–411 B.C.

24 πάντων χρημάτων ἄνθρωπον μέτρον εἶναι.
          Man is the measure of all things.
          Quoted by Plato in Theaetetus, 160d

PIERRE-JOSEPH PROUDHON
1809–1865

25 La propriété c'est le vol.
          Property is theft.
          Qu'est-ce que la propriété? ch. 1

FATHER PROUT [FRANCIS SYLVESTER MAHONY] 1804–1866

1 'Tis the bells of Shandon,
That sound so grand on
The pleasant waters
Of the River Lee.
The Bells of Shandon

JOHN PUDNEY 1909–

2 Do not despair
For Johnny head-in-air;
He sleeps as sound
As Johnny underground.
For Johnny, st. 1

PUNCH

3 Advice to persons about to marry.—'Don't.' *Punch*, vol. viii, p. 1. 1845

4 You pays your money and you takes your choice. *Ib.* vol. x, p. 17. 1846. *A quotation from what appears to be a peepshow rhyme. See V. S. Lean, Collectanea (1902–4).*

5 Never do to-day what you can put off till to-morrow. *Ib.* vol. xvii, p. 241. 1849

6 Who's 'im, Bill?
A stranger!
'Eave 'arf a brick at 'im.
Ib. vol. xxvi, p. 82. 1854

7 What is Matter?—Never mind.
What is Mind?—No matter.
Ib. vol. xxix, p. 19. 1855

8 '*Peccavi*—I've Scinde' wrote Lord Ellen so proud.
More briefly Dalhousie wrote—'*Vovi*—I've Oude'.
Ib. vol. xxx, p. 141. 1856

9 It ain't the 'unting as 'urts 'un, it's the 'ammer, 'ammer, 'ammer along the 'ard 'igh road.
Ib. vol. xxx, p. 218. 1856

10 Mun, a had na' been the-erre abune two hours when—*bang*—went saxpence!!! *Ib.* vol. liv, p. 235. 1868

11 Go directly—see what she's doing, and tell her she mustn't.
Ib. vol. lxiii, p. 202. 1872

12 There was one poor tiger that hadn't *got* a Christian.
Ib. vol. lxviii, p. 143. 1875

13 Here was an old owl liv'd in an oak
The more he heard, the less he spoke;
The less he spoke, the more he heard
O, if men were all like that wise bird!
Ib. p. 155. 1875

14 It's worse than wicked, my dear, it's vulgar. *Ib.* Almanac. 1876

15 'Is Life worth living?' . . . he suspects it is, in a great measure, a question of the Liver. *Ib.* vol. lxxiii, p. 207. 1877

16 What sort of a doctor is he?
Oh, well, I don't know very much about his ability; but he's got a very good bedside manner!
Punch, vol. lxxxvi, p. 121. 1884

17 I used your soap two years ago; since then I have used no other.
Ib. p. 197. 1884

18 Don't look at me, Sir, with—ah—in that tone of voice.
Ib. vol. lxxxvii, p. 38. 1884

19 Oh yes! I'm sure he's not so fond of me as at first. He's away so much, neglects me dreadfully, and he's so cross when he comes home. What *shall* I do? Feed the brute!
Ib. vol. lxxxix, p. 206. 1886

20 Nearly all our best men are dead! Carlyle, Tennyson, Browning, George Eliot!—I'm not feeling very well myself. *Ib.* vol. civ, p. 210. 1893

21 I'm afraid you've got a bad egg, Mr. Jones.
Oh no, my Lord, I assure you! Parts of it are excellent!
Ib. vol. cix, p. 222, 1895

ISRAEL PUTNAM 1718–1790

22 Men, you are all marksmen—don't one of you fire until you see the whites of their eyes.
Bunker Hill, 1775. Frothingham, *History of the Siege of Boston* (1873), ch. 5, note. *Also attr. to William Prescott (1726–95)*

ERNIE PYLE 1900–1945

23 The worm's eye point of view.
Here Is Your War

FRANCIS QUARLES 1592–1644

24 We spend our midday sweat, our midnight oil;
We tire the night in thought, the day in toil. *Emblems*, bk. ii, No. 2, l. 33

25 Be wisely worldly, be not worldly wise.
Ib. l. 46

26 Our God and soldiers we alike adore
Ev'n at the brink of danger; not before:
After deliverance, both alike requited,
Our God's forgotten, and our soldiers slighted. *Epigram*

27 My soul, sit thou a patient looker-on;
Judge not the play before the play is done:
Her plot hath many changes; every day
Speaks a new scene; the last act crowns the play.
Epigram. Respice Finem

1 He that had no cross deserves no
crown.   *Esther*, Sect. 9, Medit. 9

FRANÇOIS QUESNAY 1694–1774

2 Laissez faire, laissez passer.
> No interference, and complete free-
> dom of movement.
> *Of Government interference. Also
> attr. to Marquis d'Argenson,
> Mémoires* (1736)

SIR ARTHUR QUILLER-COUCH
1863–1944

3 Know you her secret none can utter?
Hers of the Book the tripled Crown?
Poems. *Alma Mater*

FRANÇOIS RABELAIS 1494?–1553

4 L'appétit vient en mangeant.
> The appetite grows by eating.
> *Gargantua*, I. v

5 Fay ce que vouldras.
> Do what thou wilt.   *Ib.* I. lvii

6 Tirez le rideau, la farce est jouée.
> Ring down the curtain, the farce
> is over.
> *Attr. to Rabelais on his death-bed*

7 Je m'en vais chercher un grand peut-
être.
> I go to seek a great perhaps.   *Ib.*

8 Vogue la galère!
> Let her rip!
> [Literally, the words mean 'loose
> the galley' or 'hoist sail'.]
> *Works*, bk. i, ch. 40

JEAN RACINE 1639–1699

9 Elle flotte, elle hésite; en un mot, elle
est femme.
> She is all wavering and hesitation:
> in short, she is a woman.
> *Athalie*, iii. 3

10 Ce n'est plus une ardeur dans mes
veines cachée:
C'est Vénus tout entière à sa proie
attachée.
> It is no longer a passion hidden in
> my veins: it is the goddess Venus
> herself fastened on her prey.
> *Phèdre*, I. iii

11 Point d'argent, point de Suisse.
> No money, no Swiss [soldiers].
> *Les Plaideurs*, I. i

THOMAS RAINBOROWE d. 1648

12 The poorest he that is in England hath
a life to live as the greatest he.
> *In the Army debates at Putney,
> 29 Oct. 1647.* Peacock, *Life of
> Rainborowe*

SIR WALTER RALEGH 1552?–1618

13 Give me my scallop-shell of quiet,
My staff of faith to walk upon,
My scrip of joy, immortal diet,
My bottle of salvation,
My gown of glory, hope's true gage,
And thus I'll take my pilgrimage.
> *The Passionate Man's Pilgrimage*

14 Fain would I climb, yet fear I to fall.
> *Line Written on a Window-Pane.*
> Queen Elizabeth wrote under it,
> 'If thy heart fails thee, climb
> not at all.' Fuller, *Worthies*
> (1840), i. 419

15 Even such is time, which takes in
trust
Our youth, our joys, and all we have,
And pays us but with age and dust,
Who in the dark and silent grave,
When we have wandered all our ways,
Shuts up the story of our days.
And from which earth, and grave, and
dust,
The Lord shall raise me up, I trust.
> *Written the night before his death.
> Found in his Bible in the Gate-
> house at Westminster*

16 O eloquent, just, and mighty Death!
whom none could advise, thou has
persuaded; what none hath dared,
thou hast done; and whom all the
world hath flattered, thou only hast
cast out of the world and despised:
thou hast drawn together all the far-
stretched greatness, all the pride,
cruelty, and ambition of man, and
covered it all over with these two
narrow words, *Hic jacet*.
> *A History of the World*, bk. v,
> ch. vi, § 12

17 [Feeling the edge of the axe before his
execution:]
'Tis a sharp remedy, but a sure one for
all ills.
> Hume, *History of Great Britain*
> (1754), vol. i, ch. iv, p. 72

18 [When asked which way he preferred
to lay his head on the block:]
So the heart be right, it is no matter
which way the head lies.
> W. Stebbing, *Sir Walter Raleigh*,
> ch. xxx

SIR WALTER A. RALEIGH
1861–1922

19 I wish I loved the Human Race;
I wish I loved its silly face;
I wish I liked the way it walks;
I wish I liked the way it talks;
And when I'm introduced to one
I wish I thought *What Jolly Fun!*
> *Laughter from a Cloud* (1923),
> p. 228. *Wishes of an Elderly Man*

JULIAN RALPH 1853–1903

1 News value.
Lecture to Brander Matthews's
English Class, Columbia, 1892.
Thomas Beer's *Mauve Decade*

JEREMIAH EAMES RANKIN
1828–1904

2 God be with you, till we meet again,
By His counsels guide, uphold you,
With His sheep securely fold you:
God be with you, till we meet again.
Hymn

CHARLES READE 1814–1884

3 Courage, mon ami, le diable est mort!
The Cloister and the Hearth,
ch. 24, and *passim*

4 Sow an act, and you reap a habit.
Sow a habit, and you reap a character.
Sow a character, and you reap a
destiny.
Attr. See Notes and Queries,
9th series, vol. 12, p. 377

ERICH MARIA REMARQUE
1898–

5 Im Westen nichts Neues.

All Quiet on the Western Front.
Title of Novel. Trans. by A. W.
Wheen

EBEN REXFORD 1848–1916

6 Darling, I am growing old,
Silver threads among the gold
Shine upon my brow to-day;
Life is fading fast away.
Silver Threads among the Gold

FREDERIC REYNOLDS 1764–1841

7 How goes the enemy? [Said by Mr.
Ennui, 'the time-killer'.]
The Dramatist, I. i

ARCHBISHOP WALTER
REYNOLDS [De REYNEL or
REGINALD] d. 1327

8 Vox Populi, vox Dei.

The voice of the people, the voice
of God.
Text of Sermon when Edward III
ascended the throne, 1 Feb. 1327.
Walsingham, *Historia Anglicana*
(ed. 1863), i. 186

CECIL JOHN RHODES 1853–1902

9 So little done, so much to do.
Last words. L. Michell, *Life,*
vol. ii, ch. 39

GRANTLAND RICE 1880–1954

10 For when the One Great Scorer comes
To write against your name,
He marks—not that you won or lost—
But how you played the game.
Alumnus Football

SIR STEPHEN RICE 1637–1715

11 Sir Stephen Rice . . . having been
often heard to say, before he was a
judge, that he will drive a coach and
six horses through the Act of Settle-
ment.
W. King, *State of the Protestants*
of Ireland (1672), ch. 3, § 3,
par. 6

ROBERT LEROY RIPLEY
1893–1949

12 Believe it or not.
Title of newspaper feature

ANTOINE DE RIVAROL 1753–1801

13 Ce qui n'est pas clair n'est pas
français.

What is not clear is not French.
De l'universalité de la langue
française (1784)

SIR BOYLE ROCHE 1743–1807

14 He regretted that he was not a bird,
and could not be in two places at once.
Attr.

15 Mr. Speaker, I smell a rat; I see him
forming in the air and darkening the
sky; but I'll nip him in the bud.
Attr.

DUC DE LA ROCHEFOUCAULD
1613–1680

16 Dans l'adversité de nos meilleurs amis,
nous trouvons quelque chose qui ne
nous déplaît pas.

In the misfortune of our best friends,
we find something which is not
displeasing to us.
Maximes supprimées, 583

DUC DE LA ROCHEFOUCAULD-
LIANCOURT 1747–1827

17 LOUIS XVI: C'est une révolte?
LA ROCHEFOUCAULD-LIANCOURT: Non,
Sire, c'est une révolution.

LOUIS XVI: Is it a revolt?
LA R.-LIANCOURT: No, Sire, it is a
revolution.
When the news arrived at Ver-
sailles of the Fall of the Bastille,
1789

JOHN WILMOT, EARL OF ROCHESTER 1647–1680

1 A merry monarch, scandalous and poor.
   Works (1926). A Satire on King Charles II for which he was banished from the Court, l. 19

2 Here lies a great and mighty king
   Whose promise none relies on;
   He never said a foolish thing,
   Nor ever did a wise one.
   The King's Epitaph. An alternative version of the first line is:
   'Here lies our sovereign lord the King.'

E. W. ROGERS

3 Ev'ry member of the force
   Has a watch and chain, of course;
   If you want to know the time,
   Ask a P'liceman!   *Ask A P'liceman*

JAMES EDWIN THOROLD ROGERS 1823–1890

4 While ladling butter from alternate tubs
   Stubbs butters Freeman, Freeman butters Stubbs.
      Attr. in Hutton's Letters of Bishop Stubbs

SAMUEL ROGERS 1763–1855

5 Think nothing done while aught remains to do.   *Human Life, l. 49*

6 But there are moments which he calls his own,
   Then, never less alone than when alone,
   Those whom he loved so long and sees no more,
   Loved and still loves—not dead—but gone before,
   He gathers round him.   *Ib. l. 755*

7 Sheridan was listened to with such attention that you might have heard a pin drop.   *Table Talk*

MME ROLAND 1754–1793

8 O liberté! O liberté! que de crimes on commet en ton nom!
   O liberty! O liberty! what crimes are committed in thy name!
      Lamartine, Histoire des Girondins, bk. li, ch. 8

9 The more I see of men, the better I like dogs.   *Attr.*

JAMES ROLMAZ

10 'Where did you get that hat?
   Where did you get that tile?
   Isn't it a nobby one, and just the proper style?
   I should like to have one just the same as that!'

Where'er I go they shout, 'Hello! Where did you get that hat?'
      Where Did You Get That Hat?

PIERRE RONSARD 1529–1585

11 Quand vous serez bien vieille, au soir, à la chandelle,
   Assise auprès du feu, dévidant et filant,
   Direz, chantant mes vers, en vous émerveillant,
   Ronsard me célébrait du temps que j'étais belle.
   When you are very old, and sit in the candle-light at evening spinning by the fire, you will say, as you murmur my verses, a wonder in your eyes, 'Ronsard sang of me in the days when I was fair.'
      Sonnets pour Hélène, ii. 43

FRANKLIN DELANO ROOSEVELT 1882–1945

12 I pledge you—I pledge myself—to a new deal for the American people.
      Speech at Convention, Chicago, 2 July 1932. (New York Times, 3 July, sect. 1, p. 8, col. 7.)
      E. K. Lindley, *The Roosevelt Revolution, ch. 1*

13 Let me assert my firm belief that the only thing we have to fear is fear itself.
      First Inaugural Address, 4 March 1933

14 In the field of world policy; I would dedicate this nation to the policy of the good neighbour.   *Ib.*

15 I see one-third of a nation ill-housed, ill-clad, ill-nourished.
      Second Inaugural Address, 20 Jan. 1937

16 We must be the great arsenal of democracy.
      Fireside Chat, 29 Dec. 1940

17 In the future days, which we seek to make secure, we look forward to a world founded upon four essential freedoms.
   The first is freedom of speech and expression—everywhere in the world.
   The second is freedom of every person to worship God in his own way—everywhere in the world.
   The third is freedom from want. . . .
   The fourth is freedom from fear.
      Speech, 6 Jan. 1941

THEODORE ROOSEVELT 1858–1919

18 Speak softly and carry a big stick.
      Speech, Minnesota State Fair, 2 Sept. 1901

1 The first requisite of a good citizen in this Republic of ours is that he shall be able and willing to pull his weight.
Speech, New York, 11 Nov. 1902

2 The men with the muck-rakes are often indispensable to the well-being of society; but only if they know when to stop raking the muck.
Ib. At the laying of the Corner-stone of the Office Building of House of Representatives, 14 Apr. 1906

3 There can be no fifty-fifty Americanism in this country. There is room here for only 100 per cent. Americanism, only for those who are Americans and nothing else.
Ib. Republican Convention, Saratoga

4 We demand that big business give the people a square deal; in return we must insist that when any one engaged in big business honestly endeavors to do right he shall himself be given a square deal.
Autobiography (1913), p. 615

ARCHIBALD PHILIP PRIMROSE, EARL OF ROSEBERY
1847–1929

5 There is no need for any nation, however great, leaving the Empire, because the Empire is a Commonwealth of Nations.
Speech at Adelaide, 18 January 1884

6 I must plough my furrow alone.
Speech, City of London Liberal Club, 19 July 1901

ALAN STRODE CAMPBELL ROSS 1907–

7 U and non-U.
'Upper Class English Usage', *Bulletin de la Société neo-philologique de Helsinki* (1954). *See also Nancy Mitford,* 'The English Aristocracy', *Encounter* (September 1955)

CHRISTINA GEORGINA ROSSETTI 1830–1894

8 My heart is like a singing bird
Whose nest is in a watered shoot;
My heart is like an apple-tree
Whose boughs are bent with thickset fruit;
My heart is like a rainbow shell
That paddles in a halcyon sea;
My heart is gladder than all these
Because my love is come to me.
A Birthday

9 In the bleak mid-winter
Frosty wind made moan,
Earth stood hard as iron,
Water like a stone;
Snow had fallen, snow on snow,
Snow on snow,
In the bleak mid-winter,
Long ago. *Mid-Winter*

10 In the bleak mid-winter
A stable-place sufficed
The Lord God almighty,
Jesus Christ. *Ib.*

11 Better by far you should forget and smile
Than that you should remember and be sad. *Remember*

12 When I am dead, my dearest,
Sing no sad songs for me;
Plant thou no roses at my head,
Nor shady cypress tree:
Be the green grass above me
With showers and dewdrops wet;
And if thou wilt, remember,
And if thou wilt, forget.
Song: When I am Dead

13 Does the road wind up-hill all the way?
Yes, to the very end.
Will the day's journey take the whole long day?
From morn to night, my friend.
Up-Hill

DANTE GABRIEL ROSSETTI 1828–1882

14 Mother of the Fair Delight,
Thou handmaid perfect in God's sight.
Ave, l. 1

15 The blessed damozel leaned out
From the gold bar of Heaven;
Her eyes were deeper than the depth
Of waters stilled at even;
She had three lilies in her hand,
And the stars in her hair were seven.
The Blessed Damozel, i

16 Her hair that lay along her back
Was yellow like ripe corn. *Ib. ii*

ROUGET DE LISLE 1760–1836

17 Allons, enfants de la patrie,
Le jour de gloire est arrivé.
Come, children of our country, the day of glory has arrived.
La Marseillaise

JEAN-JACQUES ROUSSEAU 1712–1778

18 L'homme est né libre, et partout il est dans les fers.
Man was born free, and everywhere he is in chains.
Du Contrat Social, ch. 1

1 'Monseigneur, il faut que je vive,'
disait un malheureux auteur satirique
au ministre qui lui reprochait l'in-
famie de ce métier. 'Je n'en vois pas la
nécessité,' lui repartit froidement
l'homme en place.

'My Lord—I must live'—once said
a wretched author of satire to a
minister who had reproached
him for following so degrading a
profession. 'I fail to see why,'
replied the Great Man coldly.
Émile, iii (*see 10:14*)

MARTIN JOSEPH ROUTH
1755–1854

2 You will find it a very good practice
always to verify your references, sir!
Burgon, *Memoir of Dr. Routh.
Quarterly Review* (July 1878),
vol. cxlvi

NICHOLAS ROWE 1674–1718

3 The evening of my age.
The Fair Penitent, IV. i

4 I feel the pangs of disappointed love.
Ib.

5 Is this that haughty, gallant, gay
Lothario? *Ib.* v. 1

'RED ROWLEY'

6 Mademoiselle from Armenteers,
Hasn't been kissed in forty years,
Hinky, dinky, parley-voo.
Song of the First World War

DAMON RUNYON 1884–1946

7 More than somewhat. *Title of Book*

JOHN RUSKIN 1819–1900

8 [On Whistler's 'Nocturne in Black and
Gold']
I have seen, and heard, much of
Cockney impudence before now; but
never expected to hear a coxcomb ask
two hundred guineas for flinging a
pot of paint in the public's face.
Fors Clavigera, letter lxxix,
18 June 1877

9 All violent feelings . . . produce in us
a falseness in all our impressions of
external things, which I would
generally characterize as the 'Pathetic
Fallacy'.
Modern Painters (1888), vol. iii

10 There is really no such thing as bad
weather, only different kinds of good
weather. *Quoted by Lord Avebury*

LORD JOHN RUSSELL 1792–1878

11 Among the defects of the Bill, which
were numerous, one provision was
conspicuous by its presence and
another by its absence.
*Speech to the electors of the City of
London, Apr. 1859*

SIR WILLIAM HOWARD
RUSSELL 1820–1907

12 [The Russians] dash on towards that
thin red line tipped with steel.
*The British Expedition to the
Crimea* (1877), p. 156

W. ST. LEGER 1850–c. 1915

13 There is a fine stuffed chavender,
A chavender, or chub,
That decks the rural pavender,
The pavender, or pub,
Wherein I eat my gravender,
My gravender, or grub.
The Chavender, or Chub, st. 1

CHARLES-AUGUSTIN
SAINTE-BEUVE 1804–1869

14 Et Vigny plus secret,
Comme en sa tour d'ivoire, avant
midi rentrait.

And Vigny more reserved,
Returned ere noon, within his ivory
tower.
Quoted in Paléologue's *Vigny*,
p. 71

'SAKI' [HECTOR HUGH MUNRO]
1870–1916

15 The cook was a good cook, as cooks go;
and as cooks go she went.
*Reginald. Reginald on Besetting
Sins*

16 Women and elephants never forget
an injury. *Ib.*

ROBERT CECIL, LORD
SALISBURY 1830–1903

17 By office boys for office boys.
Remark about The Daily Mail.
See H. Hamilton Fyfe, *North-
cliffe, an Intimate Biography*,
ch. 4

SALLUST 86–34 B.C.

18 Pro patria, pro liberis, pro aris atque
focis suis.

On behalf of their country, their
children, their altars, and their
hearths. *Catiline*, 59

1 Urbem venalem et mature perituram,
si emptorem invenerit.

> The venal city soon to perish, if
> a buyer can be found.
> *Jugurtha*, 35

2 Punica fide.

> With Carthaginian faith [i.e. treach-
> ery.] *Ib.* 108, 3

EPES SARGENT 1813–1880

3 A life on the ocean wave,
A home on the rolling deep.
A Life on the Ocean Wave

SIEGFRIED SASSOON 1886–1967

4 If I were fierce and bald and short of
breath,
I'd live with scarlet Majors at the
Base,
And speed glum heroes up the line
to death. *Base Details*

5 And when the war is done and youth
stone dead
I'd toddle safely home and die—in
bed. *Ib.*

6 Everyone suddenly burst out singing.
Everyone Sang

7 The song was wordless;
The singing will never be done. *Ib.*

RICHARD SAVAGE d. 1743

8 No tenth transmitter of a foolish
face. *The Bastard*, l. 8

HENRY J. SAYERS d. 1932

9 Ta-ra-ra-boom-de-ay!
Title of Song (1891)

FRIEDRICH VON SCHELLING
1775–1854

10 Architecture in general is frozen
music. *Philosophie der Kunst*

FRIEDRICH VON SCHILLER
1759–1805

11 Freude, schöner Götterfunken,
Tochter aus Elysium,
Wir betreten Feuertrunken,
Himmlische, dein Heiligtum.
Deine Zauber binden wieder,
Was die Mode streng geteilt,
Alle Menschen werden Brüder
Wo dein sanfter Flügel weilt.

> Thou radiance sprung from God
> Himself,
> Thou daughter of Elysium, Joy,
> Thy shrine we tread, Thou Maid
> Divine,
> Though light's excess our sense
> destroy.

> What harsh world-use has rent
> apart,
> Thy healing spells restore again;
> Where'er Thy gentle wings may
> rest,
> Brothers we find our fellow-men.
> *An die Freude*

12 Die Sonne geht in meinem Staat nicht
unter.

> The sun does not set in my
> dominions.
> [Philip II.] *Don Carlos*, Act 1, sc. 6

13 Mit der Dummheit kämpfen Götter
selbst vergebens.

> With stupidity the gods themselves
> struggle in vain.
> *Jungfrau von Orleans*, III. vi

14 Die Weltgeschichte ist das Welt-
gericht.

> The world's history is the world's
> judgement.
> *First lecture as Professor of His-
> tory, Jena, 26 May 1789*

MAX SCHNECKENBURGER
1819–1849

15 Die Wacht am Rhein.

> The watch on the Rhine.
> *Title of Song*

LOUIS SCHNEIDER

16 O Tannenbaum, O Tannenbaum,
Wie grün sind deine Blätter!

> O pine-tree, O pine-tree,
> How green are thy leaves!
> *Der Kurmärker und die Picarde*

CHARLES PRESTWICH SCOTT
1846–1932

17 Comment is free but facts are sacred.
In the Manchester Guardian, *6 May
1926*

ROBERT FALCON SCOTT
1868–1912

18 For God's sake look after our people.
Journal, 25 March 1912

19 Had we lived, I should have had a tale
to tell of the hardihood, endurance,
and courage of my companions which
would have stirred the heart of every
Englishman. These rough notes and
our dead bodies must tell the tale.
Message to the Public

SIR WALTER SCOTT 1771–1832

20 Come fill up my cup, come fill up my
can,
Come saddle your horses, and call
up your men;

Come open the West Port, and let me
  gang free,
And it's room for the bonnets of
  Bonny Dundee!'
      *Bonny Dundee. (The Doom of
      Devorgoil, Act II, sc. ii)*

1 But answer came there none.
      Bridal of Triermain, can. III. x

2 He is gone on the mountain,
    He is lost to the forest,
  Like a summer-dried fountain,
    When our need was the sorest.
        The Lady of the Lake, can. III. xvi

3 Like the dew on the mountain,
    Like the foam on the river,
  Like the bubble on the fountain,
    Thou art gone, and for ever!   *Ib.*

4 The way was long, the wind was cold,
  The Minstrel was infirm and old;
  His wither'd cheek and tresses grey,
  Seem'd to have known a better day.
  The harp, his sole remaining joy,
  Was carried by an orphan boy,
  The last of all the Bards was he,
  Who sung of Border chivalry.
        *The Lay of the Last Minstrel,
        introduction, l. 1*

5 If thou would'st view fair Melrose
    aright,
  Go visit it by the pale moonlight;
  For the gay beams of lightsome day
  Gild, but to flout, the ruins grey.
        Ib. c. II. i

6 Breathes there the man, with soul so
    dead,
  Who never to himself hath said,
    This is my own, my native land!
  Whose heart hath ne'er within him
    burn'd,
  As home his footsteps he hath turn'd
    From wandering on a foreign strand!
  If such there breathe, go, mark him
    well;
  For him no Minstrel raptures swell;
  High though his titles, proud his
    name,
  Boundless his wealth as wish can
    claim;
  Despite those titles, power, and pelf,
  The wretch, concentred all in self,
  Living, shall forfeit fair renown,
  And, doubly dying, shall go down
  To the vile dust, from whence he
    sprung,
  Unwept, unhonour'd, and unsung.

  O Caledonia! stern and wild,
  Meet nurse for a poetic child!
  Land of brown heath and shaggy
    wood,
  Land of the mountain and the flood,
  Land of my sires! what mortal hand
  Can e'er untie the filial band
  That knits me to thy rugged strand!
        Ib. can. VI. i–ii

7 That day of wrath, that dreadful day,
  When heaven and earth shall pass
    away.
    The Lay of the Last Minstrel, can. VI. xxxi

8 O, young Lochinvar is come out of the
    west,
  Through all the wide Border his steed
    was the best. *Marmion, can. V. xii*

9 So faithful in love, and so dauntless in
    war,
  There never was knight like the young
    Lochinvar.   *Ib.*

10 For a laggard in love, and a dastard
     in war,
   Was to wed the fair Ellen of brave
     Lochinvar.   *Ib.*

11 'O come ye in peace here, or come ye
     in war,
   Or to dance at our bridal, young Lord
     Lochinvar?'   *Ib.*

12 O what a tangled web we weave,
   When first we practise to deceive!
        Ib. can. VI. xvii

13 O Woman! in our hours of ease,
   Uncertain, coy, and hard to please,
   And variable as the shade
   By the light quivering aspen made;
   When pain and anguish wring the
     brow,
   A ministering angel thou!   *Ib. xxx*

14 You . . . whirl'd them to the back o'
   beyont.   *The Antiquary, ch. 2*

15 Look not thou on beauty's charm-
     ing,—
   Sit thou still when kings are arming,—
   Taste   not   when   the   wine-cup
     glistens,—
   Speak not when the people listens,—
   Stop thine ear against the singer,—
   From the red gold keep thy finger;—
   Vacant heart and hand, and eye,—
   Easy live and quiet die.
        The Bride of Lammermoor, ch. 3

16 [He] was ever after designated as a
   'stickit minister'.
        Guy Mannering, ch. 2

17 The ancient and now forgotten pastime of high jinks.   *Ib. ch. 36*

18 Proud Maisie is in the wood,
     Walking so early,
   Sweet Robin sits in the bush,
     Singing so rarely.
        The Heart of Midlothian, ch. 40

19 Come, trowl the brown bowl to me,
     Bully boy, bully boy,
   Come, trowl the brown bowl to me:
     Ho! jolly Jenkin, I spy a knave in
       drinking,
   Come, trowl the brown bowl to me.
        Ivanhoe, ch. 20

20 But, my lord, there is a Southern proverb,—fine words butter no parsnips.
        The Legend of Montrose, ch. 3

1 But with the morning cool repentance came.   *Rob Roy, ch. 12*

2 There's a gude time coming.
    Ib. ch. 29, note

3 Fair, fat, and forty.
    St. Ronan's Well, ch. 7

4 The play-bill, which is said to have announced the tragedy of Hamlet, the character of the Prince of Denmark being left out.
    The Talisman, introduction. For an earlier report of this anecdote see Times Literary Supplement, *3 June 1939*

5 The Big Bow-Wow strain I can do myself like any now going; but the exquisite touch, which renders ordinary commonplace things and characters interesting, from the truth of the description and the sentiment, is denied to me. [On Jane Austen.]
    Journal, 14 Mar. 1826

6 I would like to be there, were it but to see how the cat jumps.
    Ib. 7 Oct. 1826

7 From the lone shieling of the misty island
    Mountains divide us, and the waste of seas—
Yet still the blood is strong, the heart is Highland,
    And we in dreams behold the Hebrides!
Fair these broad meads, these hoary woods are grand;
But we are exiles from our fathers' land.
    Canadian Boat Song. Of disputed authorship. See Times Literary Supplement, *23 Dec. 1904,* G. M. Fraser's *article.*

SCOTTISH METRICAL PSALMS
1650

8 The Lord's my shepherd, I'll not want.
    He makes me down to lie
In pastures green: he leadeth me
    the quiet waters by.
My soul he doth restore again;
    and me to walk doth make
Within the paths of righteousness,
    ev'n for his own name's sake.

Yea, though I walk in death's dark vale,
    yet will I fear none ill:
For thou art with me; and thy rod
    and staff me comfort still.
My table thou hast furnished
    in presence of my foes;
My head thou dost with oil anoint,
    and my cup overflows.
    Psalm xxiii. 1

9 The race that long in darkness pin'd have seen a glorious light.
    Paraphrase 19. Isaiah ix. 2–8

EDMUND HAMILTON SEARS
1810–1876

10 It came upon the midnight clear,
    That glorious song of old,
From Angels bending near the earth
    To touch their harps of gold;
'Peace on the earth, good will to man
    From Heaven's all gracious King.'
The world in solemn stillness lay
    To hear the angels sing.
    The Christian Register (1850).
    That Glorious Song of Old

ALAN SEEGER 1888–1916

11 I have a rendezvous with Death
    At some disputed barricade.
    I Have a Rendezvous with Death

SIR JOHN ROBERT SEELEY
1834–1895

12 We [the English] seem, as it were, to have conquered and peopled half the world in a fit of absence of mind.
    The Expansion of England, Lecture I

JOHN SELDEN 1584–1654

13 Ignorance of the law excuses no man; not that all men know the law, but because 'tis an excuse every man will plead, and no man can tell how to confute him.   *Table Talk, p. 99. Law*

14 Take a straw and throw it up into the air, you shall see by that which way the wind is.   *Ib. 105. Libels*

15 Pleasure is nothing else but the intermission of pain.   *Ib. 132. Pleasure*

WALTER CARRUTHERS SELLAR 1898–1951
and
ROBERT JULIAN YEATMAN
contemporary

16 1066, And All That.   *Title of Book*

17 The Roman Conquest was, however, a *Good Thing.*
    1066, And All That, ch. 1

18 Napoleon's armies always used to march on their stomachs, shouting: 'Vive l'Intérieur!'   *Ib. ch. 48*

19 A Bad Thing: America was thus clearly top nation, and History came to a .   *Ib. ch. 62*

SENECA d. A.D. 65

20 Contra bonum morem.
    Against good custom.
    Dialogues, vi. i. 2

ROBERT WILLIAM SERVICE
1874–

1 The lady that's known as Lou.
Songs of a Sourdough. The Shooting of Dan McGrew

EDWARD SEXBY d. 1658

2 Killing no Murder Briefly Discourst in Three Questions.
Title of Pamphlet (1657)

RICHARD SHACKLOCK c. 1575

3 Proud as peacocks.
Hatchet of Heresies (1565), p. 26b

THOMAS SHADWELL 1642?–1692

4 'Tis the way of all flesh.
The Sullen Lovers, v. ii

5 And wit's the noblest frailty of the mind. *A True Widow*, II. i

6 I am, out of the ladies' company, like a fish out of the water. *Ib.*

WILLIAM SHAKESPEARE
1564–1616

In the references the line number is given without brackets where the scene is all verse up to the quotation and the line number is certain. It is given in square brackets where prose makes it variable, and the references are to the Oxford Standard Authors Shakespeare in one volume.

7   It were all one
That I should love a bright particular star
And think to wed it, he is so above me.
All's Well That Ends Well, I. i. [97]

8 My friends were poor but honest.
Ib. iii. [203]

9 They say miracles are past.
Ib. II. iii. [1]

10 A young man married is a man that's marred. *Ib.* [315]

11 I know a man that had this trick of melancholy sold a goodly manor for a song. *Ib.* III. ii. [8]

12 Where's my serpent of old Nile?
Antony and Cleopatra, I. v. 25

13   My salad days,
When I was green in judgment. *Ib.* 73

14 I do not much dislike the matter, but The manner of his speech.
Ib. II. ii. 117

15 The barge she sat in, like a burnish'd throne,
Burn'd on the water; the poop was beaten gold,
Purple the sails, and so perfumed, that The winds were love-sick with them, the oars were silver,
Which to the tune of flutes kept stroke, and made
The water which they beat to follow faster,
As amorous of their strokes. For her own person,
It beggar'd all description; she did lie
In her pavilion,—cloth-of-gold of tissue,—
O'er-picturing that Venus where we see
The fancy outwork nature; on each side her
Stood pretty-dimpled boys, like smiling Cupids,
With divers-colour'd fans, whose wind did seem
To glow the delicate cheeks which they did cool,
And what they undid did.
Antony and Cleopatra, II. ii. [199]

16 Age cannot wither her, nor custom stale
Her infinite variety; other women cloy
The appetites they feed, but she makes hungry
Where most she satisfies. *Ib.* [243]

17 Let's have one other gaudy night.
Ib. III. xi. 182

18 Unarm, Eros; the long day's task is done,
And we must sleep. *Ib.* IV. xii. 35

19 I am dying, Egypt, dying; only
I here importune death awhile, until
Of many thousand kisses the poor last
I lay upon thy lips. *Ib.* xiii. 18

20   A Roman by a Roman
Valiantly vanquished. *Ib.* 57

21   O! see my women,
The crown o' the earth doth melt. My lord!
O! wither'd is the garland of the war,
The soldier's pole is fall'n; young boys and girls
Are level now with men; the odds is gone,
And there is nothing left remarkable
Beneath the visiting moon. *Ib.* 62

22   What's brave, what's noble,
Let's do it after the high Roman fashion,
And make death proud to take us.
Ib. 86

23 Finish, good lady; the bright day is done,
And we are for the dark.
Ib. v. ii. 192

24   Antony
Shall be brought drunken forth, and I shall see
Some squeaking Cleopatra boy my greatness
I' the posture of a whore. *Ib.* 217

1 I know that a woman is a dish for the gods, if the devil dress her not.
Antony and Cleopatra, v. ii. [274]

2   I have
Immortal longings in me.   *Ib.* [282]

3   Husband, I come:
Now to that name my courage prove my title!
I am fire and air; my other elements
I give to baser life.   *Ib.* [289]

4 CLEOPATRA:
          Come, thou mortal wretch
With thy sharp teeth this knot intrinsicate
Of life at once untie; poor venomous fool,
Be angry, and dispatch. O! couldst thou speak,
That I might hear thee call great Cæsar ass
Unpolicied.
CHARMIAN:
          O eastern star!
CLEOPATRA: Peace! peace!
Dost thou not see my baby at my breast,
That sucks the nurse asleep? *Ib.* [305]

5 Now boast thee, death, in thy possession lies
A lass unparallel'd.   *Ib.* [317]

6 It is well done, and fitting for a princess
Descended of so many royal kings.
Ib. [328]

7 Well said: that was laid on with a trowel. *As You Like It*, I. ii. [113]

8 Hereafter, in a better world than this,
I shall desire more love and knowledge of you.   *Ib.* [301]

9 Sweet are the uses of adversity,
Which like the toad, ugly and venomous,
Wears yet a precious jewel in his head;
And this our life, exempt from public haunt,
Finds tongues in trees, books in the running brooks,
Sermons in stones, and good in everything.   *Ib.* II. i. 12

10 Ay, now am I in Arden; the more fool I. When I was at home I was in a better place; but travellers must be content.   *Ib.* iv. [16]

11   As true a lover
As ever sigh'd upon a midnight pillow.
Ib. [26]

12 Thou speakest wiser than thou art ware of.   *Ib.* [57]

13 Under the greenwood tree
Who loves to lie with me,
And turn his merry note
Unto the sweet bird's throat,
Come hither, come hither, come hither:
    Here shall he see
    No enemy
But winter and rough weather.
As You Like It, II. v. 1

14 I can suck melancholy out of a song as a weasel sucks eggs.   *Ib.* [12]

15 Who doth ambition shun
And loves to live i' the sun,
Seeking the food he eats,
And pleas'd with what he gets.
Ib. [38]

16 'Call me not fool till heaven hath sent me fortune.'
And then he drew a dial from his poke,
And, looking on it with lack-lustre eye,
Says very wisely, 'It is ten o'clock;
Thus may we see,' quoth he, 'how the world wags.'   *Ib.* vii. 19

17 And so, from hour to hour, we ripe and ripe,
And then from hour to hour, we rot and rot:
And thereby hangs a tale.   *Ib.* 26

18 A worthy fool! Motley 's the only wear.
Ib. 34

19 If ever you have look'd on better days,
If ever been where bells have knoll'd to church,
If ever sat at any good man's feast,
If ever from your eyelids wip'd a tear,
And know what 'tis to pity, and be pitied,
Let gentleness my strong enforcement be.   *Ib.* 109

20   All the world's a stage,
And all the men and women merely players:
They have their exits and their entrances;
And one man in his time plays many parts,
His acts being seven ages. At first the infant,
Mewling and puking in the nurse's arms.
And then the whining schoolboy, with his satchel,
And shining morning face, creeping like snail
Unwillingly to school. And then the lover,
Sighing like furnace, with a woful ballad
Made to his mistress' eyebrow. Then a soldier,
Full of strange oaths, and bearded like the pard,
Jealous in honour, sudden and quick in quarrel,
Seeking the bubble reputation
Even in the cannon's mouth. And then the justice,

In fair round belly with good capon
  lin'd,
With eyes severe, and beard of formal
  cut,
Full of wise saws and modern in-
  stances;
And so he plays his part. The sixth
  age shifts
Into the lean and slipper'd pantaloon,
With spectacles on nose and pouch on
  side,
His youthful hose well sav'd a world
  too wide
For his shrunk shank; and his big
  manly voice,
Turning again towards childish treble,
  pipes
And whistles in his sound. Last scene
  of all,
That ends this strange eventful history,
Is second childishness, and mere
  oblivion,
Sans teeth, sans eyes, sans taste, sans
  everything.
              As You Like It, II. vii. 139

1 Blow, blow, thou winter wind,
  Thou art not so unkind
      As man's ingratitude:
  Thy tooth is not so keen,
  Because thou art not seen,
      Although thy breath be rude.
  Heigh-ho! sing, heigh-ho! unto the
    green holly:
  Most friendship is feigning, most
    loving mere folly.
      Then heigh-ho! the holly!
      This life is most jolly.

2 Freeze, freeze, thou bitter sky,
  That dost not bite so nigh
      As benefits forgot:
  Though thou the waters warp,
  Thy sting is not so sharp
      As friend remember'd not. *Ib.* 174

3 Run, run, Orlando: carve on every tree
  The fair, the chaste, and unexpressive
    she.   *Ib.* III. ii. 9

4 Thou art in a parlous state.   *Ib.* [46]

5 Let us make an honourable retreat;
  though not with bag and baggage, yet
  with scrip and scrippage.   *Ib.* [170]

6   Down on your knees,
  And thank heaven, fasting, for a good
    man's love.   *Ib.* v. 57

7 Dead shepherd, now I find thy saw of
    might:
  'Who ever lov'd that lov'd not at first
    sight?'   *Ib.* 81

8 For now I am in a holiday humour.
                      Ib. IV. i [70]

9 When you were gravelled for lack of
    matter.   *Ib.* [76]

10 Men have died from time to time, and
   worms have eaten them, but not for
   love.   *Ib.* [110]

11 Men are April when they woo,
   December when they wed: maids are
   May when they are maids, but the
   sky changes when they are wives.
              As You Like It, IV. i. [153]

12 It was a lover and his lass,
     With a hey, and a ho, and a hey
       nonino,
   That o'er the green cornfield did pass,
     In the spring time, the only pretty
       ring time,
   When birds do sing, hey ding a ding,
       ding;
   Sweet lovers love the spring.

   Between the acres of the rye,
     With a hey, and a ho, and a hey
       nonino,
   These pretty country folks would lie,
     In the spring time, &c. *Ib.* v. iii. [18]

13 An ill-favoured thing, sir, but mine
   own.   *Ib.* iv. [60]

14 The retort courteous . . . the quip
   modest . . . the reply churlish . . . the
   reproof valiant . . . the countercheck
   quarrelsome . . . the lie circumstantial
   . . . the lie direct.   *Ib.* [96]

15 He uses his folly like a stalking-horse,
   and under the presentation of that he
   shoots his wit.   *Ib.* [112]

16 If it be true that 'good wine needs no
   bush', 'tis true that a good play
   needs no epilogue.   *Ib. Epilogue* [3]

17   They threw their caps
   As they would hang them on the
     horns o' the moon,
   Shouting their emulation.
              Coriolanus, I. i. [218]

18 Hear you this Triton of the minnows?
   mark you
   His absolute 'shall'?   *Ib.* III. i. 88

19 If you have writ your annals true, 'tis
     there,
   That, like an eagle in a dove-cot, I
   Flutter'd your Volscians in Corioli:
   Alone I did it.   *Ib.* v. v. 114

20 Hark! hark! the lark at heaven's gate
     sings,
     And Phœbus 'gins arise,
   His steeds to water at those springs
     On chalic'd flowers that lies;
   And winking Mary-buds begin
     To ope their golden eyes:
   With everything that pretty is,
     My lady sweet, arise!
              Cymbeline, II. iii. [22]

21 I have not slept one wink. *Ib.* iv. [103]

22 Fear no more the heat o' the sun,
     Nor the furious winter's rages;
   Thou thy worldly task hast done,
     Home art gone and ta'en thy wages:
   Golden lads and girls all must,
     As chimney-sweepers, come to dust.
              Ib. IV. ii. 258

1 You come most carefully upon your
hour.   *Hamlet*, I. i. 6

2 For this relief much thanks; 'tis bitter
cold,
And I am sick at heart.   *Ib.* 8

3 In the most high and palmy state of
Rome,
A little ere the mightiest Julius fell,
The graves stood tenantless and the
sheeted dead
Did squeak and gibber in the Roman
streets.   *Ib.* 113

4 It faded on the crowing of the cock.
Some say that ever 'gainst that season
comes
Wherein our Saviour's birth is celebrated,
The bird of dawning singeth all night
long;
And then, they say, no spirit can walk
abroad;
The nights are wholesome; then no
planets strike,
No fairy takes, nor witch hath power
to charm,
So hallow'd and so gracious is the
time.   *Ib.* 157

5 But, look, the morn, in russet mantle
clad,
Walks o'er the dew of yon high eastern
hill.   *Ib.* 166

6 The memory be green.   *Ib.* ii. 2

7 A little more than kin, and less than
kind.   *Ib.* 65

8 Not so, my lord; I am too much i'
the sun.   *Ib.* 67

9 Seems, madam! Nay, it is; I know not
'seems'.   *Ib.* 76

10 But I have that within which passeth
show;
These but the trappings and the suits
of woe.   *Ib.* 85

11 O! that this too too solid flesh would
melt,
Thaw, and resolve itself into a dew;
Or that the Everlasting had not fix'd
His canon 'gainst self-slaughter! O
God! O God!
How weary, stale, flat, and unprofit-
able
Seem to me all the uses of this world.
Fie on't! O fie! 'tis an unweeded
garden,
That grows to seed; things rank and
gross in nature
Possess it merely. That it should
come to this!
But two months dead: nay, not so
much, not two:
So excellent a king; that was, to this,
Hyperion to a satyr: so loving to my
mother,
That he might not beteem the winds
of heaven

Visit her face too roughly. Heaven and
earth!
Must I remember? Why, she would
hang on him,
As if increase of appetite had grown
But what it fed on; and yet, within
a month,
Let me not think on't: Frailty, thy
name is woman!
A little month; or ere those shoes were
old
With which she follow'd my poor
father's body,
Like Niobe, all tears; why she, even
she,—
O God! a beast, that wants discourse
of reason,
Would have mourn'd longer,—married
with mine uncle,
My father's brother, but no more like
my father
Than I to Hercules.   *Hamlet*, I. ii.

12 We'll teach you to drink deep ere you
depart.   *Ib.* 175

13 Thrift, thrift, Horatio! the funeral
bak'd meats
Did coldly furnish forth the marriage
tables.
Would I had met my dearest foe in
heaven
Ere I had ever seen that day, Horatio!
Ib. 180

14 In my mind's eye, Horatio.   *Ib.* 185

15 He was a man, take him for all in all,
I shall not look upon his like again.
Ib. 187

16 In the dead vast and middle of the
night.   *Ib.* 198

17 But answer made it none.   *Ib.* 215

18 A countenance more in sorrow than
in anger.   *Ib.* 231

19   All is not well;
I doubt some foul play.   *Ib.* 254

20 Do not, as some ungracious pastors do,
Show me the steep and thorny way to
heaven,
Whiles, like a puff'd and reckless
libertine,
Himself the primrose path of dalliance
treads,
And recks not his own rede.   *Ib.* iii. 47

21 And these few precepts in thy memory
Look thou character. Give thy
thoughts no tongue,
Nor any unproportion'd thought his
act.
Be thou familiar, but by no means
vulgar;
The friends thou hast, and their adoption tried,
Grapple them to thy soul with hoops
of steel;
But do not dull thy palm with enter-
tainment

Of each new-hatch'd, unfledg'd com-
rade. Beware
Of entrance to a quarrel; but, being in,
Bear't that th' opposed may beware
of thee.
Give every man thine ear, but few
thy voice;
Take each man's censure, but reserve
thy judgment.
Costly thy habit as thy purse can buy,
But not express'd in fancy; rich, not
gaudy;
For the apparel oft proclaims the man,
And they in France of the best rank
and station
Are most select and generous, chief in
that.
Neither a borrower, nor a lender be;
For loan oft loses both itself and
friend,
And borrowing dulls the edge of
husbandry,
This above all: to thine own self be
true,
And it must follow, as the night the
day,
Thou canst not then be false to any
man.
Farewell; my blessing season this in
thee!   *Hamlet*, I. iii. 58

1   You speak like a green girl,
Unsifted in such perilous circumstance.   *Ib.* 101

2 HAMLET:
The air bites shrewdly; it is very cold.
HORATIO:
It is a nipping and an eager air.
                        Ib. iv. 1

3 But to my mind,—though I am native
here,
And to the manner born,—it is a
custom
More honour'd in the breach than the
observance.   *Ib.* 14

4 Angels and ministers of grace defend
us!   *Ib.* 39

5   Unhand me, gentlemen,
By heaven! I'll make a ghost of him
that lets me.   *Ib.* 84

6 Something is rotten in the state of
Denmark.   *Ib.* 90

7   But that I am forbid
To tell the secrets of my prison-house,
I could a tale unfold whose lightest
word
Would harrow up thy soul, freeze thy
young blood,
Make thy two eyes, like stars, start
from their spheres,
Thy knotted and combined locks to
part,
And each particular hair to stand an
end,
Like quills upon the fretful porpen-
tine.   *Ib.* v. 13

8 Murder most foul, as in the best it is;
But this most foul, strange, and unnatural.   *Hamlet*, I. v. 27

9 And duller shouldst thou be than the
fat weed
That rots itself in ease on Lethe wharf.
                        Ib. 32

10   O my prophetic soul!
My uncle!   *Ib.* 40

11 But, soft! methinks I scent the morning air.   *Ib.* 58

12 Cut off even in the blossoms of my sin,
Unhousel'd, disappointed, unanel'd,
No reckoning made, but sent to my
account
With all my imperfections on my
head:
O, horrible! O, horrible! most horrible!
If thou hast nature in thee, bear it not.
                        Ib. 76

13   Leave her to heaven,
And to those thorns that in her bosom
lodge,
To prick and sting her.   *Ib.* 86

14 O most pernicious woman!
O villain, villain, smiling, damned
villain!
My tables,—meet it is I set it down,
That one may smile, and smile, and be
a villain;
At least I'm sure it may be so in
Denmark.   *Ib.* 105

15 Well said, old mole! canst work i' the
earth so fast?   *Ib.* 162

16 There are more things in heaven and
earth, Horatio,
Than are dreamt of in your philosophy.   *Ib.* 166

17 To put an antic disposition on.
                        Ib. 172

18 Rest, rest, perturbed spirit! *Ib.* 182

19 The time is out of joint; O cursed
spite,
That ever I was born to set it right!
                        Ib. 188

20 By indirections find directions out.
                     Ib. II. i. 66

21 Brevity is the soul of wit.   *Ib.* ii. 90

22 More matter with less art.   *Ib.* 95

23 That he is mad, 'tis true; 'tis true 'tis
pity;
And pity 'tis 'tis true: a foolish figure;
But farewell it, for I will use no art.
                        Ib. 97

24 Still harping on my daughter.
                        Ib. [190]

25 POLONIUS:
What do you read, my lord?
HAMLET:
Words, words, words.   *Ib.* [195]

26 Though this be madness, yet there is
method in it.   *Ib.* [211]

1 HAMLET:
Then you live about her waist, or in the middle of her favours?
GUILDENSTERN:
Faith, her privates we.
Hamlet, II. ii. 240

2 There is nothing either good or bad, but thinking makes it so. *Ib.* [259]

3 O God! I could be bounded in a nut-shell, and count myself a king of infinite space, were it not that I have bad dreams. *Ib.* [263]

4 It goes so heavily with my disposition that this goodly frame, the earth, seems to me a sterile promontory; this most excellent canopy, the air, look you, this brave o'erhanging firmament, this majestical roof fretted with golden fire, why, it appears no other thing to me but a foul and pestilent congregation of vapours. What a piece of work is a man! How noble in reason! how infinite in faculty! in form, in moving, how express and admirable! in action how like an angel! in apprehension how like a god! the beauty of the world! the paragon of animals! And yet, to me, what is this quintessence of dust? man delights not me; no, nor woman neither, though, by your smiling, you seem to say so. *Ib.* [316]

5 I am but mad north-north-west; when the wind is southerly, I know a hawk from a handsaw.[1] *Ib.* [405]

[1] = heron-shaw, or heron.

6 One fair daughter and no more, The which he loved passing well.
Ib. [435]

7 The play, I remember, pleased not the million; 'twas caviare to the general. *Ib.* [465]

8 The mobled queen. *Ib.* [533]

9 Good my lord, will you see the players well bestowed? Do you hear, let them be well used; for they are the abstracts and brief chronicles of the time: after your death you were better have a bad epitaph than their ill report while you live. *Ib.* [553]

10 Use every man after his desert, and who should 'scape whipping?
Ib. [561]

11 O, what a rogue and peasant slave am I:
Is it not monstrous that this player here,
But in a fiction, in a dream of passion,
Could force his soul so to his own conceit
That from her working all his visage wann'd,
Tears in his eyes, distraction in 's aspect,
A broken voice, and his whole function suiting
With forms to his conceit? and all for nothing!
For Hecuba!
What's Hecuba to him or he to Hecuba
That he should weep for her?
Hamlet, II. ii. [584]

12 The play's the thing
Wherein I'll catch the conscience of the king. *Ib.* [641]

13 To be, or not to be: that is the question:
Whether 'tis nobler in the mind to suffer
The slings and arrows of outrageous fortune,
Or to take arms against a sea of troubles,
And by opposing end them? To die: to sleep;
No more; and, by a sleep to say we end
The heart-ache and the thousand natural shocks
That flesh is heir to, 'tis a consummation
Devoutly to be wish'd. To die, to sleep;
To sleep: perchance to dream: ay, there's the rub;
For in that sleep of death what dreams may come
When we have shuffled off this mortal coil,
Must give us pause. There's the respect
That makes calamity of so long life;
For who would bear the whips and scorns of time,
The oppressor's wrong, the proud man's contumely,
The pangs of dispriz'd love, the law's delay,
The insolence of office, and the spurns
That patient merit of the unworthy takes,
When he himself might his quietus make
With a bare bodkin? Who would fardels bear,
To grunt and sweat under a weary life,
But that the dread of something after death,
The undiscover'd country from whose bourn
No traveller returns, puzzles the will,
And makes us rather bear those ills we have,
Than fly to others that we know not of?
Thus conscience doth make cowards of us all;
And thus the native hue of resolution
Is sicklied o'er with the pale cast of thought,

And enterprises of great pith and
moment
With this regard their currents turn
awry,
And lose the name of action.
Hamlet, III. i. 56

1   Nymph, in thy orisons
Be all my sins remember'd.   *Ib*. 89

2   For, to the noble mind,
Rich gifts wax poor when givers prove
unkind.   *Ib*. 100

3 Get thee to a nunnery.   *Ib*. [124]

4 I am myself indifferent honest.
Ib. [125]

5 Be thou as chaste as ice, as pure as
snow, thou shalt not escape calumny.
Ib. [142]

6 O! what a noble mind is here o'er-
thrown:
The courtier's, soldier's, scholar's, eye,
tongue, sword;
The expectancy and rose of the fair
state,
The glass of fashion, and the mould of
form,
The observed of all observers, quite,
quite down!
And I, of ladies most deject and
wretched,
That suck'd the honey of his music
vows,
Now see that noble and most sovereign
reason,
Like sweet bells jangled, out of tune
and harsh;
That unmatch'd form and figure of
blown youth,
Blasted with ecstasy: O! woe is me,
To have seen what I have seen, see
what I see!   *Ib*. [159]

7 Speak the speech, I pray you, as I
pronounced it to you, trippingly on the
tongue; but if you mouth it, as many
of your players do, I had as lief the
town-crier spoke my lines. Nor do not
saw the air too much with your hand,
thus; but use all gently: for in the
very torrent, tempest, and—as I may
say—whirlwind of passion, you must
acquire and beget a temperance, that
may give it smoothness. O! it offends
me to the soul to hear a robustious
periwig-pated fellow tear a passion to
tatters, to very rags, to split the ears
of the groundlings, who for the most
part are capable of nothing but inex-
plicable dumb-shows and noise: I
would have such a fellow whipped for
o'erdoing Termagant; it out-herods
Herod: pray you, avoid it. *Ib*. ii. 1

8 Be not too tame neither, but let your
own discretion be your tutor: suit the
action to the word, the word to the
action; with this special observance,

that you o'erstep not the modesty of
nature.   *Hamlet*, III. ii. [19]

9 The purpose of playing, whose end,
both at the first and now, was and is,
to hold, as 'twere, the mirror up to
nature.   *Ib*. [24]

10 To show . . . the very age and body
of the time his form and pressure.
Ib. [26]

11   Give me that man
That is not passion's slave, and I will
wear him
In my heart's core, ay, in my heart of
heart,
As I do thee. Something too much of
this.   *Ib*. [76]

12 Here's metal more attractive.
Ib. [117]

13 The lady doth protest too much, methinks.   *Ib*. [242]

14 We that have free souls, it touches us
not: let the galled jade wince, our
withers are unwrung.   *Ib*. [255]

15 What! frighted with false fire?
Ib. [282]

16 So runs the world away.   *Ib*. [289]

17 You would play upon me; you would
seem to know my stops; you would
pluck out the heart of my mystery;
you would sound me from my lowest
note to the top of my compass.
Ib. [387]

18 HAMLET:
Do you see yonder cloud that's al-
most in shape of a camel?
POLONIUS:
By the mass, and 'tis like a camel,
indeed.
HAMLET:
Methinks it is like a weasel.
POLONIUS:
It is backed like a weasel.
HAMLET:
Or like a whale?
POLONIUS:
Very like a whale.   *Ib*. [400]

19 They fool me to the top of my bent.
Ib. [408]

20 'Tis now the very witching time of
night.   *Ib*. [413]

21 Let me be cruel, not unnatural;
I will speak daggers to her, but use
none.   *Ib*. [420]

22 O! my offence is rank, it smells to
heaven.   *Ib*. iii. 36

23 Now might I do it pat, now he is
praying.   *Ib*. 73

24 How now! a rat? Dead, for a ducat,
dead!   *Ib*. iv. 23

25 Look here, upon this picture, and on
this.   *Ib*. 53

1   Speak no more;
Thou turn'st mine eyes into my very
soul. *Hamlet*, III. iv. 88

2 A king of shreds and patches. *Ib.* 102

3   Mother, for love of grace,
Lay not that flattering unction to your
soul. *Ib.* 144

4 I must be cruel, only to be kind.
Ib. 178

5 For 'tis the sport to have the engi-
ner
Hoist with his own petar. *Ib.* 206

6 How all occasions do inform against
me,
And spur my dull revenge!
Ib. IV. iv. 32

7   Rightly to be great
Is not to stir without great argument,
But greatly to find quarrel in a straw
When honour's at the stake. *Ib.* 53

8 How should I your true love know?
From another one?
By his cockle hat and staff,
And his sandal shoon. *Ib.* v. [23]

9 He is dead and gone, lady,
He is dead and gone,
At his head a grass-green turf;
At his heels a stone. *Ib.* [29]

10 Come, my coach! Good-night, ladies;
good-night, sweet ladies; good night,
good-night. *Ib.* [72]

11 When sorrows come, they come not
single spies,
But in battalions. *Ib.* [78]

12   We have done but greenly
In hugger-mugger to inter him.
Ib. [83]

13 There's such divinity doth hedge a
king,
That treason can but peep to what it
would. *Ib.* [123]

14 There's rosemary; that's for remembrance; pray, love, remember: and
there is pansies, that's for thoughts.
Ib. [174]

15 You must wear your rue with a difference. There's a daisy; I would give
you some violets, but they withered
all when my father died. *Ib.* [181]

16 They say he made a good end.
Ib. [184]

17 And where the offence is let the great
axe fall. *Ib.* [218]

18 There is a willow grows aslant a brook,
That shows his hoar leaves in the
glassy stream;
There with fantastic garlands did she
come,
Of crow-flowers, nettles, daisies, and
long purples,

That liberal shepherds give a grosser
name,
But our cold maids do dead men's
fingers call them:
There, on the pendent boughs her
coronet weeds
Clambering to hang, an envious sliver
broke,
When down her weedy trophies and
herself
Fell in the weeping brook. Her clothes
spread wide,
And, mermaid-like, awhile they bore
her up;
Which time she chanted snatches of
old tunes,
As one incapable of her own distress.
Hamlet, IV. vii. 167

19 Cudgel thy brains no more about it,
for your dull ass will not mend his
pace with beating. *Ib.* v. i. [61]

20 Alas! poor Yorick. I knew him,
Horatio; a fellow of infinite jest, of
most excellent fancy; he hath borne
me on his back a thousand times; and
now, how abhorred in my imagination
it is! my gorge rises at it. Here hung
those lips that I have kissed I know
not how oft. Where be your gibes now?
your gambols? your songs? your
flashes of merriment, that were wont to
set the table on a roar? Not one now,
to mock your own grinning? quite
chap-fallen? Now get you to my lady's
chamber, and tell her, let her paint
an inch thick, to this favour she must
come. *Ib.* [201]

21 Imperious Cæsar, dead, and turn'd to
clay,
Might stop a hole to keep the wind
away. *Ib.* [235]

22   Lay her i' the earth;
And from her fair and unpolluted
flesh
May violets spring! I tell thee, chur-
lish priest,
A ministering angel shall my sister be,
When thou liest howling. *Ib.* [260]

23 Sweets to the sweet: farewell!
Ib. [265]

24 There's a divinity that shapes our
ends,
Rough-hew them how we will.
Ib. ii. 10

25 It did me yeoman's service. *Ib.* 36

26 Not a whit, we defy augury: there's
a special providence in the fall of a
sparrow. If it be now, 'tis not to come;
if it be not to come, it will be now:
if it be not now, yet it will come: the
readiness is all. *Ib.* [232]

27 A hit, a very palpable hit. *Ib.* [295]

28   This fell sergeant, death,
Is strict in his arrest. *Ib.* [350]

1 Report me and my cause aright.
                    Hamlet, v. ii. [353]

2 I am more an antique Roman than a
   Dane.   *Ib.* [355]

3   Horatio, what a wounded name,
   Things standing thus unknown, shall
      live behind me.
   If thou didst ever hold me in thy heart,
   Absent thee from felicity awhile,
   And in this harsh world draw thy
      breath in pain,
   To tell my story.   *Ib.* [358]

4 The rest is silence.   *Ib.* [372]

5 Now cracks a noble heart. Good-
      night, sweet prince,
   And flights of angels sing thee to thy
      rest!   *Ib.* [373]

6 Let us be Diana's foresters, gentlemen
   of the shade, minions of the moon.
               King Henry IV, Part I, i. ii. [28]

7 Old father antick, the law.   *Ib.* 69

8   O! the blood more stirs
   To rouse a lion than to start a hare.
                               Ib. iii. 192

9 By heaven methinks it were an easy
      leap
   To pluck bright honour from the
      pale-fac'd moon,
   Or dive into the bottom of the deep,
   Where fathom-line could never touch
      the ground,
   And pluck up drowned honour by the
      locks;
   So he that doth redeem her thence
      might wear
   Without corrival all her dignities:
   But out upon this half-fac'd fellow-
      ship!   *Ib.* 201

10 I know a trick worth two of that.
                               Ib. II. i. [40]

11   Falstaff sweats to death
   And lards the lean earth as he walks
      along.   *Ib.* ii. [119]

12 Out of this nettle, danger, we pluck
   this flower, safety.   *Ib.* iii. [11]

13 Show it a fair pair of heels.
                               Ib. iv. [52]

14 Nay that's past praying for. *Ib.* [214]

15 No, my good lord; banish Peto, banish
   Bardolph, banish Poins; but for
   sweet Jack Falstaff, kind Jack Falstaff, true Jack Falstaff, valiant Jack
   Falstaff, and therefore more valiant,
   being, as he is, old Jack Falstaff,
   banish not him thy Harry's company:
   banish not him thy Harry's company:
   banish plump Jack and banish all the
   world.   *Ib.* [528]

16 O! monstrous! but one half-penny-
   worth of bread to this intolerable deal
   of sack!   *Ib.* [598]

17 GLENDOWER:
   I can call spirits from the vasty deep.
   HOTSPUR:
   Why, so can I, or so can any man;
   But will they come when you do call
      for them?
            King Henry IV, Part I, III. i. [53]

18 O! while you live, tell truth, and
   shame the devil!   *Ib.* [62]

19 Now I perceive the devil understands
   Welsh.   *Ib.* [233]

20 My near'st and dearest enemy.
                               Ib. ii. 123

21 Shall I not take mine ease in mine inn?
                               Ib. iii. [91]

22 But thought's the slave of life, and
   life time's fool;
   And time, that takes survey of all the
      world,
   Must have a stop.   *Ib.* IV. iv. [81]

23   Fare thee well, great heart!
   Ill-weav'd ambition, how much art
      thou shrunk!
   When that this body did contain a
      spirit,
   A kingdom for it was too small a
      bound;
   But now two paces of the vilest earth
   Is room enough: this earth, that bears
      thee dead,
   Bears not alive so stout a gentleman.
                               Ib. [87]

24   Poor Jack, farewell!
   I could have better spar'd a better
   man.   *Ib.* v. iv. [103]

25 The better part of valour is discretion.
                               Ib. [120]

26 Lord, Lord, how this world is given to
   lying! I grant you I was down and out
   of breath; and so was he; but we rose
   both at an instant, and fought a long
   hour by Shrewsbury clock.   *Ib.* [148]

27 I am not only witty in myself, but the
   cause that wit is in other men.
            King Henry IV, Part II, I. ii. [10]

28 I am as poor as Job, my lord, but not
   so patient.   *Ib.* [145]

29 He hath eaten me out of house and
   home.   *Ib.* II. i. [82]

30   Then, happy low, lie down!
   Uneasy lies the head that wears a
   crown.   *Ib.* III. i. 30

31 We have heard the chimes at midnight.   *Ib.* ii. [231]

32 I care not; a man can die but once;
   we owe God a death.   *Ib.* [253]

33 Thy wish was father, Harry, to that
   thought.   *Ib.* IV. v. 91

34 Under which king, Bezonian? speak,
   or die!   *Ib.* v. iii. [115]

1 I know thee not, old man: fall to thy
prayers;
How ill white hairs become a fool and
jester!
    King Henry IV, Part II, IV. v. [52]

2 O! for a Muse of fire, that would
ascend
The brightest heaven of invention.
    King Henry V, Chorus, 1

3   Can this cockpit hold
The vasty fields of France? or may we
cram
Within this wooden O the very casques
That did affright the air at Agincourt?
    Ib. 11

4 His present and your pains we thank
you for:
When we have match'd our rackets to
these balls,
We will in France, by God's grace,
play a set
Shall strike his father's crown into the
hazard.   *Ib.* I. ii. 260

5 Now all the youth of England are on
fire,
And silken dalliance in the wardrobe
lies;
Now thrive the armourers, and
honour's thought
Reigns solely in the breast of every
man:
They sell the pasture now to buy the
horse,
Following the mirror of all Christian
kings,
With winged heels, as English Mer-
curies.
For now sits Expectation in the air
And hides a sword from hilts unto the
point
With crowns imperial, crowns and
coronets,
Promis'd to Harry and his followers.
    Ib. II. Chorus, 1

6 He's in Arthur's bosom, if ever man
went to Arthur's bosom. A' made a
finer end, and went away an it
had been any christom child; a'
parted even just between twelve and
one, even at the turning o' the tide:
for after I saw him fumble with the
sheets and play with flowers and
smile upon his fingers' ends, I knew
there was but one way; for his nose
was as sharp as a pen, and a' babbled
of green fields. [Theobald's emen-
dation of the Folio's reading: 'A
table of green fields'.] *Ib.* iii. [9]

7 Yes, that a' did; and said they were
devils incarnate.   *Ib.* [33]

8 Once more unto the breach, dear
friends, once more;
Or close the wall up with our English
dead!
In peace there's nothing so becomes a
man

As modest stillness and humility:
But when the blast of war blows in our
ears,
Then imitate the action of the tiger;
Stiffen the sinews, summon up the
blood,
Disguise fair nature with hard-
favour'd rage;
Then lend the eye a terrible aspect.
    King Henry V, III. i. 1

9 I see you stand like greyhounds in
the slips,
Straining upon the start. The game's
afoot:
Follow your spirit; and, upon this
charge
Cry 'God for Harry! England and
Saint George!'   *Ib.* 31

10 Men of few words are the best men.
    Ib. ii. [40]

11 A little touch of Harry in the night.
    Ib. IV. Chorus, 47

12 I think the king is but a man, as I am:
the violet smells to him as it doth to
me.   *Ib.* i. [106]

13 Every subject's duty is the king's; but
every subject's soul is his own.
    Ib. [189]

14   What infinite heart's ease
Must kings neglect, that private men
enjoy!   *Ib.* [256]

15 'Tis not the balm, the sceptre and the
ball,
The sword, the mace, the crown im-
perial,
The intertissued robe of gold and pearl,
The farced title running 'fore the king,
The throne he sits on, nor the tide of
pomp
That beats upon the high shore of this
world,
No, not all these, thrice-gorgeous
ceremony,
Not all these, laid in bed majestical,
Can sleep so soundly as the wretched
slave,
Who with a body fill'd and vacant
mind
Gets him to rest, cramm'd with dis-
tressful bread;
Never sees horrid night, the child of
hell,
But, like a lackey, from the rise to set
Sweats in the eye of Phœbus, and all
night
Sleeps in Elysium; next day after
dawn,
Doth rise and help Hyperion to his
horse,
And follows so the ever-running year
With profitable labour to his grave:
And, but for ceremony, such a wretch,
Winding up days with toil and nights
with sleep,
Hath the forehand and vantage of a
king.   *Ib.* [280]

1 O God of battles! steel my soldiers'
hearts;
Possess them not with fear.
King Henry V, IV. i. [309]

2 O! that we now had here
But one ten thousand of those men in
England
That do no work to-day. *Ib.* iii. 16

3 If we are mark'd to die, we are enow
To do our country loss; and if to live,
The fewer men, the greater share of
honour. *Ib.* 20

4 He which hath no stomach to this fight,
Let him depart; his passport shall be
made,
And crowns for convoy put into his
purse:
We would not die in that man's com-
pany
That fears his fellowship to die with us.
This day is called the feast of Crispian:
He that outlives this day and comes
safe home,
Will stand a tip-toe when this day is
nam'd,
And rouse him at the name of
Crispian.
He that shall live this day, and see old
age,
Will yearly on the vigil feast his neigh-
bours,
And say, 'To-morrow is Saint Cris-
pian:'
Then will he strip his sleeve and
show his scars,
And say, 'These wounds I had on
Crispin's day.'
Old men forget: yet all shall be forgot,
But he'll remember with advantages
What feats he did that day. Then
shall our names,
Familiar in his mouth as household
words,
Harry the King, Bedford and Exeter,
Warwick and Talbot, Salisbury and
Gloucester,
Be in their flowing cups freshly re-
member'd.
This story shall the good man teach
his son;
And Crispin Crispian shall ne'er go by,
From this day to the ending of the
world,
But we in it shall be remembered;
We few, we happy few, we band of
brothers;
For he to-day that sheds his blood
with me
Shall be my brother; be he ne'er so vile
This day shall gentle his condition:
And gentlemen in England, now a-bed
Shall think themselves accurs'd they
were not here,
And hold their manhoods cheap whiles
any speaks
That fought with us upon Saint
Crispin's day. *Ib.* 35

5 Expect Saint Martin's summer, halcyon days.
King Henry VI, Part I, I. ii. 131

6 Unbidden guests
Are often welcomest when they are
gone. *Ib.* II. ii. 55

7 What stronger breastplate than a
heart untainted!
Thrice is he arm'd that hath his
quarrel just,
And he but naked, though lock'd up
in steel,
Whose conscience with injustice is
corrupted.
King Henry VI, Part II, III. ii.
232

8 Forbear to judge, for we are sinners
all.
Close up his eyes, and draw the curtain
close;
And let us all to meditation.
Ib. iii. 31

9 The first thing we do, let's kill all the
lawyers. *Ib.* IV. ii. [86]

10 And Adam was a gardener. *Ib.* [146]

11 O tiger's heart wrapp'd in a woman's
hide!
King Henry VI, Part III, I. iv.
137

12 The mirror of all courtesy.
King Henry VIII, II. i. 53

13 Orpheus with his lute made trees,
And the mountain-tops that freeze,
Bow themselves when he did sing.
Ib. III. i. 3

14 Farewell! a long farewell, to all my
greatness!
This is the state of man: to-day he
puts forth
The tender leaves of hope; to-morrow
blossoms,
And bears his blushing honours thick
upon him;
The third day comes a frost, a killing
frost;
And, when he thinks, good easy man,
full surely
His greatness is a-ripening, nips his
root,
And then he falls, as I do. I have
ventur'd,
Like little wanton boys that swim on
bladders,
This many summers in a sea of glory,
But far beyond my depth: my high-
blown pride
At length broke under me, and now
has left me
Weary and old with service, to the
mercy
Of a rude stream that must for ever
hide me.
Vain pomp and glory of this world,
I hate ye:

I feel my heart new open'd. O how wretched
Is that poor man that hangs on princes' favours!
There is, betwixt that smile we would aspire to,
That sweet aspect of princes, and their ruin,
More pangs and fears than wars or women have;
And when he falls, he falls like Lucifer,
Never to hope again.
King Henry VIII. ii. 352

1 Had I but serv'd my God with half the zeal
I serv'd my king, he would not in mine age
Have left me naked to mine enemies.
Ib. 456

2 To dance attendance on their lordships' pleasures. *Ib.* v. ii. 30

3 Mad world! Mad kings! Mad composition! *King John,* II. i. 561

4 Bell, book, and candle shall not drive me back,
When gold and silver becks me to come on. *Ib.* III. iii. 12

5 Life is as tedious as a twice-told tale,
Vexing the dull ear of a drowsy man. *Ib.* iv. 108

6 To gild refined gold, to paint the lily,
To throw a perfume on the violet,
To smooth the ice, or add another hue
Unto the rainbow, or with taper light
To seek the beauteous eye of heaven to garnish,
Is wasteful and ridiculous excess. *Ib.* IV. ii. 11

7 I beg cold comfort. *Ib.* v. vii. 42

8 This England never did, nor never shall,
Lie at the proud foot of a conqueror,
But when it first did help to wound itself.
Now these her princes are come home again,
Come the three corners of the world in arms,
And we shall shock them: nought shall make us rue,
If England to itself do rest but true.
Ib. 112

9 You blocks, you stones, you worse than senseless things!
O you hard hearts, you cruel men of Rome,
Knew you not Pompey?
Julius Cæsar, I. i [39]

10 Beware the ides of March. *Ib.* ii. 18

11 Why, man, he doth bestride the narrow world
Like a Colossus; and we petty men
Walk under his huge legs, and peep about
To find ourselves dishonourable graves.
Men at some time are masters of their fates:
The fault, dear Brutus, is not in our stars,
But in ourselves, that we are underlings. *Julius Cæsar,* I. i. 134

12 For mine own part, it was Greek to me. *Ib.* [288]

13 Let's carve him as a dish fit for the gods,
Not hew him as a carcass fit for hounds. *Ib.* II. i. 173

14 CALPHURNIA:
When beggars die, there are no comets seen;
The heavens themselves blaze forth the death of princes.
CÆSAR:
Cowards die many times before their deaths;
The valiant never taste of death but once.
Of all the wonders that I yet have heard,
It seems to me most strange that men should fear;
Seeing that death, a necessary end,
Will come when it will come.
Ib. ii. 30

15 CÆSAR:
The ides of March are come.
SOOTHSAYER:
Ay, Cæsar; but not gone. *Ib.* III. i. 1

16 If I could pray to move, prayers would move me;
But I am constant as the northern star,
Of whose true-fix'd and resting quality
There is no fellow in the firmament.
Ib. 59

17 Et tu, Brute? *Ib.* 77

18 O mighty Cæsar! dost thou lie so low?
Are all thy conquests, glories, triumphs, spoils,
Shrunk to this little measure? *Ib.* 148

19 Though last, not least in love. *Ib.* 189

20 O! pardon me, thou bleeding piece of earth,
That I am meek and gentle with these butchers;
Thou art the ruins of the noblest man
That ever lived in the tide of times.
Ib. 254

21 And Cæsar's spirit ranging for revenge,
With Ate by his side, come hot from hell,
Shall in these confines, with a monarch's voice
Cry, 'Havoc!' and let slip the dogs of war. *Ib.* 270

1 Not that I loved Cæsar less, but that
I loved Rome more.
Julius Cæsar, III. ii. [22]

2 As he was valiant, I honour him: but,
as he was ambitious, I slew him.
Ib. [27]

3 Friends, Romans, countrymen, lend
me your ears;
I come to bury Cæsar, not to praise
him.
The evil that men do lives after them,
The good is oft interred with their
bones;
So let it be with Cæsar. The noble
Brutus
Hath told you Cæsar was ambitious;
If it were so, it was a grievous fault;
And grievously hath Cæsar answer'd
it.   *Ib.* [79]

4 For Brutus is an honourable man;
So are they all, all honourable men.
Ib. [88]

5 He was my friend, faithful and just to
me:
But Brutus says he was ambitious;
And Brutus is an honourable man.
Ib. [91]

6 But yesterday the word of Cæsar
might
Have stood against the world; now
lies he there,
And none so poor to do him reverence.
Ib. [124]

7 If you have tears, prepare to shed them
now.
You all do know this mantle: I re-
member
The first time ever Cæsar put it on;
'Twas on a summer's evening, in his
tent,
That day he overcame the Nervii.
Ib. [174]

8 See what a rent the envious Casca
made.   *Ib.* [180]

9 This was the most unkindest cut of all.
Ib. [188]

10 O! what a fall was there, my countrymen;
Then I, and you, and all of us fell
down,
Whilst bloody treason flourish'd over
us,
O! now you weep, and I perceive you
feel
The dint of pity; these are gracious
drops.   *Ib.* [195]

11 I come not, friends, to steal away
your hearts:
I am no orator, as Brutus is;
But, as you know me all, a plain,
blunt man,
That love my friend.   *Ib.* [220]

12 For I have neither wit, nor words, nor
worth,

Action, nor utterance, nor power of
speech,
To stir men's blood; I only speak
right on;
I tell you that which you yourselves
do know. *Julius Cæsar*, III. ii. [225]

13   But were I Brutus,
And Brutus Antony, there were an
Antony
Would ruffle up your spirits, and put
a tongue
In every wound of Cæsar, that should
move
The stones of Rome to rise and
mutiny.   *Ib.* [230]

14 Here was a Cæsar! when comes such
another?   *Ib.* [257]

15 Let me tell you, Cassius, you yourself
Are much condemn'd to have an
itching palm.   *Ib.* IV. iii. 9

16 Remember March, the ides of March
remember.   *Ib.* 18

17 I had rather be a dog, and bay the
moon,
Than such a Roman.   *Ib.* 27

18   All his faults observ'd,
Set in a note-book, learn'd, and conn'd
by rote,
To cast into my teeth.   *Ib.* 96

19 There is a tide in the affairs of men,
Which, taken at the flood, leads on to
fortune;
Omitted, all the voyage of their life
Is bound in shallows and in miseries.
On such a full sea are we now afloat,
And we must take the current when it
serves,
Or lose our ventures.   *Ib.* 217

20 BRUTUS:
Then I shall see thee again?
GHOST:
Ay, at Philippi.
BRUTUS:
Why, I will see thee at Philippi, then.
Ib. 283

21 For ever, and for ever, farewell,
Cassius!
If we do meet again, why, we shall
smile!
If not, why then, this parting was well
made.   *Ib.* V. i. 117

22   O! that a man might know
The end of this day's business, ere it
come;
But it sufficeth that the day will end,
And then the end is known.   *Ib.* 123

23 This was the noblest Roman of them
all.   *Ib.* V. 68

24 His life was gentle, and the elements
So mix'd in him that Nature might
stand up
And say to all the world, 'This was a
man!'   *Ib.* 73

1 LEAR:
So young, and so untender?
CORDELIA:
So young, my lord, and true.
King Lear, I. i. [108]

2 This is the excellent foppery of the
world. *Ib.* ii. [132]

3 How sharper than a serpent's tooth
it is
To have a thankless child!
Ib. iv. [312]

4 Blow, winds, and crack your cheeks!
rage! blow!
You cataracts and hurricanoes, spout
Till you have drench'd our steeples,
drown'd the cocks!
You sulphurous and thought-execut-
ing fires,
Vaunt-couriers to oak-cleaving
thunderbolts,
Singe my white head! And thou, all-
shaking thunder,
Strike flat the thick rotundity o' the
world!
Crack nature's moulds, all germens
spill at once
That make ingrateful man!
Ib. III. ii. 1

5 I tax not you, you elements, with un-
kindness;
I never gave you kingdom, call'd you
children,
You owe me no subscription: then,
let fall
Your horrible pleasure; here I stand,
your slave,
A poor, infirm, weak, and despis'd old
man.
But yet I call you servile ministers,
That have with two pernicious daugh-
ters join'd
Your high-engender'd battles 'gainst
a head
So old and white as this. *Ib.* [16]

6 I am a man
More sinned against than sinning.
Ib. [59]

7 O! that way madness lies; let me shun
that. *Ib.* iv. 21

8 Poor naked wretches, wheresoe'er you
are,
That bide the pelting of this pitiless
storm,
How shall your houseless heads and
unfed sides,
Your looped and window'd ragged-
ness, defend you
From seasons such as these? *Ib.* 28

9 Take physic, pomp;
Expose thyself to feel what wretches
feel. *Ib.* 33

0 Tom's a-cold. *Ib.* [57]

11 Keep thy foot out of brothels, thy
hand out of plackets, thy pen from
lenders' books, and defy the foul
fiend. *King Lear*, III. iv. [96]

12 Thou art the thing itself; unac-
commodated man is no more but such
a poor, bare, forked animal as thou
art. *Ib.* [109]

13 The prince of darkness is a gentleman.
Ib. [148]

14 Child Roland to the dark tower came,
His word was still, Fie, foh, and fum,
I smell the blood of a British man.
Ib. [185]

15 The little dogs and all,
Tray, Blanch, and Sweet-heart, see,
they bark at me. *Ib.* vi. 65

16 I am tied to the stake, and I must
stand the course. *Ib.* vii. [54]

17 Out, vile jelly! *Ib.* [83]

18 As flies to wanton boys, are we to the
gods;
They kill us for their sport.
Ib. IV. i. 36

19 How fearful
And dizzy 'tis to cast one's eyes so
low!
The crows and choughs that wing the
midway air
Show scarce so gross as beetles; half-
way down
Hangs one that gathers samphire,
dreadful trade!
Methinks he seems no bigger than his
head.
The fishermen that walk upon the
beach
Appear like mice, and yond tall an-
choring bark
Diminish'd to her cock, her cock a
buoy
Almost too small for sight. The mur-
muring surge,
That on the unnumber'd idle pebbles
chafes,
Cannot be heard so high. *Ib.* vi. 12

20 GLOUCESTER:
Is't not the king?
LEAR:
Ay, every inch a king.
Ib. [110]

21 Give me an ounce of civet, good
apothecary, to sweeten my imagination. *Ib.* [133]

22 Get thee glass eyes;
And, like a scurvy politician, seem
To see the things thou dost not.
Ib. [175]

23 Mine enemy's dog,
Though he had bit me, should have
stood that night
Against my fire. *Ib.* vii. 36

1 Thou art a soul in bliss; but I am
  bound
Upon a wheel of fire, that mine own
  tears
Do scald like molten lead.
            King Lear, IV. vii. 46

2 I am a very foolish, fond old man,
Fourscore and upward, not an hour
  more or less;
And, to deal plainly,
I fear I am not in my perfect mind.
                        Ib. 60

3 For, as I am a man, I think this lady
To be my child Cordelia.   *Ib.* 69

4 Pray you now, forget and forgive.
                        Ib. [85]

5   Men must endure
Their going hence, even as their com-
  ing hither:
Ripeness is all.   *Ib.* v. ii. 9

6   Come, let's away to prison;
We two alone will sing like birds i' the
  cage:
When thou dost ask me blessing, I'll
  kneel down,
And ask of thee forgiveness: and we'll
  live,
And pray, and sing, and tell old tales,
  and laugh
At gilded butterflies, and hear poor
  rogues
Talk of court news; and we'll talk
  with them too,
Who loses, and who wins; who's in,
  who's out;
And take upon's the mystery of
  things,
As if we were God's spies; and we'll
  wear out,
In a wall'd prison, packs and sets of
  great ones
That ebb and flow by the moon.
                        Ib. iii. 8

7 The gods are just, and of our pleasant
  vices
Make instruments to plague us.
                        Ib. [172]

8 The wheel is come full circle.
                        Ib. [176]

9   Her voice was ever soft,
Gentle and low, an excellent thing in
  woman.   *Ib.* [274]

10 I have seen the day, with my good
  biting falchion
I would have made them skip.
                        Ib. [278]

11 And my poor fool is hang'd! No, no,
  no life!
Why should a dog, a horse, a rat,
  have life,
And thou no breath at all? Thou'lt
  come no more,
Never, never, never, never, never!
Pray you, undo this button. *Ib.* [307]

12 Vex not his ghost: O! let him pass;
  he hates him
That would upon the rack of this
  tough world
Stretch him out longer.
            King Lear, v. iii. [314]

13 Spite of cormorant devouring Time.
            Love's Labour's Lost, I. i. 4

14 He hath not fed of the dainties that
are bred in a book; he hath not eat
paper, as it were; he hath not drunk
ink.   *Ib.* IV. ii. [25]

15 Never durst poet touch a pen to
  write
Until his ink were temper'd with
  Love's sighs.   *Ib.* iii. [346]

16 From women's eyes this doctrine I
  derive:
They sparkle still the right Prome-
  thean fire;
They are the books, the arts, the
  academes,
That show, contain, and nourish all
  the world.   *Ib.* [350]

17 MOTH:
They have been at a great feast of
languages, and stolen the scraps.
COSTARD:
O! they have lived long on the alms-
basket of words. I marvel thy master
hath not eaten thee for a word; for
thou art not so long by the head as
honorificabilitudinitatibus: thou art
easier swallowed than a flap-dragon.
                        Ib. v. i. [39]

18 A jest's prosperity lies in the ear
Of him that hears it, never in the
  tongue
Of him that makes it. *Ib.* ii. [869]

19 When daisies pied and violets blue
    And lady-smocks all silver-white
And cuckoo-buds of yellow hue
    Do paint the meadows with delight,
The cuckoo then, on every tree,
Mocks married men; for thus sings he,
                        Cuckoo,
Cuckoo, cuckoo; O, word of fear,
Unpleasing to a married ear!
                        Ib. [902]

20 When icicles hang by the wall,
    And Dick, the shepherd, blows his
      nail,
And Tom bears logs into the hall,
    And milk comes frozen home in
      pail,
When blood is nipp'd and ways be
  foul,
Then nightly sings the staring owl,
                        Tu-who;
Tu-whit, tu-who—a merry note,
While greasy Joan doth keel the pot
When all aloud the wind doth blow,
And coughing drowns the parson's
  saw;
And birds sit brooding in the snow,

And Marion's nose looks red and raw,
When roasted crabs hiss in the bowl.
Love's Labour's Lost, v. ii. [920]

1 The words of Mercury are harsh after
the songs of Apollo.   *Ib.* [938]

2 FIRST WITCH:
When shall we three meet again
In thunder, lightning, or in rain?
SECOND WITCH:
When the hurly-burly's done,
When the battle's lost and won.
THIRD WITCH:
That will be ere the set of sun.
FIRST WITCH:
Where the place?
SECOND WITCH:
          Upon the heath.
THIRD WITCH:
There to meet with Macbeth.
FIRST WITCH:
I come, Graymalkin!
SECOND WITCH:
          Paddock calls.
THIRD WITCH:
Anon!
ALL:
Fair is foul, and foul is fair:
Hover through the fog and filthy air.
          Macbeth, I. i. 1

3 DUNCAN:
What bloody man is that? . . .
MALCOLM:
      This is the sergeant.   *Ib.* ii. 1

4 Disdaining fortune, with his bran-
dish'd steel,
Which smok'd with bloody execution,
Like valour's minion carv'd out his
passage.   *Ib.* 17

5 A sailor's wife had chestnuts in her
lap,
And munch'd, and munch'd, and
munch'd: 'Give me,' quoth I:
'Aroint thee, witch!' the rump-fed
ronyon cries.
Her husband's to Aleppo gone, master
o' the Tiger:
But in a sieve I'll thither sail,
And, like a rat without a tail,
I'll do, I'll do, and I'll do.   *Ib.* iii. 4

6 Sleep shall neither night nor day
Hang upon his pent-house lid.
He shall live a man forbid.
Weary se'nnights nine times nine
Shall he dwindle, peak, and pine:
Though his bark cannot be lost,
Yet it shall be tempest-tost.   *Ib.* 19

7 So foul and fair a day I have not seen.
          Ib. 38

8   What are these,
So withered, and so wild in their
attire,
That look not like th' inhabitants o'
the earth,
And yet are on 't?   *Ib.* 39

9   Two truths are told,
As happy prologues to the swelling act
Of the imperial theme.
          Macbeth, I. iii. 127

10 This supernatural soliciting
Cannot be ill, cannot be good.   *Ib.* 130

11   Present fears
Are less than horrible imaginings.
          Ib. 137

12   Come what come may,
Time and the hour runs through the
roughest day.   *Ib.* 146

13 MALCOLM:
          Nothing in his life
Became him like the leaving it; he died
As one that had been studied in his
death
To throw away the dearest thing he
owed
As 'twere a careless trifle.
DUNCAN:
          There's no art
To find the mind's construction in the
face;
He was a gentleman on whom I built
An absolute trust.   *Ib.* iv. 7

14 Glamis thou art, and Cawdor; and
shalt be
What thou art promis'd. Yet do I fear
thy nature;
It is too full o' the milk of human
kindness
To catch the nearest way; thou
wouldst be great.   *Ib.* v. [16]

15   The raven himself is hoarse
That croaks the fatal entrance of
Duncan
Under my battlements. Come, you
spirits
That tend on mortal thoughts! unsex
me here,
And fill me from the crown to the toe
top full
Of direst cruelty; make thick my
blood,
Stop up the access and passage to
remorse,
That no compunctious visitings of
nature
Shake my fell purpose, nor keep
peace between
The effect and it! Come to my
woman's breasts,
And take my milk for gall, you mur-
dering ministers,
Wherever in your sightless sub-
stances
You wait on nature's mischief! Come,
thick night,
And pall thee in the dunnest smoke of
hell,
That my keen knife see not the
wound it makes,
Nor heaven peep through the blanket
of the dark,
To cry 'Hold, hold!'   *Ib.* [38]

1 Your face, my thane, is as a book
      where men
   May read strange matters. To beguile
      the time,
   Look like the time; bear welcome in
      your eye,
   Your hand, your tongue: look like the
      innocent flower,
   But be the serpent under't.
                     Macbeth, I. v. [63]

2 DUNCAN:
   This castle hath a pleasant seat; the air
   Nimbly and sweetly recommends itself
   Unto our gentle senses.
   BANQUO:
                  This guest of summer,
   The temple-haunting martlet, does
      approve
   By his lov'd mansionry that the
      heaven's breath
   Smells wooingly here: no jutty,
      frieze,
   Buttress, nor coign of vantage, but
      this bird
   Hath made his pendent bed and pro-
      creant cradle:
   Where they most breed and haunt,
      I have observ'd,
   The air is delicate.   *Ib.* vi. 1

3 If it were done when 'tis done, then
      'twere well
   It were done quickly: if the assassina-
      tion
   Could trammel up the consequence,
      and catch
   With his surcease success; that but
      this blow
   Might be the be-all and the end-all
      here,
   But here, upon this bank and shoal
      of time,
   We'd jump the life to come. *Ib.* vii. 1

4   Besides, this Duncan
   Hath borne his faculties so meek,
      hath been
   So clear in his great office, that his
      virtues
   Will plead like angels trumpet-
      tongu'd, against
   The deep damnation of his taking-off;
   And pity, like a naked new-born babe,
   Striding the blast, or heaven's cheru-
      bim, hors'd
   Upon the sightless couriers of the air,
   Shall blow the horrid deed in every
      eye,
   That tears shall drown the wind.
   I have no spur
   To prick the sides of my intent, but
      only
   Vaulting ambition, which o'erleaps
      itself,
   And falls on the other.   *Ib.* 16

5 He hath honour'd me of late; and I
      have bought
   Golden opinions from all sorts of
      people.   *Ib.* 32

6 Letting 'I dare not' wait upon 'I
      would,'
   Like the poor cat i' the adage.
                     Macbeth, I. vii. 44

7 MACBETH:
                  If we should fail,—
   LADY MACBETH:
                        We fail!
   But screw your courage to the stick-
      ing-place,
   And we'll not fail.   *Ib.* 60

8   There's husbandry in heaven;
   Their candles are all out.   *Ib.* II. i. 4

9 Is this a dagger which I see before me,
   The handle toward my hand? Come,
      let me clutch thee:
   I have thee not, and yet I see thee still.
   Art thou not, fatal vision, sensible
   To feeling as to sight! or art thou but
   A dagger of the mind, a false creation,
   Proceeding from the heat-oppressèd
      brain?   *Ib.* 33

10 Hear it not, Duncan; for it is a knell
   That summons thee to heaven or to
      hell.   *Ib.* 64

11 Consider it not so deeply.   *Ib.* ii. 31

12 I had most need of blessing, and
      'Amen'
   Stuck in my throat.   *Ib.* 33

13 Methought I heard a voice cry, 'Sleep
      no more!
   Macbeth does murder sleep,' the in-
      nocent sleep,
   Sleep that knits up the ravell'd sleave
      of care,
   The death of each day's life, sore
      labour's bath,
   Balm of hurt minds, great nature's
      second course,
   Chief nourisher in life's feast.   *Ib.* 36

14 Glamis hath murder'd sleep, and
      therefore Cawdor
   Shall sleep no more, Macbeth shall
      sleep no more!   *Ib.* 43

15 Will all great Neptune's ocean wash
      this blood
   Clean from my hand? No, this my
      hand will rather
   The multitudinous seas incarnadine,
   Making the green one red.   *Ib.* 61

16 A little water clears us of this deed.
                                  Ib. 68

17 The primrose way to the everlasting
   bonfire.   *Ib.* iii. [22]

18 The labour we delight in physics
   pain.   *Ib.* [56]

19 All is but toys; renown and grace is
      dead,
   The wine of life is drawn, and the mere
      lees
   Is left this vault to brag of. *Ib.* [101]

20 There's daggers in men's smiles.
                               Ib. [147]

1 A falcon, towering in her pride of place,
Was by a mousing owl hawk'd at and kill'd. *Macbeth*, II. iv. 12

2 Thy soul's flight,
If it find heaven, must find it out to-night. *Ib.* III. i. 141

3 LADY MACBETH:
Things without all remedy
Should be without regard: what's done is done.
MACBETH:
We have scotch'd the snake, not killed it. *Ib.* ii. 11

4 Duncan is in his grave;
After life's fitful fever he sleeps well;
Treason has done his worst: nor steel, nor poison,
Malice domestic, foreign levy, nothing,
Can touch him further. *Ib.* 22

5 A deed of dreadful note. *Ib.* 44

6 Be innocent of the knowledge, dearest chuck,
Till thou applaud the deed. Come, seeling night,
Scarf up the tender eye of pitiful day,
And with thy bloody and invisible hand,
Cancel and tear to pieces that great bond
Which keeps me pale! Light thickens, and the crow
Makes wing to the rooky wood;
Good things of day begin to droop and drowse,
Whiles night's black agents to their preys do rouse. *Ib.* 45

7 Now spurs the lated traveller apace
To gain the timely inn. *Ib.* iii. 6

8 But now I am cabin'd, cribb'd, con-fin'd, bound in
To saucy doubts and fears. *Ib.* iv. 24

9 Now good digestion wait on appetite,
And health on both! *Ib.* 38

10 Stand not upon the order of your going,
But go at once. *Ib.* 119

11 It will have blood, they say; blood will have blood. *Ib.* 122

12 I am in blood
Stepp'd in so far that, should I wade no more,
Returning were as tedious as go o'er. *Ib.* 136

13 Double, double toil and trouble;
Fire burn, and cauldron bubble. *Ib.* IV. i. 10

14 Eye of newt and toe of frog,
Wool of bat and tongue of dog. *Ib.* 14

15 Slips of yew
Sliver'd in the moon's eclipse. *Ib.* 27

16 Finger of birth-strangled babe,
Ditch-deliver'd by a drab,
Make the gruel thick and slab.
Macbeth, IV. i. 30

17 By the pricking of my thumbs,
Something wicked this way comes.
Open, locks,
Whoever knocks. *Ib.* 44

18 How now, you secret, black, and mid-night hags! *Ib.* 48

19 A deed without a name. *Ib.* 49

20 Be bloody, bold, and resolute; laugh to scorn
The power of man, for none of woman born
Shall harm Macbeth. *Ib.* 79

21 But yet I'll make assurance double sure,
And take a bond of fate. *Ib.* 83

22 Macbeth shall never vanquish'd be until
Great Birnam wood to high Dunsi-nane hill
Shall come against him. *Ib.* 90

23 What! will the line stretch out to the crack of doom? *Ib.* 117

24 The weird sisters. *Ib.* 136

25 His flight was madness: when our actions do not,
Our fears do make us traitors.
Ib. ii. 3

26 Stands Scotland where it did?
Ib. iii. 164

27 All my pretty ones?
Did you say all? O hell-kite! All?
What! all my pretty chickens and their dam,
At one fell swoop? *Ib.* 216

28 Out, damned spot! out, I say! One; two: why then, 'tis time to do't. Hell is murky! Fie, my lord, fie! a soldier, and afeard? What need we fear who knows it, when none can call our power to account? Yet who would have thought the old man to have had so much blood in him? *Ib.* v. i. [38]

29 The Thane of Fife had a wife: where is she now? What! will these hands ne'er be clean? *Ib.* [46]

30 All the perfumes of Arabia will not sweeten this little hand. *Ib.* [56]

31 The devil damn thee black, thou cream-faced loon!
Where gott'st thou that goose look?
Ib. iii. 11

32 I have lived long enough: my way of life
Is fall'n into the sear, the yellow leaf;
And that which should accompany old age,
As honour, love, obedience, troops of friends,

I must not look to have; but, in their
   stead,
Curses, not loud but deep, mouth-
   honour, breath,
Which the poor heart would fain deny,
   and dare not.   *Macbeth*, v. iii. 22

1 MACBETH:
Canst thou not minister to a mind
   diseas'd,
Pluck from the memory a rooted
   sorrow,
Raze out the written troubles of the
   brain,
And with some sweet oblivious anti-
   dote
Cleanse the stuff'd bosom of that
   perilous stuff
Which weighs upon the heart?
DOCTOR:
             Therein the patient
Must minister to himself.
MACBETH:
Throw physic to the dogs; I'll none
   of it.   *Ib.* 40

2 Hang out our banners on the outward
   walls;
The cry is still, 'They come;' our
   castle's strength
Will laugh a siege to scorn.   *Ib.* v. 1

3 I have supp'd full with horrors.
                          Ib. 13

4 SEYTON:
The queen, my lord, is dead.
MACBETH:
She should have died hereafter;
There would have been a time for
   such a word.
To-morrow, and to-morrow, and
   to-morrow,
Creeps in this petty pace from day to
   day,
To the last syllable of recorded time;
And all our yesterdays have lighted
   fools
The way to dusty death. Out, out,
   brief candle!
Life's but a walking shadow, a poor
   player,
That struts and frets his hour upon
   the stage,
And then is heard no more; it is a tale
Told by an idiot, full of sound and
   fury,
Signifying nothing.   *Ib.* 16

5 I pull in resolution, and begin
To doubt the equivocation of the
   fiend
That lies like truth: 'Fear not, till
   Birnam wood
Do come to Dunsinane.'   *Ib.* 42

6 I 'gin to be aweary of the sun,
And wish the estate o' the world
   were now undone.   *Ib.* 49

7   Blow, wind! come, wrack!
At least we'll die with harness on our
   back.   *Ib.* 51

8 They have tied me to a stake; I cannot
   fly.
But bear-like I must fight the course.
              Macbeth, v. vii. 1

9 Why should I play the Roman fool,
   and die
On mine own sword?   *Ib.* 30

10 I bear a charmed life.   *Ib.* 41

11 And let the angel whom thou still
   hast served
Tell thee, Macduff was from his
   mother's womb
Untimely ripp'd.   *Ib.* 43

12   Lay on, Macduff;
And damn'd be him that first cries,
   'Hold, enough!'   *Ib.* 62

13 Spirits are not finely touch'd
But to fine issues.
     Measure for Measure, I. i. 35

14 And liberty plucks justice by the nose.
                  Ib. iii. 29

15 'Tis one thing to be tempted, Escalus,
Another thing to fall.   *Ib.* II. i. 17

16 Some rise by sin, and some by virtue
   fall.   *Ib.* 38

17 This will last out a night in Russia,
When nights are longest there.
                   Ib. [144]

18   O! it is excellent
To have a giant's strength, but it is
   tyrannous
To use it like a giant.   *Ib.* ii. 107

19   But man, proud man,
Drest in a little brief authority,
Most ignorant of what he's most
   assur'd,
His glassy essence, like an angry ape,
Plays such fantastic tricks before
   high heaven,
As make the angels weep.   *Ib.* 117

20   Thou hast nor youth nor age;
But, as it were, an after-dinner's sleep,
Dreaming on both.   *Ib.* III. i. 32

21   Dar'st thou die?
The sense of death is most in appre-
   hension,
And the poor beetle, that we tread
   upon,
In corporal sufferance finds a pang
   as great
As when a giant dies.   *Ib.* 75

22   If I must die,
I will encounter darkness as a bride,
And hug it in mine arms.   *Ib.* 81

23 CLAUDIO:
          Death is a fearful thing.
ISABELLA:
And shamed life a hateful.
CLAUDIO:
Ay, but to die, and go we know not
   where;

To lie in cold obstruction and to rot;
This sensible warm motion to become
A kneaded clod; and the delighted
spirit
To bathe in fiery floods, or to reside
In thrilling region of thick-ribbèd
ice;
To be imprisoned in the viewless
winds,
And blown with restless violence
round about
The pendant world!
Measure for Measure, III. i. 114

1 The weariest and most loathèd worldly
life
That age, ache, penury, and im-
prisonment
Can lay on nature, is a paradise
To what we fear of death. *Ib.* 127

2 There, at the moated grange, resides
this dejected Mariana. *Ib.* [279]

3 Take, O take those lips away,
That so sweetly were forsworn;
And those eyes, the break of day,
Lights that do mislead the morn:
But my kisses bring again, bring again
Seals of love, but seal'd in vain, seal'd
in vain. *Ib.* IV. i. 1

4 I am a kind of burr; I shall stick.
Ib. iii. [193]

5 They say best men are moulded out of
faults,
And, for the most, become much more
the better
For being a little bad. *Ib.* v. i. [440]

6 In sooth I know not why I am so sad:
It wearies me; you say it wearies you;
But how I caught it, found it, or came
by it,
What stuff 'tis made of, whereof it is
born,
I am to learn.
The Merchant of Venice, I. i. 1

7 There are a sort of men whose visages
Do cream and mantle like a standing
pond. *Ib.* 88

8 As who should say, 'I am Sir Oracle,
And when I ope my lips let no dog
bark!'
O, my Antonio, I do know of these,
That therefore only are reputed wise,
For saying nothing. *Ib.* 93

9 If to do were as easy as to know what
were good to do, chapels had been
churches, and poor men's cottages
princes' palaces. *Ib.* ii. [13]

10 It is a good divine that follows his
own instructions; I can easier teach
twenty what were good to be done,
than be one of the twenty to follow
mine own teaching. *Ib.* [15]

11 He doth nothing but talk of his horse.
Ib. [43]

12 God made him, and therefore let him
pass for a man.
The Merchant of Venice, I. ii. [59]

13 I will buy with you, sell with you,
talk with you, walk with you, and so
following; but I will not eat with you,
drink with you, nor pray with you.
What news on the Rialto? *Ib.* iii. [36]

14 How like a fawning publican he looks!
I hate him for he is a Christian.
Ib. [42]

15 If I can catch him once upon the hip,
I will feed fat the ancient grudge I
bear him. *Ib.* [47]

16 The devil can cite Scripture for his
purpose. *Ib.* [99]

17 Signior Antonio, many a time and oft
In the Rialto you have rated me.
Ib. [107]

18 For sufferance is the badge of all our
tribe. *Ib.* [111]

19 Mislike me not for my complexion,
The shadow'd livery of the burnished
sun. *Ib.* II. i. 1

20 The very staff of my age, my very
prop. *Ib.* ii. [71]

21 It is a wise father that knows his own
child. *Ib.* [83]

22 Truth will come to light; murder
cannot be hid long. *Ib.* [86]

23 But love is blind, and lovers cannot
see
The pretty follies that themselves
commit. *Ib.* vi. 36

24 My daughter! O my ducats! O my
daughter!
Fled with a Christian! O my Christian
ducats! *Ib.* viii. 15

25 The portrait of a blinking idiot.
Ib. ix. 54

26 Let him look to his bond.
Ib. III. i. [51, 52, 54]

27 Hath not a Jew eyes? hath not a Jew
hands, organs, dimensions, senses,
affections, passions! fed with the same
food, hurt with the same weapons, subject to the same diseases, healed by
the same means, warmed and cooled
by the same winter and summer, as
a Christian is? If you prick us, do we
not bleed? if you tickle us, do we not
laugh? if you poison us, do we not
die? and if you wrong us, shall we not
revenge? *Ib.* [63]

28 TUBAL:
One of them showed me a ring that he
had of your daughter for a monkey.
SHYLOCK:
I would not have given it for a wilder-
ness of monkeys. *Ib.* [126]

H

1 Tell me where is fancy bred,
 Or in the heart or in the head?
How begot, how nourished?
 Reply, reply.

It is engender'd in the eyes,
With gazing fed; and fancy dies
In the cradle where it lies.
 Let us all ring fancy's knell:
 I'll begin it,—Ding, dong, bell.
   The Merchant of Venice, III. ii. 63

2   Rash-embrac'd despair,
And shuddering fear, and green-ey'd
 jealousy.   *Ib.* 109

3 I will have my bond. *Ib.* iii. 17

4 A harmless necessary cat. *Ib.* IV. i. 55

5 The quality of mercy is not strain'd,
It droppeth as the gentle rain from
 heaven
Upon the place beneath: it is twice
 bless'd;
It blesseth him that gives and him
 that takes:
'Tis mightiest in the mightiest: it
 becomes
The throned monarch better than his
 crown;
His sceptre shows the force of tem-
 poral power,
The attribute to awe and majesty,
Wherein doth sit the dread and fear of
 kings;
But mercy is above this sceptred
 sway,
It is enthroned in the hearts of kings,
It is an attribute to God himself,
And earthly power doth then show
 likest God's
When mercy seasons justice. There-
 fore, Jew,
Though justice be thy plea, consider
 this,
That in the course of justice none of us
Should see salvation: we do pray for
 mercy,
And that same prayer doth teach us
 all to render
The deeds of mercy. *Ib.* [184]

6 A Daniel come to judgment! yea, a
 Daniel!
O wise young judge, how I do honour
 thee!   *Ib.* [223]

7 'Tis not in the bond. *Ib.* [263]

8 A second Daniel, a Daniel, Jew!
Now, infidel, I have thee on the hip.
       Ib. [334]

9   In such a night
Troilus methinks mounted the Troyan
 walls,
And sigh'd his soul towards the
 Grecian tents,
Where Cressid lay that night.
       Ib. v. i. 3

10   In such a night
Stood Dido with a willow in her hand
Upon the wild sea-banks, and waft
 her love
To come again to Carthage.
   The Merchant of Venice, v. i. 9

11 How sweet the moonlight sleeps upon
 this bank!
Here will we sit, and let the sounds of
 music
Creep in our ears: soft stillness and
 the night
Become the touches of sweet harmony.
Sit, Jessica: look, how the floor of
 heaven
Is thick inlaid with patines of bright
 gold:
There's not the smallest orb which
 thou behold'st
But in his motion like an angel sings,
Still quiring to the young-eyed cheru-
 bins;
Such harmony is in immortal souls;
But, whilst this muddy vesture of
 decay
Doth grossly close it in, we cannot
 hear it.   *Ib.* 54

12 I am never merry when I hear sweet
 music.   *Ib.* 69

13 The man that hath no music in him-
 self,
Nor is not mov'd with concord of
 sweet sounds,
Is fit for treasons, stratagems, and
 spoils;
The motions of his spirit are dull as
 night,
And his affections dark as Erebus:
Let no such man be trusted. *Ib.* 83

14 PORTIA:
How far that little candle throws his
 beams!
So shines a good deed in a naughty
 world.
NERISSA:
When the moon shone, we did not see
 the candle.
PORTIA:
So doth the greater glory dim the less.
       Ib. 90

15 Here will be an old abusing of God's
patience, and the king's English.
   The Merry Wives of Windsor,
      I. iv. [5]

16 There's the humour of it. *Ib.* II. i. [139]

17 Why, then the world's mine oyster,
Which I with sword will open.
       Ib. ii. 2

18 Marry, this is the short and the long
of it.   *Ib.* [62]

19 I cannot tell what the dickens his
name is. *Ib.* III. ii. [20]

20 As good luck would have it. *Ib.* v. [86]

21 A man of my kidney. *Ib.* [119]

1 But earthlier happy is the rose dis-
till'd,
Than that which withering on the
virgin thorn
Grows, lives, and dies, in single
blessedness.
A Midsummer Night's Dream,
I. i. 76

2 Ay me! for aught that ever I could
read,
Could ever hear by tale or history,
The course of true love never did run
smooth.   *Ib.* 132

3 A part to tear a cat in, to make all
split.   *Ib.* ii. [32]

4 I will aggravate my voice so that I
will roar you as gently as any suck-
ing dove; I will roar you as 'twere any
nightingale.   *Ib.* [84]

5 A proper man, as one shall see in a
summer's day.   *Ib.* [89]

6 Over hill, over dale,
Thorough bush, thorough brier,
Over park, over pale,
Thorough flood, thorough fire.
Ib. II. i. 2

7 But I might see young Cupid's fiery
shaft
Quench'd in the chaste beams of
the wat'ry moon,
And the imperial votaress passed on,
In maiden meditation, fancy-free.
Yet mark'd I where the bolt of Cupid
fell:
It fell upon a little western flower,
Before milk-white, now purple with
love's wound,
And maidens call it, Love-in-idleness.
Ib. 161

8 I'll put a girdle round about the
earth
In forty minutes.   *Ib.* 175

9 I know a bank whereon the wild
thyme blows,
Where oxlips and the nodding violet
grows
Quite over-canopied with luscious
woodbine,
With sweet musk-roses, and with
eglantine:
There sleeps Titania some time of the
night,
Lull'd in these flowers with dances and
delight;
And there the snake throws her
enamell'd skin,
Weed wide enough to wrap a fairy in.
Ib. 249

10 You spotted snakes with double
tongue,
Thorny hedge-hogs, be not seen;
Newts, and blind-worms, do no wrong;
Come not near our fairy queen.
Ib. ii. 9

11 Weaving spiders come not here;
Hence, you long-legg'd spinners,
hence!
Beetles black, approach not near;
Worm nor snail, do no offence.
A Midsummer Night's Dream, II. ii. 20

12 What hempen home-spuns have we
swaggering here,
So near the cradle of the fairy queen?
Ib. III. i. [82]

13 Bless thee, Bottom! bless thee! thou
art translated.   *Ib.* [124]

14 Lord what fools these mortals be!
Ib. ii. 115

15   So we grew together,
Like to a double cherry, seeming
parted,
But yet an union in partition,
Two lovely berries moulded on one
stem.   *Ib.* 208

16   Jack shall have Jill;
Nought shall go ill;
The man shall have his mare again,
And all shall be well.   *Ib.* 461

17 I have had a dream, past the wit of
man to say what dream it was.
Ib. IV. i. [211]

18 The eye of man hath not heard, the
ear of man hath not seen, man's hand
is not able to taste, his tongue to conceive, nor his heart to report, what
my dream was.   *Ib.* [218]

19 The lunatic, the lover, and the poet,
Are of imagination all compact:
One sees more devils than vast hell
can hold,
That is, the madman; the lover, all
as frantic,
Sees Helen's beauty in a brow of
Egypt:
The poet's eye, in a fine frenzy rolling,
Doth glance from heaven to earth,
from earth to heaven;
And, as imagination bodies forth
The forms of things unknown, the
poet's pen
Turns them to shapes, and gives to
airy nothing
A local habitation and a name.
Such tricks hath strong imagination,
That, if it would but apprehend some
joy,
It comprehends some bringer of that
joy;
Or in the night, imagining some fear,
How easy is a bush suppos'd a bear!
Ib. v. i. 7

20 That is the true beginning of our end.
Consider then we come but in despite.
We do not come as minding to content
you,
Our true intent is. All for your
delight,
We are not here.   *Ib.* [111]

1 Whereat, with blade, with bloody
   blameful blade,
   He bravely broach'd his boiling
     bloody breast.
   A Midsummer Night's Dream, v. i. [148]

2 The best in this kind are but shadows,
   and the worst are no worse, if imagination amend them.   *Ib.* [215]

3 Well roared, Lion.   *Ib.* [272]
   Now the hungry lion roars,
     And the wolf behowls the moon;
   Whilst the heavy ploughman snores,
     All with weary task fordone.
                           Ib. ii. 1

4   Not a mouse
   Shall disturb this hallow'd house:
   I am sent with broom before,
   To sweep the dust behind the door.
                           Ib. 17

5 He is a very valiant trencher-man.
                  Much Ado About Nothing,
                           I. i. [52]

6 BEATRICE:
   I wonder that you will still be talking,
   Signior Benedick: nobody marks you.
   BENEDICK:
   What! my dear Lady Disdain, are
   you yet living?   *Ib.* [121]

7 I will live a bachelor.   *Ib.* [256]

8 There was a star danced, and under
   that was I born.   *Ib.* II. i. [351]

9 Sigh no more, ladies, sigh no more,
     Men were deceivers ever;
   One foot in sea, and one on shore,
   To one thing constant never.
         Then sigh not so,
         But let them go,
   And be you blithe and bonny,
   Converting all your sounds of woe
   Into Hey nonny, nonny.

   Sing no more ditties, sing no mo
     Of dumps so dull and heavy;
   The fraud of men was ever so,
     Since summer first was leavy.
                           Ib. iii. [65]

10 Sits the wind in that corner? *Ib.* [108]

11 He hath a heart as sound as a bell,
   and his tongue is the clapper; for
   what his heart thinks his tongue
   speaks.   *Ib.* III. ii. [12]

12 Are you good men and true? *Ib.* iii. 1

13 Comparisons are odorous. *Ib.* v. [18]

14 A good old man, sir; he will be
   talking: as they say, 'when the age is
   in, the wit is out.'   *Ib.* [36]

15 For there was never yet philosopher
   That could endure the toothache
   patiently.   *Ib.* v. i. 35

16 But I will wear my heart upon my
   sleeve
   For daws to peck at: I am not what
   I am.   *Othello*, I. i. 64

17 Your daughter and the Moor are now
   making the beast with two backs.
                  Othello, I. i. [117]

18 The gross clasps of a lascivious Moor.
                           Ib. [127]

19 Keep up your bright swords, for the
   dew will rust them.   *Ib.* ii. 59

20   Rude am I in my speech,
   And little bless'd with the soft phrase
   of peace.   *Ib.* iii. 81

21   Yet, by your gracious patience,
   I will a round unvarnish'd tale deliver.
                           Ib. 90

22 It was my hint to speak, such was the
     process;
   And of the Cannibals that each other
     eat,
   The Anthropophagi, and men whose
     heads
   Do grow beneath their shoulders. This
     to hear
   Would Desdemona seriously incline.
                           Ib. 142

23   My story being done,
   She gave me for my pains a world of
     sighs:
   She swore, in faith, 'twas strange,
     'twas passing strange;
   'Twas pitiful, 'twas wondrous pitiful.
                           Ib. 158

24 Virtue! a fig! 'tis in ourselves that we
   are thus, or thus.   *Ib.* [323]

25 Put money in thy purse.   *Ib.* [345]

26   Do not put me to 't,
   For I am nothing if not critical.
                  Ib. II. i. 118

27 To suckle fools and chronicle small
   beer.   *Ib.* 160

28   If it were now to die,
   'Twere now to be most happy, for
   I fear
   My soul hath her content so absolute
   That not another comfort like to this
   Succeeds in unknown fate. *Ib.* [192]

29 And let me the canakin clink:
     A soldier's a man;
     A life's but a span;
   Why then let a soldier drink.
                  Ib. iii. [73]

30 'Tis pride that pulls the country down.
                           Ib. [99]

31 Silence that dreadful bell! it frights
   the isle
   From her propriety.   *Ib.* [177]

32 Thy honesty and love doth mince this
   matter.   *Ib.* [249]

33 Reputation, reputation, reputation!
   O! I have lost my reputation. I have
   lost the immortal part of myself, and
   what remains is bestial. My reputation,
   Iago, my reputation!   *Ib.* [264]

1 O! thereby hangs a tail.
     Othello, III. i. [8]

2 Talk him out of patience. *Ib.* iii. 23

3 Excellent wretch! Perdition catch my
 soul
But I do love thee! and when I love
 thee not,
Chaos is come again.   *Ib.* 90

4 Good name in man and woman, dear
 my lord,
Is the immediate jewel of their souls;
Who steals my purse steals trash; 'tis
 something, nothing;
'Twas mine, 'tis his, and has been
 slave to thousands;
But he that filches from me my good
 name
Robs me of that which not enriches
 him,
And makes me poor indeed. *Ib.* 155

5 O! beware, my lord, of jealousy;
It is the green-ey'd monster which
 doth mock
The meat it feeds on. *Ib.* 165

6   For I am declin'd
Into the vale of years. *Ib.* 265

7   O curse of marriage!
That we can call these delicate crea-
 tures ours,
And not their appetites. I had rather
 be a toad,
And live upon the vapour of a dun-
 geon,
Than keep a corner in the thing I love
For others' uses.   *Ib.* 268

8   Trifles light as air
Are to the jealous confirmations strong
As proofs of holy writ. *Ib.* 323

9   Not poppy, nor mandragora,
Nor all the drowsy syrups of the
 world,
Shall ever medicine thee to that sweet
 sleep
Which thou ow'dst yesterday. *Ib.* 331

10   O! now, for ever
Farewell the tranquil mind; farewell
 content!
Farewell the plumed troop and the
 big wars
That make ambition virtue! O, fare-
 well!
Farewell the neighing steed and the
 shrill trump,
The spirit-stirring drum, the ear-
 piercing fife,
The royal banner, and all quality,
Pride, pomp, and circumstance of
 glorious war!
And, O you mortal engines, whose
 rude throats
The immortal Jove's dread clamours
 counterfeit,
Farewell! Othello's occupation's gone!
      Ib. 348

11 But this denoted a foregone conclusion. *Othello*, III. iii. 429

12 But yet the pity of it, Iago! O! Iago,
the pity of it, Iago! *Ib.* IV. i. [205]

13   But, alas! to make me
The fixed figure for the time of scorn
To point his slow and moving finger
 at;
Yet could I bear that too. *Ib.* ii. 52

14 DESDEMONA:
    Mine eyes do itch;
Doth that bode weeping?
EMILIA:
'Tis neither here nor there. *Ib.* iii. [59]

15 It is the cause, it is the cause, my
 soul;
Let me not name it to you, you chaste
 stars!
It is the cause.   *Ib.* v. ii. 1

16 Put out the light, and then put out
 the light.   *Ib.* 7

17 Here is my journey's end, here is my
 butt,
And very sea-mark of my utmost sail.
      Ib. 266

18 Blow me about in winds! roast me in
 sulphur!
Wash me in steep-down gulfs of liquid
 fire!
O Desdemona! Desdemona! dead!
      Ib. 278

19 An honourable murderer, if you will;
For nought did I in hate, but all in
 honour.   *Ib.* 293

20 I have done the state some service,
 and they know 't;
No more of that. I pray you, in your
 letters,
When you shall these unlucky deeds
 relate,
Speak of me as I am; nothing ex-
 tenuate,
Nor set down aught in malice: then,
 must you speak
Of one that lov'd not wisely but too
 well;
Of one not easily jealous, but, being
 wrought,
Perplex'd in the extreme; of one whose
 hand,
Like the base Indian, threw a pearl
 away
Richer than all his tribe; of one whose
 subdu'd eyes
Albeit unused to the melting mood,
Drop tears as fast as the Arabian trees
Their med'cinable gum. Set you down
 this;
And say besides, that in Aleppo once,
Where a malignant and a turban'd
 Turk
Beat a Venetian and traduc'd the
 state,

I took by the throat the circumcised dog,
And smote him thus. *Othello*, v. ii. 338

1 Old John of Gaunt, time-honour'd Lancaster. *King Richard II*, I. i. 1

2 The purest treasure mortal times afford
Is spotless reputation; that away,
Men are but gilded loam or painted clay.
A jewel in a ten-times-barr'd-up chest
Is a bold spirit in a loyal breast.
Mine honour is my life; both grow in one;
Take honour from me, and my life is done. *Ib.* 177

3 We were not born to sue, but to command. *Ib.* 196

4 Teach thy necessity to reason thus;
There is no virtue like necessity. *Ib.* iii. 275

5 O, no! the apprehension of the good
Gives but the greater feeling to the worse. *Ib.* 300

6 Methinks I am a prophet new inspir'd,
And thus expiring do foretell of him:
His rash fierce blaze of riot cannot last,
For violent fires soon burn out themselves;
Small showers last long, but sudden storms are short;
He tires betimes that spurs too fast betimes. *Ib.* II. i. 31

7 This royal throne of kings, this scepter'd isle,
This earth of majesty, this seat of Mars,
This other Eden, demi-paradise,
This fortress built by Nature for herself
Against infection and the hand of war,
This happy breed of men, this little world,
This precious stone set in the silver sea,
Which serves it in the office of a wall,
Or as a moat defensive to a house,
Against the envy of less happier lands,
This blessed plot, this earth, this realm, this England,
This nurse, this teeming womb of royal kings,
Fear'd by their breed and famous by their birth,
Renowned for their deeds as far from home,—
For Christian service and true chivalry,—
As is the sepulchre in stubborn Jewry
Of the world's ransom, blessed Mary's Son:
This land of such dear souls, this dear, dear land. *Ib.* 40

8 England, bound in with the triumphant sea. *King Richard II*, II. i. 61

9 That England, that was wont to conquer others,
Hath made a shameful conquest of itself. *Ib.* 65

10 I count myself in nothing else so happy
As in a soul remembering my good friends. *Ib.* iii. 46

11 Grace me no grace, nor uncle me no uncle. *Ib.* 87

12 Not all the water in the rough rude sea
Can wash the balm from an anointed king. *Ib.* III. ii. 54

13 O! call back yesterday, bid time return. *Ib.* 69

14   Of comfort no man speak:
Let's talk of graves, of worms, and epitaphs;
Make dust our paper, and with rainy eyes
Write sorrow on the bosom of the earth.
Let's choose executors, and talk of wills. *Ib.* 144

15 For God's sake, let us sit upon the ground
And tell sad stories of the death of kings:
How some have been depos'd, some slain in war,
Some haunted by the ghosts they have depos'd,
Some poison'd by their wives, some sleeping kill'd;
All murder'd: for within the hollow crown
That rounds the mortal temples of a king
Keeps Death his court, and there the antick sits,
Scoffing his state and grinning at his pomp;
Allowing him a breath, a little scene,
To monarchize, be fear'd, and kill with looks,
Infusing him with self and vain conceit
As if this flesh which walls about our life
Were brass impregnable; and humour'd thus
Comes at the last, and with a little pin
Bores through his castle wall, and farewell king! *Ib.* 155

16 What must the king do now? Must he submit?
The king shall do it: must he be depos'd?
The king shall be contented: must he lose

The name of king? o' God's name, let
it go.
I'll give my jewels for a set of beads,
My gorgeous palace for a hermitage,
My gay apparel for an almsman's
gown,
My figur'd goblets for a dish of wood,
My sceptre for a palmer's walking
staff,
My subjects for a pair of carved saints,
And my large kingdom for a little
grave,
A little little grave, an obscure grave;
Or I'll be buried in the king's highway,
Some way of common trade, where
subjects' feet
May hourly trample on their sove-
reign's head;
For on my heart they tread now
whilst I live;
And buried once, why not upon my
head?   *King Richard II*, III. iii. 143

1 You make a leg.   *Ib.* 175

2   And there at Venice gave
His body to that pleasant country's
earth,
And his pure soul unto his captain
Christ,
Under whose colours he had fought so
long.   *Ib.* IV. i. 97

3 As in a theatre, the eyes of men,
After a well-grac'd actor leaves the
stage,
Are idly bent on him that enters next,
Thinking his prattle to be tedious.
Ib. v. ii. 23

4 Now is the winter of our discontent
Made glorious summer by this sun of
York.   *King Richard III*, I. i. 1

5 This weak piping time of peace.
Ib. 24

6 And therefore, since I cannot prove a
lover, . . .
I am determined to prove a villain.
Ib. 28

7 Was ever woman in this humour
woo'd?
Was ever woman in this humour won?
Ib. ii. 229

8 Clarence is come,—false, fleeting, perjur'd Clarence.   *Ib.* IV. 55

9 I am not in the giving vein to-day.
Ib. IV. ii. 115

10 Harp not on that string.   *Ib.* IV. 365

11 The king's name is a tower of strength.
Ib. v. iii. 12

12 A horse! a horse! my kingdom for a
horse!   *Ib.* IV. 7

13 A pair of star-cross'd lovers.
Romeo and Juliet, Prologue, 6

14 The two hours' traffic of our stage.
Ib. 12

15 Come, we burn daylight, ho!
Romeo and Juliet, I. iv. 43

16 For you and I are past our dancing
days.   *Ib.* v. [35]

17 O! she doth teach the torches to
burn bright.
It seems she hangs upon the cheek of
night
Like a rich jewel in an Ethiop's ear;
Beauty too rich for use, for earth too
dear.   *Ib.* [48]

18 My only love sprung from my only
hate!   *Ib.* [142]

19 Young Adam Cupid, he that shot so
trim
When King Cophetua lov'd the
beggar-maid.   *Ib.* II. i. 13

20 He jests at scars, that never felt a
wound.
But, soft, what light through yonder
window breaks?
It is the east, and Juliet is the sun.
Ib. ii. 1

21 See! how she leans her cheek upon her
hand:
O! that I were a glove upon that hand,
That I might touch that cheek.
Ib. 23

22 O Romeo, Romeo! wherefore art thou
Romeo?   *Ib.* 33

23 What's in a name? that which we call
a rose
By any other name would smell as
sweet.   *Ib.* 43

24 ROMEO:
Lady, by yonder blessed moon I swear
That tips with silver all these fruit-
tree tops,—
JULIET:
O! swear not by the moon, the in-
constant moon,
That monthly changes in her circled
orb,
Lest that thy love prove likewise
variable.   *Ib.* 107

25 Good-night, good-night! parting is
such sweet sorrow
That I shall say good-night till it be
morrow.   *Ib.* 184

26 O flesh, flesh, how art thou fishified!
Ib. IV. [41]

27 I am the very pink of courtesy.
Ib. [63]

28 Thy head is as full of quarrels as an
egg is full of meat.   *Ib.* III. i. [23]

29 A word and a blow.   *Ib.* [43]

30 A plague o' both your houses!
Ib. [112]

31 O! I am Fortune's fool.   *Ib.* [142]

32 Gallop apace, you fiery-footed steeds,
Towards Phœbus' lodging.   *Ib.* ii. 1

1 Give me my Romeo: and, when he
    shall die,
Take him and cut him out in little
    stars,
And he will make the face of heaven
    so fine
That all the world will be in love with
    night,
And pay no worship to the garish sun.
                Romeo and Juliet, III. ii. 21

2 Night's candles are burnt out, and
    jocund day
Stands tiptoe on the misty mountain
    tops.   *Ib.* v. 9

3 Tempt not a desperate man.
                              Ib. v. iii. 59

4   Beauty's ensign yet
Is crimson in thy lips and in thy
    cheeks,
And death's pale flag is not ad-
    vanced there.   *Ib.* 94

5   Eyes, look your last!
Arms, take your last embrace! and,
    lips, O you
The doors of breath, seal with a
    righteous kiss
A dateless bargain to engrossing
    death!   *Ib.* 112

6 And thereby hangs a tale.
            The Taming of the Shrew, IV. i.
                                        [60]

7   She shall watch all night:
And if she chance to nod I'll rail and
    brawl,
And with the clamour keep her still
    awake.
This is the way to kill a wife with
    kindness.   *Ib.* [208]

8   What seest thou else
In the dark backward and abysm of
    time?   *The Tempest*, I. ii. 49

9 Come unto these yellow sands,
    And then take hands:
Curtsied when you have, and kiss'd,—
    The wild waves whist,
Foot it featly here and there;
And, sweet sprites, the burden bear.
    Hark, hark!
          Bow, wow,
    The watch-dogs bark:
          Bow, wow,
Hark, hark! I hear
The strain of strutting Chanticleer
          Cock-a-diddle-dow.
                              Ib. 375

10 This music crept by me upon the
    waters,
Allaying both their fury, and my
    passion,
With its sweet air.   *Ib.* 389

11 Full fathom five thy father lies;
    Of his bones are coral made:
Those are pearls that were his eyes:
    Nothing of him that doth fade,

12 But doth suffer a sea-change
Into something rich and strange.
Sea-nymphs hourly ring his knell:
                    Ding-dong.
Hark! now I hear them,—ding-dong,
    bell.   *The Tempest*, I. ii. 394

13 A very ancient and fish-like smell.
                            Ib. II. ii. [27]

14 Misery acquaints a man with strange
    bedfellows.   *Ib.* [42]

15 Thou deboshed fish thou.
                            Ib. III. ii. [30]

16 Flout 'em, and scout 'em; and scout
    'em, and flout 'em;
Thought is free.   *Ib.* [133]

17 He that dies pays all debts. *Ib.* [143]

18   The isle is full of noises,
Sounds and sweet airs, that give
    delight, and hurt not.   *Ib.* [147]

19 Deeper than did ever plummet sound,
I'll drown my book.   *Ib.* v. i. 56

20 Where the bee sucks, there suck I
In a cowslip's bell I lie;
There I couch when owls do cry.
On the bat's back I do fly
After summer merrily:
Merrily, merrily shall I live now
Under the blossom that hangs on the
    bough.   *Ib.* 88

21   O brave new world,
That has such people in 't. *Ib.* 183

22   Retire me to my Milan, where
Every third thought shall be my grave.
                              Ib. [310]

23 Uncover, dogs, and lap.
            Timon of Athens, III. vi. [96]

24 We have seen better days.
                            Ib. IV. ii. 27

25 She is a woman, therefore may be
    woo'd;
She is a woman, therefore may be
    won;
She is Lavinia, therefore must be lov'd.
            Titus Andronicus, II. i. 82

26 Men prize the thing ungain'd more
    than it is.
            Troilus and Cressida, I. ii. [313]

27 Time hath, my lord, a wallet at his
    back,
Wherein he puts alms for oblivion,
A great-size'd monster of ingratitudes:
Those scraps are good deeds past;
    which are devour'd
As fast as they are made, forgot as
    soon
As done.   *Ib.* III. iii. 145

28 One touch of nature makes the whole
    world kin,
That all with one consent praise new-
    born gawds.   *Ib.* 175

1   The end crowns all,
And that old common arbitrator, Time,
Will one day end it.
Troilus and Cressida, III. iv. 223

2 If music be the food of love, play on;
Give me excess of it, that, surfeiting,
The appetite may sicken, and so die.
That strain again! it had a dying fall:
O! it came o'er my ear like the sweet
   sound
That breathes upon a bank of violets,
Stealing and giving odour! Enough!
   no more:
'Tis not so sweet now as it was before.
Twelfth Night, I. i. 1

3 A plague o' these pickle herring!
Ib. v. [127]

4 Make me a willow cabin at your gate,
And call upon my soul within the
   house.   *Ib.* [289]

5 O mistress mine! where are you roam-
   ing?
O! stay and hear; your true love's
   coming,
   That can sing both high and low.
Trip no further, pretty sweeting;
Journeys end in lovers meeting,
   Every wise man's son doth know.

What is love? 'tis not hereafter;
Present mirth hath present laughter;
   What's to come is still unsure:
In delay there lies no plenty;
Then come kiss me, sweet and twenty,
   Youth's a stuff will not endure.
Ib. II. iii. [42]

6 Is there no respect of place, persons,
nor time, in you?   *Ib.* [100]

7 SIR TOBY:
Dost thou think, because thou art
   virtuous, there shall be no more cakes
   and ale?
CLOWN:
Yes, by Saint Anne, and ginger shall be
hot i' the mouth too.   *Ib.* [124]

8 My purpose is, indeed, a horse of that
colour.   *Ib.* [184]

9 Come away, come away, death,
   And in sad cypress let me be laid;
Fly away, fly away, breath:
   I am slain by a fair cruel maid.
My shroud of white, stuck all with yew,
   O! prepare it.
My part of death no one so true
   Did share it.

Not a flower, not a flower sweet,
   On my black coffin let there be
   strown;
Not a friend, not a friend greet
   My poor corse, where my bones shall
   be thrown:
A thousand thousand sighs to save,
   Lay me, O! where
Sad true lover never find my grave,
   To weep there.   *Ib.* iv. 51

10 DUKE:
And what's her history?
VIOLA:
A blank, my lord. She never told her
   love,
But let concealment, like a worm i' the
   bud,
Feed on her damask cheek: she pin'd
   in thought;
And with a green and yellow melan-
   choly,
She sat like patience on a monument,
Smiling at grief.
Twelfth Night, II. iv. [111]

11 I am all the daughters of my father's
   house,
And all the brothers too.   *Ib.* [122]

12 But be not afraid of greatness: some
men are born great, some achieve
greatness, and some have greatness
thrust upon them.   *Ib.* v. [158]

13 Remember who commended thy
yellow stockings, and wished to see
thee ever cross-gartered.   *Ib.* [168]

14 He will come to her in yellow stockings, and 'tis a colour she abhors;
and cross-gartered, a fashion she
detests.   *Ib.* [220]

15 In the south suburbs, at the Elephant.
Ib. III. iii. 39

16 Why, this is very midsummer madness.   *Ib.* iv. [62]

17 Still you keep o' the windy side of the
law.   *Ib.* [183]

18 He is a knight dubbed with un-
hatched rapier, and on carpet consideration.   *Ib.* [260]

19 And thus the whirligig of time brings
in his revenges.   *Ib.* v. i. [388]

20 When that I was and a little tiny boy,
   With hey, ho, the wind and the rain;
A foolish thing was but a toy,
   For the rain it raineth every day.

But when I came to man's estate,
   With hey, ho, the wind and the rain;
'Gainst knaves and thieves men shut
   their gates,
   For the rain it raineth every day.

But when I came, alas! to wive,
   With hey, ho, the wind and the rain;
By swaggering could I never thrive,
   For the rain it raineth every day.

But when I came unto my beds,
   With hey, ho, the wind and the rain;
With toss-pots still had drunken
   heads,
   For the rain it raineth every day.

A great while ago the world begun,
   With hey, ho, the wind and the
   rain;
But that's all one, our play is done,
   And we'll strive to please you every
   day.   *Ib.* [401]

1 O! how this spring of love resembleth
The uncertain glory of an April day.
The Two Gentlemen of Verona,
III. iii. 84

2 Who is Sylvia? what is she,
    That all our swains commend her?
Holy, fair, and wise is she;
    The heaven such grace did lend her,
That she might admired be.

Is she kind as she is fair?
    For beauty lives with kindness:
Love doth to her eyes repair,
    To help him of his blindness;
And, being help'd, inhabits there.

Then to Silvia let us sing,
    That Silvia is excelling;
She excels each mortal thing
    Upon the dull earth dwelling;
To her let us garlands bring.
                          Ib. IV. ii. 40

3   A sad tale's best for winter.
I have one of sprites and goblins.
    The Winter's Tale, II. i. 24

4 *Exit, pursued by a bear.*
    Ib. III. iii. *Stage Direction*

5 When daffodils begin to peer,
    With heigh! the doxy, over the dale,
Why, then comes in the sweet o' the
    year;
    For the red blood reigns in the
        winter's pale.

The white sheet bleaching on the
    hedge,
    With heigh! the sweet birds, O,
        how they sing!
Doth set my pugging tooth on edge;
    For a quart of ale is a dish for a
        king.

The lark, that tirra-lirra chants,
    With, heigh! with, heigh! the
        thrush and the jay,
Are summer songs for me and my
    aunts,
    While we lie tumbling in the
        hay.   *Ib.* IV. ii. 1

6 A snapper-up of unconsidered trifles.
                          Ib. [26]

7 Jog on, jog on the foot-path way,
    And merrily hent the stile-a:
A merry heart goes all the day,
    Your sad tires in a mile-a.
                          Ib. [133]

8   Daffodils,
That come before the swallow dares,
    and take
The winds of March with beauty;
    violets dim,
But sweeter than the lids of Juno's
    eyes
Or Cytherea's breath; pale prime-
    roses,
That die unmarried, ere they can
    behold

Bright Phœbus in his strength,—a
    malady
Most incident to maids; bold oxlips
    and
The crown imperial; lilies of all
    kinds,
The flower-de-luce being one.
    The Winter's Tale, IV. iii. 118

9 Lawn as white as driven snow.
                          Ib. [220]

10 Crabbed age and youth cannot live
    together:
Youth is full of pleasance, age is full of
    care.   *The Passionate Pilgrim*, xii

11 Age, I do abhor thee, youth, I do
    adore thee.   *Ib.*

12 Shall I compare thee to a summer's
    day?
Thou art more lovely and more temper-
    ate:
Rough winds do shake the darling buds
    of May,
And summer's lease hath all too short
    a date:
Sometimes too hot the eye of heaven
    shines,
And often is his gold complexion
    dimm'd;
And every fair from fair sometime
    declines,
By chance, or nature's changing course
    untrimm'd;
But thy eternal summer shall not fade,
Nor lose possession of that fair thou
    ow'st,
Nor shall death brag thou wander'st
    in his shade,
When in eternal lines to time thou
    grow'st;
So long as men can breathe, or eyes
    can see,
So long lives this, and this gives life
    to thee.   *Sonnets*, 18

13 When in disgrace with fortune and
    men's eyes
I all alone beweep my outcast state,
And trouble deaf heaven with my
    bootless cries,
And look upon myself, and curse my
    fate,
Wishing me like to one more rich in
    hope
Featur'd like him, like him with
    friends possess'd,
Desiring this man's art, and that man's
    scope,
With what I most enjoy contented
    least;
Yet in these thoughts myself almost
    despising,
Haply I think on thee,—and then
    my state,
Like to the lark at break of day
    arising
From sullen earth, sings hymns at
    heaven's gate;

For thy sweet love remember'd such
wealth brings
That then I scorn to change my state
with kings.   *Sonnets,* 29

1 When to the sessions of sweet silent
thought
I summon up remembrance of things
past,
I sigh the lack of many a thing I
sought,
And with old woes new wail my dear
times' waste.   *Ib.* 30

2 Full many a glorious morning have
I seen
Flatter the mountain-tops with sove-
reign eye,
Kissing with golden face the meadows
green,
Gilding pale streams with heavenly
alchymy.   *Ib.* 33

3 Why didst thou promise such a
beauteous day,
And make me travel forth without my
cloak?   *Ib.* 34

4 Not marble, nor the gilded monuments
Of princes, shall outlive this powerful
rhyme.   *Ib.* 55

5 Like as the waves make towards the
pebbled shore,
So do our minutes hasten to their end.
               Ib. 60

6 When I have seen by Time's fell hand
defac'd
The rich-proud cost of outworn buried
age.   *Ib.* 64

7 No longer mourn for me when I am
dead
Than you shall hear the surly sullen
bell
Give warning to the world that I am
fled
From this vile world, with vilest
worms to dwell.   *Ib.* 71

8 That time of year thou mayst in me
behold
When yellow leaves, or none, or few,
do hang
Upon those boughs which shake
against the cold,
Bare ruin'd choirs, where late the
sweet birds sang.   *Ib.* 73

9 Farewell! thou art too dear for my
possessing,
And like enough thou know'st thy
estimate:
The charter of thy worth gives thee
releasing;
My bonds in thee are all determinate.
               Ib. 87

10 Thus have I had thee, as a dream doth
flatter,
In sleep a king, but, waking, no such
matter.   *Ib.*

11 Lilies that fester smell far worse than
weeds.   *Sonnets,* 94

12 How like a winter hath my absence been
From thee, the pleasure of the fleeting
year!
What freezings have I felt, what dark
days seen!
What old December's bareness every
where!   *Ib.* 97

13 To me, fair friend, you never can be old,
For as you were when first your eye
I ey'd,
Such seems your beauty still. Three
winters cold
Have from the forests shook three
summers' pride,
Three beauteous springs to yellow
autumn turn'd
In process of the seasons have I seen,
Three April perfumes in three hot
Junes burn'd,
Since first I saw you fresh, which yet
are green.
Ah! yet doth beauty, like a dial-hand,
Steal from his figure, and no pace
perceiv'd;
So your sweet hue, which methinks
still doth stand,
Hath motion, and mine eye may be
deceiv'd:
For fear of which, hear this, thou
age unbred:
Ere you were born was beauty's sum-
mer dead   *Ib.* 104

14 Not mine own fears, nor the prophetic soul
Of the wide world dreaming on things
to come,
Can yet the lease of my true love
control.   *Ib.* 107

15 Alas! 'tis true I have gone here and
there,
And made myself a motley to the
view.   *Ib.* 110

16 Let me not to the marriage of true
minds
Admit impediments. Love is not love
Which alters when it alteration finds,
Or bends with the remover to remove:
O, no! it is an ever-fixed mark,
That looks on tempests and is never
shaken;
It is the star to every wandering bark,
Whose worth 's unknown, although his
height be taken.
Love's not Time's fool, though rosy
lips and cheeks
Within his bending sickle's compass
come;
Love alters not with his brief hours
and weeks,
But bears it out even to the edge of
doom.
If this be error, and upon me prov'd,
I never writ, nor no man ever lov'd.
               Ib. 116

1 The expense of spirit in a waste of
     shame
  Is lust in action; and till action, lust
  Is perjur'd, murderous, bloody, full
     of blame,
  Savage, extreme, rude, cruel, not to
     trust.   *Sonnets*, 129

2 Mad in pursuit, and in possession so;
  Had, having, and in quest to have,
     extreme;
  A bliss in proof,—and prov'd, a very
     woe;
  Before, a joy propos'd; behind, a
     dream.
  All this the world well knows; yet
     none knows well:
  To shun the heaven that leads men
     to this hell.   *Ib.*

3 My mistress' eyes are nothing like the
     sun;
  Coral is far more red than her lips'
     red:
  If snow be white, why then her
     breasts are dun;
  If hairs be wires, black wires grow on
     her head.   *Ib.* 130

4 Two loves I have of comfort and de-
     spair,
  Which like two spirits do suggest me
     still:
  The better angel is a man right fair,
  The worser spirit a woman colour'd
     ill.   *Ib.* 144

5 Good friend, for Jesu's sake forbear
  To dig the dust enclosed here.
  Blest be the man that spares these
     stones,
  And curst be he that moves my bones.
        *Shakespeare's Epitaph (chosen by
        himself for his tomb at Stratford-
        on-Avon)*

6 Item, I give unto my wife my second
     best bed, with the furniture.
                          Will, 1616

DAVID TAYLOR SHAW 1813–1890

7 O Britannia, the pride of the ocean,
  The home of the brave and the free,
  The shrine of the sailor's devotion,
  No land can compare unto thee!
        *The Red, White, and Blue. First
        line changed to 'Columbia, the
        gem of the ocean', when sung by
        Shaw in America. Attr. also to
        Thomas à Becket, 1850*

GEORGE BERNARD SHAW 1856–1950

8 You can always tell an old soldier by
  the inside of his holsters and cartridge-
  boxes. The young ones carry pistols
  and cartridges: the old ones, grub.
                  Arms and the Man, Act I

9 I never apologize.
              Arms and the Man, Act III

10 You're not a man, you're a machine.
                                    Ib.

11 I'm only a beer teetotaller, not a
   champagne teetotaller.
                      Candida, Act III

12 The British soldier can stand up to
   anything except the British War
   Office.   *The Devil's Disciple*, Act III

13 Stimulate the phagocytes.
              The Doctor's Dilemma (1906),
              Act I

14 With the single exception of Homer,
   there is no eminent writer, not even
   Sir Walter Scott, whom I can despise
   so entirely as I despise Shakespeare
   when I measure my mind against
   his. . . . It would positively be a
   relief to me to dig him up and throw
   stones at him.
              Dramatic Opinions and Essays
              (1907), vol. ii, p. 52

15 Go anywhere in England, where there
   are natural, wholesome, contented,
   and really nice English people; and
   what do you always find? That the
   stables are the real centre of the
   household.
              Heartbreak House (1919), Act III

16 The greatest of evils and the worst of
   crimes is poverty.
              Major Barbara (1907), Preface

17 Wot prawce Selvytion nah? *Ib.* Act II

18 Nothing is ever done in this world
   until men are prepared to kill one
   another if it is not done. *Ib.* Act III

19 A lifetime of happiness: no man alive
   could bear it: it would be hell on
   earth.
              Man and Superman (1903), Act I

20 The true artist will let his wife starve,
   his children go barefoot, his mother
   drudge for his living at seventy,
   sooner than work at anything but his
   art.   *Ib.*

21 An Englishman thinks he is moral
   when he is only uncomfortable.
                                    Ib. Act III

22 There are two tragedies in life. One is
   not to get your heart's desire. The
   other is to get it.   *Ib.* Act IV

23 The golden rule is that there are no
   golden rules.
              Ib. Maxims for Revolutionists,
              p. 227

24 He who can, does. He who cannot,
   teaches.   *Ib.* p. 230

25 Marriage is popular because it combines the maximum of temptation
   with the maximum of opportunity.
                              Ib. p. 231

1 Home is the girl's prison and the woman's workhouse.
Man and Superman (1903),
Maxims for Revolutionists, p. 240

2 Every man over forty is a scoundrel.
Ib. p. 242

3 Not bloody likely.
Pygmalion (1912), Act II

HENRY WHEELER SHAW ['JOSH BILLINGS'] 1818–1885

4 Thrice is he armed that hath his quarrel just,
But four times he who gets his blow in fust.
Josh Billings, his Sayings (1865)

RICHARD SHEALE sixteenth century

5 For Witherington needs must I wail,
As one in doleful dumps;
For when his legs were smitten off,
He fought upon his stumps.
Ballad of Chevy Chase, pt. II, x

PERCY BYSSHE SHELLEY
1792–1822

6 I weep for Adonais—he is dead!
O, weep for Adonais! though our tears
Thaw not the frost which binds so dear a head!
Adonais, I

7 A pard-like Spirit, beautiful and swift—
Ib. XXXII

8 He has out-soared the shadow of our night;
Envy and calumny and hate and pain,
And that unrest which men miscall delight,
Can touch him not and torture not again;
From the contagion of the world's slow stain
He is secure, and now can never mourn
A heart grown cold, a head grown grey in vain.
Ib. XL

9 He is a portion of the loveliness
Which once he made more lovely.
Ib. XLIII

10 The One remains, the many change and pass;
Heaven's light forever shines, Earth's shadows fly;
Life, like a dome of many-coloured glass,
Stains the white radiance of Eternity.
Ib. LII

11 A widow bird sate mourning for her love
Upon a wintry bough;
The frozen wind crept on above,
The freezing stream below.

There was no leaf upon the forest bare,
No flower upon the ground,
And little motion in the air
Except the mill-wheel's sound.
Charles the First, sc. v, l. 10

12 The world's great age begins anew,
The golden years return,
The earth doth like a snake renew
Her winter weeds outworn;
Heaven smiles, and faiths and empires gleam,
Like wrecks of a dissolving dream.

A brighter Hellas rears its mountains
From waves serener far;
A new Peneus rolls his fountains
Against the morning star.
Where fairer Tempes bloom, there sleep
Young Cyclads on a sunnier deep.

A loftier Argo cleaves the main,
Fraught with a later prize;
Another Orpheus sings again,
And loves, and weeps, and dies.
A new Ulysses leaves once more
Calypso for his native shore.
Hellas, l. 1060

13 I arise from dreams of thee
In the first sweet sleep of night.
When the winds are breathing low,
And the stars are shining bright:
I arise from dreams of thee,
And a spirit in my feet
Hath led me—who knows how?
To thy chamber window, Sweet!
The Indian Serenade

14 Best and brightest, come away!
Fairer far than this fair day.
To Jane: The Invitation

15 O world! O life! O time!
On whose last steps I climb,
Trembling at that where I had stood before;
When will return the glory of your prime?
No more—Oh, never more! *A Lament*

16 When the lamp is shattered
The light in the dust lies dead—
When the cloud is scattered
The rainbow's glory is shed.
When the lute is broken,
Sweet tones are remembered not;
When the lips have spoken,
Loved accents are soon forgot.
Lines: When the Lamp

17 Underneath Day's azure eyes
Ocean's nursling, Venice lies,
A peopled labyrinth of walls,
Amphitrite's destined halls.
Lines written amongst the Euganean Hills, l. 94

18 I met Murder in the way—
He had a mask like Castlereagh.
The Mask of Anarchy, II

19 Ye are many—they are few.
Ib. XXXVIII

20 Swiftly walk over the western wave,
Spirit of Night!
Out of the misty eastern cave,

Where, all the long and lone daylight,
Thou wovest dreams of joy and fear,
Which make thee terrible and dear,—
Swift be thy flight!   *To Night*

1 O wild West Wind, thou breath of
  Autumn's being,
Thou, from whose unseen presence the
  leaves dead
Are driven, like ghosts from an en-
  chanter fleeing,

Yellow, and black, and pale, and
  hectic red,
Pestilence-stricken multitudes: O thou,
Who chariotest to their dark wintry
  bed

The winged seeds, where they lie cold
  and low,
Each like a corpse within its grave,
  until
Thine azure sister of the spring shall
  blow

Her clarion o'er the dreaming earth,
  and fill
(Driving sweet buds like flocks to feed
  in air)
With living hues and odours plain and
  hill:

Wild Spirit, which art moving everywhere;
Destroyer and preserver; hear, oh,
  hear!   *Ode to the West Wind, l. 1*

2 Thou who didst waken from his
  summer dreams
The blue Mediterranean, where he
  lay,
Lulled by the coil of his crystalline
  streams

Beside a pumice isle in Baiae's bay,
And saw in sleep old palaces and
  towers
Quivering within the wave's in-
  tenser day,

All overgrown with azure moss and
  flowers
So sweet, the sense faints picturing
  them.   *Ib. l. 29*

3 If I were a dead leaf thou mightest
  bear;
If I were a swift cloud to fly with
  thee;
A wave to pant beneath thy power,
  and share

The impulse of thy strength, only less
  free
Than thou, O uncontrollable! If even
I were as in my boyhood, and could be

The comrade of thy wanderings over
  Heaven,
As then, when to outstrip thy skiey
  speed
Scarce seemed a vision; I would
  ne'er have striven

As thus with thee in prayer in my
  sore need,
Oh, lift me as a wave, a leaf, a cloud!
I fall upon the thorns of life! I bleed!
          Ode to the West Wind, l. 43

4 Make me thy lyre, even as the forest is:
What if my leaves are falling like its
  own?
The tumult of thy mighty harmonies

Will take from both a deep, autumnal
  tone,
Sweet though in sadness. Be thou,
  Spirit fierce,
My spirit! Be thou me, impetuous one!

Drive my dead thoughts over the
  universe
Like withered leaves to quicken a
  new birth!
And, by the incantation of this verse,

Scatter, as from an unextinguished
  hearth
Ashes and sparks, my words among
  mankind!
Be through my lips to unawakened
  earth

The trumpet of a prophecy! O, Wind,
If Winter comes, can Spring be far
  behind?   *Ib. l. 57*

5 I met a traveller from an antique land
Who said: Two vast and trunkless
  legs of stone
Stand in the desert.   *Ozymandias*

6 My name is Ozymandias, king of
  kings:
Look on my works, ye Mighty, and
  despair!   *Ib.*

7 Nothing beside remains. Round the
  decay
Of that colossal wreck, boundless and
  bare
The lone and level sands stretch far
  away.   *Ib.*

8 The dust of creeds outworn.
          Prometheus Unbound, I. 697

9 On a poet's lips I slept
Dreaming like a love-adept
In the sound his breathing kept;
Nor seeks nor finds he mortal blisses,
But feeds on the aërial kisses
Of shapes that haunt thought's wilder-
  nesses.
He will watch from dawn to gloom
The lake-reflected sun illume
The yellow bees in the ivy-bloom,
Nor heed, nor see, what things they
  be;
But from these create he can
Forms more real than living man,
Nurslings of immortality!   *Ib. 737*

10 A traveller from the cradle to the
  grave
Through the dim night of this immortal day.   *Ib. IV. 551*

1 To suffer woes which Hope thinks
   infinite;
  To forgive wrongs darker than death
   or night;
   To defy Power, which seems omni-
    potent;
  To love, and bear; to hope till Hope
   creates
  From its own wreck the thing it con-
   templates;
   Neither to change, nor falter, nor
    repent;
  This, like thy glory, Titan, is to be
  Good, great and joyous, beautiful and
   free;
  This is alone Life, Joy, Empire and
   Victory.
        Prometheus Unbound, IV. 570

2 A Sensitive Plant in a garden grew.
        The Sensitive Plant, pt. I, l. 1

3 Hail to thee, blithe Spirit!
   Bird thou never wert,
  That from Heaven, or near it,
   Pourest thy full heart
  In profuse strains of unpremeditated
   art.   *To a Skylark*

4 Like a Poet hidden
   In the light of thought,
  Singing hymns unbidden,
   Till the world is wrought
  To sympathy with hopes and fears it
   heeded not.   *Ib.*

5 We look before and after;
   We pine for what is not;
  Our sincerest laughter
   With some pain is fraught;
  Our sweetest songs are those that tell
   of saddest thought.   *Ib.*

6 Teach me half the gladness
   That thy brain must know,
  Such harmonious madness
   From my lips would flow
  The world should listen then—as I am
   listening now.   *Ib.*

7 Rarely, rarely, comest thou,
  Spirit of Delight!
        *Song: Rarely, Rarely, Comest
        Thou*

8 An old, mad, blind, despised, and
  dying king.   *Sonnet: England in 1819*

9 Lift not the painted veil which those
   who live
  Call Life.
        Sonnet: Lift not the Painted Veil

10 Music, when soft voices die,
   Vibrates in the memory—
  Odours, when sweet violets sicken,
   Live within the sense they quicken.

  Rose leaves, when the rose is dead,
   Are heaped for the beloved's bed;
  And so thy thoughts, when thou art
   gone,
  Love itself shall slumber on.
        To——. Music, When Soft Voices

11 I fear thy kisses, gentle maiden,
   Thou needest not fear mine;
  My spirit is too deeply laden
   Ever to burthen thine.

  I fear thy mien, thy tones, thy motion,
   Thou needest not fear mine;
  Innocent is the heart's devotion
   With which I worship thine.
        To——. I Fear Thy Kisses

12 One word is too often profaned
   For me to profane it,
  One feeling too falsely disdained
   For thee to disdain it.
        *To——. One Word is too often
        Profaned*

13 The desire of the moth for the star,
   Of the night for the morrow,
  The devotion to something afar
   From the sphere of our sorrow. *Ib.*

14 And like a dying lady, lean and pale,
  Who totters forth, wrapped in a
   gauzy veil.   *The Waning Moon*

15 Poets are the unacknowledged legis-
  lators of the world.
        A Defence of Poetry

16 The rich have become richer, and the
  poor have become poorer; and the
  vessel of the state is driven between
  the Scylla and Charybdis of anarchy
  and despotism.   *Ib.*

17 Poetry is the record of the best and
  happiest moments of the happiest and
  best minds.   *Ib.*

WILLIAM SHENSTONE 1714–1763

18 Whoe'er has travell'd life's dull round,
  Where'er his stages may have been,
  May sigh to think he still has found
  The warmest welcome, at an inn.
        At an Inn at Henley

ROBERT LOWE, VISCOUNT SHERBROOKE 1811–1892

19 I believe it will be absolutely necessary
  that you should prevail on our future
  masters to learn their letters.
        *Speech in House of Commons
        (on the passing of the Reform Bill),
        15 July 1867. Popularized as
        'We must educate our masters'*

PHILIP HENRY SHERIDAN 1831–1888

20 The only good Indian is a dead Indian.
        Attr., at Fort Cobb, Jan. 1869

RICHARD BRINSLEY SHERIDAN 1751–1816

21 Not a translation—only *taken from
  the French.*   *The Critic, I. i*

1 Yes, sir, puffing is of various sorts; the principal are, the puff direct, the puff preliminary, the puff collateral, the puff collusive, and the puff oblique, or puff by implication. *The Critic*, I. ii

2 No scandal about Queen Elizabeth, I hope? *Ib.* II. i

3 Where they do agree on the stage, their unanimity is wonderful! *Ib.* ii

4 O Lord, sir, when a heroine goes mad she always goes into white satin.
Ib. III. i

5 An oyster may be crossed in love. *Ib.*

6 I loved him for himself alone.
The Duenna, I. iii

7 I was struck all of a heap. *Ib.* II. ii

8 Madam, a circulating library in a town is as an evergreen tree of diabolical knowledge! It blossoms through the year! And depend on it, Mrs. Malaprop, that they who are so fond of handling the leaves, will long for the fruit at last. *The Rivals*, I. ii

9 You gentlemen's gentlemen are so hasty. *Ib.* II. ii

10 An aspersion upon my parts of speech!
Ib. III. iii

11 If I reprehend any thing in this world, it is the use of my oracular tongue, and a nice derangement of epitaphs!
Ib.

12 She's as headstrong as an allegory on the banks of the Nile. *Ib.*

13 Too civil by half. *Ib.* iv

14 I own the soft impeachment. *Ib.* v. iv

15 You shall see them on a beautiful quarto page, where a neat rivulet of text shall meander through a meadow of margin. *The School for Scandal*, I. i

16 MRS. CANDOUR:
I'll swear her colour is natural: I have seen it come and go.
LADY TEAZLE:
I dare swear you have ma'am: it goes off at night, and comes again in the morning. *Ib.* II. ii

17 I'm called away by particular business. But I leave my character behind me. *Ib.*

18 Oh! plague of his sentiments! *Ib.* iii

19 Here's to the maiden of bashful fifteen;
Here's to the widow of fifty;
Here's to the flaunting, extravagant quean;
And here's to the housewife that's thrifty.
Let the toast pass,—
Drink to the lass,
I'll warrant she'll prove an excuse for the glass. *Ib.* III. iii. Song

20 Damned disinheriting countenance.
The School for Scandal, IV. i

21 CHARLES SURFACE:
Lady Teazle, by all that's wonderful!
SIR PETER TEAZLE:
Lady Teazle, by all that's damnable!
Ib. iii

22 It was an amiable weakness. *Ib.* v. i

23 The Right Honourable gentleman is indebted to his memory for his jests, and to his imagination for his facts.
Speech in Reply to Mr. Dundas.
T. Moore, *Life of Sheridan* (1825),
ii. 471

JAMES SHIRLEY 1596–1666

24 The glories of our blood and state
Are shadows, not substantial things;
There is no armour against fate;
Death lays his icy hand on kings:
Sceptre and crown
Must tumble down,
And in the dust be equal made
With the poor crooked scythe and spade.
The Contention of Ajax and Ulysses, I. iii

25 Only the actions of the just
Smell sweet, and blossom in their dust.
Ib.

THE SHORTER CATECHISM

26 'What is the chief end of man?'
'To glorify God and to enjoy him for ever.'

ALGERNON SIDNEY 1622–1683

27 Liars ought to have good memories.
Discourses on Government, ch. 2,
§ xv

28 'Tis not necessary to light a candle to the sun. *Ib.* § xxiii

SIR PHILIP SIDNEY 1554–1586

29 My true love hath my heart and I have his,
By just exchange one for the other giv'n;
I hold his dear, and mine he cannot miss,
There never was a better bargain driv'n. *The Arcadia*, bk. iii *ad fin.*

30 With how sad steps, O Moon, thou climb'st the skies!
How silently, and with how wan a face!
What! may it be that even in heavenly place
That busy archer his sharp arrows tries?
Astrophel and Stella, Certain Sonnets. Sonnet XXXI

1 Come, Sleep! O Sleep, the certain
  knot of peace,
    The baiting-place of wit, the balm of
    woe,
  The poor man's wealth, the prisoner's
    release,
    Th' indifferent judge between the
    high and low.
        Astrophel and Stella, Certain Son-
        nets, Sonnet XXXIX

2 With a tale forsooth he cometh unto
  you, with a tale which holdeth
  children from play, and old men from
  the chimney corner.
        The Defence of Poesy (1595)

3 Thy necessity is yet greater than mine.
    On giving his water-bottle to a
    dying soldier on the battlefield of
    Zutphen, 1586. Sir Fulke Gre-
    ville's Life (1907), ch. 12. *The*
    word 'necessity' is more often
    quoted as 'need'

SIMONIDES 556–468 B.C.

4 ὦ ξεῖν', ἄγγειλον Λακεδαιμονίοις ὅτι τῇδε
  κείμεθα, τοῖς κείνων ῥήμασι πειθόμενοι.

    Go, tell the Spartans, thou who
    passest by,
      That here obedient to their
      laws we lie.
        Select Epigrams (ed. Mackail), iii. 4

GEORGE R. SIMS 1847–1922

5 It is Christmas Day in the workhouse.   *The Dagonet Ballads*

SIR OSBERT SITWELL 1892–1969

6 The British Bourgeoisie
  Is not born,
  And does not die,
  But, if it is ill,
  It has a frightened look in its eyes.
        At the House of Mrs. Kinfoot

JOHN SKELTON 1460?–1529

7 For the soul of Philip Sparrow,
  That was late slain at Carrow
  Among the Nunnes Black,
  For that sweet soul's sake
  And for all sparrows' souls
  Set in our bead-rolls,
  Pater noster qui
  With an *Ave Mari.*
        The Sparrow's Dirge

8 The Tunning of Elynour Rumming.
        Title of Poem

CHRISTOPHER SMART 1722–1771

9 And now the matchless deed's
  achiev'd,
    Determined, dared, and done.
        Song to David, st. 86

FRANCIS EDWARD SMEDLEY
1818–1864

10 You are looking as fresh as paint.
        Frank Fairlegh, ch. 41

SAMUEL SMILES 1812–1904

11 A place for everything, and everything
  in its place.   *Thrift, ch. 5*

ADAM SMITH 1723–1790

12 To found a great empire for the sole
  purpose of raising up a people of
  customers, may at first sight appear a
  project fit only for a nation of shop-
  keepers. It is, however, a project
  altogether unfit for a nation of shop-
  keepers; but extremely fit for a
  nation that is governed by shop-
  keepers.
        Wealth of Nations, vol. II, bk. iv,
        ch. 7, pt. iii (see *1 : 2, 151 : 15*)

LOGAN PEARSALL SMITH
1865–1946

13 Thank heavens, the sun has gone in,
  and I don't have to go out and enjoy
  it.   *All Trivia.* Last Words

SAMUEL FRANCIS SMITH
1808–1895

14 My country, 'tis of thee,
  Sweet land of liberty,
    Of thee I sing:
  Land where my fathers died,
  Land of the pilgrims' pride,
  From every mountain-side
    Let freedom ring.   *America*

REV. SYDNEY SMITH 1771–1845

15 Looked as if she had walked straight
  out of the Ark.
        Lady Holland, *Memoir* (1st ed.
        1855), vol. i, ch. 7, p. 157

16 Madam, I have been looking for a
  person who disliked gravy all my life;
  let us swear eternal friendship.
        Ib. ch. 9, p. 257

17 As the French say, there are three
  sexes—men, women, and clergymen.
        Ib. p. 262

18 Serenely full, the epicure would say,
  Fate cannot harm me, I have dined
  to-day.
        Ib. ch. 11, p. 373, *Recipe for*
        Salad

19 You remember Thurlow's answer . . .
  you never expected justice from a
  company, did you? They have neither
  a soul to lose, nor a body to kick.
        Ib. p. 376

20 Deserves to be preached to death by
  wild curates.   *Ib.* p. 384

1 I never read a book before reviewing
it; it prejudices a man so.
      H. Pearson, *The Smith of Smiths*
      (1934), ch. 3, p. 5

2 ——'s idea of heaven is, eating *pâtés
de foie gras* to the sound of trumpets.
      Ib. ch. 10, p. 236

3 I am just going to pray for you at
St. Paul's, but with no very lively
hope of success.   *Ib.* ch. 13, p. 308

4 Dame Partington . . . was seen . . .
with mop and pattens . . . vigorously
pushing away the Atlantic Ocean.
The Atlantic Ocean beat Mrs. Partington.
      Peter Plymley's Letters (1929),
      p. 228

TOBIAS GEORGE SMOLLETT
1721–1771

5 That great Cham of literature, Samuel
Johnson.
      *Letter to John Wilkes, 16 Mar.
      1759. Boswell's Johnson* (1934),
      vol. i, p. 348

GEORGE HUNT SMYTTAN
1822–1870
and
FRANCIS POTT 1832–1909

6 Forty days and forty nights
Thou wast fasting in the wild,
Forty days and forty nights
Tempted, and yet undefiled.
      *Hymn: Forty Days and Forty
      Nights. The Penny Post* (1856)

SOCRATES 469–399 B.C.

7 ὦ Κρίτων, τῷ Ἀσκληπιῷ ὀφείλομεν ἀλε-
κτρυόνα. ἀλλὰ ἀπόδοτε καὶ μὴ ἀμελήσητε.

      Crito, we owe a cock to Aesculapius;
      pay it, therefore, and do not
      neglect it.
      Last words, 399 B.C. Plato,
      Phaedo, 118a

SOLON c. 640–c. 558 B.C.

8 πρὶν δ᾽ ἂν τελευτήσῃ, ἐπισχεῖν μηδὲ καλέειν
κω ὄλβιον, ἀλλ᾽ εὐτυχέα.

      Call no man happy till he dies, he
      is at best but fortunate.
      Herodotus, *Histories,* i. 32

SOPHOCLES 495–406 B.C.

9 πολλὰ τὰ δεινὰ κοὐδὲν ἀνθρώπου δεινό-
τερον πέλει.

      Wonders are many, and none is
      more wonderful than man.
      Antigone, 332. Trans. by Jebb

10 μὴ φῦναι τὸν ἅπαντα νικᾷ λόγον.

      Not to be born is best.
      Oedipus Coloneus, 1225

JOHN BABSONE LANE SOULE
1815–1891

11 Go west, young man.
      Article in the Terre Haute, In-
      diana, Express (1851)

ROBERT SOUTHEY 1774–1843

12 It was a summer evening,
    Old Kaspar's work was done,
And he before his cottage door
    Was sitting in the sun,
And by him sported on the green
His little grandchild Wilhelmine.
      The Battle of Blenheim

13 But what they fought each other for,
    I could not well make out.   *Ib.*

14 'And everybody praised the Duke,
    Who this great fight did win.'
'But what good came of it at last?'
    Quoth little Peterkin.
'Why that I cannot tell,' said he,
'But 'twas a famous victory.'   *Ib.*

15 Curses are like young chickens, they
always come home to roost.
      The Curse of Kehama. Motto

16 His coat was red and his breeches were
    blue,
And there was a hole where his tail
came through.
      The Devil's Walk, iii

17 He passed a cottage with a double
    coach-house,
    A cottage of gentility!
And he owned with a grin
That his favourite sin
    Is pride that apes humility.   *Ib.* viii

18 No stir in the air, no stir in the sea,
The ship was still as she could be.
      The Inchcape Rock

19 And then they knew the perilous rock,
And blest the Abbot of Aberbrothok.
      Ib.

20 O Christ! It is the Inchcape Rock!
      Ib.

21 Sir Ralph the Rover tore his hair;
He curst himself in his despair.   *Ib.*

22 You are old, Father William, the
    young man cried,
    The few locks which are left you are
    grey;
You are hale, Father William, a
    hearty old man,
    Now tell me the reason, I pray.
      *The Old Man's Comforts, and
      how he Gained them*

1 You are old, Father William, the young man cried
   And pleasures with youth pass away,
   And yet you lament not the days that are gone,
   Now tell me the reason, I pray.
   The Old Man's Comforts, and how he Gained them

2 The death of Nelson was felt in England as something more than a public calamity; men started at the intelligence, and turned pale, as if they had heard of the loss of a dear friend.
   The Life of Nelson, ch. 9

HERBERT SPENCER 1820–1903

3 This survival of the fittest.
   Principles of Biology, pt. iii, ch. 12, Indirect Equilibration, § 165

4 Progress, therefore, is not an accident, but a necessity. . . . It is a part of nature.   *Social Statics, pt. i, ch. 2, § 4*

5 It was remarked to me by the late Mr. Charles Roupell . . . that to play billiards well was a sign of an ill-spent youth.
   Remark. Duncan, Life and Letters of Spencer (1908), ch. 20, p. 298

STEPHEN SPENDER 1909–

6 I think continually of those who were truly great—
   The names of those who in their lives fought for life,
   Who wore at their hearts the fire's centre.
   I Think Continually of Those

7 Born of the sun they travelled a short while towards the sun,
   And left the vivid air signed with their honour.   *Ib.*

EDMUND SPENSER 1552?–1599

8 Triton blowing loud his wreathed horn.
   Colin Clout's Come Home Again, l. 245

9 A gentle knight was pricking on the plain.
   The Faerie Queene, bk. I, c. I. i

10 Sleep after toil, port after stormy seas, Ease after war, death after life does greatly please.   *Ib. c. IX. xl*

11 And all for love, and nothing for reward.   *Ib. bk. II, c. VIII. ii*

12 For all that nature by her mother wit Could frame in earth.
   Ib. bk. IV, c. X. xxi

13 Sweet Thames, run softly, till I end my Song.   *Prothalamion, l. 18*

14 At length they all to merry London came,
   To merry London, my most kindly nurse,
   That to me gave this life's first native source.   *Prothalamion, l. 127*

15 So now they have made our English tongue a gallimaufry or hodgepodge of all other speeches.
   The Shepherd's Calendar. Letter to Gabriel Harvey

REV. WILLIAM ARCHIBALD SPOONER 1844–1930

16 Kinquering Congs their titles take.
   Announcing the hymn in New College Chapel, 1879 (see 59:18)

17 You have deliberately tasted two worms and you can leave Oxford by the town drain.
   Dismissing a student. Attr.

SIR CECIL ARTHUR SPRING-RICE 1858–1918

18 I vow to thee, my country—all earthly things above—
   Entire and whole and perfect, the service of my love.   *Last Poem*

19 I am the Dean of Christ Church, Sir: There's my wife; look well at her.
   She's the Broad and I'm the High; We are the University.
   The Masque of Balliol, composed by and current among members of Balliol College, Oxford, in the late 1870's. This first couplet (identified as by C. A. Spring-Rice) was unofficially altered to:

20 I am the Dean, and this is Mrs. Liddell; She is the first and I the second fiddle.
   (See also 6:9, 20:5)

SIR JOHN COLLINGS SQUIRE 1884–

21 It did not last: the Devil howling 'Ho! Let Einstein be!' restored the status quo.
   Answer to Pope's epitaph for Sir Isaac Newton

MME DE STAËL 1766–1817

22 Tout comprendre rend très indulgent.
   To know all makes one tolerant.
   Corinne (1807), lib. iv, ch. 3

EDWARD STANLEY, EARL OF DERBY 1799–1869

23 When I first came into Parliament, Mr. Tierney, a great Whig authority, used always to say that the duty of an Opposition was very simple—it

was, to oppose everything, and propose nothing.
> *House of Commons, 4 June 1841.*
> *Hansard, 3rd ser., lviii. 1188*

1 Don't you see that we have dished the
Whigs?
> *With reference to the Reform Bill*
> *of 1867.* Monypenny and Buckle,
> *Life of Disraeli,* ii. 285

SIR HENRY MORTON STANLEY
1841–1904

2 Dr. Livingstone, I presume?
> *How I found Livingstone,* ch. 11

FRANK LEBBY STANTON
1857–1927

3 Sweetest li'l feller, everybody knows;
Dunno what to call him, but he's
mighty lak' a rose;
Lookin' at his mammy wid eyes so
shiny blue
Mek' you think that Heav'n is comin'
clost ter you.   *Mighty Lak' a Rose*

SIR RICHARD STEELE 1672–1729

4 There are so few who can grow old
with a good grace.
> *The Spectator,* No. 263

5 Though her mien carries much more
invitation than command, to behold
her is an immediate check to loose
behaviour; to love her is a liberal
education.   *The Tatler,* No. 49

6 Reading is to the mind what exercise
is to the body.   *Ib.* No. 147

JAMES KENNETH STEPHEN
1859–1892

7 Two voices are there: one is of the
deep;

And one is of an old half-witted sheep
Which bleats articulate monotony,

And Wordsworth, both are thine.
> *Lapsus Calami. Sonnet*

8 When the Rudyards cease from kip-
ling
And the Haggards ride no more.
> *Ib. To R.K.*

JAMES STEPHENS 1882–1950

9 I heard a sudden cry of pain!
There is a rabbit in a snare.
> *The Snare*

10 Little One! Oh, Little One!
I am searching everywhere!   *Ib.*

LAURENCE STERNE 1713–1768

11 They order, said I, this matter better
in France.
> *A Sentimental Journey,* l. 1

12 God tempers the wind, said Maria,
to the shorn lamb.
> *Ib. Maria. From a French pro-*
> *verb, but familiar in Sterne's*
> *form of words*

13 'Pray, my dear,' quoth my mother,
'have you not forgot to wind up the
clock?'—'Good   G——!' cried my
father, making an exclamation, but
taking care to moderate his voice at
the same time,—'Did ever woman,
since the creation of the world, inter-
rupt a man with such a silly question?'
> *Tristram Shandy,* bk. i, ch.1

14 My uncle Toby would never offer to
answer this by any other kind of
argument, than that of whistling
half a dozen bars of Lillabullero.
> *Ib.* ch. 21

15 I should have no objection to this
method, but that I think it must
smell too strong of the lamp.
> *Ib.* ch. 23

16 That's another story. *Ib.* bk. ii, ch. 18

17 The nonsense of the old women (of
both sexes).   *Ib.* bk. iv, ch. 16

18 Said my mother, 'what is all this
story about?'—
'A Cock and a Bull,' said Yorick.
> *Ib.* bk. ix, ch. 33

ADLAI EWING STEVENSON
1900–1965

19 [Mr. Stevenson] derided the Secretary
[of State] for 'boasting of his brink-
manship—the art of bringing us to the
edge of the nuclear abyss'.
> *New York Times,* 26 Feb. 1956,
> p. 1, col. 5 (reporting a speech
> by Mr. Adlai Stevenson).

ROBERT LOUIS STEVENSON
1850–1894

20 Every one lives by selling something.
> *Across the Plains,* IX. *Beggars,* iii

21 Am I no a bonny fighter? [*Alan Breck.*]
> *Kidnapped,* ch. 10

22 I have thus played the sedulous ape
to Hazlitt, to Lamb, to Wordsworth,
to Sir Thomas Browne, to Defoe, to
Hawthorne, to Montaigne, to Baude-
laire and to Obermann.
> *Memories and Portraits,* ch. 4

23 I own I like definite form in what my
eyes are to rest upon; and if landscapes were sold, like the sheets of
characters of my boyhood, one penny
plain and twopence coloured, I should

go the length of twopence every day of my life.
>   *Travels with a Donkey. Father Apollinaris*

1 Fifteen men on the dead man's chest
 Yo-ho-ho, and a bottle of rum!
Drink and the devil had done for the rest—
 Yo-ho-ho, and a bottle of rum!
>   *Treasure Island*, ch. 1

2 Tip me the black spot. *Ib.* ch. 3

3 Pieces of eight! *Ib.* ch. 10

4 Many's the long night I've dreamed of cheese—toasted, mostly. [*Ben Gunn.*]
>   *Ib.* ch. 15

5 Marriage is like life in this—that it is a field of battle, and not a bed of roses. *Virginibus Puerisque*, I. i

6 To travel hopefully is a better thing than to arrive, and the true success is to labour. *Ib.* VI. *El Dorado*

7 Though we are mighty fine fellows nowadays, we cannot write like Hazlitt. *Ib.* X. *Walking Tours*

8 You must not fancy I am sick, only over-driven and under the weather.
>   *The Wrecker*, ch. 4

9 Nothing like a little judicious levity. [*Michael Finsbury.*] *The Wrong Box*, ch. 7

10 'The "Athæneum", that was the name! Golly, what a paper!' '"Athenæum", you mean,' said Morris.
>   *Ib.* ch. 15

11 A child should always say what's true,
And speak when he is spoken to,
And behave mannerly at table:
At least as far as he is able.
>   *A Child's Garden of Verses*. V. *Whole Duty of Children*

12 The pleasant land of counterpane.
>   *Ib.* XVI. *The Land of Counterpane*

13 The friendly cow, all red and white,
 I love with all my heart:
She gives me cream with all her might,
 To eat with apple-tart.
>   *Ib.* XXIII. *The Cow*

14 The world is so full of a number of things,
I'm sure we should all be as happy as kings. *Ib.* XXIV. *Happy Thought*

15 Give to me the life I love,
 Let the lave go by me,
Give the jolly heaven above
 And the byway nigh me.
Bed in the bush with stars to see,
 Bread I dip in the river—
There's the life for a man like me,
 There's the life for ever.
>   *Songs of Travel*. I. *The Vagabond*

16 The untented Kosmos my abode,
 I pass, a wilful stranger;
My mistress still the open road
 And the bright eyes of danger.
>   *Songs of Travel*, II. *Youth and Love*

17 I will make you brooches and toys for your delight
Of bird-song at morning and star-shine at night.
I will make a palace fit for you and me
Of green days in forests and blue days at sea. *Ib.* XI

18 Bright is the ring of words
 When the right man rings them,
Fair the fall of songs
 When the singer sings them. *Ib.* XIV

19 Trusty, dusky, vivid, true,
With eyes of gold and bramble-dew,
Steel-true and blade-straight,
The great artificer
Made my mate. *Ib.* XXV. *My Wife*

20 Sing me a song of a lad that is gone,
 Say, could that lad be I?
Merry of soul he sailed on a day
 Over the sea to Skye. *Ib.* XLII

21 Mull was a-stern, Rum on the port,
 Eigg on the starboard bow;
Glory of youth glowed in his soul,
 Where is that glory now? *Ib.*

22 Go, little book, and wish to all
Flowers in the garden, meat in the hall,
A bin of wine, a spice of wit,
A house with lawns enclosing it,
A living river by the door,
A nightingale in the sycamore!
>   *Underwoods*, bk. I. i. *Envoy*

23 Under the wide and starry sky
Dig the grave and let me lie.
Glad did I live and gladly die,
 And I laid me down with a will.
This be the verse you grave for me:
'Here he lies where he longed to be;
Home is the sailor, home from sea,
 And the hunter home from the hill.'
>   *Ib.* xxi. *Requiem*

24 If I have faltered more or less
In my great task of happiness;
If I have moved among my race
And shown no glorious morning face;
If beams from happy human eyes
Have moved me not; if morning skies,
Books, and my food, and summer rain
Knocked on my sullen heart in vain:—
Lord, thy most pointed pleasure take
And stab my spirit broad awake;
Or, Lord, if too obdurate I,
Choose thou, before that spirit die,
A piercing pain, a killing sin,
And to my dead heart run them in!
>   *Ib.* xxii. *The Celestial Surgeon*

WILLIAM STEVENSON
1530?–1575

25 I stuff my skin, so full within,
 Of jolly good ale and old,

Back and side go bare, go bare,
  Both foot and hand go cold:
But belly God send thee good ale
    enough,
  Whether it be new or old.
          Gammer Gurton's Needle, Act II,
            Song

SAMUEL JOHN STONE 1839–1900

1 The Church's one foundation
    Is Jesus Christ her Lord;
  She is His new creation
    By water and the Word.
          Lyra Fidelium (1866). *The
            Church's One Foundation*

2 Yet Saints their watch are keeping,
    Their cry goes up, 'How long?'
  And soon the night of weeping
    Shall be the morn of song.   *Ib.*

HARRIET BEECHER STOWE
                                  1811–1896

3 'Who was your mother?' 'Never had
    none!' said the child, with another
    grin. 'Never had any mother? What
    do you mean? Where were you born?'
    'Never was born!' persisted Topsy.
          Uncle Tom's Cabin, ch. 20

4 'Do you know who made you?' 'No-
    body, as I knows on,' said the child,
    with a short laugh. . . . 'I 'spect I
    grow'd.'   *Ib.*

SIR JOHN SUCKLING 1609–1642

5 Why so pale and wan, fond lover?
      Prithee, why so pale?
  Will, when looking well can't move her,
      Looking ill prevail?
      Prithee, why so pale?
          Aglaura, IV. i. *Song*

6 Her feet beneath her petticoat,
    Like little mice, stole in and out,
      As if they fear'd the light.
          Ballad. Upon a Wedding, viii

7 The Prince of Darkness is a gentleman.
          The Goblins, Act III, *A Catch*

8 Out upon it, I have loved
    Three whole days together;
  And am like to love three more,
    If it prove fair weather.

  Time shall moult away his wings,
    Ere he shall discover
  In the whole wide world again
    Such a constant lover.
          A Poem with the Answer

SUETONIUS *fl. c.* A.D. 120

9 Festina lente. [σπεῦδε βραδέως.]
    Hasten slowly. *Divus Augustus*, 25

10 Ave, Imperator, morituri te salutant.
    Hail, Emperor, those about to die
    salute thee. *Life of Claudius*, 21

MAXIMILIAN DE BETHUNE,
DUC DE SULLY 1559–1641

11 Les anglais s'amusent tristement
    selon l'usage de leur pays.

    The English take their pleasures
      sadly after the fashion of their
      country.   *Memoirs, c.* 1630

ROBERT SMITH SURTEES
                                  1803–1864

12 The only infallible rule we know is,
    that the man who is always talking
    about being a gentleman never is one.
          Ask Mamma (1858), ch. 1

13 'Unting is all that's worth living for—
    all time is lost wot is not spent in
    'unting—it is like the hair we breathe
    —if we have it not we die—it's the
    sport of kings, the image of war
    without its guilt, and only five-and-
    twenty per cent. of its danger.
          Handley Cross (1843), ch. 7

14 'Unting fills my thoughts by day, and
    many a good run I have in my sleep.
    Many a dig in the rib I gives Mrs. J.
    when I think they're running into the
    warmint (renewed cheers). No man
    is fit to be called a sportsman wot
    doesn't kick his wife out of bed on
    a haverage once in three weeks!
                            Ib. ch. 11

15 Come Hup! I say, you hugly beast!
                            Ib. ch. 13

16 He will bring his nightcap with him,
    for where the M.F.H. dines he sleeps,
    and where the M.F.H. sleeps he break-
    fasts.   *Ib.* ch. 15

17 It ar'n't that I loves the fox less, but
    that I loves the 'ound more. *Ib.* ch. 16

18 Full o' beans and benevolence!
                            Ib. ch. 27

19 Hellish dark, and smells of cheese!
                            Ib. ch. 50

20 And a nod or a wink for every pretty
    maid that showed at the windows;
    for . . . , as he says, 'there is no harm
    in looking'.
          Jorrocks's Jaunts and Jollities
          (1838), No. 4. *Surrey Stag-
            Hounds*

21 No one knows how ungentlemanly he
    can look, until he has seen himself
    in a shocking bad hat.
          Mr. Facey Romford's Hounds
          (1865), ch. 9

22 He was a gentleman who was generally
    spoken of as having nothing a-year,
    paid quarterly.
          Mr. Sponge's Sporting Tour
          (1853), ch. 24

JONATHAN SWIFT 1667–1745

1 Instead of dirt and poison we have rather chosen to fill our hives with honey and wax; thus furnishing mankind with the two noblest of things, which are sweetness and light.
The Battle of the Books, preface

2 And he gave it for his opinion, that whoever could make two ears of corn or two blades of grass to grow upon a spot of ground where only one grew before, would deserve better of mankind, and do more essential service to his country than the whole race of politicians put together.
Gulliver's Travels. Voyage to Brobdingnag, ch. 7

3 With my own fair hands.
Journal to Stella, 4 Jan. 1711

4 Will she pass in a crowd? Will she make a figure in a country church?
Ib. 9 Feb. 1711

5 Not die here in a rage, like a poisoned rat in a hole.
Letter to Bolingbroke, 21 Mar. 1729

6 I have ever hated all nations, professions and communities, and all my love is towards individuals. . . . But principally I hate and detest that animal called man; although I heartily love John, Peter, Thomas, and so forth.
Letter to Pope, 29 Sept. 1725

7 What they call 'running a man down'.
Letter to a Young Lady on her Marriage (1723)

8 Promises and pie-crust are made to be broken.
Polite Conversation. Dialogue 1

9 The sight of you is good for sore eyes.
Ib.

10 You were half seas over. *Ib.*

11 I won't quarrel with my bread and butter. *Ib.*

12 I swear, she's no chicken; she's on the wrong side of thirty, if she be a day. *Ib.*

13 She wears her clothes, as if they were thrown on her with a pitchfork. *Ib.*

14 You must take the will for the deed.
Ib. Dialogue 2

15 She has more goodness in her little finger, than he has in his whole body.
Ib.

16 I know Sir John will go, though he was sure it would rain cats and dogs.
Ib.

17 There's none so blind as they that won't see. *Ib. Dialogue 3*

18 She watches him, as a cat would watch a mouse.
Polite Conversation. Dialogue 3

19 She pays him in his own coin. *Ib.*

20 All the world and his wife. *Ib.*

21 Party is the madness of many, for the gain of a few.
Thoughts on Various Subjects

22 They never would hear,
But turn the deaf ear,
As a matter they had no concern in.
Dingley and Brent, ii

23 Hail, fellow, well met,
All dirty and wet:
Find out, if you can,
Who's master, who's man.
My Lady's Lamentation, 1. 171

24 Philosophy, the lumber of the schools.
Ode to Sir W. Temple, ii

25 Walls have tongues, and hedges ears.
Pastoral Dialogue, 1. 8

26 So, naturalists observe, a flea
Hath smaller fleas that on him prey;
And these have smaller fleas to bite 'em,
And so proceed *ad infinitum*.
Thus every poet, in his kind,
Is bit by him that comes behind.
On Poetry, 1. 337

27 Ubi saeva indignatio ulterius cor lacerare nequit.

Where fierce indignation can no longer tear his heart.
Swift's Epitaph

ALGERNON CHARLES SWINBURNE 1837–1909

28 When the hounds of spring are on winter's traces,
The mother of months in meadow or plain
Fills the shadows and windy places
With lisp of leaves and ripple of rain;
And the brown bright nightingale amorous
Is half assuaged for Itylus,
For the Thracian ships and the foreign faces,
The tongueless vigil and all the pain.
Atalanta in Calydon. Collected Poetical Works (1924), vol. ii. Chorus, p. 249

29 And time remembered is grief forgotten,
And frosts are slain and flowers begotten,
And in green underwood and cover
Blossom by blossom the spring begins. *Ib. p. 250*

1 Before the beginning of years
   There came to the making of man
Time with a gift of tears,
   Grief with a glass that ran.
Pleasure with pain for leaven,
   Summer with flowers that fell,
Remembrance fallen from heaven,
   And Madness risen from hell,
Strength without hands to smite,
   Love that endures for a breath;
Night, the shadow of light,
   And Life, the shadow of death.
     Atalanta in Calydon. Collected
     Poetical Works (1924), vol. ii,
     Chorus, p. 258

2 Eyesight and speech they wrought
   For the veil of the soul therein,
A time for labour and thought,
   A time to serve and to sin;
They gave him light in his ways,
   And love, and a space for delight,
And beauty and length of days,
   And night, and sleep in the night.
His speech is a burning fire;
   With his lips he travaileth;
In his heart is a blind desire,
   In his eyes foreknowledge of death;
He weaves, and is clothed with deri-
   sion;
   Sows, and he shall not reap;
His life is a watch or a vision
   Between a sleep and a sleep.
           Ib. p. 259

3 We shift and bedeck and bedrape us,
   Thou art noble and nude and
   antique.   *Dolores*, vii

4   Change in a trice
The lilies and languors of virtue
   For the raptures and roses of vice.
               Ib. ix

5 O splendid and sterile Dolores,
   Our Lady of Pain.   *Ib.*

6 From too much love of living,
   From hope and fear set free,
We thank with brief thanksgiving
   Whatever gods may be
That no man lives forever,
   That dead men rise up never;
That even the weariest river
   Winds somewhere safe to sea.
     The Garden of Persephone

7 Swallow, my sister, O sister swallow,
   How can thine heart be full of the
     spring?
A thousand summers are over and
   dead.
   What hast thou found in the spring
     to follow?
What hast thou found in thine heart
   to sing?
What wilt thou do when the summer
   is shed?   *Itylus*

8 Glory to Man in the highest! for Man
is the master of things. *Hymn of Man*

9 Wilt thou yet take all, Galilean? but
   these thou shalt not take,
The laurel, the palms and the paean,
   the breasts of the nymphs in the
   brake;
Breasts more soft than a dove's, that
   tremble with tenderer breath;
And all the wings of the Loves, and all
   the joy before death.
          Hymn to Proserpine

10 Thou hast conquered, O pale Galilean;
   the world has grown grey from Thy
   breath;
We have drunken of things Lethean,
   and fed on the fullness of death.
Laurel is green for a season, and love
   is sweet for a day;
But love grows bitter with treason,
   and laurel outlives not May.   *Ib.*

11 There lived a singer in France of old
By the tideless dolorous midland sea.
In a land of sand and ruin and gold
There shone one woman, and none but
   she.   *The Triumph of Time*

PUBLILIUS SYRUS
               fl. first century B.C.

12 Bis dat qui cito dat.
   He gives twice who gives soon.
     Proverbial, attr. to Syrus

13 Necessitas non habet legem.
   Necessity has no law.
     Proverbial, attr. to Syrus

TACITUS *c.* A.D. 55–*c.* 117

14 Atque omne ignotum pro magnifico
est; sed nunc terminus Britanniae
patet.
   For wonder grows where knowledge
   fails. But now the very bounds of
   Britain are laid bare.
     Agricola, 30. Trans. by Fyfe

15 Ubi solitudinem faciunt, pacem ap-
pellant.
   When they make a wilderness they
   call it peace.   *Ib.*

16 Felix . . . opportunitate mortis.
   Fortune favoured him . . . in the
   opportune moment of his death.
              Ib. 45

17 Editis annalibus laudatoque M. Bruto
C. Cassium Romanorum ultimum
dixisset.
   In his history he had praised Brutus
   and had called Cassius the last
   of the Romans.   *Annals*, iv. 34

18 Elegantiae arbiter. [Petronius.]
   Judge of taste.   *Ib.* xvi. 18

1 Maior privato visus dum privatus fuit,
et omnium consensu capax imperii
nisi imperasset.

> When he was a commoner he seemed
> too big for his station, and had he
> never been emperor, no one would
> have doubted his ability to reign.
> [Servius Galba.]
> *Histories*, I. xlix. Trans. by Fyfe

CHARLES-MAURICE DE TALLEYRAND 1754–1838

2 Ils n'ont rien appris, ni rien oublié.

> They have learnt nothing, and for-
> gotten nothing.
> *Attributed to Talleyrand by the
> Chevalier de Panat in a letter to
> Mallet du Pan, Jan. 1796, 'Per-
> sonne n'est corrigé, personne n'a
> su ni rien oublier ni rien ap-
> prendre.' (Mémoires et corre-
> spondance de Mallet du Pan
> (1851), ii. 196.) See also 80:11*

3 N'ayez pas de zèle.

> Not too much zeal.
> Sainte-Beuve, *Portraits de
> femmes, Madame de Staël*, p. 131

4 Voilà le commencement de la fin.

> This is the beginning of the end.
> *On the announcement of
> Napoleon's defeat at Borodino,
> 1812*

5 War is much too serious a thing to be
left to military men.

> *Quoted by Briand to Lloyd George
> during the First World War*

NAHUM TATE 1652–1715
and
NICHOLAS BRADY 1659–1726

6 As pants the hart for cooling streams
When heated in the chase.

> *New Version of the Psalms* (1696).
> *As Pants the Hart*

7 Through all the changing scenes of
life. *Ib. Through all the Changing*

8 Fear Him, ye saints, and you will then
Have nothing else to fear. *Ib.*

9 While shepherds watch'd their flocks
by night,
All seated on the ground,
The Angel of the Lord came down,
And glory shone around.

'Fear not,' said he, for mighty dread
Had seized their troubled mind;
'Glad tidings of great joy I bring
To you and all mankind.'

> *Supplement to the New Version of
> the Psalms* (1700). *While Shep-
> herds Watched*

ANN TAYLOR 1782–1866
and
JANE TAYLOR 1783–1824

10 Twinkle, twinkle, little star,
How I wonder what you are!
Up above the world so high,
Like a diamond in the sky!

> *Rhymes for the Nursery. The
> Star. (By Jane Taylor)*

BISHOP JEREMY TAYLOR 1613–1667

11 Every school-boy knows it.

> *On the Real Presence*, § v, par. 1

JOHN TAYLOR 1580–1653

12 'Tis a mad world, my masters.

> *Western Voyage*, l. 1

ARCHBISHOP WILLIAM TEMPLE 1881–1944

13 We have ... seen that in place of the
conception of the Power-State we are
led to that of the Welfare-State.

> *Citizen and Churchmen* (1941),
> p. 35

ALFRED, LORD TENNYSON 1809–1892

14 Break, break, break,
On thy cold gray stones, O Sea!
And I would that my tongue could
utter
The thoughts that arise in me.

> *Break, Break, Break*

15 And the stately ships go on
To their haven under the hill;
But O for the touch of a vanish'd hand,
And the sound of a voice that is still!

Break, break, break,
At the foot of thy crags, O Sea!
But the tender grace of a day that is
dead
Will never come back to me. *Ib.*

16 A happy bridesmaid makes a happy
bride. *The Bridesmaid*, l. 4

17 I come from haunts of coot and hern,
I make a sudden sally
And sparkle out among the fern,
To bicker down a valley.

> *The Brook*, l. 23

18 For men may come and men may go,
But I go on for ever. *Ib.* l. 33

19 That petitionary grace
Of Sweet Seventeen. *Ib.* l. 112

20 Half a league, half a league,
Half a league onward.

> *The Charge of the Light Brigade*

21 'Forward, the Light Brigade!'
Was there a man dismay'd? *Ib.*

1 Some one had blunder'd.
    The Charge of the Light Brigade

2 Their's not to make reply,
  Their's not to reason why,
  Their's but to do and die:
  Into the valley of Death
  Rode the six hundred.   *Ib.*

3 Cannon to right of them
  Cannon to left of them,
  Cannon in front of them
    Volley'd and thunder'd.   *Ib.*

4 Into the jaws of Death,
  Into the mouth of Hell.   *Ib.*

5 When can their glory fade?
  O the wild charge they made!
  All the world wonder'd.   *Ib.*

6 Sunset and evening star,
    And one clear call for me!
  And may there be no moaning of the
    bar,
  When I put out to sea,

  But such a tide as moving seems
    asleep,
    Too full for sound and foam,
  When that which drew from out the
    boundless deep
  Turns again home.

  Twilight and evening bell,
    And after that the dark!
  And may there be no sadness of fare-
    well,
    When I embark;

  For tho' from out our bourne of Time
    and Place
    The flood may bear me far,
  I hope to see my Pilot face to face
    When I have crost the bar.
                          Crossing the Bar

7 Gray metropolis of the North. [Edin-
  burgh.]   *The Daisey,* xxvi

8 A daughter of the gods, divinely tall
  And most divinely fair.
        A Dream of Fair Women, 1. 87

9 He clasps the crag with crooked
    hands;
  Close to the sun in lonely lands,
  Ring'd with the azure world, he
    stands.
  The wrinkled sea beneath him crawls;
  He watches from his mountain walls,
  And like a thunderbolt he falls.
                          The Eagle

10 And when they buried him the little
    port
  Had seldom seen a costlier funeral.
                          Enoch Arden

11 The mellow lin-lan-lone of evening
  bells.   *Far-Far-Away*

12 Flower in the crannied wall,
  I pluck you out of the crannies,
  I hold you here, root and all, in my
    hand,

Little flower—but *if* I could understand
What you are, root and all, and all in
  all,
I should know what God and man is.
            Flower in the Crannied Wall

13 More black than ashbuds in the front
  of March.
        The Gardener's Daughter, 1. 28

14 Pray God our greatness may not fail
  Thro' craven fears of being great.
            Hands All Round, iii

15 Wearing the white flower of a blame-
    less life,
  Before a thousand peering littlenesses,
  In that fierce light which beats upon
    a throne,
  And blackens every blot.
        The Idylls of the King, Dedica-
        tion, 1. 24

16 Clothed in white samite, mystic,
    wonderful.
        Ib. 1. 284, and *The Passing of
        Arthur,* 1. 199

17 Live pure, speak true, right wrong,
    follow the King—
  Else, wherefore born?
        Ib. Gareth and Lynette, 1. 117

18 The children born of thee are sword
    and fire,
  Red ruin, and the breaking up of
    laws.   *Ib. Guinevere,* 1. 422

19 It was my duty to have loved the
    highest:
  It surely was my profit had I known:
  It would have been my pleasure had
    I seen.
  We needs must love the highest when
    we see it,
  Not Lancelot, nor another. *Ib.* 1. 652

20 God make thee good as thou art
  beautiful.   *Ib. The Holy Grail,* 1. 136

21 Elaine the fair, Elaine the loveable,
  Elaine, the lily maid of Astolat.
        Ib. Lancelot and Elaine, 1. 1

22 The shackles of an old love straiten'd
    him,
  His honour rooted in dishonour stood,
  And faith unfaithful kept him falsely
    true.   *Ib.* 1. 870

23 It is the little rift within the lute,
  That by and by will make the music
    mute,
  And ever widening slowly silence all.
        Ib. Merlin and Vivien, 1. 388

24 Man dreams of fame while woman
    wakes to love.   *Ib.* 1. 458

25 So all day long the noise of battle
    roll'd
  Among the mountains by the winter
    sea.
        Ib. The Passing of Arthur, 1. 170

1 And slowly answer'd Arthur from the
   barge:
  'The old order changeth, yielding
    place to new,
  And God fulfils himself in many ways,
  Lest one good custom should corrupt
    the world.' *The Idylls of the King.*
      The Passing of Arthur, l. 407

2 If thou shouldst never see my face
   again,
  Pray for my soul. More things are
   wrought by prayer
  Than this world dreams of. Wherefore, let thy voice
  Rise like a fountain for me night and
   day.
  For what are men better than sheep
   or goats
  That nourish a blind life within the
   brain,
  If, knowing God, they lift not hands
   of prayer
  Both for themselves and those who
   call them friend?
  For so the whole round earth is every
   way
  Bound by gold chains about the feet
   of God.   *Ib.* l. 414

3   I am going a long way
  With these thou seest—if indeed I go
  (For all my mind is clouded with a
   doubt)—
  To the island-valley of Avilion;
  Where falls not hail, or rain, or any
   snow,
  Nor ever wind blows loudly; but it
   lies
  Deep-meadow'd, happy, fair with
   orchard lawns
  And bowery hollows crown'd with
   summer sea,
  Where I will heal me of my grievous
   wound.   *Ib.* l. 424

4 Thou madest man, he knows not why,
  He thinks he was not made to die;
  And thou hast made him: thou art
   just.
    In Memoriam, prologue. (*The
    numbering of the Cantos follows
    that of the latest edition, and in-
    cludes the additional Canto No.
    xxxix, first published in 1869.*)

5 Our little systems have their day;
  They have their day and cease to be:
  They are but broken lights of thee,
  And thou, O Lord, art more than they.
                      Ib.

6 I held it truth, with him who sings
  To one clear harp in divers tones,
  That men may rise on stepping-
   stones
  Of their dead selves to higher things.
            In Memoriam, i

7   Never morning wore
  To evening, but some heart did break.
                   Ib. vi

8   The last red leaf is whirl'd away,
  The rooks are blown about the skies.
         In Memoriam, xv

9   'Tis better to have loved and lost
  Than never to have loved at all.
                Ib. xxvii

10 Oh yet we trust that somehow good
  Will be the final goal of ill. *Ib.* liv

11   But what am I?
  An infant crying in the night:
  An infant crying for the light:
  And with no language but a cry.
                  Ib. liv

12   So careful of the type she seems,
  So careless of the single life. *Ib.* lv

13 Nature, red in tooth and claw. *Ib.* lvi

14 So many worlds, so much to do,
  So little done, such things to be.
                 Ib. lxxiii

15 Dusty purlieus of the law. *Ib.* lxxxix

16   There lives more faith in honest
   doubt,
  Believe me, than in half the creeds.
                  Ib. xcvi

17 He seems so near and yet so far.
                  Ib. xcvii

18 Ring out, wild bells, to the wild sky.
                  Ib. cvi

19 Ring out the old, ring in the new,
  Ring, happy bells, across the snow:
  The year is going, let him go;
  Ring out the false, ring in the true. *Ib.*

20 Ring out old shapes of foul disease;
  Ring out the narrowing lust of gold;
  Ring out the thousand wars of old,
  Ring in the thousand years of peace.
  Ring in the valiant man and free,
  The larger heart, the kindlier hand;
  Ring out the darkness of the land;
  Ring in the Christ that is to be. *Ib.*

21   Wearing all that weight
  Of learning lightly like a flower.
        Ib. Conclusion, st. x

22 Kind hearts are more than coronets,
  And simple faith than Norman
   blood.
      Lady Clara Vere de Vere, vi

23 On either side the river lie
  Long fields of barley and of rye.
        The Lady of Shalott, pt. i

24 'Tirra lirra,' by the river
   Sang Sir Lancelot.   *Ib.*

25 She left the web, she left the loom,
  She made three paces thro' the room
  She saw the water-lily bloom,
  She saw the helmet and the plume,
   She look'd down to Camelot.
  Out flew the web and floated wide;
  The mirror crack'd from side to side;
  'The curse is come upon me,' cried
   The Lady of Shalott.   *Ib.*

1 Heard a carol, mournful, holy,
Chanted loudly, chanted lowly,
Till her blood was frozen slowly,
And her eyes were darken'd wholly,
    Turn'd to tower'd Camelot.
                The Lady of Shalott, pt. i

2 But Lancelot mused a little space;
He said, 'She has a lovely face;
God in his mercy lend her grace,
    The Lady of Shalott.'   *Ib.*

3 Airy, fairy Lilian.   *Lilian*

4 Comrades, leave me here a little,
    while as yet 'tis early morn:
Leave me here, and when you want
    me, sound upon the bugle-horn.
                    Locksley Hall, l. i

5 In the Spring a livelier iris changes on
    the burnish'd dove;
In the Spring a young man's fancy
    lightly turns to thoughts of love.
                            Ib. l. 19

6 He will hold thee, when his passion
    shall have spent its novel force.
Something better than his dog, a
    little dearer than his horse. *Ib.* l. 49

7   This is truth the poet sings,
That a sorrow's crown of sorrow is
    remembering happier things.
                            Ib. l. 75

8 For I dipt into the future, far as
    human eye could see,
Saw the Vision of the world, and all
    the wonder that would be.
                            Ib. l. 119

9 Heard the heavens fill with shouting,
    and there rain'd a ghastly dew
From the nations' airy navies grappling
    in the central blue.   *Ib.* l. 123

10 In the Parliament of man, the Fede-
    ration of the world.   *Ib.* l. 128

11 Yet I doubt not thro' the ages one in-
    creasing purpose runs,
And the thoughts of men are widen'd
    with the process of the suns.
                            Ib. l. 137

12 Knowledge comes, but wisdom lingers.
                            Ib. l. 143

13 I the heir of all the ages, in the fore-
    most files of time.   *Ib.* l. 178

14   Forward, forward let us range,
Let the great world spin for ever down
    the ringing grooves of change.
                            Ib. l. 181

15 Better fifty years of Europe than a
    cycle of Cathay.   *Ib.* l. 184

16   A land
In which it seemed always afternoon.
                    The Lotus-Eaters

17 Music that gentlier on the spirit lies,
Than tir'd eyelids upon tir'd eyes.
                    Ib. Choric Song, i

18 She only said, 'My life is dreary,
    He cometh not,' she said;
She said, 'I am aweary, aweary.
I would that I were dead!'   *Mariana*

19 Faultily faultless, icily regular, splen-
    didly null.   *Maud*, Pt. I. II

20 Come into the garden, Maud,
    For the black bat, night, has flown;
Come into the garden, Maud,
    I am here at the gate alone;
And the woodbine spices are wafted
        abroad,
    And the musk of the rose is blown.
                        Ib. XXII. i.

There has fallen a splendid tear
    From the passion-flower at the gate.
She is coming, my dove, my dear;
    She is coming, my life, my fate;
The red rose cries, 'She is near, she is
        near;'
    And the white rose weeps, 'She is
        late;'
The larkspur listens, 'I hear, I hear;
    And the lily whispers, 'I wait.'

She is coming, my own, my sweet;
    Were it ever so airy a tread,
My heart would hear her and beat,
    Were it earth in an earthy bed;
My dust would hear her and beat,
    Had I lain for a century dead;
Would start and tremble under her
        feet,
    And blossom in purple and red.
                        Ib. x–xi

21 You must wake and call me early,
    call me early, mother dear;
To-morrow 'ill be the happiest time
    of all the glad New-year;
Of all the glad New-year, mother, the
    maddest merriest day;
For I'm to be Queen o' the May,
    mother, I'm to be Queen o' the May.
                    The May Queen

22   In after-dinner talk,
Across the walnuts and the wine.
                The Miller's Daughter

23 But I knaw'd a Quaäker feller as often
    'as towd me this:
'Doänt thou marry for munny, but
    goä wheer munny is!'
            Northern Farmer. New Style

24 Bury the Great Duke
With an empire's lamentation,
Let us bury the Great Duke
To the noise of the mourning of a
    mighty nation.
        *Ode on the Death of the Duke of
        Wellington*, i

25 Foremost captain of his time,
Rich in saving common-sense,
And, as the greatest only are,
In his simplicity sublime.
O good grey head which all men knew!
                            Ib. iv

1 O fall'n at length that tower of
   strength
   Which stood four-square to all the
   winds that blew!
     *Ode on the Death of the Duke of
     Wellington, iv.*

2 Not once or twice in our rough island-
   story,
   The path of duty was the way to
   glory.   *Ib.* viii

3 O mother Ida, many-fountain'd Ida.
          Œnone, l. 22

4 Dear mother Ida, harken ere I die.
   It was the deep midnoon: one silvery
   cloud
   Had lost his way between the piney
   sides
   Of this long glen. Then to the bower
   they came,
   Naked they came to that smooth-
   swarded bower,
   And at their feet the crocus brake like
   fire,
   Violet, amaracus, and asphodel,
   Lotos and lilies.   *Ib. l. 89*

5 I built my soul a lordly pleasure-house,
   Wherein at ease for aye to dwell.
         The Palace of Art, i

6 With prudes for proctors, dowagers
   for deans,
   And sweet girl-graduates in their
   golden hair.
     The Princess, prologue, l. 141

7 As thro' the land at eve we went,
   And pluck'd the ripen'd ears,
   We fell out, my wife and I,
   O we fell out I know not why,
   And kiss'd again with tears.
   And blessings on the falling out
    That all the more endears,
   When we fall out with those we love
   And kiss again with tears!
       Ib. ii. Introd. Song

8 O hard, when love and duty clash!
         Ib. ii. l. 273

9 Sweet and low, sweet and low,
    Wind of the western sea,
   Low, low, breathe and blow,
    Wind of the western sea!
   Over the rolling waters go,
   Come from the dying moon, and
   blow,
    Blow him again to me;
   While my little one, while my pretty
    one, sleeps. *Ib. iii. Introd. Song*

10 The splendour falls on castle walls
    And snowy summits old in story:
   The long light shakes across the lakes,
    And the wild cataract leaps in
    glory.
   Blow, bugle, blow, set the wild echoes
    flying,
   Blow, bugle; answer, echoes, dying,
    dying, dying. *Ib. iv. Introd. Song*

11 O hark, O hear! how thin and clear,
    And thinner, clearer, farther going!
   O sweet and far from cliff and scar
    The horns of Elfland faintly blow-
    ing!
     The Princess, iv. Introd. Song

12 O love, they die in yon rich sky,
    They faint on hill or field or river:
   Our echoes roll from soul to soul,
    And grow for ever and for ever.
           Ib.

13 Tears, idle tears, I know not what
    they mean,
   Tears from the depth of some divine
    despair
   Rise in the heart, and gather to the
    eyes,
   In looking on the happy Autumn-
    fields,
   And thinking of the days that are
    no more.   *Ib. l. 21*

14 O tell her, Swallow, thou that knowest
    each,
   That bright and fierce and fickle is the
    South,
   And dark and true and tender is the
    North.   *Ib. l. 78*

15 Home they brought her warrior dead.
   She nor swoon'd, nor utter'd cry:
   All her maidens, watching, said,
   'She must weep or she will die.'
       Ib. vi. Introd. Song

16 Now sleeps the crimson petal, now
    the white;
   Nor waves the cypress in the palace
    walk;
   Nor winks the gold fin in the porphyry
    font:
   The fire-fly wakens: waken thou with
    me.

   Now droops the milk-white peacock
    like a ghost,
   And like a ghost she glimmers on to
    me.   *Ib. l. 61*

17 Now folds the lily all her sweetness up,
   And slips into the bosom of the lake:
   So fold thyself, my dearest, thou, and
    slip
   Into my bosom and be lost in me.
         Ib. l. 171

18 Come down, O maid, from yonder
    mountain height:
   What pleasure lives in height?
         Ib. l. 177

19   Sweet is every sound,
   Sweeter thy voice, but every sound
    is sweet;
   Myriads of rivulets hurrying thro' the
    lawn,
   The moan of doves in immemorial
    elms,
   And murmuring of innumerable bees.
         Ib. l. 203

1 Her court was pure; her life serene;
    God gave her peace; her land
       reposed;
    A thousand claims to reverence
       closed
    In her as Mother, Wife, and Queen;
      To the Queen (1851), 'Revered,
      beloved'

2   At Flores in the Azores Sir Richard
      Grenville lay,
   And a pinnace, like a fluttered bird,
      came flying from far away:
   'Spanish ships of war at sea! we have
      sighted fifty-three!'   *The Revenge,* i

3 And they blest him in their pain, that
      they were not left to Spain,
   To the thumbscrew and the stake, for
      the glory of the Lord.   *Ib.* iii

4 'Shall we fight or shall we fly?
   Good Sir Richard, tell us now,
   For to fight is but to die!
   There'll be little of us left by the time
      this sun be set.'
   And Sir Richard said again: 'We be all
      good English men.
   Let us bang these dogs of Seville, the
      children of the devil,
   For I never turn'd my back upon Don
      or devil yet.'   *Ib.* iv

5 And they praised him to his face with
      their courtly foreign grace;
   But he rose upon their decks, and he
      cried:
   'I have fought for Queen and Faith
      like a valiant man and true;
   I have only done my duty as a man is
      bound to do:
   With a joyful spirit I Sir Richard
      Grenville die!'
   And he fell upon their decks, and he
      died.   *Ib.* xiii

6 What does little birdie say
   In her nest at peep of day?
      Sea Dreams, 1. 281

7 Birdie, rest a little longer,
   Till the little wings are stronger.
   So she rests a little longer,
   Then she flies away.   *Ib.* 1. 285

8 My strength is as the strength of ten,
   Because my heart is pure.
      Sir Galahad

9 Alone and warming his five wits,
   The white owl in the belfry sits.
      Song. The Owl

10 The woods decay, the woods decay and
      fall,
   The vapours weep their burthen to the
      ground,
   Man comes and tills the field and lies
      beneath,
   And after many a summer dies the
      swan.   *Tithonus,* 1. 1

11 Here at the quiet limit of the world.
      Ib. 1. 7

12 It little profits that an idle king,
   By this still hearth, among these
      barren crags,
   Match'd with an aged wife, I mete and
      dole
   Unequal laws unto a savage race.
      Ulysses, 1. 1

13   I will drink
   Life to the lees: all times I have en-
      joy'd
   Greatly, have suffer'd greatly, both
      with those
   That loved me, and alone; on shore,
      and when
   Thro' scudding drifts the rainy Hyades
   Vext the dim sea: I am become a
      name;
   For always roaming with a hungry
      heart
   Much have I seen and known; cities
      of men
   And manners, climates, councils,
      governments,
   Myself not least, but honour'd of them
      all;
   And drunk delight of battle with my
      peers,
   Far on the ringing plains of windy
      Troy.
   I am a part of all that I have met;
   Yet all experience is an arch where-
      thro'
   Gleams that untravell'd world, whose
      margin fades
   For ever and for ever when I move.
   How dull it is to pause, to make an end,
   To rust unburnish'd, not to shine in
      use!
   As tho' to breathe were life. Life
      piled on life
   Were all too little, and of one to me
   Little remains: but every hour is
      saved
   From that eternal silence, something
      more,
   A bringer of new things.   *Ib.* 1. 6

14   This gray spirit yearning in desire
   To follow knowledge like a sinking
      star,
   Beyond the utmost bound of human
      thought.   *Ib.* 1. 30

15   My mariners,
   Souls that have toil'd, and wrought,
      and thought with me—
   That ever with a frolic welcome took
   The thunder and the sunshine, and
      opposed
   Free hearts, free foreheads—you and
      I are old;
   Old age hath yet his honour and his
      toil;
   Death closes all: but something ere
      the end,
   Some work of noble note, may yet
      be done,
   Not unbecoming men that strove with
      gods.

The lights begin to twinkle from the
rocks:
The long day wanes: the slow moon
climbs: the deep
Moans round with many voices. Come,
my friends,
'Tis not too late to seek a newer world.
Push off, and sitting well in order
smite
The sounding furrows; for my pur-
pose holds
To sail beyond the sunset, and the
baths
Of all the western stars, until I die.
It may be that the gulfs will wash us
down:
It may be we shall touch the Happy
Isles,
And see the great Achilles, whom we
knew.
Tho' much is taken, much abides;
and tho'
We are not now that strength which
in old days
Moved earth and heaven; that which
we are, we are;
One equal temper of heroic hearts,
Made weak by time and fate, but
strong in will
To strive, to seek, to find, and not to
yield.   *Ulysses*, l. 45

1   I salute thee, Mantovano,
I that loved thee since my day began,
Wielder of the stateliest measure ever
moulded by the lips of man.
                              To Virgil, x

2 Every moment dies a man,
Every moment one is born.
                        The Vision of Sin, ix

3 Sea-King's daughter from over the
sea, Alexandra!
Saxon and Norman and Dane are we,
But all of us Danes in our welcome of
thee, Alexandra!
                        A Welcome to Alexandra

4 O plump head-waiter at the Cock
To which I most resort.
                *Will Waterproof's Lyrical Mono-
                logue*, i

5 A louse in the locks of literature.
                *Said of Churton Collins to Ed-
                mund Gosse.* Evan Charteris's
                *Life and Letters of Sir Edmund
                Gosse*, ch. xiv

TERENCE c. 195–159 B.C.

6 Homo sum; humani nil a me alienum
puto.
    I am a man, I count nothing human
    alien from me.
                    Heauton Timorumenos, 77

7 Fortis fortuna adiuvat.
    Fortune aids the brave.
                            Phormio, 203

8 Quot homines tot sententiae: suo'
quoique mos.
    So many men, so many opinions; his
    own a law to each. *Phormio*, 454

TERTULLIAN A.D. c. 160–c. 225

9 O testimonium animae naturaliter
Christianae.
    O witness of the soul naturally
    Christian.   *Apol.* xvii

10 Plures efficimus quoties metimur a
vobis, semen est sanguis Christiano-
rum.
    The more ye mow us down, the
    more we grow, the blood of Chris-
    tians is seed. (*Traditionally ren-
    dered as* 'The blood of the mar-
    tyrs is the seed of the Church'.)
                            Ib. 1 *ad fin.*

11 Certum est quia impossibile est.
    It is certain because it is impossible.
                        De Carne Christi, 5

EDWARD TESCHEMACHER
                        nineteenth century

12 Where my caravan has rested,
Flowers I leave you on the grass.
                Where My Caravan Has Rested

**WILLIAM MAKEPEACE
THACKERAY** 1811–1863

13 Kind, cheerful, merry Dr. Brighton.
                        The Newcomes, bk. i

14 Rake's progress.
                Pendennis, title of ch. 19. *Used
                earlier by Hogarth*

15 Business first; pleasure afterwards.
[*Queen of Paflagonia.*]
                The Rose and the Ring, ch. 1

16 Them's my sentiments! [*Fred Bullock.*]
                        Vanity Fair, ch. 21

17 Darkness came down on the field and
city: and Amelia was praying for
George, who was lying on his face,
dead, with a bullet through his heart.
                            Ib. ch. 32

18 How to live well on nothing a year.
                        Ib. Title of ch. 36

19 There were three sailors of Bristol
City
Who took a boat and went to sea.
But first with beef and captain's
biscuits
And pickled pork they loaded she.
There was gorging Jack and guzzling
Jimmy,
And the youngest he was little Billee.
Now when they got as far as the
Equator
They'd nothing left but one split pea.
                            Little Billee

1 Says gorging Jim to guzzling Jacky,
  We have no wittles, so we must eat
    we.   *Little Billee*

2 There's little Bill as is young and
    tender,
  We're old and tough—so let's eat *he.*
                        Ib.

3 He scarce had said his Catechism,
  When up he jumps: 'There's land
    I see!
  There's Jerusalem and Madagascar,
  And North and South Ameri*key.*
  There's the British Fleet a-riding at
    anchor,
  With Admiral Napier, K.C.B.'   *Ib.*

4 Werther had a love for Charlotte
    Such as words could never utter;
  Would you know how first he met her?
    She was cutting bread and butter.

  Charlotte was a married lady,
    And a moral man was Werther,
  And for all the wealth of Indies,
    Would do nothing for to hurt her.

  So he sighed and pined and ogled,
    And his passion boiled and bubbled,
  Till he blew his silly brains out
    And no more was by it troubled.

  Charlotte, having seen his body
    Borne before her on a shutter,
  Like a well-conducted person,
    Went on cutting bread and butter.
             Sorrows of Werther

WILLIAM MAKEPEACE THAYER

5 Log-cabin to White House.
    Title of a biography (1910) of
    James Garfield (1831–1881)

BRANDON THOMAS 1848–1914

6 Brazil, where the nuts come from.
             Charley's Aunt

FRANCIS THOMPSON 1859–1907

7 I fled Him, down the nights and down
    the days;
  I fled Him, down the arches of the
    years;
  I fled Him, down the labyrinthine
    ways
    Of my own mind; and in the mist of
    tears
  I hid from Him, and under running
    laughter.   *The Hound of Heaven*

8 But with unhurrying chase,
  And unperturbèd pace,
  Deliberate speed, majestic instancy,
  They beat—and a Voice beat
  More instant than the Feet—
  'All things betray thee, who betrayest
    Me.'   *Ib.*

9 O world invisible, we view thee,
  O world intangible, we touch thee,
  O world unknowable, we know thee,
  Inapprehensible, we clutch thee!
           The Kingdom of God

10 The angels keep their ancient
    places;—
  Turn but a stone, and start a wing!
  'Tis ye, 'tis your estrangèd faces,
  That miss the many-splendoured
    thing.

  But (when so sad thou canst not
    sadder)
  Cry;—and upon thy so sore loss
  Shall shine the traffic of Jacob's ladder
  Pitched betwixt Heaven and Charing
    Cross.

  Yea, in the night, my Soul, my
    daughter,
  Cry,—clinging Heaven by the hems;
  And lo, Christ walking on the water
  Not of Gennesareth, but Thames! *Ib.*

11 It is little I repair to the matches of
    the Southron folk,
  Though my own red roses there may
    blow;
  It is little I repair to the matches of
    the Southron folk,
    Though the red roses crest the caps
    I know.
  For the field is full of shades as I near
    the shadowy coast,
  And a ghostly batsman plays to the
    bowling of a ghost,
  And I look through my tears on a
    soundless-clapping host
  As the run-stealers flicker to and fro,
    To and fro:—
  O my Hornby and my Barlow long
    ago!   *At Lord's*

WILLIAM HEPWORTH THOMPSON 1810–1886

12 We are none of us infallible—not
  even the youngest of us.
    Remark referring to G. W. Bal-
    four, then Junior Fellow of
    Trinity. G. W. E. Russell's
    Collections and Recollections, ch.
    18

JAMES THOMSON 1700–1748

13 When Britain first, at heaven's
    command,
  Arose from out the azure main,
  This was the charter of the land,
  And guardian angels sung this strain:
    'Rule, Britannia, rule the waves;
    Britons never will be slaves.'
      Alfred: a Masque (1740), Act II,
      Scene the last

14 Delightful task! to rear the tender
    thought,
  To teach the young idea how to shoot.
      The Seasons, Spring, l. 1152

1 Or sighed and looked unutterable
  things.
                The Seasons, Summer, l. 1188

2 Oh! Sophonisba! Sophonisba! Oh!
                        Sophonisba, III. iii

JAMES THOMSON 1834–1882

3 The City of Dreadful Night.
                        Title of Poem

4 As we rush, as we rush in the train,
  The trees and the houses go wheeling
      back,
  But the starry heavens above that
      plain
  Come flying on our track.
                Sunday at Hampstead, x

5 Give a man a horse he can ride,
  Give a man a boat he can sail.
                Sunday up the River, xv

HENRY DAVID THOREAU
                        1817–1862

6 As for Doing-good, that is one of the
  professions which are full. Moreover,
  I have tried it fairly, and, strange as
  it may seem, am satisfied that it does
  not agree with my constitution.
                Walden. Economy

7 The three-o'-clock in the morning
  courage, which Bonaparte thought
  was the rarest.   *Ib. Sounds*

8 It takes two to speak the truth,—
  one to speak, and another to hear.
                *A Week on the Concord and
                Merrimack Rivers, Wednesday*

9 Some circumstantial evidence is very
  strong, as when you find a trout in
  the milk.
                *Unpublished MSS. in Miscel-
                lanies, Biographical Sketch (1918),*
                vol. x, p. 30

ROSE HARTWICK THORPE
                        1850–1939

10 Curfew must not ring to-night.
                        Title of Poem

THUCYDIDES c. 460–c. 400 B.C.

11 κτῆμα ἐς ἀεί.
   A possession for ever.   *History,* i, § 4

12 ἀνδρῶν γὰρ ἐπιφανῶν πᾶσα γῆ τάφος.
   The whole earth is the sepulchre
     of famous men.   *Ib.* ii. 43, § 3

JAMES THURBER 1894–1961

13 The War Between Men and Women.
                Title of Series of Cartoons

14 Is Sex Necessary?   *Title of Book*

EDWARD, FIRST BARON THURLOW 1731–1806

15 Did you ever expect a corporation to
   have a conscience, when it has no soul
   to be damned, and no body to be
   kicked?
                Attr. See Sydney Smith, Recipe
                for Salad, *p. 376, and John
                Poynder,* Literary Extracts from
                English and Other Works *(1884)*

TIBULLUS 54?–18? B.C.

16 Iuppiter pluvius.
   Jupiter the rain-bringer.
                        Ib. I. vii. 26

THOMAS TICKELL 1686–1740

17 There taught us how to live; and
   (oh! too high
   The price for knowledge) taught us
   how to die.
                *Epitaph. On the Death of Mr.
                Addison,* l. 81. Addison's *Works*
                (1721), preface, p. xx

HARRY TILZER

18 Come, Come, Come and have a drink
   with me
   Down at the old 'Bull and Bush'.
                Song sung by Florrie Ford

19 Come, Come, Come and make eyes at
   me.   *Ib.*

TITUS VESPASIANUS
                        A.D. 39–81

20 Amici, diem perdidi.
   Friends, I have lost a day.
                Suetonius, Titus, ch. 8, i

JACOPONE DA TODI d. 1306

21 Stabat mater dolorosa
   Iuxta crucem lacrimosa.
   At the cross her station keeping
   Stood the mournful mother weeping.
                *Pacheu, Jacopone de Todi. Trans.
                in English Hymnal. Also ascribed
                to Innocent III*

LEO TOLSTOY 1828–1910

22 All happy families resemble each
   other, each unhappy family is unhappy in its own way.
                Anna Karenina, pt. i, ch. 1.
                Trans. by Maude

AUGUSTUS MONTAGUE TOPLADY 1740–1778

23 Rock of ages, cleft for me,
   Let me hide myself in thee.
                The Gospel Magazine, Oct. 1775.
                Rock of Ages

I

1 Nothing in my hand I bring,
  Simply to thy Cross I cling;
  Naked, come to thee for dress;
  Helpless, look to thee for grace;
  Foul, I to the Fountain fly;
  Wash me, Saviour, or I die.
        The Gospel Magazine, Oct. 1775.
        Rock of Ages

THOMAS TRAHERNE 1637?–1674

2 The corn was orient and immortal
  wheat, which never should be reaped,
  nor was ever sown. I thought it had
  stood from everlasting to everlasting.
        Centuries of Meditations. Cent.
        iii, § 3

JOSEPH TRAPP 1679–1747

3 The King, observing with judicious
  eyes
  The state of both his universities,
  To Oxford sent a troop of horse, and
  why?
  That learned body wanted loyalty;
  To Cambridge books, as very well
  discerning
  How much that loyal body wanted
  learning.
        *On George I's Donation of the
        Bishop of Ely's Library to Cam-
        bridge University.* Nichols's *Liter-
        ary Anecdotes*, vol. iii, p. 330.
        For the reply see 43:3

ANTHONY TROLLOPE 1815–1882

4 It's dogged as does it. It ain't thinking about it.
        Last Chronicle of Barset, ch. 61

ST. VINCENT TROUBRIDGE
1895–1963

5 There is an iron curtain across Europe.
        Sunday Empire News, 21 Oct.
        1945 (*see also* 63:5 *and* 94:11)

WALTER JAMES REDFERN
TURNER 1889–1946

6 Chimborazo, Cotopaxi,
  They had stolen my soul away!
        Romance, vii

THOMAS TUSSER 1524?–1580

7 At Christmas play and make good
  cheer,
  For Christmas comes but once a
  year.
        *Five Hundred Points of Good
        Husbandry*, ch. 12. *The Farmer's
        daily Diet*

8 It is an ill wind turns none to good.
        Ib. ch. 13. *Description of the
        Properties of Winds*

9 Who goeth a borrowing
  Goeth a sorrowing.
  Few lend (but fools)
  Their working tools.
        *Five Hundred points of Good
        Husbandry*, ch. 15. *September's
        Abstract*

10 In doing of either, let wit bear a stroke,
   For buying or selling of pig in a poke.
        Ib. September's Husbandry

11 Naught venture, naught have.
        Ib. ch. 16. *October's Abstract*

12 To dog in the manger some liken I
   could.
        Ib. ch. 28. *Against Fantastical
        Scrupleness*

13 Feb, fill the dyke
   With what thou dost like.
        Ib. ch. 34. *February's Husbandry*

14 Sweet April showers
   Do spring May flowers.
        Ib. ch. 38. *April's Husbandry*

15 Look ere thou leap, see ere thou go.
        Ib. ch. 56. *Dialogue of Wiving and
        Thriving*

16 The stone that is rolling can gather no
   moss.   *Ib. Housewifely Admonitions*

MARK TWAIN [SAMUEL LANG-
HORNE CLEMENS] 1835–1910

17 There was things which he stretched,
   but mainly he told the truth.
        *The Adventures of Huckleberry
        Finn*, ch. 1

18 The statements was interesting, but
   tough.   *Ib.* ch. 17

19 There's plenty of boys that will come
   hankering and gruvvelling around
   when you've got an apple, and beg
   the core off you; but when *they've* got
   one, and you beg for the core and
   remind them how you give them a
   core one time, they make a mouth at
   you and say thank you 'most to death,
   but there ain't-a-going to *be* no core.
        Tom Sawyer Abroad, ch. 1

20 This poor little one-horse town.
        The Undertaker's Chat

21 The report of my death was an
   exaggeration.
        *Cable from Europe to the Asso-
        ciated Press*

HENRY TWELLS 1823–1900

22 At even ere the sun was set,
   The sick, O Lord, around thee lay.
        Hymns Ancient and Modern
        (1868), Appendix. *At Even Ere
        the Sun Was Set*

EDWARD SMITH UFFORD
                              1851–1929

1 Throw out the life-line across the dark
  wave,
  There is a brother whom someone
  should save,
  Throw out the life-line, throw out the
  life-line,
  Someone is sinking to-day.
              Revivalist Hymn (1884)

MRS. C. UNWIN

2 The Hungry Forties.
                  Title of Book (1905)

RALPH R. UPTON

3 Stop; look; listen.
      *Slogan devised in 1912 to replace
      the old U.S. railway-crossing
      signs of 'Look out for the loco-
      motive'*

W. UPTON

4 This lass so neat, with smile so sweet,
  Has won my right good will,
  I'd crowns resign to call thee mine,
  Sweet lass of Richmond Hill.
      *The Lass of Richmond Hill.
      Oxford Song Book (see 137:15)*

SIR JOHN VANBRUGH 1664–1726

5 Much of a muchness.
              The Provok'd Husband, I. i

6 The want of a thing is perplexing
  enough, but the possession of it is
  intolerable.   *The Confederacy*, I. ii

HENRY VAUGHAN 1622–1695

7 My soul, there is a country
      Far beyond the stars,
  Where stands a wingèd sentry
      All skilful in the wars:
  There, above noise and danger,
      Sweet Peace is crown'd with smiles,
  And One born in a manger
      Commands the beauteous files.
              Silex Scintillans. Peace

8 If thou canst get but thither,
      There grows the flower of Peace,
  The Rose that cannot wither,
      Thy fortress, and thy ease.
  Leave then thy foolish ranges;
      For none can thee secure,
  But One, who never changes,
      Thy God, thy life, thy cure.   *Ib.*

9 They are all gone into the world of
  light,
      And I alone sit lingering here;
  Their very memory is fair and bright,
      And my sad thoughts doth clear.
              Ib. They Are All Gone

10 I see them walking in an air of glory,
      Whose light doth trample on my
      days:
  My days, which are at best but dull
      and hoary,
      Mere glimmering and decays.
              Silex Scintillans. They Are All Gone

11 I saw Eternity the other night,
  Like a great ring of pure and endless
      light,
      All calm, as it was bright;
  And round beneath it, Time in hours,
      days, years,
      Driv'n by the spheres
  Like a vast shadow mov'd; in which
      the world
  And all her train were hurl'd.
              Ib. The World

VEGETIUS *fourth century* A.D.

12 Qui desiderat pacem, praeparet bel-
   lum.
      Let him who desires peace, prepare
      for war.   *De Re Mil.* 3, prologue

PIERRE VERGNIAUD 1753–1793

13 Il a été permis de craindre que la
   Révolution, comme Saturne, dévorât
   successivement tous ses enfants.
      There was reason to fear that the
      Revolution, like Saturn, might
      devour in turn each one of her
      children.
          Lamartine, *Histoire des Giron-
          dins*, bk. xxxviii, ch. 20

PAUL VERLAINE 1844–1896

14 Et tout le reste est littérature.
      All the rest is mere fine writing.
              Jadis et Naguère

QUEEN VICTORIA 1819–1901

15 I will be good.
      *Letter from the Baroness Lehzen
      to Her Majesty, 2 Dec. 1867.*
      Martin's *The Prince Consort*
      (1875), vol. i, p. 13

16 We are not amused.
      *Notebooks of a Spinster Lady,
      2 Jan. 1900*

17 We are not interested in the possi-
   bilities of defeat.
      *To A. J. Balfour, in 'Black Week',
      Dec. 1899*

18 He [Mr. Gladstone] speaks to Me as if
   I was a public meeting.
          G. W. E. Russell's *Collections and
          Recollections*, ch. 14

ALFRED DE VIGNY 1797–1863

1 Seul le silence est grand; tout le reste est faiblesse . . .
Fais énergiquement ta longue et lourde tâche . . .
Puis, après, comme moi, souffre et meurs sans parler.

Silence alone is great; all else is feebleness . . .
Perform with all your heart your long and heavy task. . . .
Then as do I, say naught, but suffer and die. *La Mort du Loup*

FRANÇOIS VILLON b. 1431

2 Mais où sont les neiges d'antan?

But where are the snows of yester-year?
Le Grand Testament, Ballade des Dames du Temps Jadis. Trans. by D. G. Rossetti

VIRGIL 70–19 B.C.

3 Arma virumque cano, Troiae qui primus ab oris
Italiam fato profugus Lavinaque venit
Litora—multum ille et terris iactatus et alto
Vi superum, saevae memorem Iunonis ob iram.

Arms I sing, and the man, who first from the shores of Troy came, Fate-exiled, to Italy and her Lavinian strand—much buffeted he on flood and field by constraint of Heaven and fell Juno's unslumbering ire.
Aeneid, i. 1. Trans. by Jackson

4 Fidus quae tela gerebat Achates.
The weapons which loyal Achates bore.
Ib. 188

5 Forsan et haec olim meminisse iuvabit.
The day may dawn when this plight shall be sweet to remember.
Ib. 203

6 Vera incessu patuit dea.
The goddess indubitable was revealed in her step. *Ib.* 405

7 Sunt hic etiam sua praemia laudi;
Sunt lacrimae rerum et mentem mortalia tangunt.
Even here, virtue hath her rewards, and mortality her tears: even here, the woes of man touch the heart of man! *Ib.* 461

8 Mens sibi conscia recti.
A mind conscious of the right.
Ib. 604

9 Timeo Danaos et dona ferentis.
I fear the Danaans, though their hands proffer gifts. *Ib.* ii. 49

10 Horresco referens.
I shudder to recall it.
Aeneid, ii. 20

11 Dis aliter visum.
Heaven's thought was otherwise.
Ib. 428

12 Non tali auxilio nec defensoribus istis Tempus eget.
The hour calls not for such succour nor such defenders. *Ib.* 521

13 Monstrum horrendum, informe, ingens, cui lumen ademptum.
A monster fearful and hideous, vast and eyeless. *Ib.* iii. 658

14 Varium et mutabile semper Femina.
A fickle thing and changeful is woman always! *Ib.* iv. 569

15 Facilis descensus Averni:
Light is the descent to Avernus!
Ib. vi. 126

16 Procul, o procul este, profani.
Hence, O hence, . . . ye that are uninitiated. *Ib.* 258

17 Tendebantque manus ripae ulterioris amore.
Their hands outstretched in yearning for the farther shore. *Ib.* 314

18 Tu regere imperio populos, Romane, memento
(Hae tibi erunt artes), pacisque imponere morem,
Parcere subiectis et debellare superbos.
Roman, be this thy care—these thine arts—to bear dominion over the nations and to impose the law of peace, to spare the humbled and to war down the proud!
Ib. 851

19 Geniumque loci . . . precatur.
Implored the Genius of the place.
Ib. vii. 136

20 Flectere si nequeo superos, Acheronta movebo.
And if Heaven be inflexible, Hell shall be unleashed! *Ib.* 312

21 Macte nova virtute, puer, sic itur ad astra.
Good speed to thy youthful valour, child! So shalt thou scale the stars! *Ib.* ix. 641

22 Audentis Fortuna iuvat.
Fortune is ally to the brave.
Ib. x. 284

23 Experto credite.
Believe the man with experience.
Ib. xi. 283

24 Latet anguis in herba.
A snake lurks in the grass!
Eclogues, iii. 93

1 Ultima Cumaei venit iam carminis
     aetas;
  Magnus ab integro saeclorum nascitur
     ordo.
  Iam redit et virgo, redeunt Saturnia
     regna,
  Iam nova progenies caelo demittitur
     alto.
     The last age, heralded in Cumean
        song, is come, and the great
        march of the centuries, begins
        anew. Now the Virgin returns:
        now Saturn is king again, and a
        new and better race descends
        from on high.   *Eclogues,* iv. 5

2 Non omnia possumus omnes.
     All power is not to all.   *Ib.* viii. 63

3 Omnia vincit Amor: et nos cedamus
     Amori.
     Love is lord of all: yield we, too, to
        Love!   *Ib.* x. 69

4 Ultima Thule.
     Farthest Thule.
        Georgics, i. 30. *Trans. by Jackson*
                          Labor omnia vicit

5 Improbus et duris urgens in rebus
     egestas.
     Never-flinching labour proved lord
        of all, and the stress of need in
        a life of struggles.   *Ib.* 145

6   Imponere Pelio Ossam
  Scilicet, atque Ossae frondosum invol-
     vere Olympum.
     In sooth ... to pile Ossa on Pelion
        and roll leaf-crowned Olympus on
        Ossa.   *Ib.* 281

7 Felix qui potuit rerum cognoscere
     causas.
     Happy he, who has availed to read
        the causes of things.   *Ib.* ii. 490

8 Sed fugit interea, fugit inreparabile
     tempus.
     Meanwhile, Time is flying—flying,
        never to return.   *Ib.* iii. 284

9 At genus immortale manet, multos-
     que per annos
  Stat fortuna domus, et avi numerantur
     avorum.
     Yet the race abides immortal, the
        star of their house sets not
        through many years, and grand-
        sire's grandsire is numbered in
        the roll.   *Ib.* iv. 208

10 Sic vos non vobis mellificatis apes.
   Sic vos non vobis nidificatis aves.
   Sic vos non vobis vellera fertis oves.
      So you bees make your honey, not
         for yourselves.
      So you birds make nests, not for
         yourselves.
      So you sheep bear fleeces, not for
         yourselves.
         *Attr. On Bathyllus' claiming the
         authorship of certain lines by Virgil*

VOLTAIRE 1694–1778

11 Dans ce pays-ci il est bon de tuer de
   temps en temps un amiral pour
   encourager les autres.
      In this country [England] it is
         thought well to kill an admiral
         from time to time to encourage
         the others.   *Candide,* ch. 23

12 Tout est pour le mieux dans le meilleur
   des mondes possibles.
      All is for the best in the best of
         possible worlds.   *Ib.* 30

13 Cela est bien dit, répondit Candide,
   mais il faut cultiver notre jardin.
      'That is well said,' replied Candide,
         'but we must cultivate our gar-
         den.' (We must attend to our own
         affairs.)   *Ib.*

14 Le mieux est l'ennemi du bien.
      The best is the enemy of the good.
         Dict. Philosophqiue, art. *Art Dra-
         matique*

15 Si Dieu n'existait pas, il faudrait
   l'inventer.
      If God did not exist, it would be
         necessary to invent him.
         *Epîtres, xcvi. A l'Auteur du
         Livre des Trois Imposteurs*

16 Ce corps qui s'appelait et qui s'appelle
   encore le saint empire romain n'était
   en aucune manière ni saint, ni romain,
   ni empire.
      This agglomeration which was called
         and which still calls itself the Holy
         Roman Empire was neither holy,
         nor Roman, nor an empire.
         *Essai sur les Mœurs et l'Esprit
         des Nations,* lxx

17 Quoi que vous fassiez, écrasez l'in-
   fâme, et aimez qui vous aime.
      Whatever you do, trample down
         abuses, and love those who love
         you.
         Lettres. A M. d'Alembert, 28 Nov.
         1762

18 On dit que Dieu est toujours pour les
   gros bataillons.
      It is said that God is always for the
         big battalions.
         Ib. A M. Le Riche, 6 Feb. 1770

19 Le secret d'ennuyer est ... de tout dire.
      The way to be a bore [for an author]
         is to say everything.
         *Sept Discours en vers sur
         l'Homme,* vi. *Sur la Nature de
         l'Homme.* v. 174–5

20 I disapprove of what you say, but
   I will defend to the death your right
   to say it.
      *Attr. in S. G. Tallentyre, The
      Friends of Voltaire* (1907), p. 199

HENRY WALLACE 1888–

1 The century on which we are entering
—the century which will come out of
this war—can be and must be the
century of the common man.
*Address: The Price of Free World
Victory, 8 May 1942*

LEW WALLACE 1827–1905

2 Beauty is altogether in the eye of the
beholder.
The Prince of India (1893), III.
vi. 78 (*see 111:23*)

WILLIAM ROSS WALLACE
d. 1881

3 The hand that rocks the cradle
Is the hand that rules the world.
John o' London's Treasure Trove

EDMUND WALLER 1606–1687

4   Go, lovely Rose!
Tell her, that wastes her time and me,
That now she knows,
When I resemble her to thee,
How sweet and fair she seems to be.
Song: Go, Lovely Rose!

HORACE WALPOLE, FOURTH EARL OF ORFORD 1717–1797

5 [Strawberry Hill] is a little plaything-
house that I got out of Mrs. Chene-
vix's shop, and is the prettiest bauble
you ever saw. It is set in enamelled
meadows, with filigree hedges.
Letters. To Conway, 8 June 1747

6 One of the greatest geniuses that ever
existed, Shakespeare, undoubtedly
wanted taste.
Ib. To Wren, 9 Aug. 1764

7 This world is a comedy to those that
think, a tragedy to those that feel.
*Ib. To the Countess of Upper
Ossory, 16 Aug. 1776*

8 All his [Sir Joshua Reynolds's] own
geese are swans, as the swans of others
are geese.
*Ib. To the Countess of Upper
Ossory, 1 Dec. 1786*

SIR ROBERT WALPOLE, FIRST EARL OF ORFORD 1676–1745

9 They now *ring* the bells, but they will
soon *wring* their hands.
*Remark on the declaration of war
with Spain, 1739.* W. Coxe,
Memoirs of Sir Robert Walpole
(1798), vol. i, p. 618

10 All those men have their price.
Ib. p. 757

11 Madam, there are fifty thousand men
slain this year in Europe, and not one
Englishman.
Remark to Queen Caroline, 1734.
Hervey, *Memoirs* (1848), vol. i,
p. 398

12 The balance of power.
*Speech in the House of Commons,
13 Feb. 1741*

WILLIAM WALSH 1663–1708

13 I can endure my own despair,
But not another's hope.
Song. 'Of All the Torments'

IZAAK WALTON 1593–1683

14 I remember that a wise friend of mine
did usually say, 'that which is everybody's business is nobody's business.'
Compleat Angler, pt. i, ch. 2

15 Look to your health; and if you have
it, praise God, and value it next to
a good conscience; for health is the
second blessing that we mortals are
capable of; a blessing that money
cannot buy.   *Ib.* ch. 21

BISHOP WILLIAM WARBURTON 1698–1779

16 Orthodoxy is my doxy; heterodoxy is
another man's doxy.
Remark to Lord Sandwich. Priest-
ley, *Memoirs* (1807), vol. i,
p. 372

ARTEMUS WARD [CHARLES FARRAR BROWNE] 1834–1867

17 Shall we sell our birthrite for a mess of
potash?
*Artemus Ward His Book. The
Crisis*

18 Do me eyes deceive me earsight? Is
it some dreams? *Ib. Moses, the Sassy*

19 It is a pity that Chawcer, who had
geneyus, was so unedicated. He's the
wuss speller I know of.
Artemus Ward in London, ch. 4.
At the Tomb of Shakespeare

20 He [Brigham Young] is dreadfully
married. He's the most married man
I ever saw in my life.
Artemus Ward's Lecture

21 Why is this thus? What is the reason
of this thusness?   *Ib.*

MRS. HUMPHRY WARD 1851–1920

22 'Propinquity does it'—as Mrs. Thorn-
burgh is always reminding us.
Robert Elsmere, bk. i, ch. 2

SUSAN WARNER 1819–1885

1 Jesus loves me—this I know,
   For the Bible tells me so.
                              The Love of Jesus

GEORGE WASHINGTON
                              1732–1799

2 Father, I cannot tell a lie, I did it
   with my little hatchet.
              Attr. remark. Mark Twain's
              Mark Twain as George Washing-
              ton. Another version is: I can't
              tell a lie, Pa; you know I can't
              tell a lie. I did cut it with my
              hatchet.
              Weems, *Washington* (1800) (5th
              ed., 1806)

3 We must consult Brother Jonathan.
              Said to have been a frequent re-
              mark of his during the American
              Revolution, referring to Jonathan
              Trumbull, 1710–85, Governor of
              Connecticut. Norwich Evening
              Courier, 12 Nov. 1846, No. 797,
              p. 2. (Publications of the Colonial
              Society of Massachusetts (1905),
              vol. vii, p. 94)

WILLIAM WATSON 1559?–1603

4 Fiat justitia et ruant coeli.
              Let justice be done though the
              heavens fall.
              Quodlibets of Religion and State
              (1602)

SIR WILLIAM WATSON 1858–1936

5 April, April,
   Laugh thy girlish laughter;
   Then, the moment after,
   Weep thy girlish tears!   *April*

ISAAC WATTS 1674–1748

6 Let dogs delight to bark and bite,
   For God hath made them so;
   Let bears and lions growl and fight,
   For 'tis their nature too.
              Divine Songs for Children, xvi.
              Against Quarrelling

7 But, children, you should never let
   Such angry passions rise;
   Your little hands were never made
   To tear each other's eyes.   *Ib.*

8 Birds in their little nests agree
   And 'tis a shameful sight,
   When children of one family
   Fall out, and chide, and fight.   *Ib.*

9 How doth the little busy bee
   Improve each shining hour,
   And gather honey all the day
   From every opening flower!
              Ib. xx. *Against Idleness and Mis-*
              chief

10 In works of labour, or of skill,
   I would be busy too;
   For Satan finds some mischief still
   For idle hands to do.
              Divine Songs for Children, xx.
              Against Idleness and Mischief

11 Hush! my dear, lie still and slumber,
   Holy angels guard thy bed!
   Heavenly blessings without number
   Gently falling on thy head.
              Ib. xxxv. *Cradle Hymn*

12 'Tis the voice of the sluggard; I heard
   him complain,
   'You have wak'd me too soon, I must
   slumber again.'
   As the door on its hinges, so he on his
   bed,
   Turns his sides and his shoulders and
   his heavy head.
              Moral Songs, i. *The Sluggard*

13 Jesus shall reign where e'er the sun
   Does his successive journeys run;
   His kingdom stretch from shore to
   shore
   Till moons shall wax and wane no
   more.   *Psalms,* lxxii

14 Our God, our help in ages past
   Our hope for years to come,
   Our shelter from the stormy blast,
   And our eternal home.

   Beneath the shadow of Thy Throne
   Thy saints have dwelt secure;
   Sufficient is Thine Arm alone,
   And our defence is sure.

   Before the hills in order stood,
   Or earth received her frame,
   From everlasting Thou art God,
   To endless years the same.

   A thousand ages in Thy sight
   Are like an evening gone;
   Short as the watch that ends the night
   Before the rising sun.

   Time, like an ever-rolling stream,
   Bears all its sons away;
   They fly forgotten, as a dream
   Dies at the opening day.
              Ib. xc. *First line altered by John*
              Wesley to 'O God . . .'

15 There is a land of pure delight,
   Where saints immortal reign;
   Infinite day excludes the night,
   And pleasures banish pain.
              Hymns and Spiritual Songs, bk. ii,
              No. 66. *There is a Land of Pure*
              Delight

16 When I survey the wondrous Cross,
   On which the Prince of glory died,
   My richest gain I count but loss
   And pour contempt on all my pride.
              Hymns and Spiritual Songs,
              bk. iii, No. 7. *When I Survey the*
              Wondrous Cross

17 Were the whole realm of nature mine,
   That were a present far too small;
   Love so amazing, so Divine,
   Demands my soul, my life, my all. *Ib.*

FREDERIC EDWARD WEATHERLY 1848–1929

1 Where are the boys of the Old Brigade?
The Old Brigade

SIDNEY WEBB, LORD PASSFIELD 1859–1947

2 The inevitability of gradualness.
Presidential address to the annual conference of the Labour Party, 1920

WILLIAM WEBB *fl.* 1839

3 His throat they cut from ear to ear,
His brains they punched in,
His name was Mr. William Weare,
Wot lived in Lyon's Inn.
Ballad. See Lord William Lennox in The Sporting Review, July 1839, vol. ii, p. 42. Also attr. to Theodore Hook (1788–1841). See C. Hindley's Life and Times of James Catnach (1878), p. 145

DANIEL WEBSTER 1782–1852

4 There is always room at the top.
When advised not to become a lawyer as the profession was overcrowded

5 Fearful concatenation of circumstances.
Argument on the Murder of Captain Joseph White

JOHN WEBSTER 1580?–1625?

6 I am Duchess of Malfi still.
The Duchess of Malfi, IV. ii, l. 146

7 I know death hath ten thousand several doors
For men to take their exits. *Ib.* l. 222

8 Cover her face; mine eyes dazzle: she died young. *Ib.* l. 267

9 I saw him even now going the way of all flesh. *Westward Hoe*, II. ii

10 A mere tale of a tub, my words are idle. *The White Devil*, II. i. 92

11 Call for the robin redbreast and the wren,
Since o'er shady groves they hover,
And with leaves and flowers do cover
The friendless bodies of unburied men. *Ib.* v. iv. 100

12 I am i' th' way to study a long silence.
Ib. vi. l. 204

13   I have caught
An everlasting cold; I have lost my voice
Most irrecoverably. *Ib.* l. 270

ARTHUR WELLESLEY, DUKE OF WELLINGTON 1769–1852

14 It has been a damned serious business
—Blücher and I have lost 30,000 men.
It has been a damned nice thing—the
nearest run thing you ever saw in your
life. . . . By God! I don't think it would
have done if I had not been there.
Creevey Papers, ch. x, p. 236

15 All the business of war, and indeed all
the business of life, is to endeavour
to find out what you don't know by
what you do; that's what I called
'guessing what was at the other side
of the hill'.
Croker Papers (1885), vol. iii, p. 276

16 I never saw so many shocking bad
hats in my life.
On seeing the first Reformed Parliament. Sir William Fraser, Words on Wellington (1889), p. 12

17 The battle of Waterloo was won in the
playing fields of Eton.
Montalembert, De l'Avenir Politique de l'Angleterre (1855). The attribution has been refuted by the 7th Duke.

18 In refusing the dedication of a song
[the Duke of Wellington] informed
Mrs. Norton that he had been obliged
to make a rule of refusing dedications,
'because, in his situation as Chancellor
of the University of Oxford, he had
been much exposed to authors'.
G. W. E. Russell's Collections and Recollections, ch. 2

19 Hard pounding this, gentlemen; let's
see who will pound longest.
At Waterloo. Sir W. Scott, Paul's Letters (1815)

20 I used to say of him [Napoleon] that
his presence on the field made the
difference of forty thousand men.
Stanhope, Notes of Conversations with the Duke of Wellington, 2 Nov. 1831

21 What is the best to be done for the
country? How can the Government
be carried on? *Ib.* 18 May 1839

('The Queen's Government must be
carried on'—*and variants—was used
by him on several occasions.*)

22 I don't know what effect these men
will have upon the enemy, but, by
God, they terrify me.
On a draft of troops sent to him in Spain, 1809. (Also attr. to George III)

23 [*To a gentleman who accosted him in the street saying, 'Mr. Jones, I believe?'*]
If you believe that you will believe
anything. *Attr.*

1 Up Guards and at them again!
> *Attr. to Wellington during the*
> *Battle of Waterloo. Capt. Batty's*
> *letter, 22 June 1815, in Booth's*
> *Battle of Waterloo. J. W. Croker,*
> *in a letter to A. Greville, 14 Mar.*
> *1852, wrote 'Perhaps I might also*
> *venture to ask his Grace whether*
> *he did say, "Up Guards and at*
> *them".' Wellington replied in an*
> *undated letter to Croker which is in*
> Croker Correspondence and
> Diaries *(1884), vol. iii, p. 280:*
> 'What I must have said and
> possibly did say was, Stand up,
> Guards! and then gave the
> commanding officers the order to
> attack'

2 Publish and be damned.   *Attr.*

HERBERT GEORGE WELLS
1866–1946

3 'I expect,' he said, 'I was thinking
jest what a Rum Go everything is.
I expect it was something like that.'
> *Kipps, bk. iii, ch. 3, § 8*

4 The Shape of Things to Come.
> *Title of Book (1933)*

5 The Time-Machine.
> *Title of Novel (1895)*

6 The War that will end War.
> *Title of Book (1914)*

CHARLES WESLEY 1707–1788

7 'Christ, the Lord, is risen to-day,'
Sons of men and angels say,
Raise your joys and triumphs high,
Sing, ye heavens, and earth reply.
> *Hymns and Sacred Poems (1739).*
> *Christ, the Lord, is Risen To-day*

8 Jesu, Lover of my soul,
Let me to Thy Bosom fly,
While the nearer waters roll,
While the tempest still is high;
Hide me, O my Saviour, hide,
Till the storm of life is past;
Safe into the haven guide,
O receive my soul at last.
> *Ib. (1740), Jesu, Lover of My Soul*

9 Other refuge have I none;
Hangs my helpless soul on Thee.   *Ib.*

10 Cover my defenceless head
With the shadow of Thy wing.   *Ib.*

11 Thou of Life the Fountain art;
Freely let me take of Thee;
Spring Thou up within my heart,
Rise to all eternity.   *Ib.*

12 Gentle Jesus, meek and mild,
Look upon a little child;
Pity my simplicity;
Suffer me to come to thee.
> *Ib. (1742), Gentle Jesus, Meek and*
> *Mild*

13 Soldiers of Christ, arise,
And put your armour on.
> *Hymns and Sacred Poems (1749).*
> *Soldiers of Christ, Arise*

14 Lift up your heart, lift up your voice;
Rejoice, again I say, rejoice.
> *Hymns for Our Lord's Resurrec-*
> *tion (1746): Rejoice, the Lord is*
> *King*

15 Hark! the herald-angels sing
Glory to the new-born King:
Peace on earth, and mercy mild,
God and sinners reconciled.
> *Ib. Christmas Hymn: Hark! the*
> *Herald Angels Sing. First two*
> *lines altered by George Whitefield*
> *in 1753 from Wesley's original*
> Hark, how all the welkin rings,
> 'Glory to the King of kings'.

16 Lo! he comes with clouds descending.
> *Hymns of Intercession for all*
> *Mankind (1758): Lo! He Comes*
> *with Clouds. New Version of*
> *John Cennick's 'Lo! He cometh,*
> *countless trumpets', in Collection*
> *of Sacred Hymns (1752)*

17 Let saints on earth in concert sing.
> *Funeral Hymns (1759): Let saints*
> *on earth. Altered by F. H.*
> *Murray in his Hymnal for Use*
> *in the English Church (1852),*
> *from 'Let all the saints terres-*
> *trial sing'*

JOHN WESLEY 1703–1791

18 I look upon all the world as my parish.
> *Journal, 11 June 1739*

19 Let it be observed, that slovenliness
is no part of religion; that neither
this, nor any text of Scripture, con-
demns neatness of apparel. Certainly
this is a duty, not a sin. 'Cleanliness is,
indeed, next to godliness.'
> *Sermons, No. xciii. On Dress*

REV. SAMUEL WESLEY 1662–1735

20 Style is the dress of thought; a modest
dress,
Neat, but not gaudy, will true critics
please.
> *An Epistle to a Friend concerning*
> *Poetry (1700)*

MAE WEST 1893–

21 Come up and see me sometime.
> *Diamond Lil (1932)*

EDITH WHARTON 1862–1937

22 Mrs. Ballinger is one of the ladies who
pursue Culture in bands, as though it
were dangerous to meet it alone.
> *Xingu, ch. 1*

JAMES ABBOTT McNEILL WHISTLER 1834–1903

1 I am not arguing with you—I am telling you.
Gentle Art of Making Enemies

2 'I only know of two painters in the world,' said a newly introduced feminine enthusiast to Whistler, 'yourself and Velasquez.' 'Why,' answered Whistler in dulcet tones, 'why drag in Velasquez?'
O. C. Seitz, *Whistler Stories* (1913), p. 27

3 [*In answer to the question* 'For two days' labour, you ask two hundred guineas?']
No, I ask it for the knowledge of a lifetime.   *Ib.* p. 40

4 [*Answering Oscar Wilde's* 'I wish I had said that']
You will, Oscar, you will.
L. C. Ingleby, *Oscar Wilde*, p. 67

HENRY KIRKE WHITE 1785–1806

5 Oft in danger, oft in woe,
Onward, Christians, onward go.
W. J. Hall's *Mitre Hymn Book* (1836). *Adapted by Dr. W. B. Collyer from White's original* 'Much in sorrow, oft in woe'

WILLIAM ALLEN WHITE 1868–1944

6 All dressed up, with nowhere to go.
On the Progressive Party in the U.S.A. in 1916, after Theodore Roosevelt had retired from the Presidential campaign

WILLIAM LINDSAY WHITE 1900–

7 They Were Expendable.
Title of Book (1942)

GEORGE WHITEFIELD 1714–1770

8 I had rather wear out than rust out.
Attr. by Robert Southey

WILLIAM WHITING 1825–1878

9 O hear us when we cry to Thee
For those in peril on the sea.
Hymn: Eternal Father Strong to Save

WALT WHITMAN 1819?–1892

10 O Captain! my Captain! our fearful trip is done,
The ship has weather'd every rack, the prize we sought is won,
The port is near, the bells I hear, the people all exulting.
O Captain! My Captain! i

11 Exult O shores, and ring O bells!
But I with mournful tread
Walk the deck my Captain lies, Fallen cold and dead.
O Captain! My Captain! iii

12 Out of the cradle endlessly rocking,
Out of the mocking-bird's throat, the musical shuttle,

A reminiscence sing.
Out of the Cradle endlessly Rocking

13 Pioneers! O Pioneers.   *Title of Poem*

14 I think I could turn and live with animals, they are so placid and self-contain'd,
I stand and look at them long and long.
They do not sweat and whine about their condition,
They do not lie awake in the dark and weep for their sins,
They do not make me sick discussing their duty to God,
Not one is dissatisfied, not one is demented with the mania of owning things,
Not one kneels to another, nor to his kind that lived thousands of years ago,
Not one is respectable or unhappy over the whole earth.
Song of Myself, 32

15 Do I contradict myself?
Very well then I contradict myself,
(I am large, I contain multitudes.)
Ib. 50

JOHN GREENLEAF WHITTIER 1807–1892

16 'Shoot, if you must, this old gray head,
But spare your country's flag,' she said.   *Barbara Frietchie*, l. 35

17 For all sad words of tongue or pen,
The saddest are these: 'It might have been!'   *Maud Muller*, l. 105

18 Dinna ye hear it?—Dinna ye hear it?
The pipes o' Havelock sound!
Pipes at Lucknow, iv

CORNELIUS WHURR c. 1845

19 What lasting joys the man attend
Who has a polished female friend.
The Accomplished Female Friend

GEORGE JOHN WHYTE-MELVILLE 1821–1878

20 Then drink, puppy, drink, and let ev'ry puppy drink,
That is old enough to lap and to swallow;
For he'll grow into a hound, so we'll pass the bottle round,
And merrily we'll whoop and we'll holloa. *Drink, Puppy, Drink*, chorus

1 Wrap me up in my tarpaulin jacket,
And say a poor buffer lies low,
And six stalwart lancers shall carry me,
With steps solemn, mournful, and slow.   *The Tarpaulin Jacket*

BISHOP SAMUEL WILBERFORCE 1805–1873

2 If I were a cassowary
On the plains of Timbuctoo,
I would eat a missionary,
Cassock, band, and hymn-book too.
          Impromptu verse, Ascribed

ELLA WHEELER WILCOX 1855–1919

3 Laugh and the world laughs with you;
Weep, and you weep alone;
For the sad old earth must borrow its mirth,
But has trouble enough of its own.   *Solitude*

OSCAR WILDE 1854–1900

4 I never saw a man who looked
With such a wistful eye
Upon that little tent of blue
Which prisoners call the sky.
          The Ballad of Reading Gaol (1898), pt. I. iii

5 Yet each man kills the thing he loves,
By each let this be heard,
Some do it with a bitter look,
Some with a flattering word.
The coward does it with a kiss,
The brave man with a sword!
          Ib. vii

6 And the wild regrets, and the bloody sweats,
None knew so well as I:
For he who lives more lives than one
More deaths than one must die.
          Ib. III. xxxvii

7 The truth is rarely pure, and never simple.   *The Importance of Being Earnest* (1895), Act I

8 In married life three is company and two none.   *Ib.*

9 I have invented an invaluable permanent invalid called Bunbury, in order that I may be able to go down into the country whenever I choose.   *Ib.*

10 To lose one parent, Mr. Worthing, may be regarded as a misfortune; to lose both looks like carelessness.   *Ib.*

11 All women become like their mothers. That is their tragedy. No man does. That's his.   *Ib.*

12 The chapter on the Fall of the Rupee you may omit. It is somewhat too sensational.   *Ib.* Act II

13 On an occasion of this kind it becomes more than a moral duty to speak one's mind. It becomes a pleasure.
          The Importance of Being Earnest, Act II

14 Please do not shoot the pianist. He is doing his best.
          Impressions of America. Leadville

15 I couldn't help it. I can resist everything except temptation.
          Lady Windermere's Fan (1891), Act I

16 We are all in the gutter, but some of us are looking at the stars.   *Ib.* Act III

17 There is nothing in the whole world so unbecoming to a woman as a Nonconformist conscience.   *Ib.*

18 CECIL GRAHAM:
What is a cynic?
LORD DARLINGTON:
A man who knows the price of everything and the value of nothing.   *Ib.*

19 There is no such thing as a moral or an immoral book. Books are well written, or badly written.
          Picture of Dorian Gray (1891), preface

20 There is only one thing in the world worse than being talked about, and that is not being talked about.
          Ib. ch. 1

21 The only way to get rid of a temptation is to yield to it.   *Ib.* ch. 2

22 Anybody can be good in the country.
          Ib. ch. 19

23 MRS. ALLONBY:
They say, Lady Hunstanton, that when good Americans die they go to Paris.
LADY HUNSTANTON:
Indeed? And when bad Americans die, where do they go to?
LORD ILLINGWORTH:
Oh, they go to America.
          A Woman of No Importance (1893), Act I (see *10:9*)

24 The English country gentleman galloping after a fox—the unspeakable in full pursuit of the uneatable.   *Ib.*

25 One should never trust a woman who tells one her real age. A woman who would tell one that, would tell one anything.   *Ib.*

26 LORD ILLINGWORTH:
The Book of Life begins with a man and a woman in a garden.
MRS. ALLONBY:
It ends with Revelations.   *Ib.*

27 Children begin by loving their parents; after a time they judge them; rarely, if ever, do they forgive them.   *Ib.*

1 [*At the New York Custom House*]
I have nothing to declare except my
genius.
> F. Harris, *Oscar Wilde* (1918),
> p. 75

2 [*A huge fee for an operation was mentioned*]
'Ah, well, then,' said Oscar, 'I suppose that I shall have to die beyond
my means.'
> R. H. Sherard, *Life of Oscar
> Wilde* (1906), p. 421

JOHN WILKES 1727–1797

3 The chapter of accidents is the longest
chapter in the book.
> *Attr. to John Wilkes by Southey
> in* The Doctor (1837), vol. iv,
> p. 166

EMMA HART WILLARD
1787–1876

4 Rocked in the cradle of the deep. *Song*

WILLIAM III OF GREAT
BRITAIN 1650–1702

5 I will die in the last ditch.
> Hume, *History of Great Britain*,
> vol. ii (1757), p. 226. *Charles II*,
> ch. 3

6 Every bullet has its billet.
> John Wesley, *Journal*, 6 June
> 1765

HARRY WILLIAMS
and
JACK JUDGE

7 It's a long way to Tipperary, it's a
long way to go;
It's a long way to Tipperary, to the
sweetest girl I know!
Good-bye Piccadilly, Farewell Leices-
ter Square;
It's a long, long way to Tipperary, but
my heart's right there!
> *It's a Long Way to Tipperary.
> Chorus claimed by Alice Smythe
> B. Jay. Written in 1908. See
> New York Times, 20 Sept. 1907*

8 In the shade of the old apple tree.
> *Title of Song*

NATHANIEL PARKER WILLIS
1806–1867

9 At present there is no distinction
among the upper ten thousand of the
city.   *Necessity for a Promenade Drive*

W. G. WILLS *nineteenth century*

10 I'll sing thee songs of Araby,
And tales of wild Cashmere,
Wild tales to cheat thee of a sigh,
Or charm thee to a tear. *Lalla Rookh*

D. EARDLEY WILMOT
contemporary

11 It's a corner of heaven itself,
Though it's only a tumble-down
nest,
But with love brooding there, why,
no place can compare,
With my little grey home in the
west.   *My Little Grey Home*

JOHN WILSON 1785–1854
see CHRISTOPHER NORTH

THOMAS WOODROW WILSON
1856–1924

12 Armed neutrality.
> *Message to Congress, 26 Feb.
> 1917*

13 The world must be made safe for
democracy.
> *Address to Congress, 2 Apr. 1917*

ARTHUR WIMPERIS 1874–1953

14 Gilbert, the Filbert,
The Colonel of the Knuts.
> *Gilbert the Filbert*

ANNE FINCH, LADY
WINCHILSEA d. 1720

15 Now the Jonquille o'ercomes the
feeble brain;
We faint beneath the aromatic pain.
> *The Spleen*

WILLIAM WINDHAM 1750–1810

16 Those entrusted with arms . . .
should be persons of some substance
and stake in the country.
> *Speech in the House of Commons,
> 22 July 1807*

CATHERINE WINKWORTH
1829–1878

17 Now thank we all our God,
With heart and hands and voices
Who wondrous things hath done
In whom His world rejoices.
> *Trans. of* Martin Rinkart: *Nun
> danket alle Gott*

GEORGE WITHER 1588–1667

18 Shall I, wasting in despair,
Die because a woman's fair?
Or make pale my cheeks with care,
'Cause another's rosy are?
Be she fairer than the day,
Or the flow'ry meads in May;
If she think not well of me,
What care I how fair she be?
> *Sonnet*

PELHAM GRENVILLE WODEHOUSE 1881–

1 He spoke with a certain what-is-it in his voice, and I could see that, if not actually disgruntled, he was far from being gruntled.
The Code of the Woosters

2 Donning the soup-and-fish in preparation for the evening meal.
Jeeves and the Impending Doom

CHARLES WOLFE 1791–1823

3 Not a drum was heard, not a funeral note,
As his corse to the rampart we hurried.
The Burial of Sir John Moore at Corunna, i

4 We buried him darkly at dead of night,
The sods with our bayonets turning.
Ib. ii

5 But he lay like a warrior taking his rest,
With his martial cloak around him.
Ib. iii

6 Few and short were the prayers we said,
And we spoke not a word of sorrow;
But we steadfastly gazed on the face that was dead,
And we bitterly thought of the morrow.
Ib. iv

7 We carved not a line, and we raised not a stone—
But we left him alone with his glory.
Ib. viii

JAMES WOLFE 1727–1759

8 The General . . . repeated nearly the whole of Gray's Elegy . . . adding, as he concluded, that he would prefer being the author of that poem to the glory of beating the French to-morrow.
J. Playfair, *Biogr. Acc. of J. Robinson in Transactions R. Soc. Edinb. 1814*, vii. p. 499

9 Now God be praised, I will die in peace.
Dying words. J. Knox, *Historical Journal of Campaigns, 1757–60.* Published 1769. Ed. 1914, vol. ii, p. 114

THOMAS, CARDINAL WOLSEY 1475?–1530

10 Father Abbot, I am come to lay my bones amongst you.
Cavendish, *Negotiations of Thomas Wolsey* (1641), p. 108

11 Had I but served God as diligently as I have served the king, he would not have given me over in my gray hairs.
Ib. p. 113

MRS. HENRY WOOD 1814–1887

12 Dead! and . . . never called me mother.
East Lynne (dramatized version by T. A. Palmer, 1874). These words do not occur in the novel

ELIZABETH WORDSWORTH 1840–1932

13 If all the good people were clever,
And all clever people were good,
The world would be nicer than ever
We thought that it possibly could.

But somehow, 'tis seldom or never
The two hit it off as they should;
The good are so harsh to the clever,
The clever so rude to the good!
St. Christopher and Other Poems: Good and Clever

WILLIAM WORDSWORTH 1770–1850

14 A slumber did my spirit seal;
I had no human fears:
She seemed a thing that could not feel
The touch of earthly years.

No motion has she now, no force;
She neither hears nor sees;
Rolled round in earth's diurnal course,
With rocks, and stones, and trees.
A Slumber did My Spirit Seal

15 O blithe new-comer! I have heard,
I hear thee and rejoice.
O Cuckoo! Shall I call thee bird,
Or but a wandering voice?
To the Cuckoo: O Blithe New-comer!

16 Thrice welcome, darling of the Spring!
Ib.

17 Still glides the Stream, and shall for ever glide;
The Form remains, the Function never dies.
The River Duddon, xxxiv. After-Thought

18 And if, as toward the silent tomb we go,
Through love, through hope, and faith's transcendent dower,
We feel that we are greater than we know.
Ib.

19 Stern daughter of the voice of God!
O Duty! if that name thou love
Who art a light to guide, a rod
To check the erring and reprove.
Ode to Duty

20 Not in the lucid intervals of life
That come but as a curse to party strife.
Evening Voluntaries, iv. Not in the Lucid Intervals

1 Bliss was it in that dawn to be alive,
   But to be young was very heaven!
            *French Revolution, as it Appeared
            to Enthusiasts*, and *The Prelude*,
            bk. xi, l. 108

2 Who is the happy Warrior? Who is he
   That every man in arms should wish
      to be?
            Character of the Happy Warrior

3 The rapt one, of the godlike forehead,
   The heaven-eyed creature sleeps in
      earth:
   And Lamb, the frolic and the gentle,
   Has vanished from his lonely hearth.
            *Extempore Effusion upon the
            Death of James Hogg*

4 Him whom you love, your Idiot Boy.
            The Idiot Boy

5   All shod with steel
   We hissed along the polished ice, in
      games
   Confederate.
            Influence of Natural Objects and
            The Prelude, bk. i, l. 414

6   'Yet still the solitary cliffs
   Wheeled by me—even as if the earth
      had rolled
   With visible motion her diurnal round!'
            Ib. and *The Prelude*, bk. i, l. 458

7 There was a time when meadow,
      grove, and stream,
   The earth, and every common sight,
      To me did seem
   Apparelled in celestial light,
   The glory and the freshness of a dream.
   It is not now as it hath been of yore;—
      Turn wheresoe'er I may,
      By night or day,
   The things which I have seen I now
      can see no more.
            Ode. Intimations of Immortality, i

8   The rainbow comes and goes,
            And lovely is the rose,
            The moon doth with delight
   Look round her when the heavens are
      bare,
            Waters on a starry night
            Are beautiful and fair;
   The sunshine is a glorious birth:
   But yet I know, where'er I go,
   That there hath passed away a glory
      from the earth.   *Ib.* ii

9 And the babe leaps up on his mother's
      arm.   *Ib.* iv

10 —But there's a tree, of many, 'one
   A single field which I have looked
      upon,
   Both of them speak of something that
      is gone:
   The pansy at my feet
   Doth the same tale repeat:
   Whither is fled the visionary gleam?
   Where is it now, the glory and the
      dream?   *Ib.*

11 Our birth is but a sleep and a for-
      getting:
   The Soul that rises with us, our
      life's Star,
   Hath had elsewhere its setting,
      And cometh from afar:
   Not in entire forgetfulness,
   And not in utter nakedness,
   But trailing clouds of glory do we
      come
      From God, who is our home:
   Heaven lies about us in our infancy!
   Shades of the prison-house begin to
      close
      Upon the growing boy,
   But he beholds the light, and whence
      it flows,
      He sees it in his joy;
   The youth, who daily farther from the
      east
      Must travel, still is Nature's priest,
      And by the vision splendid
      Is on his way attended;
   At length the man perceives it die
      away,
   And fade into the light of common
      day.
            Ode. Intimations of Immortality, v

12 Hence in a season of calm weather
      Though inland far we be,
   Our souls have sight of that immortal
      sea
      Which brought us hither,
      Can in a moment travel thither,
   And see the children sport upon the
      shore,
   And hear the mighty waters rolling
      evermore.   *Ib.* ix

13 Though nothing can bring back the
      hour
   Of splendour in the grass, of glory in
      the flower;
   We will grieve not, rather find
   Strength in what remains behind;
   In the primal sympathy
   Which having been must ever be;
   In the soothing thoughts that spring
   Out of human suffering;
   In the faith that looks through death,
   In years that bring the philosophic
      mind.   *Ib.*

14 Another race hath been, and other
      palms are won.
   Thanks to the human heart by which
      we live,
   Thanks to its tenderness, its joys, and
      fears,
   To me the meanest flower that blows
      can give
   Thoughts that do often lie too deep
      for tears.   *Ib.* xi

15 It is a beauteous evening, calm and
      free,
   The holy time is quiet as a nun,
   Breathless with adoration.
            Miscellaneous Sonnets, pt. i, xxx.
            It is a Beauteous Evening

1 We must be free or die, who speak the
    tongue
That Shakespeare spake; the faith
    and morals hold
Which Milton held.
    *National Independence and Lib-
    erty*, pt. I, xvi. *It is not to be thought
    of*

2 I travelled among unknown men
    In lands beyond the sea;
Nor, England! did I know till then
    What love I bore to thee.
    I Travelled among Unknown Men

3 I wandered lonely as a cloud
That floats on high o'er vales and hills,
When all at once I saw a crowd,
A host, of golden daffodils;
Beside the lake, beneath the trees,
Fluttering and dancing in the breeze.
    I Wandered Lonely as a Cloud

4 Continuous as the stars that shine
And twinkle on the milky way.   *Ib.*

5 For oft, when on my couch I lie
In vacant or in pensive mood,
They flash upon that inward eye
Which is the bliss of solitude;
And then my heart with pleasure fills,
And dances with the daffodils.   *Ib.*

6 Give all thou canst; high Heaven
    rejects the lore
Of nicely-calculated less or more.
    Ecclesiastical Sonnets, pt. III,
    xliii. *King's College Chapel. Tax
    not the Royal Saint*

7 Milton! thou shouldst be living at
    this hour:
England hath need of thee; she is a fen
Of stagnant waters.
    *National Independence and
    Liberty*, pt. I, xiv. *London.
    Milton! thou shouldst*

8 Plain living and high thinking are
    no more:
    Ib. xiii. *Written in London. O
    Friend! I Know Not*

9   The cattle are grazing,
    Their heads never raising;
There are forty feeding like one!
    Written in March

10 My heart leaps up when I behold
    A rainbow in the sky:
So was it when my life began;
So is it now I am a man;
So be it when I shall grow old,
    Or let me die!
The Child is father of the Man;
And I could wish my days to be
Bound each to each by natural piety.
    My Heart Leaps Up

11 Another year!—another deadly blow!
Another mighty Empire overthrown!
And we are left, or shall be left, alone.
    *National Independence and
    Liberty*, pt. I, xxvii. *November.
    Another Year!*

12 Nuns fret not at their convent's
    narrow room;
And hermits are contented with their
    cells.
    Miscellaneous Sonnets, pt. I, i.
    Nuns Fret Not

13 The light that never was, on sea or
    land,
The consecration, and the poet's
    dream.
    *Elegiac Stanzas Suggested by a
    Picture of Peele Castle in a Storm*

14 A primrose by a river's brim
A yellow primrose was to him,
And it was nothing more.
    Peter Bell, pt. i, l. 249

15 Is it a party in a parlour?
Cramm'd just as they on earth were
    cramm'd—
Some sipping punch, some sipping
    tea,
But, as you by their faces see,
All silent and all damned!
    Ib. pt. i, l. 516 (later omitted)

16 The dew was falling fast, the stars
    began to blink;
I heard a voice; it said, 'Drink, pretty
    creature, drink!'   *The Pet Lamb*

17   Where the statue stood
Of Newton, with his prism and silent
    face,
The marble index of a mind for ever
Voyaging through strange seas of
    thought alone.
    The Prelude, bk. iii, l. 61

18 Sweet Spenser, moving through his
    clouded heaven
With the moon's beauty and the
    moon's soft pace,
I called him Brother, Englishman, and
    Friend!   *Ib.* l. 280

19 I thought of Chatterton, the mar-
    vellous boy,
The sleepless soul, that perished in his
    pride;
Of him who walked in glory and in joy,
Following his plough, along the moun-
    tain side:
By our own spirits are we deified:
We poets in our youth begin in glad-
    ness;
But thereof comes in the end des-
    pondency and madness.
    Resolution and Independence, vii

20   The good old rule
Sufficeth them, the simple plan,
That they should take, who have the
    power,
And they should keep who can.
    *Memorials of a Tour in Scotland,
    1803.* xi. *Rob Roy's Grave*

1 Scorn not the Sonnet; Critic, you have
   frowned,
Mindless of its just honours; with
   this key
Shakespeare unlocked his heart.
        Miscellaneous Sonnets, pt. II, i.
        Scorn Not the Sonnet

2   And when a damp
Fell round the path of Milton, in his
   hand
The Thing became a trumpet; whence
   he blew
Soul-animating strains,—alas! too few.
                                    Ib.

3 She dwelt among the untrodden ways
     Beside the springs of Dove,
A maid whom there were none to
   praise
     And very few to love:

A violet by a mossy stone
   Half hidden from the eye!
Fair as a star, when only one
   Is shining in the sky.

She lived unknown, and few could
   know
   When Lucy ceased to be;
But she is in her grave, and, oh,
   The difference to me!
        *She Dwelt Among the Untrodden
        Ways*

4 She was a phantom of delight
When first she gleamed upon my sight;
A lovely apparition, sent
To be a moment's ornament.
        She was a Phantom of Delight

5 A perfect woman, nobly planned,
To warn, to comfort, and command;
And yet a spirit still, and bright
With something of angelic light.   *Ib.*

6 Type of the wise who soar, but never
   roam;
True to the kindred points of heaven
   and home!   *To a Skylark*

7 Behold her, single in the field,
     Yon solitary Highland lass!
        *Memorials of a Tour in Scotland,
        1803, ix. The Solitary Reaper*

8 A voice so thrilling ne'er was heard
In spring-time from the Cuckoo-bird,
Breaking the silence of the seas
Among the farthest Hebrides.   *Ib.*

9 Will no one tell me what she sings?—
Perhaps the plaintive numbers flow
For old, unhappy, far-off things,
And battles long ago.   *Ib.*

10 Spade! with which Wilkinson hath
tilled his lands.
        To the Spade of a Friend

11 And much it grieved my heart to
    think
What man has made of man.
        Lines Written in Early Spring

12 And 'tis my faith that every flower
Enjoys the air it breathes.   *Ib.*

13 Two Voices are there; one is of the sea,
One of the mountains; each a mighty
   Voice,
In both from age to age thou didst
   rejoice,
They were thy chosen music, Liberty!
        *National Independence and
        Liberty*, xii. *Thought of a Briton
        on the Subjugation of Switzerland:
        Two Voices are There*

14 And hark! how blithe the throstle sings!
He, too, is no mean preacher
Come forth into the light of things,
   Let Nature be your teacher.
                The Tables Turned

15 One impulse from a vernal wood
   May teach you more of man,
Of moral evil and of good,
   Than all the sages can.   *Ib.*

16 I've measured it from side to side:
'Tis three feet long, and two feet wide.
        The Thorn, iii [early reading]

17   Sensations sweet,
Felt in the blood, and felt along the
heart.
        *Lines composed a few miles above
        Tintern Abbey*, l. 27

18   That best portion of a good man's
            life,
His little, nameless, unremembered
   acts
Of kindness and of love.   *Ib.* l. 33

19   I have learned
To look on nature, not as in the hour
Of thoughtless youth; but hearing
   often-times
The still, sad music of humanity,
Nor harsh nor grating, though of
   ample power
To chasten and subdue. And I have felt
A presence that disturbs me with the joy
Of elevated thoughts; a sense sublime
Of something far more deeply inter-
   fused,
Whose dwelling is the light of setting
   suns,
And the round ocean and the living air,
And the blue sky, and in the mind of
   man.   *Ib.* l. 88

20   Thou hast left behind
Powers that will work for thee; air,
   earth, and skies;
There's not a breathing of the common
   wind
That will forget thee; thou hast great
   allies;
Thy friends are exultations, agonies,
And love, and man's unconquerable
   mind.
        *National Independence and
        Liberty*, pt. I, viii. *To Toussaint
        L'Ouverture: Toussaint, the Most
        Unhappy*

1 Once did she hold the gorgeous East
in fee,
And was the safeguard of the West.
        Ib. vi. *On the Extinction of the
        Venetian Republic: Once Did
        She Hold*

2 And when she took unto herself a
Mate,
She must espouse the everlasting Sea.
                                Ib.

3 I take my little porringer
And eat my supper there.
                        We are Seven

4 Earth has not anything to show more
fair:
Dull would he be of soul who could
pass by
A sight so touching in its majesty:
This City now doth, like a garment,
wear
The beauty of the morning; silent,
bare,
Ships, towers, domes, theatres, and
temples lie
Open unto the fields, and to the sky;
All bright and glittering in the smoke-
less air.
Never did sun more beautifully steep
In his first splendour, valley, rock, or
hill;
Ne'er saw I, never felt, a calm so
deep!
The river glideth at his own sweet will:
Dear God! the very houses seem
asleep;
And all that mighty heart is lying still!
        Miscellaneous Sonnets, pt. II,
        xxxvi. *Composed upon West-
        minster Bridge*

5 The world is too much with us; late
and soon,
Getting and spending, we lay waste
our powers:
Little we see in Nature that is ours;
We have given our hearts away, a
sordid boon!
This Sea that bares her bosom to the
moon;
The winds that will be howling at all
hours,
And are up-gathered now like sleeping
flowers;
For this, for everything, we are out of
tune;
It moves us not; Great God! I'd
rather be
A Pagan suckled in a creed outworn,
So might I, standing on this pleasant
lea,
Have glimpses that would make me
less forlorn;
Have sight of Proteus rising from the
sea,
Or hear old Triton blow his wreathed
horn.
        Ib. xxxiii. *The World is Too
        Much with Us*

6 Every great and original writer, in
proportion as he is great and original,
must himself create the taste by which
he is to be relished.
                Letter to Lady Beaumont

HENRY CLAY WORK 1832–1884

7 Bring the good old bugle, boys, we'll
    sing another song;
Sing it with a spirit that will start the
    world along,
Sing it as we used to sing it—fifty
    thousand strong,
    As we were marching through
    Georgia.
            Marching Through Georgia

8 'Hurrah! hurrah! we bring the Jubilee!
Hurrah! hurrah! the flag that makes
    you free!'
So we sang the chorus from Atlanta
    to the sea,
    As we were marching through
    Georgia.   *Ib. Chorus*

9 Father, dear father, come home with
    me now,
The clock in the belfry strikes one.
            Temperance song (1864)

SIR HENRY WOTTON 1568–1639

10 How happy is he born and taught
        That serveth not another's will;
    Whose armour is his honest thought,
        And simple truth his utmost skill!
            Character of a Happy Life, i

11 This man is freed from servile bands,
        Of hope to rise, or fear to fall:—
    Lord of himself, though not of lands,
        And having nothing, yet hath all.
                                Ib. vi

12 He first deceas'd; she for a little tri'd
To live without him: lik'd it not, and
di'd.
        *Death of Sir Albertus Moreton's
        Wife*

13 You meaner beauties of the night,
        That poorly satisfy our eyes,
    More by your number, than your
        light,
        You common people of the skies,
        What are you when the moon shall
        rise?
            *On His Mistress, the Queen of
            Bohemia*

14 An ambassador is an honest man sent
to lie abroad for the good of his
country.
        *Written in the Album of Christo-
        pher Fleckmore* (1604)

SIR CHRISTOPHER WREN
1632–1723

1 Si monumentum requiris, circumspice.
> If you would see his monument
> look around.
>> *Inscription over the interior of the*
>> *North Door in St. Paul's Cathe-*
>> *dral, London. Attr. to Wren's son*

SIR THOMAS WYATT 1503?–1542

2 They flee from me, that sometime did
   me seek.   *Remembrance*

WILLIAM WYCHERLEY
1640?–1716

3 QUAINT:
  With sharp invectives—
  WIDOW:
  Alias, Billingsgate.
>> *Plain Dealer*, Act III

XENOPHON b. c. 430 B.C.

4 θάλαττα θάλαττα.
> The sea! the sea!
>> *Anabasis*, IV. vii. 24

WILLIAM BUTLER YEATS
1865–1939

5 Down by the salley gardens my love
   and I did meet;
  She passed the salley gardens with
   little snow-white feet.
  She bid me take love easy, as the
   leaves grow on the tree;
  But I, being young and foolish, with
   her would not agree.
>> *Down by the Salley Gardens*

6 I have spread my dreams under your
   feet;
  Tread softly, because you tread on my
   dreams.
>> *He Wishes for the Cloths of*
>> *Heaven*

7 Nor law, nor duty bade me fight,
  Nor public men, nor cheering crowds,
  A lonely impulse of delight
  Drove to this tumult in the clouds;
  I balanced all, brought all to mind,
  The years to come seemed waste of
   breath,
  A waste of breath the years behind
  In balance with this life, this death.
>> *An Irish Airman Foresees His*
>> *Death*

8 When I play on my fiddle in Dooney
  Folk dance like a wave of the sea.
>> *The Fiddler of Dooney*

9 I will arise and go now, and go to
   Innisfree,
  And a small cabin build there, of clay
   and wattles made:
  Nine bean-rows will I have there, a
   hive for the honey-bee,
  And live alone in the bee-loud glade.
>> *The Lake Isle of Innisfree*

10 And pluck till time and times are done
   The silver apples of the moon
   The golden apples of the sun.
>> *The Song of Wandering Ængus*

11 When you are old and gray and full of
    sleep,
   And nodding by the fire, take down
    this book,
   And slowly read, and dream of the
    soft look
   Your eyes had once, and of their
    shadows deep;
   How many loved your moments of
    glad grace,
   And loved your beauty with love
    false or true,
   But one man loved the pilgrim soul in
    you,
   And loved the sorrows of your chang-
    ing face.
   And bending down beside the glowing
    bars,
   Murmur, a little sadly, how Love fled
   And paced upon the mountains over-
    head
   And hid his face amid a crowd of
    stars.   *When you are Old*

ANDREW YOUNG 1807–1889

12 There is a happy land,
    Far, far away,
   Where Saints in glory stand,
    Bright, bright as day.
>> *Hymn: There is a Happy Land.*
>> C. H. Bateman's *Sacred Song*
>> *Book* (1843)

EDWARD YOUNG 1683–1765

13   Be wise with speed;
   A fool at forty is a fool indeed.
>> *Love of Fame*, Sat. ii, l. 281

14 How commentators each dark passage
    shun,
   And hold their farthing candle to the
    sun.   *Ib.* Sat. vii, l. 97

15 Tir'd Nature's sweet restorer, balmy
    sleep!
>> *The Complaint: Night Thoughts*,
>> Night i, l. 1

16 Procrastination is the thief of time.
>> *Ib.* l. 393

17 Man wants but little; nor that little,
    long.   *Ib.* Night iv, l. 118

18 By night an atheist half believes a
    God.   *Ib.* Night v, l. 176

1 Life is the desert, life the solitude;
Death joins us to the great majority.
The Revenge, Act IV

2 You are so witty, profligate, and thin,
At once we think thee Milton, Death,
and Sin. *Epigram on Voltaire*

ISRAEL ZANGWILL 1864–1926

3 America is God's Crucible, the great
Melting-Pot where all the races of
Europe are melting and reforming! . . .
God is making the American.
The Melting Pot, Act I

ÉMILE ZOLA 1840–1902

4 J'accuse.
I accuse.
Title of an open letter to the President of the Republic, in connexion with the Dreyfus case, published in L'Aurore, 13 Jan. 1898

INDEX

Note: "Sow an a." line reads 175:4

L

M

N

Satan (*cont.*)
  messenger of S.   36:4
  S. exalted sat   146:10
  S. finds some mischief   239:10
Satanic: dark S. mills?   38:16
Satchel: schoolboy, with his s.   183:20
Satin: always goes into white s.   216:4
Satire: author of s.   178:1
  S. or sense   165:7
Satisfied: am s.   233:6
  I shall not be s.   137:5
Satisfies: where most she s.   182:16
Satisfy: poorly s. our eyes   249:13
Saturday: betwixt a S. and Monday   55:4
  Died on S.   158:2
  S.'s child   156:17
Saturn: that the Revolution, like S.   235:13
Saturnia: redeunt S. regna   237:1
Satyr: Hyperion to a s.   185:11
Satyrs: men, like s.   138:9
Sauce: best s. in the world   59:9
  Chops and Tomata s.   75:24
  only one s.   54:19
Saucy: To s. doubts   199:8
Saul: S. and Jonathan   24:48
  S. hath slain his thousands   24:45
  S., S., why persecutest thou me?   34:35
Savage: noble s. ran   79:19
  S., extreme, rude   212:1
  s. in his blindness   101:16
  s. place!   66:14
  sooth a s. breast   68:9
  So s. and Tartarly   52:6
  unto a s. race   230:12
Save: died to s. their country   21:14
  himself he cannot s.   32:24
  One drop would s. my soul   138:14
  s. his soul   29:13, 138:14
  S. me from the lion's mouth   169:1
  s. me, oh, s. me   54:14
  someone should s.   235:1
Saved: And s. the sum of things   111:11
  by delaying s. the state   83:45
  has s. herself   162:22
  He s. others   32:24
  only s. the world   21:14
  s. from that eternal silence   230:13
Saviour: God my S.   32:37
  Hide me, O my S.   241:8
  S. of 'is country   127:21
  S. of the world was born   50:14
  'tis thy S.   70:3
  Wash me, S.   234:1
  Wherein our S.'s birth   185:4
Savoir être à soi   149:3
Savour: lost his s.   30:12
Saw: drowns the parson's s.   196:20
  ever s. in my life   238:20
  ever s. in your life   240:14
  everybody s. with joy   105:15
  God s. that it was good   23:7
  He s.; but blasted   98:11
  I find thy s. of might   184:7
  I s. a child   39:8
  I s., I conquered   53:2
  Ne'er s. I   249:4
  s. my works   170:26
  s. the swallows gathering   142:5
  vision once I s.   66:15
Saws: Full of wise s.   183:20
Saxon: ancient S. phrase   133:21
  S. and Norman   231:3
  S. is not like us Normans   126:18
Say: all their friends could s.   131:5
  always s. what's true   221:9
  disapprove of what you s.   237:20
  everyone will s.   92:21, 22
  I s. to this man, Go   31:5
  If we s. that we have no sin   37:8

  is all that they can s.   64:12
  press me to s.   149:2
  s. to all the world   194:24
  s. what you mean   56:22
  s. what you will   68:16
  Though I s. it   19:25
  When you have nothing to s.   68:1
  will s. unto him   33:22
  yet I s. unto you   30:28
  your right to s. it   237:20
Saying: For loving, and for s. so   77:19
  keep on s. it long enough   22:5
  wild waves s.   55:27
Scabbard: threw away the s.   63:25
Scabbards: leaped from their s.   47:14
Scald: mine own tears do s.   196:1
Scale: On every golden s.!   56:13
  s. the stars!   236:21
  with her lifted s.   164:1
Scallop-shell of quiet   174:13
Scan: presume not God to s.   164:18
Scandal: No s. about Queen Eliza-
    beth   216:2
Scandalous and poor   176:1
Scapegoat: a s. into the wilderness   24:11
Scar: from cliff and s.   229:11
Scarce: S. seemed a vision   214:3
  Show s. so gross   195:19
Scarcity: on the very first s.   47:17
Scare: to s. the monster   125:5
Scarf up the tender eye   199:6
Scarlet: His sins were s.   21:15
  In S. town   16:2
  sins be as s.   27:21
  though the s. line was slender   123:13
Scars: He jests at s.   207:20
  show his s.   192:4
Scatter: S., as from an unextin-
    guished hearth   214:4
  s. the good seed   53:12
Scattered: bones lie s.   147:16
  enemies be s.   170:6
  hath s. the proud   32:38
  s. his Maker's image   79:3
  snows have s. and fled   110:5
  When the cloud is s.   213:16
Scatterest: as thou s. them   170:17
Scene: Last s. of all   183:20
  little s.   206:15
  see the distant s.   153:15
  Speaks a new s.   173:27
  that memorable s.   140:8
  to leave the s.   108:13
Scenes: changing s. of life   225:7
  watch the busy s.   117:1
Scent: amber s.   147:5
  s. the morning air   186:11
Sceptic: for the s. side   164:18
  What ever s. could inquire for   49:16
Sceptre: My s. for a palmer's walk-
    ing staff   206:16
  S. and crown   216:24
  s. and the ball   191:15
  s. shows the force   202:5
Sceptred: In s. pall   144:8
  s. race!   129:19
  this s. isle   206:7
Scheme: this sorry S. of Things   86:1
Schemes: far from s. of business   108:14
Scherzando! ma non troppo   91:2
Scholar: a s. among rakes   136:24
  let a s. all Earth's volumes   59:20
  s.'s eye   188:6
  s.'s life assail   117:2
Scholars: all the lore its s. need   122:18
School: After the s. of Stratford atte
    Bowe   60:12
  microcosm of a public s.   76:22
  special reason for hating s.   20:8

GREEK INDEX

PRINTED IN GREAT BRITAIN
AT THE UNIVERSITY PRESS, OXFORD
BY VIVIAN RIDLER
PRINTER TO THE UNIVERSITY